CW01261667

THE PRIVATE RAILWAYS
OF
COUNTY DURHAM

COLIN E. MOUNTFORD

INDUSTRIAL RAILWAY SOCIETY 2004

Published by the INDUSTRIAL RAILWAY SOCIETY
at 24, Dulverton Road, Melton Mowbray, Leicestershire, LE13 0SF

© INDUSTRIAL RAILWAY SOCIETY 2004

ISBN 1 901556 29 8

Visit the Society at www.irsociety.co.uk

This book is one of a series of monographs about industrial railways published by the Industrial Railway Society. Details of the other titles currently available can be obtained by sending a stamped, self-addressed envelope to Mr.S.Geeson, Hon. Sales Officer, 24, Dulverton Road, Melton Mowbray Leicestershire, LE13 0SF.

British Library Cataloguing-in-Publication Data. A catalogue record for this book is available from the British Library.

All rights reserved. No part of this publication may be reproduced, stored in a retrieval system or transmitted in any form or by any means without prior permission in writing from the Industrial Railway Society. Within the UK, exceptions are allowed in respect of any fair dealing for the purpose of private research or private study or criticism or review as permitted under the Copyright, Designs and Patents Act 1988.

Designed and printed by Hillprint Media, Prime House, Park 2000, Newton Aycliffe, Co. Durham, DL5 6AR.
01325 245555

Front cover:
Lambton Railway 0-6-2T 5, RS 3377/1909, at Bournmoor, hauling a coal train from Lambton D Coal Preparation Plant, Fencehouses, to the Railway's exchange sidings with British Railways at Penshaw on 14th February 1969, the penultimate day before the official end of steam locomotive working on the Railway.

Back cover:
The Lambton Railway's 0-6-0 tender engine 11, whose builders are unknown, at Lambton Staiths in Sunderland and believed taken about 1882, possibly the earliest known Lambton Railway photograph. The Railway was developed by the Earls of Durham, whose initials appear on both the locomotive and its tender.

Contents

		Page
	Introduction & Acknowledgments	
Chapter 1	The Early Industrial Locomotives written by Jim Rees & Andrew Guy	1
Chapter 2	The Beamish Railway	16
Chapter 3	The Bowes Railway (formerly the Pontop & Jarrow Railway)	26
Chapter 4	The Chopwell & Garesfield Railway	63
Chapter 5	The Whittonstall Railway	91
Chapter 6	Craghead and Burnhope	101
Chapter 7	The Derwent Railway	109
Chapter 8	The Hetton Railway	114
Chapter 9	The Lambton Railway	145
Chapter 10	The Londonderry Railway	219
Chapter 11	The Pelaw Main Railway	254
Chapter 12	The Sacriston Railway	295
Chapter 13	The South Hetton Colliery Railway	306
Chapter 14	The South Shields, Marsden & Whitburn Colliery Railway	333
Chapter 15	The Harton electric system	355
Chapter 16	The Towneley Colliery Railway	379
Chapter 17	The Weatherhill & Rookhope and The Rookhope & Middlehope Railways	388
Index 1	Important people and companies	406
Index 2	Locations	408
Index 3	References to public railways	412
Index 4	Locomotives	413
Index 5	Synopsis of chapters	428

The noted photographer, Ian Carr (right), and the author at the closure of Lambton Staiths, Sunderland, on 6th January 1967, with 37, RSHN 7755/1953, the very last locomotive to leave.

Introduction

The North-East England coalfield was the first in the world to be developed commercially. In the hinterland of Newcastle upon Tyne, to the west and south of Gateshead, and the area to the east and north-east of Chester-le-Street, coal seams were close to the surface and easy to work. The rivers Tyne and Wear provided good access to the sea and small boats called keels brought the coal down to Newcastle upon Tyne, North Shields and Sunderland to be transferred into the colliers waiting to take it to London, the main market. To convey the coal from pit to river, transport was needed – not the canals that were built elsewhere in England, but an increasing network of wooden waggonways, totalling perhaps 150 miles by 1800. All were built under wayleave arrangements – a private agreement between the landowner and the colliery owner for the latter to build his line over the former's land and pay a charge for each ton of coal which was carried over it. Although by 1800 there were still variations in size, most coal was carried in "Newcastle chaldrons", waggons built to carry 53 hundredweights (20 hundredweights = 1 [short] ton). To haul these waggons, usually one at a time, horses were used, many hundreds of them.

However, by the end of the eighteenth century many of the larger colliery owners were finding that their transport arrangements were inadequate, inefficient and increasingly expensive. As the shallower pits near the rivers were worked out, new pits had to be sunk further away, so that some waggonways had to stretch up to ten miles from the river. Demand and output were rising, placing increasingly heavy demands on both a waggonway's capability and its operating methods. In addition, the Napoleonic Wars saw a marked increase in the cost of horse fodder. Faced with these problems, some owners looked for possible solutions.

The first major development was the introduction of rope haulage. Although Tyneside was not the first place to adopt the principle of using the weight of full waggons going downhill to pull the empty wagons uphill, the first gravity-worked, or self-acting, incline was constructed in 1797 at Elswick, near Newcastle upon Tyne, and their use spread rapidly. Equally, some collieries were already using stationary steam engines for pumping and winding; why not also for hauling waggons? This was first done on the new Urpeth Waggonway, near Chester-le-Street, in 1805. These two developments led to a third. Hitherto, waggonways could not be taken across the often steep-sided valleys in the North-East and had been compelled to follow the valleys of the tributaries of the River Tyne. With rope haulage now available, waggonways could be built to shipping points, or staiths, much further downstream or even close to the mouths of the two rivers, so that colliers could be loaded directly and the disadvantages of the keels could be eliminated.

And if a stationary steam engine could haul waggons on wheels, why not a put a steam engine on wheels? Thus, driven on by the needs and money of its coal industry, the North-East became the centre of the development of the steam locomotive. The weight of these machines compelled the owners keen to try them to re-lay the sections where they might be used with cast iron and later wrought iron rails, another major change, with a parallel change of name to "railways". Interestingly, the main developments took place on new lines, culminating here with the opening of the Stockton & Darlington Railway in September 1825, the world's first public railway, though still primarily built to carry coal. The "Railway Age" was born, and its growth and spread transformed industry and transport not only in Britain but throughout the world.

Here in the North-East all the strands above continued throughout the nineteenth century and well into the twentieth century. Almost all public railways were new lines; only one waggonway, the Tanfield Waggonway, was rebuilt by a public railway and even then it did not carry passengers. Initially, the public railways were mostly small local lines, although the Stockton & Darlington soon began to expand its system, either directly or through railways nominally subsidiary. The first to recognise the power of size and the economies of scale was George Hudson, the "Railway King" and M.P. for Sunderland. Various amalgamations in 1854 formed the North Eastern Railway, which then over time took over virtually all of the other railway companies in the region, including the Stockton & Darlington Railway in 1863, to give itself a powerful monopoly. This stranglehold was further aggravated by the fact that the NER insisted on supplying the coal wagons and also built its own docks and staiths, unlike the position in South Wales, for example, where the colliery owners purchased their own wagons and the railway companies merely worked them between pit and port.

Another difference between Durham and South Wales was that in Durham many landowners worked the coal under their land themselves. The leading aristocratic owners, the Earl of Durham and the Marquis of Londonderry, had no intention of allowing themselves to be dependent on the NER. They rebuilt their waggonways as railways and extended them – indeed, they had every intention of total vertical economic control, controlling their own shipments through their own staiths, developing their own shipping fleets and building their own workshops to service their collieries, their railway, their staiths and their ships. Their lead was followed to a lesser degree by all of the other leading colliery companies north of Durham City, and private railways became as extensive as the waggonways had once been. Because, with one exception, their prime aim was to carry coal, many of them incorporated rope inclines, whose technical sophistication was developed to a level probably unequalled elsewhere in Britain. Many of these railways survived to be taken over by the National Coal Board in 1947, from which most received new locomotives and wagons. The last steam locomotive worked until 1976, the last rope inclines until 1984. The private railways declined as the coal industry itself declined. Some of them worked for over 150 years, and the last closed in 1991.

Their variety was perhaps unparalleled: one has national importance in the history of railways; another was one of the largest private railways in Britain; four operated a public passenger service; two were electrified, one of them being narrow gauge (and which later replaced electrification with rope haulage); one system served one of the remotest areas of England, far from the coal industry. Several colliery companies had running powers over the NER, later the LNER, but very much on their terms, even to their traffic having precedence over NER traffic. Only one, the Londonderry Railway, was taken over by the NER, in 1900.

I first visited one of the railways in November 1961, a month after I had come to Durham University as a student. My uncle, Eric Mountford, author and authority on the railways in South Wales, wanted me to discover how many former South Wales/Great Western Railway locomotives were still working in the North-East. So on a gloomy day I set out by bus for South Hetton, and having just passed the colliery I looked down a street and saw a real Taff Vale locomotive! Over the next thirty years I was privileged to visit all the surviving railways very many times, thanks to the kindness of NCB/British Coal officials at every level, from Area Deputy Director to railway or workshop manager to loco driver. I was given access to locomotive records from Area Headquarters to railway loco shed and colliery office, rode on many locomotives, steam and diesel, and even had an official pass to travel on the rope inclines of the Bowes Railway. I met many former railwaymen and enjoyed their memories. The railways that had closed I walked, fortunately before new development obliterated many trackbeds. I recorded their work, the changes from steam to diesel, their decline and closure, and have continued to record the routes since.

In 1977 I was the joint editor, with the late Les Charlton, of the 2nd edition of *Industrial Locomotives of Durham*, published by the Industrial Railway Society in its Handbook series. In 1996 I began work, with Dave Holroyde, on a 3rd edition, which it had already been agreed would need to be two volumes. By 2000 it was clear that this limit would be exceeded; and so it was decided to create a book dealing solely with Durham's private railways, which would then be followed by two further volumes dealing with all the other Durham information.

Since 1977 a great deal more material has come into public deposit, making possible real academic research into various aspects of the private railways. The Durham Record Office was the first in the country to put all its catalogues online, making research into its records so much easier, and I would like to record special thanks to the Chief Archivist, Jennifer Gill, and all of her staff for all their help and patience in handling my many hundreds of requests. The Northumberland Record Office at Gosforth in Newcastle upon Tyne also has a considerable quantity of Durham material, as does the Tyne & Wear Archives Service and The North of England Institute of Mining & Mechanical Engineers (notably Hunt's *Mineral Statistics* and the Annual Reports of the Mines & Quarries Inspectorate), also both in Newcastle upon Tyne. The Regional Resource Centre at Beamish, The North of England Open Air Museum; Tyne & Wear Museums; the University of Durham; the University of Newcastle upon Tyne and the Local Studies Centres in the central libraries at Newcastle upon Tyne, Gateshead and Sunderland also have important material. I am especially grateful to Russell Wear for so kindly putting all the records of the Industrial Locomotive Society at my disposal, and in particular the note books of several members who visited the North-East in the 1930s and 1940s. Similarly, the late Jim Peden kindly copied me the Durham entries in the extensive notebooks of C.H.A.Townley. The members of the North Eastern Railway Association willingly investigated NER locomotive queries for me and put at my disposal the considerable archive of R.H.Inness and K.Hoole at the Darlington Railway Centre & Museum. I am especially grateful to Jim Rees, Railway Vehicles Collection Manager at the National Railway Museum, York, and Andy Guy, Research Consultant, for kindly agreeing to write a chapter on the first locomotives, based on their extensive research, which has radically changed both our knowledge and understanding of this period. Other specialists in particular fields very kindly shared their expertise, not least Derek Charlton and Chris Goldsmith, and their important research into waggonways north of the Tyne and south of the Wear respectively. Finally, I owe a great deal to Dave Holroyde for his considerable contribution, both with the indexes and commenting on the draft. Without all this help this book could not have been written, and I am sincerely grateful.

The Maps

These may be divided into plans of the systems, usually at various dates through their history and specific locations where the layout was particularly complicated, in the hope that both will help the reader to understand these more easily. All have been superbly drawn by Roger Hateley, to whom I

General Key

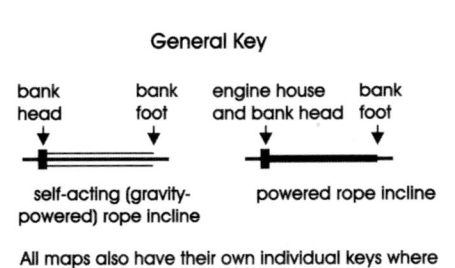

bank head | bank foot | engine house and bank head | bank foot

self-acting (gravity-powered) rope incline | powered rope incline

All maps also have their own individual keys where appropriate.

am especially grateful for his skill, commitment and patience. We were very fortunate to have the help of John Talbot of the Signalling Records Society, whose own research into North East signalling and his care in checking that our diagrams followed strictly the conventions used by signalling historians has done much to enhance the book's coverage and accuracy of the conventional signalling on the railways which used it.

Printed material used as illustrations

Where this has been used it has been included in the same Fig. No. sequence as the maps. Some of this has come from public deposit, and I am very grateful to the various organisations that have allowed me to use it. Most of them have followed the now-standard convention of requiring their reference numbers to be included in the credits, which for this list are as follows:

Beamish, The North of England Open Air Museum 32465, Fig.1; 96322, Fig.8
Durham County Record Office C255, Fig.35
F.Jones Collection/R.H.Inness Figs.58; 69; 84
C.E.Mountford Collection Fig.55
Newcastle upon Tyne City Library Figs.2; 7
Sedgefield District Council, Timothy Hackworth Victorian & Railway Museum, Shildon, with kind permission of Dr.M.Bailey and J.Glithero Fig.68
from W.W.Tomlinson, *The North Eastern Railway*, Figs. 4; 5; 6
Tyne & Wear Museums, Monkwearmouth Station Museum Collection, Sunderland J 18326, Fig.9

Photographs

Photographs of industrial railways may be roughly divided into four main categories.

1. Vernacular - taken by ordinary people years ago, many of whom worked on the railways. Some were copied in the 1940s-1960s by enthusiasts; some remain in private hands; some are now in public deposit, not least at Beamish, The North of England Open Air Museum, at its Regional Resource Centre. The Museum began collecting these when few other public bodies were willing to take them, and now has by far the biggest public collection in the region.

2 Professional - taken by professional photographers a century or more ago. The scenes that professional photographers thought could be sold as commercial postcards to be sent through the post never cease to amaze me. Many of them are now commercially traded by postcard dealers, and I am especially grateful to George Nairn, one of the leading dealers in the country, for not only allowing me to look through and use photographs from his collection but for alerting me when particularly interesting photographs came his way.

3 Enthusiast - taken by those interested in industrial railways from the 1930s onwards. Many continue in the ownership of those that took them; some are held by family relatives; some have been purchased by private individuals and some are now held by organisations such as the Industrial Railway Society, The Locomotive Club of Great Britain and The Midland Railway Trust Ltd. I would like to mention especially Ian Carr, whose main-line work has long been regarded as amongst the best in the country; but if Ian had not set out in 1959 to record thoroughly the Hetton Railway before it closed, there would be almost no later visual record of it; and Ian continued to record the industrial scene through to its close. We first met in January 1967 at the closure of Lambton Staiths, and the frontispiece is a sincere acknowledgement of his immense contribution.

4. Public Deposit – held by Beamish Museum, mentioned above, the Durham County Record Office, the Tyne & Wear Archives, Tyne & Wear Museums and Darlington Railway Centre & Museum. Some of these have come as part of larger deposits of company records; some are the collections of the work of commercial photographers, some are collections formerly in private hands.

Everyone whom I have approached has been more than willing to let me look at anything I wanted. And not just look; I was able to make photocopies, or have those I was interested in scanned on to CD for detailed consideration later.

All of this made it possible to examine literally thousands of photographs, covering a huge range of time (the earliest was taken in 1859) and of content. From these copies were made of around 500 and the total was then whittled down to the final list by Dave Holroyde and I. We wanted to include as wide and interesting a range of photographs as possible, and to achieve this we have inevitably had to include some photographs of less than top quality. Every photograph was then scanned (or transferred from its disc), cropped and then repaired as necessary, using digital techniques, by my friend Malcolm Young. We were very conscious of the ethical issues involved in undertaking this work, and our prime aim was to do nothing that would alter the view that the original photographer saw. We have therefore corrected tilt, repaired creases, scratches, hair marks, dust spots and similar marks, and we have altered the brightness or contrast where we thought it helpful; but the final result is still the view as the original photographer saw it. With so hours, and I am very grateful indeed to Malcolm for all his skill and patience, and again, without whose work this book could not have been compiled. I certainly feel that the photographs included here, many being published for the first time, are a fascinating and glorious record of the railways in their own right.

As with the printed illustrations above, those controlling photographs in public deposit insisted each photograph's reference number be included in the credits. Where photographs have come from private collections, I also thought it appropriate to include the original photographer's name, where it is known.

Beamish, The North of England Open Air Museum B584 58; B586 59; 5760 6; 6109 251; 12088 300; 15735 306; 15737 302; 17475 303; 17783 307; 19752 88; 19753 101; 19754 89; 19773 161; 20284 67; 23515 213; 32906 311; 42315 99; 80868 24
J.P.R.Bennett 262
A.J.Booth 57; 61; 246
I.S.Carr (see also Tyne & Wear Museums) Frontispiece; 91; 92; 93; 94; 104; 128; 132; 133; 142; 143; 144; 147; 153; 208 240; 243; 245; 248; 265; 266; 281; 282; 283; 284; 285; 314
R.M.Casserley Collection/A.W.Croughton 256
R.M.Casserley Collection/H.C.Casserley 134; 226; 234; 250; 258; 259; 267; 313
D.G.Charlton 217
D.G.Charlton Collection/G.H.Anderson 23; 196
D.G.Charlton Collection/T.Birkett 31; 32; 33
D.G.Charlton Collection/L.G.Charlton 4; 42; 43; 47; 49; 50; 52; 60; 73; 80; 90; 96; 131; 149; 150; 218; 221; 222; 223; 244; 272; 274; 275; 293; 295
D.G.Charlton Collection/W.Parry 268
D.G.Charlton Collection/B.Roberts 297
D.G.Charlton Collection/D.Ridley 83
D.G.Charlton Collection 16; 29; 65; 66; 129; 192; 197; 210; 260; 305; 306
J.Cook Collection 85; 86; 98
Darlington Railway Centre & Museum – Ken Hoole Study Centre
K.Hoole Vol.3 89; 236 (I.Holloway); 124 237
K.Hoole, Londonderry Railway album 162; 163; 164; 165; 166; 167; 168; 169; 170; 171; 172; 175; 176; 177; 178; 179; 180; 181
C.G.Down Collection 62; 63; 64
M.Dunnett 138
Durham County Record Office NCB3/105/5a 252
T.Ermel 13; 54; 199
T.M.Hardy Collection 271
W.J.Hatcher 289; 290
Ken Hoole Study Centre, Darlington Railway Centre & Museum 46
D.W.Holroyde 241; 247
D.W.Holroyde Collection 53
Industrial Railway Society/C.A.Appleton 302; 309; 310
Industrial Railway Society/J.Hill 154
Industrial Railway Society/C.H.A.Townley 8; 74; 124; 182; 188; 219; 291; 292; 294
R.G.Jarvis Collection, copyright the Midland Railway Trust Ltd. 30; 119; 122; 225; 227; 228; 229; 231; 232; 235

F.Jones 5; 9; 18; 48; 112; 123; 125; 127; 130; 136; 233; 280
F.Jones Collection 186; 187; 195; 216
Locomotive Club of Great Britain/Ken Nunn Collection 185; 253; 255
A.Lynn Collection 141
Professor N.McCord, by kind permission of the University of Newcastle upon Tyne 44
D.Monk-Steel 287
C.E.Mountford Front cover; 10; 11; 12; 15; 20; 25; 26; 34; 36; 37; 38; 39; 51; 56; 68; 69; 70; 71; 72; 76; 77; 78; 79; 106; 126; 135; 139; 152; 155; 156; 157; 158; 159; 160; 190; 192; 194; 203; 204; 214; 238; 239; 242; 249; 264; 276; 277; 278; 279; 286; 287; 296
C.E.Mountford Collection/T.Dolan 19; 200
C.E.Mountford Collection/E.W.Hayes 7
C.E.Mountford Collection/E.H.Jeynes 14; 17; 22; 207; 215
C.E.Mountford Collection/C.J.Kenyon 145
C.E.Mountford Collection/J.McIvor 198
C.E.Mountford Collection 21; 28; 40; 41; 80; 81; 87; 109; 202; 230; 257
G.Nairn Collection 65; 116; 174; 183; 188; 191; 201; 205; 206; 209; 211; 212; 220
Newcastle City Council 1
North Eastern Railway Association (collection housed at Ken Hoole Study Centre, Darlington Railway Centre & Museum)
R.H.Inness Vol 4 2; 27; 75; 113; 114; 115; 118; 184
R.H.Inness Vol 5 254
D.Rounthwaite Collection/T.E.Rounthwaite 298
I.M.Scrimgeour 273
Siemens Museum, Munich 269; 270
Seaham Harbour Dock Company 172
A.Slack Collection Back cover; 110; 111
A.Snowdon 263
M.J.Squire 151
N.Stead Collection/G.M.Staddon 146; 148
N.Stead Collection 45; 55
Tyne & Wear Museums, Newcastle upon Tyne C12348/21 120; C12348/22 121
Tyne & Wear Museums, Coulson Cairns Collection, Newcastle upon Tyne 1999/430 117; 1999/442 261; 1999/492/1 224
Tyne & Wear Museums, Monkwearmouth Station Museum Collection, Sunderland J18356 35; J18383 (I.S.Carr) 100; J18385 102; J18387 105; J18392 97; J18394 312; K52 95; K65 (I.S.Carr) 107; K85 (S.Teasdale) 103; K87 (I.S.Carr) 108
B.K.Twigg Collection 84
V.Wake 140
R.Wildsmith 137

These railways were an integral part of industry in Durham, yet invariably they gave a friendly welcome to those who visited them. I hope their history will be as equally interesting and enjoyable.

Colin E. Mountford

27, Glencoe Avenue,
Cramlington,
Northumberland NE23 6EH

Chapter One
The First Industrial Locomotives

Jim Rees, Railway Vehicles Collection Manager, National Railway Museum, York
and
Andy Guy, Research Consultant

Our understanding of the 'railway' is dominated by our modern perception of it as a principal transport infrastructure, managed as a major industry in its own right, with varied traffic and powered by locomotives. But for over half of its history in Britain it had a very different character. First seen in England at the very beginning of the seventeenth century, its original role – moving coal - was to be its dominant work over the next two hundred years.

These waggonways were not the 'permanent way' thought of today, but were typically a line of wooden rails laid with rough sleepers in a crude ballast of pit waste; the outstanding preserved example is the quite remarkable remains excavated in Co. Durham at Lambton D Pit near Fencehouses in 1996. The land for the waggonway was made available by a private agreement with the landowner, this 'wayleave agreement' usually including a charge for the volume of coal conveyed over it and a condition to return the land to its original state when the lease expired or was given up. Although earthworks were increasingly necessary over time, the early ways were seldom considered to be permanent works but were removed as the shallow pits became exhausted.

The North East of England developed the most intensive system of waggonway lines. By 1800 it had perhaps 150 miles of way, half the total in the whole country, and its seemingly primitive lines were handling over two million waggon movements each year. These 'Newcastle Roads' had a distinct regional character. With very few exceptions they were built and operated by the collieries to carry coal from the pit to loading staiths on the rivers Tyne and Wear, and so merely acted as the transport arm of the coal trade rather than a business in their own right. They all seem to have had a gauge of at least four feet, allowing the use of waggons large enough to hold a 'chaldron' of coal (53 hundredweights). The following twenty years would see an increasing change to cast iron though still of the edge type rather than the L-shaped plate rail often favoured elsewhere – and a growing desire by the leading coal owners to increase the productivity of their horse-worked waggonways by experimenting with new forms of motive power using gravity and steam.

Fig. 1. A horse and chaldron wagon typically found around Tyneside at the time it was drawn.

1. One of the lines of the wooden waggonway, once part of the Lambton Waggonway, which were uncovered at Fencehouses during the clearance of Lambton Coke Works in 1996 – the largest such discovery ever made in Britain.

The first rope-worked inclines in the North East were built at the turn of the eighteenth and nineteenth centuries, their fixed power helped by the fact that the full waggons were always travelling in the same direction. The first self-acting incline, where the weight of full waggons going downhill hauled the empties uphill, was constructed in the mid-1790s; the first powered incline, where a stationary engine hauled the full waggons uphill, was built in 1805. Other coal owners hoped that making the steam power mobile might provide a way forward.

Thus the first quarter of the nineteenth century saw the invention, development and first effective use of the steam locomotive. By 1825, with the Stockton & Darlington Railway and *Locomotion*, the creation of the modern railway had begun, to be consummated with the Liverpool & Manchester Railway five years later. The work up to and including the Stockton & Darlington Railway had concentrated on the development of the industrial locomotive and by far the majority of this pioneering phase had taken place in Durham and Northumberland.

The two counties cannot be conveniently discussed separately. Together they span the Great Northern Coalfield and it was this, the greatest coal production area in Britain, which stimulated the successful development of the locomotive. Many of the details of this experimental work are lost and others are, at the least, imperfectly understood, but an attempt to explore these trials is both worthwhile and fascinating. Never again would there be a situation where the most basic principles of the steam locomotive would be so profoundly considered, and it was to be here that its fundamental design was established.

The notes below, based on newly-discovered documents and a re-examination of the original sources, often differ from the information in the standard texts. They suggest that we did not know what we thought we knew; the true story of these pioneers is bigger, more complex and much more interesting that many of us used to think. However, it must equally be emphasised that few of the engines below have a clear and undisputed history.

RICHARD TREVITHICK (1771-1833)

Richard Trevithick, inventor of the railway locomotive, was one of the outstanding engineers of his time. Born in Cornwall, his early career was as a tin mine "Captain" and he showed exceptional ability from the first. He developed a successful high-pressure steam engine at the very end of the eighteenth century, very quickly appreciating that here, for the first time, was a portable engine capable of real work. To demonstrate its possibilities, he built an experimental steam carriage tried in Camborne, Cornwall. That it should have succeeded on the road but failed to survive Trevithick's celebration in the local pub seems to sum up both the ability and misfortune of the 'Cornish Giant'.

The engine was patented in 1802, with specific allowance for its use for both road and rail vehicles. A road carriage tested in London had some limited success but faced fundamental problems with steering and poor surfaces – neither of which would apply on a waggonway. In 1803/4 the first rail locomotive was built for the Coalbrookdale Ironworks in Shropshire, although the extent of Trevithick's direct role in its design remains unclear. The well-known drawing of a 'Tram Engine' is thought to be a representation of it, a four-wheeled locomotive arranged with a single horizontal cylinder working above the firebox of a return-tube boiler and transmitting drive via gears and a flywheel to a pair of wheels on just one side.

The second and more famous engine was built directly under the instructions of Trevithick for the Penydarren plateway near Merthyr Tydfil in 1804. Originally built to win a wager, and adapted from a stationary engine, more is known of its work but less of its design, although it is likely to have closely resembled the 'Tram Engine' in general arrangement. It did haul loads and it did travel some distance, but it broke so many of the fragile iron plates that it was quickly withdrawn.

Improved and simplified Patent Steam Engine.
WE, Messrs. Richard Trevithick, Andrew Vivian, and William West, of Camborne, in the County of Cornwall, respectfully inform the Public, that we have appointed Mr John Whinfield, of Gateshead, in the County of Durham, Iron and Brass Founder, our Agent, to make, sell, and erect Steam Engines, upon the Principles for which we have obtained a Patent, within the several Counties of Northumberland, Cumberland, Westmorland, Durham, Yorkshire, and Lincolnshire; and request all Orders, on that Account, to be executed in any of those Counties, may be sent to Mr Whinfield.—Signed, RICHARD TREVITHICK,
ANDREW VIVIAN,
WILLIAM WEST.

N. B. These Engines are considerably cheaper than any other Engine at present in Use. They require no Injection-Water, having neither Condenser, Air-Pump, &c. or Working Gear; have no Beam, &c. and require only a Sufficiency of Water to supply the Waste in the Boiler, which is about half a Gallon per Minute for an Engine of Ten Horses' Power. The Steam, after it has done its Office, may be condensed and returned to feed the Boiler again.

Fig. 2. The notice in the Newcastle Courant of 22nd October 1803 advertising John Whinfield of Gateshead as the local licensee of Trevithick's patent – the very beginning of the railway age in North East England.

The third locomotive – the first to be seen in the North-East and the first to be built for edge rather than plate rails - was constructed by the local agent for the Trevithick patent, John Whinfield, to the designs of Trevithick and John Steele (1). Steele was a local man, from Pontop in north-west Durham, who had worked alongside Trevithick on the Penydarren engine. Two sets of main drawings survive which, although differing in detail, show that again the general arrangement was of a single horizontal cylinder with a flywheel and gearing. The machine was demonstrated in 1805 at the maker's premises in **Pipewellgate, Gateshead**, alongside the Tyne. It had been designed specifically for Wylam Colliery in Northumberland, but apparently as a speculation rather than in response to a firm order, and Christopher Blackett, the owner of Wylam Colliery, declined to take it, so that it was subsequently adapted to blow the foundry's cupola. Trevithick, in a casual aside, suggested that more of his locomotives might be in use around Newcastle upon Tyne (though this is unproven) and there is also a suggestion (although again the evidence is weak) that the civil engineer and factory owner William Chapman may have owned a Trevithick locomotive (2) on Tyneside.

The final Trevithick locomotive was the famous *Catch Me Who Can* of 1808, built as a demonstration engine giving rides to the public in an enclosure near Euston in London. The details of this first passenger engine are uncertain; the picture on the invitation cards suggests an advanced design with a vertical cylinder directly driving the rear wheels. This venture failed to attract sufficient customers and was closed down when the engine fell off the track.

Trevithick's four engines were undoubtedly the first railway locomotives and, equally undoubtedly, they had failed in economic work. He had proved the possibility but not the practicality. It appears that he did not address the great limiting factor of the earliest engines, that of insufficient rail strength. However, he had established a number of key design points that would be used, and often claimed as original, by many of the pioneers who followed him. He had shown that a portable high pressure engine on a railway was possible. He recognised the importance of the blast pipe to raise the fire and its lack of usefulness in the early boilers. He acknowledged the difficulty of sufficient efficiency in these small self-contained engines by keeping the cylinder hot within the boiler by providing a return flue to increase the heat surface area and he used gearing to increase haulage at the expense of speed. He showed it could work on plate as well as edge rails and that the adhesion of smooth wheels could be sufficient for it to haul loads. He had demonstrated both freight and passenger engines. With his demoralised withdrawal from locomotive work many of these lessons would have to be learned anew.

The North-East locomotives
(1)   Built and tested at Whinfield's foundry in Gateshead but not sold. Two contemporary

Fig.3

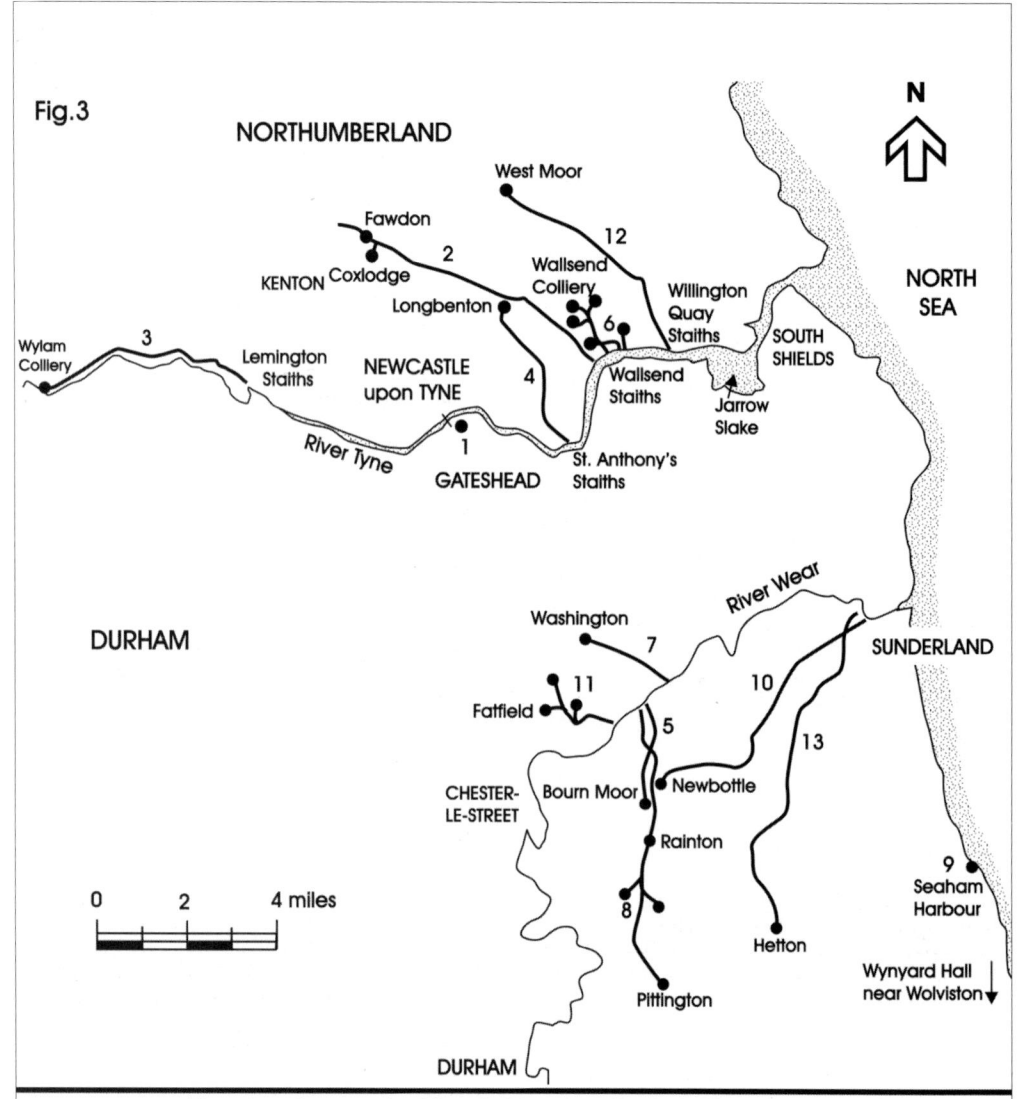

The development of the first locomotives, 1805 - 1822

1 Whinfield's Foundry, Gateshead
2 Kenton & Coxlodge Waggonway
3 Wylam Waggonway
4 Heaton Waggonway
5 Lambton Waggonway
6 Wallsend Waggonway
7 Washington Colliery Waggonway
8 Rainton Waggonway
9 Seaham Harbour
10 Newbottle Waggonway
11 Fatfield Waggonway
12 Killingworth Waggonway
13 Hetton Colliery Railway

Note that only pits at the ends of waggonways have been shown.

TREVITHICK'S GATESHEAD ENGINE.

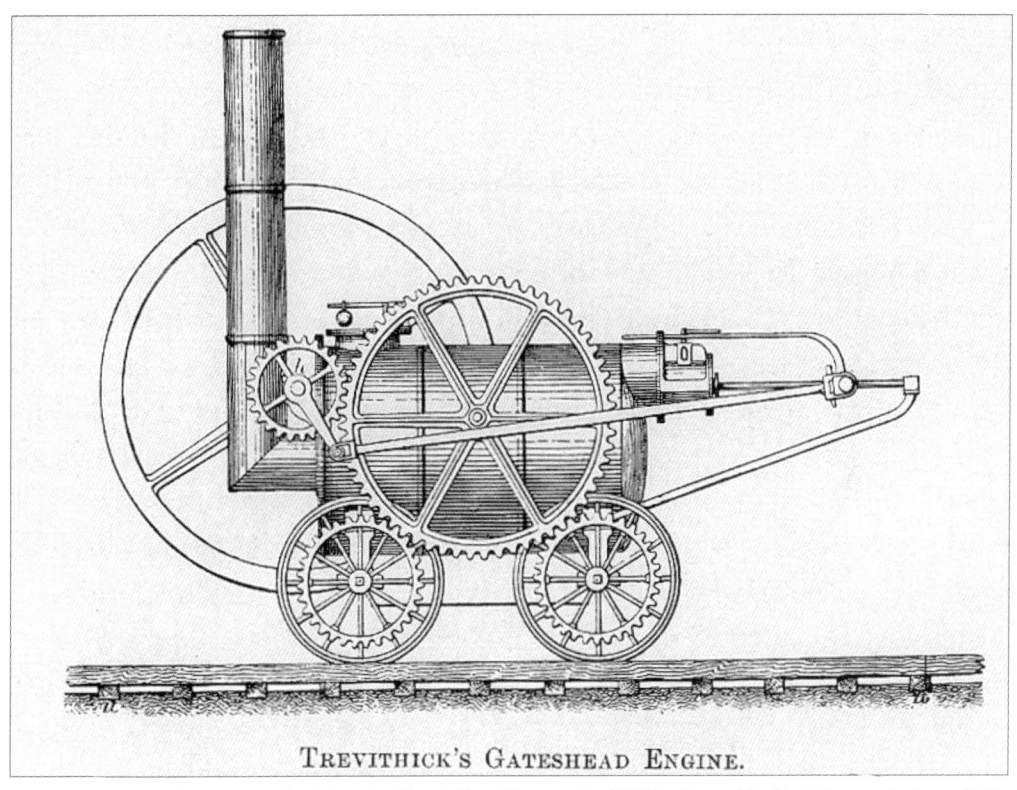

Fig. 4. The Trevithick locomotive built by John Whinfield, as illustrated in W.W.Tomlinson, The North Eastern Railway, 1915.

drawings exist for this engine, differing in wheel diameter and gear ratio; it is not clear which was used. It was a four-wheeled locomotive and had a cast iron boiler with a single return flue. The single cylinder, with slide-bar motion set horizontally into the other end of the boiler, drove through a flywheel and gear to two wheels on one side. The gauge, about five feet, would have been correct for the Wylam waggonway.

It was converted to a stationary foundry blowing engine. The single cylinder was replaced by a similar cylinder at some time during its working life and it was finally scrapped in the 1860s.

(2) A Trevithick-type locomotive, apparently fitted with roughened wheels as in the patent of 1802, may have been in store (pre-1810?) at the Willington Ropeworks, Howdon-on-Tyne, of William Chapman (see below). Its existence has not been established and its possible use and disposal are unknown.

**JOHN BLENKINSOP (1783-1831) &
MATTHEW MURRAY (?1765-1826)**
The first engines to demonstrate the economic practicability of the steam locomotive were built for the Middleton Colliery waggonway near Leeds. John Blenkinsop was the 'viewer', or mine engineer, for the colliery, but he was born and trained at Felling, east of Gateshead, and he must have known of, and may even have attended, the trials of the Trevithick locomotive there in 1805. In 1811 he patented a railway traction system by which a high pressure engine supported on wheels drove through gears a cogged wheel engaging in matching cogs on the side of a rail, similar to a modern mountain rack railway. His interest was not specifically in the design of the engine itself; that seems to have been left to Matthew Murray, a partner in the engineering firm of Fenton, Murray & Wood.

Their Round Foundry in Leeds, one of the leading works in the country, was the greatest competitor to the works of Matthew Boulton and James Watt at Birmingham. Murray, who is also believed to have been born and raised on either Tyneside or Teesside, was its engineer and he made a number of significant advances in steam engine design, including the development of the slide valve. For Blenkinsop's engine he fundamentally improved Trevithick's designs by fitting twin cylinders and arranging them as double-acting and quartered, thus removing the need for the heavy flywheel. The engine was now self-starting and potentially both more manageable and more powerful. His cylinders were placed vertically along the boiler centreline with slide bar motion giving direct drive through gearing. These features would be adopted by the engine designers who followed and it was the practical basis for a sufficiently effective, albeit slow, heavy-haulage engine.

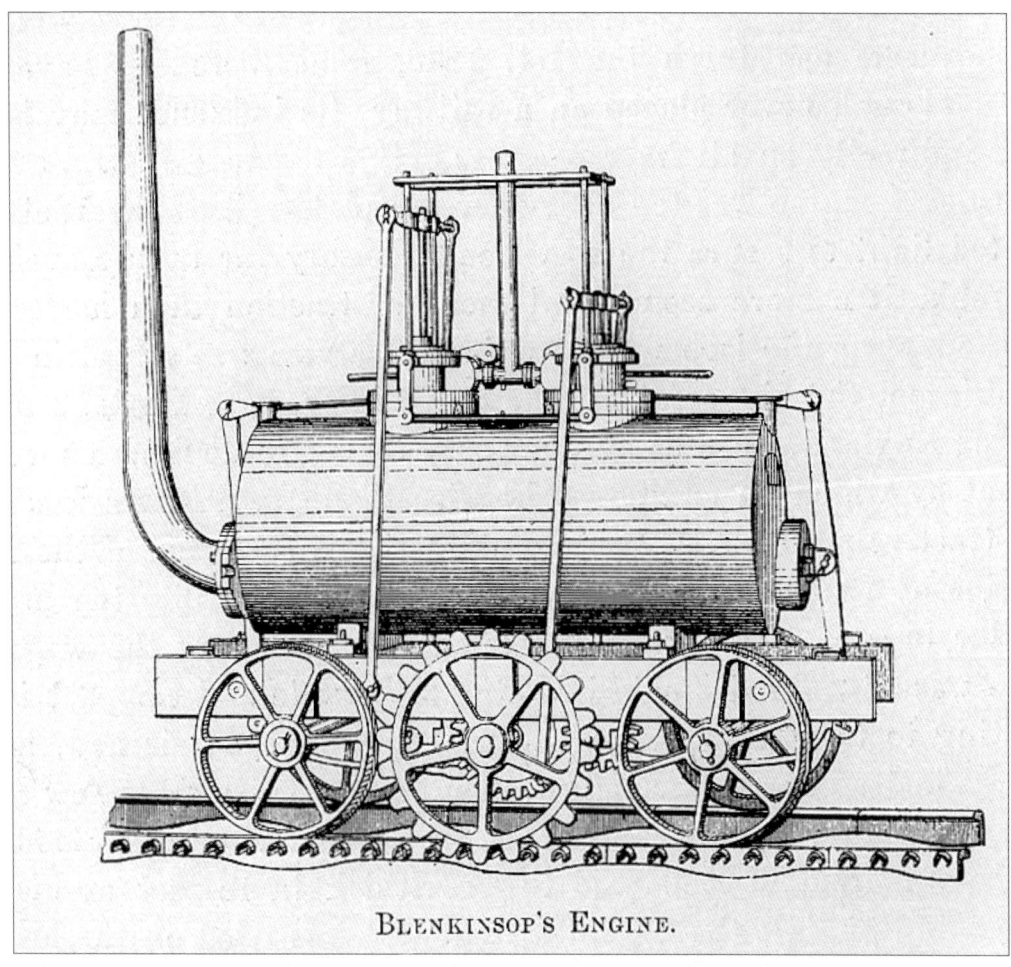

Fig. 5. 'Blenkinsop's Engine', as illustrated in W.W.Tomlinson, The North Eastern Railway, 1915.

At least three Blenkinsop/Murray engines were to be produced for the Middleton Colliery and they had a long working life. However, their significance went well beyond Leeds. Blenkinsop promoted his patent with gusto. The trials and their use were documented in the national magazines of the day; special visitors were encouraged and details of the engines sent out to interested parties. They would be the first steam locomotive design to be built in Europe, with an abortive attempt to build two in Prussia, and there is a possibility, though remote, that another was tried in Belgium. It has been suggested that one was ordered for a Welsh colliery and certainly three were built by Robert Daglish for his Orrell Colliery near Wigan.

Three more were ordered for the **Kenton & Coxlodge Waggonway** near Newcastle upon Tyne. The line from the collieries arched round the north-west of the town and then ran south to staiths on the River Tyne near Wallsend. The first locomotive (1), delivered in 1813, had originally been ordered for Middleton Colliery but was sold instead to the Owners of Kenton & Coxlodge, who were anxious to start locomotive operations on their recently-laid cogged rails. A grand public opening was held in September 1813, but the first engine was damaged almost immediately and was laid off for some time. The owners ordered two further, but larger, engines from Murray (2, 3) but all the locomotives had been laid off by the middle of 1815 following allegations of deliberate misuse and sabotage. It is uncertain if they ever worked again and the ultimate fate of the engines is unknown. The Blenkinsop track had only been laid half way towards the river staiths and when later the waggonway was rebuilt it was not fitted with the necessary cog rails. However, these engines proved the potential of steam locomotives in the region and were a dominant influence on the first designs of George Stephenson.

The locomotives

All were built to 4ft 7½in gauge and were four-wheeled, with the addition of one rack wheel on the side. The two cylinders were mounted vertically into the top centre line of the boiler, front and rear, driving down to a spur gear mounted between crankshafts beneath the boiler.

1. *Lord Wellington* (perhaps the first locomotive known to have had a formal name rather than a nickname); built by Fenton, Murray & Wood in 9/1813 for the Middleton Colliery, Leeds, but diverted here; had the same dimensions (unknown) as the Leeds engines.
2/3. Built by Fenton, Murray & Wood in 1814 and designed for the longer waggonway of the Kenton & Coxlodge Collieries, with the boilers enlarged to 7ft 1in long x 4ft 8in diameter, with the cylinders having a diameter of 8in x 24in stroke.

All three locomotives were laid aside during 1815. There may have been some limited use after 1817. Their final disposal is unknown.

WILLIAM HEDLEY (1779-1843) &
TIMOTHY HACKWORTH (1786-1850)

If the Blenkinsop/Murray design was the first practical steam locomotive, then the first engine in regular work to use adhesion has been claimed for the **Wylam Colliery waggonway**. Although Wylam Colliery's owner, Christopher Blackett, had declined the Gateshead locomotive, probably due to the waggonway's unsuitable wooden track, he rebuilt the line as an iron plateway and invited Trevithick to build him a further locomotive in 1809. The offer was declined, but Blackett persisted in his interest in the new technology. He instigated a number of experiments to establish the principles and limits of adhesion, at a period when others such as Blenkinsop, Chapman and Brunton were concentrating on alternative systems of traction. These were undertaken by his viewer, William Hedley, and foreman blacksmith, Timothy Hackworth. Satisfied that adhesion was a practicable principle, a boiler and motion was fitted on the test carriage by Thomas Waters, the successor to John Whinfield as Trevithick's local agent. Little is known of this engine (1), but it is supposed to have been a single cylinder, geared flywheel engine with many similarities to the Gateshead engine.

This first engine at Wylam proved promising, but too weak for effective work. It was followed by a new design on four wheels with twin cylinders sitting upright on the frame, flanking the boiler. Although now strong enough for work, its weight broke the waggonway's plate rails. It was then rebuilt on a very different arrangement, sitting on two four-wheeled frames, probably bogies, and was joined by two further engines to the same design. The three were reputedly named *Elisabeth*, *Jane* and *Lady Mary* (2,3,4).

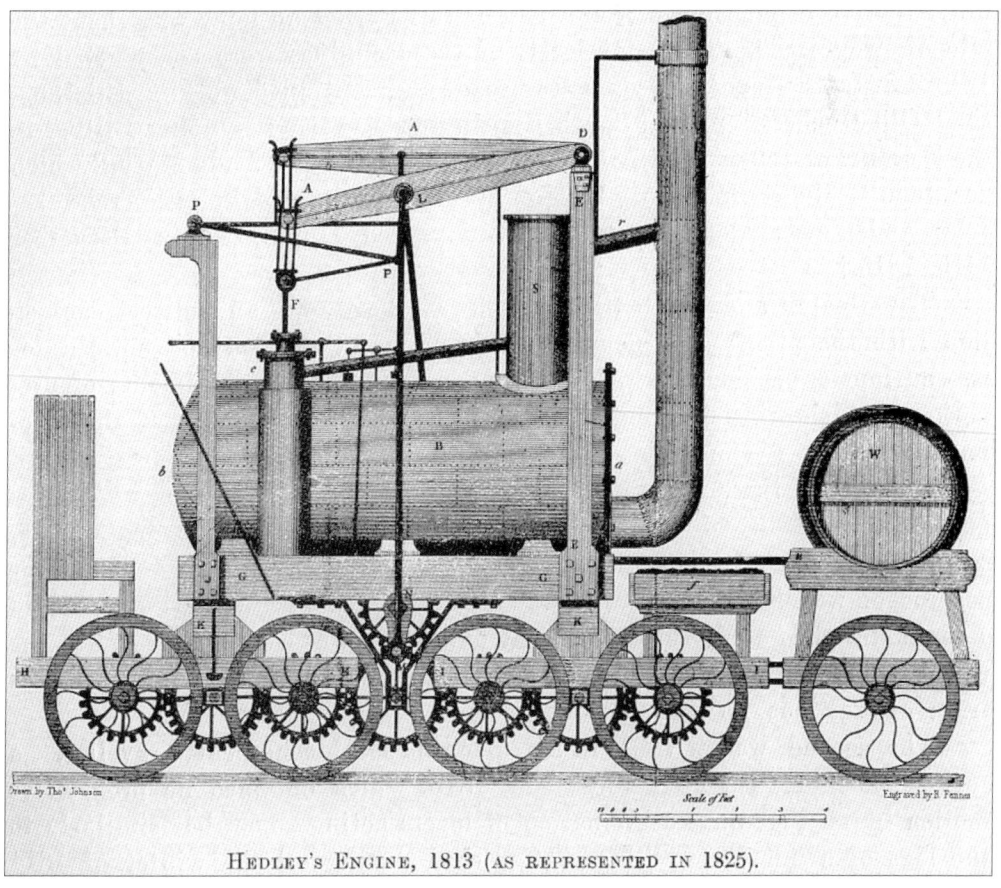

HEDLEY'S ENGINE, 1813 (AS REPRESENTED IN 1825).

Fig. 6. The Wylam 8-wheeled locomotives, as illustrated by Nicholas Wood in his Treatise on Railroads, 1825.

It is uncertain who was responsible for these locomotive designs. The families of Hedley and Hackworth have made conflicting and exclusive claims for their credit – certainly, of the two men it was Hackworth who would later have a distinguished career as a locomotive designer and builder at Shildon, whilst Hedley became a successful mine owner. The adaptation to eight wheels may well have been inspired by the designs of William Chapman (see below). The engines themselves were evidently successful, drawing all the colliery traffic over the entire six-mile waggonway and as such forming, until the 1830s, the only line wholly powered by locomotives.

When the waggonway was rebuilt for iron edge rails between 1828 and 1830 (by which time both Hedley and Hackworth had left the colliery), one engine was dismantled; but the other two were rebuilt as four-wheelers. Remarkably, both engines have survived, under their famous nicknames of *Puffing Billy* and *Wylam Dilly*.

'Billies' or 'Puffing Billies' seems to have been a common generic for early locomotives by the mid-nineteenth century and was not restricted just to this location. There is no evidence for their current names prior to preservation, but there are references to one being known as 'The Old Duchess'.

The locomotives
1. A four-wheeled Trevithick-type, single cylinder (possibly later fitted with a second cylinder), geared, with flywheel. It was 5ft 0in gauge, to work on plate rails. Built by Thomas Waters of Gateshead about 1813 on to the chassis of Hedley's adhesion carriage of 1812. Known as *Black Billy*, it worked for perhaps a year, and was then converted for stationary use.
2/3/4. These three, all also built to 5ft 0in gauge, had single return flue boilers, with two vertical cylinders mounted on the outside of the boiler. The first was built about 1813-1814 as a four wheeler, but was rapidly converted in 1814 to eight wheels, with the following two engines built as such. Unfortunately, the exact form of the 'bogies' is as yet unknown and it is therefore difficult to place these locomotives in the history of bogie development and in relation to Chapman's work. In this form they ran for approximately fifteen years. One engine, possibly *Lady Mary*, was broken up by 1832. The two remaining locomotives were converted between 1828 and 1830 from plate rail to edge and from eight wheels to four. The two preserved locomotives have Fremantle type motion; the original motion may have been the Watt type.

Puffing Billy was loaned to the Patent Office Museum in London, now the Science Museum, in 1862 and sold to them in 1865. *Wylam Dilly*, which in 1822 had been temporarily converted to a steam paddle tug for working on the River Tyne, was bought in 1869 by the Hedley family at the auction following the closure of the colliery. It was taken to Craghead Colliery, from where in 1882 it was taken to what is now the Royal Museum of Scotland, where it remains. These two locomotives are the oldest in preservation.

2. Wylam Dilly, as preserved at Craghead between 1869 and 1882, here with William Hedley Jnr (centre) and his brother George - the world's oldest preserved locomotive. This was one of a series of photographs, probably taken at Wylam before the loco was moved to Craghead, which hung in the Craghead Colliery manager's office for many years.

WILLIAM CHAPMAN (1749-1832) & JOHN BUDDLE Jnr (1773-1843)

William Chapman was a Tyneside-based civil engineer, specialising in canal, drainage and harbour works and credited with the development of the skew-arch masonry bridge. He was a skilled mechanical engineer, an authority on early steam boats and the inventor of an advanced rope-making machine. With interests in local collieries and waggonways as well, it is perhaps not surprising that his attention was drawn to steam locomotives. It has been mentioned above that as early as 1810 he may have owned a Trevithick-type engine. In 1812 he and his brother Edward patented a locomotive design that included chain haulage (an engine-driven wheel engaging a chain laid within the track) and, more importantly, the use of a bogie.

Both of these design elements were used on a locomotive built by the Butterley Company in Derbyshire for the **Heaton Colliery waggonway** near Newcastle upon Tyne (1), operated by The Owners of Heaton Colliery. Surviving plans show an arrangement of a six-wheeled engine including a four-wheeled bogie and twin vertical cylinders set closely together in what must be a return flue boiler. The drive is taken by side levers to power a drum which in turn takes up a chain loosely secured between the rails. The locomotive was assembled in 1813 and tried until Heaton Colliery was closed due to flooding in 1815, then being converted to a stationary pit engine for pumping and winding.

The Heaton engine is generally regarded as a practical failure, but it did lead to a similar design for the **Lambton Waggonway**, which served the collieries near Chester-le-Street owned by John George Lambton (see chapter 9). Built by Phineas Crowther at his Ouseburn Foundry in Newcastle-upon-Tyne in 1814, it had both chain and adhesion traction combined on an eight-wheeled frame (2). Judging from contemporary Chapman designs, it probably had all the axles coupled with gears and arranged as two four-wheeled bogies, somewhat similar to the adapted Wylam locomotives of the same year, although how the drive worked in tandem with the 'winch' mechanism is quite unknown. It must have been a machine of formidable complexity, and it was most likely the last to use the Chapman chain system. It was first tried at the end of 1814, in the Bourn Moor area, but the track proved too fragile, it was laid aside and eventually sold to Heaton Colliery.

Chapman's main collaborator was John Buddle, 'King of the Coal Trade', the greatest colliery engineer of his day, an outstanding technical innovator and one of the first 'scientific' viewers. Buddle was not only the viewer for both Heaton Colliery and the Lambton collieries, he also supervised the trials of and improvements to the locomotives tried on them, a pattern that would be continued with further Chapman engines. In 1815 a Chapman locomotive was built for **Wallsend Colliery**, with the machined parts supplied by Hawks & Co of Gateshead (3). This was to be the famous *Steam Elephant*. Initially it was a failure on the wooden waggonway at Wallsend, so in 1816 it was taken across the Tyne for trials on the **Washington Colliery waggonway**, where again it proved unsuccessful. When the Wallsend

3. The now-famous painting of the "Steam Elephant", designed by William Chapman and John Buddle, working on the Wallsend waggonway about 1826 - and drawn with sufficient accuracy that it made possible the design of a successful replica for Beamish, The North of England Open Air Museum.

waggonway was converted to cast iron rails in 1817 the engine returned and it was there that it finally entered into regular service. The *Elephant* was of a more conventional design than Chapman's previous engines, using adhesion rather than being chain-hauled, and it was fitted with six geared wheels on a single wooden frame – the first six-wheeled engine. There is evidence that a second locomotive of this type (4) was also built for Wallsend. Either *Elephant* or this possible second engine was transferred by 1825 to Hetton Colliery to work at the southern end of the **Hetton Railway** (see chapter 8). By 1834 this locomotive had been modified with a longer boiler and direct drive to the front and rear wheels but retaining gear coupling between the three axles. It is not known if it had this arrangement at Wallsend.

In 1816 a Chapman engine on two four-wheeled frames, with all the axles coupled by gears, was supplied to the Whitehaven Colliery in Cumberland. Four years later Buddle purchased the old Lambton waggonway locomotive and completely rebuilt it for his new **Heaton Colliery waggonway**, lengthening the boiler, cutting the eight-wheeled twin frames down to a single-framed four wheeler and coupling the axles with a chain (2). It was the first locomotive to use solid springs and can be recognised as the 'large travelling engine' mentioned in contemporary correspondence but unidentified for so long.

In 1822 Buddle's enginewright at Heaton, Joseph Smith, built an engine (5) of unknown design for the **Rainton Waggonway**, which served the collieries managed by Buddle for the Marquis of Londonderry (see chapter 10). It was shown to the Duke of Wellington at Rainton when he visited the collieries and the waggonway on 29th September 1827, but it appears to have had little general success.

References in Buddle's extensive correspondence show that a form of locomotive crane (6) was attempted during the construction of **Wynyard Hall** for the Marquis of Londonderry from 1828 onwards. During the construction of **Seaham Harbour**, designed by the elderly Chapman and managed by Buddle, both a rail crane and a locomotive crane (7) were used.

It was long believed that George Stephenson was alone in building locomotives between 1815 and 1825. The productions of Chapman and Buddle show conclusively that this was not the case, and that their roles in the development of the locomotive have been seriously undervalued. They produced a series of locomotives whose variety of design was unrivalled in the period, from chain-drive bogie engines on wooden rails to adhesion crane locomotives for harbour construction, and tested them on a remarkable number of waggonways. Their recognition has perhaps been hampered by the apparent restrictions on their use – Chapman's engines were used solely on Buddle-managed concerns. They appear not to have publicised their results nor sought orders elsewhere, but increasingly explored locomotives as pragmatic answers to specific site problems. It is evident that many of these experiments proved them to have limited practical application at the time.

It is likely that William Chapman influenced the successful Wylam locomotive redesign to eight wheels, that he was involved in the engine tested by John Grimshaw (see below) and advised George Stephenson on his first locomotive. John Buddle was not only the most influential colliery engineer of his generation but had the ear of government. His apparent conclusion in 1825, that locomotives were not yet a general answer to railway haulage, may have had a deep effect on the commercial and political attitudes of the time.

The locomotives

1. Heaton Colliery waggonway, Newcastle upon Tyne. The gauge was 4ft 9½in. A self-hauled, chain locomotive on six wheels, four of which were a bogie, the first locomotive to have one. Two in-line vertical 8in cylinders, with a boiler 7ft 6in long x 3ft 6in diameter. Built by the Butterley Company, Derbyshire and entered service in 1813. Converted to a stationary engine in 1815.

2. Lambton Waggonway locomotive; gauge 4ft 2in. Chapman chain system and/or adhesion, with two four-wheeled bogie frames and probably a return flue boiler. Built by Phineas Crowther of the Ouseburn Foundry, Newcastle upon Tyne in 1815. The engine was still being trialled in 1816 and does not seem to have done any useful work. It was sold to Heaton Colliery in 1820 for use on the colliery's new waggonway via Wallsend. It was rebuilt to John Buddle's specification by Joseph Smith, the foreman enginewright, to become a chain-coupled, four-wheeler on plate springs and with a lengthened boiler fitted with a single flue. No other details are known, but it worked for some years.

3,4. Wallsend Colliery waggonway; gauge 4ft 8in. This 'Steam Elephant' was designed by William Chapman and built at the colliery workshops with parts supplied by Hawks & Co of Gateshead. It had six geared wheels with two in-line cylinders and slide bar motion. Briefly tested also at Washington during 1816, then returned to Wallsend. It is likely that another of a similar type was also used at Wallsend. Either the original or its partner was at Hetton Colliery by 1825 and was still present there in 1834. By that date it had a lengthened boiler and direct drive but retained gear-coupled axles. Its eventual fate, and that of its partner, if it existed, is not known.

5. Rainton Waggonway locomotive; gauge probably 4ft 2in. Built by Joseph Smith at Heaton Colliery about 1822. An adhesion engine of unknown arrangement, it was laid aside by 1825, but under trial again in 1826. It was admired by the Duke of Wellington in

1827 (see chapter 10) and may be the locomotive that was working at Seaham Harbour in 1828. Its eventual fate is unknown.

6. The Wynyard locomotive is likely to have been a locomotive with a crane, and is possibly the same engine as (5), modified.

7. At the construction of Seaham Harbour from 1828 onwards there were two distinct Buddle/Chapman locomotives. One was possibly the Rainton (5) or Wynyard (6) locomotive fitted with a crane attachment, the other was a proper locomotive crane built in 1828. No further details are known.

WILLIAM BRUNTON (1777-1851)

Certainly the most unusual locomotive of this period was that used on the **Newbottle Waggonway**. This was a major new line, opened in 1812 by John Nesham, the owner of Newbottle Colliery, near Houghton-le-Spring. It was the first to cross the barrier of hills between Rainton and Sunderland to reach the River Wear and the deep-water port of Sunderland from the south. The line was engineered by Edward Steel, supposedly assisted by John Grimshaw (see below) and it would later form part of the Lambton Railway (see chapter 9).

In 1813 William Brunton patented an engine for canal or railway which drove steam-powered legs. His design has long been a by-word for eccentricity; but Brunton was an established engineer, heading one of the largest works in the country, the Butterley Company at Crich in Derbyshire, and he had previously directed the engine works of Boulton & Watt in Birmingham.

A small locomotive was tried at Crich Quarry, adjoining the Butterley works, apparently sufficiently promising for another to be made for Newbottle Colliery. Here it was probably used on the section of the waggonway at Philadelphia, between the pits that formed the colliery and the foot of the West Herrington incline. It worked through the winter of 1814 and was then rebuilt with a larger boiler. On its official opening day, 31st July 1815, in front of a great crowd of spectators, it blew up. This was the first railway disaster, with a dozen or more killed, apparently caused by strapping the boiler's safety valve down to give added steam pressure. The exact design of the locomotive is unknown, but it has been established that the engine shown in the patent could not have worked in that form.

The locomotive

Gauge 4ft 2in, built by the Butterley Company, Derbyshire, in September 1814 and assembled at Newbottle in October 1814. Its design is uncertain, but it probably had twin cylinders set horizontally in the boiler backplate giving drive to two jointed legs alternately pushing against the track bed outside the rails and supported on four wheels. Exploded, 31st July 1815.

JOHN GRIMSHAW (c1762-1840)

One of the most elusive and least understood engines is that attributed to John Grimshaw. Nicholas Wood, Stephenson's collaborator, himself a noted engineer and later a leading colliery owner, made a remarkable note in his private diary for 1815, in which he mentioned the trial of an engine whose design and construction predated and hence made invalid Stephenson & Dodds' locomotive patent of that year. According to Wood, the locomotive was trialled at Newbottle, but it is possible that he was in error (see below). The engine's details are unknown, but it seems possible that it used chain-coupling, for which Stephenson and Dodds had claimed rights. If so, its origins are likely to be a pamphlet by William Tindall and John Bottomley of Scarborough, who had proposed the arrangement the previous year, probably directly influenced by William Chapman. Wood goes on to say that the engine was run by Grimshaw of Fatfield and [William] Norvell of Sunderland, both of whom, like Chapman, had strong interests in the local rope-making industry; he was a partner in the first factory to produce machine-made hemp rope. He was instrumental in saving the early cast iron bridge across the Wear at Sunderland from collapse, conducted tests on rail friction and later his support for the Stockton & Darlington Railway was to be a significant factor in its establishment.

Grimshaw is mentioned in another diary as trying, and failing with, a "2 Horse Trevith[ick] Engine" at **Fatfield** the same year, and it could well be that the two are the same. Unfortunately, this description does not necessarily identify the design, as 'Trevithick Engine' was typically used at the time to describe anything that used high pressure steam. Grimshaw leased Fatfield Colliery from J.G.Lambton – whose colliery interests at this date were administered by the Lambton Board, headed by Buddle, which could be significant. Fatfield was one of a number of collieries in the area with short waggonways down to the River Wear near Washington.

> nately broken, and others sustained slight injury.
> On Monday last, a melancholy accident occurred upon the waggon-way, belonging to the owners of Newbottle Colliery. A new boiler having been procured for and annexed to the travelling steam engine, used in drawing the loaden coal waggons up the ascent of the rail-way, it was tried for the first time on the above day, when the engineer, it is supposed, too anxious for its success, had overcharged the boiler with steam which caused it to burst with a tremendous explosion. Upwards of 50 persons, men and children, we lament to say, have been wounded or scalded by the destructive accident. Three persons have already died, viz.:—Wm Sharp, the manager of the engine, who was blown to a considerable distance, and most dreadfully mangled; Wm Nesbitt, one of the overman of the colliery, and John Holmes, a pit-boy. Several others remain in a dangerous state. For the three persons who died immediately, the coroner, in case of the parish, gave permissive warrants for interment, deferring his inquest until the result of the other sufferers, now lingering, should be known.
> The Bishop of St Davids' Premium of ten pounds for

Fig. 7. The explosion of the Brunton locomotive on the Newbottle Waggonway on 31st July 1815, as reported in the Durham County Advertiser of 5th August 1815 – the world's first recorded railway disaster.

The design and fate of the locomotive remains unknown, but the horsepower, only 2, seems excessively low even for the period. Tested on 24th February 1815, it was possibly chain coupled.

GEORGE STEPHENSON (1781-1848)
George Stephenson, despite his famously humble origins, was to be doubly fortunate in his early locomotive work. Firstly, he worked for and had gained the support of his employers, the 'Grand Allies', the most powerful colliery partnership in the region. More correctly Lord Ravensworth & Partners, its members were powerful aristocrats with collieries on both sides of the River Tyne. Secondly, in the process of designing his first engine in 1813-1814, he had the opportunity to observe the nearby locomotives of Blenkinsop on the Kenton & Coxlodge waggonway, those at Wylam and Chapman's engine at Heaton; indeed, it now seems likely that he had direct assistance from both Chapman and Buddle.

The resulting engine was fundamentally that of an adhesion Blenkinsop/Murray, with the general arrangement of boiler, cylinders, motion and gearing bearing a very close relationship to the Leeds design. Completed in 1814 for the **Killingworth Colliery Waggonway**, north-east of Newcastle upon Tyne and owned by the 'Allies', *My Lord* (1) proved only a partial success as an engine but showed the advantages of a pragmatic approach by a practical 'mechanic'. There is some evidence that a second geared engine, probably known as *Blucher*, was also developed in the same year (2).

In late February 1815, Stephenson, together with the Killingworth Colliery viewer, Ralph Dodds, patented a new arrangement in which the connecting rods were coupled directly onto the wheels, with axles combined by chains or a crank. According to Stephenson's collaborator, Nicholas Wood, also employed at Killingworth at this time, a test engine (3) had been earlier tried with the crank but it had broken, and only then had the chain-coupling been developed (hence Wood's anxiety about Grimshaw's engine above) and this design was tested in early February 1815. This was undoubtedly at Killingworth, and the 'Allies' paid the patent expenses.

Stephenson was aware that the deficiencies of the rails were as great a problem as those of the locomotives. Cast iron rails were short and brittle, with a particular weakness at the numerous joints, and with unsprung engines, the jolt was breaking the rail and chipping its edges. His patent of 1816, taken out with William Losh, the owner of the Walker Ironworks in Newcastle upon Tyne, attempted a double solution. For the rail, they developed a half-lap joint to lessen the gap, and for the engine they designed a 'steam spring' which, in effect, attempted to act as a shock-absorber between boiler and axle by using steam pressure. This, with the 1815 chain-coupled direct drive, was to be the standard Stephenson arrangement for his colliery locomotives up to 1826 (4). Improved and tested over several years, the Killingworth designs developed in conjunction with Nicholas Wood were to prove practical and popular; but surprisingly, there are very few surviving details of the colliery locomotive stock at Killingworth and the actual type, number and fate of the engines used there remains speculative.

Stephenson's locomotives for the **Hetton Railway** (see chapter 8) were built on the same plan. The texts state that the railway opened in November 1822 with five of his locomotives. However, recent reseaches have thrown considerable doubt on this. It now appears that Stephenson provided only three brand new engines for the line (5,6,7), and that the total rose to four during 1823 and to five later still. These two additional engines were very possibly second-hand, one perhaps from Killingworth and the other, illustrated in an 1834 Hetton account book, (see Chapman & Buddle, 3/4 above) perhaps the *Steam Elephant*, a similar locomotive. All five had been scrapped by 1850. Research now shows that the famous '1822' Hetton engine that supposedly survived and worked until about 1911 was in fact a new-build in the early 1850s in traditional style.

It is uncertain where Stephenson's locomotives were made. Those for Killingworth are said traditionally to have been built at the colliery; however, there is some evidence that the first may have been built at the colliery's Long Benton Pit and that one or more were built at the Walker Ironworks in Newcastle on Tyne of Losh, Wilson & Bell. The Hetton locomotives could have been built at Killingworth or Walker, or possibly at the new Hetton Colliery workshops established there by George's brother Robert, although some imported skilled labour would have been needed.

The simple but effective 'Killingworth' design was to be the most successful design type of the pioneering period. One worked at Llansamlet in South Wales and another, six-wheeled and for plate rails, was made for the Kilmarnock & Troon Railway in Scotland. The problems they experienced on the Hetton Railway are detailed in chapter 8. The first six locomotives built by Robert Stephenson & Co, established at Forth Banks in Newcastle upon Tyne in 1823, were to the same general plan: *Locomotion* and the three that followed for the Stockton & Darlington Railway in 1825 incorporated parallel motion; the two for the Springwell Colliery Railway in 1826 (see chapter 3) had traditional slide bars. All used side rods for coupling, although the patent steam springs were to be later phased out.

The locomotives
All those built for the North-East were 4ft 8in/4ft 8½in gauge, had twin vertical cylinders, slide bar motion and four wheels.

For Killingworth Colliery, with 8in x 24in cylinders
1. *My Lord*, built 1814; geared; possibly converted to a stationary engine at Wallsend staiths after 1830.
2. *Blucher*, believed built in 1814 and similar to (1)

Fig. 8. A drawing of one of the Hetton locomotives, included in Thomas Tredgold, A Practical Treatise on Rail-roads and Carriages, published in 1825.

Fig. 9. A lithograph of Hetton Colliery by J.D.Harding, dated to about 1825.

3. possibly called *X Y Z*, built in 1815, chain coupled
4. possibly called *Flying Childers*, built in 1816 and similar to (3) but with steam springs

At least one of these engines was built with, or had been converted to, side-rod coupling by 1831. One engine was possibly sent to the Hetton Railway.

For the Hetton Railway, with 9in x 24in cylinders, chain coupled and steam springs and built in 1821-1822

5. *Dart*
6. *Tallyho*
7. *Star*

All of these had been scrapped by the 1850s. See also the text above.

By 1825, and the opening of the Stockton & Darlington Railway, the pioneering period of the steam locomotive was coming to an end. Robert Stephenson & Co, the first locomotive-building firm, had been established in Newcastle upon Tyne, practical engine designs and rails were available and in the following few years the railway industry was formed, with the basic principles of railway transport established. The difficult, and often unsuccessful, experimental work had been concentrated on the waggonways of Durham and Northumberland.

It had not developed easily; it would be mistaken to assume that the locomotive was instantly embraced as the logical answer to the transport problems of the day. All four of Trevithick's locomotives failed to be taken up. Two are known to have broken rails and it seems to have been a problem that he was unwilling to solve. Following the failure of *Catch Me Who Can*, there would be no further attempts at an engine to haul passengers for over twenty years, and no more locomotive experiments at all until 1812.

That these experiments should then be concentrated so markedly in the North-East is attributable to a combination of factors. The region's economy was centred on the export of coal from the Rivers Tyne and Wear, and these were served, in the complete absence of canals, almost exclusively by waggonways, with transport charges a significant expense per ton. The Napoleonic Wars led to greatly-increased costs in the use of horses, hence concentrating minds on improving efficiency and finding alternatives, especially when there was little opportunity to reduce the costs of mining itself. Conversion to iron rails and rope haulage were eventually successfully adopted; but it was the locomotive that promised savings on an epic scale. Thus the problems of its development were addressed by local colliery engineers and mechanics, and paid for by colliery owners who glimpsed the potential benefits.

By the middle of 1815 it must have seemed that the battle to establish the locomotive was nearing victory; despite many set-backs, engines were to be seen at Wylam, Heaton, Kenton & Coxlodge, Wallsend, Newbottle, Lambton and Killingworth Collieries. It turned out to be something of a false dawn; by the end of that year locomotives were only working at Wylam and Killingworth. The causes were several – explosion (Newbottle), mine closure (Heaton), alleged sabotage (Kenton & Coxlodge) and rail problems (Lambton and Wallsend). From Trevithick's time, the expense, weaknesses and brittle nature of cast iron rails had bedevilled the take-up of the locomotive. The engines were heavier than the waggons and their weight, lack of springing and operating stresses were often too much for the rails. Heavier castings were uneconomic, and so the designs of the time either had to spread the weight further (such as at Wylam and with the Chapman engines) or keep it to an absolute minimum, making water capacity and steam generation a fundamental problem until the development of the stronger malleable iron rail in the early 1820s.

The set-backs and expensive failures of 1815 were emphasized by a change in economic circumstances that same year. Following Wellington's victory at Waterloo, the end of the Napoleonic Wars saw an easing in the general costs of horse haulage. Then as iron rails replaced wood, their greatly-reduced friction enabled a horse to pull a load two or three times greater than before. Self-acting inclined planes proved to be simple and efficient, while rope haulage by stationary engine was developing increasing power and reliability. The balance had shifted against the experimental technology of the locomotive, which had proved too often to be more expensive and less dependable than had been hoped.

The development of the locomotive was now carried on only by Chapman and Stephenson, supported by their powerful sponsors, the backing of the collieries controlled by John Buddle and the 'Grand Allies' at Killingworth. Of the pioneers of these years, it would be George Stephenson who would be best remembered. The others remained colliery or general engineers; only Stephenson nailed his personal career to the mast, to the development of the locomotive and to the future as a railway engineer, appreciating the possibilities of a steam transport system rather than focussing on a local problem of traction power. Killingworth and Hetton would lead to Darlington and Liverpool, *My Lord* to *Locomotion*. It was to his great benefit to have his innate conservatism tempered by the fresh ambitions and abilities of his son Robert, allowing *Rocket* and *Planet* to spearhead a new generation of engines with abilities far beyond the slow, short-distance, heavy-haulage waggonway engine.

The development of the railway locomotive had its roots deep in Durham and Northumberland – intended for coal transport, designed by colliery engineers and paid for by coal money. Its use was to be a core feature of industry in the region until mining itself died in the 1980s and 1990s; but its influence was to shape fundamentally the Industrial Revolution as it spread world-wide.

Chapter Two
The Beamish Railway

OWNERS BEFORE 1947
The Lambton, Hetton & Joicey Collieries Ltd until 1/1/1947
James Joicey & Co Ltd until 26/11/1924
James Joicey & Co until 8/1/1886; see also below

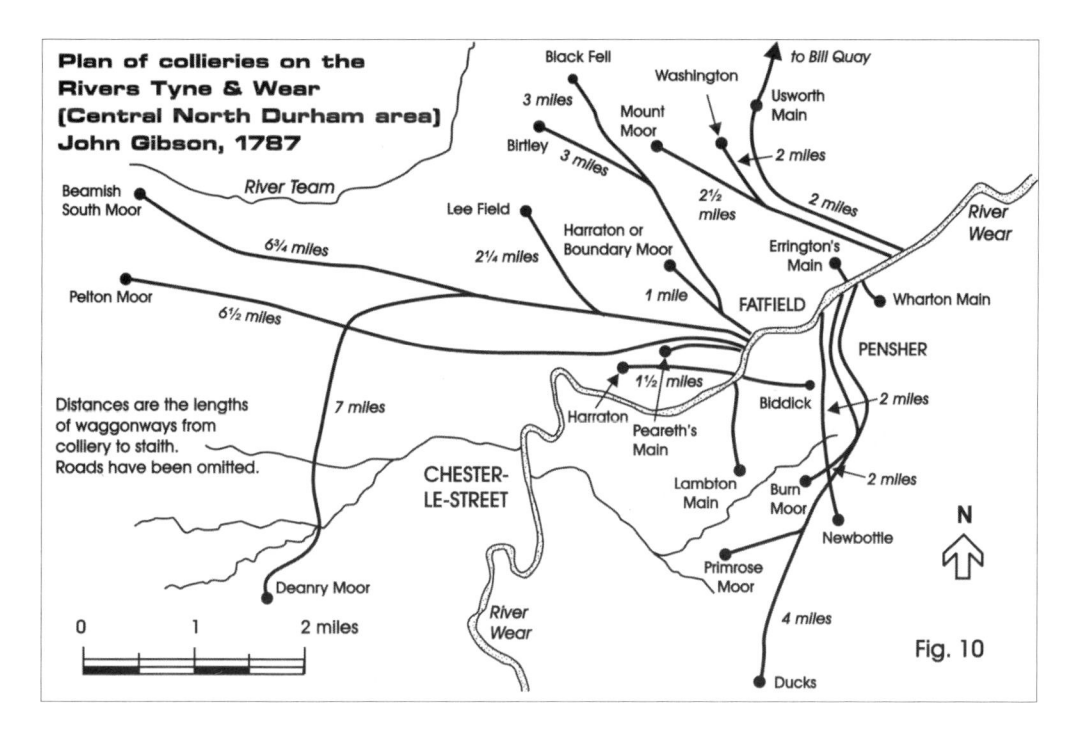

Plan of collieries on the Rivers Tyne & Wear (Central North Durham area) John Gibson, 1787

Fig. 10

This railway developed from a wooden waggonway built in 1763 to take coal from collieries in the Beamish area to staiths on the River Wear at Fatfield. It was rare amongst Durham waggonways in running west to east, whereas the vast majority ran from south to north. The earliest map to show the line is the *Plan of the Collieries on the Rivers Tyne & Wear,* by John Gibson, 1787, the first map to show the general waggonway system serving the two rivers (Fig.10). The line's far western extremity was **Beamish South Moor Colliery** near Stanley, which had previously been served by the old Shield Row Waggonway. From Beamish South Moor Colliery to the staiths is given on the map as 6¾ miles, with the line crossing the Great North Road between Chester-le-Street and Birtley. Two branches are shown, one from just west of the Great North Road running south and south-westwards for about three miles to serve **Deanry Moor Colliery**, situated between the later villages of Craghead and Waldridge, and a second branch about a mile long

running north-westwards to serve **Lee Field Colliery**, situated alongside the Great North Road about a mile north of the previously-mentioned level crossing. At this date the whole system would have been worked by horses.

The branches to Deanry Moor and Lee Field Collieries do not appear on nineteenth century maps, and were clearly short-lived. An untitled map attributed to about 1833 shows the line running to **South Moor Colliery** (but a different colliery from Beamish South Moor Colliery above) and shows two collieries in the Beamish area, one called **Beamish Colliery** and the other un-named; but eastwards from here the old route appears to have been abandoned in favour of a new line to serve **Ouston Colliery** before turning north-eastwards, where a short branch from an un-named colliery, probably **Urpeth Colliery**, joined. A little further east a system of short branches brought coal from pits comprising **Harraton Colliery** to the line, before it continued to the

15

staiths at Fatfield. This reference illustrates the difficulties in researching waggonway history, for in addition to the South Moor Colliery problem above, there is well-established evidence that Ouston and Urpeth Collieries were served by both their own line to the River Wear, and more importantly, by the Ouston Waggonway to the River Tyne (see the chapter on the Pelaw Main Railway), which this map does not show at all. If the Beamish line ever did serve Ouston and Urpeth Collieries the detour was certainly short-lived, and the original line via Pelton was soon re-instated.

By the early 1830s the Waggonway was owned by a Morton John Davison, a local landowner. In 1832 he was approached by the newly-formed Stanhope & Tyne Railroad Company, who wished to purchase the waggonway in order for it to form part of the Stanhope & Tyne's route between Stanhope and South Shields; but the two sides failed to agree a price, and the Stanhope & Tyne was compelled to construct its line slightly to the south.

According to correspondence dated 1832 quoted in W.W.Tomlinson's *The North Eastern Railway* (1915), the gauge of the line at this date was 4ft 4in, and about this time it was re-laid with iron rails. It may be that it was when this was done that the gauge was altered to 4ft 8½in, and the rope haulage described below was introduced, but firm information is lacking. The line as shown on Bell's *Map of the Great Northern Coalfield*, published in 1843, is shown in Fig.11.

The 1st edition of the Ordnance Survey maps, surveyed in 1857, shows that by this date various changes had taken place. The section between South Moor Colliery and Beamish had been lifted, Beamish Colliery then being the western extremity of the line. The O.S. map also appears to show a second extension from Beamish, also then lifted, curving northwards to a junction south of Causey with what in 1857 was the North Eastern Railway's Tanfield Branch. The northern part of this route was part of the old Tanfield Way's Causey branch, begun in 1725 and subsequently extended twice (see *A Fighting Trade – Rail Transport in Tyne Coal, 1600-1800* by G.Bennett, E.Clavering & A.Rounding, published by Portcullis Press in 1990). For it to be shown on an O.S. map the trackbed is more likely to be nineteenth than eighteenth century in origin; but the rebuilt Tanfield Waggonway was not re-opened by the Brandling Junction Railway until 26th November 1839, so if there was a link between the two lines it must again have been short-lived.

East of Pelton the waggonway was crossed by what was now the North Eastern Railway's Pontop & South Shields Branch, and the O.S. map shows that a north-facing connection had been installed between the waggonway and the northern end of the Vigo West Incline, presumably to allow Beamish coal to be shipped at South Shields, rather than Fatfield. This in turn had led to the abandonment of the waggonway east of here, except for the section still used by Harraton Colliery, owned by the Earl of Durham; the track on this section was still in place in 1921, but it would seem unlikely that any coal was shipped at Fatfield after 1890-1900.

The waggonway was also crossed just west of the Durham turnpike road by a branch from the Ouston waggonway (see chapter 11), which joined the Pontop & South Shields line at the southern end of Vigo West bank foot.

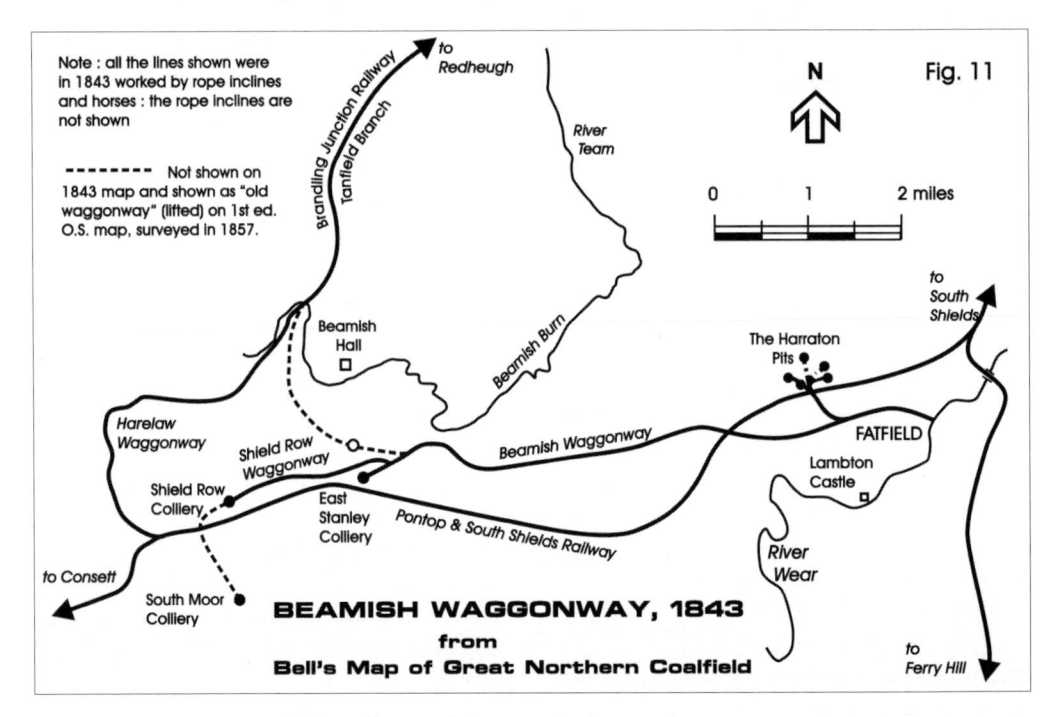

BEAMISH WAGGONWAY, 1843
from
Bell's Map of Great Northern Coalfield

Fig. 11

Fig. 12

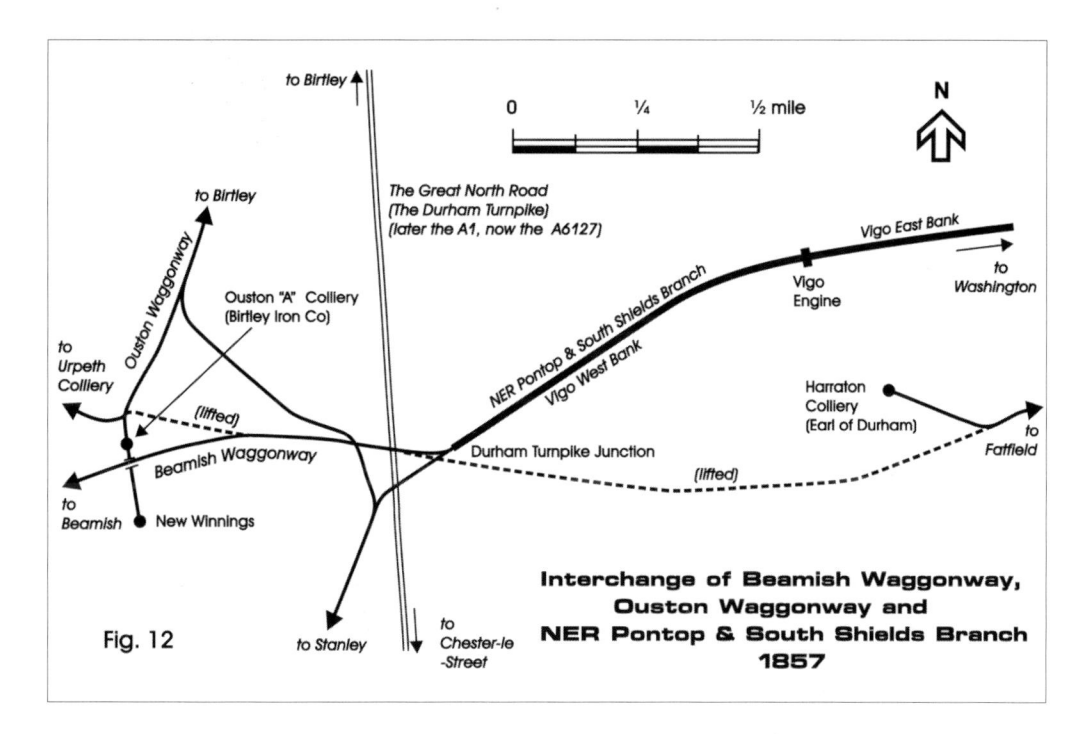

Interchange of Beamish Waggonway, Ouston Waggonway and NER Pontop & South Shields Branch 1857

In the second quarter of the nineteenth century there was an ever-increasing demand for Durham coal for steam, gas and coke making, as well as for household purposes. Not only were the Durham aristocracy and landowners often coal owners, but others, often from the working class, came forward, determined to better themselves and to succeed. One of these was James Joicey (1806-1863). The eldest son of a colliery deputy at Backworth in Northumberland, he began by opening a school in his home village. A biography in the *Newcastle Weekly Chronicle* of 19th June 1880 states that he then moved to Durham, where with an engineer called Joseph Smith he was involved in the winning of South Hetton Colliery (1833), the construction of its railway to Seaham, and 'undertook the formation of a new railway to Hartlepool', presumably the Hartlepool Dock & Railway. He next purchased a collier brig to enter the London coal trade, and prospered so well that in either 1837 or 1838 he was able to lease his first colliery, Oxhill Colliery, near Annfield Plain, later called **South Tanfield Colliery** (NZ 179521). At first this was worked jointly with Smith, but the latter left after nine months. Seeing the growing market for colliery machinery and engineering work, James and his second brother George (1813-1856) set up in 1849 the company of J & G Joicey, initially to operate a foundry in Pottery Bank, Newcastle upon Tyne; but from 1854 the firm entered the manufacture of winding engines and general colliery and engineering equipment, together with an unknown number of locomotives. In later years this firm was controlled by George's eldest son, Jacob (1843-1899); it was closed down in 1925.

Meanwhile, on 1st January 1850 James went into partnership with his third brother John (1816-1881), having by then also acquired **Twizell Colliery** (NZ 223524), near West Pelton, opened in 1844, and **Tanfield Lea Colliery** (NZ 188544), opened in 1831. These three collieries were operated under the titles of **The Owners of South Tanfield Colliery**, etc. Their next major development, sometime between 1850 and 1852, was the leasing of **Beamish Colliery**, comprising then of the Air and East Stanley Pits (see below) and its railway to Fatfield. On 1st January 1853 their youngest brother Edward (1824-1879) joined the partnership and it may be from this date that the business took the title **James Joicey & Co**; it was certainly the title used when the partnership was revised four years later. Under James Joicey's energetic ownership development was soon underway. The colliery was modernised, including the installation of a new Joicey-built winder at the Second Pit in 1855, while workshops were built nearby to service the shafts and the railway.

By the 1870s there had been radical changes in the Ouston area. The NER line southwards from Gateshead down the Team Valley to Durham had been fully opened on 1st December 1868, and this may have played a part in the decision to replace the former junction between the Beamish Waggonway and the Pontop & South Shields branch at the northern end of the former Vigo Bank Foot by a new, but northern-facing junction where the Ouston branch junction with the branch had been, the two private railways joining just west of the bridge carrying them over the NER Team Valley line. The former Ouston waggonway junction here had been known as Durham Turnpike Junction to the men, but when the Beamish Railway joined there the name was changed to Beamish Junction, although the old name continued in colloquial use.

From Beamish Junction the line rose steeply westwards, climbing some 300 feet in 3½ miles to reach the village of Pit Hill, later called Beamish. A document of April 1880 (DCRO/NCB 7/1/10) shows that for much of the first two miles the gradients varied between 1 in 22 and 1 in 38. To the west of Beamish village was the first of the three coal-producing shafts known as **BEAMISH COLLIERY (SECOND PIT)**, also known as the **CHOP HILL PIT** (NZ 221537), which was served via a ½ mile branch. The sinking of this pit had begun on 17th April 1824. About 200 yards to the west the line divided. The northern arm (½ mile) went on to serve the **AIR PIT** (NZ 212535), which was sunk in 1849. The southern arm (¾ mile) ran south-westwards to serve **EAST STANLEY COLLIERY** (NZ 213529), which appears to have been sunk by at least 1833. Served by a short spur to the line immediately north of the branch to Beamish Second Colliery was **BEAMISH ENGINE WORKS** (NZ 222537), This was a typical workshops complex of the period, with single-storey buildings flanking four sides of an open courtyard; similar examples were found at the original Lambton Engine Works (see chapter 9), at Chilton Moor Shops (see chapter 10) and at Springwell (see chapter 3), the last now preserved.

Information about the operation of the Railway during the second half of the nineteenth century is extremely scarce, almost the only source being a series of descriptions of the collieries in the Supplement to the *Mining Journal* dated 11th February 1871. The description mentions a **stationary engine at Pit Hill** (NZ 227534) and says that it worked two inclines, one 1½ miles long at 1 in 40, the other ¾ mile long on the other side by main-and-tail haulage. The longer incline is clearly that on the eastern side, and 1½ miles would place the bank foot slightly north-east of the village of Pelton, where indeed the 1st edition Ordnance Survey map shows the line becoming double track. The ¾ mile of main-and-tail haulage, thus on the western side of the engine, proves to be the distance between the engine house and the junction of the Beamish and East Stanley branches. How the branches to the Engine Works and the Second Pit fitted in to the main-and-tail working is again unknown. This leaves the two branches, and unfortunately the Supplement's descriptions are far from clear. The description of the Air Pit includes "A beam engine is used for hauling wagons near the pit", while that for East Stanley Colliery says "A beam engine, formerly a winding engine, is now used as a wagon hauling engine from the bank head to a point above the screens, 100 yards." The assumption in both cases must be that these beam engines were situated at the collieries, but the reference to "bank head" would seem incorrect, as the end of the main-and-tail haulage would have been the bank foot. Despite these problems, it would seem that in 1871 the whole system was still operated by rope haulage, certainly as far east as Pelton. How the remaining distance from the bank foot to Durham Turnpike Junction was operated is unknown, but presumably horses were used. Return 102 of the Durham Coal Owners Association (DCRO NCB1/Co/86/102), which collected information about railway operation in April 1871 and November 1876, also lists two stationary engines at Beamish Colliery in April 1871, which presumably refers to those at the Air Pit and at East Stanley.

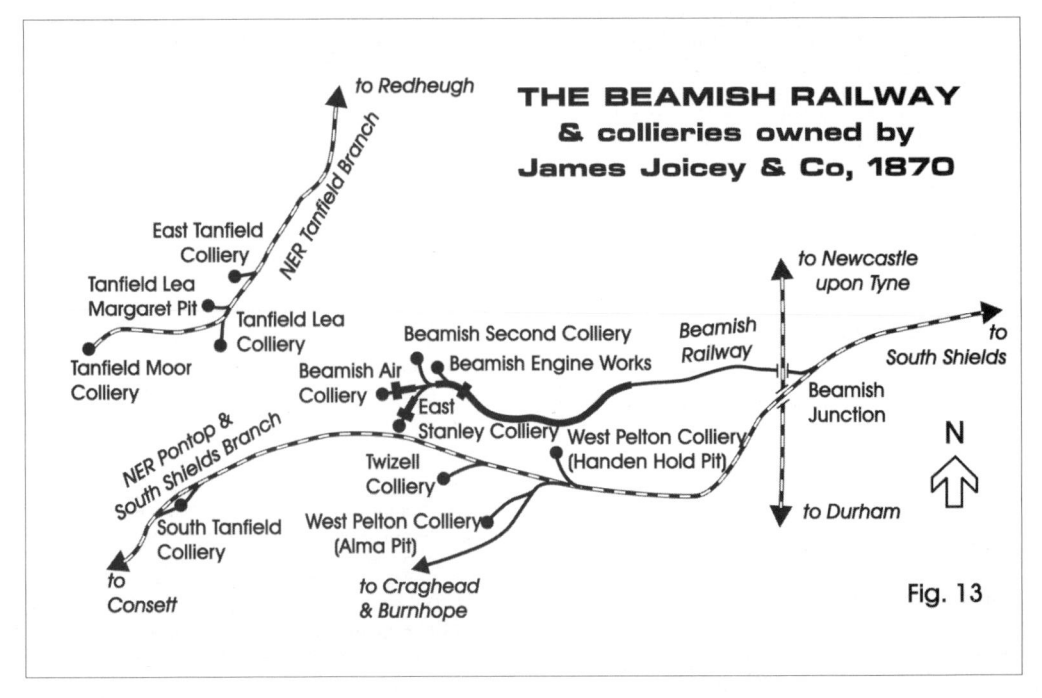

Fig. 13

4. STANLEY, RS 2014/1872, long derelict at Handen Hold Colliery, and brought to Beamish Engine Works in 1951 for an overhaul that by 22nd March 1961 was far from finished.

The visit of the Supplement's journalist in 1871 is fortunate, as in the following year what seem to be the first two locomotives arrived. The section of DCOA Return 102 for November 1876 lists two locomotives, but still lists one stationary engine. The 1880 document mentioned above, a renewal of the lease for the first two miles west from Beamish Junction, refers to rope haulage, which can only be that operated by the "Pit Hill Engine", so that presumably the engine houses replaced by locomotive working were those at East Stanley and the Air Pit. To house the locomotives one wing of Beamish Engine Works was converted into a long, one-road, **loco shed**.

In October 1883 the firm began the sinking of a new shaft, the **MARY PIT** (NZ 211536) just west of the Air Pit, the line being extended from there to serve it; the sinking was completed in December 1886. From Beamish Mary Pit to Durham Turnpike Junction was 4¾ miles. It was probably also in the 1880s that a link with the Pelaw Main Railway (which see), owned by The Birtley Iron Co, was put in just to the east of Pelton bank foot. This allowed the Iron Company to bring in traffic from the NER for destinations as far north as Birtley, including the independent firms that that Railway served, and to dispatch their traffic, though very little coal traffic was included. On 13th November 1893 the North Eastern Railway opened the remainder of the Annfield Plain deviation route, built to provide a locomotive-worked alternative to the central section of the Pontop & South Shields branch. This passed through Beamish, close to the Railway, but there was no connection between the two lines. The 2nd edition of the Ordnance Survey, published in 1896, shows that at this date the section between Chop Hill and Pelton was still a rope incline, the layout showing that fulls and empties were worked simultaneously. When locomotive haulage was introduced on this section is not known, though the purchase of an additional locomotive in 1904 could be significant.

The firm was never a major player in the Durham coke industry, but there were beehive coke ovens at Beamish, the last of these, at Beamish Mary Colliery, being closed on 31st July 1919.

In 1862 James, John and Edward Joicey were joined by William James (1836-1912), James' illegitimate son. In the following year James died, having just seen George's second son, James (1846-1936), begin working for the firm as a clerk. In 1867 he became a partner, eventually coming to control the firm and see it converted to a limited company on 8th January 1886. On 3rd July 1893 James Joicey was created a baronet, and raised to baron on 13th January 1906. On 1st July 1896 he manoeuvred the Earl of Durham into selling to him all the Lambton collieries, railways and other industrial activities (see Lambton Railway), setting up a new company, The Lambton Collieries Ltd, to run the business. In 1911 he similarly left Sir Lindsay Wood with no alternative but to sell him The Hetton Coal Co Ltd and The North Hetton Coal Co Ltd (see Hetton Railway), absorbing them to form The Lambton & Hetton Collieries Ltd. In November 1924 James Joicey & Co Ltd was put into voluntary liquidation and its business amalgamated with The Lambton & Hetton Collieries Ltd to form a new company, **The Lambton, Hetton & Joicey Collieries Ltd**, still with Lord Joicey as chairman. This new firm was

5. No.5, MAJOR, K 4294/1905, climbing the bank from Pelton to West Pelton with eleven empties, in the 1950s.

registered on 26th November 1924, although it did not purchase the assets of James Joicey & Co Ltd, for £293,246, until 18th August 1925. At this date Lambton & Hetton controlled 20,000 acres raising 2,860,000 tons and Joicey 6,000 acres raising 2,060,000 tons, making the new company the largest coal company in the world. The family retained control until nationalisation, firstly under James' elder son, Arthur (1880-1940), and then his younger son, Hugh (1881-1966), respectively 2nd and 3rd Baron Joicey.

Besides Beamish Colliery, the firm also owned **EAST TANFIELD COLLIERY** (NZ 194552) near Tanfield, closed at the end of 1913; **HANDEN HOLD COLLIERY** (NZ 233526) at West Pelton and formerly known as **WEST PELTON COLLIERY (Handenhold Pit)**; **SOUTH TANFIELD COLLIERY** (NZ 179521), near Annfield Plain, closed in November 1914; **TANFIELD LEA COLLIERY** (NZ 188544) at Tanfield Lea; **TWIZELL COLLIERY** (NZ 223524) near West Pelton, **WEST PELTON COLLIERY**, also known as **West Pelton Colliery (Alma Pit)** (NZ 232515), which was also linked by a narrow gauge tramway to **TWIZELL BURN DRIFT** (NZ 246518), and **TANFIELD MOOR COLLIERY** (NZ 171553) at White-le-Head, none of them very far from Beamish. All of these except Tanfield Moor Colliery and Twizell Burn Drift are known to have had locomotives, and it may well be that they were sent to Beamish Engine Works for repairs – at least one was sent and scrapped there – but no records of such movements survive. At Beamish the Air Pit closed in 1911, its workings being merged with the Mary Pit, and about this time the colliery was re-organised into three collieries, **BEAMISH MARY COLLIERY**, **BEAMISH SECOND COLLIERY** and **EAST STANLEY COLLIERY**.

The Joicey Group of collieries was an official sub-division of the company's activities, and these changes had little or no impact on the Beamish Railway; so far as is known, no Lambton Railway locomotives ever came to Beamish, though two old Hetton Railway locomotives were sent to Handen Hold Colliery, while no Beamish locomotives ever went to Lambton Engine Works for repairs. The normal allocation at Beamish was five locomotives. Of these, three were "lead" engines, handling the traffic between Beamish and Pelton, with two at work and one spare, washing out or under repair, while the remaining two were "pilots", handling colliery shunting, with one working and one spare.

In 1931 the company began to mine coal in the grounds of Beamish Hall, via two drifts at NZ 215552 and NZ 218543. These were administratively part of Beamish Second Colliery, which then became **BEAMISH SECOND & PARK COLLIERY**. Coal from the northernmost drift was hauled across the surface between the two drifts by an underground hauler to a landing in the second drift, whence a second hauler took them on to the Beamish Second Pit shaft bottom. The description of the working suggests that both were main-and-tail rope haulages. Both the colliery and the drifts closed later in the 1930s, but were all re-opened in 1944. On the debit side East Stanley Colliery was closed in the summer of 1939. Beamish Mary Colliery and Beamish Second & Park Colliery, together with Beamish Engine Works, were vested in NCB Northern Division No.5 (Mid-West Durham) Area on 1st January 1947.

6. 3, TWIZELL, RS 2730/1891, rounding the curve near Beamish Engine Works on empties for Beamish Mary Colliery.

7. TANFIELD, Joicey 377/1885, awaiting scrap at Beamish Engine Works, 5th May 1935.

NATIONAL COAL BOARD

Northumberland & Durham Division No.5 Area from 1/1/1964
Durham Division No.5 (Mid-West Durham) Area from 1/1/1950; this Area was divided between Nos.4 and 6 Areas on 1/1/1963, with the enlarged No.6 Area then being re-numbered No.5 Area
Northern Division No.5 (Mid-West Durham) Area from 1/1/1947

8. Beamish Engine Works loco shed, 18th November 1950.

As well as continuing to be responsible for the locomotives at Handen Hold Colliery (see above), in the organisation of No. 5 Area affairs that followed nationalisation in 1947, Beamish Engine Works was also given the responsibility for the maintenance of the locomotives on the Sacriston Railway (which see), which closed in February 1955. A locomotive from Handen Hold Colliery also travelled over the BR Pontop & South Shields branch to reach **ALMA COLLIERY** (see above), which was re-opened by the NCB and worked until 28th November 1958. Locomotives Nos.3-5, 40 and 503 received Railway Executive plates for travelling over BR lines at Durham Turnpike Junction or at Handen Hold Colliery.

In 1954 it was decided to construct a new coal washery at Handen Hold Colliery, whence coal would be dispatched down the BR Pontop & South Shields line. To allow Beamish coal to be washed here a ½ mile link was to be built between the two lines just east of Handen Hold Colliery, which in turn would allow the steeply-graded section of the Railway between West Pelton and Durham Turnpike Junction to be abandoned. This was constructed during 1954-1955, the NCB using Thos W. Ward Ltd as the contractors. It involved a reverse at the Railway end of the link, and so the former double line track at Pit Hill was converted into a run-round loop, although in practice the wagons were run past the loco by gravity in order for the loco to change ends. A cabin and a water crane were also provided here. The section east of West Pelton was closed by mid 1955 and had been lifted by March 1957. This closure also brought to an end the link with the Pelaw Main Railway at Beamish Junction, mentioned above.

Drift mining in Beamish Park ceased in 1958, and Beamish Second Colliery closed on 9th November 1962, leaving the Beamish Engine Works shed with only one locomotive duty and the whole system

9. *A major repair that Beamish Engine Works did complete: 40, RS 1919/1868, formerly Hetton Railway No.7, at Handen Hold Colliery, West Pelton, in 1953.*

10. *Looking east from the sand cabin and watering point at Chop Hill, 28th March 1966.*

needing only two working locomotives. Beamish Engine Works and its loco shed closed on 7th August 1963, the shed's one remaining duty being transferred to Handen Hold, though the buildings survived for some years afterwards. When Beamish Mary Colliery closed on 26th March 1966 the remainder of the Railway closed with it. The line was unusual amongst Durham's private railways in not having its own rolling stock, certainly not in the twentieth century, with NER/LNER and British Railways wagons being used for coal traffic.

Handen Hold Colliery continued to use a locomotive for shunting until 13th January 1967, when the work was taken over by BR. The colliery closed on 1st March 1968.

Several sections of the Railway and the waggonways mentioned are now roads. The J & G Joicey vertical winding engine, built in 1855, from Beamish Second Colliery, is now preserved in full working order (steam) in its rebuilt engine house and screens at the colliery site at Beamish, The North of England Open Air Museum, together with a curious disc signal originally located near a level crossing at West Pelton. The Mahogany Drift, the southernmost of the drifts in Beamish Park, has been re-opened for underground visits by visitors. The Museum's entrance is only a few yards from the route of the Railway.

11 (left). The disc signal guarding the level crossing between Chop Hill and West Pelton, 28th March 1966.

12. 503, RSHN 7605/1949, being coaled up outside its shed at Handen Hold Colliery, West Pelton, on 17th June 1965.

The loco sheds are coded as follows:
    BEW Beamish Engine Works, Beamish (Note: some transfers may have been for repairs in the Works)
      HH Handen Hold Colliery, West Pelton (only locomotives transferred to and from Beamish Engine Works are shown, plus the one transfer here after Beamish Engine Works had closed)

Gauge : 4ft 8½in

(1)	(BEAMISH)	0-6-0T	IC	RS	2013	1872	New		
	BEW								(1)
(2)	STANLEY	0-6-0T	IC	RS	2014	1872	New		
	BEW-HH by 5/6/1937-BEW (repairs) /1951								(2)
3	TWIZELL	0-6-0T	IC	RS	2730	1891	New		
	BEW-HH c7/1951(after 6/1951, by 9/1951)-BEW c12/1952 (after 9/1951, by 6/1952)								
	-HH /1957 (after 11/1956, by 3/1958)-BEW /1958 (after 3/1958, by 7/1958)								
	-W.G.Bagnall Ltd, Stafford, repairs, /1960-HH c1/1961-BEW c8/1961								
	-HH 29/7/1963 (NCB records gave 7/8/1963)								(3)

4	LINHOPE		0-6-0T	IC	RS	2822	1895	New	

BEW-Robert Stephenson & Co Ltd, Darlington, for repairs, by 25/6/1934
-BEW ?/?-HH by 2/4/1949-BEW ?/?-HH c/1953 (after 7/1952, by 4/1954)
-BEW c/1955 (after 30/8/1954, by 7/1956)-HH c5/1958 (after 4/1958, by 7/1958)
-BEW 15/7/1958-HH c5/1960 (after 4/1960, by 6/1960)
-BEW c6/1960 (by 7/1960)   (4)

No.5	MAJOR		0-6-0T	IC	K	4294	1905	New	
				reb	HL	2812	1931	*	

BEW-Brandon Colliery, Brandon, loan, 6/10/1949-BEW 27/3/1950
-Robert Stephenson & Hawthorns Ltd, Newcastle upon Tyne, repairs, by 7/1956
-BEW 11/1957-HH 29/7/1963 (NCB records gave 7/8/63)   (5)

	(TANFIELD)		0-4-0ST	OC	Joicey	377	1885	(a)	Scr c/1935
40			0-6-0ST	IC	RS	1919	1869		
				reb	HL	1182	1930	(b)	

HH-BEW c8/1951(after 6/1951, by 9/1951)-HH by 2/1952
-BEW /1954 for repairs (after 7/1953, by 4/1954)   Scr 11/1955

	CECIL		0-6-0T	IC	HC	1524	1924	(c)	
	BEW								(6)
503	"SACRISTON"		0-4-0ST	OC	RSHN	7605	1949	(d)	

BEW-HH after 7/1958, by 15/4/1959-BEW by 8/1959-HH c9/1959 (after 8/1959, by 10/1959)
-BEW c5/1960 (after 4/1960, by 6/1960)-HH 6/1960-BEW c/1962 (after 10/1960, by 6/1962)
-HH c8/1962 (after 6/1962, by 9/1962)   Scr 4/1969

	MARGARET		0-6-0ST	IC	AB	1005	1904		
				reb	AB	8833	1924	(e)	

BEW-HH c1/1958(by 2/1958)-BEW c4/1959 (after 15/4/1959, by 5/1959)   (7)

37			0-6-0ST	OC	HL	3528	1922	(f)	
	HH								Scr 4/1969

* after a new firebox was fitted at Robert Stephenson & Hawthorns Ltd, Newcastle upon Tyne, in 1957 the Hawthorn Leslie rebuild plate was altered to read rebuilt HL 2812/1957

(a) ex Twizell Colliery, near West Pelton, by 5/5/1935
(b) ex The Lambton, Hetton & Joicey Collieries Ltd, Handen Hold Colliery, West Pelton, 1/1/1947; formerly Lambton Railway, 40, originally Hetton Railway, 7
(c) ex Sacriston Railway, Bank Foot Loco Shed, Waldridge, 5/1955 (by 4/5/1955)
(d) ex Sacriston Railway, Sacriston Colliery, Sacriston, /1955 (after 7/1955, by 7/1956)
(e) ex Sacriston Railway, Bank Foot Loco Shed, Waldridge, 11/1955 (by 30/11/1955)
(f) ex Craghead Colliery, Craghead, 1/7/1966

(1) said to have been scrapped c/1939, but its frames and four wheels were used for many years after this as a carrier for heavy loads such as boilers; it was recorded at Handen Hold Colliery in 11/1950 and at Beamish in 1953; it was not recorded here on 30/8/1954
(2) a new boiler was purchased in 1952 and a major rebuild was begun in 1955, but the work was never completed; the loco was sold for scrap on 25/7/1961 and is believed to have been scrapped on site during 12/1961
(3) to Morrison Busty Colliery, Annfield Plain, 14/2/1968; sold to what was then called the North Regional Museum for preservation, and moved to Marley Hill Loco Shed store, Sunniside, 3/1972; now preserved at Beamish, The North of England Open Air Museum, but moved to Tanfield Railway, Marley Hill, for restoration, 10/3/1995
(4) sold for scrap to Thos W Ward Ltd, Middlesbrough, 23/7/1963; the loco may have been moved to Handen Hold Colliery for cutting up; as late as 29/12/1966 a visitor saw the locomotive's dome and wheels there
(5) to Derwenthaugh Loco Shed, Swalwell (see Chopwell & Garesfield Railway), 12/4/1966; scrapped on site by D.Sep.Bowran Ltd, Gateshead, 5/1970
(6) to Bearpark Colliery, Bearpark, 20/2/1957; thence to Brandon Colliery, Meadowfield, 13/3/1957, and to Bank Foot Coke Ovens, Crook, by 19/5/1957 (NCB records gave 13/3/1959, in error); to Roddymoor Colliery, Crook 21/11/1960 (paper transfer); thence to Brancepeth Colliery, Willington 18/10/1961, loan; made an official transfer, 26/3/1962; sold for scrap to C.Herring & Sons Ltd, Hartlepool, and dispatched from colliery, 23/11/1964
(7) to Brandon Colliery, Meadowfield, 8/1959; thence to Brancepeth Colliery, Willington, 25/1/1960; scrapped on site by Scott & Ellis, Sunderland, 6/1962

Chapter Three
The Bowes Railway
called the Pontop & Jarrow Railway between 1853 and 1932

OWNERS BEFORE 1947
John Bowes & Partners Ltd until 1/1/1947
John Bowes, Esq., & Partners until 21/7/1886; see also below

This was one of largest private railways in Durham. It was created in the mid-1850s by the linking of two older lines, the Springwell Colliery Railway and the Marley Hill Railway.

SPRINGWELL COLLIERY RAILWAY
Lord Ravensworth & Partners until 1/1/1850

This partnership of colliery owners, known locally as "The Grand Allies", was at the beginning of the nineteenth century the most powerful in the country. It had been made between the families of Wortley, Ord, Liddell and Bowes, to run for ninety nine years from November 1726. It was renewed when that term expired, the partnership by then owning collieries in both Durham and Northumberland. Sir Henry Liddell had been created Baron Ravensworth on 26th June 1747.

On 8th May 1821 the "Allies" began the sinking of **SPRINGWELL COLLIERY** (NZ 285589), about four miles south-east of Gateshead. Not far away lay another "Allies" pit – **MOUNT MOOR COLLIERY** (NZ 279577), which had been won nearly a century earlier and whose coal was carried by a waggonway 2¼ miles long to staiths on the River Wear near Washington (see Fig.10). But this involved trans-shipping the coal in keels down to colliers at Sunderland, and the Allies were determined to end this system. So they engaged John Buddle (see the chapters on the Lambton and Londonderry Railways) to develop proposals for a new waggonway between their Stanley Colliery at Stanley, via Mount Moor and Springwell Collieries, down to the River Tyne at Jarrow. Buddle proposed a line 11½ miles long, with six rope inclines and two locomotive-worked sections (NRO 3410/Bud/32/326). However, the Allies decided not to proceed with the section west of Mount Moor, and then commissioned George Stephenson, the former engine-wright at their Killingworth Colliery in Northumberland, to re-design the remainder. In the event Stephenson was heavily occupied with the construction of the Stockton & Darlington Railway, and it seems likely that the design was the work of young Joseph Locke, one of Stephenson's assistants. Coal from Mount Moor Colliery would be hauled up a 750-yard rope incline to the **Blackham's Hill Engine** (later spelling) (NZ 283581), which would then lower the waggons down to Springwell Colliery, a distance of 1170 yards. From Springwell a **self-acting incline** 1¼ miles long, one of the longest built up to this date, would work traffic down to the Leam Lane, whence locomotives would take over for the final 4¾ miles to Jarrow. A second, short "inclined plane", almost certainly self-acting, would take the waggons down to the **SPRINGWELL STAITHS** (NZ 330658). Two locomotives were ordered from the recently-established firm of Robert Stephenson & Co in Newcastle upon Tyne.

The sinking of Springwell Colliery was completed on 24th February 1824, but construction of the railway seems to have been protracted. Although the line was only completed from Jarrow to Springwell and the locomotives had not been delivered, the Allies decided to open it, using horses, on 17th January 1826. The locomotives were finally delivered in April 1826, a locomotive shed being provided at **SPRINGWELL BANK FOOT** (NZ 296605). The remaining section, between Springwell and Mount Moor, is reported to have been opened two months later.

In 1842 the line was extended for a further 2½ miles to **Kibblesworth Colliery** (NZ 243562), which was owned by George Southern and won in March 1842. This section was opened on 30th May 1842. This extension required two more inclines, again single line. The Kibblesworth Engine would lower the wagons down the 1¼ miles to Long Acre at Lamesley, from where the Black Fell Engine would haul them 1¼ miles up to Mount Moor. Whether Southern provided his own waggons and shipped his coal at Jarrow is not known.

A passenger service
Soon after this a passenger service was begun over part of the line. On 30th August 1839 the Brandling Junction Railway's line between Gateshead and Monkwearmouth (Sunderland) was opened, crossing under the colliery line near Wardley. A link between the two lines was put in on the north-west side of the crossing and a building known as **SPRINGWELL STATION** (NZ 312624) erected in the triangle of land thus created. There does not seem to have been a similar building at Jarrow at this

time; possibly the train stopped in the sidings near the staiths. It would seem that the service was begun by the Brandling Junction Railway, very probably using horses, though local tradition averred that the coach was allowed to go down to Jarrow by gravity. The earliest-known timetable is dated 1st July 1845, though the service may have begun before that. By 1849 there were five trains on weekdays and four on Sundays.

By 1849 Lord Ravensworth & Partners was in financial difficulties. One of the partners was John Bowes, whose own firm, John Bowes, Esq., & Partners, was developing a powerful colliery empire in north-west Durham under the managing partner, Charles Mark Palmer. Another partner in this firm was Nicholas Wood, who was also Agent to Lord Ravensworth & Partners. Palmer wanted to acquire the Springwell Colliery railway and its two collieries in order to prevent the line falling into the hands of the "Railway King", George Hudson, and also because he hoped to link Marley Hill to Kibblesworth and so have his own line to ship Bowes & Partners' coal at Jarrow. This duly happened in February 1850 under an agreement back-dated to 1st January 1850. The older partnership continued until the 1880s, although no longer owning any collieries.

Gauge : 4ft 8½in

No.1		0-4-0	VC	RS	1826	New	(1)
No.2		0-4-0	VC	RS	1826	New	(1)
	STRATHMORE					(a)	(1)

The two RS locomotives were almost certainly ordered before the order for the first two locomotives for the Stockton & Darlington Railway on 16th September 1824. However, they were not delivered until after the Stockton & Darlington locomotives, presumably because the latter were required urgently. What RS works numbers the Springwell locomotives were allocated has been the subject of considerable dispute, now impossible to resolve.

(a) origin and identity unknown; believed to have been here before 1850

(1) to John Bowes, Esq., & Partners, with the railway, 1/1/1850

MARLEY HILL RAILWAY

With the demand for Durham coke increasing dramatically after 1830, new collieries were being developed in north-west Durham, whose coking coal traditionally had the highest reputation. One of the major landowners in this area was John Bowes (1811-1885). In the summer of 1839, in partnership with William Hutt (1801-1882, Bowes' step-father), Nicholas Wood (1795-1865) and the Countess of Strathmore (1787-1860, Bowes' mother), he set up the **Marley Hill Coal Company**, with the aim of re-opening **MARLEY HILL**

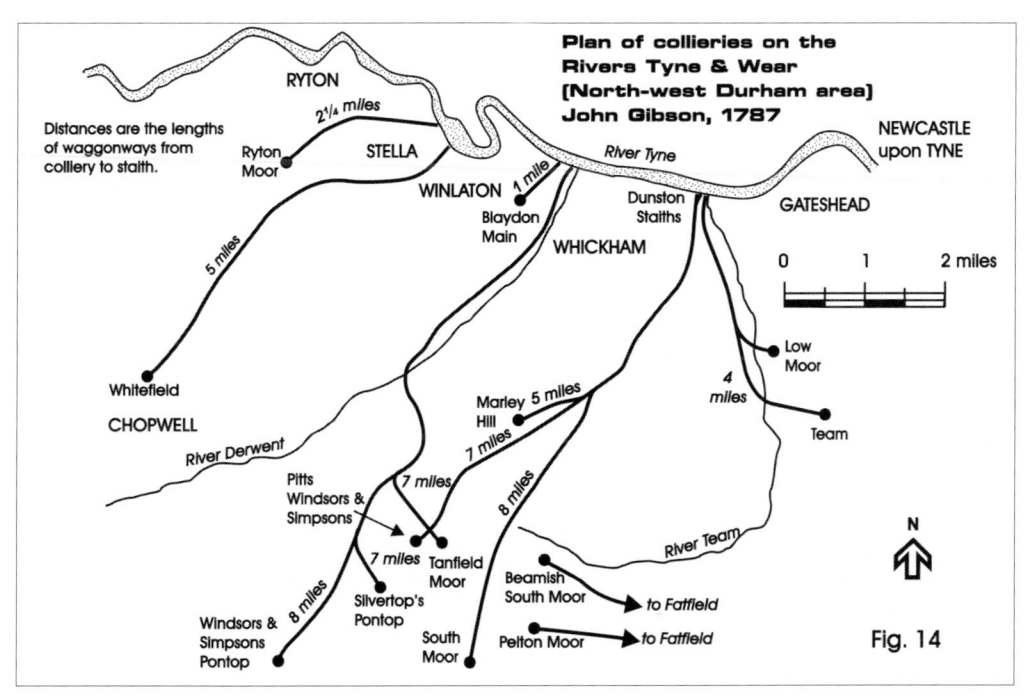

Fig. 14

COLLIERY (NZ 206575). In the last quarter of the eighteenth century this colliery had been served by the Tanfield Waggonway (see Fig. 14), and it may well be that the Brandling Junction Railway's rebuilding of this line, opened on 26th November 1839, stirred Bowes' interest in re-opening the colliery. The new sinking began on 8th January 1840 and was completed on 28th June 1841. It was linked to the Tanfield Branch just north of its Bowes Bridge Engine House by a line just under ½ mile long.

As noted above, Nicholas Wood was the Agent to Lord Ravensworth & Partners, and had been their viewer at Killingworth Colliery during George Stephenson's experiments with the miners' safety lamp and steam locomotives. He played a not insignificant part in the history of early railways, and locally was the Engineer to the Brandling Junction Railway. He also developed important colliery interests, for besides those already mentioned, he became a partner in The Hetton Coal Company and The Harton Coal Company, as well as developing his own firm, Nicholas Wood & Partners, which developed collieries east of Bishop Auckland. He was also the founder in 1852 of The North of England Institute of Mining & Mechanical Engineers in Newcastle upon Tyne. But a significant change in the management of the Marley Hill Coal Company occurred in 1844 when it was joined by Charles Mark Palmer (1822-1907), who became Managing Partner in 1846 at the age of only 24. It was an example of his ambition that in November 1847 the firm's name was changed to **John Bowes, Esq., & Partners**.

About 1842 John Berkley, a corn merchant from Newcastle upon Tyne, acquired the Hobson Pit at Burnopfield, 2½ miles south-west of Marley Hill. It would seem that at first Berkley intended to re-lay an old waggonway south-wards to link to the Tanfield Branch, from which a second link, owned by the Derwent Iron Company, would give access to the Pontop & South Shields Railway at Annfield Plain. Work is said to have been started in 1842, but was abandoned in favour of a line north-eastwards to Marley Hill. Construction, under the supervision of his son, Cuthbert Berkley (1826-1912), began in the autumn of 1844 and was completed early in 1845. The biggest engineering work on the line was the one-mile Hobson Bank, a steep, winding bank from Burnopfield down to Crookgate, for which a stationary engine proved necessary. The opening of this line also provided rail access to Crookbank Colliery, about 1½ miles south-west of Marley Hill, which was won in 1845, though its owners are unknown.

As early as 1847 Palmer was urging the partners to construct a rail link between Marley Hill and Kibblesworth, in order to be able to ship all their coal at Jarrow and free themselves from the monopoly of George Hudson, "The Railway King", and his York, Newcastle & Berwick Railway, whose supply of empty waggons frequently proved capricious. However, it took some years for all the necessary pieces to fall into place.

These began with the acquisition of **CROOKBANK COLLIERY** (NZ 187571) in December 1847 after its owners had gone bankrupt, to be followed by **BURNOPFIELD COLLIERY** (NZ 173562) and **Tanfield Moor Colliery** (NZ 171553) in November 1849 when Berkley suffered the same fate, though Tanfield Moor was sold on to James Joicey (see chapter 2) in September 1850. Palmer was now determined to acquire the Springwell Colliery line, achieving this in February 1850 by an agreement back-dated to 1st January 1850, although he found that the price unavoidably included Lord Ravensworth & Partners' Northumberland collieries. Now faced with an active, powerful adversary, George Southern soon surrendered **KIBBLESWORTH COLLIERY** (NZ 243562), in November 1851. In December 1852 the Partners re-opened **ANDREWS HOUSE COLLIERY** (NZ 205573), ½ mile east of Marley Hill. This colliery had been sunk by the Northern Coal Company in 1840, and was linked to the Tanfield Branch, but it had been abandoned in 1848 when the company went bankrupt. Thus the Partners now controlled both the Marley Hill-Burnopfield line and all three collieries on it, together with Andrews House Colliery, as well as the Kibblesworth-Jarrow line with its collieries; all that was needed now was a railway to link the two.

The work of 1853-1855

Work on the 2¼ mile link between Marley Hill and Kibblesworth began in July 1853, using direct labour and again under the direction of Cuthbert Berkley. It involved making a self-acting incline from the top of the 550ft moor called Birk Heads down to Kibblesworth, giving six consecutive rope-worked inclines between Birk Heads and Springwell Bank Foot, with a total length of just over six miles. The climb from Andrews House to Birk Heads was less steep, so that locomotives could be used, but the whole section involved cutting or embankment. In addition, the branch from Andrews House Colliery had to be altered to join the new line, the Tanfield Branch itself being crossed on the level. The link with the Tanfield Branch at Bowes Bridge was maintained. Berkley became the firm's Chief Engineer, a post he held until 1899; for many years he rode a donkey to visit the collieries.

Further west the Partners decided to sink a new colliery at **DIPTON** (NZ 158358), about 1½ miles south-west of Burnopfield, and to extend the railway to serve it. This involved further cuttings and embankments, one of the latter, at Pickering Nook, south-west of Burnopfield, including a short tunnel to allow the Lintz Colliery waggonway to White-le-Head to pass under the line. The line was ready early in 1855, but remained unused awaiting the completion of Dipton Colliery.

It was also clear that considerable improvements would have to be made to the Kibblesworth-Jarrow section in order for it to handle the considerable increase in traffic planned. During the first half of 1854 the Black Fell Incline was doubled to allow fulls and empties to be run simultaneously, whilst at Blackham's Hill a more powerful stationary

Fig. 15

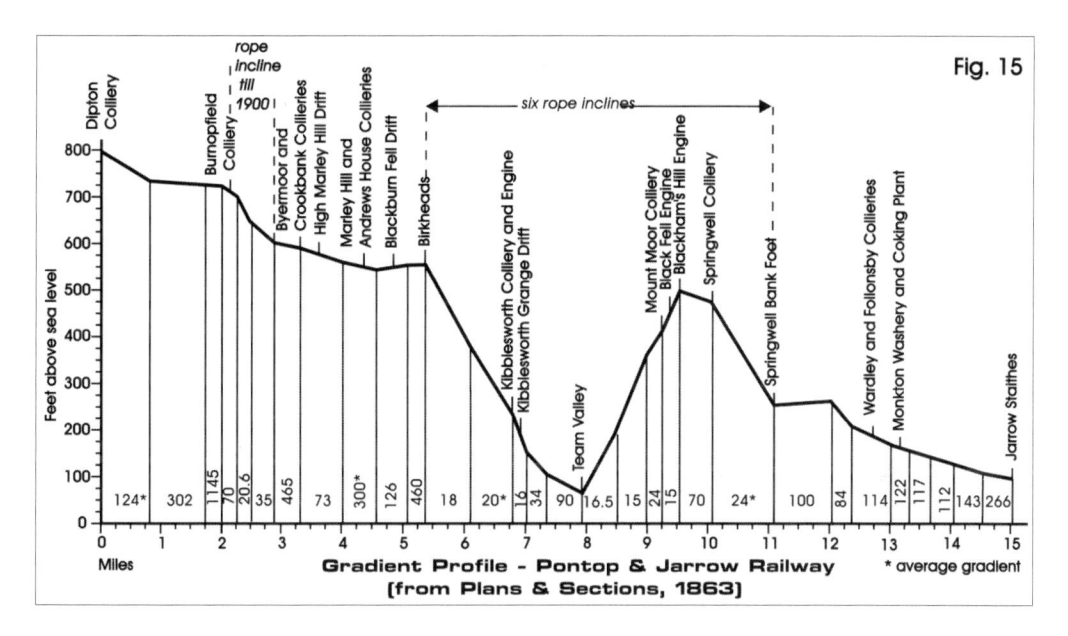

Gradient Profile - Pontop & Jarrow Railway
(from Plans & Sections, 1863)

* average gradient

engine was installed and the working of the inclines was altered, again to allow them to be operated simultaneously rather than alternately. In addition, Mount Moor Colliery was re-opened in June 1854, after standing idle for some years, this too having to be worked by the Blackham's Hill Engine. Quite clearly the old staiths of 1826 would have to be replaced, and new staiths were built ¼ mile to the west, with the line diverted at Jarrow Grange to serve them. They soon proved inadequate, and an additional staith had to be erected during the winter of 1854.

The section between Marley Hill and Kibblesworth was finally opened at the end of September 1854, though at first only coal from Andrews House was sent to Jarrow due to a severe shortage of waggons. Dipton Colliery opened in April 1855, and by mid-April 1855 the line was handling all the firm's traffic. Palmer's view of the importance of the line, now fifteen miles long, is reflected in his decision to give it the title of **PONTOP & JARROW RAILWAY** (although in fact the railway never reached Pontop Colliery – see below).

The coal from all the collieries between Marley Hill and Dipton produced excellent coke, and hundreds of beehive or rectangular coke ovens were built there. The firm operated its coke making for quite a time in the nineteenth century under the title of The Marley Hill Coke Company.

The *John Bowes*

Palmer's plans for expansion were not confined to increasing the Partners' coal and coke production and to developing the firm's private railways in Durham and Northumberland. In 1851 he leased an old shipyard at Jarrow, alongside the Partners' staiths, and there on 30th June 1852 was launched the first-ever iron screw collier, built for the Partners and named *John Bowes*. A month later she sailed for London with 530 tons of coal, and was back in only six days, compared with the fortnight taken by sailing colliers. With one brilliant stroke Palmer had revolutionised the sea-borne coal trade, and his shipyard, latterly owned by Palmers Shipbuilding & Iron Co Ltd, became one of the most famous in the world.

The Northumberland & Durham Coal Company

Palmer also set out to control much of the distribution of the firm's coal in London. In 1850 he made an agreement with the East & West India Docks & Birmingham Junction Railway, which was to run from the London & North Western Railway's goods station at Camden Town to the West India Docks at Blackwall, a line then under construction. Under this the Partners, through a fully-owned subsidiary called the Northumberland & Durham Coal Company, were to operate coal traffic over the line with their locomotives and wagons, delivering to local coal merchants, in return for an annual payment of £10,000. The Partners' first train ran on 15th October 1851, but the line did not become fully operational until about the end of February 1852. In January 1853 the railway changed its title to the North London Railway, although in practice it was controlled by the London & North Western Railway. In the event the arrangement did not prove the success that Palmer had hoped for, and on 15th December 1858 he completed an agreement with the L&WR under which the Northumberland & Durham Coal Company's rights and rolling stock were sold for £43,000. The money was paid on 3rd January 1859 and thereupon the North London Railway took possession.

The operation of the Railway : Dipton to Birkheads (5¼ miles)

Palmer brought in the first locomotives to work at Marley Hill in June 1847, and almost certainly during the work of 1853-1855 a large, two-road locomotive shed was built here, **MARLEY HILL LOCO SHED** (NZ 207573), although alongside the

PONTOP & JARROW RAILWAY in 1863

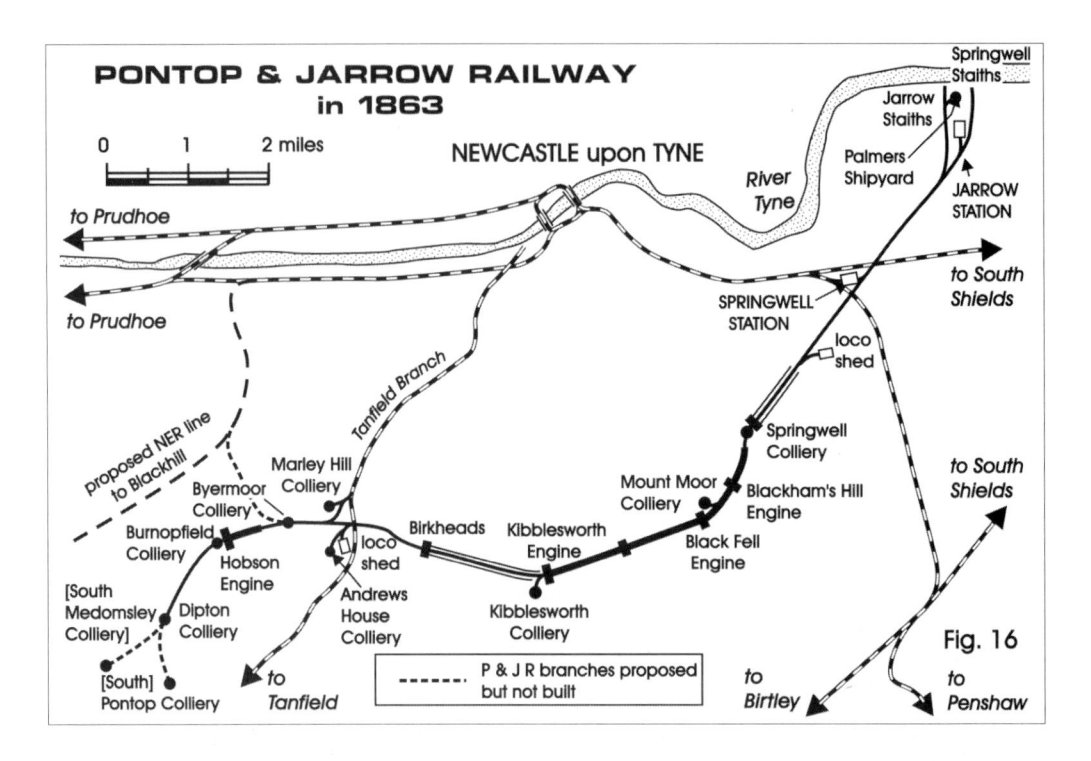

Fig. 16

branch to Andrews House Colliery. There would appear never to have been a shed specifically for locomotives working between Dipton and Burnopfield, and presumably locomotives from Marley Hill travelled out there each morning.

Rather strangely, neither the 1st nor 2nd editions of the Ordnance Survey maps record the position of the Hobson Engine. From the track layouts shown the bank foot would appear to have been at Crookgate, but there appears to be no layout suitable for a bank head. The Engine House is also not shown in *Plans & Sections of North Durham Railways* by J.F.Tone, dated November 1863, once owned by the Partners and now deposited with Tyne & Wear Archives in Newcastle upon Tyne (TWA 1312/1), which shows the Railway in plan and section to a scale of 1.7inches to the furlong. It shows a maximum gradient of 1 in 25.3, and two

13. Fulls from Burnopfield to Marley Hill Yard, limited to 20 down Hobson Bank, had to be assembled in three stages. Here 85, AB 2274/1949, the colliery's pilot, and 22, HL 3103/1915, shunt seven up to the colliery on 11th April 1968.

curves of six chains radius, while the 1st edition shows the bank as single line, which would have meant fulls and empties being run alternately. Oral tradition maintained that the hauler was a horizontal-cylindered engine built by Black Hawthorn & Co Ltd of Gateshead, although there is no evidence of this in the BH works list. However, in 1853 (i.e., in the rebuilding period) R & W Hawthorn of Newcastle upon Tyne supplied to the Marley Hill Coal Company (a curious use of the then-abandoned title) a stationary engine (RWH 866/1853) with 36in x 60in horizontal cylinders, together with three boilers measuring 30ft x 6ft, for "hauling", which may be this engine.

Oral tradition maintained that the engine was removed and the bank converted to locomotive working in 1900, although the absence of the Engine on the 2nd edition O.S. map of 1896 could mean that this work was carried out before 1900. Equally, a powerful locomotive would be needed to work up this section, which may be connected with the purchase of BH 1071 in 1892. The line was straightened somewhat and re-graded to be mostly 1 in 35, with a short section of 1 in 20.6 near the top. In 1930 The Hunslet Engine Co Ltd of Leeds designed HE 1506 specifically for this bank, this design subsequently being developed into the famous "Austerity" locomotives built during the Second World War and afterwards. When 10-ton wagons were introduced the maximum permitted load was eighteen empties up and twenty loaded wagons down, with some brakes pinned down.

14. 'Austerity' 28, VF 5298/1945, climbs the top section of Hobson Bank with materials and empties for Burnopfield Colliery in May 1965.

Branches on the western section
The *Plans & Sections* of 1863 (see above) show three branches on this western section, though there is no evidence that any of them were built. The first was a 1¼ mile link from Dipton south-east to what is shown on both the Plans and the O.S. map as **South Pontop Colliery** (NZ 162517). This was later called **Pontop Colliery**, and should not be confused with a later South Pontop Colliery, situated about ½ mile to the south. The branch to the colliery, purchased by the Partners in July 1850, would have involved a maximum gradient of 1 in 8 which was probably why it was never built, and the colliery was linked instead to the Harelaw Branch from the NER Pontop & South Shields Branch. The second proposal ran south-west from Dipton to South Medomsley Colliery (NZ 144531), which had been sunk in 1862 by D.Baker & Co; in the event this too was served by a branch from the Pontop & South Shields Branch. The third proposal, called the Low Friarside branch, would have linked Crookgate with the proposed NER Blackhill Branch between Blaydon and Consett. This line, nearly 1½ miles long, would have had even more fearsome gradients, with one section at 1 in 6.8. However, one link from this section was built at this time, a short loop at Pickering Nook to join the Lintz Colliery waggonway, which was opened in July 1867 in order to divert its traffic on to the Pontop & Jarrow Railway; however, in 1870 the Lintz company reverted to using its former line up to White-le-Head on the NER's Tanfield Branch.

In the winter of 1860 Crookbank Colliery was replaced by a new colliery nearby at **BYERMOOR** (NZ 187573), but after the site had been cleared more coke ovens were built on it (NZ 185571), so the ¼ mile branch from Crookgate was retained. The 2nd edition O.S. map shows a short branch serving quarries (NZ 184573) north of the line here, though who worked these is not known. There were also quarries further west at Mountsett, alongside the line between Burnopfield and Dipton, though nothing survives to show whether these were also rail-connected.

At first all the collieries from Marley Hill westwards had large numbers of beehive coke ovens. However, in September 1908 a new **COKE OVENS & BY-PRODUCT PLANT**, with 60 Huessener waste heat ovens, was opened at Marley Hill, and over the following few years the remaining beehive ovens were closed. To the first by-product ovens were subsequently added 30 Huessener semi-regenerative ovens (20 in 1915, and another 10 in 1919), with tar products, sulphate of ammonia and benzole being manufactured as by-products. To operate this plant a new company, the **Marley Hill Coke & Chemical Co Ltd**, was set up, probably during 1920, and this continued to operate the plant until its closure in 1938.

The operation of the Railway: the central section, all inclines (6 miles)
From Birkheads, down to the valley of the River Team and up the other side before the descent to Springwell Bank Foot, a distance of six miles, six rope inclines were used. The first, the **Birkheads Incline**, was a self-acting incline 1¼ miles long at 1 in 19, with of course fulls and empties being run simultaneously. The next, the Kibblesworth Incline, was unusual, in that although the full wagons were to travel downhill a stationary engine was used. The

15. Looking down the middle section of Hobson Bank, with the signal guarding Crookgate Crossing, on 14th November 1962; note the WHISTLE sign.

16. No.8, BH 692/1882, as delivered new to Marley Hill.

17. Marley Hill loco shed at lunch time in May 1965, with (left to right) 83, HE 3688/1949; 22, HL 3103/1915; 85, AB 2274/1949; 23, HL 2719/1907, and 28, VF 5298/1945, coming up from Byermoor.

initial gradient was 1 in 16, but towards the bottom this flattened out to a lengthy section of 1 in 90, and it was felt that a stationary engine with a flywheel would be needed to cope with this. So the **Kibblesworth Engine** (NZ 243562) was built almost alongside the Robert Pit, the engine (RWH 346) dating from 1840, though the incline was not opened until May 1842. However, soon after opening the flywheel went through the engine house roof, and while a new one was being made it was found that the incline could be worked satisfactorily without it, so the new one was never fitted.

This was a single line incline, just over a mile long, and with, from 1854, the inclines on opposite sides running sets of (latterly) six simultaneously, this incline had to run sets of (latterly) 12 in order not to be a bottleneck. This incline was one of the rare examples of needing to handle all of a colliery's traffic as well as that on the main line. Initially this was done by constructing a second kip solely for colliery traffic (to the Robert Pit) at the bank head. However, the working became even more complicated in 1914, when **KIBBLESWORTH GRANGE DRIFT** (NZ 249564) was opened alongside

18. Bowes No.20, Area No.83, HE 3688/1949, crossing British Railways' Tanfield Branch with empties from Birkheads in 1954.

the line to the south, just before the beginning of the flatter section. The Drift had its own "kip and dish" alongside the line, with sets being run in and out of here as required. To shunt wagons within the Drift yard a separate 80 h.p. hauler built by Metropolitan-Vickers Ltd and acquired second-hand was installed at its west end, with its rope attached to a wagon of scrap iron, which could then run down, dragging its rope, to whichever wagons needed to be moved.

From Kibblesworth Bank Foot at Long Acre the Railway had to climb the east side of the Team valley, up the **Black Fell Incline**, the two bank foots meeting underneath the bridges carrying the Newcastle-London main line. This incline, 1 in 30 near the bottom stiffening to 1 in 15 near the top, was 1¼ miles long and brought the wagons up to the **Black Fell Engine** (NZ 279576). When this incline was opened in 1842 it was single line, but it was doubled as part of the 1853-1855 improvements to allow the working of fulls and empties simultaneously.

To bring the line to the top of the east side of the Team valley the **Blackham's Hill Engine** (NZ 283581)

19. Empties coming over the kip at Birkheads on 21st October 1968, with Kibblesworth in the distance.

20. Fulls from Birkheads coming under the 1947 engine house at Kibblesworth, with the Robert Pit on the left and the "ball-and-chain" rapper outside the bank head cabin on the right, 14th October 1965.

21. Looking down the Kibblesworth Incline, with Kibblesworth "Drift" on the right, 25th October 1954.

22. *Pulling out the slip pin and dragging the rope out of the way of the wagons from a full set arriving at Black Fell bank head in April 1965.*

23. *The Black Fell haulerman for many years was John Humphrey, here at work in 1920, seven years after this engine, built by Robey & Co Ltd of Lincoln, was installed.*

24. The steam hauler, AB 7923/1915, at Blackham's Hill on 19th July 1950; the engine had 18in x 36in cylinders and the brake wheel in the foreground controlled the set worked to Springwell by gravity.

25. A set of empties arriving on the kip at Blackham's Hill on 11th December 1965, with the last set-rider to work on NCB inclines. The ropes for both West and East Inclines came out of the front of the engine house, the east rope (here hauling) routed eastwards round an underground return wheel.

was built, about 470 feet above sea level. This hauled the wagons up to the engine house and then lowered them to Springwell, both inclines being single line. From their opening in 1826 to 1854 this was done alternately, but from 1854 it became possible to work both inclines simultaneously, with the engine hauling on one side whilst the other side was using gravity. The **West Incline** was about 750 yards averaging 1 in 15, the **East Incline** about 1170 yards at 1 in 70. The working of these two inclines was always very complicated. On the west side the engine had to work traffic in and out of Mount Moor Colliery, latterly called **SPRINGWELL COLLIERY (VALE PIT)**. Just below Black Fell bank head the Pontop & Jarrow Railway was carried on a bridge across the Pelaw Main Railway (which see), and by the 1870s there was a link to the latter via Mount Moor Colliery, apparently to allow bricks from the brickworks at Birtley to be transferred here. This link had been removed by 1923. Besides working this link, the Blackham's Hill Engine also had to service its own boiler house and that for the Black Fell Engine, whilst on the east side it had to service a landsale depot at the bank head, work empty wagons into Springwell Colliery screens and allow for the working of traffic into the **Springwell Quarries**, worked for grindstones, first on the eastern side of the line (NZ 285587) and then on the west (NZ 283586). Various firms owned these quarries over the years; presumably their traffic was worked through to the link with the NER/LNER at Jarrow.

Springwell Colliery was unusual, in that the shafts were situated on the eastern side of the line and the screens on the western side, with a large stone coal bunker to the north of the shafts into which coal could be tipped when no Railway wagons were available (and hand-shovelled into them when they were). To the north of this bunker lay a small quarry and brickworks (NZ 285590), worked intermittently between about 1900 and 1919 by various firms. To handle the shunting at Springwell the Partners for many years kept a group of shire horses here.

The final incline, the **Springwell Incline**, was another self-acting incline, 1¼ miles long at 1 in 24. By the Second World War the kip at the bank foot comprised two lines with a capacity of 36 empty 10-ton wagons, an hour's supply for the inclines.

The operation of the Railway – Springwell Bank Foot to Jarrow (4¼ miles).

Traffic on the final section to Jarrow and its various branches was worked by locomotives from **SPRINGWELL BANK FOOT LOCO SHED** (NZ 296605). The link at Wardley with the Brandling Junction Railway, later the NER, has been noted above. It would seem that by the 1860s the passenger service between **SPRINGWELL STATION** (NZ 306620) and **JARROW STATION** (NZ 330654), situated at the western end of Great Ormonde Street (now Ormonde Street) in Jarrow was being operated by the Partners. This service was discontinued following the opening of the new NER line from Pelaw to South Shields on 1st March 1872. The link at Springwell Station, and the two stations themselves, of which no details survive, were all eventually removed.

In April 1868 the Partners acquired **WARDLEY COLLIERY** (NZ 306620) from George Elliot. Its sinking had been started in 1847 but had subsequently been abandoned. It lay only about a hundred yards from the Railway, so a branch was laid to it, and coal production was begun in April 1871. It had a rather short life, for in December 1911 coal winding ceased and it was replaced by **FOLLONSBY COLLIERY** (NZ 313608), served by another branch (¾ mile) and opened in June 1912. With the opening of this

26. Springwell Bank Head, 15th September 1974, with the Wagon Shops on the left, the kip in the centre and the Engineering Shops behind.

27. No.10, TR 252/1854, originally a tender engine but here as rebuilt to 0-6-0ST.

branch a new link was put in between it and the NER Gateshead – Washington line, the sidings becoming known as Wardley Exchange.

According to the newspaper account of the opening of the Springwell Colliery Railway in January 1826, the staiths at Jarrow (NZ 330658 – almost directly above the present Tyne Tunnel) were served by an "inclined plane". Nothing else is known about this, though it would seem likely to have been self-acting. The staiths built to replace them in 1854-1855 and served by a new ½ mile branch are said to have been worked by a stationary engine (apparently the standard practice of the period – see the staiths in Sunderland for the Lambton and Hetton Railways), but again nothing further is known. In 1882 Palmer ordered these staiths to be replaced by new staiths again further upstream, only for the latter to be burned down on 22nd May 1883 before they had been opened. These staiths, after rebuilding, were operated by gravity but with a locomotive propelling in sets of full wagons and removing the empties.

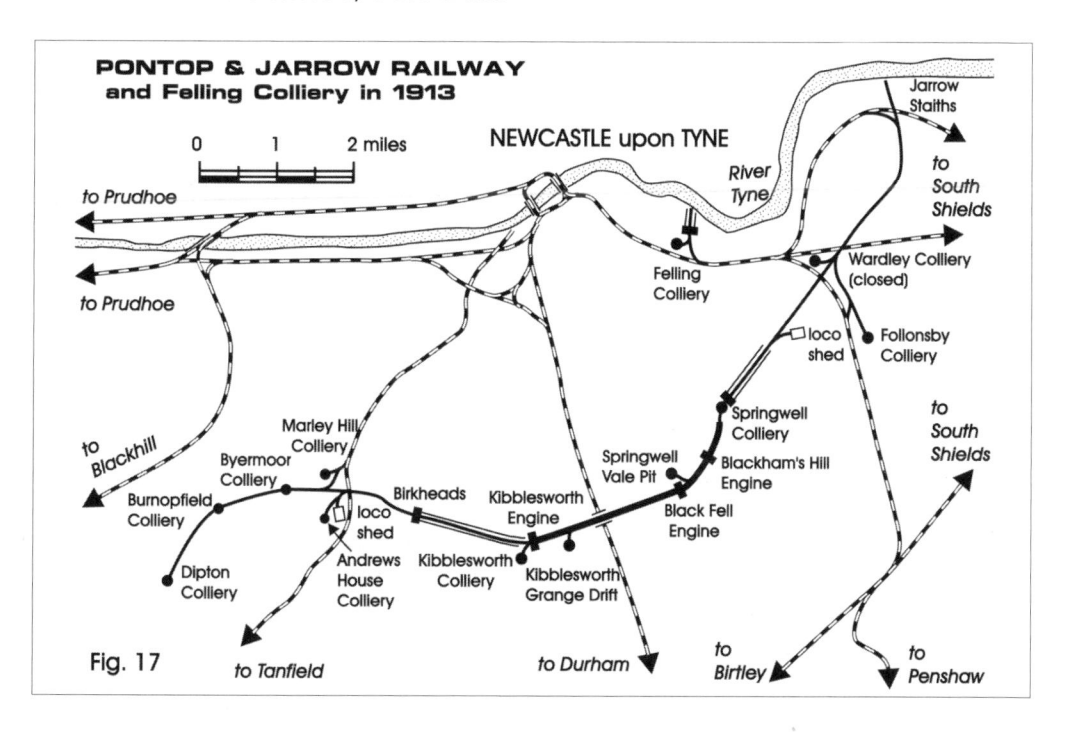

Fig. 17

28. No.3, BH 938/1888, at Jarrow, believed to be about 1898.

Links at Jarrow
The NER line between Pelaw and South Shields, opened in 1872, was carried over the Railway by a bridge, and the two were linked on the south-western side, from the NER's Pontop Junction. On the eastern side of the Railway here a branch left to serve **Palmers Shipbuilding & Iron Co Ltd** (NZ 318657-330657), which by 1900 had grown to occupy ¾ mile of river frontage. Palmers established a slag heap alongside the Railway (NZ 323645) about a mile to the south of the yard to the west of the line, linking the two by a branch line which crossed the Railway near the heap. Following the closure of Palmers in 1933 and its subsequent demolition, Sir W.G.Armstrong, Whitworth & Co (Ironfounders) Ltd built in 1937 a factory to manufacture steel castings on part of the site (NZ 321654), operated by a subsidiary company, Jarrow Metal Industries Ltd and built a second factory, to manufacture steel tubes and operated by Jarrow Tube Works Ltd, on the site of Palmers' slag heap, and retained the branch, worked by a Jarrow Metal Industries' loco, to link the two sites. There was also a link west of the 1883 staiths to the paint works of **Foster, Blackett & Wilson Ltd** (NZ 317656), and it would seem likely that P&JR locos handled traffic between this works and the NER at Pontop Junction.

Company history, 1870-1900; the end of operations in Northumberland
From the acquisition of Killingworth Colliery and its railway from Lord Ravensworth & Partners in 1850 Palmer acquired or sank new collieries in Northumberland, and in July 1872 the Partners purchased the privately-owned Brunton & Shields Railway, enabling them to integrate and rationalise their rail traffic in the area. Meanwhile, in Durham they opened Dunston Colliery in 1875, following this by purchasing in March 1882 Usworth Colliery (NZ 3155584), partly owned by Sir George Elliot, from whom in March 1883 they also purchased Felling Colliery (NZ 275623).

John Bowes and his first wife Josephine were major collectors of a wide variety of art and antiques, and to house their collections for public display they began in 1869 the construction of The Bowes Museum at Barnard Castle. In his will Bowes bequeathed a considerable sum to the still-unfinished Museum, which was eventually opened in 1892 and now has an international reputation. However, the payments required under Bowes' will forced the firm into a major appraisal of its activities. Usworth Colliery was sold in 1897, to be followed by Dunston and its associated colliery Norwood in July 1899. In Northumberland everything was sold, eventually to the Seaton Burn Coal Co Ltd in December 1899, although its predecessor the Seaton Burn Coal Syndicate took possession on 8th January 1899. This left the firm to concentrate on the collieries served by the Pontop & Jarrow Railway and Felling Colliery.

Company history, 1920-1940 : the BOWES RAILWAY
Andrews House Colliery closed in December 1920, and the economic depression after 1929 brought the closure of Felling Colliery in April 1931, Springwell (Vale Pit) in May 1931, Springwell Colliery itself in June 1932 and Kibblesworth Grange Drift in December 1932. Because of its serious financial situation the company was taken over in 1932, many of the new directors also being directors of both the Harton Coal Co Ltd and the

29. No.14, 0-6-2T CF 1158/1898 and No.1, 0-6-2ST BH 937/1888, outside Springwell Bank Foot loco shed in 1919, before the repair shop was built.

30. 9, whose original builder is unknown, is here probably at Wardley; she was scrapped in 1935.

Bedlington Coal Co Ltd in Northumberland, themselves part of other large colliery groups. However, the Bowes-Lyon family retained their interest, the 14th Earl of Strathmore (father of Queen Elizabeth The Queen Mother) latterly becoming chairman. The new management renamed the railway the **BOWES RAILWAY**.

New investment was now committed. In 1935-1936 new staiths were built, now so far upstream that they were actually in Hebburn, although they were still called **JARROW STAITHS** (NZ 318657). These incorporated conveyors and loading cranes and were operated by the Tyne Improvement Commission; they were opened on 28th July 1936. At Kibblesworth a new pit, the Glamis, was sunk, also opened in July 1936, and the colliery surface was reorganised. New screens were built on the site of the Drift and two 2ft 0in gauge endless rope systems were installed to bring the tubs from the two pits down to the screens to be tippled. A small electric hauler was installed to shunt the screens, still called "The Drift", and to deal with traffic to

31. No. 10, NBA 16628/1905, after the accident at Mill Lane Crossing, Wardley, on 16th May 1936.

and from the main line, although the operation of the main line continued as before.

Further west, about a mile east of Marley Hill, **BLACKBURN FELL DRIFT** (NZ 214573) was opened in July 1937. This lay to the north of the Railway, with tubs on a 2ft 0in gauge system being hauled out of the drift and down to the line to be tipped, unscreened, into standard gauge wagons.

In the east Wardley was developed as a major site. In the 1920s **WARDLEY DRY-CLEANING PLANT** (NZ 308622) was opened here ½ mile south of Mill Lane Crossing, and a large marshalling yard was also developed, to sort out full wagons destined for the plant and those required to go on to Jarrow. Then on 5th April 1937, immediately to the north of Mill Lane Crossing, a new coke works and by-products plant (NZ 315626) was opened, the coke being manufactured in 33 Koppers combination circulation ovens, with surplus gas supplied to Jarrow and Gateshead and crude tar, rectified benzole and sulphate of ammonia being the by-products. At first the works was known as the **BOWES COKE WORKS**, but in a very short time it was re-named **MONKTON COKE WORKS**, from the village nearby. With the opening of this works the old works at Marley Hill was closed, apparently during 1938, and the Marley Hill Coke & Chemical Co Ltd was wound up.

Also in 1937 a proposal was put forward to construct a link between Wardley and Whitehill Bank Foot near Heworth on the Pelaw Main Railway, owned by Pelaw Main Collieries Ltd. It would seem likely that the plan being considered was to use the link to bring Pelaw Main coal on the Bowes Railway to be shipped at Jarrow and allow the Pelaw Main Staiths at Bill Quay to be closed;

32. No.8, at Wardley in May 1937, was a Barry Railway 'F' class built by SS 4594/1900 and purchased from the Great Western Railway in August 1936.

33. A very rare example of a loco being loaned between railways: Lambton Railway No.39, formerly Hetton Railway No.5, RWH 1422/1867, on loan to the Bowes Railway early in 1938.

34. 15, HE 1506/1930, the predecessor of Hunslet's 'Austerity' design, at Jarrow on 17th March 1964. Note the radio-telephone apparatus fixed to the smokebox.

but although the route was surveyed, it was never constructed.

With the start of the Second World War Dipton Colliery was closed in November 1940, and thus with it the railway west of Burnopfield. In the same year Springwell Colliery was sold to The Washington Coal Co Ltd for ventilation purposes, together with Follonsby Colliery, although Bowes Railway locomotives continued to handle Follonsby traffic.

The Railway's workshops

The Railway had no locomotive workshops as such, major repairs being always undertaken at the two sheds, with boilers being sent away to local locomotive builders. Certainly by the beginning of the 20th century there was a Wagon Shop at Springwell Colliery, capable of assembling new 10-ton wagons from parts bought in, although wagons were also repaired in the open air. There was also a small Wagon Repair Shop, opened by 1894, at Birkheads and wagon repairs were also undertaken in the two loco sheds. However, when Springwell Colliery closed in 1932 the company decided to develop the site as its main workshops. The former colliery workshops on the west side of the line became **ENGINEERING WORKSHOPS**, while the former coal bunker, mentioned above, was converted into a **WAGON SHOP**. To assist with shunting this new Shop a 45 h.p. electric hauler was provided nearby, with the wagons having to be fly-shunted, with the rope detached on the move, to get them into the building.

Wagons

Like all colliery railways in the North-East, the Railway for many years used chaldron waggons for coal traffic. The long process of replacing these with 10-ton wooden hopper wagons began in the 1880s. As the number of 10-ton wagons increased the "black waggons" were confined to working through from the western collieries, until on a Sunday in the summer of 1911 those that remained were brought down to Wardley, eventually to be sold or burnt. The firm was among the first of the Durham colliery companies to eliminate its "black waggons", helped, like other local railways, by purchasing second-hand 10-ton wagons from the NER. Oral tradition maintained that the 1,200 wagons known on the Railway as "Ordinaries" were built by the company at its workshops at Springwell, but recent investigation suggests that at least the earlier of these may well have been former Stockton & Darlington Railway wagons, also purchased from the NER (its early P5 type) and then fairly extensively rebuilt at Springwell. By the 1940s the Railway had approximately 2,000 vehicles.

Liveries

When the line was called the Pontop & Jarrow Railway, P. & J.R. was painted on both the waggons and the locomotives, the latter also carrying brass numerals on the cab. When the Railway's name was changed to the Bowes Railway both the locomotives and the wagons carried BOWES, the latter in white letters three feet high.

The Bowes Railway, together with the collieries at Burnopfield, Byermoor, Marley Hill, Kibblesworth and Blackburn Fell Drift, and Monkton Coke Works, passed to NCB Northern Division No.6 Area on 1st January 1947. In addition, Bowes Railway locomotives were shunting Follonsby Colliery, latterly owned by The Washington Coal Co Ltd, via its branch from Wardley.

Reference : *The Bowes Railway*, Colin E. Mountford, published by the Industrial Railway Society, 1966, 2nd enlarged edition 1976

Source material

Not a great deal is known about the early locomotives, especially those at Marley Hill. The details given below for the first Nos.3 to 8 are based on scraps of oral tradition on the Railway that survived till the 1930s. These, fortunately, were written down by workmen on the local Railways who were also interested in their history. The majority of the detailed information is taken from the Bowes Railway Locomotive Ledger, started by the company in 1936 but containing information written up from earlier material now lost. The Ledger, together with a significant volume of other Railway material, is now deposited with the Tyne & Wear Archive Service in Newcastle upon Tyne. Additional information was also gathered from the locomotive repair books at the two sheds, also now lost.

The loco sheds are coded as follows:

	MH	Marley Hill Loco Shed
	SBF	Springwell Bank Foot Loco Shed

Gauge : 4ft 8½in

	BOWES	2-4-0?					(a)	MH (1)
	GIBSIDE	2-4-0	IC	RS			(a)	MH (1)
	RAVENSWORTH	2-4-0?					(a)	MH (1)
	STRATHMORE	?					(b)	SBF s/s
No.2	(?)	0-6-0	OC	RWH	476	1846	(c)	MH (2)

(a) the first locomotives to work at Marley Hill arrived in 6/1847, their identity and origin being unknown; whether these are linked to these locos is also not known
(b) believed to have come from Lord Ravensworth & Partners, with the Springwell Colliery Railway, 1/1/1850, but not confirmed
(c) ex North British Railway, No.29, 11/1855

(1) said to have been scrapped in the 1870s
(2) to Northumberland & Durham Coal Co (see text above), Blackwall, London, by 1/1859

No.1	"BULL"		0-4-0	VC	RS		1826	(a)

SBF-MH (via Robert Stephenson & Co, Newcastle upon Tyne, repairs) 1/1851   (1)

1			0-6-2ST	IC	BH	937	1888	New	
			reb		HL		1901		
	SBF								(2)
No.2			0-4-0	VC	RS		1826	(a)	
	SBF								(3)
No.2	(later 2)		0-6-0	IC	RS	1516	1864	New	
		reb	0-6-0ST	IC	RS	2902	1898		
			reb		HL	8243	1915		
	SBF								(4)
No.3	STREATLAM		0-4-0	OC	RS	795	1851	New	
	SBF								(5)
No.3	(later 3)		0-6-2ST	IC	BH	938	1888	New	
			reb		HL	3045	1903		
	SBF-MH 30/11/1934-SBF 19/3/1942								(6)
No.4	MARLEY HILL		0-4-0	OC	RS	816	1851	New	
	MH								s/s c/1886
No.4	(later 4)		0-6-0ST	OC	BH	891	1887	New	
	MH-SBF 31/10/1907-MH 12/6/1908								(7)
4			0-4-0ST	OC	KS	4030	1919	(b)	
	SBF								(8)
No.5	DANIEL O'ROURKE		0-4-0ST	IC	Marley Hill		1854	New	
	MH								(9)
No.5			0-6-0ST	OC	RWH	1986	1884	(c)	
			reb		HL	3593	1913		
	SBF-MH by /1904-SBF 29/1/1932								(2)
No.5			0-6-0T	IC	Ghd	7	1897	(d)	
	SBF								(10)
No.6			0-6-0	IC	RS	1074	1856	New	
	? -MH by 1885								s/s c/1890
No.6			0-4-0T	OC	FJ	125	1874	(e)	
	MH								(11)
No.6	(later 6)		0-6-0ST	OC	HL	2515	1901	New	
			reb		HL	1779	1911		
			reb		LG		1930		
	MH- Robert Stephenson & Hawthorns Ltd, Newcastle upon Tyne, repairs, 23/8/1942								
	-MH 16/5/1945-SBF 11/6/1945								(12)
No.7			?					(f)	
	?								s/s by /1874
No.7	(later 7)		0-6-0ST	IC	BH	304	1874	New	
	MH-SBF by c/1898- MH by /1904								Scr /1933
	BOWES No.7		0-4-0ST	OC	CF	1203	1901		
			reb		HL	9270	1909	(g)	
	SBF-MH 4/12/1934-SBF 13/5/1938-MH 21/11/1938-SBF 24/7/1941								(13)
No.8			?					(f)	
	?								s/s by /1882
No.8	(later 8)		0-6-0ST	IC	BH	692	1882	New	
			reb		HL	668	1910		
	MH								Scr c9/1934
No.8	(later BOWES No.8)		0-6-0ST	IC	SS	4594	1900	(h)	
	SBF								(14)
No.9	(later 9)		0-6-0ST	IC	?		?	(j)	
			reb		RS	109	1867		
			reb		RS	2821	1894		
			reb		HL	6830	1914		
			reb		Ridley Shaw		1927		
	MH-SBF ?/? - MH 31/10/1907-SBF 12/6/1908-MH 12/1/1926								
	-SBF 23/12/1927-MH 15/10/1929-SBF 29/4/1931								Scr 2/1935

45

No.9			0-6-0ST	IC	SS	4051	1894		
		reb	0-6-0PT	IC	Caerphilly		1930	(k)	
	SBF								(15)
No.10	(HARTLEPO0L)		0-6-0	IC	TR	252	1854	New	
		reb	0-6-0ST	IC	BH		1877		
	SBF								(16)
10			0-6-2ST	IC	BH	1071	1892	New	
		reb			HL		1906		
		reb			T.D.Ridley		1917		
	SBF								Scr 10/1931
	BOWES No.10		0-6-0ST	IC	NBA	16628	1905		
		reb	0-6-0PT	IC	Sdn		1924	(m)	
	SBF								(12)
No.11	(later 11)		0-6-0	IC	RS	1313	1860	New	
		reb	0-6-0ST	IC	RS		1875?		
	SBF								Scr /1915
11			0-6-0ST	OC	HL	3103	1915	New	
	MH-SBF 7/9/1945								(12)
No.12			0-6-0ST	IC	RS	1612	1864	New	
	SBF-MH after /1872								Scr /1885
12			0-6-0ST	OC	HL	2719	1907	New	
		reb			RS		1932		
	MH								(12)
No.13			0-6-0	IC	RS	1611	1864	New	
	SBF?								Scr /1896
13			0-6-0ST	IC	HL	2545	1902	New	
	SBF-MH 10/7/1931-SBF 1/11/1937								(12)
No.14			0-6-0ST	IC	RS	1800	1866	New	
	?								(17)
14			0-6-2T	IC	CF	1158	1898	(n)	
	MH-SBF 13/3/1914								Scr 9/1923
14			0-6-0ST	IC	HL	3569	1923	New	
	SBF-MH 13/2/1942								(12)
15			0-6-0T	IC	HE	1506	1930	New	
	MH								(12)
39			0-6-0ST	IC	RWH	1422	1867	(p)	
	SBF								(18)
16			0-6-0ST	IC	VF	5288	1945	(q)	
	SBF								(12)
17			0-6-0ST	IC	VF	5298	1945	(r)	
	MH								(12)
"18"	75317		0-6-0ST	IC	VF	5307	1945	(s)	
	SBF								(19)

(a) ex Lord Ravensworth & Partners, with the Springwell Colliery Railway, 1/1/1850
(b) ex Felling Colliery, Felling, 1/4/1926
(c) ex HL, Newcastle upon Tyne, 3/1886; built new in 1884 and carried RWH works plate
(d) ex LNER, 1787, Gateshead, 11/8/1936, following accident to RWH 1986/1884; LNER J79 class; previously NER H2 class
(e) ex Lord Dunsany & Partners Ltd, Pelton Colliery, Pelton Fell, c/1880 (if identification is correct)
(f) on 19/12/1854 the LNWR Southern Committee agreed the sale to Palmer of locos Nos.47 and 54. Both were 2-2-0 tender locos built by Bury, Curtis & Kennedy, No.47 in 1840 and No.54 in 1841. However, both locos seem to have survived on the LNWR until 1856, and it is not known whether either came to the Pontop & Jarrow Railway
(g) ex Felling Colliery, Felling, date unknown, but first recorded repair at SBF was 23/2/1932; ran as FELLING No.1 until 11/1934
(h) ex GWR, 713, 7/1936, via R.H.Longbotham & Co Ltd, dealers, Northwood, Middlesex; arrived 13/8/1936; previously Barry Railway, 'F' class, 52
(j) identity uncertain; may have been built by Ralph Coulthard, Gateshead; its date of arrival is also uncertain – the Bowes Railway Locomotive Ledger gave 1860, R.H.Inness gave 1862

(k)   ex GWR, 717, 11/1934, via R.H.Longbotham & Co Ltd, dealers, Northwood, Middlesex; arrived 26/11/1934; previously Barry Railway, 'F' class, 71
(m)   ex GWR, 725, 11/1934, via R.H.Longbotham & Co Ltd, dealers, Northwood, Middlesex; arrived 26/11/1934; previously Barry Railway, 'F' class, 127
(n)   ex The Harton Coal Co Ltd, South Shields, Marsden & Whitburn Colliery Railway, No.7, /1912 (after 22/7/1912), via Robert Frazer & Sons Ltd, dealers, Hebburn
(p)   hired from The Lambton, Hetton & Joicey Collieries Ltd, Lambton Railway, Philadelphia, 18/12/1937
(q)   ex War Department, 75298, Longmoor Military Railway, Liss, Hampshire, 4/1946; arrived 5/1946
(r)   ex War Department, 75308, Longmoor Military Railway, Liss, Hampshire, 4/1946; arrived 13/5/1946
(s)   ex War Department, 75317, Longmoor Military Railway, Liss, Hampshire; oral tradition claimed this locomotive worked here, but written confirmation is lacking; if she was here, she arrived between 5/1946 and 8/1946, amd was presumably on loan

(1)   the Transactions of the Institute of Mining Engineers, Vol.14, 1912-1913, p.111, states "the engines of that locomotive, which were vertical, could be seen until a few years ago driving lathes and other tools in the [Marley Hill] colliery workshops."
(2)   sold as scrap to Robert Frazer & Sons Ltd, Hebburn, 8/1936; scrapped on site, 9/1936
(3)   to Killingworth Colliery, Killingworth, Northumberland, /1863
(4)   sold as scrap to Robert Frazer & Sons Ltd, Hebburn, 2/1937; scrapped on site, 3/1937
(5)   to Killingworth Colliery, Killingworth, Northumberland, c/1880
(6)   to NCB No.6 Area, with the Railway, 1/1/1947; out of use
(7)   to Sir W.G.Armstrong, Whitworth & Co Ltd (at Lemington, Northumberland ?), /1917
(8)   returned to Felling Colliery, Felling, 14/10/1927; to SBF, 6/12/1929; to W.G.Bagnall Ltd, Stafford, Staffordshire, for repairs, 21/9/1942; to MH, 8/9/1943; to NCB No.6 Area, with the Railway, 1/1/1947
(9)   scrapped c/1885; but the saddletank survived outside Springwell Bank Foot shed until about 1954, being used to hold the clay for making firebrick arches
(10) sold as scrap to D.Sep.Bowran Ltd, Gateshead, 4/1946; scrapped, almost certainly at Follonsby Colliery, 10/1946
(11) to Felling Colliery, Felling, c/1895
(12) to NCB, No.6 Area, with the Railway, 1/1/1947
(13) loaned to The Bedlington Coal Co Ltd, Northumberland, 18/11/1942; returned to SBF, 21/8/1944; sold as scrap to D.Sep.Bowran Ltd, Gateshead, 4/1946; scrapped, almost certainly at Follonsby Colliery, 10/1946
(14) sold as scrap to D.Sep.Bowran Ltd, Gateshead, 4/1946; scrapped, almost certainly at Follonsby Colliery, 9/1946
(15) loaned to The Harton Coal Co Ltd, Boldon Colliery, 20/2/1943; returned to SBF, 14/8/1943; to MH, 24/10/1945; to NCB No.6 Area, with the Railway, 1/1/1947
(16) to Killingworth Colliery, Killingworth, Northumberland, c/1866; returned to SBF; boiler exploded at Jarrow Staithes, 14/6/1882; to MH, c/1883; to Killingworth Colliery, Killingworth, c/1886
(17) said to have been sold c/1880, possibly to a firm in Scotland
(18) returned to The Lambton, Hetton & Joicey Collieries Ltd, Philadelphia, 28/3/1938
(19) to The Weardale Steel, Coal & Coke Co Ltd, Thornley Colliery, Thornley, by 8/1946

NATIONAL COAL BOARD
North East Area from 1/4/1974
North Durham Area from 26/3/1967
Northumberland & Durham Division No.5 Area from 1/1/1964
Durham Division No.5 Area from 1/1/1963
Durham Division No.6 (North-West Durham) Area from 1/1/1950
Northern Division No.6 (North-West Durham) Area from 1/1/1947

Note: although the Railway from Black Fell to Jarrow fell inside No.1 (North-East Durham) Area, No.6 Area had the responsibility for its whole length. The Railway Manager's office remained at Springwell for some time, before moving, curiously, to Birkheads, and then Marley Hill.

Major investment
It was clear that, given that the Railway had many years of operation ahead of it, a major programme of investment was needed. By 1947 the stationary engine at Kibblesworth was 105 years old, and even before nationalisation the company had approved plans to replace it. A 350 brake horse power electric hauler was ordered from the English Electric Co Ltd, and a large new engine house, straddling the track, built alongside the old one – perhaps the last railway engine house ever to be built in Britain. The new engine started work on 9th August 1947. The stationary engines at Blackham's Hill and Black Fell were replaced during the pit holidays in 1950, the first by a 300 b.h.p. hauler from Metropolitan-Vickers Ltd and that at Black Fell by a 500 b.h.p. hauler from British Thomson-Houston Ltd. Some mechanical equipment was

also replaced, but the engine house buildings, though altered, were retained. Both new haulers began work on 30th July 1950.

New locomotives were soon ordered too, bringing the total in No.6 Area to nearly ninety. So in 1949 the Area decided to introduce a numbering scheme for its locomotives. The Area had been divided into five sub-areas called Groups, which were lettered (e.g., A Group, B Group, etc), and the numbering scheme dealt with each Group in turn. The Railway was in B Group, and the Bowes locomotives, including those that had come to the Railway since 1947, were allocated Area Nos.18-31. Locomotives purchased new by No.6 Area were numbered from 77 onwards. But the Bowes Railway's own numbering was also continued, and for many years locomotives carried both numbers.

South of Marley Hill, and served by British Railways' Tanfield Branch were East Tanfield (NZ 194552) and Tanfield Lea Collieries (NZ 188544), formerly owned by The Lambton, Hetton & Joicey Collieries Ltd, and soon after nationalisation Marley Hill Shed was given responsibility for the locomotives working here. It would also seem that the NCB may well have acquired running powers over the Tanfield Branch, not just to allow them to change locomotives when required but also to allow Bowes wagons to be worked between down to the two collieries and thus allow their coal to be brought on to the Railway. It would also seem that these trains were hauled by NCB locomotives from Marley Hill, presumably with a run-round at Bowes Bridge. How long these powers lasted is not known. East Tanfield's rail traffic was replaced by road transport in April 1958 (it closed on 9th January 1965) and Tanfield Lea Colliery was closed on 25th August 1962.

New steel wagons began to be introduced in May 1952, numbered upwards from 6001. At first these carried 13 tons, but later 14-ton and 21-ton wagons were added, although the last were not allowed to travel further west than Springwell because of narrow bridges on the inclines.

The Coal Board's drive to increase output and improve efficiency led to three important developments affecting the Railway. The first was the opening in 1948 of **HIGH MARLEY HILL DRIFT** (NZ 191572), to the west of the Railway between Marley Hill and Byermoor. Soon afterwards the NCB adopted a plan to drive a tunnel, known as Clockburn Drift (NZ 186604), between Winlaton Mill on the Chopwell & Garesfield Railway (which see) and Marley Hill Colliery, a distance of about two miles. This would incorporate locomotives and mine cars on two 3ft 6in gauge tracks to bring Marley Hill coal down to Winlaton Mill, where it would be transferred into standard gauge wagons for the ½ mile journey north to Derwenthaugh Coke Works. When this was opened, in March 1952, it reduced, but did not eliminate, Marley Hill coal dispatched on the Railway, a loss that would have been greater if the planned extension of the Drift on to Byermoor and Burnopfield Collieries had gone ahead. The Drift was regarded as part of Marley Hill Colliery, as were the locomotives, though the loco shed was at Winlaton Mill. Then in 1956 the Wardley dry-cleaning plant was replaced by a large new coal washery on the opposite side of the Railway to Monkton Coke Works, known at first as **WARDLEY WASHERY** and latterly as **MONKTON COAL PREPARATION PLANT** (NZ

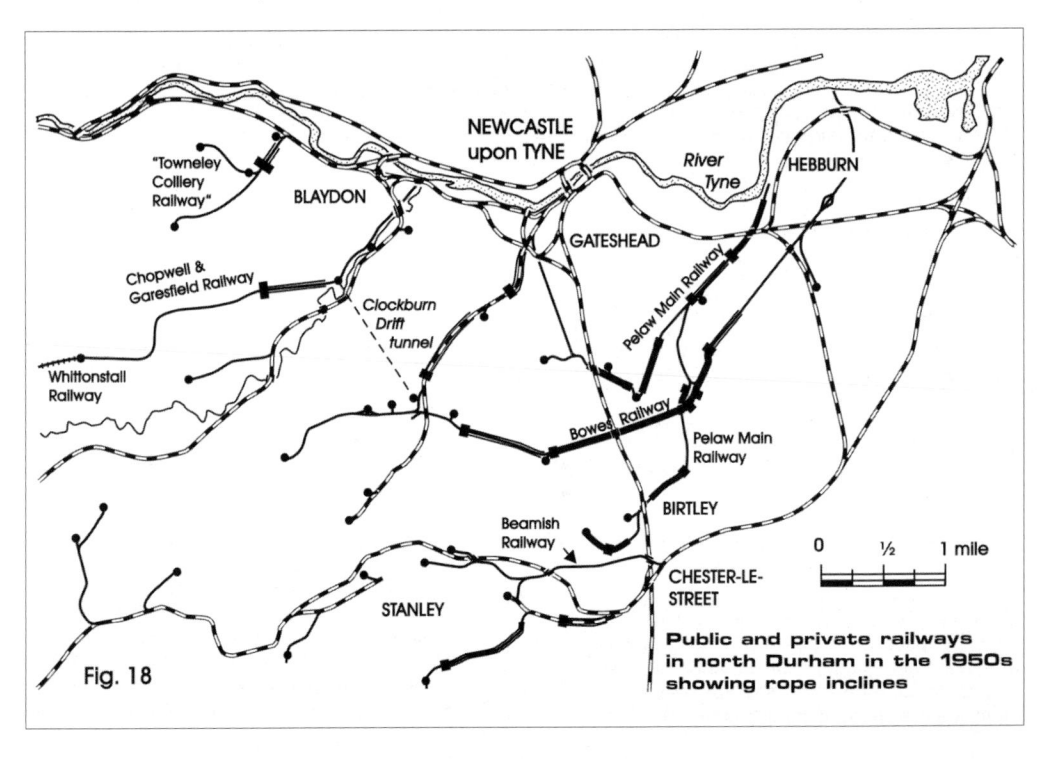

Fig. 18

Public and private railways in north Durham in the 1950s showing rope inclines

35. Springwell Bank Foot loco shed in the early 1950s, with (left to right) 13, HL 2545/1902; 6, HL 2515/1901, as rebuilt by Lingford Gardiner of Bishop Auckland in 1930, and 14, HL 3569/1923, with the repair shop on the left.

36. Springwell Bank Foot loco shed at lunch time on 24th October 1974, with (left to right) 104, S 10158/1963, outside the new diesel repair shop; 0-4-0DH AB 478/1963 and No.503, HE 6614/1965.

314627). Although Railway locomotives brought in fulls and took away empties, wagons were run through the plant by gravity. At the Coking Plant 33 new Koppers ovens were built in 1956 and started up on 11th September 1956, though the original ovens were not shut down until 1961.

Although single semaphore signals were installed at several places between Springwell Bank Foot and Jarrow, there was no conventional signalling on the Railway, and drivers avoided problems by recognising the sound of locomotive whistles and knowing the turns which each locomotive was working. Such a system has its weaknesses, and perhaps because of the complex shunting now being undertaken at Wardley, with its marshalling yard, Washery and Coke Works, radio-telephone apparatus was fitted to all the steam locomotives at Springwell Bank Foot in 1957, controlled from a weigh cabin at Wardley. New apparatus was installed when the final batch of diesel locomotives was delivered in 1965.

On at least two occasions in the 1950s and 1960s the cost of operating the Railway was compared with the costs of using road transport, on both occasions the Railway coming out significantly cheaper. Even in the early 1960s the inclines were handling over one million tons of coal per year.

The amalgamation with the Pelaw Main Railway
A proposal of 1937 to link the two railways has been noted above. In 1949 the NCB applied for permission to build a link between Heworth on the Pelaw Main Railway and Wardley; but this was rejected by the Ministry of Town & Country Planning because it would have passed close to land scheduled for domestic housing. However, at Blackham's Hill the two lines were only about 100 yards apart, and in 1955 the NCB built a link here, from near the top of the Eighton Banks Incline on the Pelaw Main Railway round to a point about half way down the Blackham's Hill East Incline, where the gradient into Springwell, at 1 in 70, was acceptable for locomotive working.

For some years this link was rarely used; but in January 1959 Ouston E Colliery, the last working colliery in the Birtley area, was closed, bringing the volume of Pelaw Main traffic down to a level which the Bowes inclines could handle, and so the two Railways were amalgamated. Major sections of the Pelaw Main Railway were closed, and the remainder, about eight miles long, became a branch of the Bowes Railway. Responsibility for the locomotives working here passed to Springwell Bank Foot shed.

The working of the Pelaw Main branch
The history of this line will be found in the chapter dealing with the Pelaw Main Railway. At the end of the branch, on the western side of the Team Valley, a locomotive was used between **RAVENSWORTH PARK DRIFT** (NZ 242588) and the bank foot of the Allerdene Incline, where there was a loco shed, known as the **SHOP PIT LOCO SHED** (NZ 253587). From a junction 100 yards north of the Shop Pit shed a second line crossed the viaduct over the southern end of the Team Valley Trading Estate before turning northwards to run through the Estate to Dunston, where there was a coal depot and also a link to British Railways' Tanfield Branch. This line, about 1½ miles long, was owned by North Eastern Trading Estates Ltd, with the NCB

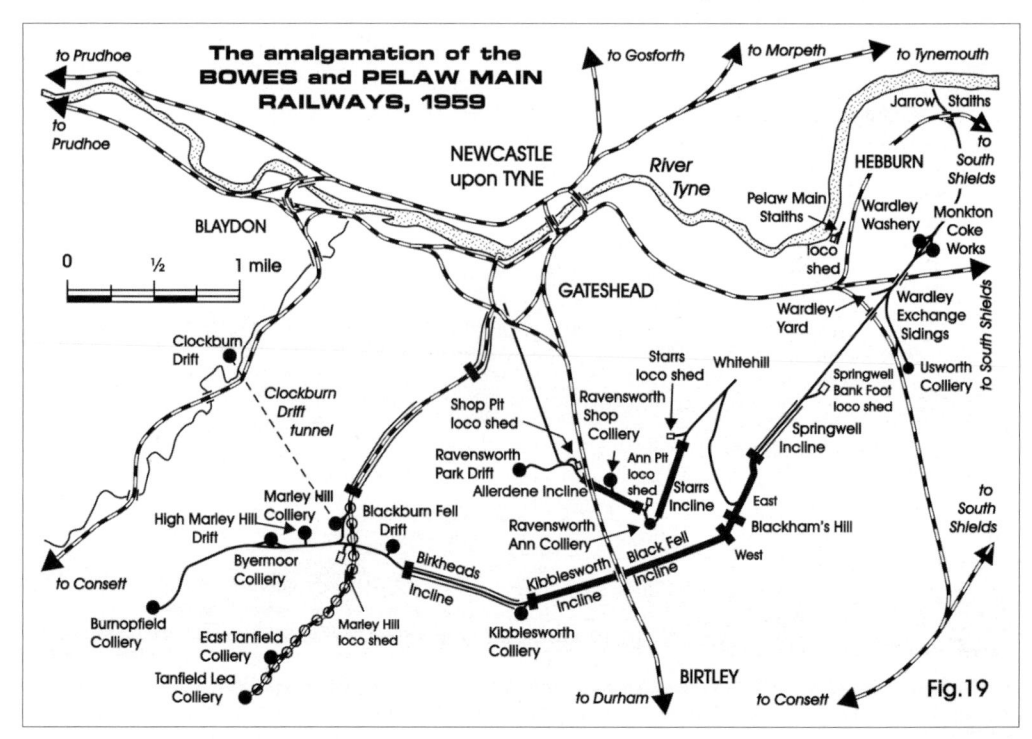

Fig.19 The amalgamation of the BOWES and PELAW MAIN RAILWAYS, 1959

exercising running powers over it. This link to BR had once been very important, but by the late 1950s it was little used.

In May 1963 the working here was re-organised. The NCB gave up its running powers and traffic between Ravensworth Park Drift and Allerdene Bank Foot was taken over by a loco hired from North Eastern Trading Estates, though the Shop Pit shed continued to be used for locomotive repairs until August 1964, when it closed. The shed was re-opened temporarily between 6th and 21st September 1965 when a landslip prevented access by the Team Valley locomotive, and in May 1966 it was restored to full working when the NCB resumed full control of the traffic, due to North Eastern Trading Estates contracting their own shunting to BR.

From the Shop Pit sidings wagons then ascended the single-line Allerdene Incline, bringing them to **RAVENSWORTH ANN COLLIERY** at Harlow Green, alongside the A1 road. This incline was operated by the **King's Engine** (NZ 265581), a 225 b.h.p. electric hauler set well above the bank head. This engine also had to handle all the traffic to and from **RAVENSWORTH SHOP COLLIERY** (NZ 258586), about half way down the incline, and all the colliery waste sent to the **MEADOWS DISPOSAL POINT** (NZ 264580), just to the west of the tunnel under the A1. Ravensworth Ann Colliery was shunted by a locomotive from the **ANN PIT LOCO SHED** (NZ 264581), co-ordinating its work with that of the next incline, the Starrs Incline, whose bank foot lay on the eastern side of the colliery yard.

From here the full wagons ascended the Starrs Incline, again single line, which brought them to the **Starrs Engine** (NZ 273594) at Wrekenton, a 500 b.h.p. electric hauler. Opposite the Engine House was the **STARRS LOCO SHED** (NZ 273593), from which two locomotives were normally in use to work the traffic between Starrs and Whitehill, where there was a large marshalling yard and the **WHITEHILL WASHERY** (NZ 277599), which was closed in 1962. From here trains were propelled to Eighton Banks, round on to the Blackham's Hill East Incline and into Springwell, where the fulls were left and a set of empties collected. Pelaw Main trains could only be accommodated in this way when the rope-hauled Blackham's Hill East empties were above the Pelaw Main junction. The working on this section was made safer in January 1971, when the reverse at Whitehill was replaced by a curve, allowing the locomotive to haul for the whole distance.

Pelaw Main Staiths
In addition to the branch, a small section of track was retained at **PELAW MAIN STAITHS** (NZ 300632) at Bill Quay. These staiths could only be reached via a **self-acting incline**, so that rail traffic had to continue. Coal was brought here by road, and then locomotives from **PELAW MAIN STAITHS LOCO SHED**, near the top of the incline, handled the traffic between the loading point and the incline. The staiths were closed in May 1964.

In March 1968 Ravensworth Ann Colliery was re-organised. Coal winding at the shaft here ceased, its coal being drawn instead via Ravensworth Park Drift, which was re-named Ravensworth Ann Colliery. As a result the Ravensworth Ann loco shed was closed on 8th March 1968, although the extra traffic from the former Park Drift meant two shifts having to be introduced at the Shop Pit loco shed.

37. Wardley Coal Preparation Plant (left) and Monkton Coking Plant (right), with the Bowes main line bisecting them, 2nd June 1971.

The introduction of diesel locomotives

No.6 Area purchased its first two diesel locomotives in 1959 to work the section of the Pelaw Main branch between Starrs and Springwell, though in practice they proved under-powered and prone to breakdown, and a steam locomotive was often substituted. Meanwhile more and more domestic housing was being built near the Railway, eventually reaching the fence at Springwell Bank Foot loco shed. So in 1962 the NCB decided to replace all the steam locomotives at Springwell Bank Foot with diesels, the programme of six locomotives being completed in 1965. The last steam locomotive left the shed on 22nd September 1966, ending 140 years of steam locomotives there.

Closures west of Kibblesworth

In the west High Marley Hill Drift closed on 29th June 1963, but the 1967 colliery closure programme saw Byermoor Colliery close on 2nd February 1968 and Burnopfield Colliery follow on 9th August 1968, the last resulting in the closure of the Railway between Burnopfield and the marshalling yard west of Marley Hill Colliery. In March 1969 the section between Blackburn Fell Drift and Kibblesworth Bank Head was closed, leaving only coal from Kibblesworth Colliery still being dispatched over the remaining five Bowes inclines. On 30th March 1970 rail transport to/from Blackburn Fell Drift was replaced by road transport by converting the Railway east of the Tanfield branch crossing up to the Drift into a road. This left only the track around Marley Hill Colliery, where a small amount of coal was still being wound up the shaft, transhipped into railway wagons and then taken down to Marley Hill Yard to be transhipped again into road transport. This ceased on 30th July 1970, though Marley Hill Loco Shed remained open to complete locomotive repairs until November 1970. Blackburn Fell Drift was merged with Marley Hill Colliery in April 1973 (one source gives 3rd March 1979, in error), although its buildings remained, derelict, for many years afterwards. Marley Hill Colliery itself, with all its coal now going out via Clockburn Drift, finally closed on 4th March 1983.

The closures of 1973-1974

In April 1973 Ravensworth Ann Colliery was merged with Kibblesworth Colliery, closing the former Ravensworth Park Drift, and with it the whole of the Pelaw Main branch, with its two rope inclines and two loco sheds, which ceased work on 18th April 1973.

USWORTH COLLIERY (formerly Wardley No.1 Colliery, and once John Bowes & Partners' Follonsby Colliery) ceased production on 8th August 1974, but the Railway's Follonsby branch remained open to handle traffic exchanged with BR via the Wardley Exchange sidings, while materials for the Railway were also transhipped from road to rail in the colliery yard. Rather confusingly, the colliery site was then re-named Wardley.

Kibblesworth Colliery closed on 4th October 1974, bringing to an end the working of four of the remaining rope inclines, though the Springwell Incline remained operational to handle wagons completing repairs at Springwell Wagon Shops. A fortnight before closure the south side of the Black Fell Incline had been narrowed to 3ft 0in gauge (making the working of standard gauge sets over the incline alternate, rather than simultaneous) in preparation for the creation of the **BLACK FELL UNDERGROUND LOCOMOTIVE TRAINING SITE**, the intention being to use an underground

38. The teeming shed at Jarrow on 17th March 1964, with fulls entering the three-road discharging points and empties coming out from the lifts, with 104, S 10158/1963.

39. The new loco shed at the former Wardley No.1 (Follonsby) Colliery, with the new loco repair shop behind on the right, 24th July 1978.

locomotive here to train drivers on steep gradients. After closure a locomotive shed was made by roofing over one of the dishes at the bank head and putting doors on each end, and a 3ft 0in gauge vehicle brought in. The test track was commissioned in January 1975, but in the following month there was a serious run-away on the 1 in 15 gradient, and it was not used again. The track was finally lifted in 1981.

Meanwhile a new **WAGON SHOP** was built at Wardley (formerly Follonsby), allowing the old Shops and the Springwell Incline to close in November 1974. The Engineering Shops, where a bay had been opened in August 1964 to handle locomotive repairs, closed on 9th March 1975.

Preservation schemes
After briefly lying empty, Marley Hill Loco Shed and its sidings were taken over as a store by the incipient North of England Open Air Museum at Beamish, which needed a site to which to bring its major railway exhibits. In 1973 the Stephenson & Hawthorn Locomotive Trust also came there, with the Museum eventually removing its locomotives to Beamish. From that small beginning has developed the Tanfield Railway, the largest preservation scheme in North-East England. It first relaid the track between the shed, Bowes Bridge and Sunniside, and then worked southwards down the former Tanfield Branch, re-instating Marley Hill signal box at the former Tanfield crossing, building a major two-platformed station at Andrews House, and then extending further south to Causey Arch, adjacent to the oldest railway bridge in the world (1726) and on to East Tanfield. A widely-varied collection of locomotives, including narrow gauge examples, has been brought to Marley Hill, where the shed remains at the centre of the Tanfield Railway's operations. 32 (AB 1659/1920), which worked on the Railway here, was saved after the closure of the Pelaw Main branch and is now preserved here.

Further east, the then newly-formed Tyne & Wear County Council funded the filming of the Railway between Kibblesworth and Jarrow before it closed (*The Bowes Line*, by Amber Films, Newcastle, available as a video). The 1¼ miles between Black Fell to Springwell was part of the original Springwell Colliery Railway, and 150 years after its opening, in January 1976, the County Council, in conjunction with the Tyne & Wear Industrial Monuments Trust, acquired this section. The Black Fell Engine and the Springwell Bank Head brake cabin and wheel were to be only static exhibits, but the Blackham's Hill Engine and its two inclines were to be kept in full working order and demonstrated as the world's only preserved rope inclines. For this a full range of the Railway's historic wagons, over 40 in all, was chosen from the remaining fleet in 1975. Once a locomotive has taken a set of wagons to Blackham's Hill the inclines can be operated, although alternately rather than simultaneously, as in NCB days. Three former Bowes Railway locomotives, No.22 (AB 2274/1949), 101 (FH 3922/1959) and No.503 (HE 6614/1965 – see below) are housed here, preserved on the Railway for which they were purchased. The whole site is a Scheduled Ancient Monument, and strict rules applied to the Bowes Railway material – for example, all the locomotives and wagons carry genuine Bowes Railway liveries of the early 1960s. In 1977 the County Council also acquired the former Engineering and Wagon Shops at Springwell. This not only preserved the last remaining workshops courtyard in the North-East, together with much historic machinery, but also provided the facilities for restoration work. In 1979-1980 these were used by Locomotion Enterprises Ltd to build the replicas of *Rocket* and *Novelty* for the re-creation of the 1830 Rainhill Trials, near Manchester. Meanwhile, a spur was laid on to the Pelaw Main curve in 1979 in order to build a passenger platform there and allow a passenger service to be introduced between Springwell and Blackham's Hill, and this was subsequently extended over the Pelaw Main trackbed almost to the Vicarage Crossing at Wrekenton. With the abolition of Tyne & Wear County Council in 1986 ownership was divided between Sunderland and Gateshead Councils, working in conjunction with the Bowes Railway Co Ltd, whose volunteers manage what is now called the Bowes Railway Centre. In the 1990s other locomotives, wagons and colliery equipment was brought to the Centre, and in 2002 the Centre applied for Museum status.

Springwell Bank Foot loco shed, the oldest locomotive shed site in the world, has also been preserved, following its abandonment by the NCB in 1978 (see below), becoming the base of vehicles owned by the North East Bus Museum.

Despite the various closures and two preservation schemes up to 1975, the section of the Railway northwards from Springwell Bank Foot was still being operated commercially by the NCB, a unique juxta-position. Partly because the new scheme was calling itself the Bowes Railway preservation scheme, the NCB decided to re-name its remaining section **MONKTON RAILWAYS**. For the history of this section under this title see the notes following the Bowes Railway loco lists.

In addition to their Bowes Railway responsibilities, additional responsibilities were undertaken as follows:
Marley Hill Loco Shed : for the locomotives at East Tanfield and Tanfield Lea Collieries; later for Clara Vale Colliery and Morrison Busty Colliery, Annfield Plain.
Springwell Bank Foot Loco Shed : repairs to locomotives at Boldon Colliery, between 1968 and 1972.
Bowes Railway Manager : for the railway operation, locomotives and wagons at Derwenthaugh Loco Shed, Swalwell, from 1970s.

In the locomotive list below the following abbreviations are used:

Bowes Railway

      MH   Marley Hill Loco Shed, Marley Hill
      SBF   Springwell Bank Foot Loco Shed, Wardley
      SW   Springwell Engineering Shops, Springwell (repairs only)

Pelaw Main branch (allocations from 30/1/1959 only; for earlier Pelaw Main Railway allocations see the chapter for the Pelaw Main Railway

      BF   Blackhouse Fell Loco Shed, near Birtley
      OE   Ouston E Pit shed, Ouston
      OEW Ouston E Workshops, Ouston
      PMS   Pelaw Main Staiths, Bill Quay
      SP   Shop Pit Loco Shed, Lamesley
      RA   Ravensworth Ann Colliery, Low Fell
      S   Starrs Loco Shed, Wrekenton

The NCB numbering is shown in the first column. 3 (BH 938/1888) was scrapped before the No.6 Area numbering scheme was introduced, whilst No.10 (NBA 16628/1905) never carried its Area number. The Bowes Railway numbers were removed from most locomotives in the 1960s.

Gauge : 4ft 8½in

-	3		0-6-2ST	IC	BH	938	1888		
				reb	HL	3045	1903	(a)	
	SBF								(1)
18	(BOWES No.4)		0-4-0ST	OC	KS	4030	1919	(b)	

MH-Tanfield Lea Colliery 8/4/1948-MH 15/9/1949-East Tanfield Colliery 17/5/1950 -Tanfield Lea Colliery 20/10/1950-MH 3/4/1951-Tanfield Lea Colliery 28/1/1953 -East Tanfield Colliery 20/2/1953-MH 6/3/1953-Tanfield Lea Colliery 3/11/1954 -MH 17/12/1955-Tanfield Lea Colliery 7/5/1959-MH 24/8/1962   (2)

19	(BOWES No.) 6	0-6-0ST	OC	HL	2515	1901		
			reb	LG		1930	(b)	
	SBF							(3)
20	(BOWES No.) 9	0-6-0PT	IC	SS	4051	1894		
			reb	Caerphilly		1930	(b)	
	MH-SBF 15/5/1947							(4)

[21]	BOWES No.10	0-6-0PT reb	IC	NBA Sdn	16628	1905 1924	(b)		
	SBF							(5)	
22	(BOWES No.) 11	0-6-0ST	OC	HL	3103	1915	(b)		

SBF-Robert Stephenson & Hawthorns Ltd, Newcastle upon Tyne, repairs, /1950
-MH 8/9/1950   Scr 5/1970

| 23 | (12) | 0-6-0ST reb | OC | HL RS | 2719 | 1907 1932 | (b) | | |

MH-Derwenthaugh 5/12/1950-MH 18/12/1951
-Robert Stephenson & Hawthorns Ltd, Newcastle upon Tyne, repairs, /1952
-MH by 26/4/1952   (6)

| 24 | (BOWES No.) 13 | 0-6-0ST | IC | HL | 2545 | 1902 | (b) | | |

SBF-Robert Stephenson & Hawthorns Ltd, Newcastle upon Tyne, repairs, 31/3/1953
-SBF 6/1954-Derwenthaugh, loan, 6/6/1958-SBF, 20/6/1958-SW, to stand, 9/10/1965   Scr 6/1968

| 25 | (14) | 0-6-0ST | IC | HL | 3569 | 1923 | (b) | | |

MH-SBF 23/6/1947
-Robert Stephenson & Hawthorns Ltd, Newcastle upon Tyne, repairs, 6/1953
-SBF /53-SW, to stand, 9/10/1965   Scr 6/1968

| 26 | (15) | 0-6-0T | IC | HE | 1506 | 1930 | (b) | | |

MH-SBF 18/9/1949-Hunslet Engine Co Ltd, Leeds, repairs, 4/10/1949-SBF, 5/1950
-Hunslet Engine Co Ltd, Leeds, repairs, 1/1959-SBF by 8/59-SW, to stand, 9/10/1965 Scr 6/1968

27	(BOWES No.) 16	0-6-0ST	IC	VF	5288	1945	(b)		
	SBF							(7)	
28	(BOWES No.) 17	0-6-0ST	IC	VF	5298	1945	(b)		
	MH							(8)	
29	(BOWES No.) 18	0-6-0T	OC	HC	1255	1917	(c)		

SBF-W.G.Bagnall Ltd, Stafford, repairs, 3/1961-SBF by 7/1962   (9)

| 30 | (BOWES No.) 19 | 0-4-0ST | OC | AB | 1883 | 1927 | (d) | | |

MH-Blaydon Burn 1/1948-SBF 12/3/1948-Axwell Park Colliery 17/12/1948
-Craghead Colliery c1/1949-Blaydon Burn by 3/4/49-Craghead Colliery by 23/8/49
-MH 28/8/1949-SBF 24/9/1953-Bradley Central Workshops, Leadgate, repairs, 17/5/1957
-SBF 29/11/1957-RA 20/5/1963 -S 24/5/1963   (10)

83	(BOWES No.) 20	0-6-0ST	IC	HE	3688	1949	New		
	MH							(11)	
31	BOWES No.21	0-4-0ST	OC	HL	2481	1900	(e)		

(EDEN until 5/1949)
MH-Tanfield Lea Colliery 15/9/1949-MH 12/12/1950-Tanfield Lea Colliery 3/4/1951
-MH 11/1951-Tanfield Lea Colliery 1/1952-MH 28/1/1953-Tanfield Lea Colliery by 1/2/1953
-MH 3/11/1954-Tanfield Lea Colliery 17/12/1955-MH c7/1957
-Tanfield Lea Colliery c1/1958-MH 7/5/1959-Tanfield Lea Colliery 17/11/1959
-MH 24/8/1962   (12)

| 85 | (BOWES No.22) | 0-4-0ST | OC | AB | 2274 | 1949 | (f) | | |

SBF-East Tanfield Colliery 24/7/1954-Tanfield Lea Colliery 2/10/1957
-East Tanfield Colliery c11/1957-Tanfield Lea Colliery 23/4/1958
-MH 17/11/1959   (13)

| 32 | (STANLEY No.1); later (No.1) | 0-4-0ST | OC | AB | 1659 | 1920 | (g) | | |

MH-Andrew Barclay, Sons & Co Ltd, Kilmarnock, repairs, 5/1950-MH 6/1950
-East Tanfield Colliery 20/10/1950-MH 24/7/1954-SBF 4/5/1968-S 18/5/1968
-SP 1/1971-SW, to stand, 19/4/1973   (14)

86	(BOWES No.) 23	0-6-0ST	IC	RSHN	7751	1953	New		
	SBF							(15)	
90	(BOWES No.) 24	0-6-0ST	IC	HE	3833	1955	New		
	SBF							(16)	
63	1308	0-4-0T	IC	Ghd	37	1891	(h)		

RA-OEW by 8/1959-OE (stored) by 7/1/1960   (17)

| 64 | 1310 | 0-4-0T reb | IC | Ghd Ouston Shops | 38 | 1891 1950 | (h) | | |
| | OE | | | | | | | (18) | |

62	TYNE	0-4-0ST	OC	AB	786	1896			
			reb	AB		1940	(h)		
	PMS								(19)
61	DERWENT	0-6-0ST	OC	AB	970	1903			
			reb	RSHN		1945	(h)		
	SP-OEW by 7/1960-SP by 4/1961-S 5/1963								(20)
69	CHARLES PERKINS	0-4-0T	OC	HL	2986	1913	(h)		
	PMS								(19)
D54		0-4-0ST	OC	HL	3467	1920	(h)		
	OE-S c/1959-BF (salvage work) 6/1/1960-OEW 7/1960 -SBF 4/2/1961-S 22/9/1962-SBF c11/1962-RA 24/5/1963								(21)
66	CHARLES NELSON	0-4-0ST	OC	P	1748	1928	(h)		
	S-SP by 6/1/1960-RA by 7/1960-OEW by 8/1960-RA by 4/1961-SP by 8/1961 -RA c1/1963-SP (repairs) 4/1964-S 8/1964-RA 6/9/1965-S 21/9/1965 -RA 2/4/1966-S 5/1966-RA 5/3/1967-S 11/3/1967-SP 4/1967-S 1/1971 -SP 30/9/1972-S 12/4/1973-SW, to stand, 17/4/1973								(22)
67	NCB-PELAW	0-4-0ST	OC	P	2093	1947	(h)		
	S-RA by 6/1/1960-SP by 7/1960-RA after 4/1961, by 8/1961-SP (repairs) 5/1963 -RA 4/1964-SP 6/9/1965-RA 21/9/1965-S (repairs) 2/4/1966 -RA 5/1966-S (repairs) 5/3/1967-RA 11/3/1967-S 21/2/1968-SW, to stand, 16/5/1968								(23)
81		0-4-0ST	OC	RSHN	7604	1949	(h)		
	S-SBF 12/5/1962-SW 9/10/1965-S 10/10/1965-RA 19/2/1968 -SP 8/3/1968 (SBF gave 23/3/1968)-SW, to stand, 8/7/1972								(24)
68	CLAUDE	0-4-0ST	OC	HL	2349	1896	(j)		
	OE								(25)
101		4wDM		FH	3922	1959	New		
	S-SBF (repairs), 4/11/1962-S by 9/1963-SBF (repairs)14/3/1964-S c8/1964 -SP 11/3/1967-S 11/3/1967-SBF (repairs) 12/1967-S 6/9/1968-SBF 7/1970 -SW (repairs, not done) 7/1972-S 9/1972-SBF (repairs) 21/9/1972 -SW 11/1972-SBF 1/1973-S 12/4/1973-SW 25/4/1973								(26)
102		4wDM		FH	3923	1959	New		
	S-SBF (repairs) 9/1963-S 16/3/1964-SBF c6/1964 -Kibblesworth (breakdown of Drift hauler) 1/10/1964-SBF 9/10/1964-S 6/9/1965 -SW (repairs) 13/12/1965-SBF 5/2/1966-S 12/1967-SBF (repairs) 7/9/1968 -S 15/7/1969-SBF 9/1/1971-S 5/10/1971-SBF c4/1972-SW (repairs) 15/7/1972 -SBF c8/1972-S 21/9/1972-SBF (repairs) 2/11/1972-S c12/1972-SBF 25/1/1973 -SW c10/1973								(27)
68029		0-6-0ST	IC	HE	3215	1945	(k)		
	SBF (almost certainly)								(28)
60	*	0-6-0ST	IC	HE	3686	1948	(m)		
	SBF								(29)
103		0-6-0DH		S	10157	1963	New		
	SBF								(30)
104		0-6-0DH		S	10158	1963	New		
	SBF								(30)
36		0-6-0ST	OC	HL	2956	1912	(n)		
	SW (repairs)								(31)
4		0-4-0ST	OC	HC	1514	1923	(p)		
	MH (repairs)								(32)
No.500		0-6-0DH		HE	6611	1965	New		
	SBF								(30)
No.502		0-6-0DH		HE	6613	1965	New		
	SBF								(30)
No.503		0-6-0DH		HE	6614	1965	New		
	SBF								(30)

34		0-6-0ST	OC	RSHN	6943	1938	(q)	
	MH (repairs)							(31)
No.504		0-6-0DH		HE	6615	1965	New	
	SBF							(30)
52		0-4-0ST	OC	HL	3474	1920	(r)	
	SP-SW, to stand, 22/2/1968							(25)
No.509		0-6-0DH		AB	514	1966	(s)	
	SBF (repairs)							(32)
No.506		0-6-0DH		HE	6617	1965	(t)	
	SBF (repairs)							(33)
No.501		0-6-0DH		HE	6612	1965	(u)	
	SBF (repairs)							(34)
-		0-4-0DH		AB	478	1963	(v)	
	SBF-S 11/7/1972-SW 9/1972-S c24/11/1972-SW, to stand, 12/4/1973-SBF 17/4/1973							(30)

* No.2 Area numbering; fitted with Hill-Bigwood mechanical stoker

(a) ex John Bowes & Partners Ltd, with the Railway, 1/1/1947; out of use
(b) ex John Bowes & Partners Ltd, with the Railway, 1/1/1947
(c) ex Port of London Authority, No.61, 25/11/1947; sent from London to Hudswell, Clarke & Co Ltd, Leeds, for a new firebox; delivered to SBF, 7/8/1948; to BR, Tyne Dock Loco Shed, to be turned, 12/8/1948, and returned
(d) ex Imperial Chemical Industries Ltd, LOCH RANNOCH, Ardeer Works, Ayrshire, Scotland, /1947; sent from Scotland to Ridley, Shaw & Co Ltd, Middlesbrough, Yorkshire (NR), for repairs; delivered to MH, 12/12/1947; name painted out, 1/1948
(e) ex Tanfield Lea Colliery, near Stanley, by 3/4/1949
(f) ordered for East Tanfield Colliery, near Stanley, but delivered New to Springwell Bank Foot Loco Shed, 20/10/1949
(g) ex East Tanfield Colliery, near Stanley, 1/5/1950
(h) ex Pelaw Main Railway in merger, 30/1/1959
(j) ex Watergate Colliery, near Sunniside, c12/1959
(k) ex British Railways, Tyne Dock Motive Power depot, Tyne Dock, 2/1962, hire
(m) ex Lambton Engine Works, Philadelphia, 7/9/1962, for trial of mechanical stoker
(n) ex Craghead Colliery, Craghead, for repairs, 10/1964
(p) ex Clara Vale Colliery, Clara Vale, for repairs, 23/12/1964
(q) ex Morrison Busty Colliery, Annfield Plain, for repairs, 8/7/1965
(r) ex Leadgate Loco Shed, Leadgate, 5/5/1966
(s) ex Whitburn Colliery, Whitburn, for repairs, 3/1968
(t) ex Boldon Colliery, for repairs, 31/10/1968
(u) ex Wearmouth Colliery, Sunderland, for repairs, 16/3/1970
(v) ex Hylton Colliery, Sunderland, 5/7/1972

(1) scrapped at Follonsby Colliery by D.Sep. Bowran Ltd, Gateshead, 3/1947
(2) to Clara Vale Colliery, Clara Vale, 1/4/1964; scrapped there, 5/1966
(3) worked as 2-4-0ST from 6/1962 after left-hand coupling rod fractured; scrapped at shed by D.Sep. Bowran Ltd, Gateshead, 4/1964
(4) scrapped at Springwell Bank Foot shed by D.Sep. Bowran Ltd, Gateshead, 4/1964
(5) sent to Marple & Gillott Ltd, Gateshead, for scrap, 8/2/1950
(6) scrapped at Marley Hill shed by Robinson & Hannon Ltd, Blaydon, 1/1971
(7) to Derwenthaugh Loco Shed, Swalwell, 16/6/1965; scrapped on site by D.Sep.Bowran Ltd, Gateshead, 3/1971
(8) to Morrison Busty Colliery, Annfield Plain, 12/11/1968; scrapped on site by J.C.Wight Ltd, Sunderland, 8/1971
(9) to Derwenthaugh Loco Shed, Swalwell, 24/10/1963 (Derwenthaugh records gave 10/10/1963); scrapped on site by D.Sep.Bowran Ltd, Gateshead, 4/1966
(10) to Leadgate Loco Shed, Leadgate, 21/1/1964; scrapped on site by J.A.Lister & Sons Ltd, Consett, 8/1965
(11) to Morrison Busty Colliery, Annfield Plain, 18/11/1970; scrapped on site, 7/1974
(12) to Leadgate Loco Shed, Leadgate, 1/12/1962; scrapped by The Consett Iron Co Ltd, 4/1964
(13) to Thomas Ness Ltd, St.Anthony's Tar Distillation Plant, Walker, Newcastle-upon-Tyne, 27/10/1970; to Tyne & Wear Industrial Monuments Trust, Bowes Railway preservation scheme, Springwell, 18/6/1976
(14) sold to member of Stephenson & Hawthorn Locomotive Trust, Marley Hill Loco Shed, Sunniside, 12/7/1973
(15) to Derwenthaugh Loco Shed, Swalwell, 8/9/1965; scrapped on site by Bowburn Metals Ltd, Bowburn, 3/1968

(16) to Derwenthaugh Loco Shed, Swalwell, 22/9/1966; scrapped on site by Derwenthaugh staff, 10/1970
(17) sent to stand in Ravensworth Colliery yard, Low Fell, after 8/1960, by 6/5/1961; scrapped on site by D.Sep. Bowran Ltd, Gateshead, 10/1963
(18) to Watergate Colliery, near Sunniside, after 8/1959, by 6/1/1960; sold to Steam Power Trust 1965 for preservation on the Middleton Railway, Leeds, and moved, 6/1965
(19) scrapped on site by D.Sep. Bowran Ltd, Gateshead, 10/1964
(20) to Derwenthaugh Loco Shed, Swalwell, 20/8/1964; to Clara Vale Colliery, Clara Vale, 8/9/1965; scrapped on site, 4/1966
(21) scrapped on site by D.Sep. Bowran Ltd, Gateshead, 12/1965
(22) scrapped on site by D.Sep. Bowran Ltd, Gateshead, 7/1973
(23) scrapped on site by Thos W.Ward Ltd, Middlesbrough, Yorkshire (NR), 12/1968
(24) scrapped on site by D.Sep. Bowran Ltd, Gateshead, 10/1972
(25) sent to stand in Ravensworth Colliery yard, Low Fell, after 8/1960, by 6/5/1961; scrapped on site by D.Sep. Bowran Ltd, Gateshead, 11/1963
(26) to East Hetton Colliery, Quarrington Hill, 15/9/1973; to South Hetton Loco Sheds, South Hetton, 10/1973; to Thornley Coal Preparation Plant, Thornley, 31/10/1974; to Wearmouth Colliery, Sunderland, 12/3/1976; to Dudley Colliery, Dudley, Northumberland, 14/4/1976; to Lambton Loco Sheds, Philadelphia, Lambton Railway, 19/4/1977; to Tyne & Wear Industrial Monuments Trust, Bowes Railway preservation scheme, Springwell, 8/1979, and moved on 13/8/1979
(27) repairs stopped; sold for scrap to A Ogden & Sons Ltd, Bowburn, 22/5/1975 and cut up on site, 9/1975
(28) returned to British Railways, Gateshead Motive Power depot, Gateshead, ex hire, 17/6/1962
(29) to Sherburn Hill Colliery, Sherburn Hill, 1/10/1962
(30) to Monkton Railways, /1975 (see below)
(31) repairs stopped; scrapped on site, 4/1966
(32) to Morrison Busty Colliery, Annfield Plain, 5/7/1965
(33) to Morrison Busty Colliery, Annfield Plain, 13/1/1966
(34) to Boldon Colliery, Boldon, 5/5/1968; ex Boldon Colliery to SBF for repairs, 11/3/1971; to Boldon Colliery, 25/5/1972
(35) to Lambton Railway Loco Sheds, Lambton Railway, 13/2/1969; ex Derwenthaugh Loco Shed, Swalwell, to SBF for repairs, 11/1972; to Derwenthaugh Loco Shed, Swalwell, 16/1/1973
(36) to Derwenthaugh Loco Shed, Swalwell, 6/10/1970

A visitor to Springwell Bank Foot shed on 26/10/1947 also recorded a 4-wheeled steam rail crane built by Booth in 1906. No other record of this crane is known.

Demonstration Locomotives
Locomotives owned by their makers on trial at Springwell Bank Foot Loco Shed, 1958-1962

Gauge : 4ft 8½in

		0-6-0DH	NBQ	27717	1957	(a)	(1)
		0-6-0DE	YE	2668	1958	(b)	(2)
		0-6-0DM	HE	4551	1956	(c)	(3)
No.5		0-6-0DM	WB	3123	1957	(d)	(4)
		0-4-0DE	BT	102	1958		
			BP	7859	1958	(e)	(5)
		0-6-0DM	WB	3160	1959	(f)	(6)
		0-6-0DH	S	10072	1961	(g)	(7)

(a) ex North British Locomotive Co Ltd, Glasgow, 7/3/1958; identity not confirmed, but almost certainly as shown here
(b) ex Yorkshire Engine Co Ltd, Sheffield, Yorkshire (WR), 21/4/1958
(c) ex Hunslet Engine Co Ltd, Leeds, Yorkshire, 9/5/1958
(d) ex West Midlands No.2 (Cannock Chase) Area, Littleton Colliery, Staffordshire, 9/1958
(e) ex Brush Electrical Engineering Co Ltd, Loughborough, Leicestershire, 6/12/1958; identity not confirmed, but almost certainly as shown here
(f) ex W.G.Bagnall Ltd, Stafford, Staffordshire. 9/1959
(g) ex No.2 Area, Lambton Railway Loco Sheds, Philadelphia, Lambton Railway, 28/3/1962;

(1) returned to North British Locomotive Co Ltd, Glasgow, 1/4/1958
(2) to Northern Division (Northumberland & Cumberland Division, No.3 (North Northumberland) Area, Ashington, Northumberland for trials, 3/5/1958
(3) returned to Hunslet Engine Co Ltd, Leeds, Yorkshire, 5/6/1958
(4) to West Midlands No.2 (Cannock Chase) Area, Hilton Main Colliery, Staffordshire, 10/1958
(5) returned to Brush Electrical Engineering Co Ltd, Loughborough, Leicestershire, 19/12/1958
(6) returned to W.G.Bagnall Ltd, Stafford, Staffordshire, c9/1959
(7) to West Midlands No.1 (North Staffordshire) Area, Hem Heath Colliery, Staffordshire, 26/7/1962

MONKTON RAILWAYS

Following the closure of the section of the Railway between Kibblesworth Colliery and Springwell Bank Foot in October 1974 and the closure of the Springwell Incline in the following month, the section still open comprised the main line between Springwell Bank Foot and Jarrow and the Follonsby branch, with locomotives continuing to be housed in the loco shed at Springwell Bank Foot. However, the line no longer served any collieries, all coal having now to be brought to the line for treatment at Monkton (formerly Wardley) Coal Preparation Plant and Monkton Coking Plant, either by rail via the link with the BR Leamside Branch at Wardley or via Pontop Junction at Jarrow, or by road via a transfer point just north of Monkton Coking Plant. With one preservation scheme established at Marley Hill and another being developed at Springwell, the remainder of the Railway was still be operated commercially, a unique juxta-position. Partly because Tyne & Wear County Council's scheme based at Springwell was being called the Bowes Railway preservation scheme, the NCB in 1975 re-named their section **MONKTON RAILWAYS**, and MONKTON was painted on the wagons following repair.

The NCB decided to establish their facilities at the former Usworth (originally Follonsby) Colliery, where the colliery buildings and screens remained, although rather confusingly the NCB called the site Wardley. The new Wagon Shop (see above) began handling repairs in February 1975. The Railway Manager's office was also moved here, and a coal stocking site was developed.

The section of track between Springwell Bank Foot and the Old Sunderland Road level crossing at Wardley was now only used by locomotives travelling to and from the shed, so to eliminate this part of the former colliery screens were converted to form a two road locomotive shed, known as **WARDLEY LOCO SHED** (NZ 313608). This allowed the line south of the Old Sunderland Road level crossing to be closed. The locomotives were transferred on 10th July 1978. In addition, a one-road locomotive repair shop was provided by converting a former compressor house nearby. By this time locomotives handling Monkton Coking Plant traffic were on hire to the owners of the plant, **National Smokeless Fuels Ltd** (an NCB subsidiary company). At the Coking Plant the Koppers ovens started in 1956 had been replaced in 1972 by 33 Woodall-Duckham Becker Regenerative ovens, to which were added in 1985 33 Gibbons Wilputte Regenerative ovens. Soon afterwards the plant became NSF's last working plant in the region.

On 19th July 1985 Monkton Coal Preparation Plant

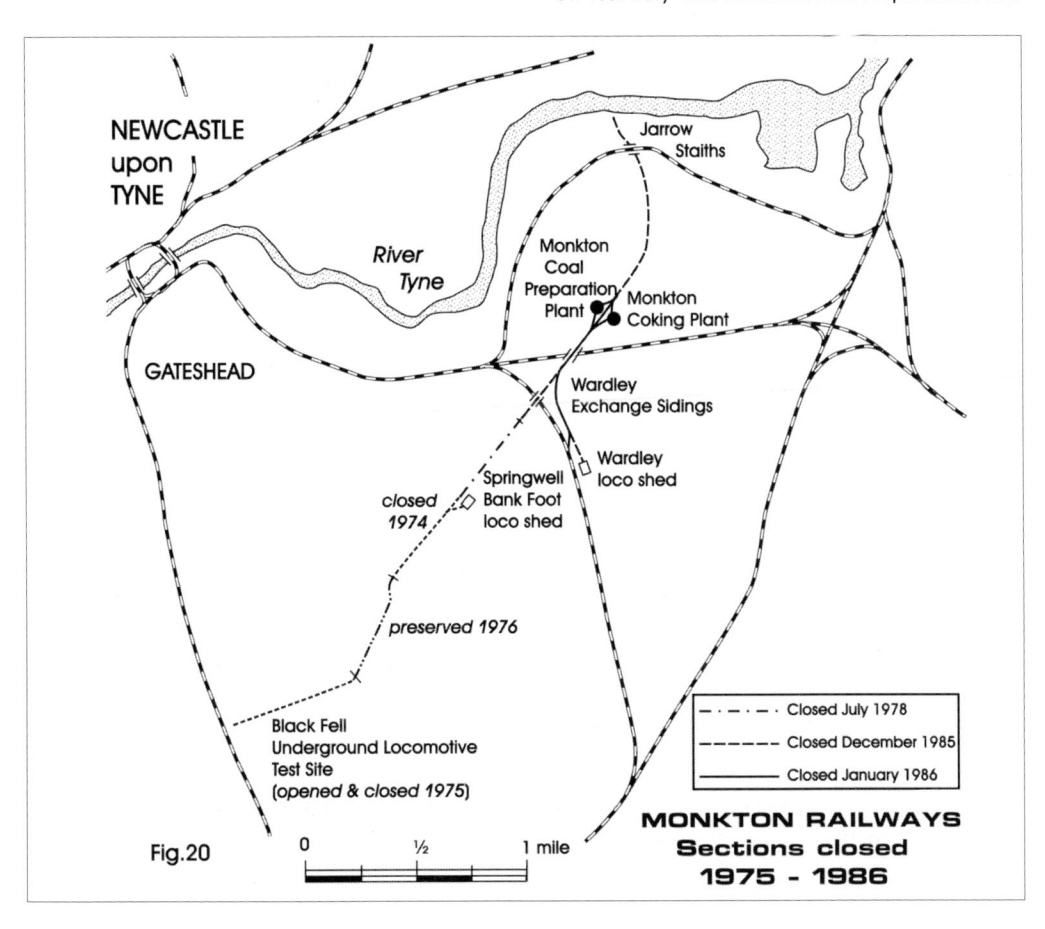

Fig.20 **MONKTON RAILWAYS Sections closed 1975 - 1986**

closed, and on the same day the hire of North East Area locomotives by National Smokeless Fuels Ltd ended. The NCB locomotives at Wardley loco shed were thus redundant, and were dispersed immediately. However, the shed itself remained open, as from 5th August 1985, after the pit holiday fortnight, NSF hired a Class 08 locomotive from BR Gateshead Motive Power Depot, the loco working for NSF for a week and being stabled in the shed before being changed for another of the same class.

With the Port of Tyne Authority opening new staiths for coal and coke at Tyne Dock, the Jarrow Staiths closed in December 1985, and so on 20th December 1985 the sections of the main line between the Old Sunderland Road level crossing and the Follonsby branch junction, and Monkton to Jarrow Staiths, closed, together with Wardley Yard and the Follonsby branch south of Wardley Exchange sidings and the NCB shed. This left the Monkton Coking Plant served by a line about a mile long from the junction at Wardley Signal Box with the BR Leamside branch. NSF continued to hire a Class 08 loco, which now had to be stabled in the open, although this was only a short-term measure pending the transfer of coking plant traffic to road haulage. Rail traffic ended on 10th January 1986, the end coming almost precisely, all but a week, 160 years after George Stephenson's Springwell Colliery Railway had been opened.

The former Follonsby Colliery buildings were mostly cleared early in 1988 to make way for the development of Wardley Disposal Point, operated by Johnsons (Chopwell) Ltd, with opencast coal being brought to the Point by road for onward dispatch by rail. Monkton Coking Plant ceased production in October 1990, ending a long history of coke manufacture in North-East England. The plant was mothballed from 29th December 1990. The closure was made permanent about March 1992 and the site was cleared during 1993. The two preservation schemes apart, much of the Railway's route between Dipton and Marley Hill survives as a trackbed, while most of the route between Marley Hill and Jarrow is now a landscaped public footpath, though with a deviation at Kibblesworth, while from Oak Street at Jarrow northwards the route has disappeared under new development. Similarly, some parts of the Pelaw Main branch have been redeveloped, while some sections of the trackbed remain largely untouched.

In the locomotive list below the following abbreviations are used

        SBF   Springwell Bank Foot Loco Shed
        Wa   Wardley Loco Shed

Gauge : 4ft 8½in

-		0-4-0DH	AB	478	1963	(a)
SBF-East Hetton Colliery 2/9/1976-Derwenthaugh 3/11/1976-SBF 11/5/1977 -Wa 10/7/1978						(1)
103		0-6-0DH	S	10157	1963	(a)
SBF-Wa 10/7/1978-Lambton Engine Works, Philadelphia, (repairs) 9/12/1983 -Wa 29/4/1985						(2)
104		0-6-0DH	S	10158	1963	(a)
SBF-Wa 10/7/1978						(3)
No.500		0-6-0DH	HE	6611	1965	(a)
SBF-Wa 10/7/1978						(4)
No.502		0-6-0DH	HE	6613	1965	(a)
SBF-Wa 10/7/1978						(5)
No.503		0-6-0DH	HE	6614	1965	(a)
SBF-Wa 10/7/1978						(6)
No.504		0-6-0DH	HE	6615	1965	(a)
SBF-Wa 10/7/1978						(7)
-		0-4-0DH	RR	10201	1964	(b)
Wa						(8)
2120/211		0-6-0DH	AB	514	1966	(c)
Wa						(9)
2233/242 [carried in error for 2333/242]	0-4-0DH	AB	524	1967	(d)	
Wa						(10)
No.71		0-6-0DH	AB	584	1973	(e)
Wa-Lambton Engine Works, Philadelphia, (repairs) 19/1/1984-Wa 6/3/1985						(11)
20/109/89		0-6-0DH	AB	647	1979	(f)
Wa						(12)

(a)   ex Bowes Railway, /1975
(b)   ex Vane Tempest Colliery, Seaham, 9/1/1980
(c)   ex Lambton Engine Works, Philadelphia, 17/11/1980
(d)   ex Seaham Colliery, 15/6/1982
(e)   ex South Hetton Loco Sheds, South Hetton, 6/12/1983
(f)   ex Lambton Engine Works, Philadelphia, 20/1/1984

(1)   to Westoe Colliery, South Shields, 4/10/1978; to Lambton Engine Works, Philadelphia, for repairs, 27/8/1979 (Plant Pool records gave 1/9/1979); to Westoe Colliery, South Shields, 18/4/1980; to C.F.Booth (Steel) Ltd, Rotherham, South Yorkshire, 21/10/1985, arrived 9/11/1985 and used as works shunter; to Shropshire Locomotive Collection, near Wellington, Shropshire, for preservation, c11/1991 and moved on 20/12/1991; offered for auction in 2001 and sold to S&D Locomotive Co, but not moved from site; to McLarens Antiques, Oswestry, Shropshire, for display, by 8/6/2002
(2)   to Lambton Engine Works, Philadelphia, as works shunter, 19/7/1985; to Sutton Colliery, Sutton-in-Ashfield, Nottinghamshire, 13/7/1987; to Coventry Colliery, Keresley, Warwickshire, c/1989; to Shropshire Locomotive Collection, for preservation, and moved on 15/9/1993 to Atcham, near Shrewsbury, Shropshire; offered for auction in 2001 and sold to S&D Locomotive Co, but not moved from site; re-sold to Harry Needle Railroad Co, 2002; still on same site, 6/2004
(3)   to Lambton Engine Works, Philadelphia, repairs, 8/3/1985; repairs cancelled; moved to Philadelphia Loco Sheds, Lambton Railway, to stand, c7/1985; scrapped on site by C.F. Booth (Steel) Ltd, Rotherham, West Yorkshire, 11/1985
(4)   to Lambton Engine Works, Philadelphia, to stand, 1/6/1985; sold for scrap to C.Herring & Son Ltd, Hartlepool, 15/11/1985 and cut up on site, 11/1985
(5)   to Wearmouth Colliery, Sunderland, 19/7/1985; to Booth Roe Metals Ltd, Rotherham, South Yorkshire, for scrap, 9/1991; cut up at Rotherham, 10-11/1991
(6)   to Wearmouth Colliery, Sunderland, 23/7/1985; to P.Dawe, for preservation at Bowes Railway preservation scheme, Springwell, 5/1994 and moved on 15/5/1994
(7)   to Westoe Colliery, South Shields, 22/7/1985; to Wearmouth Colliery, Sunderland, to be used as source of spares for similar locos, 2/1988; to Booth Roe Metals Ltd, Rotherham, South Yorkshire, for scrap, 8/1990 and cut up at Rotherham, 9/1990
(8)   to Derwenthaugh Loco Shed, Swalwell, 22/4/1981; to National Smokeless Fuels Ltd, Derwenthaugh Coking Plant, Axwell Park, 2/10/1985 (official date, but actually moved well before this date); to Rutland Railway Museum, Cottesmore, Leicestershire, for preservation, 4/1986 and moved on 25/4/1986
(9)   to Vane Tempest Colliery, Seaham, 21/8/1985; to Ashington Colliery, Northumberland, 28/11/1985; to Hawthorn Combined Mine, Murton, to be used as source of spares for similar locos, 15/2/1988; scrapped on site by M.J.K.Demolition Ltd, Esh Winning, 5/1992
(10) to Wearmouth Colliery, Sunderland, 23/2/1984; to C.H.Newton (Jnr) & Co Ltd, Durham, for scrap, 9/1985, with cutting up on site completed in 11/1985
(11) to Whittle Colliery, Newton-on-the-Moor, Northumberland, 16/7/1985; to Andrew Barclay, Sons & Co Ltd, Kilmarnock, Ayrshire, for overhaul and modifications, 23/3/1987 (reb. AB 6718/1987); to Ellington South Coal Preparation Plant, Lynemouth, Northumberland (part of Ellington Combined Mine), 29/2/1988; to Hunslet-Barclay Ltd, Kilmarnock, Ayrshire, by 10/8/1990 (reb AB 6917/1990); returned to Ellington South Coal Preparation Plant, Lynemouth, Northumberland, c10/1990; to RJB Mining (UK) Ltd, with site, 30/12/1994
(12) to South Hetton Loco Sheds, South Hetton, 11/7/1985; to Hawthorn Combined Mine, Murton, c12/1988; for subsequent history see chapter 13

Locomotives used at Monkton Coking Plant, but only to shunt the coke car
National Smokeless Fuels Ltd from 1/4/1973
NCB Coal Products Division from 1/1/1963
previously **NCB Durham No.6 Area**

Gauge : 4ft 8½in

-		0-4-0WE	RSHN	8093	1959	New	Scr 7/1987
"No.18"		0-4-0DM	RH	243081	1948	(a)	Scr 5/1972
1	D.P.WELLMAN	0-4-0DM	RH	319295	1953	(b)	Scr 5/1979
2		0-4-0DM	RH	313391	1952	(c)	Scr c1/1984
-		0-4-0WE	GB	2047	1946	(d)	Scr 7/1987
-	(03099)	0-6-0DM	Don		1960	(e)	(1)
1	(D2139)	0-6-0DM	Sdn		1960	(f)	(2)
-		0-6-0DH	HE	7305	1973	(g)	(3)
-		4wWE	TH	313V	1985	New	(3)

(a)   ex River Wear Commissioners, South Dock, Sunderland, 12/1970
(b)   ex North Western Gas Board, Bradford Road Gas Works, Manchester, 2/1972
(c)   ex North Western Gas Board, Warrington Gas Works, Warrington, Cheshire, 2/1972

(d) ex Norwood Coking Plant, Dunston, 29/5/1980, as spare to RSHN 8093/1959
(e) ex Fishburn Coking Plant, Fishburn, 26/2/1981, as further spare to RSHN 8093/1959
(f) ex Coed Ely Coking Plant, Tonyrefail, Mid-Glamorgan, 12/1983
(g) ex Lambton Coking Plant, Fencehouses, 17/6/1986

(1) to South Yorkshire Railway Preservation Society, Sheffield, South Yorkshire, 4/1992; moved, 23/4/1992
(2) to South Yorkshire Railway Preservation Society, Sheffield, South Yorkshire, 4/1992; moved, 24/4/1992; to Peak Rail, Rowsley, Derbyshire, property of Harry Needle Railroad Co Ltd, 3/2002
(3) to Cwm Coking Plant, Llantwit Fardre, Mid-Glamorgan, 10/4/1992

Locomotives hired from British Rail from 5th August 1985 to work traffic between Monkton Coking Plant and Jarrow until December 1985 and Monkton and Wardley Exchange sidings until January 1986.

Gauge : 4ft 8½in

08085	0-6-0DE	Derby	1955	(a)	(1)
08176	0-6-0DE	Dar	1956	(b)	(2)
08159	0-6-0DE	Dar	1955	(c)	(3)
08797	0-6-0DE	Derby	1960	(d)	(4)
08802	0-6-0DE	Derby	1960	(d)	(4)
08808	0-6-0DE	Derby	1960	(d)	(4)

(a) ex British Rail, Gateshead Motive Power Depot, Gateshead, c8/1985, hire
(b) ex British Rail, Gateshead Motive Power Depot, Gateshead, 8/1985, hire
(c) ex British Rail, Gateshead Motive Power Depot, Gateshead, 10/1985
(d) ex British Rail, Gateshead Motive Power Depot, Gateshead; date of arrival not known and use here unconfirmed

(1) returned to British Rail, Gateshead Motive Power Depot, Gateshead, 11/1985
(2) to National Smokeless Fuels Ltd, Lambton Coking Plant, Fencehouses, still on hire, 10/1985
(3) returned to British Rail, Gateshead Motive Power Depot, Gateshead, c10/1985
(4) returned to British Rail. Gateshead Motive Power Depot, Gateshead, date unknown, by 1/1986

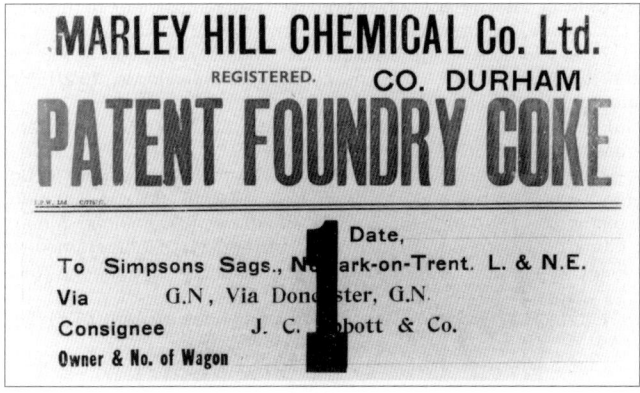

40. Wagon ticket for Marley Hill Chemical Co Ltd (red on white).

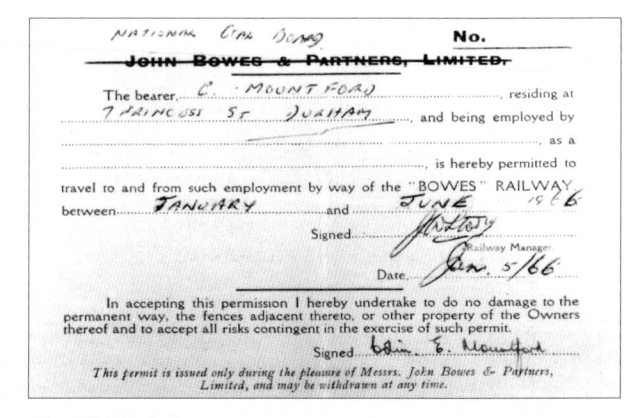

41. A Bowes Railway passenger pass.

Chapter Four
The Chopwell & Garesfield Railway

OWNERS BEFORE 1947
The Consett Iron Co Ltd until 1/1/1947; see also below

This title is found on Ordnance Survey maps attributed to the railway between Derwenthaugh, on the River Tyne near Swalwell, Garesfield and Chopwell, opened by The Consett Iron Co Ltd in 1899. "Garesfield & Chopwell Railway" is also found on O.S. maps, while "Garesfield Railway" is sometimes found in contemporary literature. When the construction of the line between Garesfield and Chopwell began in 1891 the name "Garesfield & Chopwell Railway" is used in the company's Directors' Minutes; from the appointment of a new company secretary in 1895 Chopwell & Garesfield Railway is used. The title seems to have faded away in NCB days, and it vanished altogether after the closure of more than half of the route in 1961. After this the remainder of the system was known by the National Coal Board as "Derwenthaugh Railways". Locomotives carried no railway identity; for wagon liveries see below.

The origin of the railway can be traced back to an early nineteenth century waggonway called the Garesfield Waggonway, which in turn incorporated part of a much earlier waggonway.

GARESFIELD WAGGONWAY
Marquis of Bute until 1/1/1890

As can be seen on the north-western sector of Gibson's *Plan of the Collieries of the Rivers Tyne & Wear*, 1787, (Fig. 14), one of the main waggonways in this area ran from collieries at Pontop northwards to the River Tyne near its confluence with the River Derwent. This line is now known by waggonway historians as "Western Way III". The next such map, by W. Casson in 1801, shows that from what is nowadays called Lockhaugh, two miles south of the Tyne, a branch about a mile long had been built to serve a pit at Thornley. By the time of the next map in 1812, the line from Pontop to Lockhaugh is not shown, and presumably it had been abandoned by then. However, between 1812 and the 1820s the Thornley line was extended for about 1½ miles to serve pits near the hamlet of High Spen. This was **Garesfield Colliery**, owned by the 2nd **Marquis of Bute** (1793-1848), the grandson of the 1st Marquis of Bute. The latter (1744-1814), the 4th Earl of Bute until raised to the marquessate in 1796, acquired considerable property in north west Durham through his first marriage, in 1766. This included Pontop Colliery, mentioned above. Early in the nineteenth century he purchased more land at Chopwell from Earl Cowper. His coal interests in Durham appear to have been held in some kind of partnership with the Simpson family of Bradley Hall, not far from Medomsley, near Consett, though this may not have continued in the second half of the nineteenth century.

In May 1819 George Hill of Gateshead was commissioned to recommend improvements to the line. He describes it (Northumberland County Record Office, NRO 3410 East/1) as being 7779 yards long, or nearly 4½ miles; No.4 Pit to No.1 Pit was 1592 yards; No.1 Pit to "above the works at Winlaton Mill" (presumably the ironworks started here by Ambrose Crowley in 1691, which became famous for its steel swords) 1518 yards; the bank at Winlaton Mill down to the River Derwent 410 yards, and Winlaton Mill to the staith at Derwenthaugh 3463 yards" [curiously, this adds up to only 6983 yards]. At this time the whole line was horse worked, with oral tradition claiming that on the bank north of Rowlands Gill down to Winlaton Mill "dandy carts" were used – that is, that when the loaded waggons were descending the bank by gravity the horse pulling them rode down in a specially-built empty waggon at the rear of the train. Hill recommended retaining horses on some sections, but proposed two self-acting inclines and the introduction of a steam locomotive on the section between Winlaton Mill and Derwenthaugh, a very progressive suggestion for 1819. However, there is no evidence that any of his proposals were implemented. In 1828 it was reported that the line was still worked entirely by horses and that 5400 yards had been re-laid with iron rails, but that 2681 yards were still laid with wooden rails. Some wooden rails were reported as still in use in the 1840s, which if correct would almost certainly make the line the last timber-built line in use in the North-East.

In 1837 the Marquis opened a new **GARESFIELD COLLIERY** (NZ 139598) (sometimes called **Garesfield Colliery (Bute Pit)** or **Spen Colliery**), and the old waggonway was extended to serve it. Fortunately, from the research of C.H.A.Townley in 1949, some of which was almost certainly used by L.G.Charlton in an article for the Industrial Locomotive Society *Journal*, Vol.XV, No.3 (1960), the Durham Coal Owners Association Return 102 (DCRO NCB/1/Co/86/102), which records railway operation at collieries in April 1871 and November 1876, a volume of NER Sidings Maps dated 1885/1894 at Darlington Railway Centre & Museum and Ordnance Survey maps, it has been possible to reconstruct its operation. Garesfield Colliery itself was shunted by horses for many years; but in the later years of its ownership by the Marquis, a

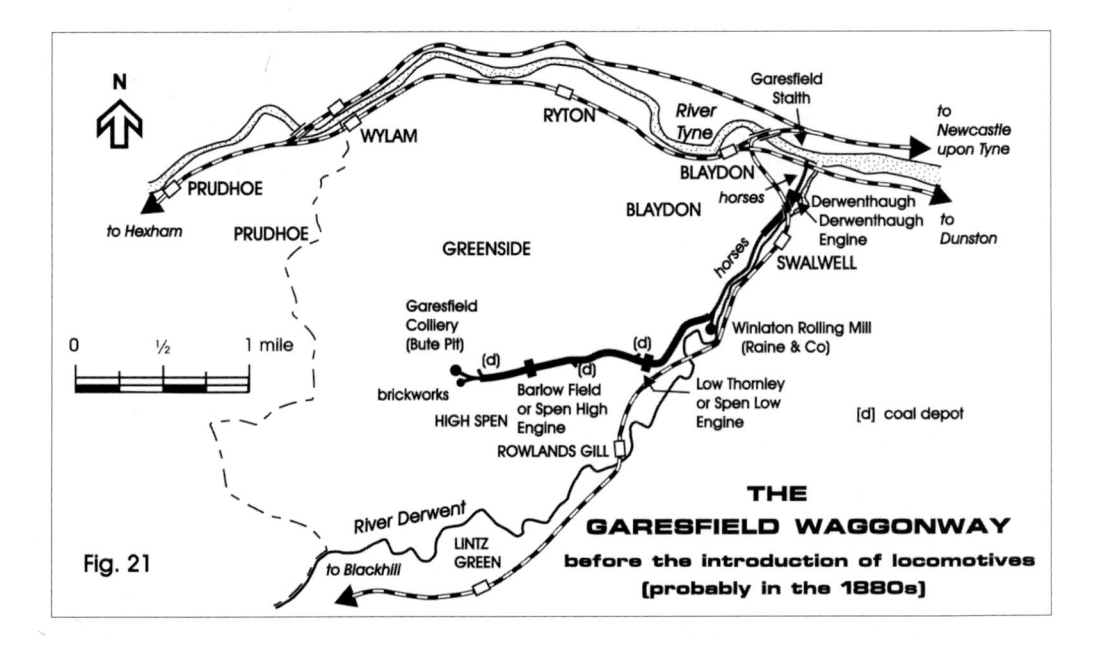

Fig. 21 — THE GARESFIELD WAGGONWAY before the introduction of locomotives (probably in the 1880s)

stationary engine was installed at the colliery, which lowered the fulls down to the bank foot of the first main incline and hauled the empties back above the screens, under which they passed by gravity. The first stationary engine on the line itself was a twin cylinder horizontal engine situated about ¼ mile east of the colliery called the **Barlowfield** or **Spen High Engine**, as it is termed on the NER map of 1894 (NZ 153598). This hauler worked rope inclines on either side of it, but had only one drum, so that the same rope had to be used for all the operations. The loaded wagons were hauled up from the bank foot near the colliery to the engine house, where the rope was released and the wagons run forward by momentum. The same rope was then attached to the rear for the 1¼ miles' descent to Low Thornley. Here the rope was attached to empties and the same process followed to work these back through to the pit. The **Low Thornley**, or **Spen Low Engine** (NZ 174598), worked the mile-long incline down to Winlaton Mill (NZ 185607), again a single line bank with full and empty sets worked alternately. The 1½ miles between Winlaton Mill and Swalwell Bridge (NZ 197623) was worked by horses, four being used for each set of waggons. Over the next ½ mile the waggons were worked by the **Derwenthaugh Engine** (NZ 203629) using a main-and-tail system, with a return wheel at Swalwell Bridge. This engine is said to have had one vertical and one horizontal cylinder, which probably means that it was a beam engine which had been compounded by the addition of a high pressure horizontal cylinder attached to the crank shaft. The final 220 yards was again worked by horses, bringing the full waggons to the **GARESFIELD STAITH** (NZ 204632), which also had beehive coke ovens nearby. Originally the Garesfield line crossed what became the NER on the level; later a link was put in to join the NER just west of its bridge over the River Derwent, and interchange sidings were developed here. The DCOA Return 102 confirms the use of three hauling engines on the line for both April 1871 and November 1876, with no locomotives.

However, the NER Sidings map of 1894 shows only the Spen High and Low Engines, and the existence of only two engines in the line's final years is confirmed by J.R.Gilchrist, the Consett Iron Co Ltd's Viewer for Garesfield and Chopwell from 1892, who wrote a lengthy descriptive article in the *Colliery Guardian* of 27th November 1896 and who also presented a paper entitled *The Garesfield Railway and Incline* to the Institution of Mining Engineers on 17th September 1902, published in Volume XXIV of the Institute's *Transactions, 1902-1903*. Clearly the Derwenthaugh Engine had ceased to work; given that it would appear to have been working in 1876, it might well have been the last in Durham to operate regularly standard gauge main-and-tail rope haulage. No locomotive is known before 1885, and despite the clear indications that it might well have been used at Derwenthaugh, Townley's informant specifically stated that a locomotive was used at Garesfield Colliery, as does Charlton in his article. However, in reviewing the railway for the directors of the Consett Iron Co Ltd in 1889 (DCRO D/Co/6), a report from the company's Chief Engineer states that Garesfield Colliery was then still being shunted by a stationary engine, presumably the one described above; and whilst locomotive haulage at Derwenthaugh is not mentioned, rope haulage here is also not mentioned, which strongly suggests that a locomotive was used between Winlaton Mill and the Tyne; indeed, the 2nd edition of the O.S. maps suggests that the former engine house building had become a **locomotive shed** (NZ 203629). In addition to the colliery traffic, the line also served the **Winlaton Ironworks** (NZ 186604), developed from the former Crowley ironworks mentioned above and latterly owned by **Crowley, Millington & Co**. In 1885 this works was acquired by **B.W. & G. Raine**, later **Raine & Co Ltd**.

The 2nd Marquis died in 1848, leaving a son only a few months old. His business affairs, much better known for his interests in South Wales, including the development of Cardiff Docks, were thus put into the hands of Trustees, who confirmed their position in law with the passing of The Marquis of Bute Estate Act in August 1848. Despite the 3rd Marquis (1847-1900) attaining his majority in 1868, he allowed his Trustees to continue to administer his business affairs. In October 1881 Garesfield Colliery and its royalty was offered for sale for £100,000, but in the midst of a severe economic depression there were no buyers.

By the mid 1880s the largest coal owner in the area was The Consett Iron Co Ltd. Whilst with its huge works at Consett, the firm was one of the major iron and steel manufacturers in North-East England, it was also an important producer of coal and coke for general sale. Its Directors' Minutes (DRO D/Co/6) show that in 1888 it controlled royalties north of the River Derwent estimated to contain nearly 14 million tons of coal, while the Marquis of Bute controlled an area estimated to contain a further 11 million tons. The company was keen to acquire this, and the other smaller royalties nearby, with a view to developing two new collieries, while the Marquis was still keen to sell. The sale was agreed on 3rd July 1889 at a price of £140,000, and contracts exchanged and some money paid, although with the Marquis retaining possession until 1st January 1890.

Gauge: 4ft 8½in

GARESFIELD	0-4-0ST	OC	BH	854	1885	New	(1)
BURLEY	0-6-0ST	OC				(a)	(2)

(a) said to have been hired from a contractor at Leeds, Yorkshire (WR), while BH 854 was under repair; however, it could also be the locomotive of unknown identity hired from Hudswell, Clarke & Co Ltd of Leeds in 1898 – see the list for The Consett Iron Co Ltd ownership below

(1) to The Consett Iron Co Ltd, with colliery and railway, 1/1/1890
(2) returned to hirer

The conversion of the Garesfield Waggonway into the Chopwell & Garesfield Railway

The company began its development of its new enlarged area by major investment at Garesfield Colliery to improve both its coal and coke production, with new surface buildings, new coke ovens and the abandonment of the stationary engine that had shunted the colliery, the latter presumably replaced by a locomotive, though no details are known. This work was carried out in 1890-1891.

However, the development of the large area of coal further west depended on a new colliery being sunk on a green field site, and this in turn depended on providing a rail link to it. The Consett directors had begun to review this problem well before the purchase from the Marquis of Bute. Four possible schemes were considered. The first involved a line from the proposed new colliery to the NER Newcastle-Carlisle line; but this seems never to have got beyond the brain-storming stage. The second involved an old rope-worked tramway serving the former Milkwellburn Colliery (NZ 111575), which had been opened about 1874 by a Mr.Carr and was better known locally as Carr's Pit, though it was actually a drift. Its coal was taken via the tramway, its gauge not known, down to and across the River Derwent by a trestle bridge and then up the valley side to an exchange siding alongside the NER Blackhill Branch near High Westwood Station. Mr.Carr went bankrupt about 1880, and the Consett Iron Co Ltd had acquired the royalty, though not re-opening the colliery. However, rebuilding this tramway was soon dismissed.

The third proposal was worked up in some detail. This was to construct a new line 3½ miles long to High Hamsterley on the NER Blackhill Branch. However, this route would involve gradients of 1 in 50 either side of the River Derwent, with bridges over both the Derwent and the Millwell Burn. The alternative was to link the new colliery to Garesfield Colliery and its waggonway. Of itself this would mean constructing a line about 2½ miles long on much easier gradients than to High Hamsterley, but the existing waggonway would have to be extensively rebuilt to be able to handle the much-increased volume of traffic; however, this would be off-set because most of the output was expected to be destined for West Cumberland, to which a junction at Derwenthaugh was closer than a junction at High Hamsterley, whilst a shipping point at Derwenthaugh – after more investment – would not only provide the company with export facilities on the Tyne but also offer the possibility of its iron ore from Spain being imported here. So the Garesfield route was chosen, albeit with the capital costs spread over nearly ten years.

W.G.Laws of Newcastle upon Tyne was appointed Engineer for the new line westwards from Garesfield and John Jackson of Darlington was awarded the contract for the work, which began on 17th June 1891. The work was not finally finished until 4th September 1894, a curiously-excessive amount of time for a straightforward contract, even allowing for sidings at the new sinking and a new locomotive shed at Garesfield. The cost was reported to the Board as just under £30,000, although this did not include any locomotives.

Locomotive believed to have been used by John Jackson in the construction of the railway between Garesfield and Chopwell:

Gauge : 4ft 8½in

    BETTY   (a)   (1)

(a)   identity and date of arrival unknown; L.G.Charlton understood that it was a "four-wheeled type" and had a "launch-type boiler"

(1)   the loco was apparently acquired by The Consett Iron Co Ltd, presumably at the end of the contract, but was not taken into Consett stock; see the entry for the 'B' class below

Work at what was to be called **CHOPWELL COLLIERY** began with drainage drifts and a great deal of other preparation. The sinking of No.1 Pit (NZ 118584) began on 13th May 1894, with No.2 Pit a few yards to the north-west soon afterwards; Gilchrist in his 1896 article states that the planning provided for the sinking to be commenced as soon as the railway had been completed. At the same time the company now turned its attention to the modernising of the railway between Garesfield and Derwenthaugh. The company would have preferred a locomotive-worked line throughout, but decided against this because its length would have been double the route finally decided on and the cost would have been high. Instead the old route from Garesfield, now to be loco-worked, was retained to just west of Garesfield farm, not far from the Spen High Engine. From here a new line, running north of the farm, was to be constructed, the majority of this being a huge self-acting incline 1½ miles long and almost the last rope-worked incline ever built in Co. Durham. This would take the line down from 506 feet above sea level to only 46 feet above sea level, with gradients of 1 in 15 on the upper section, 1 in 21 around the meetings and 1 in 19.4 on the lower section. The brief to the consulting engineers was that the incline should be capable of running sets of six 10½-ton full wagons, and of handling up to 3,000 tons of coal in a 10½ hour shift. Most self-acting inclines in Durham used a single rope wound round a braked return wheel at the bank head; but the consultants decided that this system would not provide sufficient braking power here, and instead they went back to the early nineteenth-century design of two drums and ropes, with two brakes on each drum, mounted in a drum house constructed over the track. The two drums were 15 feet in diameter and 6 feet wide. Rather unusually, the kips each side at the bank head (NZ 160602) were for fulls, with the empties road, straddled by the drum house, itself topped by a large water tank to replenish the locomotives, in the middle and incorporating an excavated dish. Between the meetings and the bank foot two tracks were maintained, to reduce the risk of disruption to traffic by an operational problem. To permit the upward haulage of loaded wagons of materials, a stationary engine was also included in the original design, but in the event it was found that the incline could handle these wagons amongst the up-coming empties, and so it was never installed. The journey time for sets was normally between 12 and 15 minutes, including the time needed to attach and detach the rope.

The construction of the new line, which involved the excavation of 170,000 cubic yards of earth, the building of eleven bridges and links to the old route at both the top and bottom of the new incline, was let to the contractor John Scott, of Darlington. The contract may well have also included alterations to the route between Winlaton Mill and Derwenthaugh, and the eventual dismantling of the old route and its stationary engines. It would seem that work did not begin until the late summer of 1895, apparently held up by negotiations for the wayleaves needed.

Locomotives believed to have been used by John Scott on this contract:

Gauge : 4ft 8½in

WILLIAM BLACK	0-6-0ST	IC	BH	1115	1895	(a)	(1)
TYNESIDER	0-6-0ST	IC	BH	1116	1895	(a)	(1)
DERWENTHAUGH	0-6-0ST	IC	MW	1313	1896	New	(2)

(a)   the BH Order Book shows these locos built for John Scott "for Derwentwater & Consett Railway". Given that such a railway never existed, "Derwentwater" would appear to be a clerical error for Derwenthaugh, although the line that Scott was to construct did not go near Consett either. This confusion apart, the two locomotives are believed to have worked on this contract

(1)   to the contractor's contract to construct the Hisehope Reservoir, near Waskerley, for the Consett Waterworks Co

(2)   this locomotive also went to Scott's contract to build the Hisehope Reservoir near Waskerley, but was apparently used first on a contract for the NER to construct the "Blaydon Loop" in 1897-1898

42. *The western side of the drumhouse at the top of the Garesfield/Thornley Incline on 28th October 1959. Note the water tank on the roof and the heavy buttressing used after it was first built to counter-act vibration and land subsidence.*

43. *Looking down the Garesfield/Thornley Incline from the drumhouse, with the rope attached to the left-hand full set and the double track beyond, 28th October 1959.*

Chopwell Colliery eventually began production in January 1897, though initially it was on a very limited scale due to a lack of men and strike action. At this stage all traffic east of Garesfield was still travelling down the old route. Despite the construction of the new line beginning in 1895, it was not until the spring of 1898 that the order was placed with The Grange Iron Co Ltd of Durham for the drums required for the Garesfield drum house, while the question of new locomotives for Derwenthaugh was not considered until even later in 1898. The line was reported to the Consett directors as "virtually complete" in May 1898, and on 24th August 1898 the requirement that the contractor maintain the line for six months after completion was activated. Despite this, there was a protracted delay in delivering the drums, and even then a rope installed in April 1897 on an incline on the old route had to be taken off and installed on the new incline. Not until 17th July 1899 were the directors told that the line was at last ready to start work. The section of the old route no longer required was then closed and abandoned. The distance between Chopwell and Derwenthaugh by the new route was approximately 7¼ miles. Thus was completed the last new colliery railway to be built in Co. Durham. The uncertainty surrounding its title has been noted above.

At the same time that the new line was being completed an addition to the new **DERWENTHAUGH STAITHS** was under construction. These were on the site of the former 74 beehive coke ovens, which had closed on 23rd May 1891, and were completed in September 1898.

Locomotive sheds
No documentary evidence has yet come to light concerning the construction of the three locomotive sheds that were to serve the line. Chopwell was initially provided with a small one-road shed south of No.2 Pit, later enlarged, apparently in the 1920s. Garesfield Colliery, on the other hand, had a sizeable two-road shed to the south-eastern side of the fulls roads at the screens, and from the known locomotive transfers here it would certainly appear that at least in the early part of the twentieth century the six-coupled engines working on this section were shedded here, rather than Chopwell. At Derwenthaugh another **two-road shed** (NZ 204630) was built about ½ mile north of what is explained above is believed to have been the original shed.

The Consett Locomotive Department carried out all major repairs to the company's locomotives in its workshops at Templetown, within the Consett Works area, but the Locomotive Registers show that minor repairs were undertaken at all three locations, sometimes with spares required urgently being sent out from Consett via passenger train. Eventually a repair shop was added to the Derwenthaugh shed.

Wagons
It would seem that in the early years of Consett ownership the 4½ ton chaldron wagons comprised most, if not all, of the wagon fleet. However, 130 second-hand "main line" coal and coke wagons, presumably of 10½ ton capacity, were purchased from the Darlington Wagon Co Ltd in February 1899, while in February 1900 100 chaldrons were sent to Robert Frazer & Sons Ltd of Hebburn in exchange for 20 10½ ton wagons. In the years before the First World War various-sized batches of wagons were purchased, apparently all second-hand NER wagons. In July 1907 the directors authorised the construction of a new Wagon Shop at Garesfield Colliery.

The wagons used on the line seem to have had their own numbering series. Initially they carried CONSETT IRON COMPANY in large white letters on the second and third planks from the top, subsequently replaced by CONSETT and IRON Co Ltd on the top plank, and later still by C.I.Co Ltd across the middle. A company photograph of Garesfield Colliery in 1925 shows the wagons there carrying GARESFIELD COLLIERY, though whether this was put on to all wagons on the system is not known. Subsequently the Garesfield wagon shop was replaced by a large wagon repair shop near Derwenthaugh loco shed.

A passenger service
Even with a new village being built at Chopwell, it was difficult to recruit men willing to live in such an isolated area, to the extent that the shortage of men affected the output of the colliery. Even when families moved there, it remained difficult for them to get to places like Consett or Newcastle for shopping or social activities. So in November 1899 the directors agreed to purchase an old 3rd class carriage from the NER, which was to run between Chopwell and Garesfield "at certain times". Whilst it is assumed that this was done, it is not known for how long this service was operated. The company also approached the NER to provide a station on the Blackhill branch, but not until 1st July 1909 did the NER eventually open High Westwood Station, some two miles from Chopwell.

Chopwell Coke Ovens
These comprised two sets of two batteries of beehive ovens, believed to be the last of this type to be built in Co. Durham. They lay immediately to the east of No.1 Pit. Production began about 1897, although the final batch of ovens, bringing the total up to 230, was not completed until 1905. However, about 1901 an electric vehicle, built by the engineers M.Coulson & Co of Spennymoor, was introduced to work on top of the ovens, using an overhead wire supply. For many years it was believed that this was a locomotive; but in *Chopwell's Story* by Les Turnbull, published in 1978, the Chopwell men stated that "the coal car was an electric truck powered from an overhead line. It had two hoppers and was capable of filling an oven with one load... There was a tunnel in from each bench of coke ovens for the coal car to go in, get filled up, come along the bank of ovens it was feeding and fill the empty oven." The gauge of its track was 4ft 0in. After the closure of the ovens in 1941 it lay derelict, and was not finally scrapped until about 1951.

Developments up to 1947
To serve the new colliery and the village the company built an **Electricity Generating Station** at Chopwell, on the opposite side of the railway from No.1 Pit. Its output was developed to supply, initially at 5000 volts AC, not only the machinery and equipment for Chopwell Colliery and Whittonstall Drift and its railway (see chapter 5), and also street and domestic lighting in Chopwell village; a distribution grid was developed to serve Garesfield, Langley Park and Medomsley Collieries, and also the Templetown area of Consett.

Chopwell No.2 Pit, initially only a ventilation shaft, began coal-drawing in 1906. Having completed its initial developments, the company turned next to the Whittonstall Royalty to the west of Chopwell. Here a drift mine was opened in 1908, served by a narrow gauge electric railway, the **Whittonstall Railway**; for its history see chapter 5. In February 1909 the company began the sinking of No.3 Pit (NZ 113586). This began production in September 1911, with its tubs taken via a gantry to No.2 Pit for screening and loading.

To handle the volume of coal that the company was now exporting from the three collieries on the system, the next improvement was a major rebuilding and extension of **DERWENTHAUGH STAITHS** (NZ 204632), opened in December 1913. These comprised two berths for ships up to about 9,000 tons, with 20ft of water at low tide. They included a short **self-acting incline** between the normal railway level and the tipplers on the staiths. There was also a signalbox at these staiths, with equipment supplied by Henry Williams Ltd of Darlington, but no other information is known. Before the First World War the company also gave serious consideration to developing Derwenthaugh to replace Tyne Dock as its delivery point for its iron ore from Spain, acquiring land for the purpose, and it also considered the construction of a steel plant here; but in the event neither plan went forward.

Coke making
Whilst the beehive ovens at Chopwell continued in production, the last 25 beehives at Garesfield closed in May 1924. Chopwell No.2 Pit ceased work with the beginning of the Chopwell miners' strike on 22nd June 1925, and never drew coal again. However, in 1928-1929 the company built **DERWENTHAUGH COKE WORKS** (NZ 193615), opened about ½ mile south of Winlaton Mill in the spring of 1929, its last major investment on the system. These comprised three batteries of Otto twin regenerative ovens (10+28+28), the first of this design in Britain, with the by-products being tar, sulphate of ammonia and rectified benzole. A battery of 20 Simon-Carves Otto twin regenerative

44. Aerial view of Derwenthaugh about 1970, looking south. At the bottom of the picture are Derwenthaugh Staiths, with the BR Redheugh Branch running across and the BR Swalwell Branch running southwards on the far left. The buildings of Derwenthaugh shed and wagon shops can be seen in the centre of the picture.

ovens was added in 1936. Semaphore signalling, with signal boxes near both ends of the coke works, was introduced on this section of the line, possibly at the same time as the coke works was opened, in order to avoid conflict between coke works traffic and 'main line' working. The Chopwell ovens were closed down in 1941. Latterly a signal was also provided on the Chopwell side of a level crossing west of Garesfield Colliery.

On 1st January 1947 the Railway, together with Chopwell Colliery, its Power Station and the closed Whittonstall Drift, Garesfield Colliery and its brickworks, latterly producing only common bricks, Derwenthaugh Coke Works and Derwenthaugh Staiths, passed to NCB Northern Division No.6 Area.

The locomotives, and locomotive transfers
The Consett Iron Co Ltd divided its locomotives and cranes into classes designated by a letter. With the exception of the first four locomotives, the 'A' class consisted entirely of six-coupled, long-boilered pannier tanks. As each time a new locomotive was ordered the firm involved was sent the original Kitson drawings to work from, the class was identical, with interchangeable parts. The 'B' class consisted of four-coupled saddletanks, later developed into three basic types - those with 12"x19" (later 13"x19") cylinders, those with 14"x22" cylinders and those with 16"x24" cylinders. None of the 'C' class, a short-lived group of four-coupled saddletanks, ever came to the Railway. The 'D' class was originally intended for crane tanks but some four-wheeled cranes were later included, while the 'E' class consisted entirely of vertical-boilered cranes.

The company's Locomotive Department maintained very detailed Locomotive Registers, those that survive recording locomotive transfers from the late 1880s onwards. Transfers to and from Consett are meticulously recorded, but these must be interpreted with some care. Firstly, whilst transfers going back to the 1880s from volumes now lost were copied up into later volumes, it may be that there were other transfers before 1914 that have not survived; this would certainly appear to be the case in the 'B' class list below. Secondly, the Registers do not in general record transfers between different locations on the Railway. Such information as is known about these from the 1940s onwards came from repair books kept by the locomotive foreman at Derwenthaugh, and inspected in the 1960s. Thirdly, there has to be a suspicion that sometimes the Registers regard a location as synonymous with the Railway itself, so that, for example, a locomotive sent to "Derwenthaugh" might actually have been sent to Chopwell once it arrived at Derwenthaugh. In addition, short-term transfers to Consett were nearly always for major overhaul in the Locomotive Repair Shop, followed by a short period of running-in; only transfers of longer than 9-12 months should regarded as a transfer that involved working at Consett. Finally, a study of the list below will show that the Locomotive Department clearly regarded certain locomotives as allocated to the Railway, though these did change over time.

The first written record of a Consett locomotive sent to Chopwell occurs in the Order Book for Black, Hawthorn & Co Ltd of Gateshead. Consett's B No 19, BH1113/1895, ordered by Consett on 4th April 1895, was sent new to Chopwell. What locomotives worked between Garesfield and Chopwell before this is not known.

Other than the 0-4-0ST taken over from the Marquis of Bute, nothing is known about the locomotives that worked at Derwenthaugh between 1890 and 1898. Then on 6th August 1898 the directors agreed to order a new 'A' class locomotive for here, followed by a second in November 1898. The second order was to be conditional on the successful builder providing a second hand locomotive on hire until delivery, but it would seem that this did not take place. Instead, at the directors' December 1898 meeting it was reported that a locomotive had been hired from Hudswell, Clarke & Co Ltd of Leeds, which would be used until the arrival of a locomotive purchased second-hand. The two 'A' class locomotives did not arrive until 13th October and 6th November 1899.

It would seem that the normal allocation from at least the 1920s onwards was two 'A' class locomotives at Chopwell, with one 'B' class locomotive shunting at Garesfield Colliery, with three 'A' class locomotives at Derwenthaugh, three 'B' class locomotives (whose main work was the staiths and the landsale depot here) and a crane. The locomotives carried no ownership identity other than their class numberplates. Latterly they were painted black with red lining.

Locomotive transfers are given below between the following locations:

- AP   Axwell Park; transfers here, rather than to Derwenthaugh, are specifically named in the Locomotive Repair Registers, and it would appear that they are associated with the Derwenthaugh Coke Works, which was situated here
- Ch   Chopwell Colliery, Chopwell
- C   Consett Iron Works, Consett (Templetown Sheds and Workshops)
- D   Derwenthaugh Loco Shed, Swalwell
- G   Garesfield Colliery, High Spen

In order to provide the complete history of a locomotive within the time span of the transfers listed below, two transfers to Langley Park Colliery, near Lanchester (*LP*) have also been included.

Gauge : 4ft 8½in

D						(a)	(1)
A No.9 TAFF	0-6-0ST	IC	SS	2260	1872	(b)	
D							(2)
A No 7	0-6-0PT	IC	K	3905	1899	New	

G**–C ?/?-D 14/11/1919-G ?/?-C 17/1/1924-D 28/5/1924-C 13/10/1927
-D 27/1/1928-C 31/5/1929-C 1/4/1932-D 11/5/1932   (3)

A No.8	0-6-0PT	IC	K	3906	1899	New	

G**   (4)

A No 4	0-6-0ST	IC	K	1998	1874		
		reb	HL		1892	(d)	

G-C /1905-D 16/3/1906   (5)

A No 10	0-6-0PT	IC	K	4051	1901	(d)	

G##-C 7/10/1908-G 8/1910-C 9/1911-D 25/10/1911-C 11/1/1927
-D13/10/1927-C 25/9/1930-D 21/11/1930-C 21/12/1933-D 26/6/1934
-C 28/10/1937-D 19/1/1938-C 20/6/1941-D 19/11/1945-Ch ?/?
-D (reps) 25/2/1946-Ch 1/3/1946-D 23/7/1946   (6)

A No.12	0-6-0PT	IC	HC	809	1907	New	

D-C 3/11/1911-G 29/3/1912-C 16/1/1913-D 6/1914-C 16/1/1922-D 16/3/1922
-C 14/3/1929-D 18/7/1929-C 17/1/1935-D 29/5/1935-G 10/5/1940-D 12/7/1940
-G 15/7/40   (7)

A No 13	0-6-0PT	IC	NLE	249	1908	New	

G-C ?/?-D 30/4/1914-C 7/6/1914-D 16/2/1920   (8)

A No 2	0-6-0ST	IC	K	1844	1872	(e)	

G-C 22/7/1920-D 31/5/1929   (9)

A No 6	0-6-0PT	IC	K	2510	1883		
		reb	RS	2915	1899	(f)	

D-C 1/10/1923-D 9/1/1924-Ch ?/?-C 12/9/1929-Ch 28/2/1930-C 8/11/1934
-Ch 4/1/1935-C 8/11/1940-D 3/1/1941-C 2/4/1943-D 23/5/1944   (10)

A No 17	0-6-0PT	IC	HC	1449	1921	(g)	

D-C 18/1/1923-D 25/5/1923-C 12/7/1929-D 18/9/1929-C 16/3/1931
-D 28/9/1932-C 3/6/1936-D 13/8/1936-C 11/1938-D 2/6/1939-C 23/4/1945
-D 4/9/1945   (11)

A No 5	0-6-0PT	IC	K	2509	1883		
		reb	HC		1900	(h)	

D-C 25/10/1928-D 22/2/1929-C 29/5/1935-D 3/6/1936-C 10/10/1940
-Ch 2/12/1941-G ?/?-D 3/3/1944-G 22/3/1944-D 21/6/1945-G 22/9/1945
-D (reps) 19/3/1946-G 26/3/1946-Ch ?/?-D between 24/7/1946 and 13/8/1946
-G 16/8/1946-Ch ?/?-D 23/9/1946-G 25/9/1946-Ch by 12/1946   (6)

A No 11	0-6-0PT	IC	HL	2641	1906	(j)	

D-C 25/5/1923-D 24/9/1923-C 8/3/1927-D 19/12/1933-C 13/8/1936
-D 28/10/1937-C 11/10/1938-D 25/11/1938-C 9/1/1945-D 16/5/1945   (6)

A No 14	0-6-0PT	IC	HL	3080	1914	(k)	

D##-C 5/12/1930-D 14/3/1931-C 11/5/1932-D 11/10/1938-C 26/5/1944
-D 9/1/1945   (6)

A No 2	0-6-0PT	IC	RSHN	7028	1941	(m)	
D							(12)

A No 9	0-6-0PT	IC	HL	3891	1936	(n)	
D-Ch 23/8/1946							(6)

A No 3	0-6-0PT	IC	HL	3951	1938	(p)	
D							(13)

** ordered for Derwenthaugh, but according to the Locomotive Registers they were new to Garesfield; this could of course be a generic entry for the Railway overall
ordered for Derwenthaugh, but according to the Locomotive Registers new to Consett Works

(a) hired from Hudswell, Clarke & Co Ltd, Leeds, Yorkshire (WR), by 13/12/1898; almost certainly a six-coupled engine; this locomotive could well be the loco BURLEY, included in the Marquis of Bute list above, which was also said to have been a six-coupled locomotive hired from Leeds
(b) the minutes of The Consett Iron Co Ltd's directors record that a second-hand locomotive with 17" cylinders had been purchased for Derwenthaugh by 13/12/1898; this locomotive had 17" cylinders and almost certainly the record refers to it, yet allegedly it was not sold by the Brecon & Merthyr Railway to the Bute Works Supply Co, Cardiff, Glamorgan, until 2/1899, being previously Brecon & Merthyr Railway, 29, RHYMNEY; it would appear from the Consett minutes that the locomotive needed minor repairs before delivery, which would suggest that it did not arrive until January or February 1899
(c) ex Consett Works, Consett, 14/11/1901
(d) ex Consett Works, Consett, 15/3/1907
(e) ex Consett Works, Consett
(f) ex Consett Works, Consett, 6/1919
(g) ex Consett Works, Consett, 8/6/1921
(h) ex Consett Works, Consett, 6/12/1922
(j) ex Consett Works, Consett, 14/1/1923
(k) ex Consett Works, Consett, 25/9/1930
(m) ex Consett Works, Consett, 27/6/1941
(n) ex Consett Works, Consett, 19/7/1946
(p) ex Consett Works, Consett, 18/12/1946

(1) presumably returned to Hudswell, Clarke & Co Ltd, Leeds, Yorkshire (WR), at end of hire period, probably early in 1899
(2) to Consett Works, Consett, almost certainly before 1904, when it was rebuilt by AB
(3) to Consett Works, Consett, 30/5/1934
(4) to Consett Works, Consett, 23/11/1899
(5) to Consett Works, Consett, 9/7/1907
(6) to NCB Northern Division No. 6 Area, with Railway, 1/1/1947
(7) to Consett Works, Consett, 16/11/1945
(8) to Consett Works, Consett, 7/6/1924
(9) to Consett Works, Consett, 18/9/1929
(10) to Consett Works, 19/7/1946
(11) not included in transfer of Railway to NCB Northern Division No.6 Area, 1/1/1947; worked from Derwenthaugh loco shed for NCB until returned to Consett Works, Consett, 2/7/1947
(12) to Consett Works, Consett, 18/12/1946
(13) not included in transfer of Railway to NCB Northern Division No.6 Area, 1/1/1947; worked from Derwenthaugh loco shed for NCB until returned to Consett Works, Consett, 16/10/1947

B No 18	0-4-0ST	OC	BH	854	1885	(a)	
D-C /1904-G 15/12/1904							(1)
BETTY						(b)	(2)
B No 19	0-4-0ST	OC	BH	1113	1895	New	
Ch-C /1904-G 15/4/1904							(3)
B No 21	0-4-0ST	OC	HL	2377	1897	New	
G							(4)
B No 22	0-4-0ST	OC	CF	1163	1898	(c)	
	reb		HL	4077	1919		
D-C ?/?- numerous transfers not connected with Railway; C-D 20/12/1946							(5)
B No 30	0-4-0ST	OC	HL	3022	1913	(d)	
D-G by 1/1/1915-D ?/?-C 19/8/1921-D 20/2/1923-C 4/9/1934-LP 18/10/1935							
-C 13/11/1935-D 11/12/1935-C 19/1/1938-D 18/3/1938-C 24/5/1940-D 26/9/1940							(6)
B No 26	0-4-0ST	OC	HL	2639	1905	(e)	
G-C after 23/8/1919-D 2/12/1920-C 2/12/1921-D 20/2/1929-C 16/10/1929							
-D 4/2/1930-C 11/2/1935-D 3/2/1937-C 2/12/1942-D 30/6/1943							(5)
B No 36	0-4-0ST	OC	HL	3471	1921	(f)	
D-C 6/5/1941-D 2/4/1942							(7)
B No 38	0-4-0ST	OC	HL	3496	1921	(g)	
D							(8)
B No 2	0-4-0ST	OC	BH	326	1874		
	reb		HL		1893		
	reb		HL		1914	(h)	
D							(9)

B No 12	0-4-0ST	OC	BH	698	1882	(j)	
D (for G)-G ?/?-D ?/?							(10)
B No 27	0-4-0ST	OC	HL	2640	1905	(k)	
D							(11)
B No 19	0-4-0ST	OC	HL	3752	1930	New	
D-C 17/3/1934-D 30/5/1934-C 2/4/1937-D 30/6/1937							
-C 5/2/1941-D 22/4/1941-G ?/?-D 25/9/1946							(5)
B No 32	0-4-0ST	OC	HL	3251	1917	(m)	
G							(12)
B No 17	0-4-0ST	OC	HL	3753	1930	(n)	
D-C 21/3/1934-D 17/4/1934-C 12/2/1937-D 2/4/1937-C 3/5/1939							
-D 23/8/1939-C 24/4/1940-D 7/4/1941							(13)
B No 25	0-4-0ST	OC	HC	702	1904	(p)	
D-C 28/9/1932-D 15/2/1933-C 3/7/1934-LP 17/7/1934-C 28/8/1934-D 4/9/1934							(14)
B No 11	0-4-0ST	OC	HL	3391	1919	(q)	
D-C 23/3/1937-D 4/9/1941-Ch by 6/1946-D 21/7/1946							(5)
B No 10	0-4-0ST	OC	HL	3476	1920	(r)	
D							(15)
B No 31	0-4-0ST	OC	HL	3023	1913	(s)	
D							(16)
B No 20	0-4-0ST	OC	HL	3745	1930	(t)	
D							(17)
B No 29	0-4-0ST	OC	HL	3004	1913	(u)	
D							(18)
B No 37	0-4-0ST	OC	HL	3472	1921	(v)	
D							(19)

(a) ex Marquis of Bute, with the Railway, 1/1/1890
(b) believed to have been ex John Jackson, contractor for extension from Garesfield to Chopwell, which was completed on 4/9/1894; said to have been a "four-wheeled type" with a "launch–type boiler"; identity unknown; not taken into The Consett Iron Co Ltd's locomotive stock
(c) according to the company's Directors' minutes, this loco was ordered new for Langley Park Colliery at Witton Gilbert; the Consett Locomotive Registers give it new to Consett, while oral tradition claimed that it was the first B class locomotive at Derwenthaugh
(d) ex Consett Works, Consett, 28/2/1914
(e) ex Consett Works, Consett, by 16/4/1915
(f) ex Consett Works, Consett, 29/8/1921
(g) ex Consett Works, Consett, 23/11/1921
(h) ex Consett Works, Consett, 20/1/1928
(j) ex Consett Works, Consett, 11/10/1928
(k) ex Consett Works, Consett, 13/10/1929
(m) ex Consett Works, Consett, 6/3/1930
(n) ex Consett Works, Consett, 25/9/1931
(p) ex Consett Works, Consett, 18/3/1932
(q) ex Consett Works, Consett, 20/3/1930
(r) ex Consett Works, Consett, 23/3/1937
(s) ex Consett Works, Consett, 28/10/1938
(t) ex Consett Works, Consett, 3/5/1939
(u) ex Consett Works, Consett, 26/6/1941
(v) ex Consett Works, Consett, 23/4/1945

(1) to Ashes Quarry, Stanhope
(2) said to have been used as a pumping engine at the Garesfield Coke Ovens (beehives), Derwenthaugh, which were replaced by new staiths in 1898; s/s
(3) to Consett Works, Consett, 30/11/1906
(4) to Consett Works, Consett, 13/6/1912
(5) to NCB Northern Division No.6 Area, with the Railway, 1/1/1947
(6) to Consett Works, Consett, 4/9/1945
(7) to Consett Works, Consett, 20/12/1946
(8) to Consett Works, Consett, 3/3/1927

(9)   to Consett Works, Consett, 20/3/1930
(10) to Consett Works, Consett, 6/3/1930
(11) to Consett Works, Consett, 1/11/1938
(12) to Consett Works, Consett, 4/9/1941
(13) to Consett Works, Consett, 15/9/1943
(14) to Consett Works, Consett, 10/10/1939
(15) to Consett Works, Consett, 29/6/1943
(16) to New Jarrow Steel Co Ltd, Jarrow (a subsidiary company of The Consett Iron Co Ltd), 6/7/1943
(17) to Consett Works, Consett, 23/8/1939
(18) to Consett Works, Consett, 18/8/1943
(19) to Consett Works, Consett, 16/5/1945

D10	4wCr	TS	5784	1900	(a)	
D- C ?/?-D 27/9/1921						(1)
D No 18	4wCr	TS	9586	1920	New	
D						(2)

(a)   ex Consett Works, Consett, 16/3/1900

(1)   to Consett Works, Consett, 20/11/1943
(2)   to Consett Works, Consett, 11/10/1921

E No 14	0-4-0VBCr OC	CoS	4101	1920	(a)	
AP-C 19/1/1933-AP 30/6/1933-D ?/?-C 17/10/1933-AP 24/7/1934-D ?/?						(1)
E No 7	0-4-0VBCr OC	BH	1051	1892	(b)	
AP						(2)
E No 13 ROSE	0-4-0VBCr OC	HL	2984	1913	(c)	
D						(3)

(a)   ex Consett Works, Consett, 19/6/1928
(b)   ex Consett Works, Consett, 25/9/1928
(c)   ex Consett Works, Consett, 18/10/1932

(1)   to Consett Works, Consett, 23/8/1934
(2)   to Consett Works, Consett, 13/2/1929
(3)   to NCB Northern Division No.6 Area, with Railway, 1/1/1947

NATIONAL COAL BOARD
North East Area from 1/4/1974
North Durham Area from 26/3/1967
Northumberland & Durham Division No.5 Area from 1/1/1964
Durham Division No.5 Area from 1/1/1963
Durham Division No.6 (North-West Durham) Area from 1/1/1950
Northern Division No.6 (North-West Durham) Area from 1/1/1947

The structure of the NCB was very hierarchical, with each Division divided into Areas and each Area divided into Groups. The Railway became part of D Group; but because Derwenthaugh had better facilities for locomotive repairs than all the surrounding collieries in both its Group and A Group, it became the main repair centre for both Groups' locomotives, although eventually this function was taken over by the Bradley Workshops at Leadgate, near Consett, also taken over from The Consett Iron Co Ltd.

Clockburn Drift
With the urgent need to develop coal resources in the years following the Second World War, No.6 Area's main development in North-West Durham was **CLOCKBURN DRIFT** (NZ 186604) at Winlaton Mill. The site of Raine's old foundry, closed in 1918, was re-developed to provide offices and workshops, from which the River Derwent was crossed on a girder bridge. From here a tunnel, large enough to take two 3ft 6in tracks, was driven for two miles to **Marley Hill Colliery** (NZ 207463), served by the Bowes Railway (which see). This would allow Marley Hill's excellent coking coal to be used at Derwenthaugh Coke Works, although new workings could be developed from the tunnel, the most notable being the Three Quarter Drift, about ¾ mile from the entrance. The plan was to continue the tunnel to Byermoor Colliery and perhaps even to Burnopfield Colliery, but this was not proceeded with. Underground diesel locomotives hauled trains of mine cars out to a tippler, where the coal was discharged into standard gauge wagons, either to be taken down to the coke works or for stock-piling. The locomotives,

45. 48, formerly A No 14, HL 3080/1914, painted black with red lining and red and gold-shaded lettering - the latter Consett Iron Co. livery applied in early NCB days.

46. The same livery as applied to the B Class engines: 59, formerly B No 28, HL 3003/1913, with 13in x 19in cylinders, at Derwenthaugh.

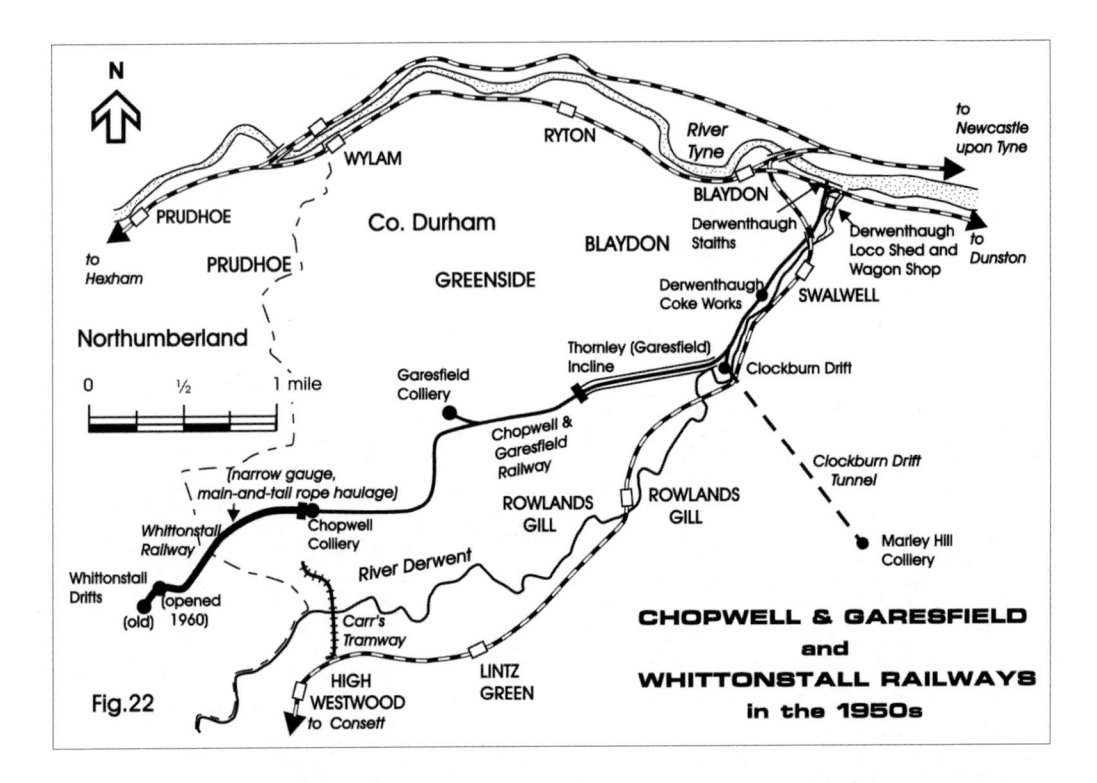

CHOPWELL & GARESFIELD and WHITTONSTALL RAILWAYS in the 1950s

Fig.22

two at first but gradually increased to six, worked from a shed near the workshops, the original small shed being later replaced by a much larger building. Man-riding trains were also run. Although having its own facilities, the Drift was always regarded as a part of Marley Hill Colliery. In addition, Whittonstall Drift (see Chapter 5) was re-opened in 1953, and over the next four years its railway was considerably up-graded.

Also in 1952 a ten-mile gas pipeline was built from Norwood Coke Works at Dunston to Derwenthaugh Coke Works and then to Consett Iron Works for the gas to be used in steel production there. At the Coke Works itself the 20 Simon-Carves Otto regenerative ovens were rebuilt and re-lit on 22nd September 1953. With the rapid decline in sales of blast furnace and industrial coke, much of it exported to Scandinavia through Derwenthaugh Staiths, the three batteries of Otto ovens were rebuilt in 1958-1959 to produce foundry coke, though reducing the overall total to 85. From 1964 this was reduced to 65 with the closure of No.4

47. *The larger 14in x 22in design, HL 3391/1919, as Area No.53 but still carrying its B No 11 plates, at Derwenthaugh on 6th August 1954.*

48. The 0-4-0VB crane E No 13, HL 2984/1913, also named ROSE, working near the southern end of Derwenthaugh Coke Works in 1953.

battery, but raised to 85 again in 1972 after a second rebuilding of the Simon Carves Otto ovens, re-lit on 6th June 1972.

The former Consett locomotives continued to work most of the traffic for some time, and to be repainted in the Consett livery of black with red lining and red and yellow shaded lettering. The only major investment in locomotives came in 1955 with three 200 h.p. Sentinel locomotives, though these proved as short-lived here as elsewhere in Durham. New wagons, all 21-ton steel hoppers, also began to replace the worst of the former Consett wagons, though wooden hoppers, some even retaining end brakes, continued in use well into the 1960s. All coal wagons were painted in the Durham Division's standard livery of chestnut enamel with white lettering, those here carrying DERWENTHAUGH in the top right-hand corner.

Derwenthaugh Staiths

In June 1951 a fire caused considerable damage to the wooden trestle carrying the top section of the incline serving the staiths, and it was were not re-opened until January 1953. Part of the staiths was

49. The livery used in the late 1950s and early 1960s - lime green with black lining and gold lettering shaded red, and a rare photograph at Chopwell: 44, formerly A No 9, HL 3891/1936, on 20th May 1957.

50. No.6 Area purchased three 200 h.p. vertical-boilered Sentinel locomotives for Derwenthaugh in 1955, but they worked only a few years. 87, S 9584/1955, is here working at Derwenthaugh on 29th April 1956.

51. 88, S 9584/1955, ceased work in May 1961, but in 1963 she was sent to Thomas Hill of Rotherham for rebuilding as a 308 h.p. diesel loco, returning as TH 135C/1964. She stands here outside the Derwenthaugh repair shop on 29th October 1971 after repairs.

then abandoned, although not dismantled until 1955. With the planned closure of collieries and the rapid decline of sales of blast furnace coke to Scandinavia the staithes were no longer needed and the last ship was loaded on 23rd March 1960. All traffic was now exchanged with British Railways, with BR locos working in to the now extensive sidings alongside the loco shed, known as Derwenthaugh Yard.

The closure of Garesfield and Chopwell Collieries
Coal production was also declining. To the north of Chopwell village, the Hutton Drifts closed in 1955. Chopwell Power Station was closed on 7th March 1959 after a major programme to re-wire the colliery houses and connect them to the national grid, and this was followed by coal-winding at Chopwell No.3 Pit on 15th May 1959 and the closure of Garesfield Colliery on 29th January 1960. By this time the Chopwell workings were so far west that it was considered more economic to draw the coal at Whittonstall. On 18th August 1960 a new drift was opened there and four days later coal-winding at Chopwell No.1 Pit ended, although the demolition of the buildings was not completed until 1966. The Railway remained open temporarily while road transport facilities were installed at Chopwell, but on 22nd October 1960 the line west of Winlaton Mill was closed, and with it the Garesfield Incline, latterly more commonly called the Thornley Incline. Production at Whittonstall continued for only a few more years, ending on 25th November 1966. The whole unit was officially abandoned on 28th January 1967.

Locomotive working from Derwenthaugh Shed
The closure of the western section left only the 2¾ miles between Winlaton Mill and Derwenthaugh, worked by locomotives from Derwenthaugh Shed and now called by the NCB "Derwenthaugh Railways". Despite this, Derwenthaugh shed continued to require five working engines during the week and two at weekends. The roster for 9th May 1968 was:

Coke Works east end	6am-2pm; 2pm-10pm; 10pm-6am
Coke Works west end	6am-2pm
Coke Works Tar Tanks	6pm-2pm
Clockburn Stockheaps	6pm-2pm
Derwenthaugh Yard	7pm-3pm,

with the weekend roster being:

Coke Works east end	6am-2pm; 2pm-10pm; 10pm-6am
Coke Works west end	6am-1pm

At this time all of the turns were still steam worked, except for the tar tanks duty, which was worked by 4wDH TH 135C/1964. The Yard turn was discontinued in the early 1970s. The last Consett engine, formerly A No 5, ceased work in 1968 after 85 years, and was deservedly preserved, a unique example of a 19th century long-boilered design. By this time the heavy work was mostly in the hands of 0-6-0ST 'Austerity' locomotives, arriving here after being displaced by diesels on other railways. As these in their turn were withdrawn, the North East Area Plant Pool established a fleet of 311 h.p.

52. 60, HL 3752/1930, was rebuilt at Derwenthaugh in 1960 with a spare Hudswell Clarke boiler and a home-made cab and painted green with red lining, here at Derwenthaugh on 14th June 1961.

53. With the closure of other railways, locomotives were often transferred to Derwenthaugh for a few more years' work: 65, formerly HENRY C. EMBLETON, HL 3766/1930, from the Pelaw Main Railway and No.5, MAJOR, K 4294/1905, from the Beamish Railway, stand out of use at Derwenthaugh in the spring of 1969.

54. 'Austerity' 7, HE 3820/1954, formerly a Lambton Railway loco, hauls a train of full hoppers southwards past Derwenthaugh Coke Works in the summer of 1969.

six-coupled Hunslet diesels here, plus one four-coupled loco for the Tar Tanks turn. On 1st April 1973 the Coke Works passed to National Smokeless Fuels Ltd, which thenceforth hired locomotives from Derwenthaugh shed to handle its traffic.

In the same way that closures elsewhere saw the arrival of redundant locomotives at Derwenthaugh, so they also resulted in redundant wagons being sent here, notably from Crookhall at Consett and from the Lambton Railway. The Coke Works also acquired second-hand tank wagons, notably from the Tar Works at Caerphilly in South Wales and some very early tanks from the Bank Foot Works at Crook.

Final closures
Clockburn Drift, together with Marley Hill Colliery, was closed on 4th March 1983, making the Coke Works entirely dependent on coal brought in by rail or road. It equally left the shed entirely dependent on Coke Works traffic, and NSF soon decided that it would be cheaper to hire in BR Class 08 locomotives from Gateshead Depot to handle its traffic. As a result two Derwenthaugh turns were terminated on 22nd October 1983 and the shed, together with the Wagon Shop, closed on 5th November 1983. However, NSF was then obliged to take over the railway and also its maintenance, using one of its own locomotives on platelaying trains. The miners' strike of 1984-5 delayed the removal of the final locomotives at Derwenthaugh, but the site was largely derelict by the spring of 1985. The strike had seen NSF lose much of its export trade, and the end of coke-making in Durham soon followed. Derwenthaugh Coke Works closed on 20th December 1985, bringing to an end railway working along the western bank of the River Derwent that could be traced back some 200 years.

Between Chopwell and High Spen much of the trackbed runs through Chopwell Wood, run by Forest Enterprise, and in June 2001 the Friends of Chopwell Wood placed two 20-ton steel hopper wagons on a short length of track (NZ 134585) to commemorate the line. However, between High Spen and Winlaton Mill it is difficult to trace either of the routes. The area between Winlaton Mill and the site of Derwenthaugh Coke Works has been reclaimed and landscaped to create "Derwenthaugh Park", part of the Derwent Walk Country Park, and the route of the old "Western Way III" northwards from the coke works is now included in the National Cycle Network Railpath 14. The site of Derwenthaugh Yard and its loco shed and wagon shop was waste ground in 2004, although the site of Derwenthaugh Staiths was occupied by a Holiday Inn.

55. Derwenthaugh loco shed, with the repair shop to the left beyond, with (left to right), an A Class engine (possibly 41, K 2509/1883), 60, HL 3752/1930 and 78, RSHN 7538/1949.

56. The large Derwenthaugh Wagon Shop, with Derwenthaugh 11-ton hopper No.861 and four 14-ton hoppers transferred from the Lambton Railway, on 21st August 1975.

57. Steam was eventually replaced by diesel, with the Area Plant Pool concentrating the standard 311 h.p. Hunslet 0-6-0DHs here; one of them, HE 6662/1966, Plant No. 9101/66, in dark blue livery, stands at Clockburn on 27th June 1979.

Locomotives on the Chopwell & Garesfield Railway, 1947-1960

Between 1947 and 1960 locomotives were transferred between the following locations:

	A	Addison Colliery, Ryton
	BB	Blaydon Burn Colliery, near Blaydon
	BW	Bradley Workshops, Leadgate, near Consett
	Ch	Chopwell Colliery, Chopwell
	D	Derwenthaugh Loco Shed, Swalwell
	G	Garesfield Colliery, High Spen
	H	Hamsterley Colliery, Hamsterley
	MB	Morrison Busty Colliery, Annfield Plain
	S	Stargate Colliery, Stargate, near Ryton
	VG	Victoria Garesfield Colliery, Rowlands Gill

Gauge : 4ft 8½in

    A No 3   0-6-0PT IC HL 3951 1938 (a)
D   (1)

    A No 17   0-6-0PT IC HC 1449 1921 (a)
D   (2)

41 (A No 5)   0-6-0PT IC K   2509 1883
                                 reb HC   1900 (b)
Ch-D 23/6/1947-Ch 27/6/1947-D 10/1/1948-G* 4/2/1948-D 2/7/1948-G 10/7/1948
-D 19/11/1948-G 22/11/1948-D 11/2/1949-G 14/2/1949
-Ch /1952 (after 8/1951, by 21/3/1953)-D 16/1/1954-BW (repairs) 8/1956
-D 11/1956-BW (repairs) 10/1/1961-D 28/10/1962   (3)

* the Derwenthaugh locomotive records for this locomotive gave all the transfers from Derwenthaugh between 4/2/1948 and 14/2/1949 as "to High Spen", which is here interpreted as Garesfield Colliery, rather than Chopwell Colliery, because Garesfield Colliery was situated at High Spen village.

44 (A No 9)   0-6-0PT IC HL 3891 1936 (b)
Ch-D, after 9/10/1949, by 12/1949-Ch by 4/2/1950-D by 8/1951-Ch by 6/1952
-D by 8/1954-Ch by 6/1957-D 7/1960-MB 9/11/1960-D 6/3/1961   (4)

45 (A No 10) 0-6-0PT IC K   4051 1901 (b)
D   (4)

    A No 11   0-6-0PT IC HL 2641 1906 (b)
D   (5)

48 (A No 14) 0-6-0PT IC HL 3080 1914 (b)
D-Ch, after 6/1957, by 9/1957-D 6/9/1957-Ch 23/9/1957
-D c10/1960 (after 7/1960, by 4/1961)   (4)

53 (B No 11) 0-4-0ST OC HL 3391 1919 (b)
D-Ch 8/2/1947-D by 3/1951-Ch 6/2/1952-D 20/2/1952-G 7/7/1953-D 9/10/1953   (6)

60 (B No 19) 0-4-0ST OC HL 3752 1930 (b)
D-Ch 30/8/1952-D 10/10/1952-BB 6/9/1957-D 18/12/1957
                               reb D'haugh   1960 #   (7)

57 (B No 22) 0-4-0ST OC CF 1163 1898
                               reb HL   4077 1919 (b)
D-G 6/1949-D 11/1949-G by 4/2/1950-D by 8/1951-G 19/12/1952-D 20/1/1953
-G 22/1/1953-D 12/2/1953-A 7/5/1956-VG by 6/1957-D 3/4/1962   (8)

58 B No 26   0-4-0ST OC HL 2639 1905 (b)
D-H 3/1948-D 6/1948-L 1/1950-D by 30/6/1950-L 15/3/1951-D by 8/1951   (9)

    E No 13 ROSE   0-4-0VBCr OC HL 2984 1913 (b)
D   (10)

42 (A No 6)   0-6-0PT IC K   2510 1883
                               reb RS   2915 1899 (c)
D-Ch 16/1/1954-D by 4/1954-Ch by 8/1954-D by 9/1955-BW (repairs) 1/1956
-D 3/1956 (repairs till 2/1957)-Ch 17/4/1957-D 21/6/1957-Ch 20/1/1958-D 4/2/1958   (11)

    B No 21   0-4-0ST OC HL 2377 1897 (d)
D   (12)

73	HASWELL	0-6-0T	IC	HC	1251	1917	(e)	
	D-VG /1949-D by 30/6/1950							(13)
	HAMSTERLEY No.1	0-4-0ST	OC	HL	3467	1920	(f)	
	D							(14)
	B No 7	0-4-0ST	OC	HL	3474	1920	(g)	
	Ch-D 7/1948							(15)
59	(B No 28)	0-4-0ST	OC	HL	3003	1913	(h)	
	D-L by 9/1950-D-8/3/1951-G /1952-D 19/12/1952 -G 20/1/1953-D 22/1/1953							
	-G 12/2/1953-D 7/7/1953-G 9/10/1953-D 3/11/1953-VG 1/12/1953							
	-D 3/1954-S 1/1955-D 3/1956							(16)
	A No 16	0-6-0PT	IC	HC	1448	1921	(j)	
	D							(17)
82	(D1)	0-6-0ST	IC	HE	3689	1949	New	
	D							(18)
4	BLAYDON BURN No.2	0-4-0ST	OC	HC	1514	1923	(k)	
	Ch-D 27/11/1950-BB /1951-D 8/2/1952-Ch 14/3/1952-D by 21/3/1953							
	-VG 7/4/1955-D 22/8/1956							(19)
23	12	0-6-0ST	OC	HL	2719	1907	(m)	
	D							(20)
12	STELLA	0-4-0ST	OC	HL	2583	1904		
			reb	HL		1931	(n)	
	D (for repairs)							(21)
89	(86 until 10/1955)	4wVBT	VCG	S	9581	1955	New	
	D							(22)
87		4wVBT	VCG	S	9583	1955	New	
	D							(23)
88		4wVBT	VCG	S	9584	1955	New	
	D							(24)
36	HOLMSIDE No.3	0-6-0ST	OC	HL	2956	1912	(p)	
	D							(25)
No.3	ASHINGTON	0-4-0ST	OC	B	303	1883		
			reb	RS	2987	1900	(q)	
	D							(26)
24	13	0-6-0ST	IC	HL	2545	1902	(r)	
	D							(27)
5	ENERGY	0-4-0ST	OC	HC	764	1906		
			reb	HL	8860	1934	(s)	
	D							(28)
8	GEORGE	0-4-0ST	OC	HC	1190	1916	(t)	
	D							(29)
65	HENRY C EMBLETON	0-6-0T	OC	HL	3766	1930	(u)	
	D-W.G.Bagnall Ltd, Stafford, Staffordshire, for repairs, 7/6/1961-D 30/12/1962							(30)
6		0-4-0ST	OC	HC	749	1906	(v)	
	D							(31)

Locomotives sent to Derwenthaugh Loco Shed after closure of the line west of Winlaton Mill and the dieselisation of other railways and collieries:

78		0-4-0ST	OC	RSHN	7538	1949	(w)	(32)
29	No.18	0-6-0T	OC	HC	1255	1917	(x)	(33)
-		4wDH		TH	135C	1964	(y)	(34)
61	DERWENT	0-6-0ST	OC	AB	970	1903	(z)	(35)
27	16	0-6-0ST	IC	VF	5288	1945	(aa)	(18)
86	23	0-6-0ST	IC	RSHN	7751	1953	(ab)	(36)
No.5	MAJOR	0-6-0T	IC	K	4294	1905		
			reb	HL	2812	1931	(ac)	(37)
90	24	0-6-0ST	IC	HE	3833	1955	(ad)	(38)
6		0-6-0ST	OC	RSHN	7603	1949	(ae)	(39)
58		0-6-0ST	IC	VF	5299	1945	(af)	(39)

59	0-6-0ST	IC	VF	5300	1945	(af)	(39)
7	0-6-0ST	IC	HE	3820	1954	(af)	(39)
No.501	0-6-0DH		HE	6612	1965	(ag)	(40)
12060	0-6-0DE		Derby		1949	(ah)	(41)
12098	0-6-0DE		Derby		1952	(aj)	(42)
209	0-6-0DH		HE	6617	1965	(ak)	(43)
No.157	0-4-0DH		HE	6676	1967	(am)	(44)
2120/210	0-6-0DH		HE	6618	1965	(an)	(45)
-	0-4-0DH		AB	478	1963	(ap)	(46)
9101/66	0-6-0DH		HE	6662	1966	(aq)	(47)
21201/208 *	0-6-0DH		HE	6616	1965	(ar)	(48)
-	0-6-0DH		AB	498	1965	(as)	(49)
-	0-4-0DH		RR	10201	1964	(at)	(50)

\# locomotive fitted with new boiler and firebox supplied by Hudswell, Clarke & Co Ltd, Leeds, Yorkshire (WR) for HC 764/1906, together with a new cab made at Derwenthaugh; loco out of traffic between 6/1959 and 2/1961

* carried incorrectly for 2120/208 (its NCB Plant number)

In addition to the above, a photograph exists of a 200hp Sentinel steam locomotive believed to be on trial at Derwenthaugh before the purchase of the three Sentinels listed above. Its identity is unknown, but it may be 4wVBT VCG S 9538/1952, which was on trial at Dorman, Long & Co, Middlesbrough, Yorkshire (NR) in 2/1954 and whose next known trial was at the Cargo Fleet Works of the South Durham, Steel & Iron Co Ltd, also in Middlesbrough, in 6/1954.

(a)   not included in transfer of Railway to NCB Northern Division No.6 Area on 1/1/1947, but worked for the NCB until the return of locomotives at Consett for repairs
(b)   ex The Consett Iron Co Ltd, with the Railway, 1/1/1947
(c)   under repair at the The Consett Iron Co Ltd, Consett Works, Consett, on 1/1/1947, when transferred to NCB Northern Division No.6 Area; returned to Derwenthaugh, 14/10/1947
(d)   ex Templetown Loco Sheds, Consett (loco owned by NCB No.6 Area, but working from The Consett Iron Co Ltd's sheds), 13/11/1947
(e)   ex Norwood Coke Works, Dunston, 27/1/1948
(f)   ex Hamsterley Colliery, Hamsterley, 3/1948, for repairs at Derwenthaugh
(g)   ex Templetown Loco Sheds, Consett (loco owned by NCB No.6 Area but working from The Consett Iron Co Ltd's sheds), c/1948
(h)   ex Templetown Loco Sheds, Consett (loco owned by NCB No.6 Area but working from The Consett Iron Co Ltd's sheds) by 17/10/1948
(j)   ex Templetown Loco Sheds, Consett (loco owned by NCB No.6 Area but working from The Consett Iron Co Ltd's sheds), 6/12/1948, for repairs at Derwenthaugh
(k)   ex Blaydon Burn Colliery, Blaydon, by 9/1950
(m)   ex Bowes Railway, Marley Hill Loco Shed, Marley Hill, 5/12/1950
(n)   ex Clara Vale Colliery, Clara Vale, after 3/1953, by 20/12/1953, for repairs
(p)   ex Morrison Busty Colliery, Annfield Plain, 7/9/1957 (loan whilst HL 3752/1930 was under repair)
(q)   ex Blaydon Burn Colliery, Blaydon, 1/4/1958, "to stand"
(r)   ex Bowes Railway, Springwell Bank Foot Loco Shed, Wardley, 6/6/1958, loan
(s)   ex Blaydon Burn Colliery, Blaydon, 13/6/1958
(t)   ex Blaydon Burn Colliery, Blaydon, 17/11/1958, "to stand"
(u)   ex Pelaw Main Railway, Ouston E Workshops, Ouston, 4/2/1959
(v)   ex Blaydon Burn Colliery, Blaydon, 25/11/1959
(w)   ex Addison Colliery, Ryton, 19/1/1961
(x)   ex Bowes Railway, Springwell Bank Foot Loco Shed, Wardley, 10/10/1963 (Bowes Railway records give date of transfer as 24/10/1963)
(y)   rebuilt from S 9584/1955 (see above); received from TH, 3/2/1964
(z)   ex Bowes Railway, Pelaw Main branch, Starrs Loco Shed, Wrekenton, Gateshead, 20/8/1964
(aa)   ex Bowes Railway, Springwell Bank Foot Loco Shed, Wardley, 16/6/1965
(ab)   ex Bowes Railway, Springwell Bank Foot Loco Shed, Wardley, 8/9/1965
(ac)   ex Handen Hold Colliery, West Pelton, 12/4/1966
(ad)   ex Bowes Railway, Springwell Bank Foot Loco Shed, Wardley, 22/9/1966
(ae)   ex Boldon Colliery, Boldon Colliery, 29/7/1968
(af)   ex Lambton Railway, Philadelphia Loco Sheds, Philadelphia, 6/3/1969
(ah)   ex British Railways, 12060, Class 11, Newton Heath Motive Power Depot, Lancashire, 27/3/1971
(aj)   ex British Railways, 12098, Class 11, Newton Heath Motive Power Depot, Lancashire, 27/3/1971
(ak)   ex Lambton Railway, Philadelphia Loco Sheds, Philadelphia, 8/4/1971
(am)   ex Silksworth Colliery, Silksworth, near Sunderland, 11/4/1972
(an)   ex Boldon Colliery, Boldon Colliery, 12/6/1972
(ap)   ex East Hetton Colliery, Kelloe, 3/11/1976

(aq) ex Lambton Railway, Philadelphia Loco Sheds, Philadelphia, 15/3/1978 (Area Plant Pool records gave 17/4/1978)
(ar) ex Lambton Engine Works, Philadelphia, after repairs, 2/2/1979; previously at Westoe Loco Shed, South Shields
(as) ex Lambton Engine Works, Philadelphia, after repairs, 1/9/1980; previously at Easington Colliery, Easington Colliiery
(at) ex Monkton Railways, Wardley Loco Shed, Wardley, 22/4/1981

(1)   to The Consett Iron Co Ltd, Consett Works, Consett, 10/1947
(2)   to The Consett Iron Co Ltd, Consett Works, Consett, 7/1947
(3)   did not work after 6/9/1968; to North of England Open-Air Museum, Marley Hill Store, Marley Hill, 4/1972, for preservation; subsequently restored to working order in Consett livery at Tyne & Wear Museums, Middle Engine Lane, North Shields, Tyne & Wear
(4)   scrapped on site by D.Sep. Bowran Ltd, Gateshead, 6/1964
(5)   to Leadgate Loco Shed, Leadgate, 3/1949; scrapped there by Thos W.Ward Ltd, Middlesbrough, Yorkshire (NR), 6/1966
(6)   scrapped on site by D.Sep. Bowran Ltd, Gateshead, 9/1962
(7)   scrapped on site by D.Sep. Bowran Ltd, Gateshead, 4/1966
(8)   scrapped on site by D.Sep. Bowran Ltd, Gateshead, 10/1962

(9)   to Leadgate Loco Shed, Leadgate, by 6/1952; to South Medomsley Colliery, near Dipton, by 10/1955; returned to Leadgate Loco Shed, c6/1956; to West Auckland Coal Preparation Plant, West Auckland – officially sold on 26/1/1957, but may have been moved there in 10/1956; to No.4 Area Central Workshops, Tursdale, for repairs, 11/1961; repairs not proceeded with, and sold for scrap to Thos W.Ward Ltd, Middlesbrough, Yorkshire (NR), 2/1963, being cut up on site in 6/1963
(10) no repairs recorded after /1951; scrapped by 3/1957
(11) withdrawn from traffic, 6/1966 and cannibalised to repair K 2509/1883; remains scrapped on site by D.Sep. Bowran Ltd, Gateshead, 8/1968
(12) withdrawn from traffic, 9/1949; scrapped, except for tank, 3/1951; tank put on HL 3003/1913, 12/1954
(13) scrapped on site by D.Sep. Bowran Ltd, Gateshead, 10/1952
(14) returned to Hamsterley Colliery, Hamsterley, after repairs, 6/1948
(15) to Templetown Loco Sheds, Consett (loco owned by NCB No.6 Area but working from The Consett Iron Co Ltd's sheds), 9/1948; to Chopwell Colliery, Chopwell, by 4/2/1950; to Leadgate loco shed, Leadgate, by 9/1950
(16) no repairs recorded after 6/1956; sold for scrap to Thos W. Ward Ltd, Middlesbrough, Yorkshire (NR), 5/1960; scrapped on site, 9/1960
(17) to Leadgate Loco Shed, Consett, after repairs, 9/2/1949
(18) scrapped on site by D.Sep. Bowran Ltd, Gateshead, 3/1971
(19) to Stargate Colliery, Stargate, near Ryton, 12/1956; to Addison Colliery, Ryton, initially for repairs, after 2/1959, by 8/1959; to Greenside Colliery, Greenside, 3/5/1960; to Addison Colliery, Ryton, after 4/1961, by 8/1961; to Clara Vale Colliery, Clara Vale, 12/11/1962; to Marley Hill Loco Shed, Marley Hill, Bowes Railway, for repairs, 23/12/1964; to Morrison Busty Colliery, Annfield Plain, 5/7/1965; scrapped on site, 9/1973
(20) returned to Bowes Railway, Marley Hill Loco Shed, Marley Hill, 18/12/1951
(21) returned to Clara Vale Colliery, Clara Vale, /1954
(22) withdrawn from traffic, 4/1961; scrapped on site by D.Sep. Bowran Ltd, Gateshead, 1/1965
(23) withdrawn from traffic, 8/1962; scrapped on site by D.Sep. Bowran Ltd, Gateshead, 1/1965
(24) withdrawn from traffic, 5/1961; frames stripped for rebuilding, 5/1963, and sent to Thomas Hill (Rotherham) Ltd, Rotherham, Yorkshire (WR), 6/1/1964; rebuilt as TH 135C/1964 (which see)
(25) to Craghead Colliery, Craghead, 18/12/1957
(26) scrapped on site by D.Sep. Bowran Ltd, Gateshead, 4/1959
(27) returned to Bowes Railway, Springwell Bank Foot Loco Shed, Wardley, 20/6/1958
(28) new boiler for this loco purchased from Hudswell, Clarke & Co Ltd, Leeds, /1960, but fitted instead to HL 3752/1930; scrapped on site by Derwenthaugh staff, 12/1960
(29) scrapped on site by D.Sep. Bowran Ltd, Gateshead, 4/1959
(30) scrapped on site by D.Sep. Bowran Ltd, Gateshead, 2/1970
(31) scrapped on site by D.Sep. Bowran Ltd, Gateshead, 26/11/1962-4/12/1962
(32) scrapped on site by Thos W. Ward Ltd, Middlesbrough, Yorkshire (NR), 3/1971
(33) scrapped on site by D.Sep. Bowran Ltd, Gateshead, 4/1966
(34) scrapped on site by T.J.Thomson & Son Ltd, Dunston, 2/1981
(35) to Clara Vale Colliery, Clara Vale, 8/9/1965; scrapped on site, 4/1966
(36) scrapped on site by Bowburn Metals Ltd, Bowburn, 3/1968
(37) withdrawn from traffic by 30/11/1966; scrapped on site by D.Sep. Bowran Ltd, Gateshead, 5/1970
(38) scrapped on site by Derwenthaugh staff, 10/1970
(39) scrapped on site by D.Sep. Bowran Ltd, Gateshead, 10/1972

(40) to Lambton Engine Works, Philadelphia, for repairs, 14/3/1978 (Area Plant Pool records gave date as 5/4/1978); to Lambton Railway, Philadelphia Loco Sheds, Philadelphia, for running-in trials, 20/12/1979; to Wearmouth Colliery, Sunderland, 8/1/1980; to Tanfield Railway, Marley Hill, for preservation, 5/1994 and moved on 13/5/1994

(41) to Lambton Railway Loco Sheds, Philadelphia, 16/4/1971; to C.H.Newton (Jnr) & Co Ltd, Durham, for scrap, but re-sold to C.F.Booth (Steel) Ltd, Rotherham, South Yorkshire, who completed the work in 12/1985

(42) to Lambton Railway Loco Sheds, Philadelphia, 16/4/1971; to National Smokeless Fuels Ltd, Lambton Coking Plant, Fencehouses, 9/1985; sold for scrap, c5/1986; acquired by P.Millar, Durham City, for preservation, c11/1986, and moved to North Tyneside Council, proposed Museum of Land Transport, Middle Engine Lane, North Shields, Tyne & Wear, 1/1987 (now Tyne & Wear Museums); for further history see chapter 9

(43) to Bowes Railway, Springwell Bank Foot Loco Shed, Wardley, for repairs, 11/1972; returned to Derwenthaugh, 16/1/1973; ceased work, 22/10/1983; to Lambton Engine Works, Philadelphia, 3/1985, to stand (Area Plant Pool records gave date, incorrectly, as 15/2/1984); scrapped on site by C.H.Newton (Jnr) & Co Ltd, Durham, 12/1985

(44) latterly out of use; scrapped on site, 2/1984

(45) to Dawdon Colliery, Seaham, 24/6/1983; to C.F.Booth (Rotherham) Ltd, Rotherham, South Yorkshire, for scrap, 11/1987

(46) to Monkton Railways, Springwell Bank Foot Loco Shed, Wardley, 11/5/1977; to Wardley Loco Shed, Wardley, 10/7/1978; to Westoe Colliery, South Shields, 4/10/1978; to Lambton Engine Works, Philadelphia, for repairs, 27/8/1979 (Plant Pool records gave 1/9/1979); to Westoe Colliery, South Shields, 18/4/1980; to C.F.Booth (Steel) Ltd, Rotherham, South Yorkshire, 21/10/1985, arrived 9/11/1985 and used as works shunter; to Shropshire Locomotive Collection, near Wellington, Shropshire, for preservation, c11/1991 and moved on 20/12/1991; for subsequent history see chapter 3

(47) ceased work, 22/10/1983; to Lambton Engine Works, Philadelphia, for repairs, 13/2/1984; to Vane Tempest Colliery, Seaham, 5/11/1985; to Seaham Colliery, Seaham, c4/1986; returned to Vane Tempest Colliery, Seaham, c7/1986; to Booth Roe Metals Ltd, Rotherham, South Yorkshire, for scrap, 1/1992 and moved there in week ending 21/2/1992

(48) ceased work, 5/11/1983; to Lambton Engine Works, Philadelphia, for repairs, 2/1985 (Area Plant Pool records gave date, incorrectly, as 15/2/1984); to Ashington Colliery, Ashington, Northumberland, 19/12/1985; to Wearmouth Colliery, Sunderland, 19/2/1988; to Booth Roe Metals Ltd, Rotherham, South Yorkshire, for scrap, 8/1990

(49) to Bates Colliery, Blyth, Northumberland, 6/10/1980; to Lambton Engine Works, Philadelphia, for repairs, 12/2/1983; to Bates Colliery, Blyth, Northumberland, 27/5/1983; scrapped on site late in 9/1985

(50) ceased work, 5/11/1983; sold to National Smokeless Fuels Ltd, Derwenthaugh Coking Plant, Winlaton Mill, 2/10/1985, although actually moved there well before this date

Locomotives at Clockburn Drift, Winlaton Mill

These worked out to the surface at Winlaton Mill, their shed being on the western bank of the River Derwent. The first four were "single-ended" locomotives (with a cab only at one end), the last two were double-ended locomotives, with a cab at both ends. The longer numbers were the Area Plant numbers, allocated by Area Headquarters from 1957 onwards.

Gauge : 3ft 6in

632	2620/21	0-6-0DMF	HC	DM632	1947	(a)	(1)
639	2620/22	0-6-0DMF	HC	DM639	1947	(a)	(2)
709	2620/23	0-6-0DMF	HC	DM709	1955	New	(3)
993	2620/24	0-6-0DMF	HC	DM993	1956	New	(4)
-	2620/25	0-6-0DMF	HC	DM1063	1957	New	(5)
No.1428	20/280/21	0-6-0DMF	HC	DM1428	1977		
			HE	8525	1977	New	(5)

(a) ex No.1 (Fife & Clackmannan) Area, Rothes Colliery, Thornton, Fifeshire, Scotland, /1950; installed, 3/1952

(1) to Ashington Central Workshops, Ashington, Northumberland, 23/3/1983; stripped for spares; remains written off, 9/1983 and scrapped on site by 31/12/1983

(2) to Ashington Central Workshops, Ashington, Northumberland, for repairs, 3/1977; returned, 2/1978; to Ashington Central Workshops, Northumberland, 23/3/1983; scrapped on site, 4/1985

(3) to Ashington Central Workshops, Ashington, Northumberland, for repairs, 7/1979; returned, 9/1980; to Ashington Central Workshops, Northumberland, 6/1983; stripped for spares; remains written off, 9/1983, and scrapped on site by 31/12/1983

(4) to Ashington Central Workshops, Ashington, Northumberland, for repairs, 11/1977; returned, 1/1979; to Ashington Central Workshops, Northumberland, 6/1983; stripped for spares; remains written off, 9/1983, and scrapped on site by 31/12/1983

58. The entrance to Clockburn Drift over the bridge crossing the River Derwent, with either HC DM632/1947 or HC DM639/1947 on a short train of side-tipping hoppers soon after the Drift opened, 29th April 1952.

59. HC DM632/1947 and HC DM639/1947, acquired from Scotland, outside the original loco shed, with a side-tipping hopper wagon in the distance, 29th April 1952.

60. Double-ended HC DM1063/1957, 100h.p. like all the locomotives at Clockburn Drift, on the man-riding train on 27th September 1957.

61. Single-ended No. 993, HC DM993/1956, hauls a train of full mine cars from the Drift through the Clockburn buildings on 27th June 1979.

(5) to Ashington Central Workshops, Ashington, Northumberland, 22/3/1983; stripped for spares; remains written off, 9/1983, and scrapped on site by 31/12/1983

Locomotives used at Derwenthaugh Coking Plant to shunt the coke car
National Smokeless Fuels Ltd from 1/4/1973
NCB Coal Products Division from 1/1/1963
previously **NCB Durham Division No.6 (North-West Durham) Area**

Gauge : 4ft 8½in

-	0-4-0WE	RSHN	7882	1957	New	(1)
-	0-4-0DH	HE	6263	1964	(a)	(2)
No.1	0-4-0DH	HE	6688	1968	(b)	(3)
-	0-4-0DH	RR	10201	1964	(c)	(4)

(a) ex South Western Gas Board, Exeter Gas Works, Exeter, Devon, 5/1971 (left Exeter by road, 18/5/1971); purchased to shunt the coke car during the rebuilding of some of the ovens, 1971-1972
(b) ex Norwood Coking Plant, Dunston, 11/10/1983
(c) sold to NSF by North East Area, 2/10/1985, but actually moved here well before this date

(1) scrapped on site by R.E. & P.Seagrave, Bishop Auckland, 7/1986
(2) to Norwood Coking Plant, Dunston, 9/1972; to Hawthorn Coking Plant, Murton, 1/1973; to Bowes Railway Co Ltd, Springwell, 11/1988, for preservation, and moved 7/12/1988
(3) to Rutland Railway Museum, Cottesmore, near Oakham, Rutland, for preservation; sold and moved, 9/10/1987
(4) to Rutland Railway Museum, Cottesmore, near Oakham, Rutland, for preservation; sold, 4/1986 and moved, 25/4/1986

Locomotives hired by National Smokeless Fuels Ltd from British Rail between October 1983 and December 1985 to handle traffic between Derwenthaugh Yard and Derwenthaugh Coking Plant.

Normally only one loco was hired at a time, and so far as is known, it returned to Gateshead MPD at weekends. From the details below it, with a gap between October 1983 and October 1985, would appear that the list is incomplete. Interestingly, NSF also used a locomotive of its own from the previous list in this period, latterly RR 10201/1964, to assist in platelaying work.

Gauge : 4ft 8½in

08148	0-6-0DE	Derby	1956	(a)	(1)
08577	0-6-0DE	Crewe	1959	(b)	(2)
08170	0-6-0DE	Dar	1956	(c)	(3)
08254	0-6-0DE	Dar	1956	(d)	(4)

(a) ex British Rail, Gateshead Motive Power Depot, Gateshead, 10/1983, hire
(b) ex British Rail, Gateshead Motive Power Depot, Gateshead, by 21/10/1985, hire
(c) ex British Rail, Gateshead Motive Power Depot, Gateshead, 4/11/1985, hire
(d) ex British Rail, Gateshead Motive Power Depot, Gateshead, 12/1985, hire

(1) returned to British Rail, Gateshead Motive Power Depot, Gateshead, c10/1983
(2) returned to British Rail, Gateshead Motive Power Depot, Gateshead
(3) returned to British Rail, Gateshead Motive Power Depot, Gateshead, 11/11/1985
(4) returned to British Rail, Gateshead Motive Power depot, Gateshead, 12/1985

Chapter Five
The Whittonstall Railway

OWNERS
NCB Northumberland & Durham Division No.5 Area from 1/1/1964
NCB Durham Division No.5 Area from 1/1/1963
NCB Durham Division No.6 (North-West Durham) Area from 1/1/1950
NCB Northern Division No.6 (North-West Durham) Area from 1/1/1947
The Consett Iron Co Ltd until 1/1/1947

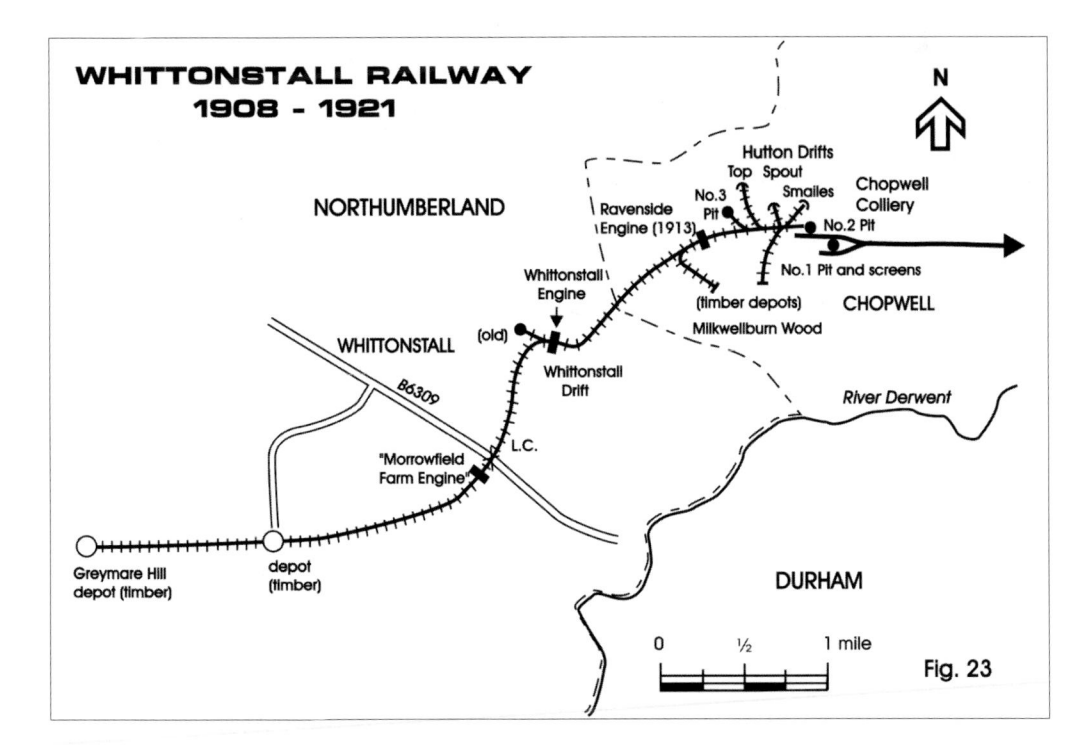

Fig. 23

In the spring of 1907, but back-dated to 23rd November 1906, The Consett Iron Co Ltd leased the adjacent Whittonstall royalty to the west of Chopwell. Even before the lease had been signed, in March 1907, the company's Engineer for the area had begun the construction of a 2ft 2in gauge tramway from Chopwell towards the drifts that were planned on the Whittonstall royalty. There were to be two drifts here to assist proper ventilation, the Three Quarter Drift and the Brockwell Drift (NZ 087572), the latter being the coal haulage drift, linked to Chopwell by a tramway about two miles long. Sadly, the company's Directors minutes do not reveal how they came to decide that the tramway should be electrified. However, the fact that the Engineer was one of a group which visited Germany early in 1907 may well be significant. The contract for the supply of trolley and transmission wires and one locomotive was agreed with Siemens Brothers Dynamo Works Ltd at Stafford on 5th November 1907. There is no record of a contract for the construction of the line itself, which would suggest that this was undertaken by the company's own men. In the haste to bring the line into use, several wooden trestle viaducts were built as a temporary measure until proper embankments could be made. Other than two short sections at 1 in 12, the maximum gradient was 1 in 20, whilst power at 500 volts DC was supplied from a double overhead wire rigged from iron lineside posts.

This was the first electrically-operated railway using an overhead wire system to be built in Durham, and so the company was very much leading the field; indeed, it remained the only electric narrow gauge line ever built in the county.

62. *The railway being constructed in Chopwell Woods, looking towards Whittonstall in 1908. Note the base of one of the overhead wire support columns lying beside the line.*

63. *As a temporary measure, wooden trestle viaducts were built until embankments could be made. The photograph dates from 1908, but the exact site, possibly just west of Chopwell No.3 Pit, is uncertain.*

64. The site of this extensive construction work is not known, but it is almost certainly at Chopwell, presumably in the winter of 1907-1908.

The official opening date is given as 11th September 1908; however, 100 tons a day was being worked from Whittonstall by 2nd June 1908, when the directors also agreed to purchase a second locomotive, or "car". The normal load was thirty full tubs, a total weight of about 18 tons, although the theoretical maximum was 25 tons. Miners were carried to and from Whittonstall in empty tubs. Coal from the tubs passed on to screens at Chopwell No.2 Pit, where it was loaded into standard gauge wagons. A car shed for the locomotives was also provided at No.2 Pit.

In February 1909 the sinking of Chopwell No.3 Pit began, some 500 yards west of No.2 Pit. This was linked to the Whittonstall line by a short branch to enable its tubs to be taken to No.2 Pit for tippling.

The first locomotive had proved "very unsatisfactory" as early as March 1909, and it seems that Siemens Brothers were unable to remedy the problems, especially with braking and lubrication. A larger and more powerful locomotive was ordered in May 1910, which interposed a jackshaft and counterweight between the wheels of each bogie in order to improve the balancing. This loco was known as "The Big Car", because it could haul 35 full tubs, equalling 21 tons. When it began work at the end of 1910 it appeared satisfactory and the company hoped that the Whittonstall output would be increased to 700 tons per day. These hopes were clearly dashed, and in the second half of 1912 the company decided to spend £1500 on replacing most of their use by main-and-tail rope haulage. In February 1913 a stationary engine known as the **Ravenside Engine** (NZ 113586), its name taken from a nearby house, was installed just to the west of the junction of the branch to No.3 Pit. This hauled a set of sixty tubs from Whittonstall to a landing just west of the engine house, a set of sixty empties then being taken back. The locomotives then split the fulls into thirties for the remaining distance to the screens. The rope haulage was also now used for conveying miners to and from Whittonstall in empty tubs.

Because of the First World War, and the loss of men to the army, Whittonstall Drift was shut down early in 1915 to enable the remaining men to be concentrated at Chopwell. However, the railway was not closed, for about 1916 a three mile extension was built from Whittonstall to Greymare Hill (NZ 047554) in order to transport timber for pit props from the company's forests there. From the Greymare Hill railhead temporary tracks were laid into the various forests and fitted with small electric haulers to pull the tubs. Timber was also brought to the railhead by lorry.

The working of this extension was quite complicated. The first ¾ mile from the railhead to the first level crossing, downhill with the load, was worked as a self-acting incline. The next 1¼ miles were worked by a hauler situated near Morrowfield Farm (NZ 083563 approx). From here to Whittonstall the hauler at the now closed drift entrance was used, with its ropes re-positioned, while the Ravenside hauler continued as before. Not long after the line was opened the self-acting

65. WHITTONSTALL No.1 or No.2 on a train of empties for Whittonstall, probably soon after the opening in 1908.

66. *WHITTONSTALL No.3, Hanomag 5968/Siemens 460, soon after delivery in 1910. For a 2ft 2in gauge locomotive she gives a massive impression.*

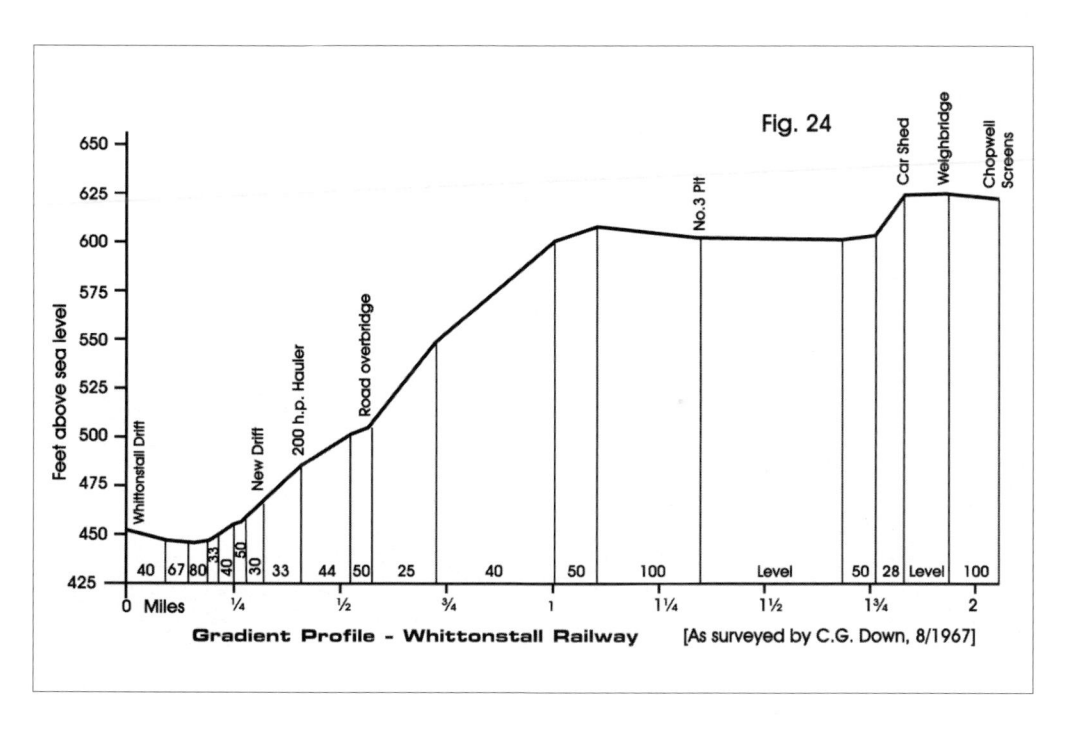

Fig. 24 — Gradient Profile - Whittonstall Railway   [As surveyed by C.G. Down, 8/1967]

67. *WHITTONSTALL No.3 paused in woods east of Whittonstall.*

railments and a new railhead established at its bank foot. Two set riders were used at the front and rear of a set (about 20 tubs) between here and Whittonstall, to open and shut the level crossing gates. Ladies from Chopwell were sometimes allowed to travel out into the forests to pick blackberries, providing themselves with small seats to fit in the tubs. With the exhaustion of the forests this line was closed and removed about 1919, when Whittonstall Drift re-opened.

However, almost immediately a new branch was laid south-eastwards to bring timber from Milkwellburn Wood. This ran from a junction about ¼ mile west of the Ravenside hauler, with the tubs being worked by a small electric hauler. But as the felling moved eastwards this branch was closed and replaced by a new one from a point near the loco shed at No.2 Pit for about ½ mile. However, instead of installing a rope hauler a wheel was fixed to a corner of the loco shed and one end of the rope attached to one of the standard gauge four-coupled saddletanks, which then ran back and forth, pulling the tubs up and down the branch as it did so. This novel method of working lasted until sometime in 1921, when the branch was closed.

To the north of Nos 2 and 3 Pits the Hutton seam outcropped. The first drift to mine this seam, the Top Hutton Drift, was served by a short branch about half way between Nos 3 and 2 Pits and was worked by a locomotive. This was subsequently closed (see below), and replaced by the Spout Drift and the Smailes Drift, both served from short links between the former Top Hutton branch and No.2 Pit; both were worked by endless rope haulage.

About 1923 it was decided to end the use of locomotive haulage to the screens, and the Ravenside Hauler was adapted to work the entire line. This was done with a set of elbow wheels that carried the main rope back to the screens and thence around a return wheel. This left the locomotives to shunt only the screens and the Top Hutton Drift. The latter closed about 1929, after which the locomotives were scrapped. In addition No.2 Pit did not resume coal winding after the General Strike in 1926. With the advent of the Second World War Whittonstall Drift and its railway closed in 1940, being still closed when the NCB took over in 1947.

Gauge : 2ft 2in

WHITTONSTALL No.1	0-4-4-0WE	Siemens	450	1908	New	Scr c/1930
WHITTONSTALL No.2	0-4-4-0WE	Siemens	454	1909	New	Scr c/1930
WHITTONSTALL No.3	0-4-4-0WE	Hano	5968	1910		
		Siemens	460	1910	(a)	Scr c/1930

(a)   New; built by Hano, with the electrical parts supplied by Siemens

Development by the NCB

Whittonstall Drift remained closed until 1953, when it was re-opened as part of the NCB's development of Chopwell Colliery. In 1954-1955 the railway was re-graded so that 1 in 25 became the steepest gradient, and the line was re-laid with 50lb rail, spring spikes and new sleepers. To eliminate the complications of elbow and return wheels the 300 bhp Ravenside hauler was removed from its engine house near No.3 Pit and installed in the old No.2 Pit winding house. New screens were built to the west of the old ones, which enabled the "dish" and tunnel, through which the line had been carried under No.2 Pit winding house to the old screens, to be filled in and the track layout simplified. The new screens came into use about 1957, after two standard gauge sidings to them had been completed.

The NCB also decided to end man-riding in open tubs, and in November 1957 three man-riding cars, comprising a master car and two slave cars, were delivered from D Wickham & Co Ltd of Ware in Hertfordshire, makers nos.7677-7679. The master car was fitted with a governor that cut in at 9 mph to apply hydraulic brakes on the two slave cars, thus preventing runaways if the haulage rope should break. Hydraulic suspension was also fitted, as was manually-operated sanding gear, to enable the brakes to grip in wet weather. As the cars were to be used on an overland line they were fitted with fully-enclosed bodies having four doors on each side, the end two sliding and the centre two hinged, and each car had 24 wooden seats.

By the late 1950s the Chopwell workings underground had reached so far west that it was considered more economic to work them from Whittonstall and to close the shafts at Chopwell. To do this a new **WEST DRIFT** (NZ 088575) was developed, about ¼ mile east of the original drift, and this opened on 18th August 1960. At its mouth a new 200 bhp main-and-tail hauler was installed to pull sets of twenty tubs up some 500 yards on a gradient of 1 in 8 to the surface, where there were two new sidings. Sets of tubs between the Brockwell Drift and these sidings were worked by the **Brockwell Hauler**, once used to work tubs out to Morrowfield Farm (see above). At the sidings the tubs were marshalled by an endless rope system into sets of sixty for the journey to Chopwell. At Chopwell the set was split into two, each half being run down to the screens on another endless rope system. Here there was a weighbridge; a few tubs were weighed, the results then being averaged and multiplied by sixty to obtain the weight of coal in that set. On reaching the curve into the screens, the tubs were detached from the rope and from each other and then run into the tippler by hand and gravity. Once out of the tippler they were hauled up

68. The entrance to the West Drift of 1960, with the line running on to the Brockwell Drift, at Whittonstall on 19th March 1966.

on to a staging by a "creeper", a moving chain between the rails with hooks that caught on to the axles of the tubs, whence they ran down by gravity back to the sidings for re-marshalling, again by an endless rope.

A casualty of the new system was the "passenger service". With the opening of the new drift it was initially proposed to add two extra cars to the train, but in the event not only was this cancelled, but in February 1961 the whole train was taken out of service. One reason was said to have been that the rope couplings were so low that the rope cut into the sleepers, but a more potent reason was that the running of passenger trains reduced the time available for coal haulage. Instead a bus was provided to take the men as close to the drifts as it could.

The tubs used on the line
When the railway opened little wooden tubs weighing 4 hundredweights and carrying 8 hundredweights were used. The bodies of these were formed from two 9in deep larch boards and corner strapping and a continuous iron band around the top. A similar band, but formed of two identical halves, was fixed around the joint of the two planks. At each end of this middle band was a hole so that a pit pony could be yoked on to the tub. The frames were 5in deep with wheels of 10in diameter.

In 1925, following the introduction of rope haulage, larger tubs were introduced. These were constructed similarly, but the body was 4ft long and 3ft 4½in wide, each plank was 10in deep and it had a capacity of 10 hundredweights (half a ton).

The frames were 6in deep and the wheels were 12in diameter.

The NCB introduced new tubs that retained the wooden frames of the 1925 tubs but had new steel bodies. These included the pony yokes of their predecessors but had an increased weight of 5½ hundredweights, with a capacity of about 11 hundredweights, so that a full set of sixty weighed about 50 tons gross.

There were latterly also a few tubs from the now-closed Garesfield Colliery, which could be identified from two corrugations in their metal bodies. On arrival at Chopwell their sides were built up by welding in order to increase their capacity from nine hundredweights to the standard eleven hundredweights.

At maximum capacity the railway could send a full set to Chopwell every 35 minutes, though this was rarely achieved. By the mid-1960s the railway was in use between 2.00 a.m. and 7.00 p.m., bringing out thirteen full sets a day from the two drifts. This declined as closure approached, until an average of about 330 tons per day was being handled. With a maximum haulage speed of 8 mph (the hauler had a governor to prevent this being exceeded) journey time from the West Drift was 13 minutes. The railway had a unique, picturesque quality, as two visitors once described: "hardly had an empty set been re-formed at Chopwell than the main rope began to slide past one's feet, denoting the departure of another full set from the drifts. Then followed the slapping of the rope over the noisy and manically-revolving rollers, and a quarter of an hour later there was the roar of tiny wheels and a

69. Tubs filled with pit props (left) and coal (right) at Whittonstall, 19th March 1966.

70. Looking towards Chopwell, about ½ mile east of Whittonstall. The main-and-tail ropes can be seen. 19th March 1966.

71. The man-riding cars built by D. Wickham & Co Ltd of Ware in Hertfordshire in 1957, but only used until February 1961, here at Chopwell No.2 Pit on 19th March 1966.

cloud of dust as the set appeared over the brow of the rise and rattled to a halt. Within a few moments the rope ends had been transferred and the empty set was off in the direction of Whittonstall".

But despite the investment the drifts became uneconomic to work. The original Drift sent out its last coal on 1st July 1966 and the West Drift followed on 25th November 1966. The buildings survived for some years afterwards, and although the track was soon removed and some areas later bulldozed, it is still possible to trace the trackbed in places. Reference : *Industrial Railway Record*, No.33, October 1970, *The Whittonstall Railway, 1908-1966*, C.G.Down.

72. The Railway's hauler house at Chopwell No.2 Pit on 19th March 1966.

Chapter Six
Craghead & Burnhope
from Burnhope to Pelton Fell

It seems very doubtful whether this railway ever had a name in the official sense. On 19th century Ordnance Survey maps the Craghead section is called the "Craghead Waggonway" and its extension the "Burnhope Waggonway". In the Durham County Record Office there are two volumes, kept by a clerk at Craghead, which record the coal tonnage carried on the line. The first (DCRO NCB 3/90) covers 1922-1937 but records only the Burnhope traffic; it calls the northern section the "Craghead Railway" until 1933, and then the "Holmside & South Moor Railway" (after its owners) from 1935. The second volume (NCB 3/87), a ledger specially printed for Holmside & South Moor Collieries Ltd, records daily traffic for both Burnhope and Craghead from 1946 until the closure of the Burnhope extension in 1949; here the line is called the "Holmside Railway". Under NCB No.6 Area the line, if it followed the Area style used elsewhere, would have been "Craghead Railways"; in practice, the locomotives began by carrying 'N.C.B. No.6 Area', sometimes with 'D Group', but latterly merely carried 'N.C.B.'.

The coal to the south of Stanley, between Annfield Plain and Pelton, lay largely unworked during the eighteenth and early nineteenth centuries. In the west of this area various coal owners had sunk pits, but these lay at the southern extremities of the wooden waggonways running northwards to the River Tyne upsteam of Newcastle upon Tyne. For pits in the Beamish area a waggonway (see the Beamish Railway) was built to the River Wear at Fatfield; but again it was nearly seven miles long, and as on the Tyne, keels were needed to transship the coal down to waiting colliers in deeper water. The development of this area needed better transport facilities and new entrepreneurs with money.

One of those who became increasingly important in the coalfield after 1825 was William Hedley (1779-1843), the former engine-wright at Wylam Colliery in Northumberland, who had played a significant part in the early development of the steam locomotive, and who had subsequently risen to become the Viewer of the colliery. Hedley had begun to develop his coal-owning interests in Durham whilst still at Wylam, his first venture being the Coxhoe royalty, to the south-east of Durham City, which he is believed to have leased in 1824. His development of this royalty in the first half of the 1830s was greatly aided by the construction of the Clarence Railway, with its staiths at Haverton Hill, and the Hartlepool Railway & Dock Co, with its staiths at Hartlepool.

Meanwhile, in 1827 Hedley left Wylam and either in 1828 or the following year he entered a partnership headed by William Bell of Sunderland, who was already the leading owner of Shincliffe Colliery near Durham City, to take over the lease of this Stanley royalty from Lord Ravensworth & Partners (see chapter 3). Here too nothing much was done until the Stanhope & Tyne Railway was opened in 1834. This ran through the middle of the area the partners had leased and also had staiths at South Shields, removing the need for keels. Although the railway itself got into financial difficulties (see chapter 7), its arrival very much stimulated the development of collieries near to it.

The partners perhaps baulked at the cost of developing the whole of the approximately 4000 acres that they controlled, and on 31st December 1838 the lease of the southern area of the royalty was taken on by Hedley alone. This done, in 1839 both the partnership, which developed South Moor Colliery at Stanley and became The South Moor Colliery Co, and Hedley began the sinking of new pits, linking them to different sections of the Stanhope & Tyne Railway.

HOLMSIDE COLLIERY/CRAGHEAD COLLIERY, Craghead
Holmside & South Moor Collieries Ltd until 1/1/1947
Thomas Hedley & Bros Ltd until 3/1/1925
Thomas Hedley & Bros until 24/7/1889
formerly **William Hedley & Sons**; originally **William Hedley**

Hedley began work on his area by commencing the sinking of the **William Pit** (NZ 216508) on 14th January 1839 in the township of Holmside and linking it by a waggonway 1¾ miles long to the Stanhope & Tyne Railway at the western end of the Pelton Level, between the Eden and Waldridge Inclines. Horses worked the first fifty yards of the waggonway from the pit to the top of a self-acting incline. This was about 1¼ miles long on an average gradient of 1 in 26. At the bottom horses were used to shunt the remaining short section to the Stanhope & Tyne. In 1854 the Hedleys sank the **George Pit** (NZ 219510), close to the incline's bank head, and for quite some time these two pits were named **CRAGHEAD COLLIERY**, the pit village built nearby also taking the name Craghead.

Meanwhile to the south west of the village Hedley sank the **Thomas Pit** (NZ 213507) in 1841, which was joined by the **Oswald Pit** (NZ 213508) in 1878.

These were given the name **HOLMSIDE COLLIERY**, after the original township. They were served by a short ¼ mile branch running south from the waggonway.

William Hedley died on 9th January 1843 and his colliery interests were taken over by his four sons, Thomas, William, George and Oswald, though William Hedley junior became the dominant partner. They subsequently disposed of the collieries around Coxhoe, but remained in the partnership which became The South Moor Colliery Co and continued alone at Craghead and Holmside, trading as Thomas Hedley & Brothers. William junior, who lived at Burnhopeside Hall near Lanchester, died on 13th December 1888, after which the firm was converted into a limited company.

BURNHOPE COLLIERY, Burnhope
The Bearpark Coal & Coke Co (Burnhope Collieries) Ltd until 1/1/1947
Ritsons (Burnhope Collieries) Ltd until 1939
U.A.Ritson & Sons Ltd until 1936
formerly **U.A.Ritson & Sons** and previously **U.A.Ritson**; see also below

In 1845 the Hedleys opened **Burnhope Colliery** (NZ 191482), about 1½ miles north-west of the village of Lanchester, extending the waggonway south-westwards from Craghead by a further 2½ miles to serve it. However, the family only retained this colliery until about 1860, when they gave up the lease of the colliery, its 837 acres and the railway to Craghead, which all passed to Messrs Fletcher & Sowerby. In 1881 the owner became Utrick Ritson of Sunderland. He also acquired South Pontop Colliery near Annfield Plain, closed by the firm in April 1927, and Preston Colliery in North Shields, Northumberland, which was closed in 1928.

The whole of the extension of the waggonway was operated by the **Burnhope Engine** (NZ 193495), latterly known as the **Bank Top Engine**, which was situated about a mile to the north of the colliery. The engine hauled waggons up to it and then lowered them down to Craghead. It may also have shunted the colliery, or shire horses may have been used. The engine, built by Thomas Murray of Chester-le-Street, was unusual in having both a vertical cylinder (27in x 60in) and a horizontal cylinder (24in x 60in) driving on to the same crankpin, added when 10-ton wagons replaced chaldrons.

In 1855 the northern end of the waggonway was joined by but not linked to a ½ mile branch from the Pelton Level to West Pelton Colliery (Alma Pit), which the Joiceys (see the Beamish Railway) had leased two years earlier.

In 1868 Wylam Colliery in Northumberland was closed, and at the auction of its plant in January 1869 the Hedleys purchased an old Wylam engine and brought it to Craghead. It is said to have been renovated and occasionally steamed on a short section of track specially laid for it. It was proclaimed as one of the two locomotives built by Hedley at Wylam in 1813, but this is now regarded as incorrect. The Wylam waggonway was re-laid with stronger cast-iron edge rails in 1827-1832, and the locomotive is now believed to have been one of a pair built at this time to replace the original engines. In 1882 it was presented to what is now the Royal Museum of Scotland at Edinburgh, where it remains on display.

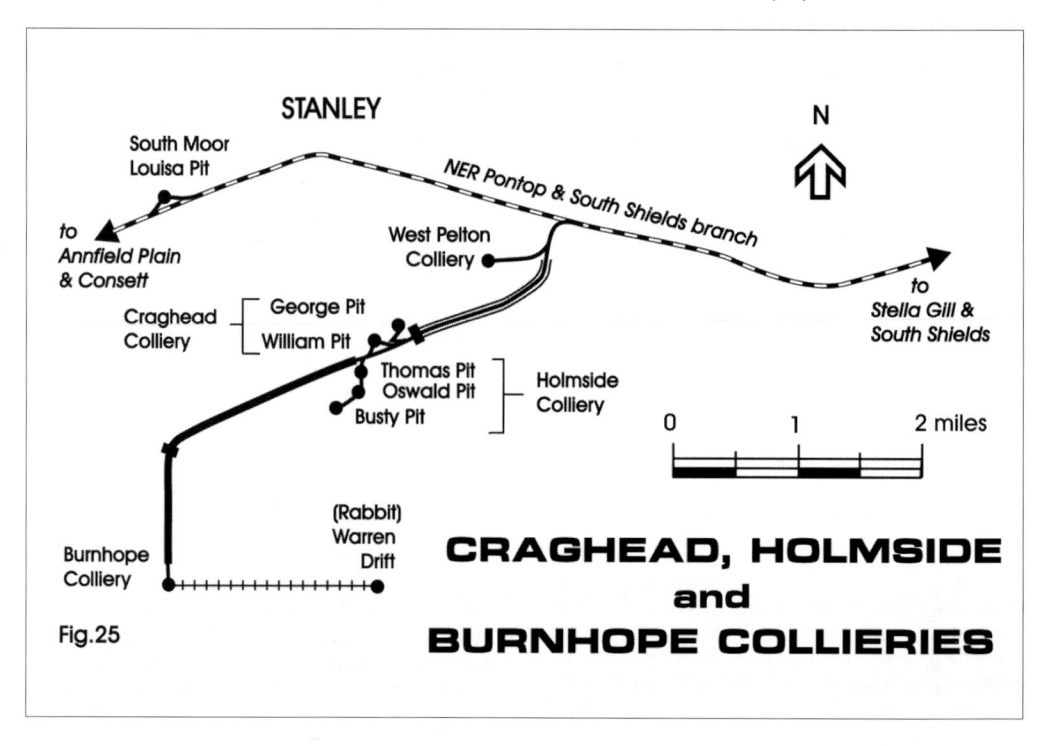

Fig.25 **CRAGHEAD, HOLMSIDE and BURNHOPE COLLIERIES**

Gauge : 5ft 0in

| | "WYLAM DILLY" | 4w | VCG | Wylam | 1827-1832 | (a) | (1) |

(a) ex The Owners of Wylam Colliery, Wylam, Northumberland, 1/1869; purchased at auction by the Hedley brothers for £16.10s 0d.

(1) exhibited at the North East Coast Exhibition of Naval Architecture & Marine Engineering, Tynemouth, Northumberland, 9/1882-10/1882; to Edinburgh Museum of Science & Art, Edinburgh, Scotland, (now the Royal Museum of Scotland), 10/1882

The date when a locomotive was first commercially used at Craghead is not known. Eventually the locomotives kept at Craghead shunted the section between the foot of the incline from Burnhope, together with Holmside Colliery, as far as the bank head of the Craghead Incline, and a locomotive also went down the incline to shunt the sidings at the bank foot which linked with the NER. As with virtually all Durham colliery companies, the company name was not carried on the locomotives, which had only a nameplate or a painted name.

A **brickworks** making common bricks was begun between the William and George Pits in 1872; it closed in 1908. The William Pit itself closed soon after the beginning of the twentieth century, to be followed by the George Pit in June 1914. The area was eventually cleared except for the loco shed, which was near to the former William Pit. However, to reach the lower seams the firm sank two new shafts immediately to the west of Holmside Colliery, the **Edward Pit** (NZ 212508) in 1909 and the **Busty Pit** (not coal-drawing) in 1916, extending the Holmside branch by another ¼ mile to serve them. The Thomas and the Edward Pits had closed by 1947.

Burnhope Colliery up to 1947
Various Returns of the Durham Coal Owners Association deal with locomotives, the earliest being Return 102. The section of this for April 1871 lists only the stationary engine described earlier, but that for November 1876 also includes a locomotive, used presumably for shunting at the colliery. Whether this was maintained continuously up to the acquisition of a new locomotive in 1904, and whether more there was more than one locomotive in this period, is not known.

Latterly, besides coal drawn via the shafts, the colliery also developed a number of drifts. The largest of these was the **Rabbit Warren Drift**, normally abbreviated to the **Warren Drift** (NZ 209481). This was begun in 1910 and was served by a narrow gauge tramway from the Annie Pit. It was 1¼ miles long and was presumably rope-worked. The drift lasted until about the Second World War. There was also an aerial ropeway 4½ miles long linking Burnhope to Langley Park Colliery at Witton Gilbert, owned by The Consett Iron Co Ltd, probably so that Burnhope coal could be used in the by-product coke ovens there.

The record of Burnhope traffic over the Craghead section between 1922 and 1937, mentioned earlier (DCRO NCB 3/90), shows that in the early 1920s the line worked six days a week and that Craghead received between 500 and 1200 tons per day from Burnhope. By 1936 this had fallen to between 275 and 400 tons per day, the latter equalling eight sets of five 10-ton wagons. Saturday working ceased after 18th March 1931, and sometimes the Burnhope section was idle for days at a time.

The colliery was taken over in 1939 by The Bearpark Coal & Coke Co Ltd, one of a number of small concerns that this firm acquired in the 1930s. However, it would appear that in the case of Burnhope the Bearpark company set up a special subsidiary company to run it, for in the printed traffic ledger for 1946-1949 the owners are shown as The Bearpark Coal & Coke Co (Burnhope Collieries) Ltd. The locomotive was sold, and the shunting of the colliery undertaken, so far as is known, by a combination of rope haulage and gravity, perhaps also with horses.

The colliery was vested in NCB Northern Division No.6 Area on 1st January 1947.

Gauge : 4ft 8½

| | - | 0-4-0ST | OC | | | (a) | (1) |
| | - | 0-4-0ST | OC | RS | 3057 | 1904 | New | (2) |

(a) details of origin, identity and arrival unknown

(1) to RS, /1904, in part exchange for new locomotive
(2) loaned to Pelaw Main Collieries Ltd, Pelaw Main Railway, in the 1930s, and returned; to South Durham Steel & Iron Co Ltd, West Hartlepool, /1939

Craghead Colliery up to 1947
On 3rd January 1925 Thomas Hedley & Bros Ltd and The South Moor Colliery Co Ltd amalgamated to form The Holmside & South Moor Collieries Ltd. Soon after this the title Holmside Colliery gave way, a little confusingly, to **CRAGHEAD COLLIERY**.

In the late 1930s it would seem that **witherite** was also mined here, albeit briefly, the same seam that was worked at the firm's Morrison North Pit at Annfield Plain. Like Burnhope, the colliery and its railway were vested in NCB Northern Division No.6 Area on 1st January 1947.

73. The overgrown single-line bank from Burnhope Colliery to the Burnhope Engine, with the engine house chimney above the trees, 3rd September 1949.

74. The Burnhope Engine in the summer of 1950, facing Burnhope, after the closure of the section between Burnhope and Craghead.

75. The Black Hawthorn catalogue photograph of BURNHOPESIDE, BH 888/1887, as prepared for the Newcastle Exhibition of 1887.

NATIONAL COAL BOARD
North Durham Area from 26/3/1967
Northumberland & Durham Division No.5 Area from 1/1/1964
Durham Division No.5 Area from 1/1/1963
Durham Division No.6 (North-West Durham) Area from 1/1/1950
Northern Division No.6 (North-West Durham) Area from 1/1/1947

Burnhope Colliery was already near the end of its working life at nationalisation in 1947. By this time, as recorded in DCRO NCB 3/87, the Burnhope traffic occasionally amounted to only 60-70 tons per day, equal to only one set of wagons, and hardly justifying the operation of a steam stationary engine and two inclines. Closure of the colliery and the railway came on 22nd July 1949, with the line carrying 223 tons on its last day.

Craghead Colliery had a long enough life-expectancy to justify some investment, and locomotive haulage was introduced underground in 1948. The traffic record above lists coal carried from Morrison North Colliery, so presumably this was being worked underground from Morrison North and wound at Craghead. The two remaining pits, the Oswald and the Busty, were merged in 1952. On the surface the railway continued much as before, with the No.6 Area numbers gradually appearing on the locomotives after 1949. The livery at this time was black with double red lining, one thick and one thin, with red numbers shaded with gold. After the closure of Burnhope Colliery only two locomotives were needed each day, one shunting the colliery and working as far as the bank head, the other going down the incline each day to work at the sidings at the bank foot and coming back up each night. The Craghead self-acting incline was unusual in that on its top section there were four rails, rather than the normal three. It was also the last NCB incline in Co.Durham to employ set-riders, one man riding on each set. Main line wagons had been used for coal traffic for many years, and this saw British Railways' 21-ton wagons introduced during the 1950s.

Shunting at the bank foot was handed over to BR in 1965. However, an increase in demurrage charges by BR for wagons waiting for loading at the colliery made the NCB decide that road transport was cheaper, and on 1st July 1966 rail traffic ceased. It was perhaps appropriate that the last locomotive to leave should be transferred to Morrison Busty Colliery at Annfield Plain, once owned by the firm. Craghead Colliery lasted for only a short time afterwards, closing on 11th April 1969.

Gauge : 4ft 8½in

	Name	Type						
	HOLMSIDE	0-6-0ST?		HH			(a)	
		reb		Dunston Engine Works Co				s/s
39	BURNHOPESIDE	0-6-0ST	OC	BH	888	1887	(b)	
		reb		HL		1931		(1)
	CRAGHEAD	0-6-0ST	OC	BH	971	1890	New	
		reb		HL		1911		(2)
	HOLMSIDE No.2	0-6-0ST	OC	CF	1204	1901	New	(3)
37	HOLMSIDE No.4 *	0-6-0ST	OC	HL	3528	1922	(c)	(4)
	BOWES No.19	0-4-0ST	OC	AB	1883	1927	(d)	(5)
80		0-6-0ST	OC	RSHN	7546	1949	(e)	(6)
36		0-6-0ST	OC	HL	2956	1912	(f)	(7)

* this was a painted name, latterly hardly visible under the grime

(a) origin and date of arrival unknown; described in the *Colliery Guardian*, 4/9/1896
(b) ordered by BH for stock, 9/1886, and exhibited at the Newcastle Exhibition of 1887 before delivery here; one source says that the locomotive was named VICTORIA when it was delivered here, but a BH catalogue photograph of the locomotive in the fully lined-out exhibition livery, included here, shows the name BURNHOPESIDE
(c) ex Morrison Busty Colliery, Annfield Plain (also owned by the firm) by 1/1/1947
(d) ex Axwell Park Colliery, Swalwell, c1/1949
(e) ex Morrison Busty Colliery, Annfield Plain, by 24/4/1950
(f) ex Derwenthaugh Loco Shed, Swalwell, 18/12/1957

(1) to Handen Hold Colliery, West Pelton, loan, after 4/1955; returned by 1/1956; scrapped by Marple & Gillott Ltd, Gateshead, 9/1959
(2) to Morrison Busty Colliery, Annfield Plain (also owned by the firm) by 30/4/1937; scrapped on site, 12/1965
(3) to Morrison Busty Colliery, Annfield Plain, by 8/1937; scrapped on site, 5/1962
(4) to Handen Hold Colliery, West Pelton, 1/7/1966; scrapped, 4/1969
(5) returned to Marley Hill Loco Shed, Marley Hill, Bowes Railway, 21/8/1949
(6) to Morrison Busty Colliery, Annfield Plain, 28/10/1966; scrapped, 6/1968
(7) to Springwell Engineering Shops, Springwell, Bowes Railway, for repairs, 10/1964, but little work done; scrapped on site, 4/1966

76. *Craghead loco shed, with the usual piles of ash, 17th June 1965.*

77. Looking towards Craghead Bank Top, with 37, HL 3528/1927, waiting to pull a load of empties off the kip, 29th June 1966.

78. Craghead Bank Top from the eastern side. Note the very tall brake cabin and the "bull" on the kip, a safety device which would catch an axle of a wagon if the set of empties should not run far enough and try to run back down the incline; 25th March 1966.

79. Sets of British Railways 21-ton steel hoppers passing on the Craghead Incline, 29th June 1966. This was the last incline in North-East England to use set-riders.

80. Craghead Bank Foot at Grange Villa, 23rd May 1957.

Chapter Seven
The Derwent Railway

OWNERS
Derwent Iron Company

The Stanhope & Tyne Railway
Following the opening of the Stockton & Darlington Railway in September 1825, plans were soon brought forward for other railway schemes in Durham. One of these began to develop from a small group of entrepreneurs perceiving an opportunity to combine the extensive limestone deposits around Stanhope for the manufacture of lime with coal in the Pontop area. Initially it would seem that their intention was to construct a railway between these two areas and then utilise the route of the former Pontop waggonway (see Fig.5) to provide access to the River Tyne upstream of Newcastle-upon-Tyne; but this was soon abandoned in favour of a much more ambitious scheme to take the line to staiths at South Shields, a distance of 33 miles, with a further 4½ miles of branches. In May 1832 the "Stanhope & Tyne Railroad Company" was formed, with William Harrison the leading promoter, his son T.E.Harrison, later to become a famous officer of the North Eastern Railway, as Engineer, and Robert Stephenson as consulting engineer.

However, desperate to keep its plans as secret as possible, the company decided against obtaining an Act of Parliament and compulsory powers, and instead set out to obtain wayleave agreements for the whole route. At first the wayleave charges were not remarkable, but the company's plans had become known by the time it began negotiations for the eastern section, and huge prices were charged here. Of the total 37½ miles, 14½ were to be worked by horses, 11 miles by stationary engines, 3 miles by self-acting inclines and 9¼ miles, between Fatfield and South Shields, by locomotives. No provision was made for any passenger traffic.

Construction began in July 1832, using fish-bellied cast iron rails supported by stone blocks of various sizes. The section between Stanhope and Annfield, a distance of 15¼ miles, was opened on 15th May 1834 and the remainder followed on 10th September 1834.

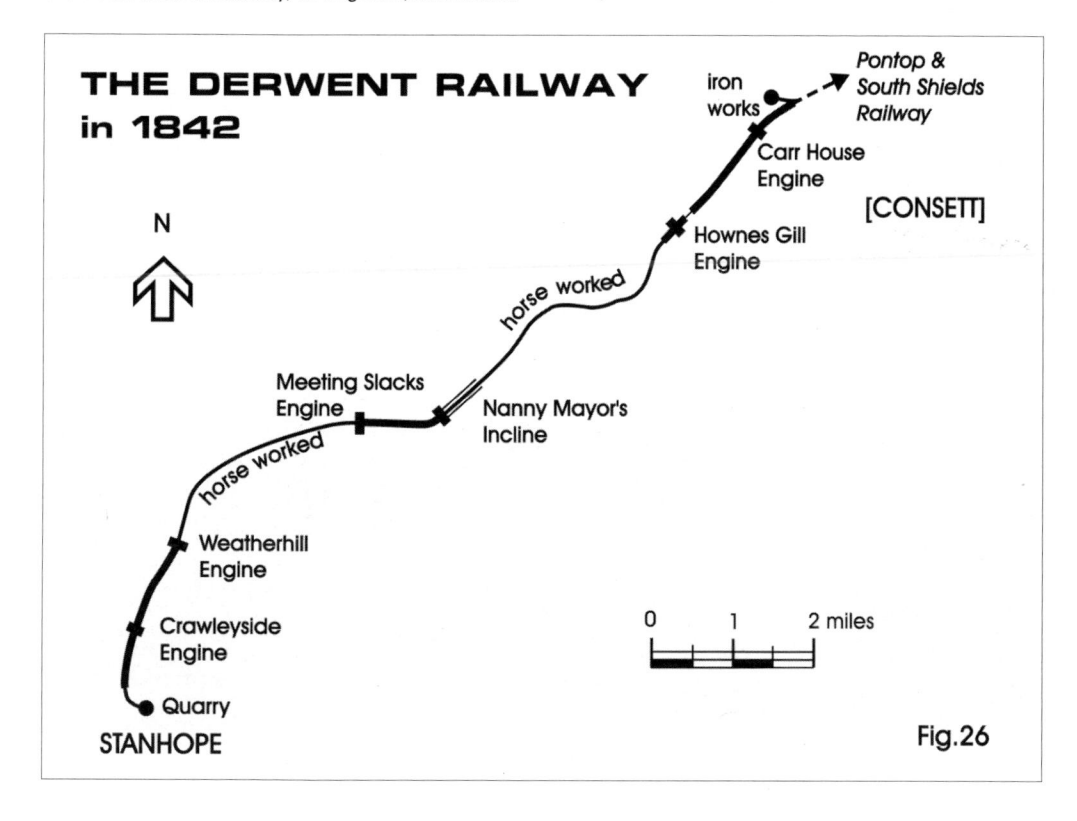

Fig.26

Fig. 27

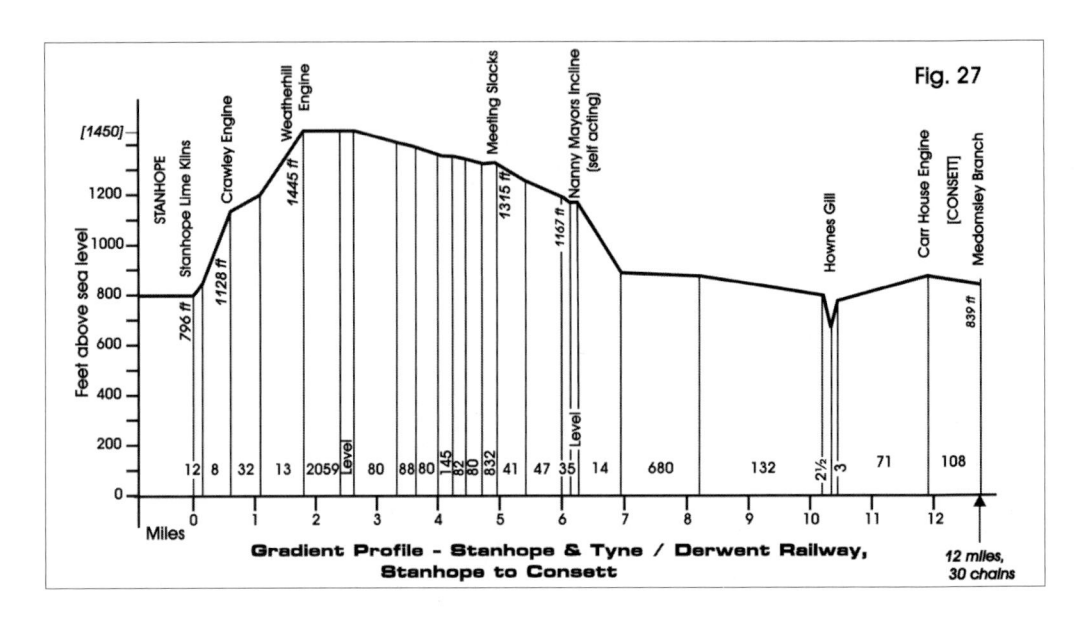

Gradient Profile - Stanhope & Tyne / Derwent Railway, Stanhope to Consett

12 miles, 30 chains

The Derwent Iron Company

The opening of the Stanhope & Tyne Railway stimulated the exploration and development of the mineral resources near its route. It was discovered that the coal measures in north-west Durham contained bands of ironstone, and of course there was limestone available from Stanhope. Documents now at the Durham County Record Office in the Consett Iron Co Ltd Collection (D/Co) show that in September 1840 William Backhouse, Charles Bigge and Edward, Caleb and William Richardson formed a partnership and built a blast furnace at Carrhouse (Carr House is also found), near Berry Edge (later called Consett), about four miles east of Annfield, the works being linked to the Stanhope & Tyne to bring in the limestone and to take away the finished products.

Events of 1840-1841

However, by 1840 the Stanhope & Tyne was facing

81. Hog Hill Tunnel, on the meetings of the Crawleyside Incline at Stanhope, about 1914.

serious financial difficulties. Due to the expense of working the section between Stanhope and Carrhouse, the company was forced in 1840 to close it and give up the making of lime, though still having to pay the rent for the quarry and the wayleave charges, and in December 1840 the company was revealed to be bankrupt. To try to avoid the personal ruin of all the shareholders, it was proposed to set up a new company, with shareholders unable to continue being allowed to drop out, escaping their liabilities with the loss of their shares. However, the new company only felt able to take over the 24½ miles between Carrhouse and South Shields. The Stanhope & Tyne company was dissolved on 5th February 1841 and the Pontop & South Shields Railway, the new name for the section east of Carrhouse, received its Act on 23rd May 1842.

Meanwhile, also in 1841 the partners at Berry Edge merged with the owners of Redesdale Iron Works in Northumberland to form the **Derwent Iron Company**, and on 14th June 1841 this new firm purchased a fully-operational iron works at Sunderland, the **Bishopwearmouth Ironworks** (NZ 388569), which was served by the Lambton Railway (which see). With the new Pontop & South Shields company unwilling to take over the former Stanhope & Tyne section west of Carrhouse, the Derwent Iron Company was compelled to purchase this section and the quarry at Stanhope in order to safeguard its supply of limestone. The exact date of the purchase is unknown, but Tomlinson (see below) attributes it to early in 1842. The new owners called their line the **DERWENT RAILWAY**.

Description of the route

The railway proper began ½ mile north of Stanhope, with the Crawleyside Incline; but from the bank foot a line ran to the west and then turned north up Stanhope Burn for about a mile to reach the **Stanhope Lead Smelter** (NY 987413), owned by the London Lead Company. A branch from this extension served **LANEHEAD QUARRY** (NY 990403), now owned by the Iron Company, at the southern end of which were the large lime kilns on which the Stanhope & Tyne had placed so much hope.

To haul wagons from Stanhope out of Weardale two fearsome inclines were needed. The Crawleyside Incline, 942 yards and worked by the 50 h.p. **Crawleyside Engine** (NY 994406), had gradients of 1 in 7¼ and 1 in 12, and passed through the short Hog Hill Tunnel, one of the very rare examples of an incline with a tunnel. The incline, including the tunnel, was double track, allowing full and empty sets to be run simultaneously, albeit only two waggons at a time. Next the **Weatherhill Engine** (NY 998423), also 50 h.p., brought the waggons up 1 mile 128 yards on an average gradient of 1 in 13 to a summit of 1,445 feet, the highest point ever reached by a public

82. *Crawleyside Bank Head, near Stanhope, about 1914.*

railway in England. The 1st edition O.S. map (1859) clearly shows a meetings, so again fulls and empties could be worked at the same time. Horses worked the next 1½ miles, which brought the waggons to the Park Head wheel house (NZ 008445 approx.). Here the tail rope of a main-and-tail system was attached, worked by the **Meeting Slacks Engine** (NZ 032454) (40 h.p.), to bring the waggons down to the engine house. The Engine also worked the incline (1 mile 453 yards) on its eastern side, lowering the waggons down over gradients from 1 in 26½ to 1 in 58 to the top of the **Nanny Mayors' Incline** (named after an eccentric woman who kept an ale-house alongside the line). This was a self-acting incline 1,122 yards long on a gradient of 1 in 14. For the next 1¼ miles the waggons were hauled by horses, which were then taken round to the rear of the train to be put into "dandy carts", so that the waggons could coast down by gravity for two miles to the edge of the Hownes Gill, a dry ravine about 150 feet deep and 266 yards across. Instead of crossing this with a bridge there was in the bottom of the ravine the **Hownes Gill Engine** (NZ 096490), given as 20 h.p. by Tomlinson, but 35 h.p. by Whittle (see below), whose purpose was to lower the waggons down one side and haul them up the other. Tomlinson describes the system as follows: "The sides of the Gill being so precipitous, 1 in 2½ and 1 in 3 respectively, it was considered necessary, in order to keep the waggons in a horizontal position, to provide cradles or trucks – one for each incline – having front and hind wheels of unequal diameter: upon these the waggons travelled side foremost. Only one waggon could be taken at a time. On arriving at the edge of the ravine, it was placed at right-angles to the line by means of a turntable, moved forward and fixed upon the incline truck, and then lowered by a rope, passing underneath between the sloping walls on which the rails were laid, to the bottom of the Gill. Here, adjoining the engine, was a rectangular platform having turntables at its four corners. Pushed off the truck towards one of these turntables, the waggon was slewed round to its ordinary position and worked forward to a turntable at another corner, which placed it once more at right-angles to the line. It was then run forward on to another truck and raised to the top of the Gill, where, after being turned round a fourth angle, it was able to proceed in a more direct fashion. The number of waggons that could be taken across Hownes Gill in a hour was twelve. Both inclines were worked at once, so that the weight of the descending waggon might assist the engine. The truck appears to have run on two pairs of rails, with width of the outer pair being 7 feet 0 1/8 inches in and of the inner pair 5 feet 1¾ inches." Though the fame of Hownes Gill attracted many visitors – one described it in 1843 as "one of the most wonderful railway rarities in existence" – no one seems ever to have sketched it.

From the eastern side of the ravine the **Carrhouse Engine** (NZ 112507) hauled the waggons up the Carrhouse West Incline, 1 mile 779 yards at 1 in 71, before lowering them down the Carrhouse East Incline, 812 yards at 1 in 108. The bank foot, to which the ironworks was linked, marked the end of the Derwent Iron Company's ownership.

It seems, however, that the Iron Company had certain powers over the next 3¼ miles, as its successor, The Consett Iron Co Ltd, was to have later. The next 2¼ miles east of Carr House East Bank Foot on what was now the Pontop & South Shields Railway were worked by horses. Then came two more rope inclines over Annfield hill, with a stationary engine on top of the hill working both the Annfield West Incline (662 yards) and East Incline, better known as the Loud Bank (1056 yards), near to Pontop Colliery.

From the foot of the Carr House East Incline a branch ran northwards for 1½ miles to serve **Medomsley Colliery** (NZ 115537). The early history of this colliery is far from clear. Whittle says that the first coal shipped at South Shields on the opening of the Stanhope & Tyne Railway on 10th September 1834 came from here, being owned by the railway company. Latimer's *Local Records 1832-1857* gives the colliery's opening date as 30th December 1839 and the owners as the Derwent Iron Co; but as this predates the founding of the iron works and the Derwent Iron Co was not formed until 1841 this may be suspect. Whittle goes on to say that the colliery was sold by the Pontop & South Shields Railway to the Derwent Iron Co "about 1844". However, it was leased to John Bowes, Esq. & Partners between July 1850 and April 1852, so it may be that the Derwent Iron Co did not acquire it until this date. Precisely who owned the colliery during the early 1840s seems impossible to state now; for the record, at this date the branch was worked by the **Derwent Engine** (NZ 115537) at the colliery.

It would seem that the Iron Company's relations with the Pontop & South Shields Railway became strained, for in December 1843 the Iron Company, in association with the Brandling Junction Railway, relaid the Tanfield Moor branch, which ran from the foot of the Annfield East Incline northwards to Harelaw to join the Brandling Junction Railway's Tanfield Branch. This meant all the Iron Company's traffic could now go via the Brandling Junction Railway to Gateshead rather than on the Pontop & South Shields Railway to South Shields, albeit travelling over part of the latter to do this.

The disposal of the Railway
Meanwhile further west the Iron Company was already looking to link up with the Stockton & Darlington Railway's Bishop Auckland & Weardale Railway, which was due to reach Crook in 1843, and put this proposal to the Stockton & Darlington in 1842. It seems that the Stockton & Darlington were circumspect about this, initially acting through three of their shareholders. The agreement provided for the Iron Company to acquire the wayleaves needed and advance £15,000 of the capital required and the Stockton & Darlington would then advance the remaining money needed to construct the 10¼ mile line,

83. The line between Weatherhill and Waskerley, showing the bleakness of the High Pennines. Local tradition claimed the water crane could be frozen for up to six months a year.

initially called the Weardale Extension Railway. In addition, the Stockton & Darlington Railway agreed to purchase the Derwent Railway from the Iron Company. Following a survey of the Derwent Railway by the Stockton & Darlington's Engineer, William Bouch, the Iron Company in 1844 replaced the horse working between Weatherhill and Parkhead by a second main-and-tail system utilising the Weatherhill Engine and (presumably) a second return wheel at Parkhead.

The Weardale Extension Railway was planned to join the Derwent Railway at the top of the Nanny Mayor's incline at Waskerley Park, soon abbreviated to Waskerley. In 1844 the contract for the work was awarded to Messrs Harris & Bray, and work began on 28th June 1844. The transfer of the wayleaves of the Derwent Railway between the Iron Company and the Stockton & Darlington Railway, together with the ownership of Lanehead Quarry at Stanhope and the Tanfield Moor branch, was completed on 1st January 1845. The "Derwent Railway" was then combined with the Weardale Extension Railway and the new system was given the name of the Weardale & Derwent Junction Railway. It was opened on 16th May 1845.

Postscript
The original ironworks partnership was reconstituted on 30th September 1844, and expansion at Consett thereafter was very rapid. In 1851 the company leased extensive ironstone deposits at Loftus in North Yorkshire. Unfortunately the Iron Company was heavily indebted to the Northumberland & Durham Bank, which failed in November 1857, and long-term stability was not re-established until the formation of The Consett Iron Co Ltd in 1864.

On the railway the Hownes Gill inclines were finally replaced by a viaduct opened on 1st July 1858, the Carrhouse inclines being also closed on the same day. The rope haulage between Weatherhill and Hownes Gill was gradually replaced by new deviation routes operated by locomotives from a shed at Waskerley; the last incline to close was the Nanny Mayor's Incline, on 4th July 1859. The Stockton & Darlington Railway amalgamated with the North Eastern Railway on 13th July 1863. Little changed then until 28th April 1951, when under British Railways the Crawleyside and Weatherhill inclines were closed. The remaining section saw traffic steadily dwindle, and it was finally closed on 1st May 1969.

References:

The North Eastern Railway, W.W.Tomlinson, Newcastle upon Tyne, 1915

The Railways of Consett & North West Durham, G.Whittle, Newton Abbot, 1971

Chapter Eight
The Hetton Railway

OWNERS BEFORE 1947
The Lambton, Hetton & Joicey Collieries Ltd until 1/1/1947
The Lambton & Hetton Collieries Ltd until 26/11/1924
The Hetton Coal Co Ltd until 8/1911
The Hetton Coal Co until 4/7/1884

The opening of Hetton Colliery on 18th November 1822 was perhaps the most significant development ever in the history of the Durham coalfield, and its associated railway, opened on the same day, was equally a major landmark in the history of railways.

In the western half of County Durham the coal seams are close to the surface and were relatively easy to work; but in the eastern half of the county there is a thick stratum of magnesian limestone and it was believed that no coal measures lay underneath it. Then in 1810 Robert Lyon, a landowner in this area near Hetton-le-Hole, began sinking a shaft on his land, only for the cost to bankrupt him. However, in 1819 one of the leading mining engineers of the time, Arthur Mowbray, left his employment as Chief Viewer to the Marquis of Londonderry and with a group of entrepreneurs took over the royalty (the Marquis had hoped to acquire it, but in the end he became a shareholder). The sinking of a new **HETTON COLLIERY**, often called **HETTON LYONS COLLIERY** after Robert Lyon (NZ 360469), began on 19th December 1820 about ¼ mile south of the village of Hetton-le-Hole. The Main Coal seam was reached on 3rd September 1822 and the Hutton seam on 6th January 1823. The Hetton Coal Company, created earlier in 1820, was the first important joint-stock coal company in Durham; its success in finding coal below the magnesian limestone led to the opening up of the whole of the eastern area of the coalfield, while its ever-increasing output, necessary to meet borrowings and provide a return on the shareholders investment, challenged the "Limitation of the Vend", the cartel of aristocratic Durham coal owners that for so many years had imposed controlled output and high prices on the London coal trade. In 1836 Nicholas Wood (1795-1865) (see also chapters 3 and 14) became the company's superintendent viewer and in 1844 the company's Managing Partner. He was succeeded by his son, Lindsay Wood (1834-1920), later Sir Lindsay Wood, who for many years was also chairman of the Harton Coal Co Ltd (chapter 14) and one of the most powerful men in the Durham coal industry.

A new inland colliery needed a waggonway to transport its coal to the nearest river. But for the Hetton Company staiths upstream on the River Wear and the cost and inconvenience of then taking coal by keel down to the river mouth to load on to sea-going colliers, as both Lambton and Londonderry were doing, were unacceptable; from the outset the Hetton company was determined to ship its coal at Sunderland directly into colliers and thus eliminate the keels.

Mowbray became interested in linking the Vane Tempest waggonway to the Newbottle line as early as 1813. When he became the leading promotor in the Hetton Coal Co he seriously considered linking Hetton Colliery to the Newbottle line (1819); but John Buddle, who disliked Mowbray intensely, was determined to keep the Newbottle line out of his hands, first by proposing to link the Vane Tempest system to it (1820) and subsequently proposing a division of the area under which Lambton got Newbottle and Londonderry got Seaham (DCRO, D/Lo/142/4), which is more or less what eventually happened. In the event the Newbottle Railway was incorporated into the Lambton Railway (see chapter 9).

Having failed to gain access to the Newbottle line, the company was thus compelled to build its own line, which was called the **HETTON RAILWAY**.

The early years of the Railway
To engineer the line the company engaged in 1819 one of the area's leading railway engineers, George Stephenson, then employed at Killingworth in Northumberland by Lord Ravensworth & Partners, known as "The Grand Allies", who allowed him to design this new line while still working for them. The result was the first railway in the world to be designed to use steam locomotives – a major pioneering step in railway development.

However, between Hetton and Sunderland lay the very real obstacle of Warden Law at 636 feet, whilst at Sunderland there were steep cliffs down to the river. So the design for the eight-mile line incorporated two locomotive-worked sections, two rope inclines worked by stationary engines and five self-acting (gravity-worked) inclines. Construction began in March 1821. A month later George Stephenson was appointed Engineer to the new Stockton & Darlington Railway, so his younger brother Robert was appointed resident engineer at Hetton; and as stated earlier, the line was opened, with due ceremony, on 18th November 1822.

The Railway proved far from satisfactory, and within only nine months of the opening the company was commissioning the first of a whole series of reports on the colliery and the Railway that were undertaken in the next ten years (these are now in public deposit, unfortunately divided between the Durham, Tyne & Wear and Northumberland Record Offices). By 1827 sections of the line had been radically altered. In addition, there is the report of two engineers from the Mining Ministry in Prussia, C. von Oeynhausen and H. von Dechen, who in 1826-1827 made an extensive survey of railways in England – *Railways in England, 1826 and 1827* (translated by E.A.Forward and published by The Newcomen Society in 1971). As part of their tour they visited the Hetton Railway, which they described as "the finest in England after the previously-described [Stockton &] Darlington Railway". It would seem that they came to Hetton in the late summer of 1827. Their report provides a very detailed description of the line. They paced the whole route, but given the vagaries of this method, their quotation of the distances given to them by the Hetton Coal Company Viewer are those given below. In addition, a very detailed plan of the line also survives, to the scale of 40 inches to the mile, undated, but almost certainly drawn in the 1840s. At this time the Railway was using "Newcastle chaldron" waggons, each holding approximately 53 hundredweights of coal, rather more than 2½ tons.

Beginning at Hetton Lyons Colliery, the first section ran for 2541 yards, just under 1½ miles, to the foot of the first incline, a place called by the Prussians the "Rough Bank", actually Rough Dene, and later known as Dene Bank Foot. The rise against the load averaged out at 1 in 334. Initially one, but by 1827 two, locomotives worked here, each for up to 14 hours a day and hauling 16 waggons at a time, full and empty, at a speed of "4 to 4½ or 5 miles an hour".

From "Rough Bank" the first of the rope inclines took the waggons up the **Copt Hill Bank**, 832 yards at 1 in 16, to the **Byer** (Byre is also found) **Engine** (NZ 355497) (60 h.p.). The section between the Byer Engine and Warden Law fell into two distinct sections, 775 yards at 1 in 91 and 775 yards at 1 in 20. It would seem that when the Railway was opened in 1822 this section was worked by only one stationary engine, at Warden Law; if so, it was soon found to be inadequate, for by the time of the Prussian engineers' visit there were two, the second being built at the change of gradient. The section to it, from the Byer Engine, soon became known as **The Flat** (later **The Flatt**), and so the stationary engine became known as the **Flat Engine** (NZ 362500) (30 h.p.) (called in the Prussian account the Warden Law Engine, incorrectly). From here the waggons were hauled up to the **Warden Law Engine** (NZ 358505) (60 h.p.). All three inclines were single line and worked sets of eight waggons alternately, at about 3 m.p.h. The hemp ropes were of 7¼ inches in circumference and lasted between 30 and 35 weeks.

From Warden Law four self-acting inclines took the waggons down to what was sometimes known as North Moor but called "The Long Run" by the men, some 2¾ miles south of Sunderland. These inclines were numbered from the top, **No.1** being 1302 yards at 1 in 30, **No.2** 1224 yards at 1 in 28½, **No.3** 716 yards at 1 in 40 and **No.4** 902 yards at 1 in 36. Sets of eight waggons, fulls and empties, were run on each simultaneously at about 10 m.p.h., the circumference of the ropes varying between 4½ and 5 inches and lasting between 36 and 59 weeks. The next 2½ miles, which included a number of rather sharp curves, divided out into two sections, 2602 yards at a fall of about 1 in 115 and 1748 yards nearly level. On this section three more of Stephenson's locomotives were employed, again hauling trains of 16 waggons. There was presumably a locomotive shed on this section, but no evidence of its location survives. The last 325 yards down to the **HETTON STAITHS** (NZ 391574) on the River Wear (see Fig.35) was operated by the Fifth or Staith Inclined Plane, a further self-acting incline at 1 in 14_, which brought sets of four fulls into the 'self-discharging depot' at the Staiths. Apart from sidings and the self-acting inclines the whole route was almost certainly single line, with fulls and empties having to be worked alternately.

The original railway was constructed using cast iron fish-bellied rail to the Stephenson & Losh patent, and manufactured by Losh, Wilson & Bell at the Walker Ironworks in Newcastle upon Tyne. Breakages soon developed at a significant level – calculated at £119-19s-8d between November 1823 and October 1824 – and a foundry opened at Hetton Colliery in 1822 was kept very busy as a result.

The opening of Elemore and Eppleton Collieries, 1827-1833

Soon after the opening the company began to plan further developments, helped by the addition to the partnership of Mr George Baker. On 25th March 1825 the sinking of **ELEMORE COLLIERY** (NZ 346356) was begun at Easington Lane on Baker's estate, coal being reached in February 1827. This colliery was linked to Hetton Colliery by a self-acting incline running northwards for about a mile. Three months after beginning the sinking of Elemore Colliery the company began the sinking of **EPPLETON COLLIERY** (NZ 364484), on 23rd May 1825. However, considerable difficulties were encountered with water in the thick bed of sand immediately below the limestone, and coal was not reached until 1833. Eppleton Colliery was linked to the main line about a mile north of Hetton by another self-acting incline, ¾ mile long.

The re-building of the northern section in 1827

As early as June 1823, only eight months after the opening, William Chapman (see chapter 1) was being invited by the company to report on the Railway, its fixed and travelling engines and the staiths (NRO 725/F/17/57). Between June and September he compiled three quite critical reports, in the second of which he noted that because of the steep gradients and severe curves on the final 1533

Fig.28 Gradient Profile - Hetton Railway in 1827

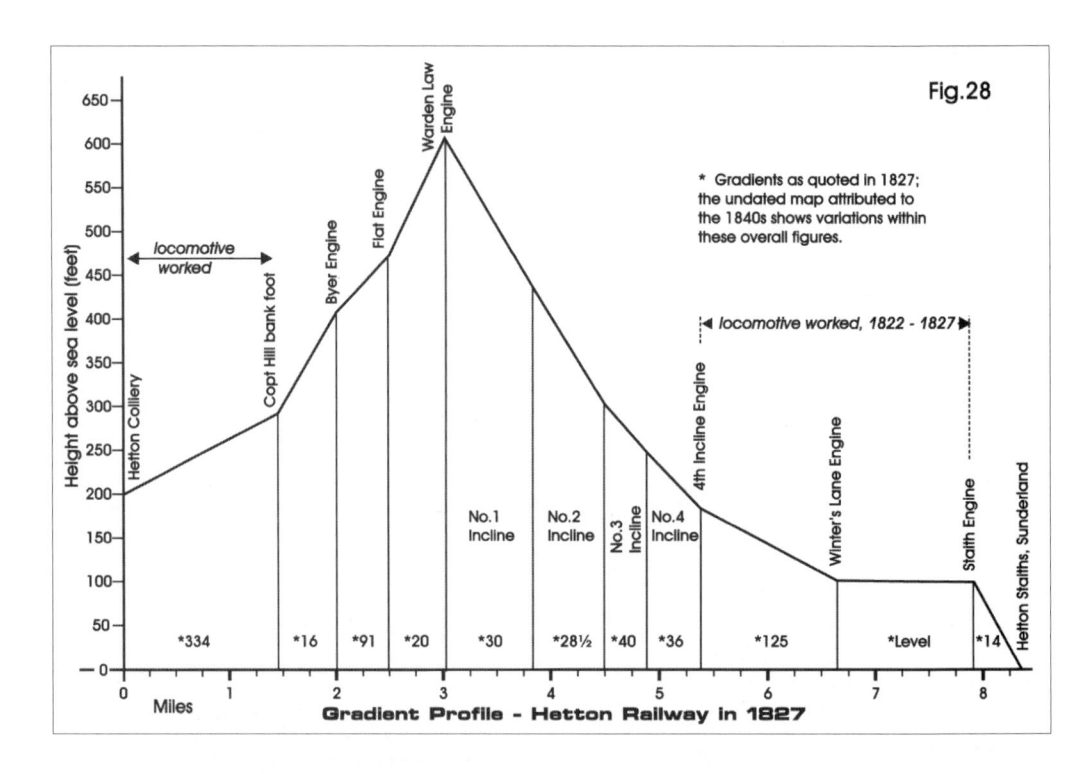

yards of the section between the top of the Staith incline and the foot of No.4 Incline, locomotives hauling trains of 16 empties from the top of the Staith Incline could not manage more than 2_-3 m.p.h., which would not be sustainable if the volume of coal were to increase. With the increase in traffic after February 1827 with the opening of Elemore Colliery, this had clearly now become critical; so the decision was taken to abandon the locomotives and replace them with rope haulage. The line was divided into two sections measuring 2550 and 1850 yards respectively. The first was worked by the Fourth Inclined Engine (NZ 373540). This originally ran a set of 16 down by gravity, braking as required; by 1832 the sets had been increased to 24, taking 10-12 minutes to cover the distance. The second and flatter section, from just south of the Sunderland-Durham Road to just south of Hylton Road, was worked by the Winter's Lane Engine (NZ 385555) and the Staith Engine (NZ 388571) together, using main-and-tail haulage, again with 24 waggons, although the Prussians saw up to 30 waggons being run. The siting of the stationary engine south of Hylton Road was presumably forced upon the company in order to avoid the problems of the rope crossing over Hylton Road and the intersection here with the Newbottle Waggonway. Research in 1998 showed that the locomotives were replaced by rope haulage at the end of May 1827. With the speed of the sets at least 10 m.p.h., the contrast with locomotive haulage was very marked.

Hetton Staiths

The original staiths, with two loading points, were 75 feet above the river at low tide and were an unusual design which required chaldrons to have an end door. On arrival at the staiths the waggons were canted forward, allowing the coal to be discharged, whence it was carried down a chute before falling vertically for 12-14 feet into the ship's hold. This method caused so much damage to the coal that it could lose up to half of its value between wagon and ship. To reduce this loss a second self-acting incline was under construction here by June 1823, presumably projecting out from the cliff, as it brought the wagons right out over the ship. By the time of yet another report on the Railway, by the company's engineer, Charles Robinson, in 1832 (NRO 725/F/17/279) there was only one self-acting incline here, working sets of four wagons to Drops Nos. 2 and 3, while the Bell Engine worked sets of two down to Drops Nos.4, 5 and 6. He added that "The Staith Engine also leads timber and goods from the Quay and ships coal from the new staith". Some staiths built later incorporated cranes for unloading materials. Nor was this the end of changes at the staiths in this period; the 1st ed. O.S. 25in map, surveyed in the mid-1850s, shows no fewer than three engine houses at the staiths (see Fig.37). What work these engines undertook is not known.

In 1840 there was yet another report into the company and its operations, this time by Nicholas Wood (Beamish, Place Collection, 2003-54.8/213). In reviewing the increased cost of wages for "leading coals", Wood states that in part this was due to "having locomotives employed instead of the fixed engine recently burned down at the Fourth Incline and having to employ extra men at the various crossings of the Turnpike Road and highways. The fixed engine being now at work, and the Warden Law Engine bank being improved [see below], the cost of labour will be partly reduced...". The accounts accompanying Wood's report show that the fire had occurred earlier in 1840. Presumably the locomotives had to be brought from Hetton, or hired – but only as a temporary measure while the engine was repaired, at a cost of over £1000.

To service the collieries and the railway the company developed extensive **Workshops** to the south of Hetton Colliery (see below). To the west of the colliery a **limestone quarry** (NZ 357471) was developed, but by 1881 this had been replaced by a **brickworks**, using seggar clay obtained underground, which made very hard common bricks. To the north-east of the colliery 120 **beehive coke ovens** (NZ 358472) were built, so that a wide range of activities was developed in quite a small area.

Links with other railways

Both Lambton and Londonderry found that their staiths on the River Wear at Pensher were inadequate and were compelled to seek outlets elsewhere to eliminate the keels and to allow a far higher volume of coal to be shipped. For Lambton this meant buying the Newbottle Waggonway, thus giving him direct access to Sunderland and then

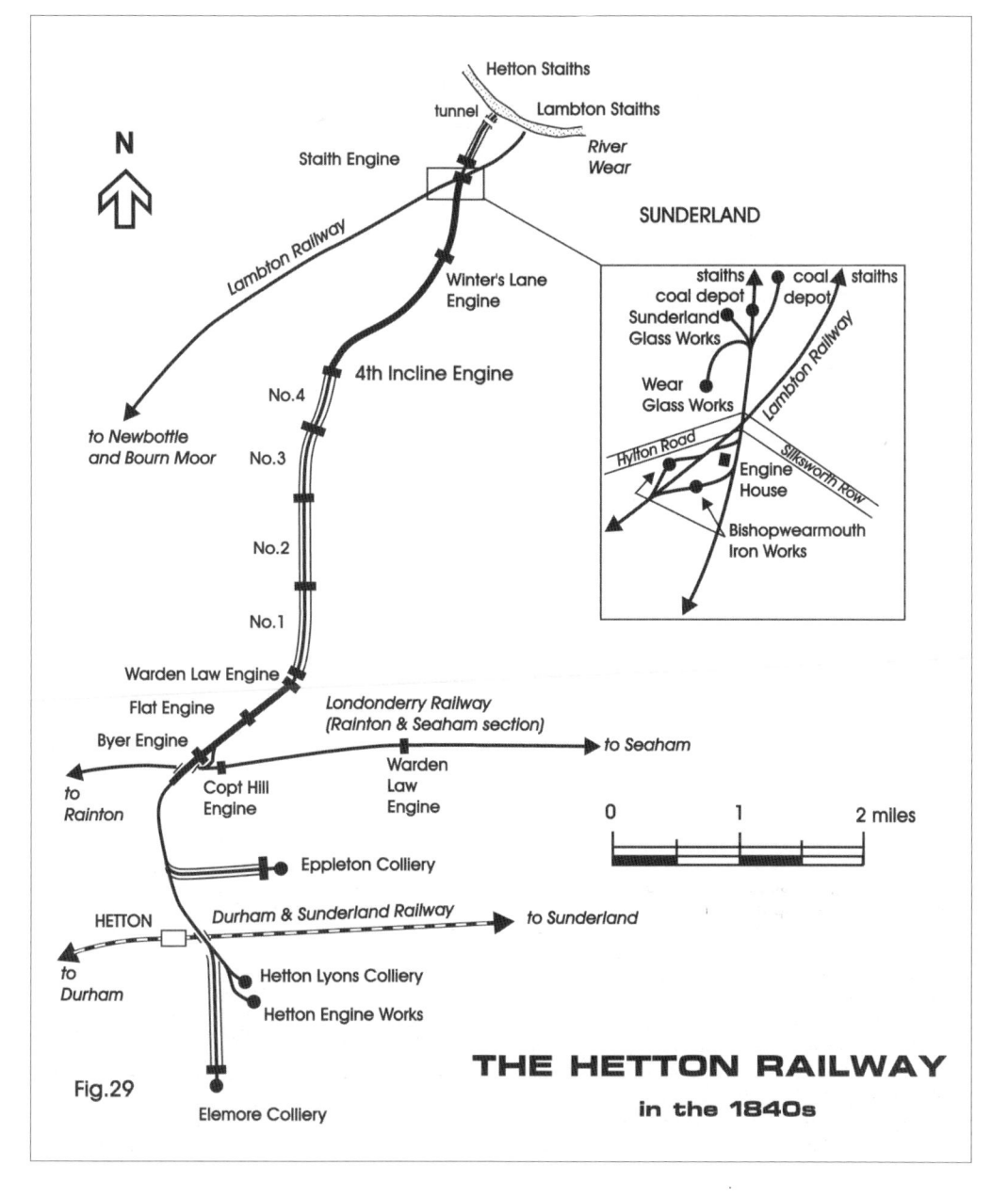

THE HETTON RAILWAY in the 1840s

Fig.29

84. "The oldest working locomotive in the world" on the Elemore self-acting incline, about 1895.

rebuilding much of it. This line, as noted above, crossed the Hetton line on the level at Hylton Road, and a link here between the two lines was soon put in. For Londonderry this meant constructing a new port at Seaham and building a line from Rainton across to it. When the Londonderry line was opened in 1831 it crossed under the Hetton Railway in a tunnel below the Copt Hill incline.

In 1843 the two firms agreed to allow small coal from North Hetton Colliery, served by the Londonderry Railway but operated by **The North Hetton Coal Co**, of which at this time The Hetton Coal Company was part-owner, to be shipped at Hetton Staiths, for which purpose a short line was constructed from north of the Byer Engine on the Hetton Railway to Copt Hill bank head on the Londonderry line, the traffic being worked presumably by the Flat Engine.

The western section of the Durham & Sunderland Railway, between Murton and Durham and opened in 1836, passed under the Hetton Railway at Hetton in a tunnel. This line was entirely rope-worked until 1858, and it seems clear that a link between the two lines, at Hetton Colliery Junction, about ¼ mile east of Hetton Station, was not put in until after the public line had abandoned rope haulage. The North Hetton line was also linked with the Durham & Sunderland line, at Moorsley. There were also at least two proposals, in 1832 and in 1838, to link Elemore Colliery to the Clarence Railway, to allow its coal to be shipped at Hartlepool, but neither was proceeded with. In addition, a map of Sunderland dated about 1835 shows a proposed line between the Winter's Lane Engine and South Dock in Sunderland, presumably again to provide extra shipping capacity, but this too was never built.

As the second-ever railway into Sunderland it was inevitable that other businessmen would site their factories alongside it to gain access to its coal. The first of these was the **Bishopwearmouth Iron Works** (NZ 388569), of which the first record occurs in January 1828, when it was owned by John White. This was situated just south of the Hylton Road crossing, and despite lying to the west of Lambton's Newbottle line it was initially served by a branch of the Hetton Railway. Later it expanded into the space between the two railways, then to be served by the Lambton Railway (which see). It was purchased by The Derwent Iron Company in 1841 and subsequently passed to The Consett Iron Co Ltd. The next development, begun in 1836, was James Hartley's **Wear Glass Works** (NZ 389573), just north of Hylton Road crossing; twenty years later it was said to have been producing a third of all the plate glass produced in Britain, and it was a major customer of the Railway for many years. Subsequently a second glass works, the **Sunderland Glass Works** (NZ 389574), was opened immediately to the north of the Wear Works; this was subsequently closed and an ironworks, the **Trimdon Iron Works**, developed on the same site. None of these works is known to have had any

85. 1, RS 1100/1857, as a 2-4-0 tender engine.

86. 1, as rebuilt at Hetton Engine Works to a 2-4-0T.

87. *37, formerly Hetton 6, RWH 1430/1868, at Hetton, probably in the 1930s. Hetton 5, RWH 1422/1867, and Hetton 7, RS 1919/1869, can be seen in photographs Nos.33 and 9, respectively.*

locomotives of their own. Besides these works the Hetton company had extensive sidings north of Hylton Road and two coal depots, so that by the mid-1850s this area was very busy indeed (see Fig. 37).

Maintenance of the line by contractors
It is clear from Wood's report of 1840 mentioned above that at the date, and for some years before it, the track had been maintained by contractors. This is the only known example of such a contract for any of the private railways in Durham, and the reasons why it was adopted are unknown, though Wood claimed it was saving the company money. Also in the Place Collection at Beamish is a complete specification for the proposed maintenance contract for 1847. Interestingly, stone blocks, rather than wooden sleepers, are still being used, at 3 cubic feet, and the schedule provides a rare specification for this type of track: there were to be eight inches of small coal or ashes below the blocks and 24 inches on each side and between the rails, to be filled up to rail level. The schedule does not include any involvement with the inclines or the locomotives, although the contractor was expected to find work for the men employed on them if they were idle.

The use of horses
Other interesting documents in the Place Collection show that in 1850 the "keep, wear & tear and upholding" of a wagon horse (i.e., used for hauling waggons) was £52-10-0 (£52 10 shillings) per year. Such a horse cost £45 'new' and could be expected to last ten years. In a comparison between horses and locomotives at Elemore Colliery dated 22nd November 1861, the cost of a new horse had risen to £50, with a new locomotive quoted as £200. Four or five horses were used here during the winter, but only three in the summer. Four horses were still being used at the staiths between 1867-1870.

Changes to the Railway and its route after 1832
As has been described already, the pressure to increase the capacity of the line had resulted in major changes by 1832. These were far from the end of the matter, not least because all the powered inclines were single line, while steam locomotives had become both more powerful and more reliable. However, complete information about the changes in the fifty years after 1832, particularly of dates and sequencing, is not available. In describing what happened it is convenient to divide the line at Warden Law.

The original steam engine at Warden Law was replaced in 1836 by a beam engine made by Thomas Murray of Chester-le-Street, a double-acting engine with a single cylinder 39in x 64in, of 97½ h.p. Almost certainly this was a condensing engine as built, although latterly it was non-condensing, albeit fitted with an economiser. It was clearly fitted with two drums as built – unusually in an open building alongside the engine house – from which it is obvious that it was installed in order to increase the capacity of the incline from the original single line operation of sets alternately to the running of fulls and empties simultaneously; it is clearly this improvement which is referred to in Nicholas Wood's report of 1840 (see above). The beam drove a flywheel 24½ft in diameter, whose shaft operated pinions which in turn drove the

88. LYONS, one of the two four-wheeled vertical-boilered locomotives built at Hetton Engine Works. On the opposite side both wheels were chain-driven.

drums. To reverse the engine the driver depressed a foot pedal, which disengaged the gab, allowing the slide vale to be worked by hand to rotate the engine back 180 degrees, at which point the gab was re-engaged. Latterly the engine was served by three Lancashire boilers set below ground level so that coal could be directed into the boiler room by a chute. The coal wagons were run into the siding by gravity but had to be hauled out using a short length of shunting rope.

In 1876 the whole section between Copt Hill Bank Foot and Warden Law Bank Foot was rebuilt. The Flatt Engine was removed (*Railway Magazine*, May 1902), though an engine was maintained here to pump water for the two remaining stationary engines. The incline up from Copt Hill Bank Foot was rebuilt to allow full and empty sets to be run simultaneously. Besides the two drums needed for this, the new Byer Engine (Grange Iron Works 125/1876) had two more drums for working the next section to Warden Law Bank Foot, now known as "The Flatts", where there was a return wheel for the rope. Normally only one of this second pair of drums was used, with sets of double the number of wagons being run alternately; but if a gale was blowing the empty wagons would not run back to Copt Hill satisfactorily, and then the Engine's fourth drum was used to implement a form of main-and-tail haulage using both drums. The fulls were hauled to the Flatts with the second rope attached to the rear end, which could then be attached to the empties needing to be hauled back, which was done by the second drum, with the first drum out of gear. The interchange at the Flatts, with a dish for the fulls and a very shallow kip for the empties, was one of the places where haulage ropes needed to cross each other, always a difficult and dangerous practice.

Both at Copt Hill and Warden Law short lengths of rope were kept, certainly in later years, to allow wagons to be shunted. For example, there was a coal depot at the Seaham road on the Copt Hill incline. To run fulls in meant hauling eight fulls (10½ or 12 tons) from the bank foot, stopping the set above the depot, then uncoupling the last three and running them into the depot by gravity. To remove the empties the normal set of five was stopped above the depot and then the short rope would be attached from the rear of the fulls to the front of the empties and the combined set hauled to the bank head. Here further short ropes were used to bring the empties on to an outside road to return to Hetton.

Further south, the rope was taken off the Elemore incline about 1895 (Elemore Colliery was closed between February 1893 and 1897) and off the Eppleton incline, by then known as the **Downs Bank**, in 1902, both being replaced by locomotive working. With the rope removed, a quarry (NZ 356484) was opened on the northern side of the branch, called at first **HIGH DOWNS QUARRY** but later **EPPLETON QUARRY**. In the 1930s this quarry is recorded as supplying sand to Hetton Loco Shed.

89. 11, HC 1412/1920, shortly after being delivered new to Hetton in August 1920, in L & HC livery.

Meanwhile, the Rainton & Seaham section of the Londonderry Railway, with its link at Copt Hill, had been closed in 1896. It has been thought in the past that the section of the Londonderry line between Rainton Bridge and Copt Hill remained open to provide a route for the North Hetton coal to reach the Hetton line; but there is no evidence that this was the case, and it is also difficult to see how it would have been handled at Copt Hill after the abandonment of the Flat Engine.

Over a considerable period of time, perhaps as much as sixty years, substantial modifications were also made north of North Moor, south of Sunderland. A print of Hartley's Glass Works dated about 1855 and reproduced on p.43 of *Railways of Sunderland*, published by Tyne & Wear County Council Museums in 1985, shows the stationary

90. 46, MW 1813/1913, outside the two-road Hetton loco shed on 6th June 1951.

engine at Hylton Road working; but on the 1st edition O.S. 6in map surveyed in 1858 the site of Winter's Lane Engine, at the other end of the main-and-tail haulage, is shown as a coal depot. It would therefore seem that the main-and-tail haulage was dispensed with in the mid-1850s and locomotive haulage resumed here. The North Moor Engine is still shown on the same O.S. map, but it too was eventually replaced by locomotive working. The link with the Lambton Railway south of Hylton Road crossing would have come to an end at the latest in 1870, when the Earl of Durham closed this line in favour of sending all of his traffic over the NER Penshaw Branch and then the Deptford Branch from Pallion to reach his staiths, his line passing under the Hetton lines in a tunnel.

Meanwhile, again at an unknown date, locomotive haulage was extended right through to the staiths. The original drops of 1822 and later were eventually replaced by staiths of the spout design. To house the locomotives working between North Moor and the staiths a two-road **loco shed** (NZ 387564) was built to the east of the line 100 yards south of the bridge carrying the Railway over Chester Road. Whether the introduction of locomotives here also resulted in the end of using horses at the staiths is not known – on balance, probably not. To the west of the line, about ¾ mile south of the same bridge, a **brickworks** (NZ 386561) was developed in the final quarter of the nineteenth century; its clay seems to have come from a small quarry next to it.

Some time during the latter part of the nineteenth century Sunderland Council came to an agreement with the coal company to establish a depot at Farringdon Row, alongside the railway, for the disposal of the town's "night soil". This was mostly dealt with at weekends. Empty chaldrons would be filled at the depot and then worked southwards as far as the bank foot of No.1 Incline. Here, just south of Burdon Lane, a loop was installed with a link into an adjacent quarry, where the refuse was tipped, using a horse to shunt the waggons. On the inclines three full waggons of refuse was balanced with eight full coal waggons descending. When this traffic ceased is not known.

The level crossing at Hylton Road clearly became an increasing inconvenience, while locomotive access to the staiths needed to be improved. So about 1890 the line between the loco shed and the throat of the staiths was replaced by a deviation. From the loco shed a double track section curved away westwards to cross the NER Penshaw Branch on a new single line bridge before curving and dividing again to pass through the site of the former Bishopwearmouth Iron Works. Here the western line went down into a cutting to enter a ¼ mile tunnel under Hylton Road known as **Farringdon Row Tunnel**, from the street alongside which the line emerged, using the route to one of the former coal depots to provide a new access to the staiths. The whole of this section, from the NER bridge to the staiths office, had a gradient of 1 in 36. The old main line – the eastern line – was retained, though shorn of its access to the staiths, to serve the Wear Glass Works and the Trimdon Iron Works, together with a large new coal depot south of Hylton Road, all of the earlier depots being closed. This was also joined by a new link east of Millfield Station on the NER. The Wear Glass Works

91. 13, HL 3055/1914, returning to Hetton loco shed through the streets at Hetton, 27th August 1959. The railway curved here, and the signal guarding the road behind the engine needed to be high in order to be seen above the nearby houses.

123

was closed in 1894 and demolished in 1896, the link with the NER also being removed. However, on most of the glass and iron works sites Sunderland Corporation built in 1900 its **Electricity Generating Station** (NZ 389574). To serve this a small yard of sidings was built south of Hylton Road, over the top of the tunnel, with the coal depot on its eastern side. Some of these were fitted with overhead wires to allow the station's electric loco (there were two, 4wWE BTH 1780/1902 and 4wWE EE 1214/1943, Bg 3054/1943) to handle the traffic between the sidings and the power station, including crossing over Hylton Road.

However, the section between this deviation and North Moor still included level crossings at Silksworth Lane and Durham Road. To eliminate this increasing inconvenience a similar solution was adopted. South of Silksworth Lane the line was diverted into a deep cutting and then taken under the Durham Road in a ¼ mile tunnel (the **Durham Road Tunnel**), before rejoining the original route. The latter work was undertaken between 1906 and 1908 by some Irish navvies. Working from opposite ends, they missed each other in the middle of the tunnel, resulting in a dog leg bend there.

The Hetton Workshops and loco sheds

It would seem almost certain that the first workshops at Hetton were built at the same time as the opening of Hetton Colliery and the Railway in 1822. Given that this was a new development on a green field site, historians have questioned whether the first major job there could have been the construction of steam locomotives. By 1855 the Workshops had expanded considerably, with two large courtyards on the north side of the Hetton to Murton road (NZ 360469), known as Colliery Lane, and a large courtyard and other buildings on the south side of the lane (NZ 360468). These were extensively rail-served, from a line running between the colliery and the quarry. Nothing has yet been found to describe the shops at this time, although the O.S. map suggests that the northern side of the northern range was used for wagon repairs at that time. Curiously, the map shows nothing which might have been a locomotive shed, though clearly there must have been one.

By 1895, when the 2nd edition O.S. survey was done, its map shows two single-road buildings which might have been locomotive sheds. One, believed to be the older, lay to the north of the colliery in the fork where lines divided to go round the colliery. The second lay to the west of the colliery, between the Minor Pit and the brickworks. By this date the line serving the two sets of workshops had been extended southwards for ¾ mile to serve a coal depot near the village of Easington Lane.

In addition, a large foundry had been built, immediately to the south of the coke ovens.

One of the families long connected with both the Hetton collieries and railway was the Gair family, and Arthur Gair describes in his autobiography, *Copt Hill to Ryhope: a colliery engineer's life*, Crichton Publishing Co, Chester-le-Street, 1982, his apprenticeship at the Engine Works between 1909 and 1914. The working hours were 6.00am to

92. 41, K 3074/1917, returning along the Dene from taking fulls to the bottom of Copt Hill Incline, 27th August 1959.

5.00pm, with breaks for breakfast between 8.00am and 8.30am and for dinner between 12 noon and 1.00pm, and there was also Saturday working [probably until 1.00pm]. He continues: "on one side was the locomotive department, and from....the fitting shop a door led into the blacksmiths' shop [which had 8 fires, with...] a large steam hammer.....adjoining this building was a large joiners' shop, a pattern shop and a large boiler shop, where locomotives' boilers were made and repaired".

The sale of the company and the Railway to Lord Joicey

One of the larger colliery companies in Durham in the last quarter of the nineteenth century, owning collieries between Chester-le-Street and Stanley, was James Joicey & Co Ltd. This had been started by James Joicey (1806-1863) and subsequently came under the control of his nephew, also named James (1846-1936). Created a baronet in 1893 and a baron in 1906, by cunning and determination he became the most powerful coal owner in Durham. The first casualty of his rise to power was the Earl of Durham, who was forced to sell out to Joicey on very favourable terms in 1896. To run this very large business Joicey set up a new company called The Lambton Collieries Ltd on 1st July 1896. Following major investments in the Lambton collieries and their Railway, Joicey turned to considering the best way of re-drawing the Durham map to his advantage. The plan eventually decided upon was to expand and consolidate mining in mid-east Durham and sell off the Lambton collieries at Sherburn, whose coal was increased in price by higher running costs to ship at Sunderland.

A letter and map still held privately by the Joicey family, undated but referring to a telephone conversation of 14th July 1902, shows that Joicey was seriously interested in acquiring The Hetton Coal Co Ltd's collieries and railway long before he actually did so in 1911. Using an intermediary to obtain information, John Watts of Robert Frazer & Sons (Newcastle upon Tyne) Ltd, the letter examines a proposal to construct a link from Herrington Colliery on the Lambton Railway to North Moor on the Hetton Railway, the first section apparently being laid on the trackbed of the former Lambton Railway route to Sunderland over Hasting Hill, closed about 1870. This link would have been about 2 miles long, and would have involved two rope inclines, the first to haul the full wagons up to Hasting Hill and the second to lower them to North Moor. The accompanying map also shows a proposed link between the Hetton Railway north of Farringdon Row Tunnel to the Lambton Staiths just east of the tunnel exit from the Deptford Branch. The letter also notes that some Hetton bridges would have to be altered to allow the passage of 10-ton Lambton wagons, and discusses the sites for new landsale depots. Clearly a lot of investigation and planning was done, but nothing came of the proposal at that time.

The Hetton Coal Co Ltd was profitable, and Sir Lindsay Wood, its owner, had dominated the Durham coal trade for many years (see also chapter 14). Knowing that Wood would never sell

93. Copt Hill bank head, with empties waiting to descend, 26th August 1959; note the signal on the right, used only to communicate with the hauler driver when a new rope was being fitted.

94. The Byer Engine House at Copt Hill, with the boiler house on left and dish and kip on right, 26th August 1959.

95. The Byer Engine, built by the Grange Iron Works, Durham, in 1876, from the driver's position. The drum on the left and another in front of it were for the Copt Hill bank; the nearer drum on the right was for the section to the Flat, with the drum in front of it used for operating the main-and-tail system when needed.

96. Looking down the Warden Law Incline, with the Flat interchange and water pump in the middle distance and the Byer Engine beyond, 20th June 1956.

willingly, Lord Joicey first bought up sufficient Hetton shares without Wood's knowledge to make it impossible for Wood to manage the company without Joicey's approval, then forced Wood to sell the remainder to him. The Hetton Coal Co Ltd, together with its subsidiary, The North Hetton Coal Co Ltd, was wound up on 29th June 1911 and Joicey took possession on 3rd July 1911. In the following month he merged all three businesses into The Lambton & Hetton Collieries Ltd. The completion of the plan saw the Sherburn collieries sold to Sir B.Samuelson & Co Ltd, the Middlesbrough steel company, on 1st January 1914.

The North Hetton branch and its collieries
This colliery comprised a group of three pits. The first two, the **Dunwell Pit** (NZ 338480) and the **Hazard Pit** (NZ 340477), completed in 1818, were originally part of **Rainton Colliery**, owned by the Marquis of Londonderry. They were served by what up to 1825 was the Londonderry Waggonway's main line, the branch for these two pits being worked by horses.

On 24th March 1825 they were sold to a partnership headed by William Russell (later Viscount Boyne) of Brancepeth Castle, which renamed them **North Hetton Colliery**. Their traffic continued to be handled by the Londonderry system. The new owners began the sinking of the **Moorsley Pit** (NZ 344466), ½ mile to the south of the Hazard Pit, on 19th April 1826, completing it on 28th May 1828. A report dated 12th December 1831 (NRO 3410/Bud/56) states that the Dunwell Pit was then not in production, and that 18 horses were employed in conveying the coal to the junction with the Londonderry Railway, whence they were taken to Pensher and then transferred on to Lord Durham's Railway to be shipped at Lord Durham's Low Lambton Staiths. The report recommended that a **stationary engine** should be installed near the Hazard Pit, the summit of the branch, to work the waggons up from the Moorsley Pit and then down to the junction with the Londonderry line. It would seem that this was done soon afterwards. It would also seem that the partnership adopted the title **The North Hetton Coal Company**, though the date is not known.

In July 1831 the Marquis of Londonderry opened his new railway between Rainton Bridge and Seaham, but the North Hetton branch was not connected to it and continued to ship its coal at Low Lambton. However, on 17th July 1836 the colliery was sold on again, this time to a partnership of the Earl of Durham, the Marquis of Londonderry and The Hetton Coal Company, and they continued the title of The North Hetton Coal Company. It would seem that the Earl was the leading shareholder. Sometime soon after this a ½ mile link was built north-eastwards from the site of the former Dunwell Pit to join the Londonderry line to Seaham at Rainton Bridge to allow its coal to be shipped at Seaham, though about ½ mile of the old route from the Dunwell Pit was retained to serve a coal depot. The length of the branch was then 1½ miles. However, in 1843 a short link was built between Copt Hill bank head on the Londonderry Railway and just north of the Byer Engine on the

97. Warden Law in the summer of 1959. A set of fulls has just come over the kip of the Warden Law Incline, and its first wagon is just being run by gravity down into the siding for the engine house boilers. The incline's two drums were housed in the open lean-to building, with the forward drum visible. In the foreground the short end of the rope for the No.1 self-acting incline can be seen, running back to the return wheel in the fenced-off pit behind the photographer, with the long end coming back underground in the boarded gulley seen in the bottom left corner. The incline's brake cabin is on the right, with the rodding to work the return wheel's brakes coming out of the cabin wall. Note the short lengths of thinner rope, used for shunting wagons at the bank heads.

Hetton Railway to allow North Hetton coal to be shipped at the Hetton Staiths in Sunderland. There was also some form of "common user" arrangement for the waggons, Londonderry, Hetton and North Hetton waggons being used indiscriminately. The construction of this link perhaps presaged a change in the ownership, for by the late 1850s, perhaps earlier, the Earl and the Marquis had withdrawn from the partnership, leaving the company solely owned by The Hetton Coal Company.

The locomotive of about 1833
The Engine Register of R & W Hawthorn of Newcastle-upon-Tyne shows that their Works number 171 was a "Locomotive" ordered by The North Hetton Coal Company. The book does not record order dates at this period, but it is likely to date from about 1833. It was one of the first locomotives ordered from the firm, but sadly no other details than "Locomotive" are given. Given the notes above one can only speculate on the purpose for which it was ordered. Perhaps the intention was to see if it could replace the horses on the line more efficiently than the stationary engine recommended in 1831. If so, presumably it proved unsatisfactory. There has also been considerable speculation over what happened to it, one suggestion being that it was transferred to the Hetton Railway, but no evidence of its use or fate survives.

Another document in the Place Collection at Beamish Regional Resource Centre gives details of all the steam engines owned by The North Hetton Coal Co in June 1863. No locomotives are listed, but by now there were two stationary engines working on the company's railway. The **Hazard Engine** is described as being a condensing engine (i.e., a Newcomen type), with a single vertical cylinder of 32in x 60in, and interestingly, it not only worked the railway but a nearby saw mill. Given the likely age of such an engine, it could well have been installed following the 1831 report. However, there was also a stationary engine at the Moorsley Pit, the **Moorsley Engine**. This was a two-cylinder horizontal engine with 14 x 20 cylinders. Another report of a similar date records that most of the coal was being dispatched via the NER Durham & Sunderland branch – thus not going northwards for shipment at Seaham, but southwards for shipment at Sunderland, and this change of traffic flow could well account for the installation of the Moorsley Engine (see Fig.52).

When these stationary engines were dispensed with is not known. The first confirmed record of a locomotive being used on this branch is dated 1902, with its loco shed at the Hazard Pit.

The North Hetton Coal Co also owned Pittington Colliery, which was served by the Londonderry Railway (see chapter 10).

98. *This device was used for the men at the bottom of an incline to inform the men at the top that their set was attached to the rope and ready to run. They pulled a wire which raised the wooden disc. Note that as the disc was raised, an arm rattled the bell on the adjacent post. Was this an early nineteenth century device once common on rope worked inclines? This one is believed to have been at Warden Law.*

Gauge : 4ft 8½in

HAZARD		0-4-0ST	OC	P	615	1896	(a)	(1)

(a) ex J.F.Wake, dealer, Darlington, /1902; previously Aberpergwm Collieries Ltd, Aberpergwm Colliery, Glyn Neath, Glamorgan, ABERPERGWM

(1) to The Lambton Collieries Ltd, with the colliery, 3/7/1911; for subsequent history see chapter 9

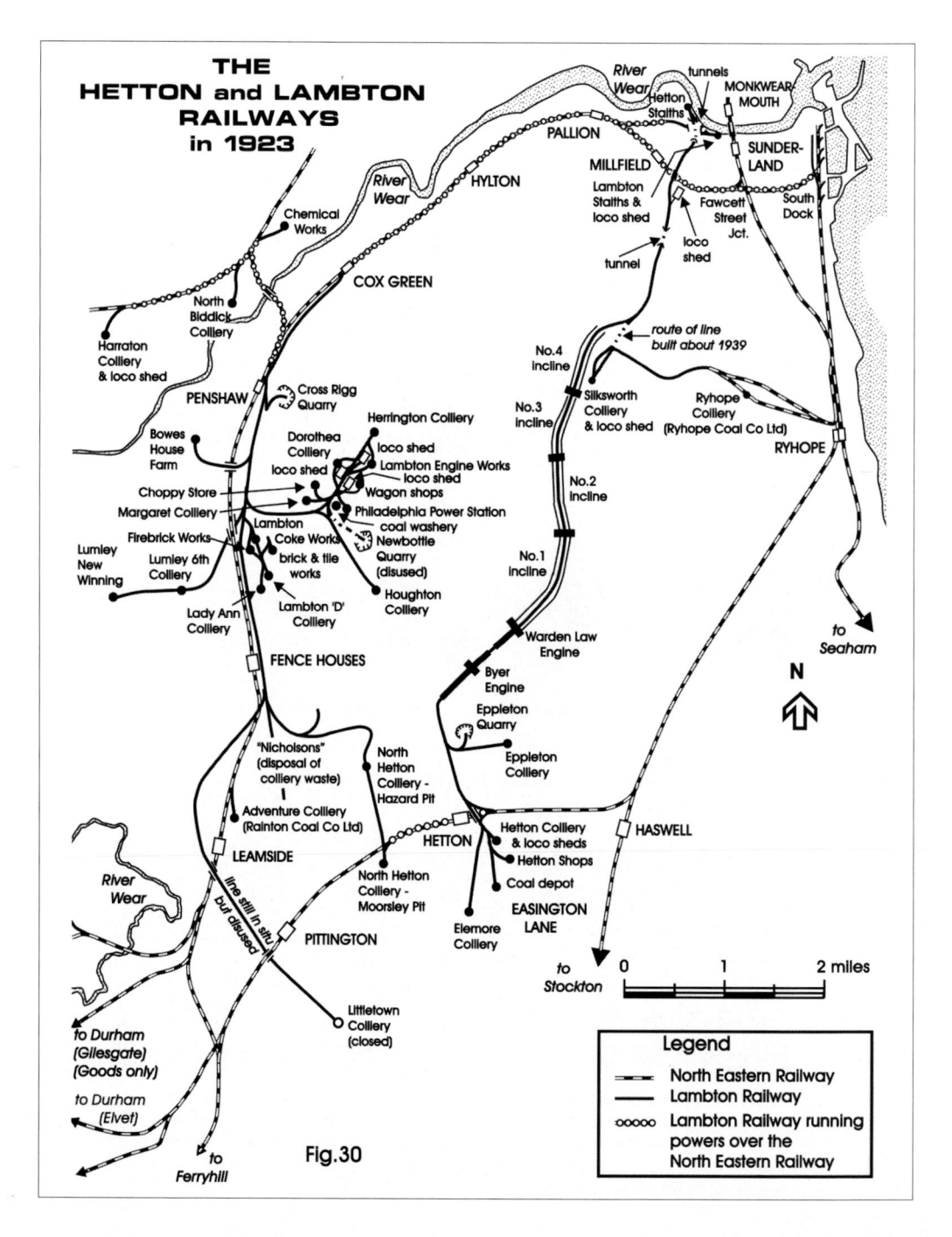

Fig.30 THE HETTON and LAMBTON RAILWAYS in 1923

Integration with the Lambton Railway
Within a few years of Joicey taking over the Hetton Railway he had integrated it with the much larger Lambton Railway (chapter 9), so that it could be operated as a combined unit. At the southern end the company's first move seems to have been to take over some of the former extensive Londonderry leases here. This area included the **Meadows Pit** (NZ 324481) and the nearby **Nicholson's Pit** (NZ 327484). The area between the two was ear-marked as the central area for the dumping of colliery waste, and to service this, a ½ mile branch was laid on the old Londonderry Railway trackbed. However, it is not currently known whether this development took place before or after the merger.

The next stage was to link this branch to the North Hetton line. The company decided to concentrate production at the Hazard Pit, and the Moorsley Pit was closed in December 1915, although the line to it was retained as far as the junction with the NER. The link between Nicholson's Pit and the Hazard Pit, about ¾ mile long, was built in 1916. This involved re-laying the track along the route of the former Londonderry Railway between Nicholson's and Rainton Bridge, and then curving round over the former North Hetton line between Rainton Bridge and the Hazard Pit. An NER map, obviously from this period but undated, shows a broken line linking Rainton Bridge with the Copt Hill Incline on the Hetton Railway itself, but this seems only to have been projected and was never built. Then in June 1916 the company acquired running powers over the NER between North Hetton Junction and its sidings and Hetton Colliery Junction (involving a reverse at North Hetton) in order to convey Hetton coal to the coke ovens at the D Pit and to the Philadelphia Generating Station and Lambton coal to the Hetton coke ovens. However, the latter traffic did not last long, as the 120 beehive ovens at Hetton were closed on 1st October 1918. Since the colliery company's loco crews were working over the NER it was necessary for them to undergo NER medical and eyesight tests and also an examination in the NER Rule Book.

At the northern end, with the two railways serving staiths adjacent to each other, it was a comparatively simple matter to join them by a ¼ mile tunnel, coming in to Lambton Staiths alongside the tunnel from the Deptford Branch. When this was done is uncertain, but it was certainly done by 1919, for in that year a large new loco shed was built at Lambton Staiths and the locomotives from the Hetton Railway shed south of the Durham Road transferred to it, although the Hetton shed remained in use for maintenance for about a further five years before being demolished. However, to avoid the need for locomotives working on the Hetton side to have to return to the Lambton Staiths shed during the day, a coaling and watering point was established alongside the lines leading to Hetton No.2 Staith (NZ 390576), almost directly above the tunnel joining the two sites. Co-incident with the new shed, the Hetton locomotives were re-numbered into the Lambton Railway list.

Six-coupled locomotives were allocated to the new shed to work "on the Hetton side" between Lambton/Hetton Staiths and North Moor, and latterly up to Silksworth Colliery (see below), and the ex Great Western Railway 0-6-2Ts acquired in the early 1930s were probably intended for and certainly worked these turns.

The two sets of staiths were controlled from the Lambton Staiths Office in Gill Road in Sunderland (overlooking the Lambton staiths), and a map there dated 2nd August 1923 showed staiths Nos.2 to 12 (no number 1) on the Lambton side and staiths 13 to 20 on the Hetton side. Of these, nine were then in use on the Lambton side and four, two "High" and two "Low", on the Hetton side. About the end of the 1920s the whole of the Hetton side was remodelled. All of the old staiths were swept away and replaced by two new staiths. At 58 feet above the river they were the highest in the North-East, and both could handle five 10 or 12-ton wagons simultaneously, making it possible to ship up to 1600 tons per hour, making them the fastest-loading in the North East also. The shutes were fitted with traps to slow the coal down. The whole of the rail layout here was also re-designed, with low level sidings to accommodate wagons carrying stone waste waiting for shipment and higher level sidings, interestingly known as "Hetton Bank Top", to which the staiths pilots brought empties from the staiths, for the 'main line' locos to assemble sets of 20 for Hetton and latterly also Silksworth Colliery (see below).

Probably in the 1930s the siding accommodation at North Moor – "The Long Run" - was also rebuilt, with fulls directed into the "high side" (west) and four long sidings, each holding 80 wagons, built on the "low side". This ensured that there was always a good supply of empties waiting to go back to the pits, in turn ensuring that the pits were not held up waiting for empties.

The Railway had continued to use chaldron waggons after the 1911 take-over. These were the larger design holding six tons, though this could be increased by a further ¾ ton by adding "greedy boards" around the top of the box, a practice followed by all of the Durham railways that used chaldrons. Their use could not become universal, as not all of the colliery screens were high enough to get them underneath, but they were welcomed when a colliery was short of empties. When waggons with "greedy boards" were being run, the inclines could run sets of seven, rather than eight, as the total weight was much the same. The new management introduced hopper wagons, starting at 10 tons, about 1921-1922, originally with wagons bought second-hand from the NER/LNER, and chaldrons ceased to be used completely in 1931. Latterly 12, 16 and then 21-ton BR wagons were used.

As it had in Sunderland, the Lambton company made a considerable investment at Hetton between the World Wars. Probably the first large new building was a new Locomotive Fitting Shop alongside Colliery Lane on its southern side. This

99. The bank head of No.2 Incline, or the "Wet Cut", with chaldron waggons, about 1900.

100. Empties leaving the bank foot of No.4 Incline at North Moor, with the sidings here beyond, in the summer of 1959. The section here was known by the men as "The Long Run".

101. 2, RWH 1969/1883, almost certainly outside the loco shed near Durham Road in Sunderland. No photograph showing this two-road building is known.

was a two-road building with ample space for four repairs at a time, with a 70-ton overhead crane. To reach it a new line was built along Colliery Lane, the volume of rail traffic presumably not causing a problem for road traffic. To replace the existing loco sheds a large new two-road loco shed was built well away from the colliery, just south of where the line crossed over the NER Hetton Tunnel. On the site of what is believed to have been a loco shed, in the fork where lines divided to pass either side of the colliery, a modern two-road Wagon Shop was built, together with its own machining and blacksmithing facilities. Once a locomotive had shunted wagons for repair up on to a kip near the colliery, each wagon was run down by gravity into the Shop, on the "running repairs" road. This could hold four wagons at a time, and handled 60-80 repairs a week. If a wagon was found to need a heavy repair, it was lifted by overhead crane across to the adjacent road, which normally held two wagons, and which handled two heavy repairs a week. Completed wagons were then run out of the Shop by gravity down towards the loco shed into a long siding holding 80 wagons, from where they were picked up by a locomotive and returned to traffic.

The depression of the 1930s brought about a much more severe rationalisation between the two Railways. Hetton Engine Works closed during the winter of 1934-1935 and locomotive repairs were concentrated at the Lambton Engine Works at Philadelphia, to which the men and much of the equipment were transferred. However, the Loco Fitting Shop at Hetton was re-opened (or perhaps never closed?) with repairs there continuing into NCB days. However, the Hetton Wagon Shops remained open. North Hetton Colliery (the Hazard Pit) was closed in March 1935, but the running powers over the LNER between Hetton and North Hetton were retained to enable the transfer of locomotives between Hetton and Philadelphia to be maintained.

The branch to Silksworth Colliery, 1938-1939
Silksworth Colliery (NZ 377451) had been opened in January 1873 by the 5th Marquis of Londonderry, and was served by a steeply-graded extension of the Londonderry Railway's branch to Ryhope Colliery. When the Londonderry Railway was taken over by the NER in October 1900 the 2¼ miles between Ryhope and Silksworth passed to Londonderry Collieries Ltd, although the traffic over it was to be worked by the NER. The colliery was situated on a long "peninsula" of the Londonderry royalty and was some distance from the other Londonderry collieries and close to the Hetton royalty. Negotiations by Joicey after the First World War saw it taken over by The Lambton & Hetton Collieries Ltd in 1920, probably on 1st February, together with the ownership of the railway down to Ryhope.

With the Hetton Railway so close, a link between the two had obvious advantages, not least in allowing Silksworth coal to be shipped at Hetton or Lambton Staiths. So in 1938-1939 a line about ¾ mile long was built from the colliery down to the Hetton Railway near Silksworth Lane, about ½ mile north of North Moor (NZ 381547). Much of the branch was graded at 1 in 40, so a six-coupled engine was essential for working the empties back up to the colliery. This had its own loco shed

Fig.31

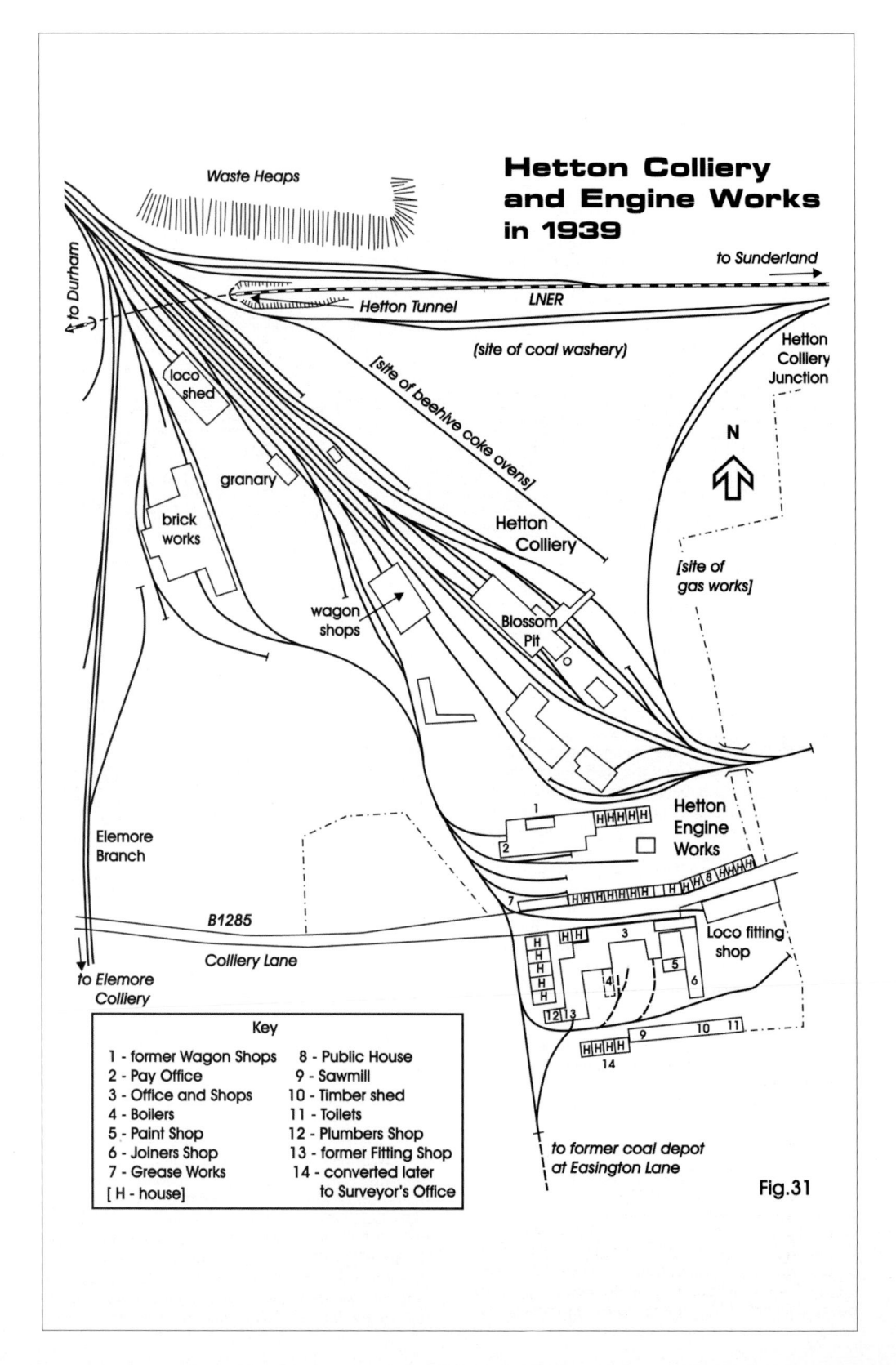

housing the two locomotives normally kept there for shunting the pit.

Signalling

The rope inclines retained to the end what was clearly a very early, even original, form of signalling for men at the bottom and top of each incline to communicate with each other. A lever at the bank foot, when operated, pulled a wire up to the bank head, where a large disc in a slotted post was hauled up. This was the sign that the wagons were attached to the rope at the bottom, and the set could be released when ready. A photograph of one of these discs shows a dark diamond in its centre, and an arm attached to it that operated a small bell, to warn the men that the disc was moving. Large red discs, some on poles up to 25ft high, were operated at level crossings. Most of these did not have gates, and to stop road traffic a red flag on a stand was placed in the road by the crossing keeper. When the crossing was clear for rail traffic the red disc did not show, but when the crossing was barred the disc was rotated through 90 degrees.

In later years, perhaps after Lambton Collieries took over, lower quadrant semaphore signalling was installed in certain places, including at Elemore Colliery, over at least one of the level crossings through the streets of Hetton, at the southern end of Farringdon Row Tunnel, guarding the junction with the branch from Hylton Road, and at Hetton Staiths. The records of The Westinghouse Brake & Signal Co Ltd of Chippenham in Wiltshire list a four-lever signal box being installed by the firm on 31st January 1923 where the Houghton to Seaham road crossed the Copt Hill Incline; but men who worked on the line in later years did not remember any signals here, and none appear visible on the only known photograph of this section. The man on duty here operated the crossing gates and worked the ropes on wagons serving the adjacent landsale depot. There was however a lower semaphore signal at Copt Hill, although it was only used when a rope was being changed. There were also a number of single lower semaphore signals between North Moor and Hetton Staiths.

The Railway, together with Hetton, Eppleton, Elemore and Silksworth Collieries, the various Hetton Workshops and Hetton Brickworks, passed to NCB Northern Division No.2 Area on 1st January 1947.

NATIONAL COAL BOARD
Durham Division No.2 (Mid-East Durham) Area from 1/1/1950
Northern Division No.2 (Mid-East Durham) Area from 1/1/1947

There were still very large reserves of coal in mid-east Durham, both in the Hetton royalty and in the former South Hetton royalty at Murton, to the east. To develop these, the NCB decided on by far its biggest single capital programme in Durham. A large new shaft was to be sunk near Murton, from which two mining horizons would link Murton, Eppleton and Elemore Collieries. These would be served by extensive locomotive-worked, fully-signalled systems using battery locomotives at Murton and Eppleton and diesels at Elemore. On the surface large washery, coking and by-products plants were planned. The complex was to be sited alongside the railway from South Hetton to Seaham, allowing coal and washery waste to be shipped via Seaham Docks as well as via the links with the BR Sunderland-Stockton line at South Hetton.

Early nineteenth century technology, with its six inclines and two steam stationary engines dating from 1836 and 1876 respectively, had no place in such a huge development, which would allow the Hetton Railway between Hetton and North Moor in Sunderland to be closed. Hetton Colliery too had no part in the plans, and it was closed on 22nd July 1950. By this time the workshop buildings north of what was now the B1285 housed the Building Department, responsible for the maintenance of the colliery buildings and colliery houses, while those to the south of the road handled mainly colliery work. Repairs in the Loco Fitting Shop ended in 1952. Hetton Brickworks survived until 1958. However, the loco shed and the Wagon Shop were to remain open until the closure of the line.

Soon after the closure of Hetton Colliery the operation of the Byer Engine at Copt Hill was altered, to run full and empty sets on the Copt Hill incline alternately and abandoning the main-and-tail back-up for section to the Flatts. This allowed two drums to be taken out of commission and simplified the rope arrangements at the two bank heads.

With coal from Elemore, Eppleton and Silksworth Collieries all needing to come down to the staiths, the "main line" engines based at the shed at Lambton Staiths, were kept busy. Three were needed daily, and if shipping was brisk each would need to make four round trips per shift. One unusual traffic was a shipment of 1100 tons per week of Elemore "Wallsend", or household, coal to Aberdeen.

The sinking of what became known as the **Hawthorn Combined Mine** (NZ 390458) at Murton began in July 1952. The coking and by-products plant was opened in November 1958, and with the first coal from the Mine drawn (from Murton Colliery) on 31st August 1959, it was decided that the Hetton Railway's line to North Moor would close on 9th September 1959. Representations were made that the 1836 beam engine at Warden Law should be preserved, and this was left in situ, to be dismantled in 1962. It was eventually included in the collection of the North of England Open Air Museum at Beamish, although forty years on it has yet to be restored and re-erected. Track-

102. 52, NR 5408/1899, (ex GWR 426, Taff Vale Railway 85), with fulls of stone from Silksworth to Sunderland, derailed at Chester Road Bridge in Sunderland after the points had been interfered with in darkness, 11th April 1954.

103. 55, K 3069/1887, (ex GWR 159, Cardiff Railway 28), on empties near Silksworth Lane, Sunderland, in the mid-1950s; the loco had just had a new cab and bunker fitted at Lambton Engine Works, and carries the new livery of black with red lining and gold lettering shaded red.

104. The first diesel in No.2 Area: 1, NBQ 27410/1955, a 400 horse power diesel hydraulic, emerges from the southern end of the Durham Road tunnel in Sunderland on a train of empties in the late 1950s.

lifting began immediately after closure and most of the locomotives at Hetton Shed were dispersed; the last track at Hetton was lifted on 20th November 1960. The Combined Mine was officially opened on 2nd January 1960.

At its closure the Railway employed 136 people, of whom 40 were locomotive staff (including shed men), 26 were incline and stationary engine men, 29 were platelaying staff, 11 were crossing minders and signalmen and 19 worked in the Wagon Shops, with a further 5 being classed as clerical & supervisory and 6 as miscellaneous (DCRO, NCB30 Box 185/20).

Silksworth to Sunderland : the final section

The northern section, between North Moor and Sunderland, survived the 1959 closure because of the NCB's contract to supply the large landsale depot at Hylton Road in Sunderland. The last coal from Hetton Staiths was shipped in the early autumn of 1962. Silksworth traffic continued to be handled by a six-coupled locomotive from Lambton Staiths, but the closure of Lambton Staiths on 6th January 1967 brought further changes. The section of the Hetton Railway between Hylton Road and the staiths was closed, the line lifted and the staiths dismantled. With the closure of Lambton Staiths loco shed, traffic over the remaining section, between Silksworth and the landsale depot, was taken over by a locomotive based at Silksworth Colliery. This continued after the closure of the colliery on 5th November 1971, though now special trains of landsale coal had to be worked by BR up to Silksworth, where the NCB took them over to work down to Hylton Road. Inevitably this circituous system could not last long, and rail traffic over this final section of the Hetton Railway ceased on 30th June 1972, almost exactly 150 years since the opening of the Railway. The track was lifted during March 1973.

Elemore Colliery was closed on 1st February 1974. Eppleton Colliery was merged with Murton Colliery and Hawthorn Combined Mine to form a new Murton Colliery on 30th March 1986, and production on the Eppleton side did not long survive this. This new Murton Colliery was closed on 29th November 1991.

The Hetton Coal Company locomotives

The first steam locomotives to work on the line are discussed in Section 1. Despite the apparently unimpeachable provenance of the account of the opening on 18th November 1822 in the *Newcastle Courant*, it is now clear that the Railway did not have five locomotives when it opened. In a letter of October 1821 George Stephenson said that he was about to start building three locomotives for a local colliery, this clearly being Hetton. Some have suggested that they were built at Hetton; but given that the sinking of the colliery did not begin until December 1820, it would seem unlikely that workshop facilities with the necessary skilled staff would have been available to tackle three locomotives by the autumn of 1821. Construction at Killingworth in Northumberland, where Stephenson's earlier locomotives had been built, would seem more likely.

However, a Hetton valuation undertaken by Nicholas Wood in September 1823 (T&WA

105. The last two Hetton staiths, reputed to be the highest, and the fastest, in North-East England. Five wagons could be unloaded simultaneously on each staith.

106. The sidings at the former Hetton Staiths on 16th February 1966, with 'Austerity' 51, RSH 7101/1943, leaving with seven 21-ton BR wagons of coal for the depot at Railway Row, Sunderland.

DF/WF/28/1 p.335) records four locomotives, and five are reported in a valuation of 1825 (NCL L.920/5836). Was it that it was always planned to have five (and hence the *Newcastle Courant* report), and two more had been built after the opening in 1822? Or were the additional two purchased second-hand? Jim Rees, in *Early Railways: The Strange Story of the Steam Elephant*, argues that the illustration of a six-coupled locomotive on Hetton documents in the 1830s suggests that a six-coupled engine worked on the line, and that the locomotive concerned was almost certainly the six-wheeler designed by John Buddle and William Chapman built at Wallsend in 1814-1815. The fifth was also probably second-hand, perhaps from Killingworth but possibly elsewhere.

Three of the five are said to have worked on the northern section, and when they were replaced by rope haulage about the end of May 1827 it is clear from the reports on the Railway that they were taken down to the southern section, though normally only two were in use there. In 1829 one of the five was involved in a trial to examine the effectiveness of burning coke. Four locomotives were said to be serviceable in 1832.

Further information comes from two accounts, one by Roger Lawson, who started work on the Railway at the age of 11 about 1853, whose autobiographical material dated June 1908 is included in *Hetton – The Development of a Community*, published by the Hetton Community Association in 1973, the second by W.H.Lambton in letters to the local press in 1906; he was then a senior official in the Durham Miners Association, but he too had started work in the 1850s, in Hetton Shops.

Lawson says that three of the "old locomotives" were named FOX, LADY BARRINGTON and LYONS. The report of the coke burning experiment in 1829 records the name of the locomotive involved as TALLY-HO. J.U.Rastrick, in his report to the directors of the Liverpool & Manchester Railway dated March 1829, also gives this name and two more, DART and STAR. It would appear from what Lawson says that "the old engines" continued working into the early 1850s, apparently without any other locomotives joining them. If so, they were not unique, as similar early locomotives were still working at Springwell (see chapter 3) and at Wylam in Northumberland.

This brings us to the problem of the "old locomotive" which worked at Hetton until about 1909, was donated to the York Railway Museum in 1926 and which is now housed at Beamish, The North of England Open Air Museum. At the end of its working life it was widely hailed as "The World's Oldest Locomotive", and was believed to be one of those built for the opening of the line in 1822. Lambton stated emphatically that he saw this locomotive being built at Hetton Shops in 1851-1852 and that it was called LYON, naming the men who did the work. Lawson too states that it was a new locomotive, although he says that it was built in 1848 and called LYONS. In 1877 it was rebuilt to a slightly more modern design at Hetton. Whether the engine now preserved is a rebuild of one of the 1822 engines, or was a new build in 1851-1852, perhaps incorporating some parts of an 1822 loco, awaits a detailed technical examination similar to those undertaken on a number of the surviving very early locomotives.

Lambton went on to say that with LYON built, they "soon after" built a second, called LADY BARRINGTON. Lawson describes the explosion of this locomotive at the end of 1858. He continues that in the previous year the first "up to date" engine had arrived (clearly RS 1100), and that this was followed in 1860 by a second-hand locomotive called WASHINGTON, about which nothing is known at all. It would seem from both of these accounts that all of these locomotives worked at the Hetton end of the line. With the end of rope haulage from North Moor to Sunderland, it is clear that locomotives must have been bought to work on this section in the same period, but no information about them survives. Investigation in 1948 recorded that Nos.2, 6 and 8 normally worked at the Sunderland end.

A numbering scheme clearly replaced the names, but again precise details are confused. It may be that the LYON(S) was regarded as 3, though all known photographs of this loco show it carrying neither name nor number. One might assume that a locomotive acquired in 1860 would have survived long enough to have been given a number, but again nothing is known (unless it was an earlier 2).

In the list below the numbers in the first column are Lambton Railway numbers, while those in the second column are the original Hetton numbers. 2 RWH 1969/1884, 2 in the Hetton list, retained her number in the re-numbering of 1919 as 2 in the Lambton Railway list was vacant.

Gauge : 4ft 8½in

For a discussion of the early locomotives here, see above and Chapter 1.

	(LYON or LYONS)	0-4-0	VC	Hetton		c1852	New		(1)
		reb		Hetton		1877	(a)		
	LADY BARRINGTON	0-4-0	VC	Hetton		c1854	New		(2)
	No.1 later 1	2-4-0	OC	RS	1100	1857	New		
	reb	2-4-0T	OC	Hetton				s/s by /1919	
	WASHINGTON						(b)	s/s	
	4	0-6-0	IC	RS	1649	1865	New		
	reb	0-6-0ST	IC	Hetton					(3)

139

107. At Silksworth Colliery: No.157, HE 6676/1967, stands on the branch to the Hetton Railway, whilst British Rail's D2071 and D2074, both built at Doncaster in 1959, arrive from Ryhope with a train of fulls from Sunderland, in the summer of 1970.

108. 514, built at Derby in 1950 as BR 12084, propels fulls from Silksworth under the bridge carrying the Queen Alexandra Road in Sunderland en route for the coal depot at Railway Row on 26th May 1972, a few days before the closure of this final section of the Railway.

39	(5)		0-6-0ST	IC	RWH	1422	1867	New		(4)
		reb			HL	2378				
37	(6)		0-6-0ST	IC	RWH	1430	1868	New		(5)
40	(7)		0-6-0ST	IC	RS	1919	1869	New		
		reb			HL	1182	1930			(6)
38	(8)		0-6-0ST	IC	RWH	1478	1870	New		(7)
	2		0-6-0ST	IC	RWH	1969	1884	New		Scr c /1939
	LYONS		4wVBT	VC	Hetton				(c)	Scr c /1914
	EPPLETON		4wVBT	VC	Hetton				(d)	Scr c /1914

(a) rebuilt with vertical frame plates and new boiler
(b) arrived in 1860; origin and identity unknown
(c) assembled from various parts, not all locomotive in origin, with chain drive outside the frame to one axle on one side and linking both axles on the other side. An article in *The Locomotive* in 1901 suggests that LYONS had not long been built; however, Arthur Gair in his autobiography (see above) says that LYONS was designed by his great-grandfather's brother, James Gair, who was the company's Chief Engineer in the mid nineteenth century, and that it was built about 1870
(d) believed to be similar to LYONS, but no photograph is known. LYONS and EPPLETON worked as shunters, one, probably LYONS, at Hetton Engine Works
(1) one source claimed that the loco was withdrawn about 1908-1909, while another source recorded that the loco worked until 9/7/1911; when it was withdrawn from traffic it was put to work driving machinery in the saw mill at Hetton Workshops. It headed the Stockton & Darlington Railway centenary procession in steam on 27/9/1925 and was presented to LNER, Railway Museum, York, Yorkshire (NR), for preservation, 7/1926
(2) exploded, 28/12/1858; s/s
(3) last recorded repair was 6/1912; s/s
(4) recorded at Hetton in 1930; to Lambton Railway Loco Sheds, Philadelphia; for subsequent history see chapter 9
(5) to Beamish Group, Tanfield Lea Colliery, Tanfield Lea; to NCB Northern Division No.6 Area, with colliery, 1/1/1947; to Morrison Busty Colliery, Annfield Plain, c5/1947; allocated No.40 in No.6 Area's numbering scheme, /1949, but not carried; returned to Lambton Railway Loco Sheds, Philadelphia, 10/1949; scrapped, /1951
(6) to Beamish Group, Handen Hold Colliery, West Pelton, by 4/6/1937; for subsequent history see the Beamish Railway
(7) to Beamish Group, Tanfield Lea Colliery, Tanfield Lea, 5/1938; to Handen Hold Colliery, West Pelton; to NCB Northern Division No.5 Area, with colliery, 1/1/1947; scrapped, 10/1951

Integration with the Lambton Railway, 1911-1947

The locomotive records that survived at Lambton Engine Works into the 1960s and 1970s included repair books and individual locomotive cards, but none offered any record of transfers between the Lambton and Hetton Railways. One is therefore forced back on oral tradition and photographs. Photographs said to have been taken at Hetton in this period are rare, and appear to be non-existant for the northern shed in Sunderland and the locomotives allocated there. From what little is known, it would seem that the poorest of the locomotives taken over in 1911 were soon scrapped. The remainder were re-numbered into Lambton Railway stock in 1919, and some may well have continued to work at Hetton until the 1930s. However, the company appears to have sent new or almost new locomotives to Hetton soon after taking over, and it may well be that the second-hand locomotives acquired between 1920 and 1923 were also purchased for the Railway (see Lambton Railway loco list). A similar reason may also have been behind the purchase of the ex-Great Western Railway 0-6-2Ts in the 1930; certainly some of them were allocated to Lambton Staiths for working up to North Moor, and later Silksworth Colliery. Only one of them is known to have worked at Hetton (see below).

The records of the Industrial Railway Society list only four locomotives at Hetton when the NCB was created on 1st January 1947. Given that the railway work to be covered included shunting three collieries, with their boilers, stone heaps and landsale depots, Hetton Workshops and brickworks and the main line as far as Dene Bank Foot, this would seem too low a number. Eight locomotives were recorded here on 11th May 1946 and the same number in September 1948.

Gauge : 4ft 8½in

13	0-4-0ST	OC	HL	3055	1914	(a)	(1)
14	0-4-0ST	OC	HL	3056	1914	(a)	(2)
11	0-4-0ST	OC	HC	1412	1920	(b)	(2)
46	0-6-0T	IC	MW	1813	1913	(c)	(3)

24	0-4-0ST	OC	BH	832	1885	(d)	(4)
43	0-4-0ST	OC	GR	769	1920	(d)	(4)
23	0-4-0ST	OC	BH	688	1882	(e)	(4)
47	0-4-0ST	OC	HL	3543	1923	(f)	(4)
54	0-6-2T	IC	Cdf	311	1897	(f)	(4)
12	0-4-0ST	OC	HL	2789	1912	(g)	(2)
32	0-4-0ST	OC	HL	2826	1910	(g)	(1)
34	0-4-0ST	OC	HL	2954	1912	(g)	(2)
48	0-4-0ST	OC	HL	3544	1923	(g)	(1)
58	0-6-0ST	IC	VF	5299	1945	(h)	(1)

(a) New to Hetton? (perhaps to replace LYONS and EPPLETON? – see above)
(b) New to Hetton?
(c) came to Hetton soon after purchase in 1/1923 (see Lambton Railway list); here on 11/5/1946
(d) recorded here in interview with loco driver born in 1918
(e) recorded here "between the Wars" by loco driver in written biography
(f) both here on 18/9/1944, when they collided on Dene Bank (Eppleton Colliery to main line), according the locomotive cards at Lambton Engine Works; their dates of arrival are unknown
(g) here on 11/5/1946
(h) ex Philadelphia, after 11/5/1946, by 31/12/1946

(1) to NCB Northern Division No.2 Area, with Railway, at Hetton Loco Shed, 1/1/1947
(2) recorded here on 11/5/1946; to NCB Northern Division with Railway, at Hetton Loco Shed, 1/1/1947?
(3) to Philadelphia, after 11/5/1946, by 31/12/1946?
(4) no departure date from Hetton is known

North Hetton Colliery (closed in 1935)

As noted above, there was a small locomotive shed here, with HAZARD 0-4-0ST P 615/1896 its sole occupant in 1911. An oral tradition recorded in 1949 said that it left for Hetton in 1914 (and apparently never returned; it became Lambton Railway 36 in 1919), and was followed by 16 (0-4-0ST HCR 96/1870), 17 (almost certainly 0-4-0ST HCR 130/1873), 11, 22 (0-4-0ST HC 230/1881), 21 (0-4-0ST RS 2308/1876), 32, 33 (0-4-0ST OC HL 2827/1910), 34, 43 (0-4-0ST GR 769/1920), 52 (0-6-2T NR 5408/1899), 54 (0-6-2T Cdf 311/1897), 23, 24 and 12 (for other makers' details see the list above). The inclusion of two 0-6-2Ts in this list seems odd; the operating procedure would normally appear to have been one 0-4-0ST shunting the colliery with a larger engine bringing empties and taking away fulls.

NCB No.2 Area, Hetton Shed, 1/1/1947 to closure, 9/1959

Again, almost all the locomotives and movements listed below arise from visitors' observations, rather than NCB documentation. The Area introduced its own numbering scheme in 1948, with the Lambton locomotives keeping their original numbers.

Perhaps the most significant development of this final period was No.2 Area's decision to purchase for the Railway the NCB's first-ever diesel locomotive in Co.Durham, a 400 h.p. machine built by the North British Locomotive Co Ltd. After extensive trials on the Lambton Railway it was purchased on 20th July 1956 for £25,000 and put into traffic at Philadelphia on 16th August 1956, before being transferred to Hetton on 1st September 1956. This too was temporary, for the intention was to utilise it on the northern section, where it was anticipated that it would replace two locomotives working between the staiths and Silksworth Colliery. It worked on this duty for some time, and was the basis on which three similar, but slightly more powerful, diesels were subsequently ordered for the Hawthorn Combined Mine.

Even after the closure of Hetton Colliery, up to eight locomotives were normally still kept at Hetton. Two months before the closure six of the eight were out working, four 0-4-0STs and four six-wheeled locomotives, with one of each spare.

In the list below the following abbreviations have been used:

H   Hetton Loco Shed, Hetton
LEW   Lambton Engine Works, Philadelphia, Lambton Railway (for repairs only)
LS   Lambton Staiths Shed, Sunderland, Lambton Railway
P   Lambton Railway Loco Sheds, Philadelphia
SH   South Hetton Loco Sheds, South Hetton

For the history of the locomotives below before they came to Hetton and after they left Hetton (with the exception of 83), please see the Lambton Railway locomotive lists in chapter 9.

Gauge : 4ft 8½in

No.	Type		Builder	Works No.	Year	Origin	Ref
11	0-4-0ST	OC	HC	1412	1920	(a)	

H-Hudswell, Clarke & Co Ltd, Leeds, for rebuild, /1948-P ?/? (or direct to H)
-H by 19/9/1948-P by 9/1950-H by 5/1951-LEW after 4/1954, by 4/1955
-P by 25/8/1955-H after 11/1956, by 28/4/1957 (1)

| 12 | 0-4-0ST | OC | HL | 2789 | 1912 | (a) | |

H-P after 19/9/1948, by 14/5/1949-LEW after 7/1949, by 7/1950
-H 7/1950-LEW by 28/2/1954-H by 4/1954
-LEW after 8/1956, by 11/1956-H by 22/5/1957 (2)

| 13 | 0-4-0ST | OC | HL | 3055 | 1914 | (a) | |

H-LEW by 19/9/1948-H by 5/1951-LEW after 6/1952, by 3/1953
-H by 16/10/1953-LEW after 22/5/1957, by 4/1958-H by 7/1958 (3)

| 14 | 0-4-0ST | OC | HL | 3056 | 1914 | (a) | |

H-P after19/9/1948, by 9/1950-H after 4/1952, by 6/1952 (4)

| 32 | 0-4-0ST | OC | HL | 2826 | 1910 | (a) | |

H-LEW 1/1947-P c/1947-H by 19/9/1948-LEW by 3/1949-H c6/1949 (5)

| 34 | 0-4-0ST | OC | HL | 2954 | 1912 | (a) | (6) |
| 48 | 0-4-0ST | OC | HL | 3544 | 1923 | (a) | |

H-RSHN (reps) by 2/1948-H by 19/9/1948-LEW after 4/1952, by 6/1952-H by 9/1952
-LEW after 3/1956, by 4/1956-H by 8/1956-SH 8/4/1957-H 11/4/1957 (7)

| 58 | 0-6-0ST | IC | VF | 5299 | 1945 | (a) | |

H-P by19/9/1948-H by 9/1950 (8)

| 41 | 0-6-0T | OC | KS | 3074 | 1917 | (b) | |

H-P after19/9/1948, by 7/1949-LEW /1951-H by 6/1951
-LEW after 10/1953, by 28/2/1954-H after 9/1954, by 4/1955
-LEW after 8/1956, by 28/4/1957-H after 9/1957, by 4/1958 (9)

| 46 | 0-6-0T | IC | MW | 1813 | 1913 | (b) | |

H-LEW after 19/9/1948, by 3/1949-H after 9/1950, by 6/6/1951
-LEW after 4/1952, by 6/1952-H by 9/1952
-LS after 4/1954, by 4/1955-LEW after 8/1956, by 11/1956-H by 28/41957 (10)

| 47 | 0-4-0ST | OC | HL | 3543 | 1923 | (c) | |

H-P by 7/1949-H by 9/1950 (11)

52	0-6-2T	IC	NR	5408	1899	(d)	(12)
49	0-4-0ST	OC	MW	2035	1924	(e)	(13)
17	0-4-0ST	OC	MW	2023	1923	(f)	(14)
33	0-4-0ST	OC	HL	2827	1910	(g)	(15)
No.39	0-4-0ST	OC	RSHN	7757	1953	(g)	(16)
59	0-6-0ST	IC	VF	5300	1945	(h)	

H-LS by 4/1955-H 4/1955 (17)

83	0-4-0ST	OC	AB	1724	1922	(j)	(18)
45	0-6-0ST	IC	HL	2932	1912	(k)	(19)
1	0-6-0DH		NBQ	27410	1955	(m)	(20)
60	0-6-0ST	IC	HE	3686	1948	(n)	(21)
72	0-6-0ST	IC	VF	5309	1945	(p)	(22)

It is believed that 55 0-6-2T K 3069/1887 also worked at Hetton for a short period. 52 and 55 were only used here in emergency. There are also known to have been short-term transfers of 0-4-0STs between Lambton Staiths loco shed and Hetton loco shed via the inclines, but details were not recorded.

(a) ex The Lambton, Hetton & Joicey Collieries Ltd, with the Railway, 1/1/1947
(b) ex Lambton Railway Loco Sheds, Philadelphia, by 19/9/1948
(c) this loco was at Robert Stephenson & Hawthorns Ltd, Newcastle upon Tyne, for repairs, 5/1948; either ex here or ex Lambton Railway Loco Sheds, Philadelphia, by 9/1948
(d) ex Lambton Railway Loco Sheds, Philadelphia, by /1949 (photographic evidence)
(e) ex Lambton Staiths Loco Shed, Lambton Railway, Sunderland, after 8/1951, by 4/1952, when it was involved in a collision at Hetton (frame buckled at rear end)
(f) ex Lambton Engine Works, Philadelphia, after 6/1952, by 9/1952
(g) ex Lambton Railway Loco Sheds, Philadelphia, by 10/1953
(h) ex Lambton Staiths Loco Shed, Lambton Railway, Sunderland, after 10/1953, by 4/1954

(j)   ex Seaham Colliery, Seaham, after 4/1955, by 4/1956
(k)   ex Lambton Railway Loco Sheds, Philadelphia, after 11/1955, by 4/1956
(m)   ex Lambton Railway Loco Sheds, Philadelphia, 1/9/1956
(n)   ex Lambton Railway Loco Sheds, Philadelphia, after 11/1956, by 5/1957
(p)   ex South Hetton Loco Sheds, South Hetton, after 7/1958, by 3/1959

(1)   at Hetton on closure of section, 9/9/1959; to Lambton Railway Loco Sheds, Philadelphia, after 10/1959, by 12/1959
(2)   to Lambton Engine Works, Philadelphia, after 7/1958, by 4/1959
(3)   at Hetton on closure of section, 9/9/1959; to Vane Tempest Colliery, Seaham, by 7/1960
(4)   at Hetton on closure of section. 9/9/1959; to Dawdon Colliery, Seaham, after 7/1960, by 24/1/1961
(5)   to Lambton Engine Works, Philadelphia, after 10/1953, by 4/1954
(6)   to Lambton Staithes Loco Shed, Sunderland, 6/1949
(7)   at Hetton on closure of section, 9/9/1959; to Lambton Staiths Loco Shed, Lambton Railway, Sunderland, after 10/1959, by 4/1960
(8)   to Lambton Railway Loco Sheds, Philadelphia, after 9/1950, by 6/1951
(9)   at Hetton on closure of section, 9/9/1959; to Brandon C Colliery, Meadowfield, 21/11/1959
(10) to Lambton Staiths Loco Shed, Lambton Railway, Sunderland, after 4/1958, by 5/1958
(11) to Lambton Engine Works, Philadelphia, after 8/1952, by 9/1952
(12) to Lambton Staiths Loco Shed, Lambton Railway, Sunderland, by 7/1950
(13) to Lambton Engine Works, Philadelphia, 4/1952?
(14) to Lambton Staiths Loco Shed, Lambton Railway, Sunderland, after 12/1952, by 4/1954
(15) at Hetton on closure of section, 9/9/1959; to Lambton Staiths Loco Shed, Sunderland, after 10/1959, by 4/1960
(16) to Lambton Railway Loco Sheds, Philadelphia, after 4/1954, by 4/1955
(17) to Lambton Railway Loco Sheds, Philadelphia, after 5/1957, by 9/1957
(18) to Seaham Colliery, Seaham, after 4/1956, by 5/1956
(19) to Lambton Railway Loco Sheds, Philadelphia, 2/1958
(20) to Lambton Staiths Loco Shed, Lambton Railway, Sunderland, 13/12/1956
(21) at Hetton on closure of section, 9/9/1959; to Lambton Railway Loco Sheds, Philadelphia, after 10/1959, by 11/1959
(22) believed to be still at Hetton on closure of section, 9/9/1959; to South Hetton Loco Sheds, South Hetton, by 10/1959 (?)

Working from Silksworth Colliery to Sunderland, 1967-1972

Gauge : 4ft 8½in

| No.157 | 0-4-0DH | HE | 6676 | 1967 | New | (1) |
| 514 | 0-6-0DE | Derby | | 1950 | (a) | (2) |

(a)   ex Lambton Railway Loco Sheds, Philadelphia, 7/4/1972

(1)   to Derwenthaugh Loco Shed, Swalwell, 11/4/1972
(2)   to Hylton Colliery, Castletown, Sunderland, 7/1972

At Hetton a significant number of the workshop buildings, including some from the nineteenth century, survive (2004). The former Loco Fitting Shop, now a garage, retains its glorious trussed roof with elliptically-chamfered beams and its large arched doors. Nearby, with a commemorative plaque, is the cottage occupied by Robert Stephenson when he came to live at Hetton in 1822. North of the road a major complex survives, including the wagon shop used before the LHJC shop and the pattern store, although everything was not in use. The LHJC Wagon Shop also survives, again little altered internally – even with the rails still in the floor, although the original floor of oak blocks has been replaced by concrete; incredibly, it is still in railway use as part of the premises of the railway contractors Hall & Blenkinsop Ltd. Although the Warden Law Engine is now at Beamish, the North of England Open Air Museum, it still awaits re-assembly. Some of the route between Hetton and Sunderland has been landscaped and levelled, but much of it can still be traced, with commemorative plaques to mark the route of George Stephenson's famous contribution to early railway development.

Chapter Nine
The Lambton Railway

OWNERS BEFORE 1947
The Lambton, Hetton & Joicey Collieries Ltd until 1/1/1947
The Lambton & Hetton Collieries Ltd until 26/11/1924
The Lambton Collieries Ltd until 8/1911
The 3rd Earl of Durham until 1/7/1896
The 2nd Earl of Durham until 27/11/1879
The 1st Earl of Durham until 28/7/1840; see also below

This was by far the largest of the private railways in County Durham, and it served in turn the two most powerful colliery owners in the county, the Earls of Durham – the Lambton family – and then Sir James Joicey, later Lord Joicey.

The Lambton family had been prominent in Co. Durham for centuries. The first of the family perhaps worthy of note is General John Lambton, who died in 1794. His son, William Henry, died only three years later, leaving his son, John George Lambton, born on 12th April 1792, only five years old. John George went on to have an outstanding political and diplomatic career, as a result being created Baron Durham on 29th January 1828 and the first Earl of Durham on 23rd March 1833. He died on 28th July 1840, to be succeeded by his son, George Frederick D'Arcy (1828-1879), with in turn his son, John George, (1855-1928) becoming the 3rd Earl. Compared with their local aristocratic contemporaries such as the Londonderrys or Bowes, it would seem that the Lambtons took far less colliery profit out of their business to use on developing their private property and ploughed much more back into the business, although ironically it was financial problems that brought about the sale of the business to James Joicey, the only man capable of buying it.

Neither the Lambton nor the Joicey family papers have been placed on public deposit (though some Lambton documents have found their way into the Durham County Record Office), and the extent to which family records of their industrial interests survive is not known. Piecing together from other primary sources even a fairly basic account of their vast empire is thus very difficult. The Lambton family's development of mining on its estate would appear to date back to the fifteenth century, though the real expansion seems to begin in the first quarter of the eighteenth century. From 1784 the Lambton collieries were operated by "undertakers", or sub-contractors, Featherstonehaugh & Company from 1784 to 1803 and Fenwick & Company from 1803 to 1813. In 1806 John Buddle, who was to become the most famous engineer in the North East coal trade, succeeded his father as Viewer (a combination of Managing Director and Chief Engineer) to the Lambton family. On 1st January 1813 Lambton took over direct control, but in April 1813 he created a three-man Board, with Buddle one of its members, to run the Lambton collieries and their waggonways. This Board met monthly until July 1819, and the records of most of its meetings survive (copies are held at the Regional Resource Centre of Beamish, The North of England Open Air Museum). In 1819 Buddle left Lambton to join Charles Stewart, later Marquis of Londonderry, and the Board was abolished, though Buddle continued to undertake occasional consultancy work for Lambton. Fortunately, the extensive papers of Buddle and his father, as well as those of other leading viewers of the time, eventually found their way into the North of England Institute of Mining and Mechanical Engineers in Newcastle upon Tyne. Most are now deposited at the Northumberland County Record Office, with others in the Tyne & Wear Archives Service, and these give information and insights invaluable in the absence of other deposits.

The origins of the Railway can be traced back to two very early waggonways and a third built at the beginning of the nineteenth century.

The Lambton Waggonway
The Lambtons initially developed mining on their estates around Lambton Castle, north-east of Chester-le-Street, and developed a waggonway system to bring coal to be loaded on to keels at Lambton High Staith (NZ 304529). Although this system continued in use until the last quarter of the eighteenth century, it was not able to cope with steadily increasing output. So in 1725 a new waggonway was built northwards to Lambton land near the hamlet of Pensher, 2½ miles downstream of the High Staith, the spot being called Low Lambton (NZ 321546).

Not all of the Lambton mines were served by this waggonway. There were also several mines in the areas of Harraton and Fatfield, to the north-west of Lambton Castle and its Park. These had their own waggonways and staiths (see below).

Then in the agreement with Featherstonehaugh in

1784 (see above) the latter undertook to begin mining in the Bourn Moor (later Bournmoor and latterly Burnmoor – as with Pensher below, the contemporary spelling of the particular period has been adopted throughout) area between Chester-le-Street and Houghton-le-Spring, and in this same year the Lambton waggonway was extended southwards from Pensher (later Painshaw and latterly Penshaw) to serve this, and also to link to the Lumley Waggonway (see below). Also in 1784 General Lambton agreed to plate some of the wooden rails with iron.

In 1996 archaeological investigations at Burnmoor revealed the most extensive remains of a wooden waggonway ever discovered in Britain (see Photo 1). These comprised 150m in lines of various lengths adjacent to the D Pit (see below), at a gauge about 4ft 3in, and they were adjudged from documentary evidence to date between 1812 and 1817 (for a full description see *Industrial Archaeology Review*, Vol. XX, 1998, pp.5-22).

In 1813 the Lambton Board was installing cast iron rails, presumably on the "main line", and undoubtedly this was a factor that led to the waggonway becoming another upon which an early steam locomotive was tested. On 24th December 1814 the world's first articulated steam locomotive, designed by William Chapman and built at the Ouseburn Foundry in Newcastle upon Tyne, was tried on the line (see chapter 1). It hauled 18 waggons up a gradient of 1 in 115, almost certainly the section between Bourn Moor and Pensher. However, the Board appears to have lost interest and soon replaced it with horse haulage.

At the beginning of the nineteenth century the main output of collieries in the North-East was domestic coal for the London market. Pits, usually not very deep, were relatively short-lived, though sometimes they were re-opened after a period of closure. At Pensher mining was concentrated on **PENSHER COLLIERY** (NZ 323539), whose sinking began on 10th May 1792. As mining in this area was divided between the Lambton and Tempest families (the Tempest land later coming under the control of Lord Londonderry – see the Londonderry Railway), the latter's colliery became known as **Old Pensher Colliery** and the Lambton Colliery as **New Pensher Colliery**, which has sometimes led to understandable confusion. Going south, the next branch of the waggonway served first the **BEANYFIELD PIT**, opened about 1797, and the **HOUGHTON GATE**, or Union Pit, sunk in 1801, both on the boundary of Lambton Park. Further south, at Bourn Moor, **BOURN MOOR COLLIERY** was a collective title for the **A to E Pits**, the **William Henry Pit** and the **Lady Ann Pit**. The sinking of the A Pit was begun in 1785, the C Pit in 1791, the D Pit in 1792 and the William Henry Pit in 1799.

Of the pits above, the Beanyfield Pit, Bourn Moor A, B and E Pits, the William Henry Pit and the Lady Ann Pit had all been closed by 1817. Houghton Gate Pit (NZ 298514) was laid in on 10th February 1817, Pensher Colliery on 31st May 1817, the C Pit (NZ 317520) on 10th July 1818 and the D Pit (NZ 318508) about 1821. The only mining still taking place in this area after these closures was the **MORTON WEST PIT** (NZ 318497), near Fence Houses. This was opened in the spring of 1814, the waggonway being extended to serve it. However, the D Pit and the Lady Ann Pit were later to be re-opened (see Fig.32).

The Lumley Waggonway

The Earls of Scarborough owned the major estate in the Lumley area, south-west of Bourn Moor. Mining is recorded here as early as the sixteenth century, and a waggonway is known to have operated between about 1704 and 1730. The 4th Earl revitalised mining, and on 10th November 1776 the sinking of a new Lumley 1st Pit was begun and a new waggonway built to the River Wear. Thereafter pits in the area were numbered. The colliery ran into difficulties, and in 1784 General Lambton leased it from the 5th Earl. His undertakers in their first lease agreed to sink two new pits here and to work Lumley and Bourn Moor as one area; the sinking of the 5th Pit was started on 9th November 1791. As noted above, the Lumley waggonway was joined to the Lambton waggonway at this time, at Elba, near the first sinkings at Bourn Moor. This in turn must mean that the two waggonways were built to the same gauge, about 4ft 2ins.

In the Lumley area **LUMLEY COLLIERY'S** 1st Pit, 2nd Pit and 4th Pit were all laid in by 1811, the 5th Pit following on 29th April 1812 and the 6th Pit about 1814. This left the **3RD PIT** (NZ 296503), re-opened in July 1811, and the **7TH PIT** (NZ 307507), which was probably opened between 1800 and 1805, as the working pits. However, this was the area where the Board planned most of its new production. The sinking of the **8TH PIT** (NZ 308492) started in the late summer of 1816 and this was followed by the sinking of the **GEORGE PIT** (NZ 302486) on 2nd June 1817, the Hutton seam at the latter being reached on 5th April 1819. To serve them a new branch of the waggonway was constructed during the late summer of 1818, leaving the branch to the 3rd Pit near the 7th Pit.

Amongst the Buddle-Atkinson Collection at the Northumberland Record Office is a detailed measurement of the whole waggonway system as it was on 14th September 1814 (NRO 3410/Bud/50/22). The "Main Way" – which is clearly regarded as the "main line" - is listed first, namely: "from branch ends of [Lumley] 6 & 7th Pits to D branch [end] 1172.6 yards; from D Pit branch to C Pit branch 699.8 yards; from C Pit branch to Pensher [Colliery branch] 2167.4 yards; from Pensher [Colliery branch] to Staith 1170.4 yards. Total 5210 yards, or 2 miles 1690 yards", while the branches are listed as follows: "from the 3rd Pit to 6 & 7th Pit branches 1903 yards; 6th Pit branch 150.26 yards; 7th [Pit branch] 88 yards; Morton W[est] Pit to Main Way 1696 yards; William Henry Pit branch to [Main Way] 1212 yards; D Pit branch to [Main Way] 844.5 yards; Pensher [Pit branch] to [Main Way] 146.96 yards;, a total of 4 miles 1496

Fig.32

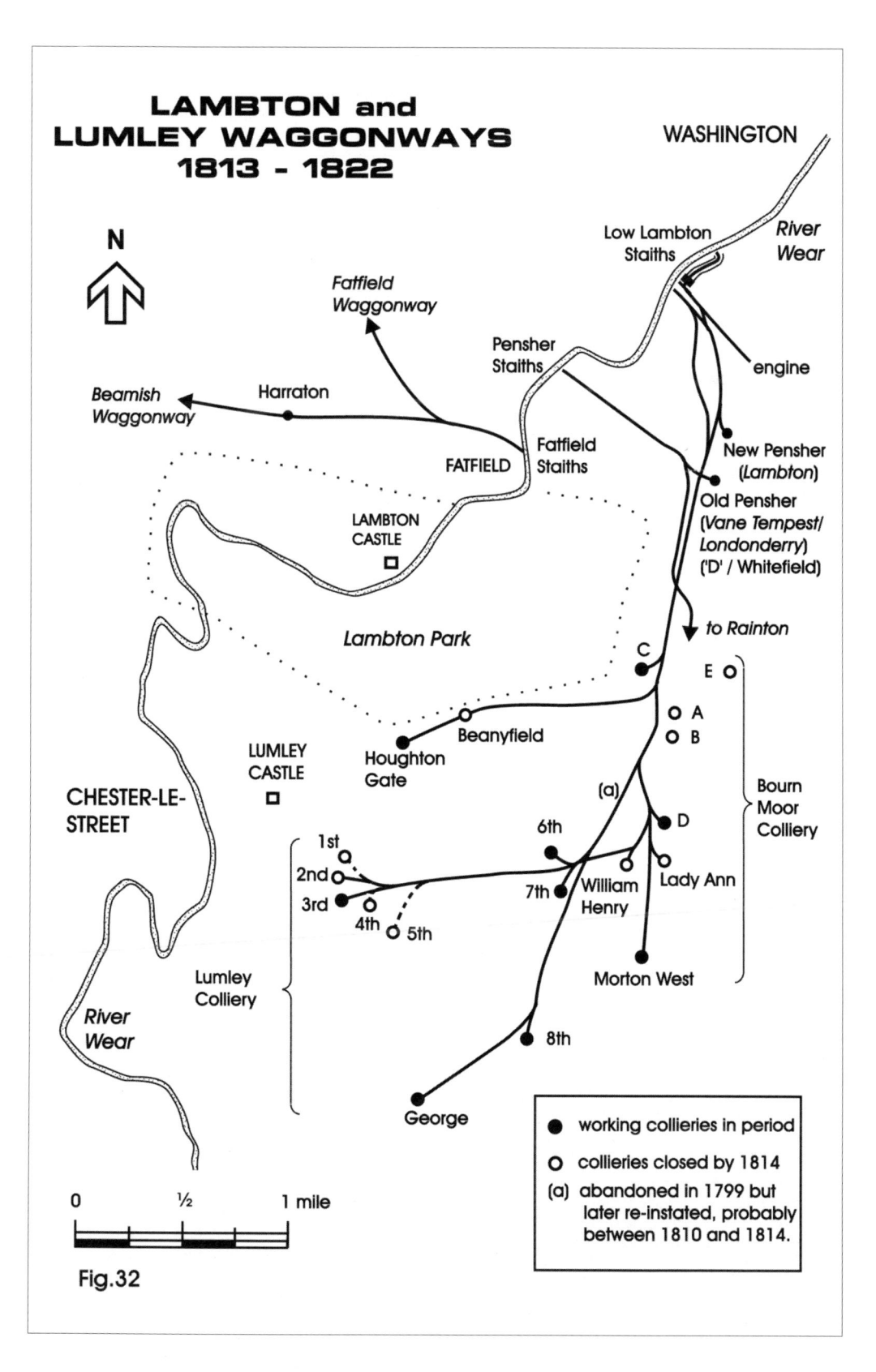

yards. The various closures reduced the system, but the new branch to the George Pit added a further 1¾ miles. In a document about the same date at this measurement Buddle gives the "breadth of way" as 4ft 2ins. At this date the whole system was horse-worked (see Fig.32).

As mentioned earlier, the Lambtons also owned a number of other pits (most sub-let), the most important of which was **HARRATON COLLIERY**, north-west of the village of Fatfield on the north side of Lambton Castle. Again, there had been early workings here; but a new sinking had been completed about 1765 and this was linked to the Beamish Waggonway, which ran from the Beamish area to a staith on the River Wear at Fatfield; by a coincidence this was later also purchased by the Joicey family (see James Joicey & Co Ltd). **HARRATON 5TH PIT** (NZ 291539) began production on 13th June 1816. The Board's minutes suggest that a radical alteration was being considered in the following year. About a mile downstream from Fatfield was the staith at the end of the Urpeth Waggonway, abandoned when its owners, Harrison, Cooke & Co, went bankrupt (see the Pelaw Main Railway). In March 1817 the Board apparently purchased this staith, together with the **self-acting incline** serving it, with the intention of linking Harraton to it; but there is no subsequent evidence that this was actually carried out.

Despite this, perhaps this purchase influenced the Board's subsequent thinking, for in June 1819 the Board decided to instal **a self-acting incline at Low Lambton**, serving a new staith downstream of the existing staith. This incline, which took the route of an old waggonway known as the Pensher Old Way to avoid any interruption to existing traffic, was 280 yards long and was designed to lower down four waggons at a time. Construction work began in July 1819. This was almost certainly the first rope incline on the Lambton system. The Board was clearly determined to increase the capacity of the waggonway, for at the same time a section of the waggonway from about ½ mile north of Bourn Moor to Pensher Stables was replaced by a new line immediately west of the existing one, but with flatter gradients, to allow a horse to pull two waggons rather than one.

However, the Board had already been reviewing the limitations of its system as a whole, not least no doubt because of the bottleneck caused by having staiths at Fatfield and thus having to use keels on the River Wear to transport coal to Sunderland, and on 9th July 1817 the construction of a waggonway running direct to Sunderland was discussed, though nothing was done. However, nearby such a waggonway already existed.

The Newbottle Waggonway
About 1¼ miles north-east of Bourn Moor Colliery (and 100 feet higher) lay the **NEWBOTTLE COLLIERY**; like Bourn Moor, this was a collective title for a number of pits. John Nesham, in partnership with John Hylton of Hylton Hall near Sunderland, acquired the lease of this area in 1734. One of the pits opened was the **SUCCESS PIT** (NZ 331520), which first drew coal on 9th November 1750 and was served by a newly-built waggonway running north and then north-west to the River Wear, crossing the Lambton waggonway en route to reach its own staith at Pensher, about ½ mile upstream from the Lambton staith. Five pits were sunk, all but the first named after John Nesham's daughters, though by about 1810 only the Success Pit and the **MARGARET PIT** (NZ 332519) were being worked.

Then about this time John Douthwaite Nesham decided on a very major investment and change of policy. A new pit, the **DOROTHEA PIT** (NZ 335524) was to be sunk about ½ mile north east of the Margaret Pit, and a new waggonway, 5¾ miles long, built to Sunderland to handle both the increased output and to eliminate the need for keels. It was to be laid with cast iron rails to a gauge about 4ft 0in. As it was to be almost entirely horse-worked it had to make a large detour eastwards to avoid the hilly ground, rising to over 400 feet in places, which barred a more direct route. The biggest problem was at Sunderland itself. The unoccupied ground closest to the mouth of the River Wear lay upstream of the Iron Bridge (built in 1779); but access to it was barred by a deep ravine called Galley's Gill. The only way of reaching the river was by constructing **a self-acting incline**; but for this a steeply-inclined wooden viaduct had to be built down the ravine, followed by a short tunnel to reach the edge of the river.

The sinking of the Dorothea Pit began in July 1811. From the wayleave dates listed in the Auction Catalogue of 1822, the opening of the waggonway probably took place on 22nd August 1812. This was the first waggonway to the River Wear at Sunderland from the south. The old waggonway, from the Jane Pit to Pensher Staith, may have become disused, and by November 1815 it had been leased to the trustees of Lady Frances Anne Vane Tempest and subsequently became part of the Londonderry Railway (NRO 3410/Wat/3/59/II/7).

It is perhaps not surprising that the progessive owner of a new waggonway laid with cast iron rails almost immediately took an interest in the early steam locomotives then being designed, and a Brunton locomotive was brought to Newbottle in 1813 (see chapter 1). However, 1815 proved a disaster for Nesham. On 20th March a large body of keelmen, seeing their livelihood being threatened by the new waggonway, pulled down the wooden viaduct at Sunderland and set fire to neighbouring buildings, causing one death, numerous injuries and £6000 of damage. Then on 30th July the Brunton locomotive exploded, causing more deaths. The viaduct was replaced by an earth embankment; but the locomotive experiment was terminated. On the credit side the sinking of the Dorothea Pit was completed in March 1816; but Nesham and his partners now faced serious financial difficulties.

By early in 1818 it would seem that the output from the Dorothea Pit was equalling the combined output of the Success and Margaret Pits, causing

NEWBOTTLE WAGGONWAY as purchased by J.G.Lambton in 1822

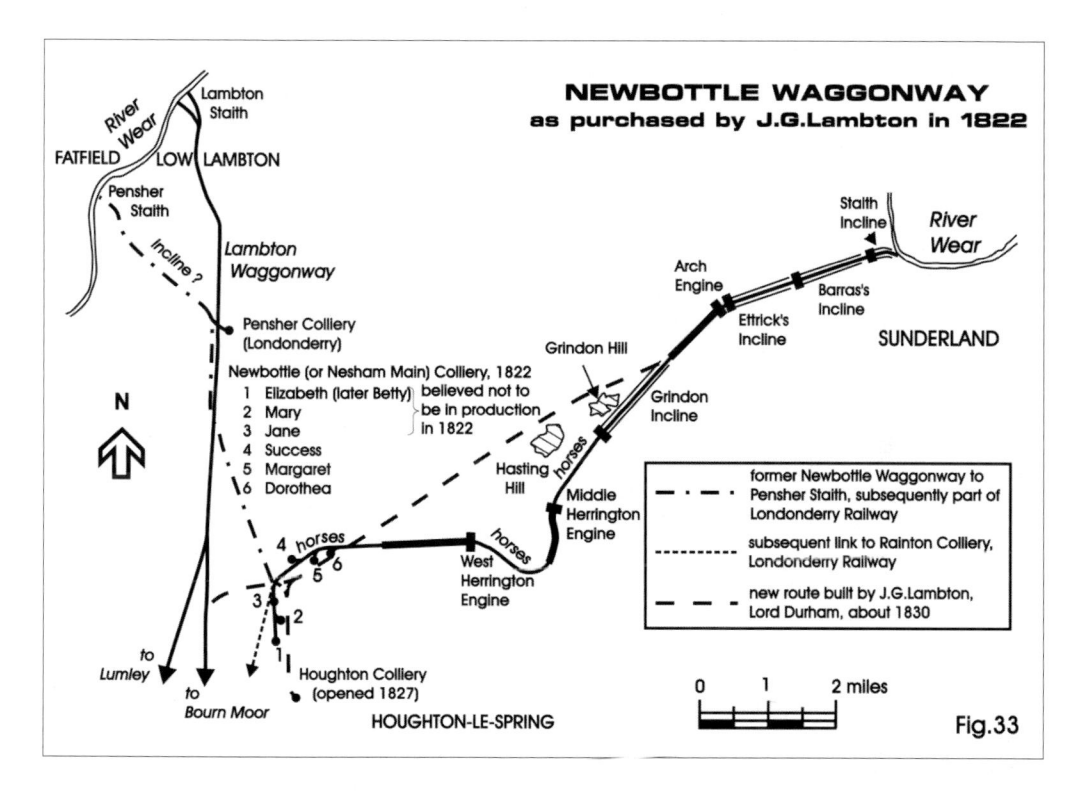

Fig.33

Nesham to look at ways of increasing the capacity of the waggonway. The result was a report from George Hill of Gateshead dated 26th May 1818 (NRO 3410/East/1/142) proposing the installation of rope haulage on certain sections. Certainly some rope haulage had been introduced by April 1819, bringing about a huge reduction in operating costs; but a description of the line in 1822 shows major differences from the proposals of 1818.

Nesham was now to find that he owned a waggonway of strategic interest to three of his neighbours, all of whose enterprises were to make them the leading colliery owners in the county. The first was Arthur Mowbray, who as Agent to the trustees of Lady Frances Anne Vane Tempest had first shown an interest in 1813 with a proposal to link the Vane Tempest waggonway to the Newbottle line. In 1819 he had joined the new Hetton Coal Company, which badly needed a line direct to Sunderland for shipping its coal, and to provide this Mowbray proposed buying Newbottle Colliery and its waggonway. This idea foundered, and the Hetton company was compelled to build its own line to Sunderland. The second was Charles Stewart, to become the 3rd Marquis of Londonderry in 1822. In April 1819 he had married Lady Frances Anne Vane Tempest and so gained control of her collieries at Rainton and Pensher and their waggonway, and he had Buddle, who had replaced Mowbray, as his Agent. In February 1820 Buddle put forward a proposal for a 500-yard line to link the Rainton line to the Newbottle line at the Success Pit to gain access to Sunderland; but this plan also came to nothing, and Stewart began to consider building a new railway eastwards to the coast (see the Londonderry Railway). Finally, to the west lay the collieries owned by John George Lambton. John Buddle, who disliked Mowbray intensely, was determined to keep the Newbottle line out of his hands, firstly by the proposal above and then, after the construction of the Hetton Railway had begun, by proposing a division of the area under which Lambton got Newbottle and Londonderry got Seaham (DRO, D/Lo/142/4), which is more or less what then happened.

Because of Nesham's financial difficulties, by early in 1822 Newbottle Colliery, its waggonway and associated farms had passed into the hands of trustees, who, unusually in Co. Durham colliery history, decided to offer everything as one lot for auction in Sunderland on 2nd July 1822. Buddle and Stewart were determined that they should not fall into Mowbray's hands; and so Lambton was the successful bidder.

As stated earlier, the waggonway as described in 1822 (Fig.33) differs considerably from Hill's proposals of 1818; but it is possible that the first three miles were the same. The first 1232 yards, serving the Success, Margaret and Dorothea Pits, was horse-worked, the calculations at that time being that a horse would work for 12 hours a day at 2 m.p.h. This brought the waggons to the West Herrington Incline, 1308 yards at 1 in 72, where sets of 12 were hauled up by the 30 h.p. **West Herrington Engine** (NZ 347529). Hill's proposals continue ".... a horse must be employed to assist the return of the empty waggons, the descent of the Plane not being enough to enable them to descend with the rope attached to them". If this did in fact happen it would be the first recorded example of an incline where a stationary engine hauled uphill and a horse pulled the empties and the rope back down.

The next 1181 yards were horse-worked, skirting between Herrington Hill and Hasting Hill to reach Middle Herrington, where the line next curved round 180 degrees to climb the southern side of Hasting Hill. This incline was 557 yards at 1 in 54, worked by the **Middle Herrington Engine** (16 h.p. – NZ 357534). Then followed another horse-worked section, 920 yards long, to bring the wagons to **Grindon Bank Head** (NZ 358540), on the south-west side of Grindon Hill. Here Hill had proposed a short self-acting incline followed by more horse-working; but by 1822 this section was the **Grindon Incline**, about 1610 yards long at 1 in 36 to 1 in 48, taking the waggons down to the foot of the Arch Bank. From here they were hauled up an incline 620 yards long at 1 in 48 by the **Arch Engine** (16 h.p. - NZ 366557). Then followed three more self-acting inclines. The first was **Ettrick's Incline** (about 980 yards), followed by **Barrass's Incline** (about 1740 yards). At the foot of this, at Hylton Road, the line was crossed by the Hetton Railway, to be opened in November 1822. Finally there was the original **Staith Incline**, about 150 yards, down to staiths at the river (NZ 394574 approx). The whole line was calculated at 10192 yards, or 5.79 miles.

The new route to Sunderland

Yet in little more than ten years Lambton had abandoned two-thirds of this route, replacing it with a completely new line, and had radically rebuilt the remainder – a very rare example of one largely rope-worked railway being replaced by another rope-worked line. His reasons are not known, but they may well have included a desire to rid himself of extortionate wayleave payments and a need to increase the capacity of the line. No detailed records of this work seem to have survived. However, in 1835 Buddle was commissioned to produce a comprehensive report on the Earl's collieries and railways and their working expenses (NRO 3410/Bud/28), and this gives extensive details about the railway (though not the length of each incline). Whilst one cannot be sure that everything that Lambton did in the 1820s was the same in 1835, it is reasonable to assume that much of it was. Buddle gives a figure of 49,141 chaldrons as shipped in the half year ending 30th June 1835, which, assuming that these were chaldrons of 53 hundredweight capacity, gives a total of 130,222 tons, or an annual figure of 260,444 tons, a not inconsiderable figure for 1835.

With the obvious advantages of shipping his coal at Sunderland it is very likely that Lambton began at the southern end by linking the Newbottle Railway (as it is now called on contemporary maps) to his own system. However, the gauge of his waggonways was 4ft 2in/4ft 3in, while the gauge of the Newbottle line was 4ft 0in, if contemporary accounts are correct; if the gauge of the Newbottle line was altered (it would have to be the Newbottle line to be altered – see below), no record survives. With the pits at Bourn Moor not producing coal at this period, the connection was made by means of a curved link running north-eastwards from Elba. One source suggests that this had been done by 1829. By the time of the Buddle report in 1835 the first section was worked by the **Bourn Moor Engine** (NZ 324516), situated at the junction with the former branch to the D and Lady Ann Pits. Then followed a steep climb of just under ½ mile from Bourn Moor to Newbottle, a length known perhaps from this beginning as **Junction Bank** and worked by the **Junction Engine** (NZ 331507). The installation of the stationary engines may date from about 1831, for about this time Lord Durham ordered two stationary engines from R & W Hawthorn in Newcastle upon Tyne. RWH 133 was a 56 h.p. engine for "Phillidelphy" and 136 a 64 h.p. engine for "Bunkers Hill" (the names Philadelphia and Bunker Hill, the site of the colliery offices nearby, were both chosen by Nesham, a strong supporter of the American War of Independence) and it could be that these two engines were installed on the Railway. Perhaps at this date, perhaps later, the section of the old Lambton waggonway at Bourn Moor that this new line crossed was lifted.

Lambton also wasted no time in opening up the large area of coal between Newbottle and Houghton-le-Spring. The sinking of **HOUGHTON COLLIERY** (NZ 338504) was begun on 29th April 1823 and completed in April 1827. It was served by a branch 1506 yards long from just north of Junction Bank, a point known latterly as Houghton Junction, the gradient stiffening towards the colliery to 1 in 90. By 1835 the branch was worked by the **Houghton Engine** at the colliery. However, the colliery was closed in 1837 and remained so until 1849.

Between the top of Junction Bank and Sunderland Lambton either replaced or rebuilt almost all of the original Newbottle line; but this work was clearly done in two, probably three, separate sections and not all at the same time – indeed, the maps of the period clearly show that the changes north of the Arch Engine precede the completely new route further south. However, in order to understand the route clearly it is better to take the line consecutively, working from the southern end.

Even between Junction Bank Top and a point just north of the Dorothea Pit at Philadelphia, Lambton built a new line, some 50 yards south of the old one, with the Success Pit linked by a short branch and the Margaret and Dorothea Pits alongside the line. Buddle's Report of 1835 records this section as worked by horses. Certainly in later years there was a stationary engine at the Dorothea Pit itself, for a description of the Pit in the Supplement to the *Mining Journal* dated 25th February 1871 recorded that "a 8in horizontal engine near the pit hauls empty wagons from the siding to a point above the screens by means of a return wheel, whence they descend by gravity". When this was installed, and when it was replaced by locomotive working, is not known. Later the "main line" was again re-routed to have the "main line" by-pass the colliery, which was then served by sidings alongside.

From Philadelphia Lambton took this new line on northwards to Arch Bank Foot. On the top of the first high ground he put the **Herrington Engine** (NZ 342534). This hauled wagons up **Herrington West Bank**, a single line incline about 950 yards long, and then lowered them down **Herrington East Bank**, also single line but shorter at about 800 yards. From this point, known as The Bottoms, they were worked up the **Foxcover Bank**, again about 800 yards and almost entirely an embankment, to what Buddle calls the **Hayston Hill Engine,** but on the 1st ed. O.S. map twenty years later is called the **Foxcover Engine** (NZ 350540); from the O.S. map it would appear that fulls and empties on this bank were worked simultaneously. From this summit the line descended the **Grindon self-acting incline**. Then followed what Buddle calls the "Grindon Planes", worked by the **Grindon Engine** (NZ 363553). This almost certainly means that there was an Incline on both sides of the engine. Since powered inclines of less than 400 yards are not known at this period, it would seem likely that the Grindon self-acting incline was about 1000-1100 yards, the Grindon West Incline about 500 yards and the East Incline, down to Arch Bank Foot, about 600 yards. However, it is possible that the reorganisation of this section also included an earlier Grindon Engine, about 50 yards south of the later engine, as the 1st ed. O.S. map shows a reservoir alongside the old line at this point which may well have served a stationary engine.

It used to be thought that this new line was built about 1834. However, the R & W Hawthorn Engine Book shows that Lord Durham ordered three "Hauling Engines for waggons, Newbottle Railway", two at 56 h.p., works Nos. 110 and 111, and one at 80hp, Works No.120. These were ordered before the dates when orders were received were entered in the Engine Book, but the orders are likely to date from about 1830, a date which would appear to be supported by a letter from Buddle dated 3rd April 1830 (NRO 3410/Bud/19/127) regarding wayleave charges for the new line across Grindon Farm.

Continuing their journey, the full waggons were then hauled up to the **Arch Engine** (NZ 366557) and then descended the **Ettrick's self-acting incline** as before. From here Lambton's thinking is not clear; for he replaced the former Barras's self-acting incline with a stationary engine, the **Glebe Engine** (NZ 381565). This would appear to have been about 1100 yards from the Arch Engine, so perhaps Ettrick's Incline was lengthened slightly. The Glebe Engine lowered the full waggons down some 950 yards to Hylton Road.

Just south of Hylton Road the line served **Bishopwearmouth Iron Works** (NZ 388569), which had formerly been served by the Hetton Railway (which see). This works passed through several hands and by the 1850s, when it was owned by the Derwent Iron Company, it had expanded into a much larger area on the opposite side of the line. When this happened the Lambton Railway was modified to work traffic into this new section, with links to the original buildings being carried over the Railway on bridges (see Fig.37). The works had closed by 1871. From the southern link to the western side of the works an extension curved away to serve **Millfield Quarry**; its owners are not known, but it was probably owned by the iron works. At Hylton Road the line was still crossed by The Hetton Coal Company's line. Finally, there was the self-acting incline down to the staiths, called by Buddle the **Low Incline**. By the 1850s the short tunnel had gone and the number of loading points expanded to 11, a measure of the volume of coal being handled. However, these were still of the design (called "drops") where the waggon was lowered out on a counter-balanced platform over the ship's hold and the bottom doors released to discharge the coal. The waggon then returned upwards, while trimmers in the hold shovelled the coal level ready for the next waggonload. The 1st ed. O.S. 25in map shows an **Engine House** near the entrance to drops Nos. 1-8 (see Fig.26), which may well have worked perhaps two waggons at a time to whichever drop needed them, but this is not confirmed. One **stationary engine** (NZ 393573) that did survive here for many years was used to work wagons to and from Chatt's landsale depot in Galley's Gill. This lay slightly to the south of the loco shed, and had two drums, each with a rope, and seems to have operated a main-and-tail system. It may well have lasted into the 1940s.

Gauge differences
As has been noted above, the gauge of the Lambton and Lumley system was 4ft 2ins (with the proviso that the 1996 discoveries showed a gauge of 4ft 3ins), while the gauge of the Newbottle waggonway was 4ft 0in. Although there is no evidence through the 1820s and 1830s of any alterations to gauge, it would seem very likely that when Lambton built his new Newbottle line it would be to the same gauge as the Lambton and Lumley system. It was certainly not built to 4ft 8½in gauge, for on 27th August 1840 Buddle records in his Journal (NRO 3410/Bud/48/12/160) that he had attended a meeting at Pensher to discuss the conversion of both the Lambton and Londonderry Railways to the "Parliamentary gauge" (4ft 8½ins). The Lambton Railway he lists as totalling 28 miles and using 1100 waggons. When the conversion was carried out is not known; it did not take place on the Londonderry Railway until 15th-18th May 1843. If the Lambton conversion took place before this then it would have brought to an end the Marquis of Londonderry's traffic to Sunderland via the Jane Pit (see below).

The old route to Low Lambton Staiths
Despite having his newly modernised route to Sunderland, Lambton still retained most of the old route to Low Lambton Staiths. Curiously, it would seem that the section between Bourn Moor and Pensher continued to be worked by horses,

perhaps because the volume of traffic was quite low. However, the ¼ mile between Pensher and the throat of the staiths was worked by the **Pensher Engine** (NZ 323539), with horses shunting the staiths themselves, as they did also at Sunderland. However, whilst the self-acting incline of 1819 may have been retained, it would appear almost certain that a **stationary engine** was installed to work the line on to the original staith. The O.S. 1855 map shows "site of old engine" at NZ 324544, while RWH 154 was a 5 h.p. engine for "Low Lambton". In fact, Lambton continued to ship coal at these staiths for many years.

Whilst dealing with the line between Bourn Moor and Pensher it is convenient to look at the branches from it. Two of these served quarries at Pensher.

The Cross Rigg Quarry branch
This limestone quarry (NZ 325539 approx.) lay on Lambton land about half way between New Pensher Colliery and Old Pensher village. It was probably begun in the 1840s, and was served by a ½ mile extension of the branch that had once served New Pensher Colliery. On a NER map of 1894 it would appear that the quarry was then called **Long Pasture Quarry,** and the line also served **Robertson's Slate Yard** and a **Tadcaster Brewery Company** store. In 1902 the lessees of the quarry are listed as Horn and Scott. It was still being worked in the 1920s, by which time it was a sizeable area. It would seem that its traffic was always worked by the Lambton Railway.

The Pensher Quarry branch
This limestone quarry (NZ 321517 approx.) lay on Londonderry land north of the village of Shiney Row, about ½ mile to the south of Cross Rigg Quarry. It was originally worked by the Londonderry Railway via an extension of the line to Old Pensher Colliery. It was leased out by March 1860, and is believed to have been linked to the Lambton Railway as part of the construction of the Union Railway (see below). The branch was approximately ¾ mile long. How long the quarry was operated is not known.

The Wapping branch
Despite the closure of the Houghton Gate Pit in 1817 (see above) it would seem that the first ½ mile of the branch that had served it was retained to serve the hamlet of Wapping. However, whilst the line is shown on the 1st ed. O.S. map (1855), it is not shown on Bell's *Map of the Great Northern Coalfield*, published in 1843, so it may have been closed and then re-laid. It supplied a coal depot provided for the villagers. Subsequently Wapping grew into the village of Bournmoor. By the 1890s its branch had been modified to form the Bowes House Farm Branch (see below).

The Lumley branch
This branch had been converted to rope haulage by the time of Buddle's report in 1835. The one stationary engine on it, about half way along near Lumley Thicks, Buddle called the **Lumley 2nd Pit Engine**, but the 1st ed. O.S. map calls it the **Black Row Engine** (NZ 304505). It was built straddling the track. This had the **Nickey Nack Bank** on its west side and the **Black Row Bank** on its east side, both about ½ mile long. The engine stood at the highest point on the branch, so it is likely that it worked both of the inclines. It would appear that Black Row bank foot was situated at the junction with the Cocken branch. From here the **New Lambton self-acting incline** took the waggons down to the foot of the incline up to the Bourn Moor Engine (see above). The collieries served by this branch which were working in 1819 (see above) had all been closed by 1835 and **LUMLEY 2ND PIT** (NZ 295504) had been re-opened, presumably sunk deeper. A new development soon afterwards was **LUMLEY 9TH PIT** (NZ 292512), sometimes known as the **Whitehouse Pit**. This lay much to the north of the others, its sinking beginning on 18th September 1841. It was served by a 1 mile branch from a junction near the 2nd Pit, though how this branch was worked is not known. However, it had closed by 1855, although by then **LUMLEY 3RD PIT** (NZ 296503) had been re-opened to replace it. There was also a short branch of perhaps 150 yards running south from the engine house to the hamlet of Lumley Thicks, again presumably serving a coal depot and probably worked by horses.

The Cocken branch
As has been described above, this was built in the summer of 1818 to serve the new 8th Pit and the George Pit. This line too was converted to rope haulage, again at an unknown date, except that the initial installation seems to have been rebuilt. The 1st ed. O.S. map records a **"Pea Flatts Old Engine"** (NZ 305498) the name was taken from a nearby farm). It would seem certain that this had something to do with the railway, and one can only speculate both as to its function and to why it was replaced by a new Pea Flatts Engine slightly further north (NZ 305500) (Buddle consistently calls it the **Peal Flatts Engine**). Neither engine lay at the junction with the Lumley branch, and how the traffic was worked between the engine(s) and the bank head of the New Lambton Incline is not known.

The second engine <u>may</u> be connected with the extension of the branch further south. It would seem from the O.S. map that the 1818 line was initially extended to serve the **CHARLES PIT** (NZ 296481), and then extended again to serve **COCKEN COLLIERY** (NZ 298474), opened in 1823. To work these the **Cocken Engine** (NZ 298483) was built, and it would seem clear from Buddle's report of 1835 that the engine worked both collieries, hauling the full waggons up to its bank head and then the Pea Flatts Engine taking them on to its bank head. Both the 8th Pit and the George Pit had closed by 1835, to be replaced by what Buddle terms the **LUMLEY PIT** and the O.S. map calls **LUMLEY WEST PIT** (NZ 293485); this, the Charles Pit and the 2nd Pit forming "Lumley Colliery". The West Pit was served by a ½ mile branch from a junction about 300 yards west of the Cocken Engine; how it was worked and how it was integrated into the operations of the Cocken Engine are not known. There were also other developments on this branch. At the bend where the lines to the Charles Pit and Cocken Colliery parted the O.S. map shows **LUMLEY SHOPS** (NZ 296482), a row of buildings on the west side of the line; one can only assume that these were workshops serving the various collieries in the Lumley area. Just west of the junction at Lumley Shops was **TOAD HOLE QUARRY** (NZ 295482), and

the line then ran northwards for nearly a mile to Great Lumley village, presumably to serve another coal depot. The O.S. map calls this line the "Lumley Waggonway".

Developments at Littletown and Sherburn

With most, if not all, of the work on the new route to Sunderland finished about 1830, Lambton now

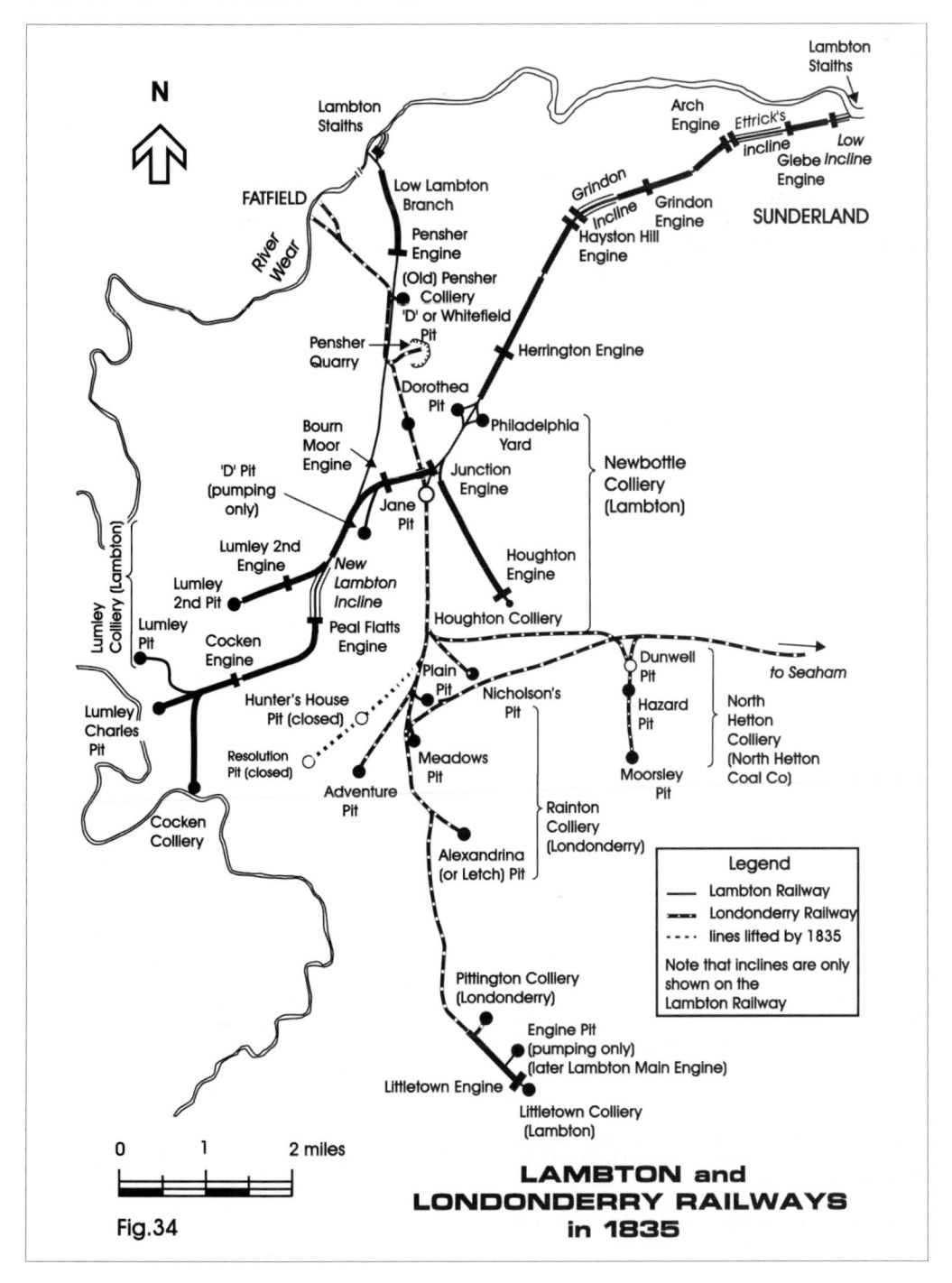

Fig.34 LAMBTON and LONDONDERRY RAILWAYS in 1835

turned to developing a large area of coal east-north-east of Durham City, some 4½ miles south of Bourn Moor. In 1831 he began the sinking of what was sometimes called **LAMBTON COLLIERY**, but which was usually called **LITTLETOWN COLLIERY** (NZ 339435). The Marquis of Londonderry had already acquired the royalty immediately to the east, opening Pittington Colliery in 1827 and extending his line from Rainton to serve it. Littletown Colliery was ready for production in 1833 or 1834 – and then became part of a collaboration unparalleled in the Durham coalfield, though whether all the elements were negotiated at the same time is not known.

The results of this collaboration are shown in Buddle's report of 1835. Firstly, Lambton linked Littletown Colliery to the Londonderry line at Pittington. Although the full waggons were to go downhill, this ½ mile branch, later known as the **Littletown Bank**, was worked by a stationary engine at the colliery, the **Littletown Engine**. The 1855 O.S. map shows a 3-4-2 rail layout on this bank, indicating that fulls and empties were run simultaneously – and a rare curiosity; for from the meetings a ¼ mile facing branch ran north to serve what was later called the **Lambton Main Engine** (NZ 337437), a pumping engine. How this branch was worked is unknown. The Littletown Engine took the waggons down to the bank head (NZ 328444) of the Pittington Incline of the Londonderry Railway, where the line from Londonderry's Pittington Colliery joined. The Earl's waggons then travelled over the Londonderry Railway for some five miles northwards to Newbottle, and the side of the Jane Pit (NZ 326516), one of Nesham's Newbottle pits. Here the Earl built a 406-yard curve round to join his line about 200 yards south of the Junction Engine, which worked the traffic on this link as well as the traffic to and from Bourn Moor (TWA DF/WF/28/1/328). And not just Lambton traffic; for despite the opening of his line from Rainton to Seaham in July 1831, the Marquis of Londonderry used this curve too (and paid for the incline rope) to send about 17,000 chaldron waggons a year, about 45,000 tons, over the Earl's line to be shipped at Sunderland. And more: for Buddle's report shows that while some coal from North Hetton Colliery, by this time owned by The North Hetton Coal Company, was going east to Seaham, a sizeable quantity was sent north on to the Londonderry Railway at Rainton and transported up to Pensher, where it was transferred to the Earl's Railway to be shipped at Low Lambton Staiths, the Earl keeping four horses there specifically to shunt this traffic. The North Hetton coal was being dispatched from Low Lambton by 1831; when the Marquis' traffic began is not known; both were still continuing in 1839.

Even before Lambton/Littletown Colliery was opened, Lambton had begun sinking a second colliery ½ mile to the south, called initially **SHERBURN COLLIERY** (NZ 336427), which began production in the second half of 1835. This was linked to the Littletown line by a self-acting incline that joined at the foot of Littletown Bank, a point known later as Bird-in-the-Bush Junction (named after a local public house). Its coal too went northwards via the Londonderry Railway. But then the Marquis opened two more pits in the area, Broomside Colliery and the Lady Seaham Pit, and it would seem obvious that his line could no longer handle the volume of traffic, particularly as the Earl was planning another colliery at Sherburn. It was thus unavoidable that the Lambton traffic had to have a line of its own.

Again the sequencing and dating are difficult. Whether the Frankland branch (see below) or the new line to Pittington came first is not known, and it would also seem unlikely that such a major extension of the system as the two lines were would pre-date the conversion to 4ft 8½in gauge. It could well have been built in 1844, for the wooden bridge over the Newcastle & Darlington Junction Railway near Leamside is recorded as being built in this year, the same year in which Sherburn House Colliery (see below) was also opened. Taking the Pittington line first, a line nearly six miles long was built from Elba down through Fence Houses. Here it utilised the trackbed of the former Londonderry waggonway branch to the Hunter's House and Resolution Pits (now closed), before turning south-east to climb the ridge near West Rainton. Here it passed under the Durham to Sunderland road in a short tunnel before dropping down to Pittington.

How the southern end of this line was worked is far from clear, and in some respects the 2nd edition of the O.S., surveyed in 1895, does not help. It would seem that the Littletown Bank remained as before. The 1895 map then shows two short banks, first the **Buddle Bank** and then the **Pittington Bank**, separated by the **Buddle Engine** (NZ 336438) – but none of this is shown on the 1st edition map. On the face of it the Buddle Engine worked the banks on either side of it. The Buddle Engine <u>may</u> be linked to the order to RWH dated 18th July 1840, in which the Earl ordered a steam engine with 15in cylinders for the "Transit of coals, Lambton Colliery"; it was allocated RWH Works No.325. From the foot of Pittington Bank the waggons were hauled for about a mile up to the Durham to Sunderland road by the **Belmont Engine** (NZ 318458). In later years, apparently referring towards the end of the nineteenth century, oral tradition maintained that this incline was operated by main-and-tail haulage; but whether that was true from the beginning is not known. From the other side of the tunnel a self-acting incline called **Belmont Bank** took the fulls down to near Pit House Lane, about ¼ mile south of the former Resolution Pit. From here there is no evidence of rope haulage, and it seems unlikely that horses would be used for the long section up to Elba, so perhaps this was one of the first places where locomotives were used (first introduced in 1842).

In 1844 **SHERBURN HOUSE COLLIERY** (NZ 322415) was opened south of the village of Sherburn, and the system was extended to serve it. About ¼ mile south of Sherburn Colliery was a **"Standing Engine"** (NZ 332424); its name has not survived.

Fig.35. The "Sunderland Coal Drops", drawn by T.H.Hair in 1839; the Hetton Staiths lie in the foreground, with the Lambton Staiths beyond.

109. How the cradle loading shown on Hair's drawing worked - Lambton Staiths in the mid-nineteenth century.

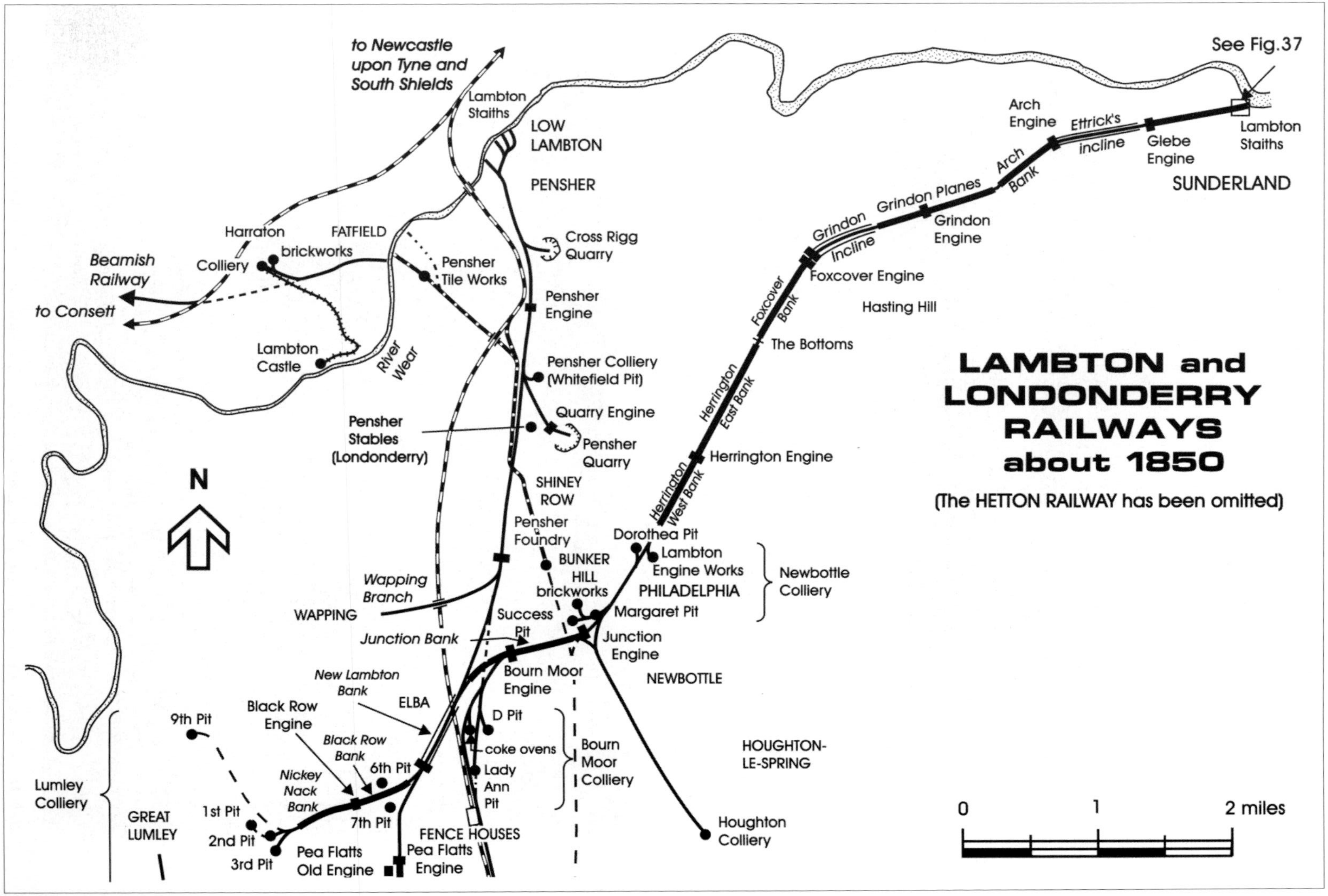
LAMBTON and
LONDONDERRY
RAILWAYS
about 1850
(The HETTON RAILWAY has been omitted)
See Fig.37
Lambton Staiths
SUNDERLAND
Glebe Engine
Ettrick's incline
Arch Engine
Arch Bank
Grindon Planes
Grindon Engine
Grindon Incline
Foxcover Engine
Hasting Hill
Foxcover Bank
The Bottoms
Herrington East Bank
Herrington Engine
Herrington West Bank
Dorothea Pit
Lambton Engine Works
PHILADELPHIA
Newbottle Colliery
Margaret Pit
Junction Engine
NEWBOTTLE
HOUGHTON-LE-SPRING
Houghton Colliery
Bourn Moor Engine
D Pit
coke ovens
Lady Ann Pit
Bourn Moor Colliery
FENCE HOUSES
Pea Flatts Engine
Pea Flatts Old Engine
7th Pit
6th Pit
Black Row Bank
Nickey Nack Bank
New Lambton Bank
ELBA
Black Row Engine
1st Pit
2nd Pit
3rd Pit
9th Pit
GREAT LUMLEY
Lumley Colliery
Junction Bank
Success Pit
WAPPING
Wapping Branch
BUNKER HILL brickworks
Pensher Foundry
SHINEY ROW
Pensher Quarry
Quarry Engine
Pensher Colliery (Whitefield Pit)
Pensher Stables (Londonderry)
Pensher Engine
Cross Rigg Quarry
PENSHER
LOW LAMBTON
Lambton Staiths
to Newcastle upon Tyne and South Shields
Pensher Tile Works
FATFIELD
Harraton Colliery
brickworks
Beamish Railway
to Consett
Lambton Castle
River Wear
N
0
1
2 miles

Fig.36

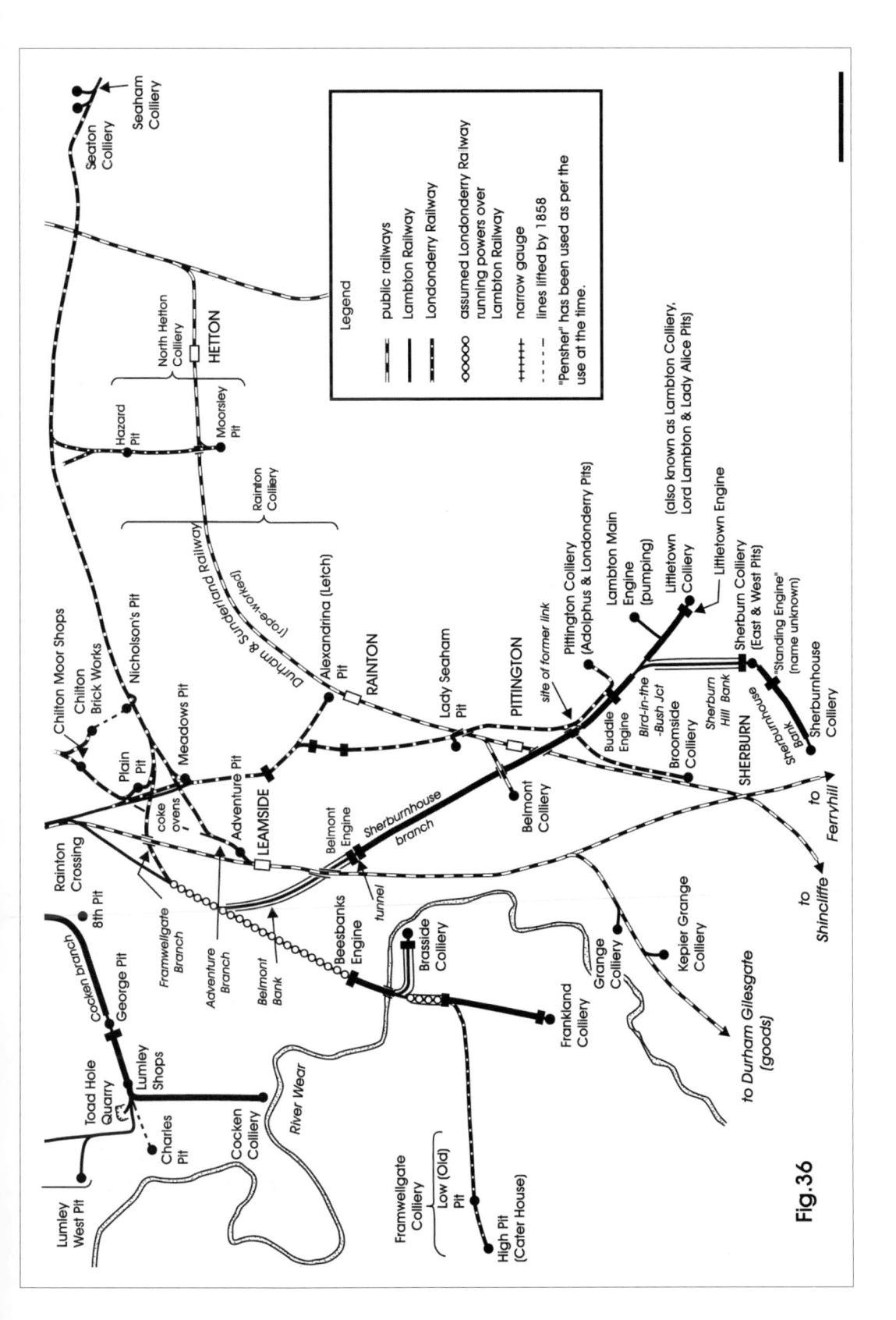

The 2nd ed. O.S. 25in map, surveyed in 1895, shows that part of this engine, almost certainly the drum house, straddled the track and that this engine was situated at the summit of the branch. It would seem very likely that this engine hauled fulls up from Sherburn House and then lowered them into Sherburn Hill. This extension also changed the name of the whole branch from the **Littletown branch** to the **Sherburnhouse branch**.

The Frankland branch

As mentioned above, at the same time that the new line to Pittington was being built the area of coal north-east of Durham City but west of the River Wear was being opened up. The first sinking here was **FRANKLAND COLLIERY** (NZ 296452), opened in 1842, and to serve it a branch about 2 miles long was built from the site of the Resolution Pit. By 1855 the line had been extended for ¼ mile to serve the nearby miners' cottages. In 1846 **BRASSIDE COLLIERY** (NZ 305458) was added, served by a ½ mile branch. However, the main branch was yet another example of Lambton and Londonderry co-operation, though again the precise details are not known. In 1838 the Northern Coal Mining Company began the sinking of Framwellgate Colliery, which lay 1½ miles north-west of Frankland; the first shipment of coal took place in May 1841. At some point Londonderry became involved, and then Lambton as well. It was agreed that Framwellgate coal would be shipped at Seaham, and to achieve this the Northern Coal Mining Company built a branch to join the Lambton line ¾ mile from Frankland Colliery. The Framwellgate coal then travelled over the Lambton Railway to the site of the former Hunter's House Pit, from where Londonderry carried it over a specially-built link to join his line to Seaham east of Rainton Meadows. These links are not shown on Bell's *Map of the Great Northern Coalfield* of 1843, but must date from this period. The Northern Coal Mining Company went bankrupt in 1848, and in August 1859 the Marchioness of Londonderry bought Framwellgate Colliery, so that it was now Londonderry traffic which was being carried over the Lambton Railway, possibly using a Londonderry Railway locomotive for the latter part of its journey. This traffic ended in 1873, when the colliery was sold and its traffic was dispatched via a link with the NER at Frankland.

Fortunately, the supplement to the *Mining Journal*

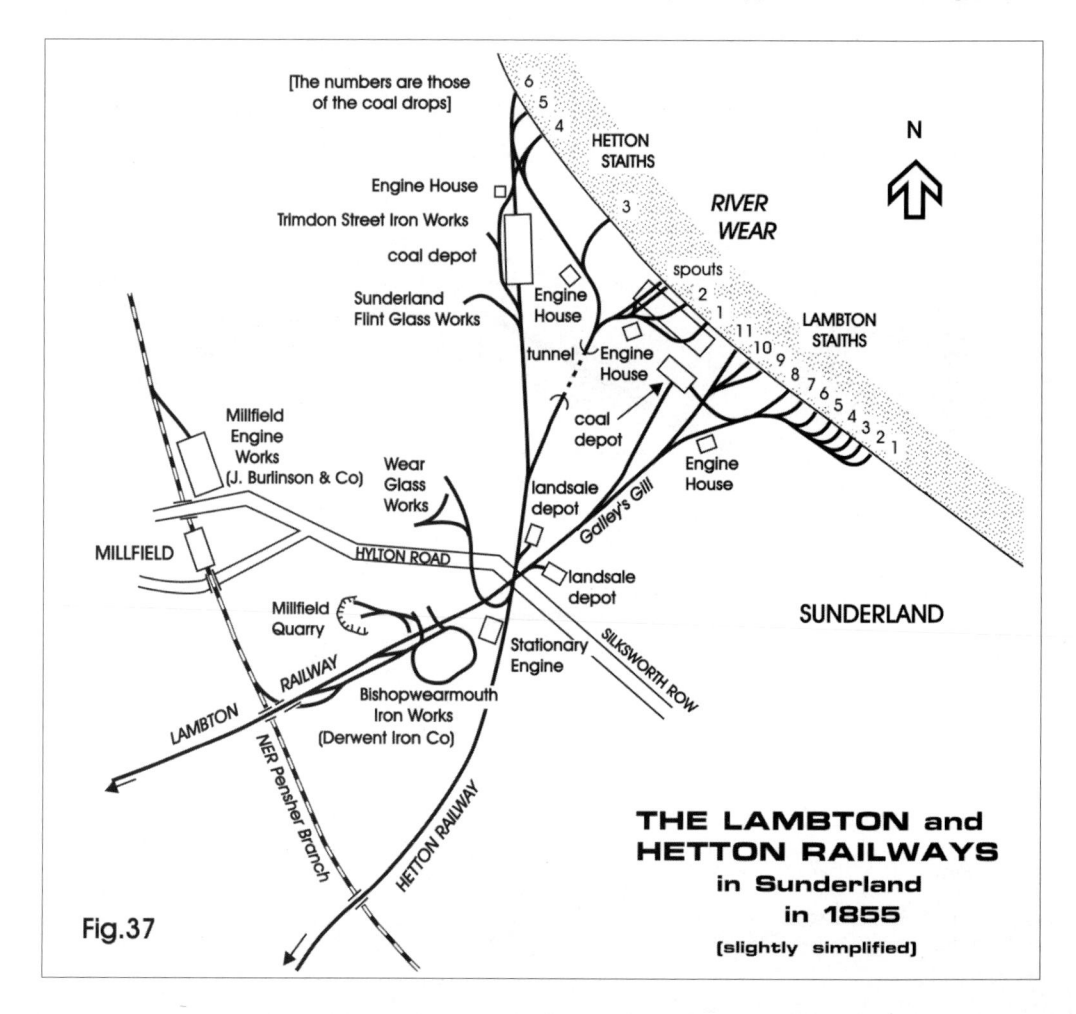

Fig.37 **THE LAMBTON and HETTON RAILWAYS** in Sunderland in **1855** (slightly simplified)

Harraton Colliery, 1855

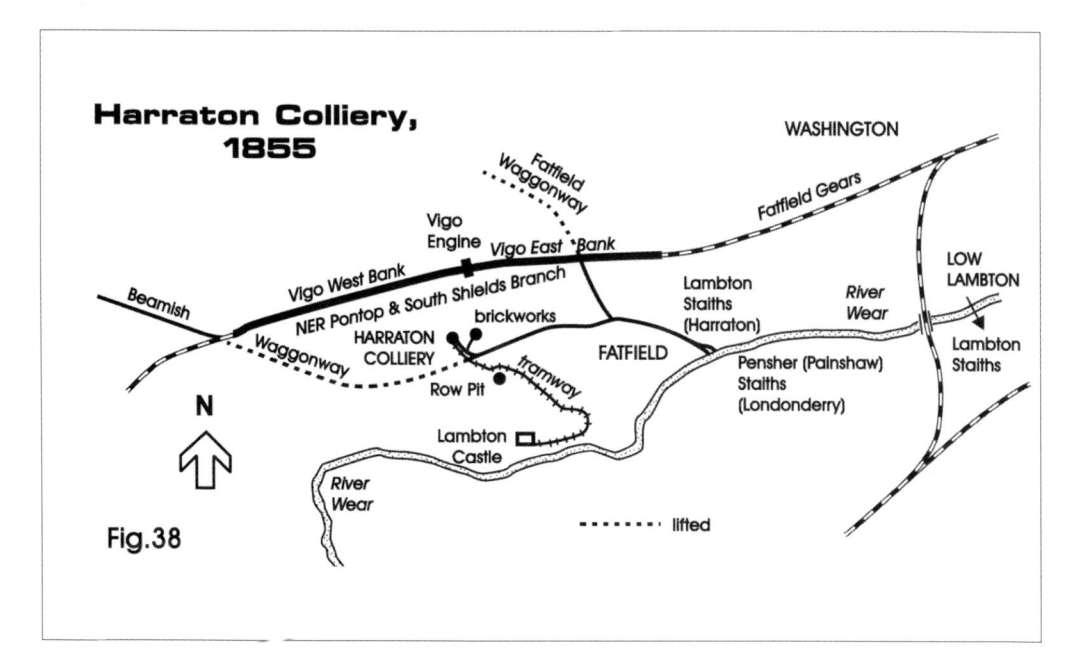

Fig.38

-------- lifted

dated 22nd April 1871 describes the working of this line, and it provides a very rare example of the winding engine for the pit also being used to work a railway on the surface: "**the haulage beam engine for the pit** [Frankland] is used to haul the waggons on the branch railway for ¾ mile by **main-and-tail**, to the top of a **self-acting incline**". This was the junction of the line from Framwellgate Colliery, and this ½ mile long self-acting incline was very unusual in having two bank heads, one for Frankland and one for Framwellgate coal. At the bank foot alongside the river the line was joined by the ½ mile **self-acting incline** from Brasside Colliery. From here the waggons "are drawn over a wooden viaduct and up the opposite bank by a stationary engine, three waggons ascending and descending together". This was the **Beesbanks Engine** (NZ 302466), named after a local farm, the incline being about ¼ mile long. From here the traffic was almost certainly locomotive-hauled latterly, though possibly horse-hauled initially.

Harraton Colliery
Throughout this period this colliery continued to be the only Lambton pit not linked to the Lambton Railway. By the 1850s the working pit (NZ 291539), with a brickworks next to it, lay to the north of the Beamish Waggonway. After the opening of the Stanhope & Tyne Railway in 1834, latterly the NER Pontop & South Shields Branch, the Waggonway had been linked to it at Vigo Bank Foot (later Beamish Junction) near Ouston, to allow its coal to be shipped at South Shields, and thus ceased to use the remaining length to Fatfield. Presumably the Earl of Durham acquired the section between Harraton and the staith in order to continue shipping Harraton coal at Fatfield, but how this line was worked is not known. The 1st ed. O.S. map shows that by 1855 a narrow gauge tramway ran from Harraton for 1¼ miles on a long curving route through Lambton Park to LAMBTON CASTLE (NZ 298526), presumably to carry coal for use at the castle and worked by horses. The line from Harraton to Fatfield is still shown in situ on the 3rd edition O.S. map, surveyed in 1919, though whether it was still in use is not known.

Workshops
Thus by the mid-1840s the Earl of Durham had developed a railway system totalling some forty route miles, most of it worked by rope haulage of some kind, including at least 16 stationary engines. This was easily the most extensive private railway in North-East England, and served a considerable number of pits, quarries and brickworks. When the Earl first began to develop his own shipping fleet is not known, but this would add further to the engineering work needed. The existence of Lumley Shops has already been mentioned, but the Earl's major workshop development was to be at Philadelphia, opposite the Dorothea Pit, the workshops which became known as **LAMBTON ENGINE WORKS** (NZ 336525). It would seem that the first facilities were already in use by 1835, for Buddle's Report lists various men employed at what he calls **Philadelphia Yard**. They developed into far more than simple workshops, with pattern makers, iron and brass foundries and rolling mills, boiler and machine shops and many others, even to leather workers (see Figs. 39 and 40).

The development of public railways in the area
By the mid-1830s public railways were beginning to spread into east Durham. The first was the Durham & Sunderland Railway, opened in 1836. This crossed under the Littletown branch at Pittington, but no connection was made, perhaps not surprisingly, as the whole of this line was rope-

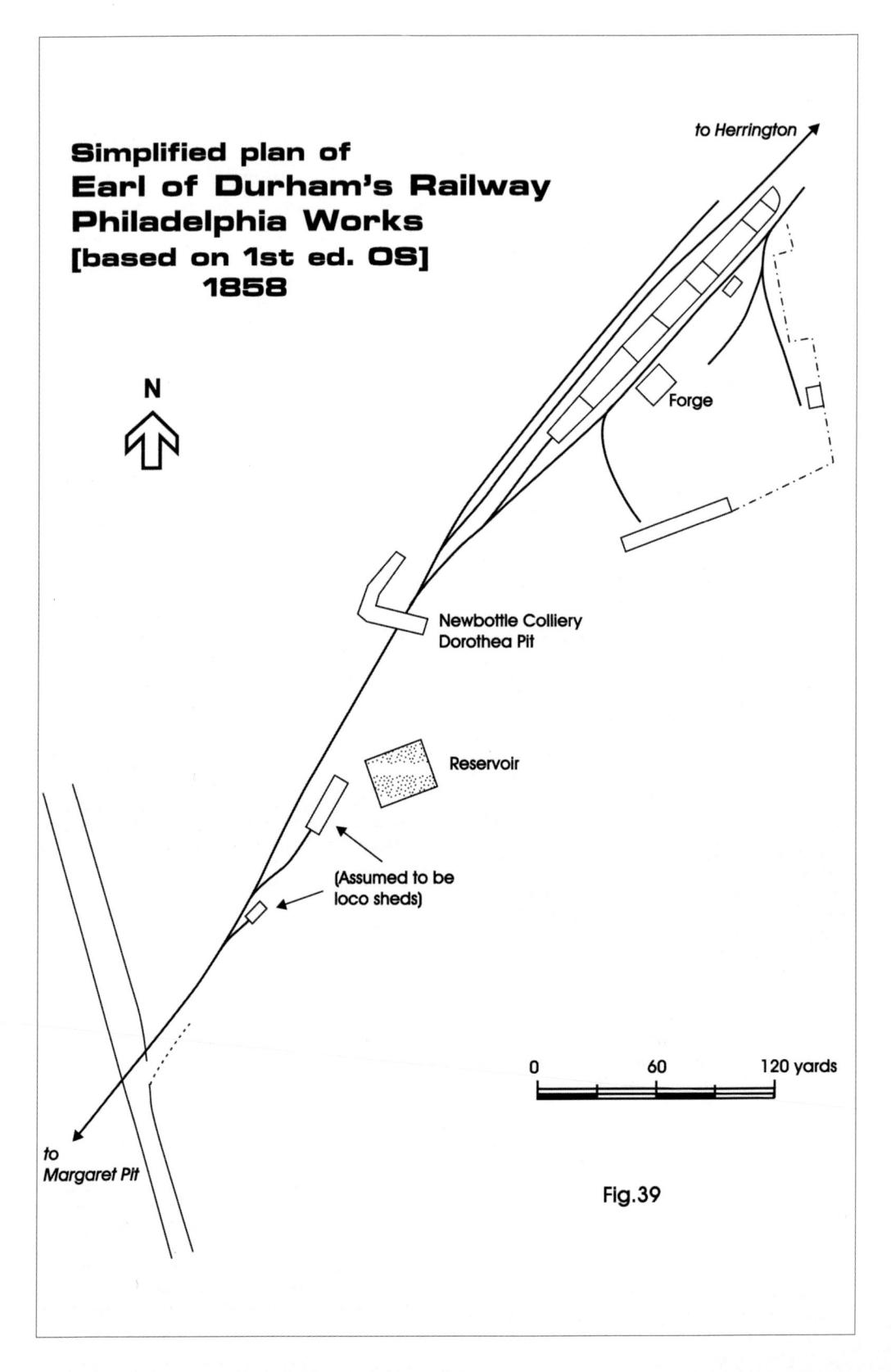

Simplified plan of Earl of Durham's Railway Philadelphia Works
[based on 1st ed. OS]
1858

to Herrington

N

Forge

Newbottle Colliery
Dorothea Pit

Reservoir

(Assumed to be loco sheds)

to Margaret Pit

0   60   120 yards

Fig.39

Fig.40

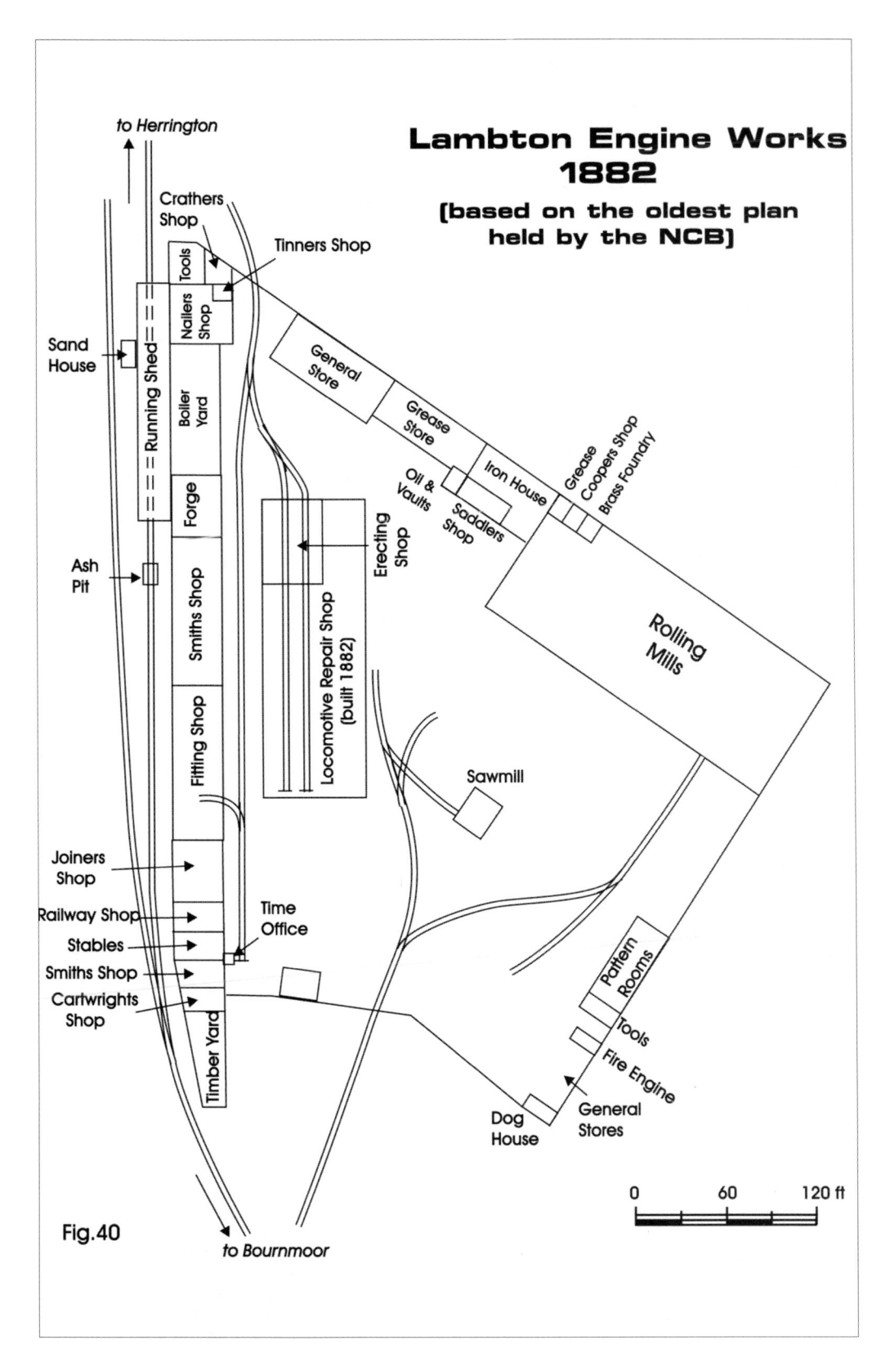

worked when it was opened. The next was the Newcastle & Darlington Junction Railway, the final link in the first route between London and Newcastle upon Tyne, which opened in 1844. This crossed under the Belmont Bank to run alongside the Lambton Railway through Fence Houses Station, just south of Bourn Moor, before continuing northwards through Pensher to cross over the River Wear just south of the staiths at Low Lambton. So Fence Houses Station became the first major interchange point with the public system.

The introduction of locomotives
It would seem very unlikely that any locomotives were acquired before the conversion to 4ft 8½in gauge. Equally, the central area of the system around Bourn Moor, together with the nearer sections of the lines running from it, all relatively level, would seem almost certain to be where locomotives were first used – northwards from Black Row bank foot on the Lumley branch, eliminating the New Lambton Incline; northwards from the Pea Flatts Engine on the Cocken branch and from the Beesbanks Engine on the Frankland branch, including the short distance from Belmont Bank Foot on the Sherburnhouse branch, and then on either to Bourn Moor bank foot or even to the foot of Junction Bank for the traffic going to Sunderland, or up to the Pensher Engine for traffic going to Low Lambton. Another section where locomotives may well have replaced horses at an early date could be the section between Junction Bank Top and Herrington West bank foot, together with the branch down to Houghton Colliery after this was re-opened in 1849. Robert Young's *Timothy Hackworth and the Locomotive* (1923) states (p.316) that about 1842 Hackworth supplied a locomotive named "Prince Albert" for the Earl of Durhams railway. This was a six-coupled tender engine, and it may well be that there were others of this design. It would seem likely that the **locomotive shed** needed for these first locomotives would be part of Lambton Engine Works, and indeed an early plan of the works, undated but believed to date from the 1850s but also subsequently over-written, shows what is probably a loco shed on its western side, alongside the line (Fig.40).

The Pensher Branch (YN&BR/NER)
In 1851 the York, Newcastle & Berwick Railway began the construction of a branch seven miles long from Pensher, through central Sunderland, with a station at Fawcett Street, and on to link up to the former Durham & Sunderland line at Hendon and so provide access to Sunderland's South Dock, opened in 1850. This line left the YN&B main line almost alongside the Pensher Engine and crossed the Lambton Railway again east of the proposed Millfield Station. It was opened for goods on 20th December 1852 and for passengers on 1st June 1853. This was perhaps the biggest single factor in the development of the Lambton Railway, for the implication was obvious. Even before the branch was opened the Earl had approached the YN&B for permission to send his coal over the line, for the minutes of their Board meeting on 29th October 1852 record that "Mr. Harrison [their Engineer] reported that he thought some arrangement might be made by which Lord Durham's coals might be brought on to the Pensher Branch, on payment of a toll to the Railway Company, the Owner finding waggons and employing his own locomotive power. The Board approved generally of the principle and requested Mr. Harrison to see Mr. Morton, Lord Durham's Agent, on the matter." There is no further reference in the Board minutes of this period, but by 1855 a link had been put in east of Millfield Station to join the Lambton Railway just south of Bishopwearmouth Iron Works and clearly an agreement had been made for the Earl to have running powers between Pensher and Millfield to run his trains into Lambton Staiths; he also purchased another six-coupled tender locomotive in 1852 and two more in 1853-1854. Despite this, the rope-hauled route over Grindon Hill continued in use, and indeed shipments also continued at Low Lambton. Equally, these running powers may have been cancelled, for on 23rd May 1863 the NER Board considered the matter again, and resolved that "Lord Durham's engines be allowed to run over the Pensher Branch to Sunderland with coal from his Lordship's collieries for shipment."

Other changes in the 1850s
One of these was a further small extension at the far south of the system. To the west of Sherburn village the Earl had been sinking **SHERBURN COLLIERY** (NZ 315425), also called the **Lady Durham Pit**, which began production in August 1854, only days after the creation of the North Eastern Railway. The colliery was connected to the Sherburnhouse branch by a ½ mile link called the **Sherburn branch**, joining the system about 200 yards north-east of Sherburn House Colliery, with loops to both north-east and south-west. The colliery also lay alongside the NER Washington to Ferryhill line, to which it was also connected. DCOA Return 102 records two locomotives being used here in April 1871 and presumably down to Sherburn House; when the first locomotive arrived here is unknown. A small **loco shed** was built at the southern end of the colliery yard. Equally, it seems unlikely that much coal went out via the NER link, where the NER built Sherburn Colliery Station, though no doubt it was used to bring goods on to the system. After about 1904 it also became the normal way of exchanging locomotives between Philadelphia and Sherburn, not using running powers but purely on an "as required" basis between Fence Houses and Sherburn Colliery Stations; previously locomotives had been exchanged internally, until the wooden bridge which carried the Belmont Incline over the NER south of Leamside Station was deemed unsafe to carry locomotives. The opening of Sherburn Colliery also led to the former Sherburn Colliery being re-named **SHERBURN HILL COLLIERY**, taking its name from the village that had grown up south of it, and the branch to it from the north being called latterly the **Littletown & Sherburn branch**.

110. 0-6-0 11, whose builders are unknown, at Lambton Staiths, Sunderland, believed to have been taken about 1882.

111. 5, a very different 0-6-0, built by Hudswell & Clarke, 30/1864, again at Lambton Staiths, Sunderland, probably taken about 1890. With 11 above, these are the only known photographs showing letters and numbers on the tenders. This practice clearly did not last very long.

112. *A very different Hudswell & Clarke design, built only two years later, but photographed seventy years later: 1, H&C 71/1866, being coaled at the coaling stage at Philadelphia in 1952.*

113. *0-6-0 10, almost certainly built by Thomas Richardson at Hartlepool, at Philadelphia, probably in the 1890s.*

The new **LAMBTON D PIT** (NZ 318508) at Bourn Moor is also believed to have been opened in 1854, and the re-opening of the **LADY ANN PIT** (NZ 318507) may also date from this time. Their re-opening meant the re-laying of the ½ mile branch to them from near the Bourn Moor Engine. In 1864 the new **LUMLEY 6TH PIT** (NZ 309506) was re-opened after standing idle since about 1814, probably replacing the 3rd Pit, the closure of which seems to have occurred about this time. In 1880 a **brickworks** was also developed near the colliery, its products extending to a very wide range of clay-based items.

The "Union Railway"

The 1st ed. O.S. maps of the mid-1850s show that the links which had brought Londonderry and North Hetton traffic on to the system had been lifted, and indeed the section of the Londonderry Railway between Chilton Moor and Pensher Foundry had also been lifted, severing the link between Rainton and Pensher. But the close co-operation between the two aristocratic families was to continue. On 26th November 1861 the Earl and the Marchioness of Londonderry made an agreement to double the track between the coke ovens at Bournmoor and Pensher Station, a distance of 3168 yards and known as the "Union Railway". The Marchioness linked this section at its southern end to the Londonderry Railway at Chilton Moor and built a separate link to Pensher Station at the northern end. However, each party was to work its own traffic, using its own locomotives and waggons, though to Lambton Railway rules. In November 1864 the Marchioness transferred most of her rights under this agreement to her new lessee of Pensher Colliery, George Elliot (see below).

The Deptford Branch (NER)

Then on 1st October 1865 the NER opened its 1¼ mile freight-only Deptford Branch, from a junction east of Pallion Station on the Pensher Branch. From the end of it the NER authorised on 16th December 1864 a ¼ mile extension through a tunnel to Lambton Staiths, which was built by contract with two-thirds of the cost paid by the Earl of Durham. The tunnel was bored to a restricted gauge, so that in later years most of the Lambton Railway locomotives had to carry cut-down cabs in order to pass through. This new line avoided all the difficulties of the crossing of the two railways at Hylton Road and allowed the Earl to work his own traffic between Pensher and Lambton Staiths almost entirely over the public system. It was presumably opened in 1865.

The Earl also gained running powers over the remainder of the Pensher Branch via Fawcett Street Junction through to Hendon, allowing him to ship his coal at the Hudson Dock of the River Wear Commissioners, on which body he was represented. The Earl seems to have begun shipping here in 1864. He also obtained running powers from Pensher North Junction on to the Pontop & South Shields Branch, with a reverse at Washington South Junction, to gain access to Harraton Colliery in order to integrate its railway operation with the rest of the system. It may well be that these powers were granted in a comprehensive agreement between the NER and the Earl of Durham dated 24th August 1871.

These running powers over the Deptford Branch, to South Dock and to Harraton Colliery brought the Lambton Railway's route mileage to about 55 miles, making it one of the largest private railways in the country.

However, the opening of the Deptford route in 1865 spelled the end for the rope-worked system over Grindon Hill, and it seems very likely that this closed almost immediately; the Glebe Engine was sold in 1867 to the adjacent Sunderland Union Workhouse, which erected a new building over the course of the line in the following year. The closure of this route also allowed a major new colliery to be sunk – **NEW HERRINGTON COLLIERY**, later shortened to **HERRINGTON COLLIERY** (NZ 341533), which was opened in 1874 about ¾ mile north-east of the Dorothea Pit. Subsequently a **brickworks** was developed to the west of the colliery. The volume of coal now going out via Pensher was so great that a large interchange yard with the NER was developed north of the station, from which a double line track ran alongside the NER for about ¾ mile before joining the NER at Cox Green Junction, slightly less than ½ mile southwest of Cox Green Station.

Branch and colliery closures

After 1875 a major depression hit the coal, iron & steel and associated industries, and the Earl was of course affected. The first colliery to close was Lumley 2nd Pit, on 13th June 1877, which closed the Lumley branch beyond the 6th Pit, though the track may have remained in place. The next colliery to close was Frankland Colliery about 1878, together with its line south of the River Wear; the rest of this line, south of the Resolution Pit, closed with the end of Brasside Colliery in 1881. In this same year Cocken Colliery closed, all three collieries being officially abandoned in January 1883. However, a NER map dated June 1894 shows the line to Great Lumley village still in place, beginning with sidings, presumably for household coal, at Pea Flatts, the George Pit, the Shop House at Lumley Shops and terminating in the depot at the village. On the 1895 O.S. map the engine houses are shown as disused, and oral evidence from the late 1940s stated that traffic over this section was worked by horses. Curiously, the line to the north between Penshaw and the staiths at Low Lambton was also still in use until at least 1897, for James Paterson's *A Guide to Sunderland*, published in that year, refers to the Painshaw Staiths and its continuing use of keels, presumably for conveying coal down to premises on the river bank at Sunderland lacking rail access. This traffic, together with the branch, seems to have closed soon afterwards. Equally, Harraton Colliery retained its old route down to the staith at Fatfield after its own link to the NER Pontop & South Shields line was built and the running powers

114. 0-6-0 12, whose builders are unknown, although one well-informed source stated that she was built by Blair & Co of Stockton for a railway in Spain, but the order was cancelled and she was purchased for the Lambton Railway about 1868.

115. Nos. 6 to 8 are attributed to Ralph Coulthard & Co of Gateshead. 7 shows the superb livery and finish of the Earl's locomotives in the nineteenth century.

116. 3, BP 550/1865 and unusually still carrying its worksplate, probably at Penshaw.

117. 4, BH 17/1866, but "constructed from material supplied by the Earl of Durham", outside the four-road shed at Philadelphia which had formerly been the Wagon Shops, probably in the 1930s.

mentioned above were acquired; this route seems to have lasted until the 1920s. Meanwhile at Newbottle, although the Success Pit is not listed on official returns of the late 1870s, it must have subsequently re-opened, for it closed in 1909, together with the Jane Pit, although the latter may have ceased to be a coal-drawing shaft before this. The management of the Margaret and Dorothea Pits was subsequently combined, although both remained coal-drawing. Similarly, no date is known for when the Junction Engine was replaced by locomotive working, although this would appear to have happened by the 1880s. Junction Bank remained single line, with all its dangers for locomotive working, until it was doubled in 1920-1921.

However, there was a major re-modelling at the bottom of Junction Bank. No date is known for this, though it would seem unlikely that it happened before the end of rope haulage in the area. From about 100 yards south of the junction with the Wapping/Bowes House branch a new, straighter route was laid down to the Lambton D Pit, with the junctions to Philadelphia and Lumley modified accordingly. In addition, a link was put in from the bottom of Junction Bank round to the Fencehouses line, creating a triangle here, though the map evidence appears to show that this link was subsequently lifted and then re-instated.

North Biddick Colliery

In November 1864 Old Pensher Colliery (Whitefield Pit) (see above) had been taken over by Sir George Elliot, once Chief Agent to the Marquis of Londonderry and latterly a coal owner on his own account. Under Elliot's agreement with the Marchioness of Londonderry he was allowed to run his traffic over the "Union Railway" in order to ship his coal at Seaham, but had to find his own waggons and use his own locomotives as far as the junction with the Londonderry Railway. There is no evidence that he ever owned locomotives here, so it would seem that Lambton Railway locomotives worked his traffic as far as Chilton Moor. It may well be that he did not acquire wagons either, for two photographs of the colliery show Lambton wagons here. It would seem that also in 1864 he took over the Earl's Pensher royalty, presumably to work the two as one unit. He subsequently opened North Biddick Colliery (NZ 307542) near the opposite bank of the River Wear, and linked it by a ¼ mile branch to the NER Pontop & South Shields branch ¼ mile south of Washington South Junction. The colliery's steep railway link up to the NER was worked by a stationary engine situated at the bank head near the NER junction; later this engine was replaced by a new engine built in the pit yard, with a return wheel for the rope at the bank head. Penshaw Colliery was closed in 1879. Whether the Earl acquired the Londonderry share in the "Union Railway" then, or only did so after the closure of the Rainton & Seaham section of the Londonderry Railway in 1896, is not known. Sir George died in December 1893, and in the following year **NORTH BIDDICK COLLIERY** was acquired by the Earl, who then modified his running powers to Harraton Colliery to include working in to North Biddick Colliery.

The Penshaw Foundry branch

The Penshaw Foundry (NZ 327520) had originally been served by the Londonderry Railway (see chapter 10). When the foundry ceased to be served by the former Londonderry line from the north the Earl of Durham linked it to the Lambton Railway near the top of Junction Bank by re-using the trackbed of the former Londonderry line which had run down to Chilton Moor. Latterly the owners were the Penshaw Foundry Co, and it closed between 1910 and 1914.

The Bowes House Farm branch

It would appear that by 1894 the former Wapping branch (see above) had been re-modelled and extended for ¼ mile to **BOWES HOUSE FARM** (NZ 310520). This new line left the Burnmoor - Penshaw line a few yards north of Burnmoor Crossing to run alongside an estate road before curving north to reach the farm. Whilst the reason for the branch can only be speculation, most colliery railways in North East England had vans which carried fodder, known as "choppy", to the collieries for the many hundreds of pit ponies used underground. It may well be that Bowes House Farm was the source of the choppy for the Lambton collieries, and hence the reason for the branch to it. A siding was retained to serve what was probably a coal depot in what was now officially called Burnmoor village, rather than Wapping. In the twentieth century a central **CHOPPY STORE** (NZ 332521) was established at Bunker Hill, behind the company offices there, and was served by a short branch running north from opposite the Margaret Pit coal washery (see below).

More quarrying activities

The next quarry after those at Penshaw described above was almost certainly **NEWBOTTLE QUARRY** (NZ 335514). This lay on the north-west side of Newbottle village and was quarried for limestone. It was served by a ½ mile branch from the north-east to south-east chord at Houghton Junction, at the top of Junction Bank. When quarrying began is not known, but the quarry was closed and the branch lifted by 1895. However, work had re-commenced by 1897 and continued, probably intermittently, at least as long as 1937. Also by 1897 the company had begun **SHERBURN HILL QUARRY**, adjacent to the colliery, and probably served by a short link. This quarry seems to have been short-lived.

The Littletown and Sherburn branch

The developments and closures above left no rope haulage north of Belmont Bank Foot on what latterly was called the Littletown and Sherburn branch. Then probably early in the 1890s a new link was built between Sherburn Hill Colliery and Littletown Colliery, curving round eastwards to join the Littletown branch just below the colliery. Clearly this was done in order to by-pass the Sherburn Hill incline and to allow locomotive working (both lines are shown on the 2nd ed. O.S. map). There would be little point in having a short

118. 15, HCR 169/1875, at Philadelphia, probably in the 1890s.

119. 18, BH 32/1867, at Philadelphia on 17th July 1935; note the LH&JC lettering.

120. The Lambton Engine Works yard, with the Locomotive Repair Shop in the centre and on the left the two-storey Fitting Shop, with the Boiler Shop at the far end, while the Rolling Mills are on the right: one of the 'Mines de Lambton' set of photographs, taken in 1891.

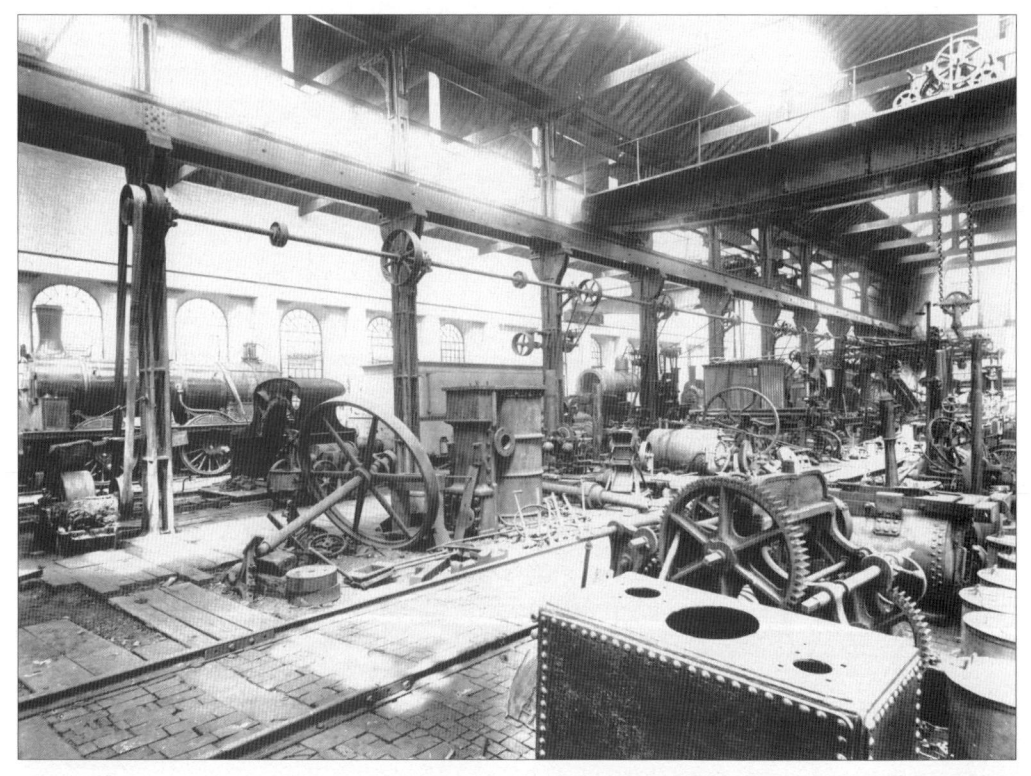

121. The interior of the Locomotive Repair Shop in 1891. The tender engine under repair would appear to be one of Nos.6-8, while the two small "boilers", actually lying upside down, come from two of the compressed air locomotives used underground at Newbottle and Lambton D Collieries.

122. 19, MW 344/1871, at Philadelphia in July 1935.

123. 21, RS 2308/1876, at Philadelphia in 1952, still carrying its brass letters and number.

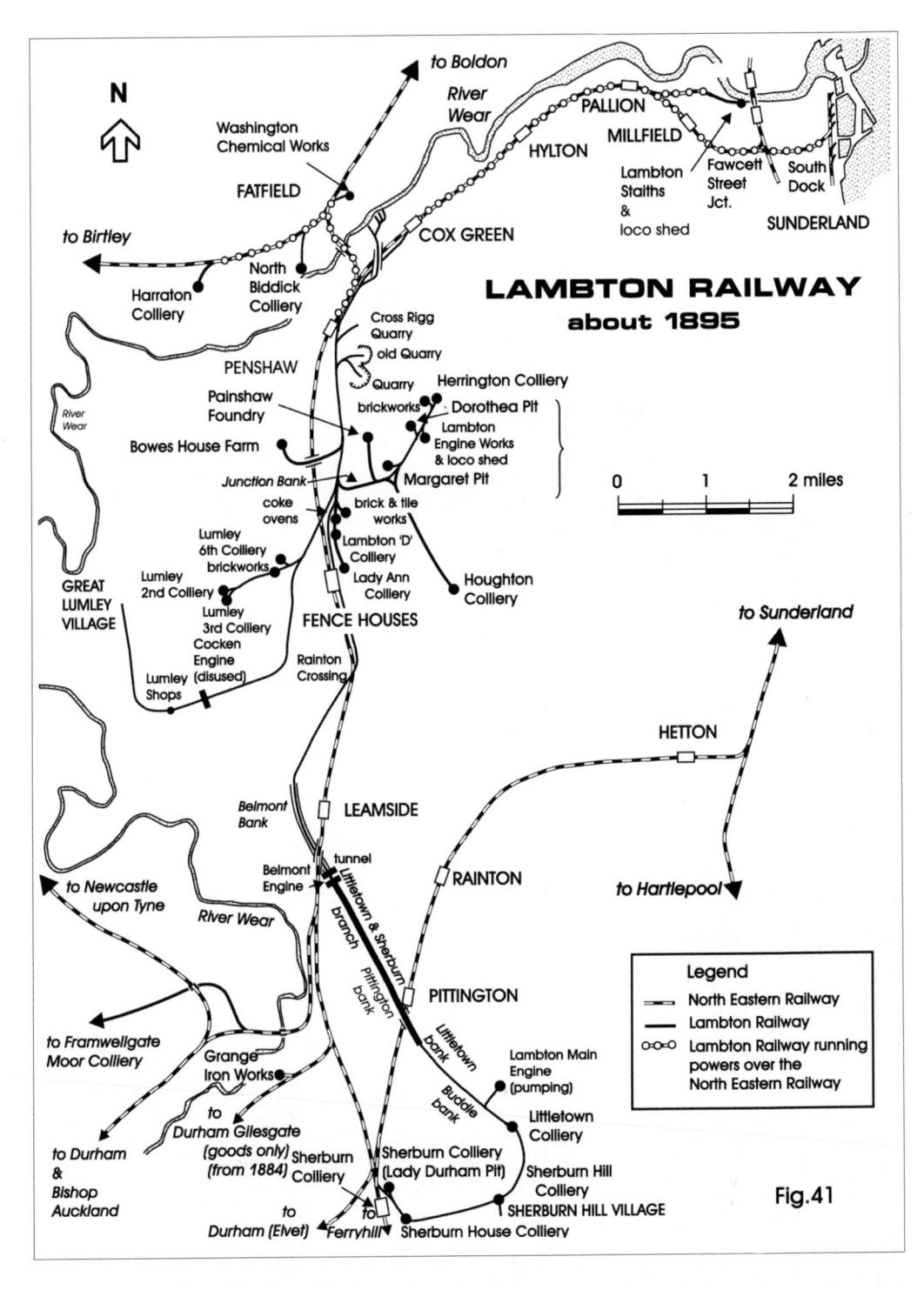

loco-worked section between two rope-worked sections, and almost certainly this new link was part of a scheme which removed rope working between Sherburn House and Sherburn Hill and also between Littletown Colliery, Pittington village and up to the bank head of the Belmont Incline. In these later years oral tradition maintained that the Belmont Engine operated main-and-tail haulage; it would seem to have been abandoned no later than 1904. Given the gradients involved, some powerful locomotives would be needed, and it would seem that at least one tender locomotive was kept at Sherburn from this period. Meanwhile, a set of coke ovens had been built on the north side of Sherburn Colliery by 1895, as had a ¼ mile line serving **Sherburn Hill village**, presumably to carry coal to the houses and perhaps remove night refuse. The NER map of 1894 mentioned above also records that lime from Running Waters Quarry near Shadforth (not owned by the Earl) was loaded in NER wagons at Sherburn House Colliery, though it does not record whether NER or the Earl's locomotives worked this traffic between Sherburn House and the junction with the NER at Sherburn Colliery.

Acquisition by Sir James Joicey

By the mid-1890s the 3rd Earl of Durham faced financial problems in maintaining his huge empire. His collieries needed investment, and he was vulnerable, like all coal owners, to the loss of major contracts for coal. He also intensely disliked Sir James Joicey (1846-1936), whose family's rise to power in the coal industry is outlined in the section describing the Beamish Railway. The dislike was mutual; and Joicey saw his opportunity to become the most powerful coal owner in the North-East. The Earl was forced to sell; only Joicey had the money to buy, and he named his price - £800,000, allegedly a great deal less than their true value. It would appear that the date of sale was 16th May 1896 but that Joicey did not take possession until 1st July 1896. He set up a new company, The Lambton Collieries Ltd, to run this business, but keeping his original company, James Joicey & Co Ltd, separate. By a curious co-incidence, it was in the same year the Marquis of Londonderry gave up his coal interests at Rainton and his railway between Rainton and Seaham was closed, thus providing Joicey with the opportunity to move in there too if he wished. However, if other coal owners now felt that Joicey was satisfied they were to be mistaken.

In 1897 Joicey appointed a new Chief Engineer, Samuel Tulip, and the major investment programme began. The Railway shared in this, for Joicey was well aware of the importance of the railway to the profitability of his business. The first changes were almost certainly the end of shipments from Painshaw Staiths and the work needed to end rope haulage in the Pittington and Sherburn areas, both noted above. Another change soon after 1896 was the replacement of the Black Row Engine on the Lumley branch by locomotive working.

A description of the problems in operating the Railway between June 1904 and January 1906 is given in the *Industrial Railway Record* No.124 (March 1991), also published by the Industrial Railway Society. This also includes the only known reference to a "railway carriage", presumably a vehicle used only for special purposes; the Railway never operated a passenger service of any kind.

By-product coke making

The company was not a major player in the Durham coke industry, but it still made a significant contribution. It was concentrated near Lambton D Pit. In 1902 six of Kay's Patent ovens, about which little is known, were started here, but only lasted three years. These were replaced by 30 Semet-Solvay waste heat ovens, which began production about April 1907. They were joined by 35 Simplex regenerative ovens, which began production about October 1918. The Semet-Solvay ovens were closed down in 1935, the Simplex ovens following early in 1938. To replace all these 15 Collin regenerative ovens were completed in October 1935, to which 15 more were added in July and August 1936 and a further 30 in January 1938. **LAMBTON COKE WORKS** (NZ 317513) also included a by-products plant manufacturing tar, sulphate of ammonia, crude benzole and gas; over 1 million cubic feet of gas was being supplied annually to Sunderland in the mid-1940s (selling surplus gas to local councils was a very profitable business). Close to Lambton D Pit were both a **FIREBRICK WORKS** (NZ 317509) and a large **BRICK & TILE WORKS** (NZ 318510); the latter was well-established by 1891.

The Philadelphia Power Station branch

With the ever-increasing use of electricity the company was amongst the first to build its own electricity generating station. **PHILADELPHIA POWER STATION** (NZ 334520), designed to supply 10,000kW, was built on a site east of the level crossing at Philadelphia and was served by a ¼ mile branch. Construction began in 1905 and the station began generation in 1907 or 1908, serving not only collieries but also the Engine Works and colliery houses, and Sunderland District Tramways, whose depot lay between the Railway and the power station. The firm's then Managing Director, Austin Kirkup, writing in 1946, said "This station, in which the Colliery Company were [sic] at first only shareholders, soon became their sole property. Much of the output was used for central pumping stations to clear waterlogged workings." The company soon decided that the station's operation would be better in the hands of a specialist firm, and on 1st April 1907 it was leased to the **Newcastle upon Tyne Electric Supply Co Ltd** (NESCO), which added the station's distribution system on 1st May 1908 and the whole of the Lambton distribution system on 13th October 1913. Although Lambton locomotives worked the coal into the station, the station had its own battery locomotive from 1918, the first battery locomotive to work in the North-East. For many years it was thought to have been purchased by NESCO, but an early photograph of it suggests that it was almost certainly new to The Lambton & Hetton Collieries Ltd. A special shed was built to house it, and presumably to re-charge the batteries, alongside one of the steam loco sheds at Philadelphia. It was numbered into the Lambton loco list proper in 1925, and lasted until the station was closed in 1936.

Another major development from this period was the reopening as a modern colliery of **LUMLEY 3RD PIT** (NZ 295503), later officially known as **LUMLEY**

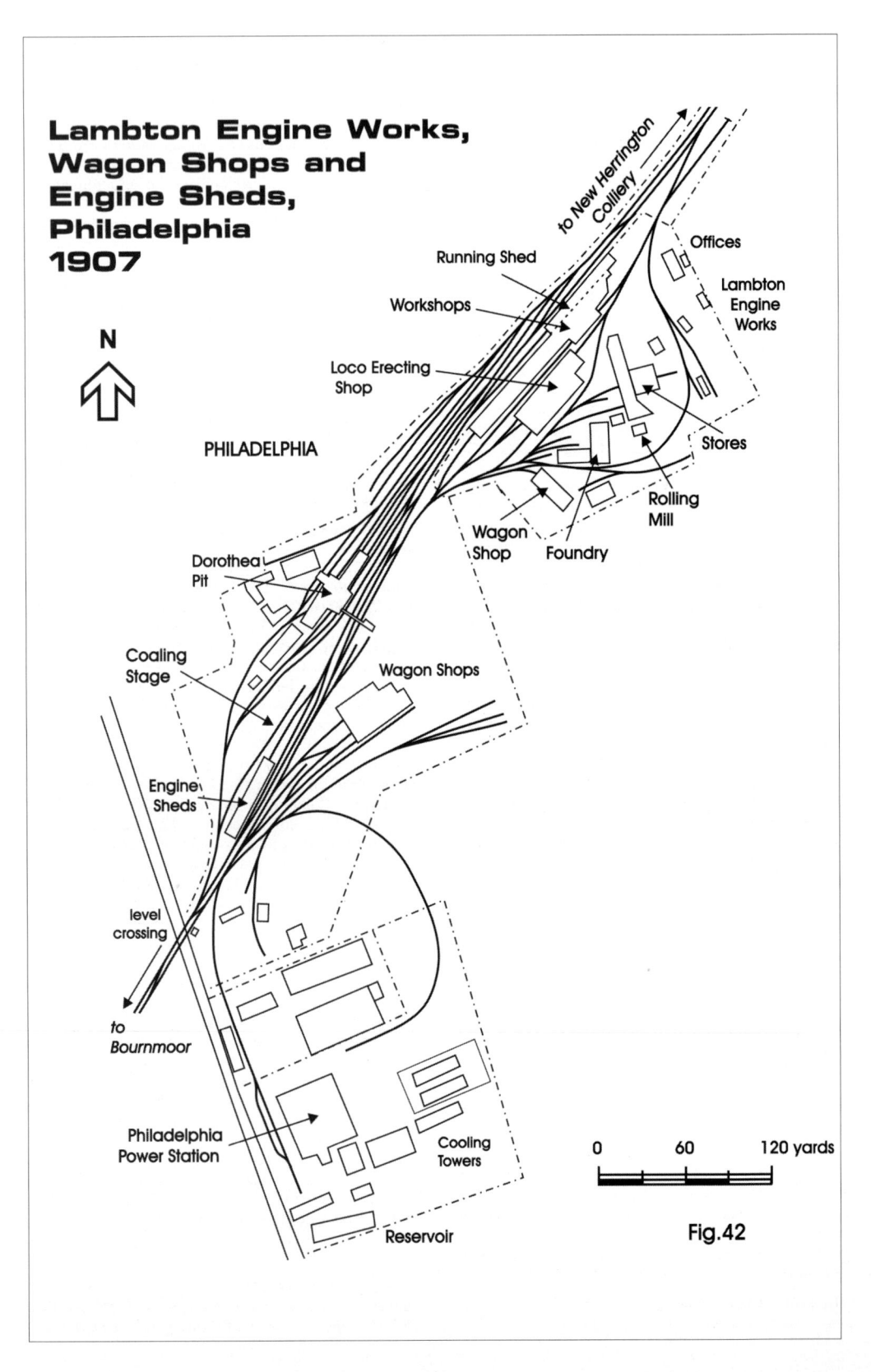

Lambton Engine Works, Wagon Shops and Engine Sheds, Philadelphia 1907

Fig.42

124. The main feature on the Littletown & Sherburn branch, abandoned in 1914, was the Belmont Tunnel at Rainton Gate. This was still intact on 16th October 1949, but was subsequently obliterated in a road-widening scheme.

NEW WINNING. The former branch from near Lumley 6th Pit was re-laid to serve it (1¼ miles) and production began about October 1908. On the debit side the Lady Ann Pit at Burnmoor closed in 1910, almost certainly being combined with Lambton D Colliery.

But the biggest changes were still to come. In the period between 1911 and 1924 Joicey transformed the company, consolidating it in the area between Chester-le-Street, Houghton-le-Spring and Hetton-le-Hole, in addition to the collieries being worked by his original company, James Joicey & Co Ltd.

Lord Joicey's plans for expansion
Already established as the region's most powerful coal owner, Joicey saw clearly the benefits of consolidating a large compact area in central and east Durham under a single management. To the east of the Lambton area lay the large royalty controlled by The Hetton Coal Co Ltd under Sir Lindsay Wood. As noted in the history of the Hetton Railway, as early as 1902 Joicey was considering a link between the Lambton Railway at Herrington and the Hetton Railway at North Moor, clearly part of a larger plan. But the Hetton company was profitable, and Joicey knew that Wood, as autocratic as he, would never sell. He then set about buying secretly enough Hetton shares to make it impossible for Wood to manage the company without Joicey's approval, forcing Wood, in fury, to sell the company to him. The Hetton company, together with its subsidiary, The North Hetton Coal Co Ltd, was wound up on 29th June 1911 and Joicey took possession on 3rd July 1911. In the following month he merged all three businesses into The Lambton & Hetton Collieries Ltd.

The next stage was to rid himself of the Sherburn collieries, which now lay some way south of the new company's main area, and whose coal was less profitable due to the long haul up to Sunderland. Attracting the interest of one of the leading Middlesbrough iron & steel companies proved the best way forward. Littletown Colliery was closed in 1913 and on 1st January 1914 the remaining Sherburn collieries were sold to Sir B. Samuelson & Co Ltd for £180,000. The new owners of course took over the section of the Lambton Railway between Sherburn Hill Colliery and the NER at Sherburn Colliery, together with four Lambton Railway locomotives. The long section north from Sherburn Hill to Fence Houses Station was no longer needed, but it seems to have remained in situ for perhaps as long as ten years, as it is shown on the 3rd edition O.S. map surveyed in 1921.

With the First World War past, the next stage was to consider the position of **SILKSWORTH COLLIERY** (NZ 377541), opened in 1873 and owned by The Londonderry Collieries Ltd, headed by the Marquis of Londonderry. This was rather distant from the other Londonderry collieries, but lay adjacent to the Hetton royalty. It came into Joicey's hands in 1920, probably on 1st February. The final stage was to merge The Lambton & Hetton Collieries Ltd with his original company, James Joicey & Co Ltd, which was done by the larger purchasing the smaller and then the creation, on 26th November 1924, of a new company, The Lambton, Hetton &

125. 24, BH 832/1885, at the Dorothea Pit, Philadelphia, in 1954.

Joicey Collieries Ltd, easily the largest coal company in the North-East. This new company divided its holdings into two Groups, Lambton & Hetton and Joicey, though the latter, not physically connected to the former, seems to have operated almost separately from it. Thus the Beamish Railway and its Engine Works were largely unaltered by the amalgamation, whereas further east railway integration was very much the aim.

The Hetton Railway in 1911
The 7-mile long Hetton Railway between Hetton and Sunderland used locomotives at its southern and northern ends but with seven rope inclines for the 3¾ miles between them. From the **loco shed** near **HETTON COLLIERY** (NZ 360469) locomotives also shunted the coke ovens here, together with **HETTON ENGINE WORKS** (NZ 360469) and **HETTON WAGON SHOPS** (NZ 360468). From Hetton they worked the first 1½ miles through the streets of the town to Dene Bank Foot, also working the 1 mile branch to **ELEMORE COLLIERY** (NZ 346356) and the ¾ mile branch to **EPPLETON COLLIERY** (NZ 364484), with its link to **HIGH DOWNS QUARRY** (NZ 356484), later re-named **EPPLETON QUARRY**. Next came the **Copt Hill Bank**, 832 yards at 1 in 16, worked by the **Byer Engine** (NZ 355497) (Grange Iron Works 125/1876), with fulls and empties being run simultaneously using two drums. The Byer Engine also worked the next 775 yards northwards, a section known as **The Flatt**, to Warden Law Bank Foot, where there was a return wheel for the rope. Sets of double the number were worked alternately, normally using one drum; but if a gale was blowing the wagons would not run properly, and then a fourth drum was used to implement a form of main-and-tail haulage using both drums on this side. Latterly sets of five 10-ton wagons were run on the southern side, with sets of ten on The Flatt.

The next incline, the **Warden Law Bank**, 775 yards at 1 in 20, was worked by the **Warden Law Engine** (NZ 358505) (Thomas Murray 1836), again with sets being worked simultaneously. The Warden Law Engine, at about 600 feet, was the summit of the line. From here four self-acting inclines took the line down to North Moor, **No.1** being 1302 yards at 1 in 30, **No.2** 1224 yards at 1 in 28½, **No.3** 716 yards at 1 in 40 and **No.4** 916 yards at 1 in 36. Locomotives then took over for the final 1¾ miles between North Moor, where there was extensive siding accommodation, and Hetton Staiths. There were tunnels at Durham Road and Farringdon Row, the latter 650 yards long. The two-road **loco shed** (NZ 387564) for this section was situated in Sunderland just south of the bridge carrying the line over Chester Terrace. Hetton Staiths lay immediately upstream of the Lambton Staiths. From south of Hylton Road in Sunderland a ½ mile branch ran northwards, crossing Hylton Road to serve the **Electricity Power Station** (NZ 389574) owned by Sunderland Corporation. There were links with the NER east of Hetton Station on the Durham & Sunderland branch and east of Millfield Station on the Penshaw branch.

The North Hetton branch
The early history of this line can be found in the chapters dealing with the Hetton and Londonderry Railways. **NORTH HETTON COLLIERY** latterly consisted of two pits, the southernmost being the **Moorsley Pit** (NZ 344466). From here the line crossed over the NER Durham & Sunderland branch, to which it was linked by a south to east

126. 27, built as a 2-4-0 tender engine by Robert Stephenson in 1845, was purchased from NER (No.30) as a 0-6-0ST in 1898 and rebuilt to this form at Lambton Engine Works in 1904. She is here at Philadelphia on 21st February 1962, resting at lunchtime from her duties as Houghton Colliery pilot.

chord. Half a mile north-west of the Moorsley Pit was the **Hazard Pit** (NZ 340477), north of which the line divided, one arm going on to serve a coal depot, the other curving north-east to join the Hetton Railway, giving a total length of 1½ miles. Despite the obvious advantages of linking to the locomotive-worked section at the southern end of the Hetton Railway, it would seem almost certain that the junction was at the meetings of the Copt Hill incline, and that rope working on this incline extended down to Rainton Bridge. From 1902 the North Hetton company had had its own locomotive based at the Hazard Pit.

127. 43, purchased, unusually, from the small firm of Grant, Ritchie & Co Ltd at Kilmarnock in 1920, Works No.769, at Philadelphia in 1954.

177

The union of the Lambton and Hetton Railways
It was clearly to the company's advantage for the two railways and the North Hetton branch to be worked as one unit, and eventually they were linked at both their northern and southern ends; but the chronology of how this happened is unclear.

The most extensive development was at the southern end, where the first move seems to have been to take over the former extensive Londonderry leases here. This area included the **MEADOWS PIT** (NZ 324481), initially used as a ventilation shaft, and the nearby **NICHOLSON'S PIT** (NZ 327484), long disused but then re-opened as a

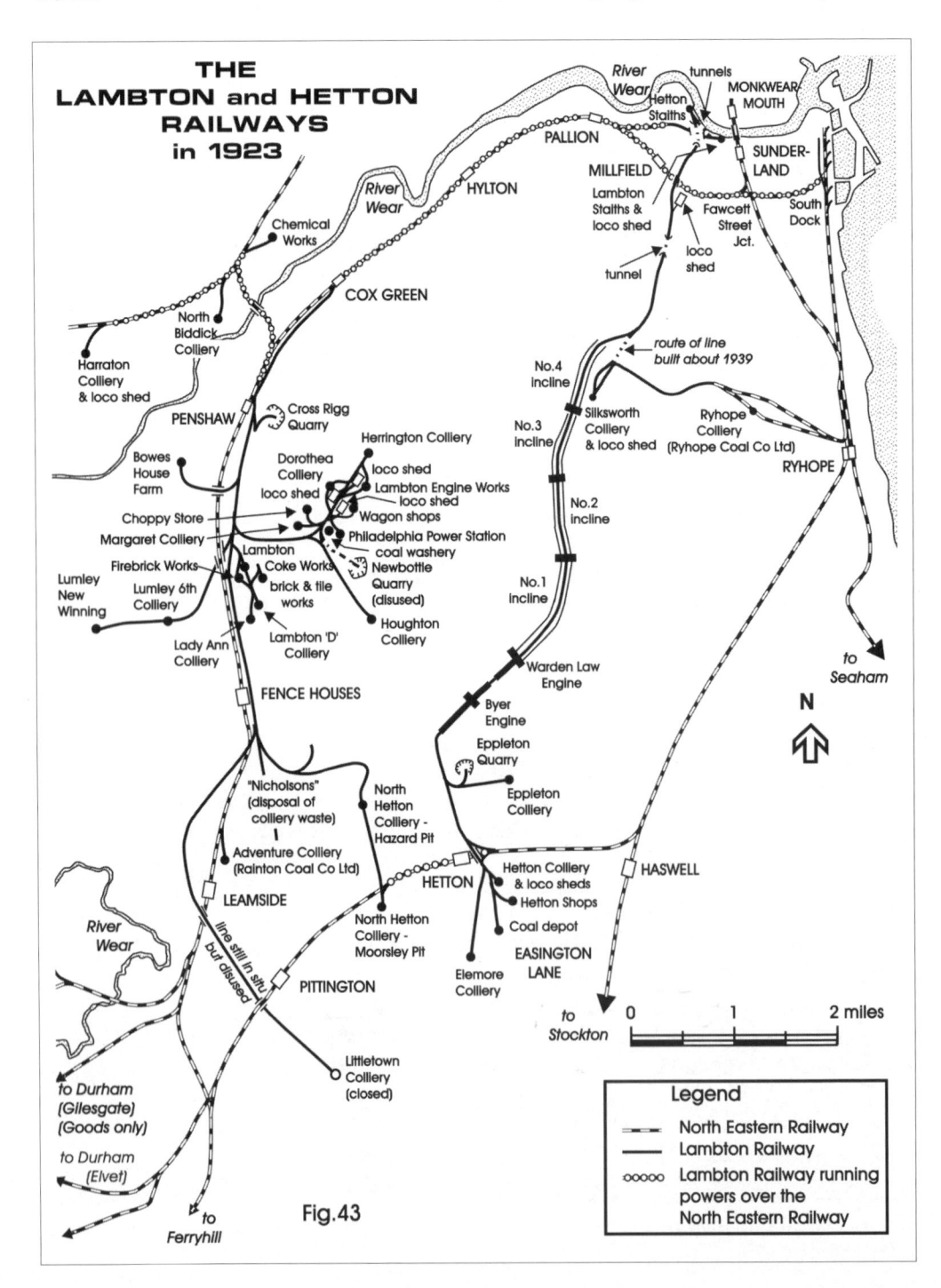

THE LAMBTON and HETTON RAILWAYS in 1923

Fig.43

Legend
- - - North Eastern Railway
——— Lambton Railway
ooooo Lambton Railway running powers over the North Eastern Railway

pumping station. The area between the two was ear-marked as the central area for the dumping of colliery waste, and to service this area a ½ mile branch was laid on the old Londonderry Railway trackbed. This site became colloquially known as **"Nicholson's"** and became sufficiently busy to warrant its own shunting turn. On balance, it would seem likely that this branch was built before the next development, though whether it was built before the merger of the two companies in 1911 is not known.

The next stage was to build a link between the branch to Nicholson's and the North Hetton line. The 3rd edition of the O.S., surveyed in 1915, shows the North Hetton link to the Hetton Railway already lifted, so that by then North Hetton coal must have been going out via the NER. The company then decided to concentrate production at the Hazard Pit, and the Moorsley Pit was closed in December 1915, though the railway between the Hazard Pit and North Hetton Junction was retained. The link to the Hazard Pit from the Lambton Railway, constructed in 1916, meant re-laying the track along the route of the former Londonderry Railway between Nicholson's and Rainton Bridge, and then curving round over the former North Hetton line between Rainton Bridge and the Hazard Pit to join the branch. Finally, in June 1916 the company acquired running powers over the NER between North Hetton Junction and Hetton Colliery Junction (involving a reverse at North Hetton) in order to convey Hetton coal to the coke ovens at the D Pit and to the Philadelphia Generating Station and Lambton coal to the Hetton coke ovens.

At their northern ends the two railways were joined by the simple process of driving a tunnel through the rock dividing the two sets of staiths. This was driven to the north of the tunnel to the Deptford branch, with a reverse on the Hetton side to gain access to that railway's higher level. The connection of the two staiths allowed for further rationalisation in the 1930s.

With these links the two Railways were worked as one unit. For a time the Hetton locomotives stayed on their own line, and they were not re-numbered into the Lambton list until 1919. But new locomotives were soon being ordered for Hetton, and Hetton's chaldron wagons were gradually replaced with Lambton wagons.

Silksworth Colliery and its branches
Silksworth Colliery, acquired in 1920, was originally served by a 2½ mile extension of the Londonderry Railway (Seaham & Sunderland section) branch to Ryhope Colliery. When the NER had taken over the Londonderry Railway in October 1900 the ownership of the section of line between Ryhope and Silksworth was specifically excluded, though the NER continued to work the traffic. The ownership of this line thus passed to The Lambton & Hetton Collieries Ltd. However, in 1911, whilst rebuilding the colliery, Londonderry Collieries had purchased a locomotive to shunt the colliery itself. This passed into Lambton stock and was immediately re-numbered. However, despite being close to the Hetton Railway, the company did not link the two until 1938-1939, when a ½ mile branch, steeply graded at 1 in 40, was built

128. 45, HL 2932/1912, acquired from Londonderry Collieries Ltd with Silksworth Colliery in 1920, shunts at Lumley Colliery on 7th January 1966. Note the chocks to stop wagons running away over the road.

between the colliery and about ¼ mile north of North Moor yard. This allowed Silksworth coal to be shipped through Lambton Staiths, but it is not known whether this was started before nationalisation in 1947.

An important improvement undertaken in 1920-1921 was the re-grading and doubling of Junction Bank, between Bournmoor and Newbottle, which had become a serious bottleneck to traffic. About the same time a **COAL WASHERY** (NZ 333519) was built at Newbottle on the opposite side of the line to the Margaret Pit, which presumably generated considerable traffic, with coal from the various pits being brought here for washing and the washed coal taken away. This work was followed by changes to the arrangements with the LNER between Penshaw and Cox Green. The relief ("independent") lines between the two places were replaced by a new double line "mineral branch" on the southern side of the LNER lines and apparently owned by LHJC, with the LNER's Cox Green Junction and Cox Green signal boxes being replaced by a new box at Cox Green Station, while Penshaw North Junction was also re-modelled. These new arrangements, which considerably simplified the working for both companies, were opened in November 1931.

By this time the whole of the "main line" between Herrington Colliery, Burnmoor, Penshaw and Cox Green was double track (and fully signalled), as was the route from Burnmoor through Fencehouses down to Nicholsons.

New locomotive sheds and repair facilities

The single line loco shed at Lambton Engine Works soon proved inadequate as the number of locomotives expanded. To assist the situation a large complex of buildings was gradually developed between the Dorothea Pit and Philadelphia level crossing. The 1st edition of the O.S. maps shows what may well have been two small loco sheds here. By the early years of the twentieth century a coal gantry had been built here between the main line and the southern entry to the Dorothea Pit yard, possibly alongside another shed building. With further accommodation needed, in 1917 the old shed on the Dorothea side of the line was replaced by a two-road shed incorporating the coal gantry with its two coaling shutes, which became the main running shed, while on the opposite side of the line was another one-road building. A further small shed was subsequently built alongside the one-road shed to house the battery loco used at the Electricity Works, this shed thus becoming known as the "electric shed". With the construction of the new Wagon Shop to the east of the Engine Works in the 1930s, the old shops, only a few yards from the loco foreman's office, were converted into a large 4-road loco shed, at last providing covered accommodation for the majority of the still-growing fleet. Meanwhile, the original shed at the Engine Works was expanded first to the north and then after 1939 also to the south and became the shed for washing out boilers.

In Sunderland the small loco shed at Lambton Staiths and the two-road shed on the Hetton Railway south of Durham Road were replaced in 1919 by a large two road shed, **LAMBTON STAITHS LOCO SHED** (NZ 393574), at Galley's Gill, near to the Deptford branch tunnel. Up to eight locomotives were allocated here, working both

129. 51, the four-wheeled battery electric loco used to shunt the Philadelphia Power Station until its closure in 1936.

130. 54, built by the Taff Vale Railway at its West Yard Works at Cardiff in 1897 as Taff Vale 64, at Lambton Staiths, Sunderland, in 1954.

131. 57, the last of the 0-6-2Ts built for the Railway, HL 3834/1934, at Philadelphia on 2nd October 1958, in the early 1950s livery of lime green with black lining edged white and gold lettering shaded red.

132. With the end of the Second World War the Railway began to acquire 'Austerity' locomotives: 58, VF 5299/1945, stands outside the Washing Out Shed (the Railway's original loco shed) at Philadelphia while 51, RSH 7101/1943, comes past with a train from Herrington Colliery, on 18th April 1968.

133. Two of the standard RSH 16in 0-6-0STs were also acquired, 63, RSHN 7600/1949, coming from South Hetton in 1958. Here it stands outside the former "electric shed" on 5th August 1966.

134. 20, RS 2260/1876, now with a double side-window cab, has come up Junction Bank from Burnmoor with a train of empties and passes the signals protecting Philadelphia level crossing on 30th April 1952.

135. Looking north from near the same point as the photograph above on 16th March 1966, with Philadelphia Crossing and its signal box, the loco sheds beyond and Lambton Engine Works in the distance to the right.

136. 26, the last of the three six-coupled tender engines built at Lambton Engine Works, in 1894, but now carrying one of the new wedge-shaped cabs adopted by the Works from the early 1950s and also fitted with a round-topped tender, passes between the Philadelphia loco sheds, with Dorothea Colliery behind, in the mid 1950s.

sets of staiths, together with the Hetton main line as far as North Moor and the branch to Silksworth Colliery after 1939. The purchase of five 0-6-2Ts from the GWR in 1929-1931 allowed the company to provide more powerful locomotives for this section. Locomotives on main line working from Penshaw could be watered here, but there were no coaling facilities other than for the shed's own allocation. The old Hetton shed was used for repairs for about a further five years, and was then demolished.

One four-coupled saddletank was also outstationed at Harraton and two at Silksworth. It is probable that another was kept at North Biddick Colliery until it closed, but this is not confirmed.

Lambton Engine Works was developed into a very major facility, growing throughout the later nineteenth century and well into the twentieth. A large Fitting Shop was built in 1882 capable of handling five or six repairs at a time. Indeed, so good were the facilities that the Engine Works built three 0-6-0 tender locomotives between 1877 and 1894 and the works also made its own new boilers, although they were more commonly bought in. The rolling mills were dispensed with and other facilities developed, including both iron and brass foundries, enabling the Works to handle not only work for the collieries, coke ovens and railways but also the company's fleet of ships and its hundreds of houses. Although all major work was carried out at the Engine Works, workshop facilities were also established at Littletown Colliery to serve the Sherburn group of collieries and the locomotives working there. After the acquisition of The Hetton Coal Co Ltd the Engine Works at Hetton was retained, and between the Wars both a new loco fitting shop and a new wagon shop were built there. Parts of the Hetton Works was closed in the winter of 1934-1935 as an economy measure and its work, together with much of its equipment and some of the men, transferred to Philadelphia; but wagon repairs at Hetton continued, and locomotive repairs, if they were stopped for a time, subsequently resumed (see chapter 8).

The wagon fleet and its repair

The gradual replacement of the 4½ ton chaldron waggons by 10/10½ ton wooden hopper wagons was begun in March 1903. By January 1905 the Railway had 719 of these, all former NER wagons, and the Railway's stock was capable of handling 13,000 tons of coal. By this time the company had built quite a large four-road **WAGON SHOP** (NZ 335523) on the southern edge of the Engine Works. The acquisition of the Hetton Railway came with a further large fleet of chaldrons, and as these did not need to work over the NER, they survived longer, the last being withdrawn in 1931. To handle this combined fleet, between the wars a large new **WAGON SHOP** (NZ 337524) was built to the east of Lambton Engine Works. This had three roads holding in total sixty wagons, with two roads for running repairs and one for major overhauls. By 1938 the company was building its own 12-ton wooden hopper wagons, as well as developing a fleet of over a hundred vans and other types of wagon for general maintenance. 67 hours was allowed for building a coal wagon, and two teams of men turned out two per week. The company also built a new Wagon Shop at Hetton, which had two roads and normally handled between 60-80 running repairs and two heavy overhauls per week. For many years, probably since the latter part of the nineteenth century, there was also a small wagon shop at Lambton Staiths, near No.9 staith. This had begun life as a tin chapel, though it was subsequently cladded in brick and then completely rebuilt. It was a one-road building capable of handling five wagons at a time and dealt with wagons arriving at the staiths and needing repair before being allowed to travel out on to the NER/LNER. In later years the building became a first aid facility, and wagons were repaired in the open air on a siding.

By 1937 Lambton Engine Works employed 228 people, which rose to 303 in 1946, with the Wagon

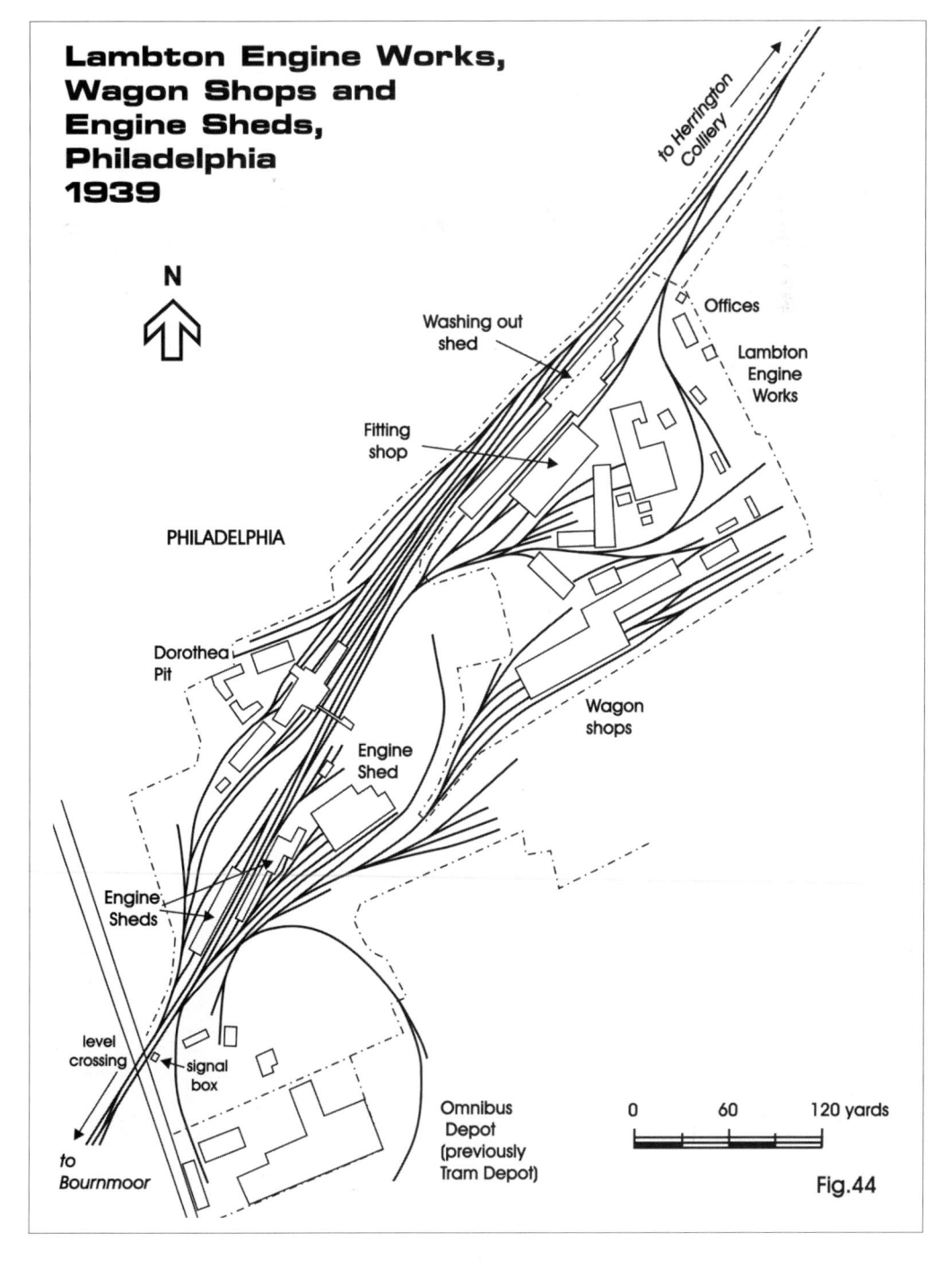

Fig.44

Shops adding 37 in 1937 rising to 45 in 1946, out of a total of 11,173 people employed overall by the company in the last year before nationalisation.

Signalling on the Railway

The 2nd edition Ordnance Survey map, dated 1898, shows signal posts at various places on the system, with no fewer than five around the bottom of Junction Bank at Burnmoor. A building here in the vee of the junction between the lines from Fencehouses and Lumley was reputed in later years to have once been a signalbox. The first "modern" signal box on the Railway was built about 50 yards to the north at **Burnmoor Crossing** in the summer of 1904, with a 22-lever frame being supplied by McKenzie & Holland Ltd of Worcester.

It would seem likely that at least three other signal boxes were built before 1914. One was situated in the vee of the junction between the line southwards from Burnmoor to Fencehouses and the Lumley branch, to control traffic here and at the bottom of Junction Bank. The second was built at the top of Junction Bank, at the points for the north-east/south-east curve to the Houghton branch, while a third was installed at Philadelphia Crossing, just south of the loco sheds. Not far from the Lambton Staiths tunnel on the NER Deptford Branch there was a further box, Deptford Junction Signal Box, which, although it also controlled access to other works and sidings on the remainder of the Deptford branch as well as the tunnel entrance to Lambton Staiths, was from at least 1911 operated by a Lambton signalman.

Important signalling installations were resumed after 1920, the most important arising from the

137. The interior of Junction Bank Top signal box, once called the Crossing Minders Signal Box, in June 1967, with its rotary train describer modified to act also as a 3-position double-line block signalling instrument (the controls were off picture).

LAMBTON & HETTON COLLIERIES JUNCTION BANK

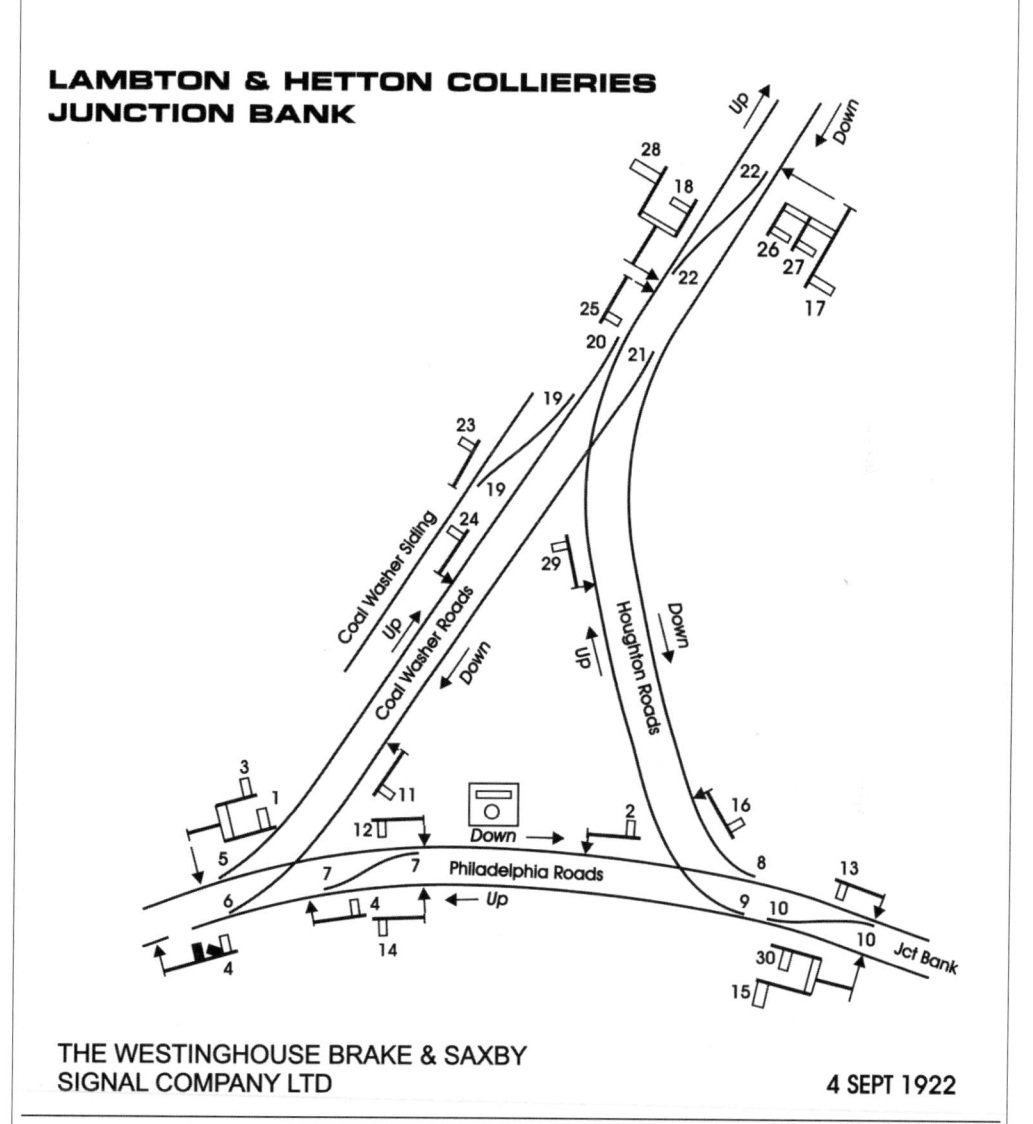

THE WESTINGHOUSE BRAKE & SAXBY SIGNAL COMPANY LTD

4 SEPT 1922

Fig.45

INTERLOCKING DRAWING L20053 BY WESTINGHOUSE (FOR "CROSSING MINDER'S CABIN")	27 JUNE 1922
SIGNAL BOX DIAGRAM, REDRAWN FROM A COPY AND A PHOTOGRAPH BY JOHN TALBOT	
FRAME TYPE 1914 "A". APPARATUS No.9306 — 12 SIGNAL READS 2 WAYS. PLUS EXTRA SEQUENTIAL LOCKING ONLY ON 1, 15, 17, 30 (NEED 2, 14, 16, 29 RESPECTIVELY)	
ADDITIONAL SLOTTED ARM ADDED, DRAWING NCBS 69-08	BY 1969
No.18 DISPENSED WITH, LEVER MADE SPARE, DRAWING NCBS 69-09	BY 1969

138. 'Austerity' 7, HE 3820/1954, passes the signal box at the top of Junction Bank, with signals 11 and 14 visible (see Fig.45) and the branch to Houghton Colliery curving away left.

much-needed doubling of Junction Bank between Newbottle and Burnmoor and the first section of the Houghton branch. The box at the top of the bank was replaced by a much larger one inside the junction triangle. This box, curiously called Crossing Minder's Cabin in the Westinghouse records but latterly known as Junction Bank Top Signal Box, contained 30 levers and was completed on 27th June 1922. Signalboxes controlling all three sides of a triangle were very rare in Britain, and the one here was the only example on an industrial railway. Curiously, this junction seems never to have had a regular name, and was also known as Houghton Junction, Philadelphia Junction or simply "The Triangle". Burnmoor Crossing box was enlarged to 28 levers on 2nd July 1924, almost certainly allowing the earlier box at the junction of the Lumley branch to be closed. Near the other end of this branch a small four-lever box was completed on 1st April 1925 to guard the road which crossed the exit from Lumley Sixth Colliery's yard. Meanwhile, the Philadelphia Crossing box's eight levers were re-locked on 16th February 1923, and according to Westinghouse records a four-lever box was installed at "Herrington Crossing" on 11th January 1926, although it is not shown on the 1939 O.S. map and in later days the men could not remember it. There is also said to have been a signal box between the Penshaw Weigh Office and Penshaw Station. This seems likely to have been in the "Dispatch Office", which contacted either Penshaw North Signal Box or Control at Newcastle upon Tyne to advise on Lambton trains running to Harraton or to the Staiths. There was also a signalbox on the branch to Harraton Colliery, guarding a road level crossing, about ¼ mile from the main line. The final box of this period was installed on the Copt Hill incline of the Hetton Railway, where it is discussed. In addition, by 1920 there were a further sixteen signal posts, mostly at level crossings and operated from the crossing cabins, around the main system, and another one at Lambton Staiths.

Closures of the 1920s and 1930s

Lumley New Winning closed in the late summer of 1924 (although it was not abandoned until August 1928), together with the Lumley branch west of the 6th Pit, although in 1937 the latter gained a new customer with the opening of a brickworks nearby (NZ 307503) owned by Lumley Bricks Ltd, with the coal being delivered to the kilns direct from the pit by a short tramway. The long-lived Margaret Pit was closed about July 1927. North Biddick Colliery followed in June 1931 and North Hetton Colliery in March 1935, although the link between the Lambton and the Hetton Railways via North Hetton was retained until the closure of the Hetton Railway in 1959. Probably in the early 1930s the old Hetton Staiths were demolished and replaced by two very high staiths capable of handling five wagons each simultaneously, the fastest-loading in the North-East.

The Philadelphia Generating Station, latterly owned by The North-Eastern Electric Supply Co Ltd, was closed on 22nd August 1936. However, in this same year there was a throw-back to the past, when the **MEADOWS PIT** at Rainton (NZ 324481), the former Londonderry pit, was re-opened for man-riding, and converted for coal production ten years later. Eppleton Quarry was still being worked in 1937, but may well have closed down a few years afterwards. Another casualty was Lumley 6th Brickworks, which closed in 1937. The Lambton brickworks near the D Pit closed because of the Second World War in 1940; it was re-opened in 1946. The changes on the traffic side have been noted above.

The Railway's locomotives

Almost nothing is known about the first locomotives that were used on the Railway other than what was passed down by oral tradition. According to the Supplement to the *Mining Journal* dated 4th April 1871 the Earl had 18 locomotives at this date. However, whatever records of these early locomotives had once existed at Lambton Engine Works, they did not survive into the last forty years of the twentieth century, and even though a few photographs survive they tell us little about some of the builders. This problem is made worse by the facilities at Lambton Engine Works, for the photographs suggest a strong "house" look to boilers, cabs and splashers, with the result that the inside cylinder tender engines look very similar. It seems very likely that the numbering system was introduced sometime between 1866 and 1870, with the tender locomotives being numbered first and then the tank locomotives. One source gives the original Nos.10-13 as listed below, which if correct would make it likely that No.9 was the loco rebuilt by Richardson in 1852 (and thus likely to be an early disposal); but some of the other locomotives listed in the first section must have been disposed of very quickly if the fleet did indeed consist of 18 locomotives in 1871 (i.e., before the arrival of No.19), and any attempt to re-construct the original list of Nos.15-17 can be no more than speculation. Repair books dating from before the First World War did survive at Lambton Engine Works until the 1970s, and these proved useful in establishing information about some of the locomotives at that time, but so far as is known these too are now lost.

For many years the Railway used 0-6-0 tender locomotives for its main line work; but in 1904 it followed developments on the NER and on the railways in South Wales by purchasing its first 0-6-2T. Whilst the tender locomotives continued in use, the 0-6-2Ts steadily increased in number, latterly also sharing the traffic on the northern end of the Hetton Railway.

Although the name "Lambton Railway" was official and was being used as early as the 1850s, this was never carried on the locomotives. The original locomotives carried E and D with the locomotive number between them, all in brass, with the tenders too having E X D painted on them. By the 1890s the latter practice had been discontinued, presumably because of the nuisance this caused when tenders had to be changed. The tradition of brass letters continued under The Lambton Collieries Ltd, the letters becoming L and C. Later the letters and numbers were simply painted on, e.g. L. & H.C., then L.H.J.C, or occasionally L.H. & J.C. On the tender locomotives this lettering went on the tender, leaving just the number on the cab side. However, some locomotives were still carrying their original plates in 1947. Almost all locomotives carried the simple number on the side of the locomotive, latterly on the cab, but carried "No.X" on the front buffer beam.

The locomotives were always treated as a common pool and moved around as required. However, this was always confined to the Lambton and Hetton Railways; and whilst some Hetton locomotives were subsequently transferred to the Joicey collieries after the amalgamation in 1924, the locomotives on the Beamish Railway and at the other Joicey collieries were always regarded as completely separate, both in numbering and for repairs.

For the locomotives which were noted as working at Hetton loco shed and at North Hetton Colliery between 1911 and 1947 please see the chapter on the Hetton Railway.

Gauge : 4ft 8½in

PRINCE ALBERT	0-6-0	OC	Hackworth		c1842	New	s/s
EARL GREY						(a)	s/s
LAMBTON CASTLE						(a)	s/s
ALBERT EDWARD	0-6-0		RWH	308	1839	(b)	s/s
-	0-6-0	IC				(a)	
	reb		TR	213	1852		(1)
-	0-6-0	IC	TR	236	1853	New	(1)
-	0-6-0	IC	TR	251	1854	New	(1)
-	0-6-0ST	IC	H&C	21	1865	New	(2)
DURHAM	0-6-0ST	IC	MW	152	1865	New	(3)
-	0-6-0ST	IC	H&C	76	1866	New	(4)
-	0-6-0	IC				(c)	
reb	0-6-0ST	IC	H&C	98	1870		(3)

(a) origin and identity unknown
(b) ex The Wingate Coal Co, Wingate Grange Colliery, Wingate
(c) origin and identity unknown; H&C records for this order give "converting 17 x 24 into a Tank Engine for Earl of Durham", presumably from a tender engine

(1) presumably included in numbering scheme below, which see
(2) presumably included in numbering scheme below; to HCR; rebuilt as HCR 170/1875 and re-sold to Commondale Brick & Tile Co, Commondale, Yorkshire (NR), 7/1875
(3) presumably included in numbering scheme below; s/s
(4) presumably included in numbering scheme below; to HCR; rebuilt as HCR 171/1875 and re-sold to Stanton Iron Works Co Ltd, Teversal Colliery, Nottinghamshire, 11/1875

1		0-6-0	IC	H&C	71	1866	New	(1)
2		0-6-0	IC	H&C	72	1866	New	(2)
2		0-6-0ST	IC	RWH	1969	1884	(a)	Scr c/1939
3		0-6-0	IC	BP	550	1865	New	(1)
4		0-6-0	IC	BH	17	1866	(b)	(1)
5		0-6-0	IC	H&C	30	1865	New	Scr c/1909
5		0-6-2T	IC	RS	3377	1909	New	(1)
6		0-6-0	IC				(c)	(1)
7		0-6-0	IC				(c)	(1)
8		0-6-0	IC				(c)	(1)
9		0-6-0	IC				(d)	s/s
9		0-6-0	IC	Earl of Durham		1877	New	(1)
10		0-6-0	IC	TR?			(e)	Scr c/1909
10		0-6-2T	IC	RS	3378	1909	New	(1)
11		0-6-0	IC				(f)	(3)
11		0-4-0ST	OC	HC	1412	1920	New	(1)
12		0-6-0	IC	Blair		1865?	(g)	Scr c/1912
12		0-4-0ST	OC	HL	2789	1912	New	(1)
13		0-4-0ST	OC	H&C	79	1866	New	(2)
13		0-4-0ST	OC	HL	3055	1914	New	(1)
14		0-6-0ST	IC	H&C	78	1866	New	(2)
14		0-4-0ST	OC	HL	3056	1914	New	(1)
15							(h)	s/s
15		0-4-0ST	OC	HCR	169	1875	New	(1)

16							(h)	s/s
16		0-4-0ST	OC	H&C	96	1870	New	(1)
17							(h)	s/s
17		0-4-0ST	OC	HCR	130	1873	New	(4)
17		0-4-0ST	OC	MW	2023	1923	New	(1)
18		0-6-0	OC	BH	32	1867	(j)	
	reb 0-6-0ST	OC						
		reb	HL	1491	1935			(1)
19		0-4-0ST	OC	MW	344	1871	New	(1)
20		0-6-0	IC	RS	2260	1876	New	(1)
21		0-4-0ST	OC	RS	2308	1876	New	(1)
22		0-4-0ST	OC	HC	230	1881	New	(1)
23		0-4-0ST	OC	BH	688	1882	New	(1)
24		0-4-0ST	OC	BH	832	1885	New	(1)
25		0-6-0	IC	Earl of Durham		1890	New	(1)
26		0-6-0	IC	Earl of Durham		1894	New	(1)
27		2-4-0	IC	RS	491	1845		
	reb 0-6-0	IC	Ghd		1864			
	reb 0-6-0ST	IC	Ghd		1873	(k)		
	reb 0-6-0T	IC	LEW		1904			(1)
28		0-4-0ST	OC	HL	2530	1902	New	(1)
29		0-6-2T	IC	K	4263	1904	New	(1)
30		0-6-2T	IC	K	4532	1907	New	(1)
31		0-6-2T	IC	K	4533	1907	New	(1)
32		0-4-0ST	OC	HL	2826	1910	New	(1)
33		0-4-0ST	OC	HL	2827	1910	New	(5)
34		0-4-0ST	OC	HL	2954	1912	New	(1)
35		0-4-0ST	OC	HL	3024	1913	New	(1)
36	(HAZARD)	0-4-0ST	OC	P	615	1896	(m)	(1)
37		0-6-0ST	IC	RWH	1430	1868	(n)	(6)
38		0-6-0ST	IC	RWH	1478	1870	(p)	(7)
39		0-6-0ST	IC	RWH	1422	1867		
		reb	HL	2378		(q)		(8)
40	(later No.40)	0-6-0ST	IC	RS	1919	1869	(r)	
		reb	HL	1182	1930			(9)
41		0-6-0T	OC	KS	3074	1917	(s)	(1)
42		0-6-2T	IC	RS	3801	1920	New	(1)
43		0-4-0ST	OC	GR	769	1920	New	(1)
44		0-6-0ST	OC	MW	1934	1917	(t)	(1)
45		0-6-0ST	IC	HL	2932	1912	(u)	(1)
46		0-6-0T	IC	MW	1813	1913	(v)	(1)
47		0-4-0ST	OC	HL	3543	1923	New	(1)
48		0-4-0ST	OC	HL	3544	1923	New	(1)
49		0-4-0ST	OC	MW	2035	1924	New	(1)
50		0-4-0ST	OC	MW	2036	1924	New	(1)
51	(No.1 until /1925)	4wBE		DK		1918	(w)	Scr c/1937
52		0-6-2T	IC	NR	5408	1899	(x)	(1)
53		0-6-2T	IC	Cdf	302	1894	(y)	(1)
54		0-6-2T	IC	Cdf	311	1897	(z)	(1)
55		0-6-2T	IC	K	3069	1887	(aa)	(1)
56		0-6-2T	IC	K	3580	1894	(ab)	(1)
57		0-6-2T	IC	HL	3834	1934	New	(1)
58		0-6-0ST	IC	VF	5299	1945	(ac)	(1)
59		0-6-0ST	IC	VF	5300	1945	(ad)	(1)

At Vesting Day on 1st January 1947 it is believed that Nos. 11, 12, 13, 14, 32, 34, 48 and 58 were at Hetton loco shed, and Nos. 17, 23, 35, 49, 50, 53, 55 and 56 were at Lambton Staiths loco shed. All of the remainder were allocated to the Lambton loco sheds at Philadelphia except for those working at Harraton and Silksworth Collieries; which these were is not known.

(a) ex Hetton Railway, 2; included in Lambton Railway list, 1919
(b) BH records give "constructed from material supplied by the Earl of Durham"; one source suggested that it might be a rebuild of a RS loco
(c) almost certainly second-hand, origin unknown, in /1864; one source suggested that the locomotives were built between 1853 and 1855
(d) existence assumed, but identity and origin unknown; could have been one of the TR locomotives above

(e) precise identity and origin unknown; Samuel Tulip (see text), interviewed in 1950, said that "some Richardson engines were at work in his day"; photographic evidence suggests that this loco could well have been one of them; one source suggests that it was TR 236/1853

(f) identity and origin unknown; Samuel Tulip (see text), interviewed in 1950, said that "some Richardson engines were at work in his day", and one source suggests that it was TR 251/1854; however, photographs of the locomotive would appear not to show any known Richardson features

(g) one source stated that 12 was a Blair loco, while another stated that the loco was built for a Spanish railway, but that it was not delivered, and was acquired by the Earl of Durham c/1868; equally, given Samuel Tulip's remark quoted in (f) and (g), this could be another Richardson engine, perhaps the one rebuilt as TR 213/1852

(h) the existence of these locomotives is assumed, if the statement about the introduction of the numbering scheme above is correct

(j) BH records give "rebuild of loco for Earl of Durham"; the origin and identity of the original loco are unknown

(k) ex NER, 8/1898. This loco was built new as a 2-4-0 for the Newcastle & Darlington Railway, No.22. It became NER 30 when the NER was formed in 1854, subsequently being re-numbered 1899 and then 1761. It was rebuilt as an 0-6-0 in 1864 and as an 0-6-0ST in 1873. Built new with 14in x 22 in cylinders and 5ft 7¼in wheels, it had 15in x 20in cylinders and 4ft 0½in wheels when purchased

(m) ex The North Hetton Coal Co Ltd, with North Hetton Colliery, 3/7/1911; it may have run as NORTH HETTON No.1 for a time; re-numbered in 1919

(n) ex Hetton Railway, 6; re-numbered in 1919

(p) ex Hetton Railway, 8; re-numbered in 1919

(q) ex Hetton Railway, 5; re-numbered in 1919

(r) ex Hetton Railway, 7; re-numbered in 1919

(s) ex ROD, 606, c/1920

(t) ex War Office, Inland Waterways & Docks Dept, Sandwich, Kent, 23, c/1920

(u) ex The Londonderry Collieries Ltd, with Silksworth Colliery, No.1 SILKSWORTH, c2/1920

(v) ex Ebbw Vale Steel, Iron & Coal Co Ltd, Monmouthshire, (exact location uncertain), 1/1923

(w) almost certainly New to The Lambton & Hetton Collieries Ltd; purchased to shunt the Philadelphia Power Station; numbered into Lambton Railway stock in 1925. Note: the "works number" 9537 quoted in Lambton records is erroneous

(x) ex GWR, 426, withdrawn in 1/1927 and put on Sales List; acquired per R.H.Longbotham & Co Ltd, 4/1929; originally Taff Vale Railway O2 class, 85

(y) ex GWR, 448, sold from running stock to R.H.Longbotham & Co Ltd, 2/1930, for LHJC; originally Taff Vale Railway, O class, 26

(z) ex GWR, 475, sold from running stock to R.H.Longbotham & Co Ltd, 2/1930, for LHJC; originally Taff Vale Railway, O1 class, 64

(aa) ex GWR, 159, sold from running stock to R.H.Longbotham & Co Ltd, 2/1931, for LHJC; originally Cardiff Railway, 28

(ab) ex GWR, 156, sold from running stock to R.H.Longbotham & Co Ltd, 2/1931, for LHJC; originally Cardiff Railway, 1

(ac) ex War Department, Longmoor Military Railway, Hampshire, 75309, 4/1946; arrived by 11/5/1946

(ad) ex War Department, Longmoor Military Railway, Hampshire, 75310, 4/1946; arrived by 11/5/1946

(1) to NCB No.2 Area, with Railway, 1/1/1947

(2) to Sir B.Samuelson & Co Ltd, with the Sherburn collieries, 1/1/1914

(3) last recorded repair at Lambton Engine Works was 6/1914; s/s

(4) last recorded repair at Lambton Engine Works was 7/1921; s/s

(5) loaned to William Doxford & Sons Ltd, Pallion, Sunderland, during 1939-1945 War, and returned; to No.2 Area, with Railway, 1/1/1947

(6) to Tanfield Lea Colliery, Tanfield Lea; for subsequent history see Hetton Railway list

(7) to Tanfield Lea Colliery, Tanfield Lea, 5/1938; for subsequent history see Hetton Railway list

(8) hired to John Bowes & Partners Ltd, Springwell Bank Foot loco shed, Bowes Railway, 18/12/1937; returned, 28/3/1938; loaned to War Department, Central Ordnance Depot, Derby, Derbyshire, 10/1940; overhauled at LMS Derby Works, 1941-1942 (here on 12/5/1941); returned to Lambton Railway, Philadelphia; to NCB No.2 Area, with Railway, 1/1/1947

(9) to Handen Hold Colliery, West Pelton, by 4/6/1937; for subsequent history see Hetton Railway list

NATIONAL COAL BOARD
North East Area from 1/4/1974
North Durham Area from 26/3/1967
Northumberland & Durham Division No.1 Area from 28/3/1965
Northumberland & Durham Division No.2 Area from 1/1/1964
Durham Division No.2 (Mid-East Durham) Area from 1/1/1950
Northern Division No.2 (Mid-East Durham) Area from 1/1/1947

The Lambton and Hetton Group of The Lambton, Hetton & Joicey Collieries Ltd formed by far the largest part of the NCB Northern Division's No.2 Area, and Lambton Engine Works was easily the largest such establishment in the Division, which covered the whole of North-East England and Cumberland. At Area level Walter Tulip, who had succeeded his father as LHJC's Chief Engineer in 1935, became Area Engineer, and the Lambton Railway numbering scheme was applied to locomotives at South Hetton (Nos.61-72, and to replacements sent there) and to those at the Londonderry collieries Vane Tempest, Seaham and Dawdon at Seaham (Nos.81-87). For a while there was a Divisional spare locomotive, based at Philadelphia, and locomotives from South Hetton and Seaham and occasionally from collieries outside No.2 Area were brought to Lambton Engine Works for repairs.

The early years of nationalisation

Initially Lambton Engine Works introduced a programme of improvements to the locomotives. New and larger cabs and tenders with improved sighting for running tender first were fitted to some of the tender engines, and an elaborate and attractive livery of middle green with black lining and white edges and gold shaded lettering, with red rods and buffer beams, was adopted. Several locomotives were rebuilt, and the Works built another "new" locomotive, a 0-6-0PT constructed from the parts of three withdrawn locomotives. Nevertheless, a steady programme of investment saw the slow withdrawal of the tender engines, though a few lasted into the 1960s. The stock was modernised by the purchase of standard RSH types and 0-6-0ST 'Austerity' locomotives, though the latter were not used for main line work, this passing entirely to the 0-6-2Ts.

However, in 1955 the NCB pioneered new development by taking on extended trials a 400 b.h.p. 0-6-0DH locomotive built by the North British Locomotive Co Ltd, the most powerful shunting design then available to British industry. It was eventually purchased in July 1956 specifically to replace two steam locomotives working between Silksworth and Sunderland on the Hetton line. In the 1950s-1960s the Works Manager of the time, Major T. Lawson, favoured the installation of American "chime" whistles on the locomotives, while a special group of boilersmiths was set up to carry out boiler repair work at the Area's collieries, rather than bring the locomotives into the Works.

By the 1950s there were only nine loading points on the Lambton side at Sunderland, with Nos. 1 and 5 having been removed and No.4 converted into conveyor belt loading, with on the Hetton side the two fast-loading high staiths and a belt for loading stone. No.7 staith on the Lambton side also became solely used for stone traffic, which was dumped 3½ miles out at sea. Three berths were available on the Lambton side, the ships turning in the mouth of the river and being hauled stern first by the tug on to the berth, so that the ship could leave immediately it was loaded and without a tug. At maximum capacity the Lambton side could load 2800 tons per shift on each berth (about 55,000 tons per week), and when this was needed the locomotives worked very hard. With BR locomotives banned from entering Deptford Tunnel, coal traffic in BR wagons, latterly mainly for landsale depots, was worked over BR between Deptford sidings and the staiths by NCB locomotives.

The loco roster at the Lambton Staiths shed in the 1950s required five locomotives in steam daily through the week:

Staiths pilot	0-4-0ST	6.00 am – 10.00 pm
Staiths pilot	0-4-0ST	6.00 am – 10.00 pm
Hetton side	six-coupled loco	6.00 am – 10.00 pm
Hetton side	six-coupled loco	7.00 am – 11.00 pm
Staiths pilot	0-4-0ST	8.00 am – 4.00 pm

With two men starting at 5.00 am to coal, water and generally prepare the locomotives.

139. At Burnmoor, with Junction Bank curving away to the left, the lines to Lambton D Colliery, Lambton Coke Works, Lambton Washery and Nicholson's waste disposal point straight ahead and the branch to Lumley Colliery leaving in front of the water tanks, 5th July 1966.

140. The last of the first three 0-6-2Ts, bought from Kitson of Leeds between 1904 and 1907, and taken at Fencehouses, a rarely-photographed location: 31, K 4533/1907, with a new angled cab, hauls empties back from the Nicholson's disposal point at Rainton.

141. 33, 0-4-0ST HL 2827/1910, hauling a train of main-line wagons, approaches Burnmoor Crossing, with the Lambton D Pit complex in the background.

142. 42, RS 3801/1920, with a long train from Harraton Colliery, passes under the elevated Penshaw North signalbox prior to propelling back to the Penshaw sidings.

143. 5, RS 3377/1909, takes water at Penshaw before departing for Sunderland, 14th May 1965.

144. 10, RS 3378/1909, approaches Cox Green Station with a train for Sunderland on British Railways' Penshaw Branch, 27th August 1965.

145. Lambton Staiths, Sunderland, in July 1966, with the Staiths Office in the top left corner, the loco shed, the two tunnels (the Deptford branch to the left and to the Hetton Staiths to the right), rows of empties awaiting return to Penshaw and the last two very high Hetton Staiths on the far right.

146. 17, MW 2023/1923, pulls empties off No.11 Staith at the western end of Lambton Staiths on 31st May 1955.

147. Lambton Staiths loco shed, with No.39, RSHN 7757/1953, taking water, on 26th April 1964. For the return trip to Penshaw first the brake van and then the empties were run down by gravity to the eastern end of the staiths for the loco to back down on to. When the Deptford signalman had set the route, the 30ft signal here was pulled off to tell the loco driver 100 yards away that the Deptford tunnel was cleared.

148. 29, K 4263/1904, the first 0-6-2T to be purchased and retaining its original rounded cab and railed bunker, passes through Pallion Station with empties for Penshaw on 4th August 1956.

198

The men on the "main line" locomotives working between Penshaw and the Staiths were paid on bonus by the number of wagons they handled, and got a very good wage if they made four round trips in a 8¼ hour shift; some even made five round trips. "Main line" locomotives always faced Sunderland and returned tender/bunker first. All trains comprised 36 wagons. Leaving Philadelphia shed at 6.00 am (see below), the first loco driver away expected to be waiting with his fulls outside the staiths tunnel by 6.30 am. The brake van was then detached and run by gravity through the tunnel under signals and down to the eastern end. The loco would then bring in the remainder of the train, and the pilots would take off the fulls and put empties on the van. After the main line loco had taken water, if it was needed, it would back down on to its train and be cleared to leave. Although the aim was a turn-round of twenty minutes, if no water was needed and the empties were ready waiting, the turn-round could be as little as five minutes, and the empties were on their way back to Penshaw. In addition, the three "main line" locomotives working on the Hetton side would also be expected to do at least four round trips per shift, working traffic from the Hetton main line and from Silksworth Colliery. Thus all of the "runners", working internally to Penshaw, from Penshaw to Sunderland and all the locomotives based at the Staiths shed, were worked very hard indeed.

In addition to loading coal, seven of the Lambton staiths were fitted with cranes, to enable pit props to be unloaded from ships into wagons for outward traffic to the collieries.

If one of the 0-4-0STs working at Hetton failed, then in an emergency a replacement would be sent from Sunderland over the inclines. The water would be checked and the fire lit, and the locomotive would then be dispatched from the Lambton Staiths shed as a light engine, but without a crew, going over the inclines as part of a set of empties. Going up to Warden Law a 0-4-0ST was equivalent to five descending full wagons. The loco would then arrive at Hetton virtually ready to work.

The Wagon Shops at Philadelphia continued to build 12 ton wooden hopper wagons, but in the mid 1950s the shop went over to building steel wagons, first 15 or 16-ton wagons and then 20-ton wagons. Depending on the volume of repair work, the target was 24 new steel wagons per month. The wagon shop at Lambton Staiths continued its repair work too, aided by repairs done in the open air on a siding alongside the cliff almost directly under the Staiths Office, while the Hetton wagon shop also continued to handle repair work.

The end of the Hetton Railway

Hetton Colliery itself was the first colliery in the local area to close, on 22nd July 1950, and this led to the operation of the Byer Engine being simplified (see chapter 8). But with the need to increase production and also very much improve the output per man shift came the Hawthorn Combine, the biggest development project in Durham. A large shaft was to be sunk south of Murton village and the collieries of Murton, Eppleton and Elemore linked to it at two horizon levels. Alongside this Hawthorn Combined Mine would be a large new washery and a new coking plant. The site had good links with British Railways and with the sea at Seaham Harbour, and it meant the majority of the Hetton Railway, with its six inclines and two old stationary engines, could be closed, leaving only the section between Silksworth and Sunderland still in use. The last coal from Hetton over the inclines was worked on 9th September 1959 and the track was soon lifted, though the Warden Law Engine, built by Thomas Murray of Chester-le-Street in 1836, was dismantled for preservation; it is now part of the collection of Beamish, The North of England Open Air Museum. Hetton Wagon Shops were no longer needed, and these closed early in 1960, though the main building continues (2004) in industrial use. However, the two remaining Hetton Staiths were retained until 1962, in order to ship Silksworth's gas coal. These were said to be the highest and the fastest staiths in North-East England, able to handle five emptying wagons simultaneously on each staith.

The closures of the 1960s

In an area where coal had been mined for at least 200 years, colliery closures were inevitable. Lambton D Colliery was the first to close, on 27th February 1965, though its coal washery remained open to serve the adjacent coking plant. Harraton Colliery followed on 29th May 1965, ending working over British Railways to serve it, and Lumley 6th Colliery and its branch closed on 22nd January 1966. The loss of these collieries severely reduced the tonnage handled by Lambton Staiths, and on 6th January 1967 these closed too. The 0-6-2T 42 worked the last train from the Staiths, with 0-4-0ST 37 the last locomotive to leave. With all Silksworth coal now being dispatched via the branch to Ryhope, the only traffic left on the Hetton line was the domestic coal for the large coal depot at Railway Row, near Hylton Road. Silksworth Colliery closed on 5th November 1971, with the domestic coal hanging on until 3rd June 1972, when this last section of the Hetton Railway closed.

The end of "main line" running over BR reduced the work available for the 0-6-2Ts down to traffic between Herrington Colliery, Lambton D Washery and Penshaw, while the other closures meant far fewer 0-4-0STs were needed. At the same time the NCB found that BR was disposing of surplus Class 14 0-6-0DH and Class 11 0-6-0DE locomotives cheaply, and so a number of each were purchased, to eliminate steam on the Railway. However, up to six steam locomotives were in use daily in the last week of steam working, which officially ended on 15th February 1969. Despite this, at least two were used in the following week because of diesel failures due to the severe weather, but then the NCB prohibited this and instead hired diesels from British Railways until mid-March 1969, when the crisis was past.

The dramatic change in the Railway's operating requirements is well shown by these two rostering sheets for the loco sheds at Philadelphia:

149. 44, MW 1934/1917, at the Philadelphia coaling stage on 22nd May 1957, after the extraordinary rebuild at Lambton Engine Works which gave it a fake tapered boiler and Belpaire firebox and replaced its saddletank with round-topped side tanks. It is carrying the new livery of black with red lining and red lettering shaded with gold.

150. 6, the six-coupled pannier tank built at Lambton Engine Works between 1955 and 1958 from the parts of two tender engines and a 0-6-0ST, here at Philadelphia on 13th May 1959.

151. Locomotives under repair in Lambton Engine Works' Fitting Shop on 22nd August 1968 – 5, RS 3377/1909, 29 K 4263/1904, with on its frames the cab from 11, HC 1412/1920, whose frames lie behind.

152. A Taff Vale locomotive (albeit with a new cab) receiving a major overhaul, including a new firebox - in 1962? 53, built at the Taff Vale Railway's West Yard Works at Cardiff in 1894, stands in the Lambton Engine Works yard on 6th December 1962, painted now in unlined black with yellow lettering; under the number the lettering was 'No.2 Area'.

29th April 1963
Day shift

Locomotive working	Loco	Type	Time off shed
Spare loco : 51 0-6-0ST		Washing out	
Herrington Colliery	52	0-6-2T	12 midnight
Runners (internal main line to Penshaw Yard)	57	0-6-2T	5.00am
Runner for washed coal ("duff")	3	0-6-0ST	5.30am
Pilot at Lambton D Washery	6	0-6-0PT	5.30am
Pilot at Lambton D Colliery	33	0-4-0ST	5.30am
Stone traffic to Nicholsons (stone heap)	63	0-6-0ST	5.30am
MAIN LINE (Penshaw Yard to Sunderland)	10	0-6-2T	6.00am
Runners (internal main line to Penshaw Yard)	30	0-6-2T	6.00am
MAIN LINE (Penshaw Yard to Sunderland)	29	0-6-2T	7.00am
Pilot at Lumley 6th Colliery	45	0-6-0ST	7.30am
Pilot at Houghton Colliery	2	0-6-0ST	7.30am
Pilot at Lambton Coke Works	53	0-6-2T	8.00am
Pilot at Philadelphia	11	0-4-0ST	8.00am
Pilot at Philadelphia Yard	28	0-4-0ST	8.00am
Herrington Colliery (2nd shift)	52	0-6-2T	8.00am
Runners (internal main line to Penshaw Yard)	69	0-6-0ST	9.00am

Night shift

MAIN LINE (Penshaw Yard to Sunderland)	57	0-6-2T	1.00pm
Runner for washed coal ("duff")	3	0-6-0ST	1.00pm
Pilot at Lambton D Washery	6	0-6-0PT	1.00pm
Pilot at Lambton D Colliery	33	0-4-0ST	1.00pm
Runners (internal main line to Penshaw Yard)	51	0-6-0ST	1.00pm
Stone traffic to Nicholson's (stone heap)	63	0-6-0ST	1.30pm
MAIN LINE (Penshaw Yard to Sunderland)	30	0-6-2T	2.00pm
Runners (internal main line to Penshaw Yard)	53	0-6-2T	3.00pm

In the event it was decided to undertake a boiler inspection on 51 while she was cold from washing out, and with no spare loco available the foreman was compelled to re-organise the work to allow 52 to take 51's shift, meaning that 52 worked a 24-hour shift on this day. The locomotives working the Main Line (British Railways), which of course included trips to Harraton Colliery, worked 32 trains on this day. Each shift was 8 hours long, and all the jobs that were allocated to six-coupled locomotives, except to 0-6-0PT 6, were regarded as "heavy work".

17th February 1969
Day shift

Locomotive working	Loco	Type	Time off shed
Pilot at Lambton D Washery	12120	0-6-0DE 350hp	4.00am
Runners (from Houghton Colliery)	D9504	0-6-0DH 650hp	5.30am
Runners (from Herrington Colliery)	D9540	0-6-0DH 650hp	5.30am
Pilot at Lambton Coke Works	12119	0-6-0DE 350hp	6.00am
Pilot at Philadelphia	D9525	0-6-0DH 650hp	7.00am

All shifts were 8¼ hours. Note that with only five diesels purchased, there was no spare locomotive in the event of a failure.

153. In 1963 the Railway acquired three large 18in RSH locos from Dorman Long's Acklam Works at Middlesbrough; here 8, RSHN 7691/1951, passes between the former Dorothea shaft on the left and Lambton Engine Works with a train of BR wagons from Herrington Colliery.

154. 9, built at Lambton Engine Works in 1877, but here with the side-window cab and tender cab fitted in the 1950s, being used as a stationary boiler at Brancepeth Colliery, Willington, on 22nd May 1964 - the last NCB tender locomotive in North East England.

155. Part of the loco shed area at Philadelphia looking south on 7th June 1968, with the loco foreman's office on the far left and a 0-4-0ST outside the Running Shed. The same view can still be seen, albeit without the track or the coaling stage.

156. Some of the Railway's other wagons at Philadelphia on 4th June 1971: on the left is Van 21, then flat wagon 75 and Van 20, with Vans 13 and 11 on the right.

157. The end of steam: 59, VF 5300/1945, leaves Burnmoor with fulls for Penshaw, with 7, HE 3820/1954, and 5, RS 3377/1909, in the distance, on 10th February 1969.

158. The end of steam: three generations - the former British Railways Class 14 650 h.p. D9504, built at Swindon in 1964; 29, K 4263/1904, and 'Austerity' 58, VF 5299/1945, stand outside the four-road shed at Philadelphia at lunchtime on 11th February 1969.

With a much smaller system and diesel haulage the Railway operated through the 1970s, with the only loss being the replacement of rail traffic to Houghton Colliery by road haulage in February 1975; the colliery finally closed on 2nd October 1981. The other main change of this period was the control of the locomotives. Following the formation of the North East Area in 1974 an area organisation known as the Plant Pool was set up at its Team Valley Headquarters in Gateshead. This not only issued plant numbers, a system begun in 1957 but rarely carried by locomotives before 1974, but also controlled transfers, overhauls and the purchase of new locomotives. Eventually the Pool decided to concentrate locomotives of the same design at specific locations, which at Philadelphia meant transferring the 650 b.h.p. Class 14s to Northumberland and concentrating on the Class 11s, although a number of locomotives also spent a short time here after repairs at Lambton Engine Works.

The final closures

Herrington, the last colliery serving the line, went over to road transport on 5th March 1984, finally closing on 20th November 1985. The loss of its traffic left the remaining loco shed still open at Philadelphia dependent on the hire of a locomotive by National Smokeless Fuels Ltd to work traffic between Lambton Coke Works and the junction with BR at Penshaw. This hire was terminated on 19th July 1985, closing the shed. The final section of the Railway closed with the Coke Works in January 1986.

The closure of Lambton Engine Works

The reductions in the Railway's work had a major impact on the Engine Works. On 26th March 1967 it was transferred to the NCB's new national Workshops Division, and in the years that followed there were two major changes to its locomotive work. Steam locomotive repairs came to an end on 17th October 1969 with the completion of the repair to 0-6-0ST RSHN 7412/1948 for Norwood Coke Works at Dunston. Thereafter only diesel repairs were handled, including some brought from as far away as South Wales, though the vast majority of the work was for the North East Area, including a few narrow gauge diesels used in stockyards on the surface of collieries. Secondly, the works became the sole local centre for the repair of underground battery locomotives, again with a handful coming from outside the North East.

But the decline in the coal industry could not but affect the Works, despite valiant efforts to attract work from outside the industry. With the Lambton wagons dispersed and all traffic now handled in BR 21-ton hoppers, the Wagon Shops closed on 28th February 1981. Rail traffic to the Works ended in March 1984, although 400 yards of track at the northern end of the site was left in place to test repaired locomotives. With the closure of the last loco shed in July 1985, it was decided that a locomotive was needed to act as a works shunter, S 10157/1963 being obtained. From 31st July 1985 the repair of battery locomotives ceased when the work was transferred to the workshops at Ashington in Northumberland. The Works was handed back to the day-to-day control of the North East Area on 1st August 1985, but in October 1985 both the iron and non-ferrous foundries were closed. Locomotive repairs ceased in May 1987, and the Works was finally closed on 22nd December 1989.

On 1st January 1947 the Railway had 54 locomotives, comprising 10 0-6-0 tender engines, 12 0-6-2Ts, six 0-6-0STs, three 0-6-0Ts and 23 0-4-0STs. Their specific allocation on that date is unknown, although all of the tender engines were at Philadelphia. The records of the Industrial Railway Society list four locomotives at Hetton, but there were almost certainly more than this, possibly up to eight. Lambton Staiths probably had eight, possibly nine. Which 0-4-0STs were at Harraton Colliery, which had one, and Silksworth Colliery (possibly two) is unknown. Details of transfers between the five sheds, if they were recorded, seem not to have survived into the 1960s, and information up to the mid 1960s given below is derived more from observations than from official records. The introduction of the Planned Maintenance scheme by the NCB in 1957 required a Plant Registry to be set up, with each item having its own card. These began to record transfers between locations, a system continued when Plant Control was created, but not maintained when Plant Pool converted to a computer system. Thus whilst information and dates given below from the 1950s onwards were almost always obtained from official sources, those that are known to be inaccurate are indicated and there may be others.

Given below is the number shown on the side of the cab of the locomotive, although on the front buffer beam the locomotive carried "No.X".

In the list below transfers are shown in italics below each locomotive entry whilst it was still regarded as a Lambton Railway locomotive. These include short-term loans to other collieries not connected to the Lambton system. The history of a locomotive once it left the Lambton system for good is shown in the disposal footnote.

159. 0-6-0DE 509, built at Darlington in 1952 as British Railways' 12119, approaches the loco foreman's office at Philadelphia on a train from Herrington Colliery on 21st October 1969.

160. Lambton Engine Works became the only NCB works in North East England which handled the repair of surface locomotives: No.52 (0-6-0DE, formerly BR D4070) from Shilbottle Colliery, and No.66 0-6-0DH HE 6662/1966, from Bates Colliery, Blyth, both in Northumberland, await overhaul, while 20/110/702, 0-6-0DH NBQ 27589/1957 (far left), awaits dispatch to Blackhall Colliery after repair, 21st October 1975.

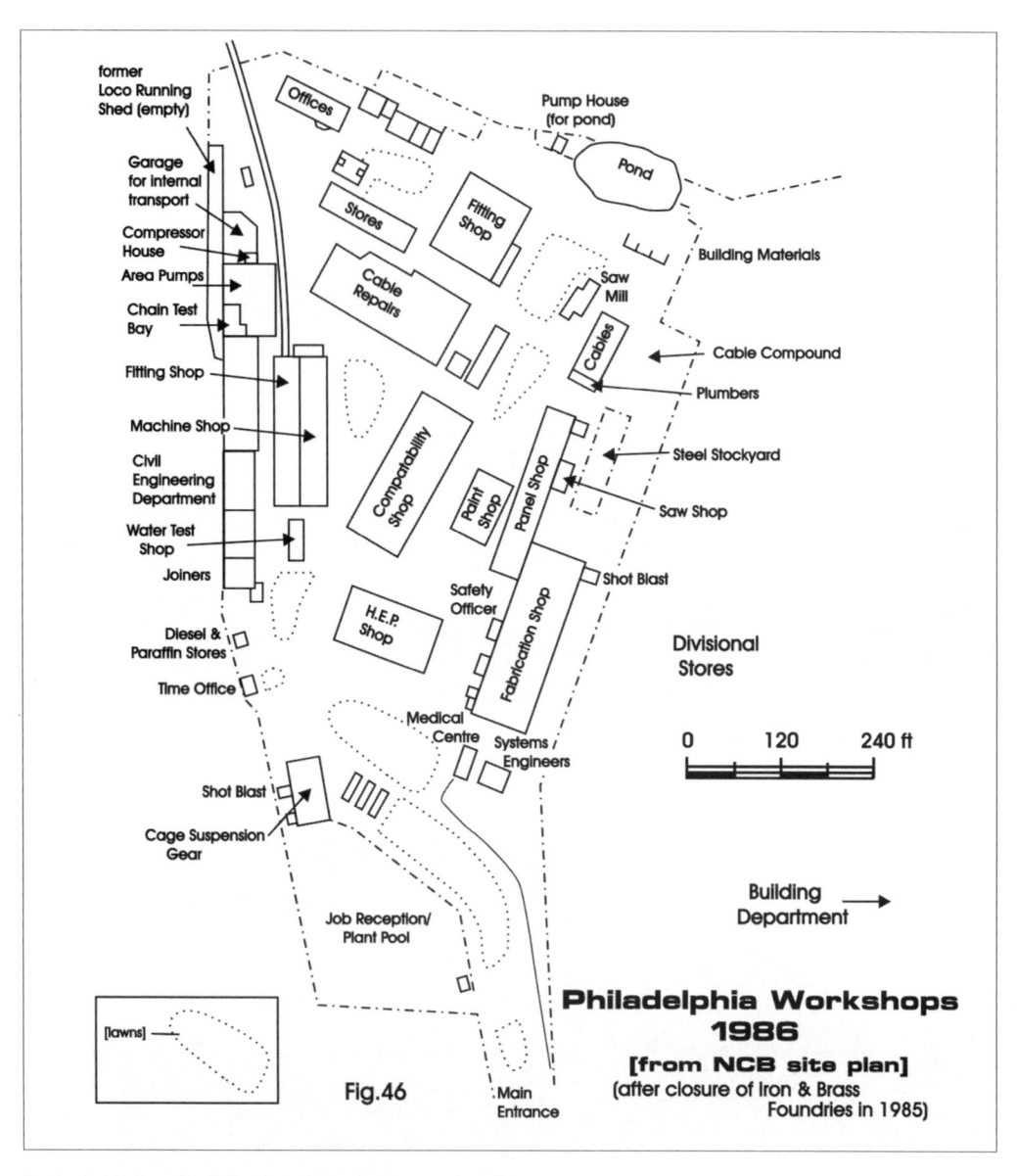

Fig.46 Philadelphia Workshops 1986
[from NCB site plan]
(after closure of Iron & Brass Foundries in 1985)

In the list below the following abbreviations are used:

Bl	Blackhall Colliery, Blackhall
Da	Dawdon Colliery, Seaham
E	Easington Colliery, Easington Colliery
H	Hetton Loco Shed, Hetton (Hetton Railway)
Ha	Harraton Colliery, Harraton
Ho	Horden Colliery, Horden
LEW	Lambton Engine Works, Philadelphia (repairs only)
LS	Lambton Staiths Loco Shed, Sunderland
Se	Seaham Colliery, Seaham
SHill	Sherburn Hill Colliery, Sherburn Hill
SBF	Springwell Bank Foot loco shed, Wardley, Bowes Railway
SH	South Hetton Loco Sheds, South Hetton
Sk	Silksworth Colliery, Silksworth
VT	Vane Tempest Colliery, Seaham
Wm	Wearmouth Colliery, Sunderland
Wt	Whittle Colliery, Newton-on-the-Moor, Northumberland

Gauge : 4ft 8½in

1 P		0-6-0	IC	H&C	71	1866	(a) Scr 8/1954
3 P		0-6-0	IC	BP	550	1865	(a) (1)
4 P		0-6-0	IC	BH	17	1866	(a) Scr 10/1954
5 P		0-6-2T	IC	RS	3377	1909	(a) (2)
6 P		0-6-0	IC				(b) (3)
7 P		0-6-0	IC				(b) Scr 2/1952
8 P		0-6-0	IC				(b) (4)
9	##	0-6-0	IC	Earl of Durham		1877	(a) (5)

P-LS c/1952-P by 10/1952

10	0-6-2T	IC	RS	3378	1909	(a)

P-Robert Stephenson & Hawthorns Ltd, Newcastle upon Tyne, for repairs, by 15/6/1957
-P ?/?   (6)

11	0-4-0ST	OC reb	HC HC	1412	1920 1948	(a)

H-Hudswell, Clarke & Co Ltd, Leeds, for rebuild, /1948-P ?/?(or direct to H)-H by 19/9/1948
-P by 9/1950-H by 5/1951-LEW after 4/1954, by 4/1955-P by 25/8/1955
-H after 11/1956, by 28/4/1957-P after 10/1959, by 12/1959   (7)

12	0-4-0ST	OC	HL	2789	1912	(a)

H-P by 14/5/1949-LEW after 7/1949, by 7/1950-H 7/1950-LEW by 28/2/1954
-H by 10/1953-LEW after 8/1956, by 11/1956-H by 22/5/1957
-LEW after 7/1958, by 4/1959   (8)

13	0-4-0ST	OC	HL	3055	1914	(a)

H-LEW by 19/9/1948-H by 5/1951-LEW after 6/1952, by 3/1953
-H by 16/10/1953-LEW after 22/5/1957, by 4/1958-H by 7/1958   (9)

14	0-4-0ST	OC	HL	3056	1914	(a)

H-P after 19/9/1948, by 9/1950-H after 4/1952, by 6/1952-VT after 7/1960, by 1/1961
-P 24/1/1961-Se 27/1/1961, arrived 1/2/1961-P 9/5/1961, arrived 10/5/1961
-Da c11/1962 (officially on 17/10/1962 but still at P on 26/11/1962)
-LEW 22/7/1965-P 5/10/1965-VT 23/10/1965(official date was 30/10/1965)
-Se 25/12/1965 (official date)-VT 27/10/1966 (official date, but loco at VT by 9/8/1966)(10)

15	0-4-0ST	OC	HCR	169	1875	(a)

P-LEW by 8/1948   (11)

16 P	0-4-0ST	OC	HCR	96	1870	(a) Scr 2/1952
17	0-4-0ST	OC	MW	2023	1923	(a)

LS-LEW after 4/1952, by 6/1952-H by 9/1952
-LS after 12/1952, by 17/4/1954-P after 9/1957, by 4/1958   Scr 8/1960

18	0-6-0ST	OC reb	BH HL	32 1491	1867 1935	(a)

P-VT 5/1958-P after 7/1958, by 4/1959   (12)

19 P	0-4-0ST	OC	MW	344	1871	(a) (13)
20 P	0-6-0	IC	RS	2260	1876	(a) Scr c8/1960
21	0-4-0ST	OC	RS	2308	1876	(a)

P-Ha after 9/50, by 5/1951-P by 4/1952   (14)

22	0-4-0ST	OC	HC	230	1881	(a)

P-Ha after 19/9/1948, by 13/5/1950-P by 9/1950   (15)

23		0-4-0ST	OC	BH	688	1882	(a)	

LS-Sk by 14/11/1948-LS by 4/1950-Sk after 9/1951, by 10/1951
-Ha by 4/1952-P by 6/1952   Scr 1/1963

24		0-4-0ST	OC	BH	832	1885	(a)	

P-Ha after 1/1949, by 14/5/1949-P by 7/1949-Ha by 10/6/1953
-P by 4/1954   (16)

25		0-6-0	IC	Earl of Durham		1890	(a)	
P								Scr 5/1960

26	##	0-6-0	IC	Earl of Durham		1894	(a)	
P								Scr 12/1962

27		2-4-0	IC	RS	491	1845		
	reb	0-6-0	IC	Ghd		1864		
	reb	0-6-0ST	IC	Ghd		1873		
	reb	0-6-0T	IC	LEW		1904	(c)	

P-SH 17/3/1952-P 4/9/1953   (17)

28	#	0-4-0ST	OC	HL	2530	1902	(a)	
P								(18)

29		0-6-2T	IC	K	4263	1904	(a)	
P								(19)

30		0-6-2T	IC	K	4532	1907	(a)	

P-LS /1958 (after 8/6/1958)-P /1961   (20)

31	#	0-6-2T	IC	K	4533	1907	(a)	
P								(21)

32		0-4-0ST	OC	HL	2826	1910	(a)	

H-LEW 1/1947-P c/1947-H by 19/9/1948-LEW by 3/1949-H c6/1949
-LEW after 10/1953, by 4/1954-VT by 4/1955-P by 25/8/1955-Ha by 11/1955
-P after 5/1956, by 8/1956-LS 8/1962-P 12/1962-LS 1/1963   (22)

33		0-4-0ST	OC	HL	2827	1910	(a)	

LS-Ha by 7/12/1952?-H by10/1953-P by 28/2/1954-H by 4/1954-LEW by 29/1/1955
-H by 4/1955-LS after 10/1959, by 4/1960-P after 7/1960, by 4/1961
-Sk 8/1961-P by 12/1961-Wm 12/1966-P 12/6/1967 (one version gave by 5/1967)   (18)

34		0-4-0ST	OC	HL	2954	1912	(a)	

H-LS 6/1949-P after 7/12/1952, by 4/3/1953-Ha by 21/4/1954-P by 30/4/1954
-LS after 4/1960, by 7/1960-Sk by 8/1962-LS by 9/1962-LEW 4/12/1962-P 3/6/1964
-LS later in 6/1964 (after 16/6/1964)-Sk 12/1966   (23)

35		0-4-0ST	OC	HL	3024	1913	(a)	

LS-LEW after 4/1954, by 4/1955-LS after 11/1955, by 22/4/1956-P c6/1960
-LEW c6/1960-P 23/5/1961-LS 30/5/1961-Sk after 10/1961, by 8/1962-LS by 9/1962
-LEW 26/11/1962-LS /1963-LEW 3/6/1965-LS 28/6/1965-Sk 7/1966   (23)

36 #		0-4-0ST	OC	P	615	1896	(a)	

P-SH 17/3/1948-P after 9/1950, by 6/1951-VT after 9/1957, by 4/1958-Se by 5/1958
-P after 8/1959, by 11/1959-VT 29/5/1961-P 10/4/1962-Se 11/5/1962-P 6/6/1962   Scr 1/1963

39		0-6-0ST	IC	RWH	1422	1867		
		reb		HL	2378		(a)	
P								(24)

41		0-6-0T	OC	KS	3074	1917	(a)	

P-H by 19/9/1948-P by 7/1949-LEW /1951-H by 6/1951
-LEW after 10/1953, by 28/2/1954-H after 9/1954, by 4/1955
-LEW after 8/1956, by 28/4/1957-H after 9/1957, by 4/1958   (25)

42		0-6-2T	IC	RS	3801	1920	(a)	
P								(26)

43		0-4-0ST	OC	GR	769	1920	(a)	

P-Sk after 8/1951, by 6/1952-P by 4/1954-Sk by 18/3/1956-LEW by 5/1957
-LS by 4/1958-Sk by 5/1958-LS by 4/1959
-Sk by 8/1959-LS after 10/1959, by 5/1960-Sk by 4/1961   (27)

44		0-6-0ST	OC	MW	1934	1917	(a)	
	reb	0-6-0T	OC	LEW		1951		

LS-P after 26/6/1949, by 7/1949-LEW for rebuilding ?/?-P by 6/1951
-LS after 4/1952, by 9/1952-P after 17/4/1954, by 29/1/1955   (28)

45		0-6-0ST	IC	HL	2932	1912	(a)

P-SH 30/11/1949-P after 8/1951, by 6/1952-H by 7/12/1952
-P by 28/2/1954-H after 11/1955, by 4/1956-P 2/1958 (29)

46		0-6-0T	IC	MW	1813	1913	(a)

P-H by 19/9/1948-LEW by 3/1949-H after 9/1950, by 6/1951
-LEW after 4/1952, by 6/1952-H by 9/1952-LS after 4/1954, by 4/1955
-LEW by 18/3/1956-H by 28/4/1957-LS after 4/1958, by 5/1958-P by 6/1958   Scr 4/1960

47		0-4-0ST	OC	HL	3543	1923	(a)

P-Robert Stephenson & Hawthorns Ltd, Newcastle upon Tyne, for repairs, by 5/1948
-either to P ?/? or to H by 19/9/1948-P by 7/1949-H by 9/1950-LEW after 8/1952, by 9/1952
-LS ?/?-Sk by 7/12/1952-P by 10/1953(?)-LS by 17/4/1954-LEW 5/2/1959
-P 29/9/1960-LS 10/1960-P by 5/1964(?)-LS by 6/1964-P by 25/6/1965
-LS 6/2/1966-P 6/1/1967 (30)

48		0-4-0ST	OC	HL	3544	1923	(a)

H-LEW by 26/10/1947
-Robert Stephenson & Hawthorns Ltd, Newcastle upon Tyne, for repairs, by 2/1948
-H by 19/9/1948-LEW after 4/1952, by 6/1952-H by 9/1952-P by 28/2/1954
-LEW after 18/3/1956, by 4/1956-H by 8/1956-SH 8/4/1957-H 5/1957
-LS after 10/1959, by 4/1960-P (to await overhaul) c6/1960-LEW 5/6/1961
-Ha 28/3/1962-P (to await overhaul) c17/10/1964-LEW 20/11/1964
-P 18/1/1965 (31)

49 #		0-4-0ST	OC	MW	2035	1924	(a)
			reb	LEW		1959	

LS-LEW by 19/9/1948
-Robert Stephenson & Hawthorns Ltd, Newcastle upon Tyne, for repairs, 6/1949-LS 6/1949
-H after 8/1951, by 4/1952(accident)-LEW ?/?-LS by 7/1952-P by 28/2/1954
-LS by 30/5/1956-LEW by 28/4/1957-LS 5/1957-P after 9/1957, by 4/1958
-LEW 1/7/1958-P 26/8/1959-Ha by 21/4/1961-P 3/1962 (32)

50 #		0-4-0ST	OC	MW	2036	1924	(a)
			reb	LEW		1957	(d)

LS-Robert Stephenson & Hawthorns Ltd, Newcastle upon Tyne, for repairs, by 5/1947
-LEW by 19/9/1948-LS by 13/1/1949-P after 4/1952, by 6/1952-LS by 9/1952
-P by 28/2/1954-LEW 1/2/1956-LS 4/1957-VT 11/1958-P 2/5/1961 (33)

52 **		0-6-2T	IC	NR	5408	1899	(a)

LS?-P by 19/9/1948-H /1949-LS by 9/1950-SH 11/1950-P 1/1951-
LS after 11/1952, by 11/4/1954-P by 25/8/1955-LEW 3/1956-LS by 5/1956
-P after 8/1956, by 11/1956-LS after 7/1958, by 4/1959-P after 8/1959, by 4/1960 (34)

53 **		0-6-2T	IC	Cdf	302	1894	(a)

LS-LEW by 19/9/1948-LS by 13/1/1949-P after 4/1952, by 6/1952-LEW 17/11/1954
-LS 3/1955-P by 28/4/1957-LS 5/1957-P after 4/1958, by 5/1958   Scr 10/1966

54		0-6-2T	IC	Cdf	311	1897	(a)

LS-LEW by 26/10/1947-P by 14/5/1949-LS after 9/1950, by 6/1951
-P after 9/1952, by 12/1952-LS after 10/1953, by 17/4/1954
-P by 29/9/1954-LEW 4/1955 (35)

55 **		0-6-2T	IC	K	3069	1887	(a)

P-LS after 14/5/1949, by 7/1949-P after 9/1950, by 6/1951-LS by 17/10/1951-P by 4/1952
-LS after 8/1952, by 7/12/1952-P by 10/1953-LS after 11/1955, by 22/4/1956
-P after 7/1958, by 3/1959 (36)

56		0-6-2T	IC	K	3580	1894	(a)

P-LS by 19/6/1949-P after 9/1950, by 6/1951 (37)

57		0-6-2T	IC	HL	3834	1934	(a)

P   Scr 5/1964

58		0-6-0ST	IC	VF	5299	1945	(a)

H-P by 19/9/1948-H by 9/1950-P after 9/1950, by 6/1951
-LS after 4/1954, by 6/7/1955-P by 4/1956-LS 8/1959-P by 18/4/1962
-LEW by 4/1963-LS 7/1963-LEW 29/7/1963-LS 8/1963-LEW 7/1964-LS 4/1965
-Wm 9/1966-P 10/3/1967 (38)

59		0-6-0ST	IC	VF	5300	1945	(a)

P-LS 12/1952 (by 7/12/1952)-H after 10/1953, by 4/1954-LS by 4/1955
-H 4/1955-P by 28/4/1957-H 5/1957, by 9/1957-SH 15/1/1959-LS 4/4/1962-P 1/1964 (38)

51 (60 till c3/1949) P	0-6-0ST	IC	RSHN	7101	1943	(e)	(39)

60   0-6-0ST   IC   HE   3686   1948   New
P-H after 11/1956, by 22/5/1957-P after 10/1959, by 11/1959-LS after 4/1960, by 5/1960
-P after 7/1960, by 8/1960-LEW 24/2/1961, where as part of overhaul fitted with
mechanical stoker-P 10/3/1962-SBF 7/9/1962-SHill 1/10/1962-Bl 3/1963-P 6/4/1965   (40)

2 (formerly No.2)   0-6-0ST   OC   RSHN   7599   1949   New
P-Wm /1951, after 9/1950-P by 8/1951-SH after 11/1956, by 28/4/1957-P 5/1957
-Da 24/1/1961-P c4/1961-E 14/4/1967-P 24/6/1967   (41)

37   0-6-0ST   IC   RWH   1430   1868   (f)
P   Scr /1951

No.37   0-4-0ST   OC   RSHN   7755   1953   New
LS-P after 11/1956, by 28/4/1957-LS 12/1960-P 5/12/1963-LS by 5/1964
-Sk by 30/6/1964-LS by 15/2/1966-Sk 2/12/1966-LS 12/1966-P 6/1/1967   (42)

38 (formerly No.38)   0-4-0ST   OC   RSHN   7756   1953   New
LS-VT 6/2/1961-P 25/6/1961-Ha 10/1964-P 6/1965   (43)

No.39   0-4-0ST   OC   RSHN   7757   1953   New
P-H after 10/1953, by 28/2/1954-P by 29/9/1954-LS after 7/1958, by 4/1959
-Sk by 30/5/1961-LS by 10/1961-P 13/6/1963-LS 18/6/1963-Sk 9/1963
-LS after 5/1964, by 6/1964-P 3/1966-LEW c4/1966   (44)

7   0-6-0ST   IC   HE   3820   1954   New
P   (45)

81 SEAHAM   0-4-0ST   OC   HL   2701   1907   (g)
P-LEW by 4/1955   (46)

84 CASTLEREAGH   0-4-0ST   OC   AB   1885   1926   (h)
P-LEW by 4/1955   (47)

72   0-6-0ST   IC   VF   5309   1945   (j)
P-LEW by 4/1955   (48)

1   0-6-0DH   NBQ   27410   1955   (k)
P-H 1/9/1956-LS 13/12/1956-P after 5/1957, by 9/1957-LS by 4/1958
-LEW by 8/6/1958-LS by 7/1958-LEW 22/5/1963
-LS 22/10/1963-LEW 22/1/1965-LS 18/2/1966-P 23/12/1966   (49)

6 ##   0-6-0PT   IC   LEW   1958   (m)
P   Scr 10/1964

63 (formerly No.63)   0-6-0ST   OC   RSHN   7600   1949   (n)
P-LS after 7/1960-P by 4/1961   (50)

68   0-6-0ST   IC   HE   3784   1953   (p)
P   (51)

62   0-6-0ST   IC   HE   3689   1949   (q)   (52)

2505/78   4wDM   FH   3852   1957   (r)
P   (53)

69   0-6-0ST   IC   HE   3785   1953   (s)
                              reb   HE   59222   1964
P-LEW 30/5/1963-Hunslet Engine Co Ltd, Leeds, Yorkshire, for rebuilding, 17/10/1963;
fitted with HE mechanical stoker; returned from HE, 2/5/1964-P 5/1964   (54)

3   0-6-0ST   OC   RSHN   7687   1951   (t)
LEW-P 2/1963   (18)

4   0-6-0ST   OC   RSHN   7688   1951   (u)
LEW-P 2/1963   Scr 12/1968

8   0-6-0ST   OC   RSHN   7691   1951   (v)
LEW-P after 27/3/1963   (55)

After 1967 all locomotives below were based at the Railway's locomotive sheds at Philadelphia. Loans from Philadelphia are still shown (in italics).

10   0-6-0ST   IC   RSHN   7294   1945   (w)
P   (56)

506   (D9504 till 8/1969)   0-6-0DH   Sdn   1964   (x)
      P-Ho 21/8/1973-P 7/9/1973   (57)

507	(D9525 till 8/1969)	0-6-0DH	Sdn		1965	(y)	(58)
508	(D9540 till 8/1969)	0-6-0DH	Sdn		1965	(z)	(59)
509	(12119 till 8/1969)	0-6-0DE	Dar		1952	(aa)	(60)
510	(12120 till 8/1969)	0-6-0DE	Dar		1952	(ab)	
	P-Wt 23/6/1978-P 21/11/1978						(61)
511	(12133 till 8/1969)	0-6-0DE	Dar		1952	(ac)	(60)
512	(12060 till 5/1971)	0-6-0DE	Derby		1949	(ad)	(62)
513	(12098 till 6/1971)	0-6-0DE	Derby		1952	(ae)	(63)
12050		0-6-0DE	Derby		1949	(af)	(64)
514	(12084 till 12/1971)	0-6-0DE	Derby		1950	(ag)	(65)
	SAM	0-6-0DM	HE	5647	1960	(ah)	(66)
No.52	(D4070)	0-6-0DE	Dar		1961	(aj)	(67)
	-	0-4-0DH	RR	10201	1964	(ak)	(68)
101		4wDM	FH	3922	1959	(am)	(69)
9101/66		0-6-0DH	HE	6662	1966	(an)	(70)
9101/65		0-6-0DH	EEV	D1121	1966	(ap)	(71)
20/109/89		0-6-0DH	AB	647	1979	New	
	P-Wt 23/1/1980-P 5/6/1980						(72)
2100/522		0-6-0DH	AB	585	1973	(aq)	(73)
No.53	(D4072)	0-6-0DE	Dar		1961	(ar)	
	P-SH 7/6/1982-LEW 27/9/1982						
	-P 17/12/1982 (official date, although loco still in LEW yard on 10/1/1983)						(74)
20/110/705		0-6-0DH	AB	604	1976	(as)	(75)
	D3088	0-6-0DE	Derby		1954	(at)	(76)
	-	0-4-0DH	AB	523	1967	(au)	(77)

  # rebuilt with angled cab
  ## rebuilt with angled cab and tender cab (two different designs)
  ** rebuilt with angled cab with side window, and new bunker

Note : locomotives from other sites sent to Lambton Engine Works for repairs were quite often sent to the Lambton Railway loco sheds at Philadelphia afterwards for a few days running in; these have not been included in the list above.

In addition to the above locomotives, 85 0-6-0ST OC RS 4113/1935 was brought from Vane Tempest Colliery, Seaham, to Lambton Engine Works for repairs in August 1960. The locomotive was partly dismantled and the boiler removed, but it was then decided that the repairs required were uneconomic and they were cancelled. The frame and its wheels were then transferred to the Lambton Railway loco sheds at Philadelphia. These were officially withdrawn in December 1962 and scrapped on site in January 1964.

(a) ex The Lambton, Hetton & Joicey Collieries Ltd, with the Railway, 1/1/1947
(b) ex The Lambton, Hetton & Joicey Collieries Ltd, with the Railway, 1/1/1947; makers' details unknown (see pre-1947 list above)
(c) ex The Lambton, Hetton & Joicey Collieries Ltd, with the Railway, 1/1/1947; for earlier history see pre-1947 list
(d) rebuilt in /1957 with boiler from 24 BH 832/1885
(e) ex War Department, Antwerp, Belgium, 6/1947, 75065 (presumably via a WD depot in Britain); purchased to be the Divisional Spare Locomotive, although numbered in the Lambton Railway list
(f) ex Morrison Busty Colliery, Annfield Plain, 10/1949 (a Lambton Railway locomotive, originally from the Hetton Railway)
(g) ex Dawdon Colliery, Seaham, by 29/1/1955 (may well have been out of use, awaiting entry to Lambton Engine Works)
(h) ex Vane Tempest Colliery, Seaham, by 29/1/1955 (may well have been out of use, awaiting entry to Lambton Engine Works)
(j) ex South Hetton Loco Sheds, South Hetton, by 29/1/1955 (may well have been out of use, awaiting entry to Lambton Engine Works)
(k) NBQ demonstration locomotive; NCB records gave "received at Philadelphia, 20/7/1956", but evidence suggests that it was undergoing extensive trials before this date, which may well be the date it was purchased by the NCB; it was acquired "to replace two steam locomotives between Silksworth and Sunderland"; put into traffic on 16/8/1956
(m) official records gave this loco as constructed at Lambton Engine Works between 16/7/1957 and 30/7/1958, although the frames and wheels were being prepared in LEW as early as 29/1/1955; it incorporated parts from withdrawn locomotives 0-6-0 6 (boiler), 0-6-0 8 (cylinders) and 0-6-0ST 39; the frames were from an 0-6-0 tender engine, possibly 6; tanks, cab and bunker were new
(n) ex South Hetton Loco Sheds, South Hetton, 11/1958
(p) South Hetton locomotive: ex Lambton Engine Works, Philadelphia, for trials, 6/10/1960

(q)   ex South Hetton Loco Sheds, South Hetton, after 8/1960, by 4/1961
(r)   ex Brandon Pit House Colliery, near Meadowfield, 26/2/1962 (official date of sale between Nos.5 and 2 Areas; actual date of transfer not recorded)
(s)   South Hetton locomotive; ex South Hetton Loco Sheds, South Hetton, 1/3/1963
(t)   ex Dorman Long (Steel) Ltd, Acklam Works, Middlesbrough, Yorkshire (NR), 1; purchased, 12/1962; to Lambton Engine Works, Philadelphia, for minor repairs and re-numbering, 24/1/1963
(u)   ex Dorman Long (Steel) Ltd, Acklam Works, Middlesbrough, Yorkshire (NR), 2; purchased, 12/1962; to Lambton Engine Works, Philadelphia, for minor repairs and re-numbering, 31/1/1963
(v)   ex Dorman Long (Steel) Ltd, Acklam Works, Middlesbrough, Yorkshire (NR), 5; purchased, 12/1962; to Lambton Engine Works, Philadelphia, for minor repairs and re-numbering, 31/1/1963
(w)   ex Lambton Engine Works, Philadelphia, c7/1968 (after 6/6/1968); previously at Wearmouth Colliery, Sunderland
(x)   ex British Railways, Dairycoates Motive Power Depot, Hull. Yorks (ER)), 27/11/1968 (official NCB records gave 2/12/1968); Class 14, D9504, withdrawn 4/1968
(y)   ex British Railways, Dairycoates Motive Power Depot, Hull Yorks (ER), 28/11/1968 (official NCB records gave 2/12/1968); Class 14, D9525, withdrawn 4/1968
(z)   ex British Railways, Dairycoates Motive Power Depot, Hull, Yorks (ER), 29/11/1968 (official NCB records gave 2/12/1968); Class 14, D9540, withdrawn 4/1968
(aa) ex British Railways, Hull, Yorkshire (ER), 6/2/1969; Class 11, 12119, withdrawn 12/1968
(ab) ex British Railways, Hull, Yorkshire (ER), 6/2/1969; Class 11, 12120, withdrawn 1/1969
(ac) ex British Railways, Immingham, Lincolnshire, 9/5/1969; Class 11, 12133, withdrawn 1/1969
(ad) ex Derwenthaugh Loco Shed, Swalwell, 16/4/1971; ex British Railways, Newton Heath Motive Power Depot, Lancashire, 27/3/1971; Class 11, 12060, not officially withdrawn until 4/1971
(ae) ex Derwenthaugh Loco Shed, Swalwell, 16/4/1971; ex British Railways, Newton Heath Motive Power Depot, Lancashire, 27/3/1971; Class 11, 12098, not officially withdrawn until 4/1971
(af) ex British Railways, location not known, 4/1971; Class 11. 12050, withdrawn 7/1970; purchased for spares only
(ag) ex Burradon Colliery, Burradon, Northumberland, 25/11/1971; ex British Railways, c10/1971; Class 11, 12084, withdrawn 5/1971
(ah) ex Lambton Engine Works, Philadelphia, c1/1975, after being found in very poor condition; ex Askern Main Colliery, Askern, North Yorkshire, 12/1974; originally BR D2598, Class 05
(aj) ex Lambton Engine Works, Philadelphia, for trials, 13/9/1976
(ak) ex Lambton Engine Works, Philadelphia, 14/4/1977
(am) ex Dudley Colliery, Dudley, Northumberland, 19/4/1977
(an) ex Lambton Engine Works, Philadelphia, 26/5/1977
(ap) ex Shilbottle Colliery, Shilbottle, Northumberland, 12/7/1979
(aq) ex Lambton Engine Works, Philadelphia, 29/9/1981
(ar) ex Lambton Engine Works, Philadelphia, 10/1981
(as) ex Lambton Engine Works, Philadelphia, 25/6/1982
(at) ex Lambton Engine Works, Philadelphia, 3/11/1982
(au) ex Lambton Engine Works, Philadelphia, 17/12/1982

(1)   withdrawn from traffic, 12/1953, but may have ceased work some time before this; scrapped on site, 10/1954
(2)   withdrawn from traffic, 15/2/1969; to Mr & Mrs B Jones, c/o North Eastern Locomotive Preservation Group, 31/7/1970; moved to British Railways' Thornaby Motive Power Depot, Thornaby, Yorkshire (NR), 7/8/1970 and then to the North Yorkshire Moors Railway, Yorkshire (NR), 28/8/1970
(3)   dismantled by 10/1950; some parts subsequently used in the construction of a new 0-6-0PT, for which see below, and the remaining parts scrapped except for the tender, which was sold to Northumberland No.2 Area in 1950 for use with their No.6, 0-6-0 RS 2917/1899, whose tender had been damaged in an accident
(4)   derelict by /1951; most parts were scrapped in 1952, but some were retained for use in the construction of a new 0-6-0PT, for which see below
(5)   withdrawn from traffic, 10/1952, but retained for use as a stationary boiler for heating colliery baths; to Brandon Colliery, Meadowfield, for this purpose, 28/8/1961, and returned to Philadelphia, 12/2/1962; to Brancepeth Colliery, Willington, similarly, 14/9/1962; scrapped at Brancepeth Colliery, 8/1965 (the last NCB tender locomotive in North East England)
(6)   withdrawn from traffic, 10/1965, after repairs were cancelled; scrapped at loco sheds, 1/1969
(7)   to Hylton Colliery, Sunderland, 17/3/1969; scrapped there, 6/1972
(8)   to Dawdon Colliery, Seaham, after 10/1959, by 4/1960; to Lambton Railway loco sheds, Philadelphia, 19/11/1962, and returned to Dawdon Colliery, Seaham, 26/11/1962; sold for scrap to J.A.Lister & Sons Ltd, Consett, 1/12/1967 and cut up on site later than month
(9)   to Vane Tempest Colliery, Seaham, after 10/1959, by 7/1960; to Lambton Engine Works, Philadelphia, for repairs, 6/2/1961; to Vane Tempest Colliery, Seaham, 18/8/1961; to J.Hanratty & Co Ltd, Bishop Auckland, for scrap, 8/1966
(10) to Lambton Railway loco sheds, Philadelphia, 8/10/1968 (official records gave 28/9/1968) and withdrawn from traffic; to North Regional Open Air Museum, Marley Hill Store, 7/12/1972, for preservation, and subsequently to North of England Open Air Museum, Beamish

(11) loaned to Horton Grange Colliery, Bebside, Northumberland, after 9/1948; returned to Lambton Railway loco sheds, Philadelphia, by 9/1950; scrapped on site, 2/1952
(12) to The Seaham Harbour Dock Co. Seaham, 2/1960; scrapped there, 12/1963
(13) to South Hetton Loco Sheds, South Hetton, 5/11/1947; withdrawn from traffic, 11/1952; scrapped on site by D.Sep. Bowran Ltd, Gateshead, 8/1954
(14) scrapped, /1954 (after 4/1954)
(15) official records gave sold for scrap to R. Frazer & Sons Ltd, Hebburn, 14/1/1957, and Industrial Railway Society records gave scrapped c8/1957; but loco was seen at Philadelphia on 20/5/1958 and is believed to have been scrapped c6/1958
(16) boiler removed by 11/1955 for use in rebuilding 50 MW 2035/1924; officially withdrawn from traffic, 9/1957; frames and wheels scrapped on site, 5/1959
(17) firebox condemned, /1963 but disposal of loco suspended in the hope of preservation: no offer was forthcoming; scrapped on site by T.W.Ward Ltd, Middlesbrough, Yorkshire (NR), 11/1968
(18) scrapped on site by T.W.Ward Ltd, Middlesbrough, Yorkshire (NR), 10/1968
(19) withdrawn from traffic, 15/2/1969; to Lambton No.29 Locomotive Syndicate, for preservation, 19/6/1970 and moved to British Railways' Thornaby Motive Power Depot, Thornaby, Yorkshire (NR), 20/6/1970; moved to North Yorkshire Moors Railway, Yorkshire (NR), 25/6/1970
(20) withdrawn from traffic in second half of 1965; scrapped on site, 1/1969
(21) scrapped on site by Thos W.Ward Ltd, Middlesbrough, Yorkshire (NR), 11/1968
(22) scrapped on site by J.C.Wight Ltd, Pallion, Sunderland, 8/1967
(23) scrapped on site by Cox & Danks Ltd, Gateshead, 2/1970
(24) derelict by 3/1949; majority scrapped on site in /1951, but some parts retained for use in construction of new 0-6-0PT (see above)
(25) became spare loco available for loan to any NCB Area in the North-East; to Brandon Colliery, Meadowfield, 21/11/1959, and returned to Philadelphia, 15/2/1961; to Horden Colliery, Horden, 21/2/1961 and returned to Philadelphia, 4/5/1961; to Morrison Busty Colliery, Annfield Plain, 31/5/1961, and returned to Philadelphia, 15/7/1961; to Blackhall Colliery, Blackhall, 13/4/1962, and returned to Philadelphia, 13/7/1962; to Lambton Engine Works, Philadelphia, c8/1962; to Brandon Pit House Colliery, near Meadowfield, 12/1962 (after 2/12/1962; Area Plant Registry gave 31/11/1962, in error), and returned to Philadelphia by 27/3/1963 (Area Plant Registry gave 31/12/1963, in error); to Lambton Engine Works, Philadelphia, by 29/4/1963; repair work halted; loco scrapped at Philadelphia, 10/1964
(26) withdrawn from traffic, 15/2/1969; scrapped on site by D.Sep. Bowran Ltd, Gateshead, 5/1970
(27) to Seaham Colliery, Seaham, 9/5/1961 and arrived 10/5/1961; scrapped on site, 2/1967
(28) to The Seaham Harbour Dock Co, Seaham, 2/1960; scrapped on site, 7/1963
(29) withdrawn from traffic, 10/2/1969; scrapped on site, 12/1970
(30) to Hylton Colliery, Sunderland, 12/1968; out of use by 20/10/1969; scrapped on site, 6/1972
(31) to Seaham Colliery, Seaham, 28/4/1965; sold for scrap to J.A.Lister & Sons Ltd, Consett, 12/1968 and cut up on site, 5/1969
(32) to Dawdon Colliery, Seaham, 6/5/1964; scrapped on site by J.A.Lister & Sons Ltd, Consett, 12/1967
(33) to Vane Tempest Colliery, Seaham, 8/5/1961; to Blackhall Colliery, Blackhall, 11/7/1967; sold for scrap to C.Herring & Son Ltd, Hartlepool, 3/4/1968
(34) withdrawn from traffic by 25/10/1967; sold for preservation and moved to Keighley & Worth Valley Railway, Yorkshire (WR), 2/1971
(35) repairs cancelled; officially withdrawn from traffic, 5/1958, and scrapped on site, 9/1958, though boiler retained for loan to collieries for steam raising
(36) withdrawn from traffic, 10/1959; official date of scrapped not recorded, but seen at Philadelphia in 3/1961, and believed to have been cut up shortly afterwards
(37) officially withdrawn from traffic, 12/1962, but out of use before this; scrapped on site, 1/1964
(38) to Derwenthaugh Loco Shed, Swalwell, 6/3/1969; scrapped on site by D.Sep. Bowran Ltd, Gateshead, 10/1972
(39) as Divisional Spare Locomotive, to Rising Sun Colliery, Wallsend, Northumberland, by 3/1949; to Seaton Delaval Loco Sheds, Seaton Delaval, Northumberland, c6/1949; to Chilton Colliery, Chilton Buildings, 1/11/1949; to Brandon Colliery, Meadowfield, 7/1/1950; to Chilton Colliery, Chilton Buildings, 23/6/1950; to Dean & Chapter Colliery, Ferryhill, 26/6/1950; returned to Lambton Railway Loco Sheds, Philadelphia, 4/1952; to South Hetton Loco Sheds, South Hetton, 16/7/1952; returned to Lambton Railway Loco Sheds, Philadelphia, 12/1955, and henceforth regarded as a Lambton Railway locomotive; to Lambton Staiths loco shed, Sunderland, after 25/6/1965, by 15/2/1966; to Lambton Railway Loco Sheds, Philadelphia, 18/2/1966; to Morrison Busty Colliery, Annfield Plain, 8/1969; scrapped on site by D.Sep. Bowran Ltd, 3/1971
(40) underfeed mechanical stoker latterly disconnected; to Dawdon Colliery, Seaham, 22/7/1965; to Lambton Engine Works, Philadelphia, 19/7/1967; to Dawdon Colliery, Seaham, 29/2/1968; to Strathspey Railway, Highland, Scotland, for preservation, 4/5/1976, leaving Dawdon c16/7/1976
(41) scrapped on site by a Chesterfield firm, 2/1970
(42) to Dawdon Colliery, Seaham, 26/1/1967; sold for scrap to C.Herring & Son Ltd, Hartlepool, 17/11/1967 and scrapped on site, 12/1967
(43) to Seaham Colliery, Seaham, 21/7/1965; sold to J.A.Lister & Sons Ltd, Consett, for scrap, 13/3/1968, but not proceeded with; re-sold for scrap to W.Willoughby, Ashington, Northumberland and removed from site on 5/9/1968, being cut up at Ashington in 10/1968

(44) to Wearmouth Colliery, Sunderland, 3/3/1967; to Hylton Colliery, Sunderland, c10/1968; scrapped on site, 12/1972
(45) to Derwenthaugh Loco Shed, Swalwell, 6/3/1969; scrapped on site by D.Sep. Bowran Ltd, Gateshead, 10/1972
(46) to Dawdon Colliery, Seaham, after 5/1956, by 8/1956
(47) to Seaham Colliery, Seaham by 11/1955
(48) to South Hetton Loco Sheds, South Hetton, after 11/1955, by 4/1956; for subsequent history see chapter 13
(49) to Wearmouth Colliery, Sunderland, 23/1/1968; to Lambton Engine Works, Philadelphia, 28/4/1977, but found to beyond economic repair; cannibalised, and remains scrapped 5/1977
(50) scrapped on site by D.Sep. Bowran Ltd, Gateshead, 5/1970
(51) to South Hetton Loco Sheds, South Hetton, 25/1/1961; for subsequent history see chapter 13
(52) to South Hetton Loco Sheds, South Hetton, after 4/1961, by 10/1961; for subsequent history see chapter 13
(53) rarely used at Philadelphia; to Hylton Colliery, Sunderland, 13/9/1965; to Wearmouth Colliery, Sunderland, 12/1968; to Hylton Colliery, Sunderland, 1/1969; scrapped c7/1970
(54) to South Hetton Loco Sheds, South Hetton, 20/5/1964
(55) scrapped on site by a Chesterfield firm, 3/1970
(56) to Wearmouth Colliery, Sunderland, 11/1968
(57) to Boldon Colliery, Boldon Colliery, 2/1974; left Boldon Colliery, 17/12/1974, for Backworth Colliery, Backworth, Northumberland; at BR Cambois Motive Power Depot, near Blyth, Northumberland, by 3/1/1975; arrived at Backworth after 6/1/1975; to Burradon Colliery, Burradon, Northumberland, 29/1/1975; to Weetslade Coal Preparation Plant, Weetslade, Northumberland, 3/1/1976; to Lambton Engine Works, Philadelphia, 21/4/1981; to Ashington Colliery, Ashington, Northumberland, 11/9/1981; sold to Kent & East Sussex Railway, Rolvenden, Kent, for preservation, 9/1987; to Nene Valley Railway, Wansford, Cambridgeshire, 25/2/1998, for repairs; returned to Kent & East Sussex Railway, 21/4/1999; to Channel Tunnel Rail Link, Beechbrook Farm Depot, Ashford, Kent, by 10/2001, on hire; to World Naval Base, The Historic Dockyard, Chatham, Kent, c2/2003; to Nene Valley Railway, Wansford, Cambridgeshire, for repairs, 4/4/2003
(58) to Burradon Colliery, Burradon, Northumberland, 7/3/1975; to Ashington Colliery, Ashington, Northmberland, 14/3/1975; to Backworth Colliery, Backworth, Northumberland, 15/12/1975; to Ashington Colliery, Ashington, Northumberland, 15/8/1980; to Weetslade Coal Preparation Plant, Weetslade, Northumberland, 1/981; returned to Ashington Colliery, Ashington, Northumberland, 24/4/1981; to Lambton Engine Works, Philadelphia, 25/7/1983; to Ashington Colliery, Ashington, Northumberland, 7/2/1984; sold to Kent & East Sussex Railway, Rolvenden, Kent, for preservation, 9/1987
(59) to Burradon Colliery, Burradon, Northumberland, 25/11/1971; to Weetslade Coal Preparation Plant, Weetslade, Northumberland, 3/1/1976; to Ashington Colliery, Ashington, Northumberland, 24/4/1981; scrapped on site by D.Short Ltd, North Shields, Tyne & Wear, 1/1984
(60) sold for scrap to C.H.Newton (Jnr) & Co Ltd, Durham City, but actually scrapped on site by C.F.Booth (Steel) Ltd, Rotherham, West Yorkshire, 11/1985
(61) being cannibalised for spares by 30/8/1979; remainder scrapped on site by L.Marley, Stanley, 3/1980
(62) sold for scrap to C.H.Newton (Jnr) & Co Ltd, Durham City, but actually scrapped on site by C.F.Booth (Steel) Ltd, Rotherham, West Yorkshire, 12/1985
(63) to National Smokeless Fuels Ltd, Lambton Coking Plant, Fencehouses, 9/1985; for subsequent history see below
(64) dismantled by 4/6/1971; remainder scrapped later in 1971
(65) to Silksworth Colliery (closed), 7/4/1972, for working last remaining section of the Hetton Railway between Silksworth and Sunderland, which closed 3/6/1972; to Hylton Colliery, Sunderland, 7/1972; to Lambton Railway Loco Sheds, Philadelphia, 3/3/1975; to Easington Colliery, Easington Colliery, 22/12/1975; to Blackhall Colliery, Blackhall, 5/1/1976; to Bates Colliery, Blyth, Northumberland, 5/4/1976; to Lambton Engine Works, Philadelphia, 25/2/1983; but work did not make loco useable, and moved to Lambton Railway Loco Sheds, Philadelphia, 21/10/1983, for use as source of spares; scrapped on site by C.F.Booth (Steel) Ltd, Rotherham, South Yorkshire, 11/1985
(66) did no work; written off, 24/2/1975, and subsequently scrapped (date not known)
(67) to Bates Colliery, Blyth, Northumberland, 12/11/1976
(68) to Seaham Colliery, Seaham, 5/1979; for subsequent history see chapters 3 and 4
(69) not used during its time at Philadelphia; to Tyne & Wear Industrial Monuments Trust, Bowes Railway, Springwell, for preservation, 8/1979, and moved to Springwell, 13/8/1979
(70) to Derwenthaugh Loco Shed, Swalwell, 15/3/1978
(71) permission to scrap given, 11/1979; scrapped early in 1980 (Lambton Engine Works incorrectly gave the scrap date as 9/8/1979)
(72) to South Hetton Loco Sheds, South Hetton, 23/6/1980; for subsequent history see chapter 13
(73) to Seaham Colliery, Seaham, 12/1981; ex Ashington Colliery, Ashington, Northumberland, to Lambton Railway Loco Sheds, Philadelphia, 2/11/1982; to Bates Colliery, Blyth, Northumberland, 1/5/1983
(74) scrapped on site by C.F.Booth (Steel) Ltd, Rotherham, South Yorkshire. 11/1985

(75) to South Hetton Loco Sheds, South Hetton, 27/9/1982; for subsequent history see chapter 13
(76) to Bates Colliery, Blyth, Northumberland, 15/2/1983; scrapped here by C.H.Newton (Jnr) & Co Ltd, Durham, 11/1985
(77) to Seaham Colliery, Seaham, 4/3/1983; scrapped here by C.Herring & Son Ltd, Hartlepool, 11/1985

Demonstration locomotives
Locomotives owned by their makers on trial at the Lambton Railway Loco Sheds, Philadelphia, during 1962. None of these trials resulted in a locomotive of these designs being purchased, or indeed any diesel locomotive being purchased, by NCB Durham No.2 Area.

Gauge : 4ft 8½in

-	0-6-0DH	S	10072	1961	(a)	(1)
-	4wDH	S	10097	1962	(b)	(2)
-	4wDH	TH	105V	1962	(c)	(3)

(a) ex Park Hill Colliery, Wakefield, Yorkshire (NR), 20/2/1962
(b) ex Western Rhyn Loco Shed (NCB), Shropshire, 3/4/1962
(c) ex Tees Side Bridge & Engineering Co Ltd, Middlesbrough, Yorkshire (NR), 10/9/1962

(1) to Springwell Bank Foot Loco Shed, Wardley, Bowes Railway, for trials, 28/3/1962
(2) to Washington Chemical Co Ltd, Washington, for trials, 19/6/1962
(3) believed sent to Lambton Staiths loco shed, Sunderland, and to Seaham Colliery, Seaham, for trials, and returned to Philadelphia; to Tees Side Bridge & Engineering Co Ltd, Middlesbrough, Yorkshire (NR), 27/9/1962

Locomotives hired from British Railways for use on the Lambton Railway
The first three were hired in the crisis following the end of steam locomotive working in February 1969, the fourth during a shortage of locomotive power while locomotives were under repair.

Gauge : 4ft 8½in

D2102	0-6-0DM	Don		1960	(a)	(1)
12078	0-6-0DE	Derby		1950	(b)	(2)
D3140	0-6-0DE	Dar		1955	(c)	(3)
(D)3516	0-6-0DE	Derby		1958	(d)	(4)

(a) ex British Railways, Darlington Motive Power Depot, Darlington, Class 03, 21/2/1969
(b) ex British Railways, Tyne Dock Motive Power Depot, Tyne Dock, Class 11, 28/2/1969
(c) ex British Railways, Thornaby Motive Power Depot, Thornaby-on-Tees, Yorkshire (NR), Class 10, 10/3/1969
(d) ex British Railways, Doncaster Motive Power Depot, Doncaster, Yorkshire (NR), Class 08, 16/4/1973

(1) returned to British Railways, Darlington Motive Power Depot, Darlington, 28/2/1969
(2) returned to British Railways, Tyne Dock Motive Power Depot, Tyne Dock, 10/3/1969
(3) returned to British Railways, Thornaby Motive Power Depot, Thornaby-on-Tees, Yorkshire (NR), 21/3/1969
(4) returned to British Railways, Doncaster Motive Power Depot, Doncaster, Yorkshire (NR), 24/4/1973

Locomotive used as works shunter at Lambton Engine Works
North East Area from 1/8/1975
previously **NCB Workshops Division**

Gauge : 4ft 8½

No.103	0-6-0DH	S	10157	1963	(a)	(1)

(a) ex Wardley Loco Shed, Wardley, Monkton Railways, 19/7/1985; for earlier history see chapter 3

(1) to Sutton Colliery, Sutton-in-Ashfield, Nottinghamshire, 13/7/1987; for subsequent history see chapter 3

Locomotives used at Lambton Coking Plant, Fencehouses
National Smokeless Fuels Ltd from 1/4/1973
NCB Coal Products Division from 1/1/1963
previously **NCB Durham No.2 Area**

The first locomotive in the list was the coke car locomotive; the others were acquired either as a standby for use with the coke car when the coke car locomotive was unavailable, or to shunt the plant after the closure of the Lambton Railway loco sheds at Philadelphia in July 1985. Despite the locomotives below, Class 08 locomotives were also hired from British Rail's Gateshead MPD; there were almost certainly more than the two listed below. The plant closed in January 1986 and was quickly demolished.

Gauge : 4ft 8½

	-	0-4-0WE	RSHN	7804	1954	New	(1)
42		0-4-0DE	RH	384141 *	1955	(a)	(2)
No.1		0-6-0DM	HE	5382	1958	(b)	(3)
41		0-6-0DE	RH	421438	1958	(c)	(4)
513		0-6-0DE	Derby		1952	(d)	(5)
	08176	0-6-0DE	Dar		1956	(e)	(6)
-		0-6-0DH	HE	7305	1973	(f)	(7)
	08164	0-6-0DE	Dar		1956	(g)	(8)

* carried 384161 in error

(a) ex Weetslade Coal Preparation Plant, Weetslade, Northumberland, 12/1979
(b) ex Fishburn Coking Plant, Fishburn, 2/9/1983 (left Fishburn, 1/9/1983)
(c) ex Vane Tempest Colliery, Seaham, 16/11/1983
(d) ex Lambton Railway Loco Sheds, Philadelphia, loan, 9/1985
(e) on hire from British Rail, but ex National Smokeless Fuels Ltd, Monkton Coking Plant, Wardley, by 21/10/1985
(f) ex Thomas Hill (Rotherham) Ltd, Rotherham, South Yorkshire, 7/11/1985, after overhaul; previously at Birch Coppice Colliery, Dordon, Warwickshire, until 10/4/1985
(g) ex British Rail, Gateshead Motive Power Depot, Gateshead, by 12/1/1986, hire

(1) to Lambton Engine Works, Philadelphia, for repairs, c6/1968, and returned, /1968; to Thomas Hill (Rotherham) Ltd, Rotherham, South Yorkshire, for repairs, 3/1984; returned, 28/8/1984; to Smithywood Coking Plant, Chapeltown, South Yorkshire, 1/1986
(2) sold for scrap to Henry Boot Ltd, but then re-sold to C.F.Booth (Steel) Ltd, Rotherham, South Yorkshire, and moved there on 8/7/1986
(3) sold for scrap to Henry Boot Ltd, but then re-sold to C.F.Booth (Steel) Ltd, Rotherham, South Yorkshire, and moved there on 26/6/1986
(4) sold for scrap to Henry Boot Ltd, but then re-sold to C.F.Booth (Steel) Ltd, Rotherham, South Yorkshire, and moved there on 7/7/1986
(5) sold for scrap, c5/1986; acquired by P.Millar, Durham City, for preservation, c11/1986, and moved to North Tyneside Council, proposed Museum of Land Transport, Middle Engine Lane, North Shields, Northumberland, 1/1987; to Harry Needle Railroad Co and moved to South Yorkshire Railway Preservation Society, Sheffield, South Yorkshire, 9/12/1997; sold for scrap to European Metal Recycling Ltd, Kingsbury, Warwickshire, c7/2001
(6) withdrawn from traffic by BR, 24/11/1985 (after a breakdown?) and stored at Lambton Coking Plant until 3/1986, when moved to British Rail, Doncaster Motive Power Depot, Doncaster, North Yorkshire
(7) to Monkton Coking Plant, Wardley (see Bowes Railway), 17/6/1986
(8) returned to British Rail, Gateshead Motive Power Depot, Gateshead, c1/1986

Even before steam had finished on the Railway itself, groups which had purchased locomotives for preservation were approaching the National Coal Board to ask whether their locomotives could be stored in the shed buildings. This brought LNER A4 class 60009 and LNER J27 class 65894 to Philadelphia, although only for a short time.

No fewer than five of the Lambton Railway's own steam locomotives and three of its diesel locomotives were acquired for preservation, together with a fourth diesel which never did any work at Philadelphia. All nine were subsequently restored to working order. Two of the Railway's 12 ton wooden hopper wagons, with their distinctive angled sides, Nos.1392 and 1955 (with cut down sides) survive on the Tanfield Railway, whilst a brake van that went to the Harton electric system in South Shields and was then converted into a passenger-carrying vehicle with windows, is on the Bowes Railway preservation scheme at Springwell. Vans from the Railway are preserved on the Embsay & Bolton Abbey Steam Railway in North Yorkshire.

Although the route of the Railway in built-up areas like Sunderland has now disappeared, it can be traced with the help of maps. Out in the Durham countryside the trackbeds can still be seen in many places, whilst the site of Lambton Staiths, with its two tunnels, has been landscaped to form part of the River Wear Trail. But at Philadelphia, the centre of its operations, the whole of Lambton Engine Works survives, together with the Wagon Shops (with the buildings partly rebuilt) and the nearby Area Divisional Stores, all now (2004) in the ownership of Philadelphia Estates Ltd, although sub-let to a wide variety of mainly industrial activities. Many of the buildings, including the pre-1860 range, are "listed". Nearby all of the locomotive sheds, with the exception of the four-road building but including the shed foreman's office, also continue in use, again mainly as industrial units. Nearby, the main buildings of the former Philadelphia Power Station also survive. Collectively they form a historic and important monument to one of the most important private railways in Britain.

Chapter Ten
The Londonderry Railway

OWNERS
The 6th Marquis of Londonderry from 5/11/1884
The 5th Marquis of Londonderry until 5/11/1884 (entitled **Earl Vane** until 25/11/1872)
The Marchioness of Londonderry until 20/1/1865
The 3rd Marquis of Londonderry until 6/3/1854; see also below

Although like other private railways in Durham the origins of this system can be traced back to an eighteenth century waggonway, the creation of this Railway was entirely the work of one powerful man, Charles Stewart, the 3rd Marquis of Londonderry.

The origins of the Londonderry industrial empire in Durham go back to the Vanes of Long Newton and the Tempests of Wynyard, both in south-east Durham. The last of the male line, Sir Henry Vane Tempest, owned extensive coal interests at Pensher and Rainton; but he died in 1813, leaving as his heir his only daughter, Lady Frances Anne Vane Tempest, aged 13, which meant her estates went into the Court of Chancery and the estates were administered by trustees. As the Agent for their coal mines the trustees employed Arthur Mowbray, continuing to do so despite his bankruptcy in 1816.

Charles William Stewart was born in Dublin in 1778 and had a distinguished military career under the Duke of Wellington and an equally successful diplomatic career subsequently, as did his half-brother, Viscount Castlereagh. On 3rd April 1819 he married Lady Frances, now described as the most desirable heiress in England, as his second wife; but although he took the surname Vane the marriage was against the wishes of her family, who, anxious to ensure that Stewart could not become the owner of Lady Frances' considerable estates, forced through a legal settlement to make him only her tenant, for life. He began by sacking Mowbray and engaging as his Agent John Buddle (1773-1843). Buddle, who had been Agent for the Lambton estates (see the Lambton Railway) since 1806, was the foremost Agent and mining engineer in the North-East. Then in 1821 Stewart purchased the Milbanke estate at Seaham, an acquisition that changed not only his own thinking but also the subsequent future of the Londonderrys' industrial interests in Co. Durham.

Following the death of his half-brother, Stewart became the **3rd Marquis of Londonderry** on 12th August 1822. In the 35 years following his marriage the Marquis dominated the coal trade, expanding his colliery ownership, creating new railways and building a new port and town at Seaham. He died on 6th March 1854. The title passed to the son by his first marriage, while Frances Anne, now the **Marchioness of Londonderry** and a formidable lady in her own right, took over full control of the extensive Durham estates, including those her husband had bought. She died on 20th January 1865, the Londonderry properties in Durham then passing to her eldest son, **Earl Vane**. He became the **5th Marquis of Londonderry** on the death of his half-brother on 25th November 1872, but lived mainly in mid-Wales on his wife's estate. He died on 5th November 1884, to be succeeded by his son, Charles Stewart Vane-Tempest (1852-1915), as the **6th Marquis of Londonderry**.

At this point all the collieries and railways, together with the port and town of Seaham, were still the personal property of the Marquis, to say nothing of extensive properties elsewhere in Britain and Ireland. With the decline of the old collieries and the need for extensive investment in the port at Seaham, the 6th Marquis undertook a huge re-organisation of his Durham properties between 1896 and 1901, closing or selling the railways, obtaining an Act of Parliament for the port which set up the Seaham Harbour Dock Company and converting the ownership of the collieries into a separate limited company. However, he remained their leading shareholder and chairman of both new companies, and this direct involvement, both of him and his successors, continued long into the twentieth century.

The 9th Marquis deposited a huge volume of family papers and company documents with the Durham County Record Office from 1963 onwards (the D/Lo collection), while the Buddle papers also survived and are now in the Northumberland County Record Office in Newcastle upon Tyne (NRO 3410/Bud). Between them these collections give very detailed information about the Londonderrys' activities.

When the family's private railway from Seaham to Sunderland, with its public passenger service, was opened in 1855, George Hardy (1825-1917) was placed in charge of locomotive repairs. In 1883 he became the Railway Manager, not finally retiring until 1902 at the age of 77. He then wrote an extensive autobiography, which gives a fascinating and detailed insight into the running of the Railway, especially the Sunderland section and the development and work of the Seaham workshops. This was edited and abbreviated by Charles Lee and published in 1973 by Goose & Son of Norwich as *The Londonderry Railway* under George Hardy's name; a copy of Hardy's original and much longer draft is held by Beamish, the North of England Open Air Museum in Co. Durham.

The Vane Tempest Waggonway
The origin of the system can be traced back to the first half of the eighteenth century. The Tempest family owned pits in the Pensher area, whose coal was carried by waggonway to staiths on the River Wear nearby, opposite Fatfield. Developments further south, in the Rainton area, caused the line to be extended there, probably in the 1780s. John Gibson's *Plan of the Collieries on the Rivers Tyne & Wear* (1787) shows the waggonway now serving Rainton, some four miles from the river. This basic position remained unchanged for the next thirty years, changing only in detail as pits were abandoned and new pits opened. However, the opening of the new Newbottle Waggonway to Sunderland in 1812 (see chapter 9) made the old Newbottle line to its staiths at Pensher redundant, and by November 1815 this had been leased to Lady Frances Anne's Trustees, becoming part of their system (NRO 3410/Wat/3/59/II/7).

When Buddle was appointed in 1819 the waggonway consisted of a main line of 4¾ miles with two branches and served two collieries. In the north lay **PENSHER COLLIERY** (also known as **Old Pensher Colliery**, to distinguish it from the (New) Pensher Colliery nearby, owned by J.G.Lambton. This colliery consisted of two pits, the **D or Whitefield Pit** (NZ 323534), from which ran a ¾ mile branch to the **Herrington Mill Pit** (NZ 328527). In between the two lay **Pensher Quarry** (NZ 326530). In the south lay **RAINTON COLLIERY**, which consisted of five pits. Three were served by the "main line" – the **North Pit** (NZ 329489), the **Dunwell Pit** (NZ 338480) and the **Hazard Pit** (NZ 340477), the last completed in 1818. The other two were served by a 1½ mile branch - the **Resolution Pit** (NZ 312477), whose sinking had begun on 9th January 1816 and was completed on 2nd May 1819, and the **Hunter's House Pit** (NZ 315484), begun on 15th September 1817. The two lines joined ¼ mile south of Chilton Moor, where the stables were situated, though soon afterwards a large new stables, the **Pensher Stables** (NZ 322537), were built. Curiously, he does not mention the old Newbottle line - perhaps that had been given up by 1819 – nor three other pits which were subsequently to be included in Rainton Colliery – the **Adventure Pit** (NZ 315471), also begun on 9th January 1816, and completed on 6th July 1817, the **Plain Pit** (NZ 323485), begun on 13th September 1817 and **Nicholson's Pit** (NZ 328483), begun two days later. All these are shown on Fig.47.

The original "main line" to Pensher Staiths
Buddle's dissatisfaction with the existing waggonway was soon obvious. In February 1820 he proposed a link to the Newbottle waggonway (D/Lo/B/309). In December 1821, almost immediately after Lord Stewart had acquired the Milbanke estate at Seaham, he was studying a line of railway from Rainton to Seaham (D/Lo/C/142, letter 8/12/1821). This route was given further impetus in November 1822, when a proposal for such a line was received from Benjamin Thompson, the owner of the Ouston Waggonway (see chapter 11). Over the following months this proposal was worked up into a costed plan (D/Lo/E594/5), and included two stationary engines, three self-acting inclines and two "elephants", or steam locomotives. Between November 1823 and February 1824 Buddle was actually surveying a line over Warden Law to Sunderland, and he even considered the acquisition of the Hetton Railway (D/Lo/C/142). None of these proposals came to anything; Londonderry simply did not have the money needed to fund a huge programme of sinking new pits, modernising old ones and developing a new harbour to be able to build a new railway as well. Instead Buddle had to begin by improving and developing the two collieries and the existing waggonway

His first plan, put forward in October 1819, was to build a new route between Old Pensher Colliery and the staiths. The first 660 yards of this was built alongside the Lambton waggonway and was worked by a **stationary engine** (NZ 321531) at the junction of the branch to Herrington Mill Pit; this had a trailing link from the Whitefield Pit at the bank foot. The final 760 yards to the staiths was a **self-acting incline**, the whole installation saving 16 horses. Three years later Buddle acquired a "travelling engine" for use at Rainton, though it seems to have done little work; it was still there in 1827, when the Duke of Wellington visited the line (see chapter 1, where the use of a second? locomotive as a crane, first at Wynyard and later at Seaham, is also discussed). Further south Buddle eventually got what he wanted, a new line nearly 700 yards long being built from Sedgeletch, north of Chilton Moor, to the former Jane Pit site at Newbottle (NZ 327516) and the former Newbottle Waggonway.

Although coal had been reached at the Adventure Pit in May 1817, production was delayed; the ½ mile branch to it was not completed until June 1823, and production did not begin until 1824. Branches were also laid to the Plain Pit and Nicholson's Pit. Next came the **Meadows Pit** (NZ 324479), where sinking began on 1st June 1821 and was completed on 12th June 1824; this was served by a ½ mile link south from the Plain Pit. Then came the **Alexandrina Pit**, equally known as the **Letch Pit** (NZ 334464), which was begun on 22nd October 1823 and completed in only ten months, on 4th August 1824; this was served by a 1¼ mile extension, begun in April 1824, from the Meadows Pit. Even further south lay the small village of Pittington, and a new colliery was opened here too. The sources do not agree about the details; one says that the sinking began in 1820 and the colliery began production in June 1827; another states that the sinking began on 3rd April 1826 and was completed on 19th June 1828. To serve **PITTINGTON COLLIERY** (NZ 333443) a line about two miles long ran southwards from Hetton Lane

THE VANE TEMPEST WAGGONWAY
1820

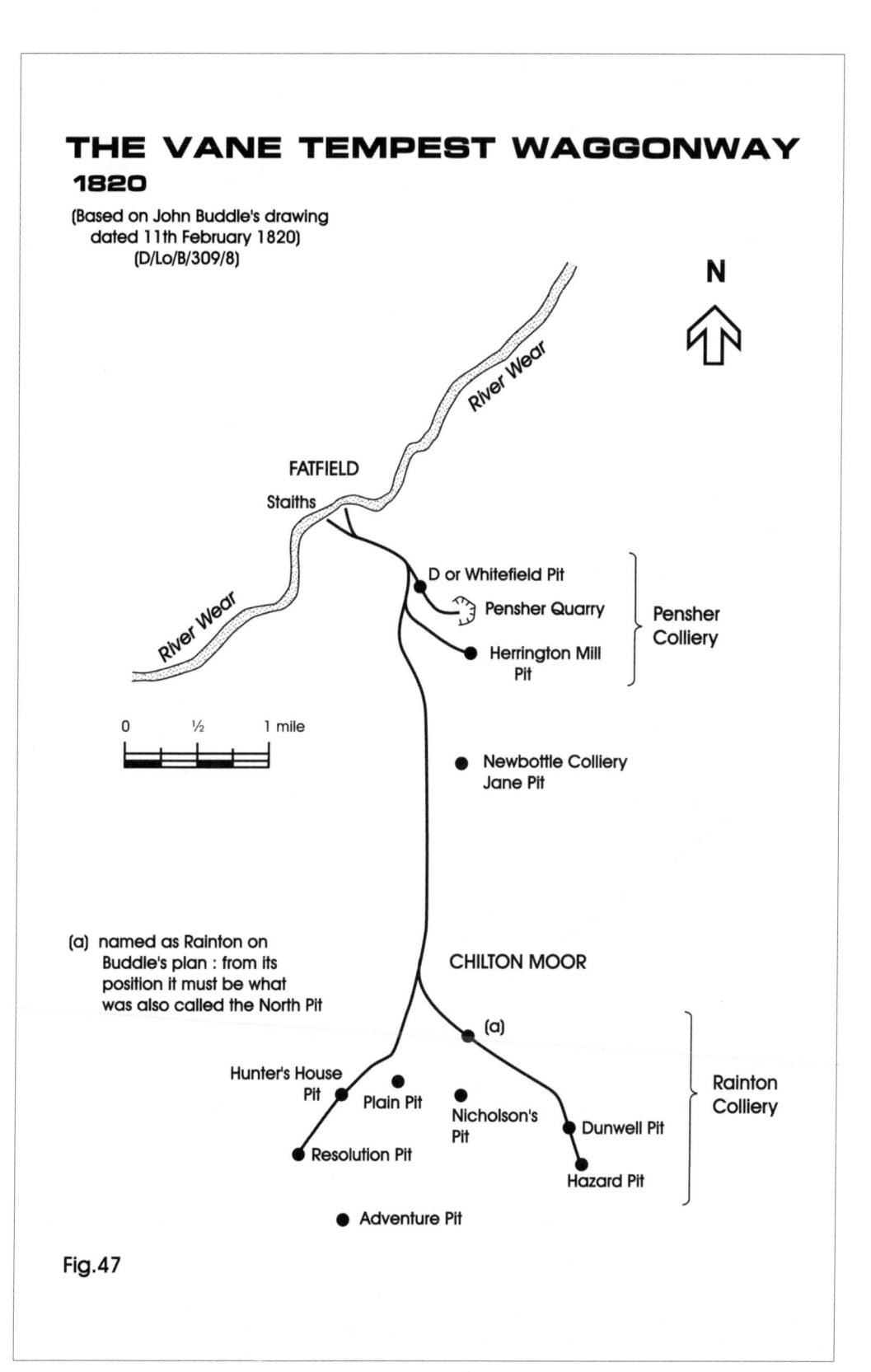

(Based on John Buddle's drawing
dated 11th February 1820)
(D/Lo/B/309/8)

N

River Wear

FATFIELD
Staiths

D or Whitefield Pit
Pensher Quarry } Pensher Colliery
Herrington Mill Pit

River Wear

0   ½   1 mile

Newbottle Colliery Jane Pit

(a) named as Rainton on Buddle's plan : from its position it must be what was also called the North Pit

CHILTON MOOR

(a)

Hunter's House Pit
Plain Pit
Nicholson's Pit
Dunwell Pit } Rainton Colliery
Resolution Pit
Hazard Pit
Adventure Pit

Fig.47

on the Alexandrina branch. On 29th September 1827 the Duke of Wellington visited the Marquis and travelled the length of what was now the main line, some six miles between Pittington and Pensher, in a special carriage built for the occasion, inspecting Pittington Colliery, travelling over the inclines, inspecting the locomotive at Rainton and later the staiths at Pensher, before dining at Buddle's house there. Then about 1835 **BROOMSIDE COLLIERY** (NZ 317437) was opened and served by a 1 mile branch from Pittington village. However on the debit side Lord Londonderry decided to dispose of the Dunwell and Hazard Pits, no doubt to help finance his huge expenditure elsewhere. On 24th March 1825 they were sold to a partnership headed by William Russell of Brancepeth Castle in Durham. They continued to send their coal over Londonderry's line to Pensher, but the two pits now became called **North Hetton Colliery**, and it may well be that it was because of this change of ownership that instead of Nicholson's Pit being served by a line from a branch which Lord Londonderry no longer owned, a new ½ mile line was built from the Plain Pit. Russell and his partners did not keep the pits long, for on 17th July 1836 they were sold to a joint partnership of Londonderry, the Earl of Durham and The Hetton Coal Company, calling itself **The North Hetton Coal Company** (see chapter 8).

Collaboration between Londonderry and Lambton
Soon after Londonderry had opened Pittington Colliery J.G.Lambton acquired the royalty immediately to the west, and in 1831 he began the sinking of what was at first called **Lambton Colliery**, but was latterly called **Littletown Colliery** (NZ 339435). The new colliery was ready for production in 1833 or 1834, but it was situated several miles from the nearest section of the Lambton Railway; and so it became part of a collaboration between two of the leading coal owners of the day that is unparralled in the Durham coalfield.

The Londonderry line to Pensher crossed under the Lambton line to Sunderland near Newbottle, just north of the Jane Pit site. So Lambton built a line from Littletown to join the Londonderry line at Pittington, while from the Jane Pit he built a 406-yard curve round to join the Junction Bank on his own line (TWA DF/WF/28/1/328). The Lambton traffic over the Londonderry line increased still further in 1835, when Lambton, now Earl of Durham, extended the line from Littletown Colliery to serve his new **Sherburn Colliery**. For his part, Londonderry saw advantages for him too; in return for Londonderry paying for the incline rope which worked the Jane Pit curve, it was agreed that Lambton would handle Londonderry traffic over his line for shipment at Sunderland – and this despite the opening of Londonderry's new line to Seaham. In 1835 17,000 Londonderry chaldrons, about 45,000 tons, went north to Sunderland. And more; for by 1831 traffic from North Hetton Colliery (see above) was going north along the Londonderry line to Pensher, where it was transferred to the Lambton system for shipment at the latter's Low Lambton Staiths. Both traffic flows were still continuing in 1839, but probably ceased in 1841, after Londonderry had obtained full control of his railway between Rainton Bridge and Seaham.

The line between Pittington and Pensher
Fortunately, amongst the Londonderry Papers at Durham is a detailed survey of the cost of operating the line between Pittington and the Jane Pit in 1839 (D/Lo/B/306/22), which includes considerable descriptive details, though these are not without their difficulties. The first section, from Pittington Colliery itself to the bank head of the first incline, was 1007 yards and was worked by seven horses. However, there was certainly a stationary engine, the **Pittington Engine**, here by 1863, for there is a description of it in the Place Collection held by Beamish Regional Resource Centre (2003-54.7/42). It is another of the rare examples of engines undertaking two functions, for besides hauling wagons on the Railway the ropes from two drums went down the shaft in boxes to go underground in the Main Coal seam for hauling the tubs – indeed, the engine, a horizontal engine with two 13¼in x 24in cylinders. provided the only powered haulage underground at the pit at that time. George Hardy also refers to this engine in his draft (p.230) in describing the fate of No.1 locomotive: "About 1863 the frame work [of this loco] with the cylinders and working gear were fixed on the Pittington wagon way and supplied with steam from a stationary boiler to haul coal wagons along the wagon way". Curiously, the engine may also have been unusual in a third way; another entry in the same Place Collection volume (2003-54.7/3) describes a boiler which had been installed at Pittington in 1854 (were the horses replaced then?), which was deliberately exploded, in steam, in 1868 in front of the Mines Inspector. This boiler had been made at the workshops of Pensher Colliery E Pit in 1811, using plates made at Lumley Forge under the supervision of Robert Oley, a German who had introduced German steel-making to the North of England.

This bank head (NZ 328444) was also the junction with the line from Lord Durham's collieries at Littletown and Sherburn. The incline itself was a self-acting bank 600 yards long on a gradient of 1 in 26, which took the line down to the road through Pittington village. At this point, called Pittington Town End, there was a stationary engine called the **Flatts Engine** (NZ 326448). This worked the branch which trailed in from Broomside Colliery, 1377 yards on a rise of 1 in 288, and the next section of the main line, **Pittington Flat**, 726 yards on a rising gradient of 1 in 576. Both of these inclines were worked by main-and-tail haulage. The waggons were then hauled up for 858 yards on a gradient of 1 in 32 to the **Pittington Bank Engine**, or **Hindmarch's Engine** (NZ 328463).

How the next 1½ miles was operated is uncertain. From Hindmarch's Engine a short bank of 484 yards at 1 in 96 took the waggons down to Hetton Lane and the junction with the trailing branch from

LONDONDERRY RAILWAY in 1840

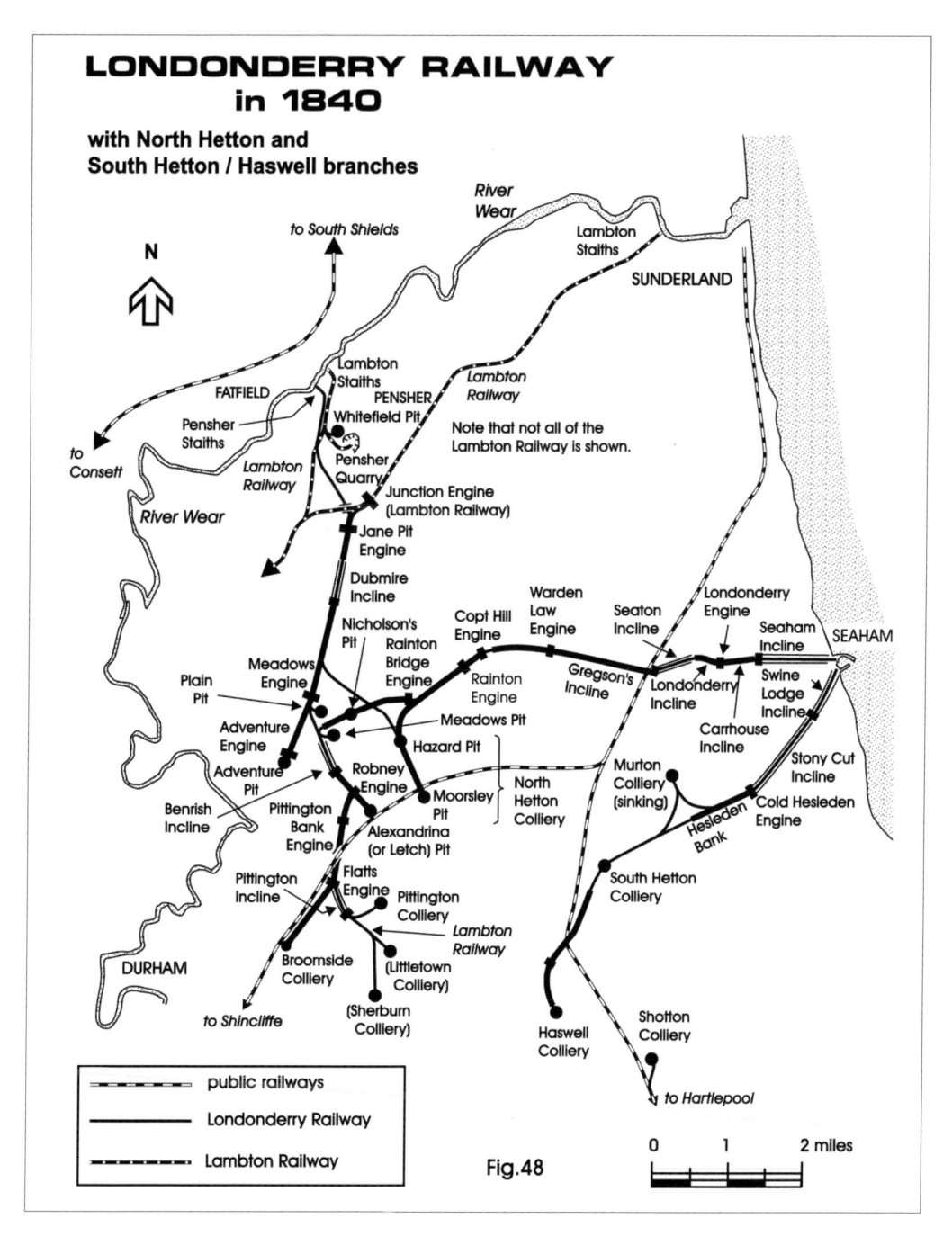

with North Hetton and South Hetton / Haswell branches

Fig. 48

the Alexandrina or Letch Pit, where the **Robney Engine** (NZ 331467) was situated. D/Lo/B/306/22 states that Hindmarch's Engine lowered them to the junction, and that a stationary engine, presumably the Robney Engine, worked the section between the Alexandrina Pit and the Benrish Inclined Plane, 1050 yards from the colliery on a rising gradient of 1 in 288. Given that this length involved the junction with the line from Pittington, it is unclear from this account how the traffic at the junction was worked. The Alexandrina branch is noted on the 1st edition O.S. map some twenty years later as the "Alexandrina Flat", while Benrish had become Benridge. However, oral tradition recorded many years later stated that the Robney Engine worked the section from Hindmarch's Engine and then took them on, allegedly by main-and-tail rope, to Benridge Bank

Rainton Area in 1857

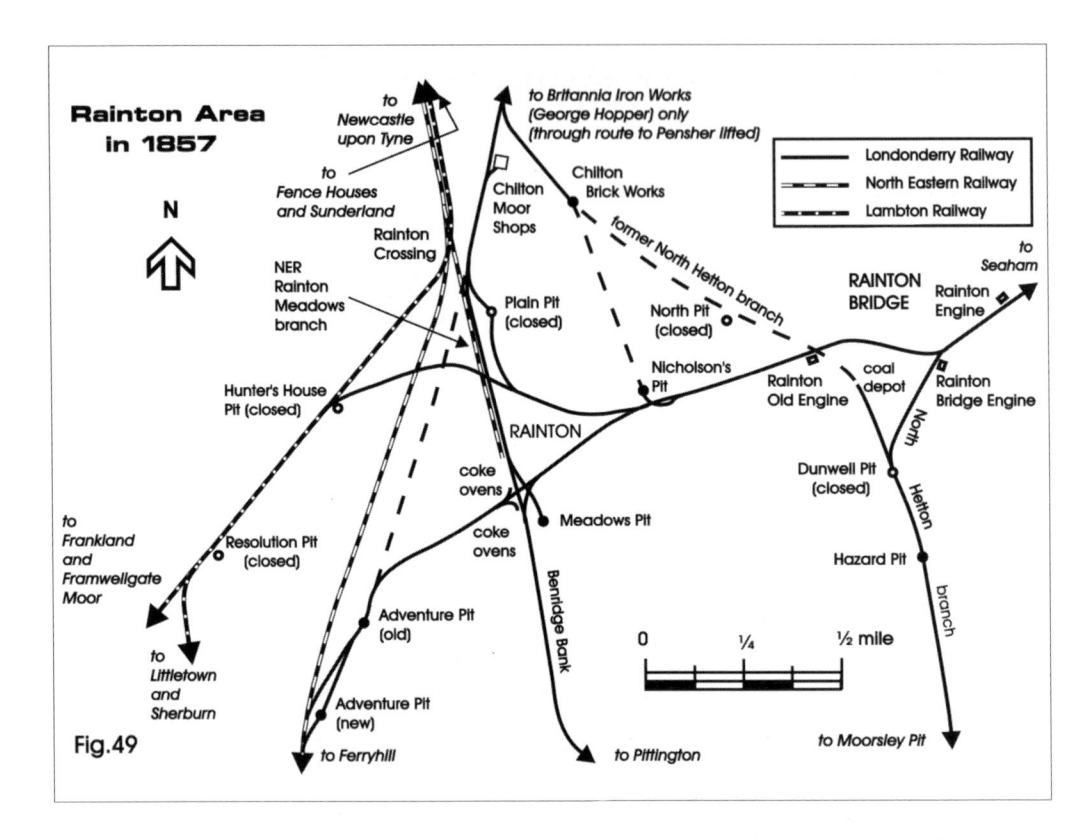

Fig. 49

[Map showing the Rainton Area in 1857 with Londonderry Railway, North Eastern Railway, and Lambton Railway routes, including locations: to Newcastle upon Tyne, to Britannia Iron Works (George Hopper) only (through route to Pensher lifted), to Fence Houses and Sunderland, Chilton Moor Shops, Chilton Brick Works, Rainton Crossing, NER Rainton Meadows branch, Plain Pit (closed), North Pit (closed), former North Hetton branch, to Seaham, RAINTON BRIDGE, Rainton Engine, Hunter's House Pit (closed), Nicholson's Pit, Rainton Old Engine, coal depot, Rainton Bridge Engine, RAINTON, coke ovens, Dunwell Pit (closed), to Frankland and Framwellgate Moor, Resolution Pit (closed), coke ovens, Meadows Pit, Hazard Pit, Benridge Bank, North Hetton branch, Adventure Pit (old), to Littletown and Sherburn, Adventure Pit (new), to Ferryhill, to Pittington, to Moorsley Pit]

Head, while horses worked the Alexandrina branch. The evidence that Hindmarch's Engine lowered the Pittington fulls down to the Alexandrina branch junction seems quite strong, as does that for horse working on the branch itself. At this distance in time such conflicting evidence is difficult to resolve.

Then followed Benrish, latterly Benridge, Bank, a self-acting incline 995 yards long, on a gradient the report gives as 1 in 11, though this would be very steep for such an incline; its trackbed, still visible in 1950, certainly appeared much less severe than 1 in 11. This incline took the fulls down alongside the Meadows Pit to the area at Rainton known as the "Meadows Crossings", where over the years a large number of beehive coke ovens was built. There was also a junction here with a short branch, opened on 24th August 1838 and worked with horses, of the Durham Junction Railway's line between Rainton and Washington.

What is described in the 1839 report had been altered considerably by the time the surveying work of the Ordnance Survey was being done here in 1857. The layout at this later date is shown in Fig. 49. However, since the lengths of the inclines in the Rainton area are given in the 1839 report it is possible to scale them out from the O.S. map.

The branch from the Adventure Pit as described in the report is clearly the line from the original Adventure Pit, which joined the main line north of the Plain Pit. This was 1333 yards on a descent of 1 in 48, and it was worked by a stationary engine, almost certainly at the Adventure Pit end. As the 1857 map shows, a new Adventure Pit was subsequently sunk some yards south of the old one, and much of the old line was abandoned in order to link the pit to the Seaham line. Just north of the Plain Pit was the **Meadows Engine** (NZ 321486) (60 h.p.), which worked the next incline north, 1920 yards at a descent of 1 in 192; this may have been operated by main-and-tail haulage. This brought the full waggons to the bank head (NZ 324500) of the self-acting **Dubmire Incline**, 990 yards at 1 in 72, which took the waggons down to Sedgeletch. From here they were hauled up the 680-yard incline at 1 in 34 to the **Jane Pit Engine** (40 h.p.) (NZ 327516). Initially the full waggons went on from here to the staiths at Pensher; but by 1831 these staiths had been closed, and the only traffic which continued to be dispatched north from the Jane Pit was that from North Hetton Colliery. This was transferred on to the Lambton Railway at Pensher and shipped at this railway's staiths at Low Lambton. The remaining fulls coming to the Jane Pit were dispatched round the curve to the Junction Bank of the Lambton Railway, to be shipped at Lambton Staiths in Sunderland. It also allowed Lambton to bring his coal from Littletown and Sherburn, which had travelled over the Londonderry line from Pittington, back on to his own system. The link was worked by the Lambton Railway's Junction Engine, though the cost of the rope was met by the Marquis.

What the gauge of this system was seems never to have been recorded. However, the fact that the Londonderry and Lambton Railway waggons travelled together over several sections of their systems suggests that the gauge of the two was the same, and at this time the Lambton system had a gauge of 4ft 2ins, possibly 4ft 3ins.

The development of Seaham and the line to it

During the 1820s the Marquis of Londonderry became one of the leading coal producers in Co. Durham, and as his output grew so did his need for direct access to a deep-water outlet for shipment. As has been noted above, buying the Hetton Railway and building a new line to Sunderland were both considered in the early 1820s, and, as noted above, the Marquis did indeed come to an agreement with Lord Durham for some of his coal to be shipped at Sunderland via the Lambton Railway.

But also noted above was the purchase of the Milbanke estate at Seaham in 1821. Here the notable engineer William Chapman (1749-1832) had already put forward a plan to develop a completely new port, 5½ miles south of Sunderland. Buddle and Londonderry were both very attracted to this idea, but they faced the major problem of how to finance both the port and its associated new town and the railway that would need to be built to it. Having failed to raise all the money needed and failed to find a reliable partner, Londonderry decided in September 1828 to go it alone in the construction of the harbour, and work began immediately. But he could not finance the new railway as well, on so on 8th November 1828 he came to an agreement with Mr. Shakespear Reed of Sunderland under which the latter would build the railway and operate it, including the provision of waggons, for a period of nine years from 1st January 1831, subsequently altered to 1st July 1831. This agreement survives in the Northumberland Record Office (NRO 3410/John/9/108). Only the Marquis' coal was to be carried, at a charge, of course, and the Marquis had the option to purchase the line when the agreement expired.

Faced with the need to find a contractor to build the line, Reed appointed in May 1829 none other than Benjamin Thompson, the same man who had put forward the original proposal for the line in 1822. He was now the managing partner of the Birtley Iron Works, and a leading advocate of rope haulage. It is thus not surprising that the new line was to be worked entirely by ropes, with all suggestion of locomotives abandoned. A detailed description of the proposed design dated about 1828 survives (D/Lo/P/202), as well as a description of the route dated 19th December 1830 (NRO 3410/For/1/17/33). As construction was well under way by the latter date it would seem highly probable that this describes the line as opened. Meanwhile Chapman (now eighty years old) and Buddle pushed on with the harbour, bringing stone from Pensher Quarry down the River Wear and then down the coast to Seaham to use in the construction of the piers. The North Dock at the harbour was duly opened on 25th July 1831, though further expenditure was needed to complete the South Dock, finally opened on 29th July 1835. The success of the new harbour did not depend solely on the Marquis' coal. A railway to South Hetton Colliery (see chapter 13) had been opened on 5th August 1833, with an extension of this to Haswell Colliery, owned by the Haswell Coal Co, brought into use on 2nd July 1835. This arrangement was converted into a formal agreement between the Marquis and The South Hetton Coal Co in 1843, with the latter also operating with its own men the staiths in the Harbour at which its coal was shipped. By 1840 the harbour was estimated to have cost £140,000 (some of it Government money), whilst the cost of constructing the railway was put at £45,586, including moveable stock (NRO 3410/John/9/116).

Besides the description of 1830 above there are detailed descriptions of the Seaham line in valuations dated 24th July 1837 (D/Lo/B/306/11), 20th August 1839 (D/Lo/B/306/13) and 12th June 1840 (NRO 3410/John/9/120). A description of the line is also given by S.A.Chapman in *The Cleveland Industrial Archaeologist* No.25 (1998), p.21, in which he quotes lengths for the inclines, all of which are noticeably less than those given in 1830 or 1840. Chapman's figures for the horse power of the engines also differ in some instances. The 1830 figures, which appear to be confirmed by scaling the O.S. maps, are given here.

The new line began officially at Rainton Bridge, a mile to the east of Rainton, and the link between Rainton and Rainton Bridge was built by the Marquis. It is assumed that at the outset this section was worked by what is shown on the O.S. maps twenty years later as the **"Rainton Old Engine"** (NZ 336486), just under ½ mile north-east of the Nicholson Pit. Given its location, it might be assumed that it worked inclines on either side, one hauling up from Rainton and the other taking the waggons on to Rainton Bridge, but there is no evidence at all about this engine. However, the same O.S. map also shows **Rainton Bridge Engine** (NZ 340485), situated to the east of the junction with the North Hetton branch. (see Fig. 49). This link was built in 1836 by the newly-established North Hetton Coal Company from the former Dunwell Pit to Rainton Bridge in order for North Hetton coal to be shipped at Seaham. Whether the Rainton Bridge Engine worked the northern section of the North Hetton branch, or whether it superceded the "Rainton Old Engine" – though its rope would have had to cross the North Hetton branch in order to work the line from Rainton – is unknown. Whatever the railway operation was here, it was short-lived, for by 1860 locomotive working had been introduced between Rainton and Rainton Bridge.

At Rainton Bridge the ownership of the contractors' section began, and here they established a waggon shop for the repair of their chaldron waggons, some 550 of them by 1840. Then followed three inclines, all worked by stationary engines, to bring the line up to the first summit near Warden Law. The first, worked by the **Rainton Engine** (NZ 351493) (82 h.p.), was a double line incline 1271 yards long at 1 in 33, almost certainly working sets of eight waggons at this time. Next was the **Copt Hill Engine** (NZ 356496) (75/82 h.p.), also working a double line incline, 715 yards long at 1 in 15½. Not far from the engine house the line passed under the Hetton Railway's Copt Hill Incline in a short tunnel. In July 1843 the construction of a link between the two lines was authorised, from Copt Hill Bank Head on the Londonderry line to the bank foot of the incline worked by the Flatt Engine on the Hetton line, and presumably worked by it. This was to allow small coal from North Hetton Colliery to be shipped at the Hetton Staiths in Sunderland. It is not known how long this link survived. The final engine house in this section was the **Warden Law Engine** (NZ 366498) (45 h.p.) – not to be confused with the Hetton Railway's Engine of the same name – which worked the inclines on either side of it. The western side, known as the **Warden Law Flatt**, was 957 yards at 1 in 120; the eastern side, known as **Gregson's Plane** and latterly as **The Long Run**, was 2970 yards on a falling gradient, again of 1 in 120. The valuation of 1840 would appear to describe a system of main-and-tail haulage for the western side. The Warden Law Engine would haul eight fulls up from Copt Hill, dragging a tail rope from the engine house there. Then Copt Hill would work a set of eight empties back, with the Warden Law rope forming the tail rope. This was repeated, and then Warden Law would run a set of 16 fulls down Gregson's Plane, hauling 16 empties back for the process to begin again.

At the bottom of Gregson's Bank was the bank head of the **Seaton Incline** (NZ 392493). The Durham & Sunderland Railway, to be opened in August 1836, was to cross the line here on the level. The self-acting Seaton Incline was 1177 yards long at 1 in 22½ and took the full waggons down to the bank foot of the **Londonderry Incline**. This was 330 yards long on a gradient of 1 in 36. A set of eight fulls was worked up to the **Londonderry Engine** (NZ 408495), which then ran sets of 16 fulls down its eastern bank, the **Carrhouse Incline**, 902 yards at 1 in 40. This brought the fulls to the bank head (NZ 414495) of the self-acting **Seaham Incline**. This was 1276 yards, about 1 in 30 at the top but flattening to 1 in 52 near the bottom, which took them down to about ½ mile from the dock. A final ½ mile **self-acting incline**, not included in the 1840 valuation and presumably regarded as part of the harbour, and for which no name is known, worked Londonderry traffic down on to the north side of the North Dock. The South Hetton traffic was shipped on the south side of the North Dock, and to work these waggons a **stationary beam engine** was built. Its use is known to have overlapped the introduction of the small locomotives Nos.16-18 in the 1870s, but when it was abandoned is not known. A second **stationary beam engine**, on the site of the later Seaham Harbour Dock Co loco shed, was provided to haul waggons of ballast up from the ships and then lower them down to the south shore for disposal.

A passenger service?
According to one local source, on Saturdays only a specially-constructed vehicle brought people from the Rainton area to Seaham to do their shopping. Presumably this was attached to normal coal traffic running over the inclines, with the return journey being run later in the day to take people home; a similar system was used over the inclines of the Durham & Sunderland Railway. This service is said to have begun with the opening of the line in 1831; how long it lasted is not known.

By the end of the initial nine-year period of the agreement between the Marquis and Shakespear Reed, the latter had died and the line was now owned by the partners forming The Birtley Iron Company. After an acrimonious dispute about its valuation the Marquis purchased the line and its stock at the end of 1840 for £22,722.

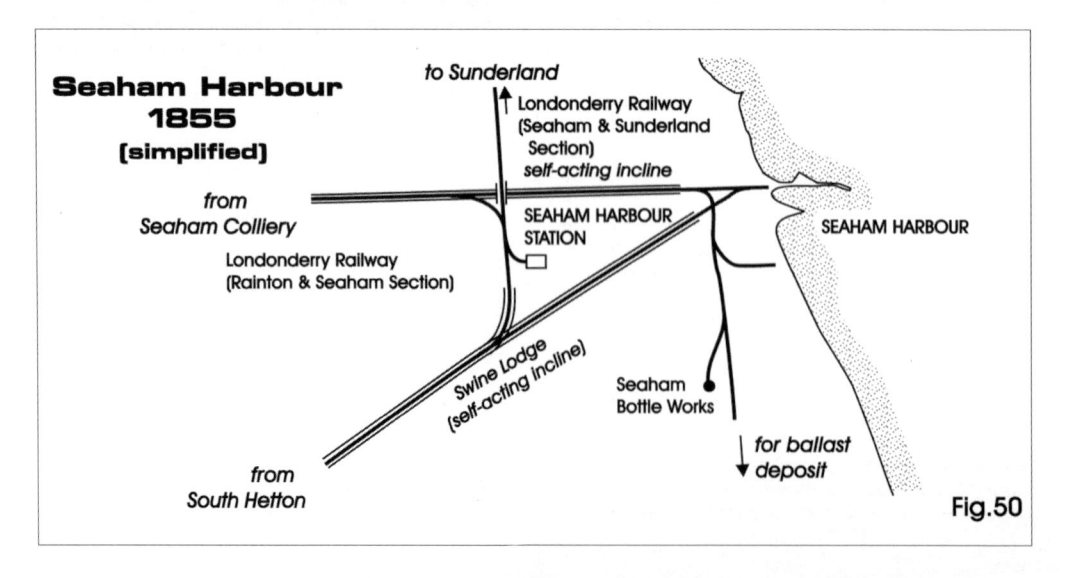

Fig.50 Seaham Harbour 1855 (simplified)

The conversion to standard gauge

It was clearly inevitable that the Londonderry system would have to be converted to "Parliamentary gauge" at some point. On 27th August 1840 Buddle attended a meeting at Pensher (NRO 3410/Bud/48/12/160) to discuss the conversion of both the Londonderry and Lambton systems, the former being listed as totalling 35 miles and using 1600 waggons. In the event the conversion of the Londonderry Railway was not carried out until 15th-18th May 1843, though the conversion of the waggons was underway at least 2½ months earlier (NRO 3410/Bud/48/15-16). The work cost £223.55.

The re-organisation/closure of the original line

The opening of the route to Seaham in 1831 considerably reduced the need for coal to go to Pensher Staiths, and it would seem that these were closed almost immediately. In addition, Buddle himself leased both the Whitefield Pit and Old Pensher Colliery from the Marquis in 1832, thus ending the Marquis' direct interest in the Pensher area. It would seem almost certain that the Whitefield Pit was now linked to the Lambton line for its coal to be shipped at Lambton Staiths at Low Lambton, and that stone from Pensher Quarry was also shipped here.

Once the Marquis had purchased the Seaham line it was clearly in his interest to have all his own coal carried down it, as well as all of the North Hetton output. This undoubtedly brought an end to sending coal on to the Lambton Railway via the link between the Jane Pit and the Junction Bank. At the same time the Earl of Durham was planning further expansion of his royalty at Sherburn, and it was clearly desirable for him to have his own line to that area. This was almost certainly built in the early 1840s, the northern end of the line being laid on the former Londonderry trackbed between the Hunter's House and Resolution Pits. This made the Jane Pit link completely redundant, and with all the North Hetton coal now going to Seaham, the old main line between Chilton Moor Shops and Pensher Foundry (NZ 327520) was closed. The system north of the Foundry was still designated as part of the Londonderry Railway on the 1st edition O.S. maps, though it is far from clear whether Londonderry still owned or operated it; for the later developments in this area see chapter 9.

Workshops

The entry in the Place Collection (Beamish 2003-54.7/7) mentioned earlier would appear to suggest that by 1811 there were workshops at Pensher Colliery E Pit capable of constructing boilers. This pit had been closed by 1819, and certainly by 1827 the **CHILTON MOOR WORKSHOPS** (NZ 323493) had been set up to the north of Rainton. These were constructed to the open courtyard design commonly used in the nineteenth century. It would seem that a large stables was built nearby, and it is possible that later the buildings here included a loco shed. When the line north of Chilton Moor was closed, the Meadows Engine also presumably ceased to work, although the line to the workshops was retained, presumably now worked by a locomotive. In addition, just south of Dubmire Bank Head, at Colliery Row, George Hopper established his **Britannia Iron Works**, probably in the mid-1850s. Hopper, originally from Houghton-le-Spring, had developed a foundry and general engineering business and needed larger premises. This new works presumably involved the re-laying of the ½ mile section northwards from Chilton Moor Shops.

Further south most of the original branch from the (old) Adventure Pit was closed and a new line built eastwards to join the Seaham line near Nicholson's Pit. Once again, the former rope haulage on this line was abandoned, probably when this change was made. Large numbers of coke ovens were built both north and west of the Meadows Pit, while on the debit side the Plain Pit was almost certainly closed by the 1850s.

The Framwellgate branch

Always eager to bring new coal to be shipped at Seaham, the Marquis concluded a complicated agreement in the early 1840s. In 1838 the Northern Coal Mining Company had begun the sinking of **Framwellgate Colliery**, north of Durham City and about 3½ miles south-west of Rainton. This consisted of two pits, the **Framwellgate/Old/Low Pit** (NZ 271455) and the **Cater House**, or **New/High Pit** (NZ 256454), a mile to the west. Shortly afterwards the Earl of Durham extended the Lambton Railway by building a branch from the former Resolution Pit (see above) to serve his new colliery at Frankland, and this offered the Framwellgate owners access to a rail system. The details and date of the complicated and unusual agreement are not known, though what happened in practice is known. The Framwellgate owners built a line 2½ miles long from the Cater House Pit to join the Lambton Railway's Frankland branch ¾ mile north of Frankland Colliery, at the top of a self-acting incline down to the River Wear. This line included a self-acting incline 1 mile long east of the Framwellgate Pit, whilst at the junction there was a separate bank head at the top of the Lambton Railway incline for the Framwellgate traffic. The waggons then travelled for nearly two miles over the Lambton system, down the self-acting incline to the River Wear, up the Beesbanks Incline worked by the Beesbanks Engine and then onwards to the site of the former Hunter's House Pit (see above). Here the Londonderry Railway built a branch, known as the Framwellgate branch, ½ mile long to join the line between the former Plain Pit and the Seaham line, immediately east of Nicholson's Pit, which allowed Framwellgate coal to be taken forward to Seaham.

Not all of the Londonderry collieries were linked to the Railway. **BELMONT COLLIERY** (NZ 319452), opened in 1835, and **OLD DURHAM COLLIERY** (NZ 292415), opened in 1849, were both served by what became the NER Durham & Sunderland branch, the latter by a ¾ mile branch, including a stationary engine, from Sherburnhouse Station, while **GRANGE COLLIERY** (NZ 301447), whose sinking began in 1844, and **KEPIER GRANGE COLLIERY** (NZ

299442) were served by what became the NER Gilesgate branch. It is believed that the coal from these four collieries came on to the Londonderry Railway via the link with what became the NER at Broomside Colliery. Only one new colliery in this area was connected to the Railway, the **LADY SEAHAM PIT** (NZ 325454), which was sunk in the late 1840s and linked from the bank foot of the Pittington Bank Engine's southern incline.

The introduction of locomotives

At some stage rope and horse working in the Rainton area was replaced by locomotive working. The area involved can be defined – to Chilton Moor Shops and the Britannia Iron Works to the north, as far east as Rainton Bridge on the Seaham line, to Benridge Bank Foot on the Pittington line, and to the Adventure Pit, to the south and certainly as far as the junction with the Lambton Railway to the west, perhaps right down to that line's Beesbanks Engine. However, when this happened is not known. Other than the locomotive of the 1820s, the Marquis is not known to have purchased any further locomotive until 1854, which, given all the changes described above, would seem rather later than is likely. If locomotives were used before 1854, no record of them has yet been found. The O.S. 2nd edition map suggests that the western wing of the courtyard forming the Chilton Moor Workshops might have been a locomotive shed, which would follow similar practice on the major systems at Philadelphia and Beamish. An oral tradition in the 1950s stated that there was, presumably in later years, a loco shed at the Meadows Crossings, though this is unsupported by documentary evidence.

The beginning of coal mining at Seaham

Up to 1845 no colliery had been sunk along the coast between South Shields, Sunderland and Seaham except for Monkwearmouth Colliery at Sunderland, which had proved difficult and expensive. The initial work at Seaham was undertaken by The North Hetton Coal Company, in which the Marquis held a part share, which on 12th August 1845 began the sinking of **SEATON COLLIERY** (NZ 409496), to the north of the Carrhouse Incline. This too proved exceptionally difficult, and coal was not won until 22nd January 1854. In the meantime the Marquis had begun the sinking of **SEAHAM COLLIERY**, a few yards to the east of Seaton Colliery, on 13th April 1849; the first coal was drawn on 27th March 1852. Seaton Colliery was subsequently acquired by The Hetton Coal Company, itself a shareholder in the North Hetton company, though the date is not known.

It was clearly essential for the two collieries to be worked together, and in an agreement dated 20th June 1860, backdated to 31st March 1860 (D/Lo/1251D/84), the Marchioness purchased Seaton Colliery from The Hetton Coal Company for £75,000. The two were then merged under the name of Seaham Colliery in November 1864, with Seaton Colliery becoming the High Pit and Seaham Colliery the Low Pit, both being coal-drawing. The colliery became the Londonderry's first venture into the gas coal market. A brickworks, known as the **LONDONDERRY BRICKWORKS** and making common bricks, was opened alongside the Railway in the area between the two pits in 1866. Gradually a colliery village grew up round the colliery, this being called New Seaham, while the original town at the coast became called Seaham Harbour. It should perhaps also be included that on 8th September 1880 there was a huge explosion at the colliery, in which 164 men and boys were killed, one of the worst disasters in Durham mining history.

Both the High and Low Pits had their own links to Seaham Bank Head. One source claimed that originally the Londonderry Engine also worked waggons into both pits, but there seems no evidence to support this. Whatever happened at the outset, for very many years empty waggons were worked into the two pits using a **stationary engine** at the Low Pit, with a separate drum and rope for each pit. The rope run between the Low Pit and Seaham Bank Head was straightforward, but to reach the High Pit the rope had apparently to be carried over the houses in Post Office Street, which divided the two sites, and then went round a return wheel. Both ropes used a box van, known to the men as a "dilly", which ran by gravity down to the bank head, dragging the rope behind it, in order for empties to be coupled on. Once at the pit the empties were run through the screens by gravity, and then run similarly down to the bank head.

The eastern half of the Durham coalfield developed considerably in the 1830s and 1840s, and despite an enlargement of the North Dock at Seaham in 1845 the port was finding it increasingly difficult to handle all the traffic. It also had competitors, not least the large new South Dock at Sunderland, which was opened on 20th June 1850. The Marquis soon saw the potential of this new dock, and from 14th September 1852 he began sending coal there via a link with the Durham & Sunderland line at Seaton Bank Head (*Newcastle Chronicle*, 17th September 1852). This arrangement clearly had severe limitations, and following agreements which once again committed the South Hetton and Haswell companies to use his facilities, the 75-year old Marquis announced that he intended to build his own railway from Seaham to Sunderland, and furthermore that this would be a public railway, also carrying passengers.

The Londonderry (Seaham & Sunderland) Railway

This was its official title, the Rainton system with its line to Seaham becoming the Londonderry (Rainton & Seaham) Railway. The contract to build the six-mile long line was awarded to Messrs. Forster & Lawton, and the Marquis cut the first turf on 8th February 1853. The southern section of the line, from Seaham northwards as far as Ryhope, was opened temporarily on 17th January 1854 (*Sunderland Herald*, 20th January 1854), the coal being transferred on to the Durham & Sunderland line via a connection at Ryhope that was then immediately removed. However, the Marquis died on 6th March 1854, and so did not live to see the

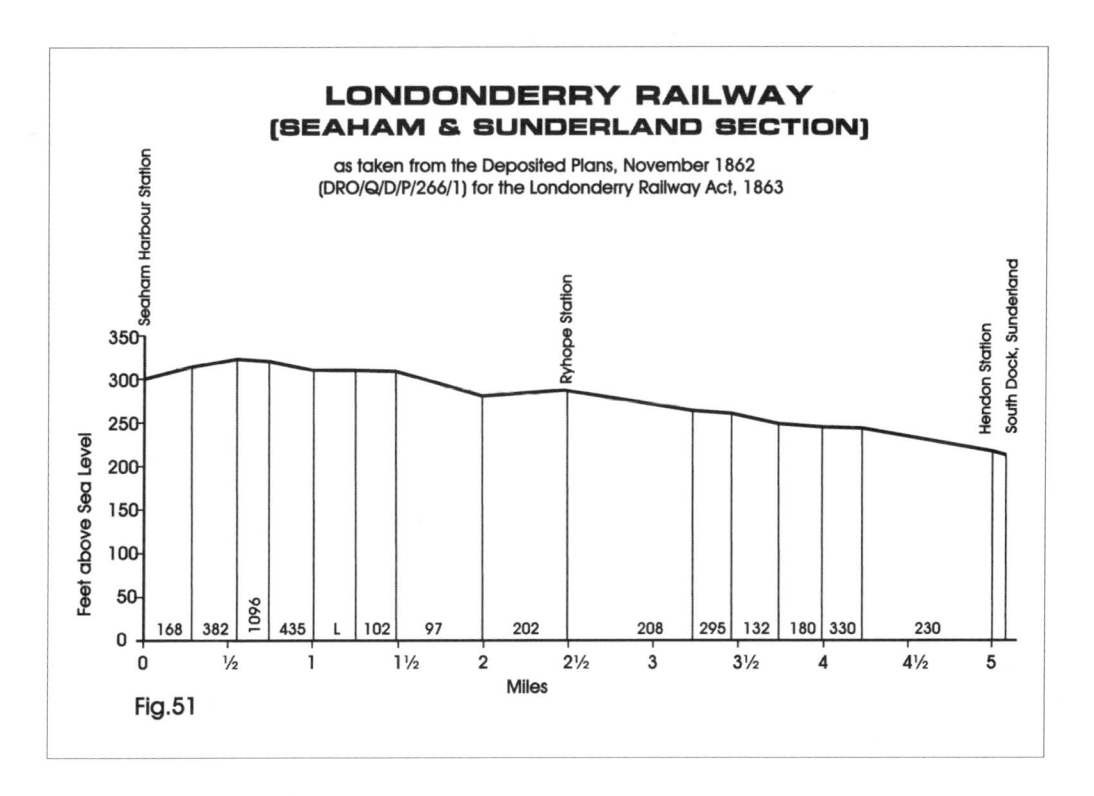

**LONDONDERRY RAILWAY
[SEAHAM & SUNDERLAND SECTION]**

as taken from the Deposited Plans, November 1862
(DRO/Q/D/P/266/1) for the Londonderry Railway Act, 1863

Fig.51

formal opening, which was undertaken by his widow, the Marchioness of Londonderry, and her son Earl Vane, on 3rd August 1854. Although not constructed under an Act of Parliament, the line was inspected by Col. Yolland of the Railway Department of the Board of Trade, and his report, dated 2nd May 1855, survives in the Public Record Office (PRO/MT 29/15/18251).

Col. Yolland's report describes the line as being 5 miles 1¾ chains long, and commencing at "Hetton bank head, Seaham", a description not found elsewhere. Beyond Seaham Station the line continued for a short distance to join the South Hetton Coal Company's line, a duplicate bank head being built at Swine Lodge Bank Head for traffic going round on to the Londonderry line. In addition, a **second self-acting incline** from Seaham Colliery, known as the **Polka Bank**, was built alongside the Seaham Incline, but ending in sidings forming a south-facing link with the line to Sunderland, just north of Seaham Station.

Col. Yolland states that the intention was to provide a double line throughout, but that at the date of his inspection the only section of double track lay between Seaham and Ryhope, other than a short distance near Seaham Harbour Station. Initially the whole line was built using wayleaves, with four miles of the new railway being over the Marquis' own land; but to avoid Seaham Hall, one of the Marquis' residences, the line took a wide curve to the west before reaching what was now the North Eastern Railway's Durham & Sunderland line at Ryhope, running alongside this for the remainder of the route. As built all five viaducts on the route were made of wood, the three largest being the Dalton, or Dawdon, viaduct (320ft, 64ft high), the Seaham Hall viaduct (200ft, 85ft high) and the Ryhope Dene viaduct (400ft, 85ft high). There were also seven other bridges, one an over-bridge. The gradients and curves over the first mile from Seaham were so severe that every coal train had to be banked from the rear until 1890. The line was laid with double-headed rails averaging between 65 and 69 lbs per yard in lengths of between 15 and 18 feet on creosoted larch and scotch fir sleepers. Col.Yolland reported that four stations had been provided, Seaham Harbour (10 chains), Seaham Colliery (20 chains), Ryhope (2 miles 40 chains) and Sunderland Dock (5 miles 1¾ chains). "Platforms have been constructed at one side of the line at each of these stations, but no station houses have yet been erected. The signals are either not yet erected or [are not] in working order. There are three Public Level Crossings at which it is intended to have Gate-Keepers; but the gates and signals are not yet put up, and there are neither Lodges nor boxes for the Policemen intended to have charge of them....". Col. Yolland refused to sanction public opening and insisted that stations must have platforms on both sides of the track where it was, or was to be, double line.

Work must have gone ahead quickly, for public passenger traffic commenced on 2nd July 1855, with the line being operated as a double line between Seaham and Ryhope and a single line between Ryhope and Sunderland; when the latter was doubled is not known. It would seem that only

LONDONDERRY RAILWAY in 1865

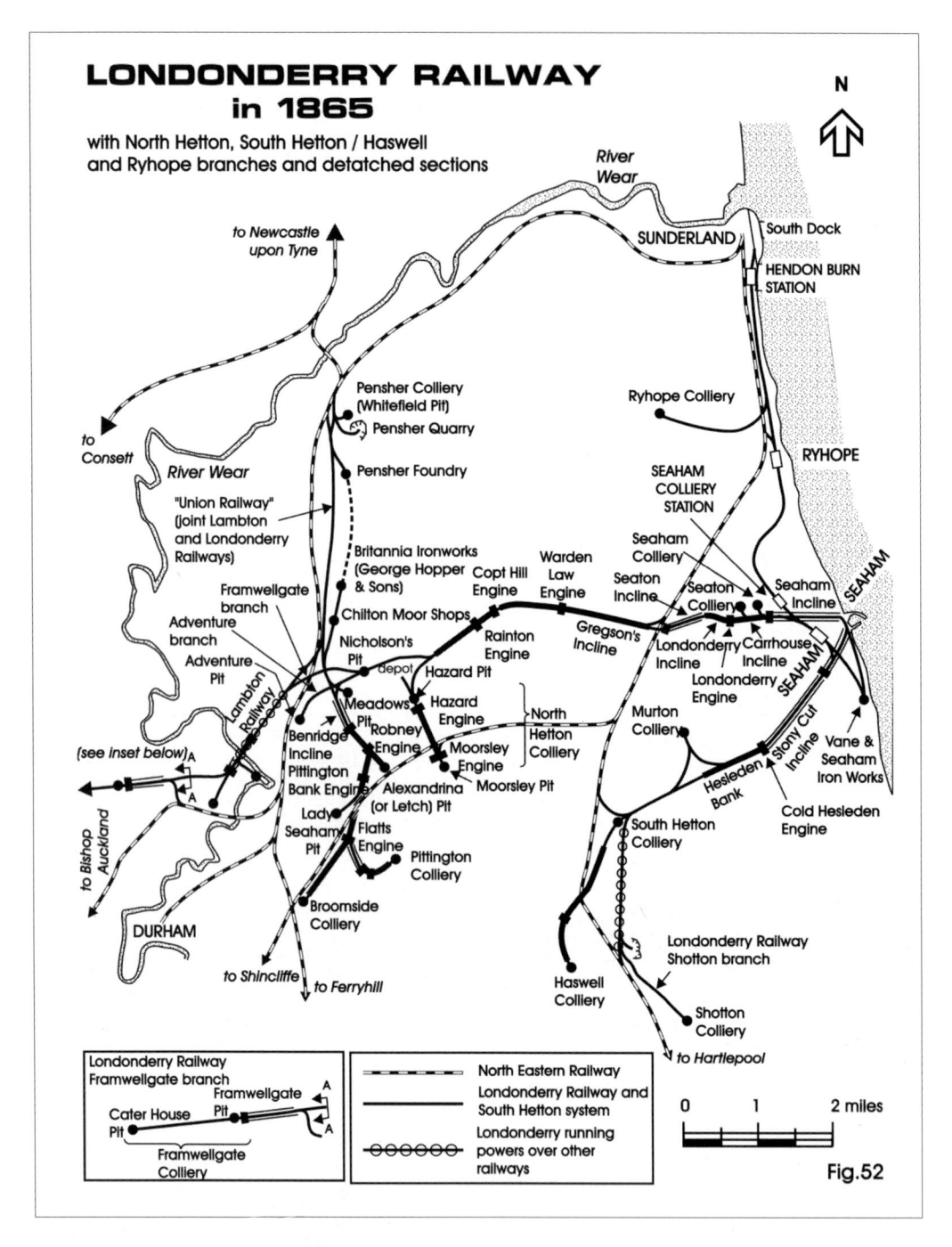

with North Hetton, South Hetton / Haswell and Ryhope branches and detatched sections

Fig.52

the stations at **SEAHAM HARBOUR** (NZ 424494) (later called **SEAHAM**) and **HENDON BURN** (NZ 409567) (rather than "Sunderland Dock") in Sunderland were opened in 1855. **RYHOPE STATION** (NZ 414527) was opened in 1858 and **SEAHAM COLLIERY STATION** (NZ 421496), just north of the bridge over the Seaham Incline, was opened by 1859. The final station was **SEAHAM HALL STATION** (NZ 414505), built for the Londonderry family's private use when staying at Seaham Hall, which was opened in 1875. The Marquis' main family house in Durham was Wynyard Hall, near Wolviston, and when on 1st March 1880 the NER opened its Castle Eden to Stockton branch it included a station at Wynyard. It is believed that the Marquis had a private train to travel between Seaham Hall and Wynyard, and that this train also travelled to Newcastle Central Station to connect with the London services. He is also said to have had to power to stop any train on request, if his private train was not available.

A varied collection of second-hand locomotives was purchased, together with some second-hand carriages from the Lancashire & Yorkshire Railway for the passenger service. There were no engineering facilities at all, all servicing and repairs being done in the open near a small brick cabin at **Polka Bank Foot** (NZ 427491), which was all that Hardy, appointed "to take charge of the mechanical requirements" in July 1855, had when he started. Slowly extra buildings were added, and Hardy's autobiography gives a graphic account of the difficulties of operating the railway in these early days. Four years later the management of the Rainton & Seaham Railway was absorbed into the management at Seaham. In 1863 the Marchioness gave the new line stronger legal status by obtaining the Londonderry (Seaham & Sunderland) Railway Act. This covered not only its main line but included the main branches (see below) and the links to the Rainton and South Hetton lines; the plans and sections are deposited at the Durham County Record Office (D/Q/D/P/266).

Industrial development at Seaham
With the Sunderland line open, the Marchioness at once began to develop the industrial base of her town. On 23rd May 1855 she leased land to John Candlish for the construction of what was at first called the **Londonderry Bottle Works**, later the **Seaham Bottle Works** (NZ 433489). This was served by an extension of what for many years was called the ballast railway, a line running south along the cliffs to handle the ballast off-loaded from ships arriving to load in the harbour. This works was owned by John Candlish until 17th March 1874, then by his brother Robert Candlish, Robert Candlish & Son (by 1882) and then Robert Candlish & Son Ltd. The works continued in production until 15th April 1921. Next came the **VANE & SEAHAM IRONWORKS** at Nose's Point, a mile south of the harbour (NZ 436478). Construction of the works, which incorporated two blast furnaces, began on 12th December 1859, and in 1860 the "ballast railway" was extended to serve it, together with a line, just over a mile long, from Polka Bank Foot. However, two years later a new line was built to the west, giving both a better junction with the South Hetton line and providing a better route to the Iron Works; this line became called the **Blastfurnace branch**. The two lines enabled a traffic flow system to be introduced, coal coming in via the Blastfurnace branch (the "west line") and finished products going out via the "east line". Coke ovens were built near the iron works and limestone obtained from quarries nearby. The works was built to be managed by the Marchioness' second son, Lord Adolphus Vane, under the title of The Seaham Iron Company. The works began production in 1863, but it was not a success, and the furnaces were put out of blast in 1865.

The next development was **Seaham Chemical Works** (NZ 434486), for the construction of which land was leased to John Watson, Francis Kipling and John Petrie on 3rd March 1865. Lying about half-way between the Bottle Works and the Iron Works, it was served by sidings from both lines, and also from a link between the two built immediately to the south of the works. Finally, a new **Seaham Gas Works** (NZ 431489) was built by the Seaham Gas Company in 1866 immediately to the west of the Bottle Works, and served by sidings from the Blastfurnace branch. None of these works had their own locomotives, all the shunting being undertaken by the Londonderry Railway.

On 1st July 1869 Watson, Kipling & Petrie leased the ironworks, the firm becoming Watson, Kipling & Co and Watson, Kipling & Co Ltd from 27th June 1877. One furnace was re-started in 1872 but was put out again in 1875, after which the works never again produced any iron and stood derelict for many years. A resolution to wind up Watson, Kipling & Co Ltd was approved on 13th June 1881, the end of the firm presumably also causing the demise of the Seaham Chemical Works.

Although not in chronological sequence, it is appropriate to include here a much later development. This was an **electrozone works** (NZ 436483), built by The British Electrozone Corporation in the mid-1890s at the southern end of the Blastfurnace branch, just before its junction with the Ballast Railway, and served by a siding from the former. 'Electrozone', and its medicinal form 'meditrina', was sea-water through which an electric current had been passed, and for which was claimed antiseptic, germicidal and disinfectant properties.

Ryhope and Silksworth Collieries and their branches
There were also developments to the north. The coal north of Seaham had been leased to the Haswell Coal Company, but as they had been unsuccessful in finding coal the lease was re-awarded in 1857 to The Ryhope Coal Company (which included some of the Haswell company's partners), which then sank **Ryhope Colliery** (NZ 399575). Coal was reached in 1859 and the first coal was drawn on 7th February 1860. This was linked to the Londonderry Railway by a 1 mile branch from Ryhope Grange. To serve what was clearly going to be a developing colliery village the Londonderry Railway at last opened **Ryhope Station** (NZ 414527) in 1858. It may be that The Ryhope Coal Co shunted the actual colliery, although the first locomotive which it is known to have owned did not arrive until 1870. The Londonderry Railway handled the traffic between the colliery and Sunderland.

Some ten years later, on 16th August 1869, Earl Vane began the sinking of **SILKSWORTH COLLIERY** (NZ 377541), work being completed on 13th January 1873. To serve this a second branch, 2¾ miles long and steeply-graded, was built from Ryhope Colliery Junction, by-passing Ryhope Colliery on its northern side. Subsequently the

161. This is said to be the scene when the first coal was drawn at Ryhope Colliery in 1859, in which case it is an exceptionally early colliery photograph. Assuming that the locomotives were Londonderry engines, the first appears be an 0-6-0, but the 0-6-0ST remains a mystery, unless it is CARADOC (see the text).

Ryhope branch was extended to join the Silksworth line ¼ mile west of Ryhope Colliery. As Silksworth was a Londonderry colliery all the railway work was handled by the Londonderry Railway.

Framwellgate Colliery
By 1859 this colliery (see above) had passed into the ownership of Richard Thompson and William Green of Durham City, who advertised it for sale in Newcastle upon Tyne on 12th July 1859. There not being a buyer, the Marchioness of Londonderry purchased it on 23rd August 1859 for £11,000, subject to an approval period of six months. Thus the branch from the two pits, with its one-mile self-acting incline east of the Low Pit, which joined the Lambton Railway north of Frankland Colliery passed into direct Londonderry control. Hardy refers to locomotives "leading coals from Framwellgate Colliery to Rainton Bridge", but this clearly cannot mean <u>between</u> the two, as the Lambton Railway worked part of the distance by rope inclines. Although there is no evidence for this, it would seem likely that the Londonderry Railway locomotives worked Framwellgate traffic between the Lambton Railway's Beesbanks Engine and Rainton Bridge and perhaps between the colliery itself and the incline east of the Low Pit.

The Shotton branch
Obviously with the intention of bringing more coal on to his Railway, the 3rd Marquis made an agreement with the Haswell Coal Company dated 5th February 1853 (D/Lo/E/378) in which he undertook to construct what was called the **Londonderry (Pespool branch) Railway**, a line estimated at 600 yards long between the South Hetton Coal Company's Pespool branch (to the Hartlepool Railway & Dock Company's line) and the Haswell Company's **Shotton Colliery** (NZ 398412). Construction would seem to have been delayed, for in a new agreement dated 17th March 1860 (D/Lo/E/378/1) between the Marchioness and the Haswell Company the branch is described as "recently constructed". The actual line was 1½ miles long, running from near the southern end of the South Hetton company's branch to the north end of Shotton Colliery. Under the agreement the Haswell company was to bear the cost of working its coal from Shotton and over the South Hetton company's railway to the South Hetton Junction with the Londonderry Railway at Seaham, be responsible for repairs to the branch and to find locomotives and waggons to work it. This was clearly altered in part almost immediately, for Hardy says (p.77 of his draft) that "at this period [1860] No.9 Engine was leading coals from Shotton Colliery by the Pesspool [sic] branch to So[uth] Hetton". This can only mean that the Londonderry Railway was working Haswell company traffic from

162. 2, originally built by the Haigh Foundry for the Manchester & Leeds Railway in 1841, after reconstruction at Seaham in 1860 for use on the passenger service; it was painted ultramarine.

163. Concerned that the NER might ban tender-first running on passenger trains over its lines between Sunderland Central Station and Hendon, Hardy rebuilt two 0-6-0s as 2-4-0 side tanks. Here 9, rebuilt at Seaham in 1880 from 0-6-0 RS 1096/1857, stands on a train at Seaham Station.

164. 4, rebuilt at Seaham in 1875 from 0-6-0 RWH 479/1846.

the branch over the South Hetton company's line as far as South Hetton, where presumably the locomotive was serviced and housed in the latter's loco shed.

The "Union Railway"
As noted above, by the mid-1850s the old Londonderry "main line" between Colliery Row and the Pensher Foundry had been lifted, leaving Pensher Colliery and the nearby Pensher Quarry isolated from the rest of the system. Then on 26th November 1861 the Marchioness made an agreement with the Earl of Durham (D/Lo/E/383/105), under which the two parties agreed to make the length of the Lambton Railway

165. 3, rebuilt at Seaham in 1876 from 0-6-0 TR 254/1855.

166. 6, built at Seaham in 1883. Note the elaborate lining on the coupling rods.

between the coke ovens at Bourn Moor and Pensher Station on the NER Pensher Branch, a distance of 3168 yards, into a double track line. At the southern end the Marchioness would build a link between Rainton and Bourn Moor (called in the agreement the Junction Railway), while at the northern end she was to construct her own link with the North Eastern Railway. Each party was to find their own locomotives and waggons, but the line was to be operated under Lambton Railway rules.

The purpose of this new line remains completely obscure. The link with the NER would suggest that the Marchioness intended to dispatch coal that way; but the NER already had a branch to the Londonderry Railway at Rainton, and any coal dispatched via Pensher would reduce the tonnage carried by her own line to Sunderland. Nevertheless it was certainly built – and almost as quickly disposed of; for on 5th November 1864 the Marchioness leased Pensher Colliery to George Elliot (her Chief Agent until 1861) and sub-let to him her rights over the Union Railway in order for him to ship his coal at Seaham. DCOA Return 102 lists a stationary engine here. How long this link and its agreement continued to be operated is unknown; Elliot closed Pensher Colliery in 1879.

The Londonderry Engine Works and Waggon Shops
The considerable expansion of the Railway in the 1850s and early 1860s, together with the Marchioness' decision to purchase her first steamer in 1857 and develop a sizeable fleet, trading to London and Europe, meant that something more than the makeshift facilities at Polka Bank Foot was desperately overdue. The initiative was at length taken by John Daglish, whom the Marchioness appointed as Chief Agent in 1863. It was he who saw that a central engineering establishment serving the whole Estate needed to be established, and that this would be best at Seaham, rather than Rainton. As a small start four waggonwrights were transferred from Chilton Moor Shops to repair waggons in the north end of Hardy's shop at Polka Bank Foot.

Daglish began in earnest in 1865 by constructing what became called the **LONDONDERRY WAGON WORKS** (NZ 428490), a building 100ft x 30ft served by a link to the South Hetton branch at Polka Bank Foot. Although given this name, the works was to do far more than repair and build waggons, including colliery "tubs, all smith work, forged work, make nails, brazier work, joinery, also chain making for every purpose…, bolt and rivet making machines, a Steam Hammer and Spring making furnace" (Hardy, draft p.100). The construction of 4-ton chaldron waggons, to replace the 53 hundredweight waggons, began at once, and soon afterwards the whole of the waggon establishment at Chilton Moor Shops was moved here too (the book of Hardy's autobiography suggests this happened in January 1866, but the hand-written draft would appear to read that this happened in January 1868). A survey of the Railway's waggons in 1867 showed that 1415 were 3-ton chaldrons and

167. 11, RS 1326/1860, possibly in as-built condition; note the coronet on the tender.

168. 15, said to have been ordered from Blair & Co of Stockton (a rare photograph of this firm's locomotives) in 1868 to help Earl Vane's prospects in the General Election that year.

169. 5, built at Seaham in 1885; note the elephant on the smokebox and the large smokebox wingplates.

170. 20, built at Seaham in 1892; Hardy seems to have preferred his tender engines to have outside frames.

171. 17, Head Wrightson 33/1873, at Seaham Bank Foot; it ran without its cab for most of its life.

172. 18, built by Stephen Lewin of Poole and probably Lewin 683/1877, in its first transformation - fitted with side tanks and a cab.

996 4-ton chaldrons. "Greedy boards", an extra plank added around the top of the box, began to be added to some waggons from the 1870s.

Opposite Seaham Station Daglish had an even larger building constructed, the **LONDONDERRY ENGINE WORKS** (NZ 423494). The main building was 135ft x 35 ft, the northern end being the locomotive running shed and the southern end a well-equipped workshop. This was a fine facility, capable not only of major renewals but also of constructing completely new locomotives. However, no foundry was included, as Robert Wright's foundry a few yards away was available. A **Grease works** was built, together with a **General Storehouse** and a **Granary** and **Stables**, the last a two-storey building delivering grain from the farms at the upper level and taking away fodder and straw at the lower level. All of these facilities, together with the **brickworks** at Seaham Colliery, also developed by Daglish, were built to service the whole Estate – the railway, the collieries, the iron works, the docks, the steam fleet, the farms and the family's two country houses in Durham, Seaham Hall and Wynyard Hall. Hardy firmly dates this construction to 1865-1866, but strangely some of the buildings at least are shown on the Deposited Plans of November 1862 (see above). But Daglish had his enemies, and he was forced to resign in 1869, except from supervising the sinking of Silksworth Colliery. Although slightly after his resignation, the introduction of small locomotives to work at the harbour instead of horses, may well also have been one of Daglish' proposals; the first of these arrived in 1870.

Retraction

By 1860 the Londonderry Railway had reached its greatest extent, bringing coal into Seaham from Framwellgate Moor in the south-west and Shotton in the south, the tonnage increased by the Haswell and South Hetton coal also coming into Seaham, the coal either then being shipped at Seaham or run to South Dock at Sunderland. But after the expansion under the 3rd Marquis and the Marchioness, their son, Earl Vane, who inherited it all after his mother's death in 1865, clearly felt that such a large industrial empire could not be sustained. The process of reducing and rationalising the empire had begun earlier, when, probably in the mid-1850s Grange Colliery and Kepier Grange Colliery were sold to The North Hetton Coal Co. The next reduction was very small - the transfer on 22nd April 1863 of the section north of Chilton Moor to George Hopper & Sons, the owners of the Britannia Iron Works at the other end. Then came the lease of Pittington Colliery was leased to The North Hetton Coal Company, according to one document on 8th October 1864, although other documents appear to show that the North Hetton company was already in possession by June 1863. Pensher Colliery was leased to George Elliot on 5th November 1864 and Broomside Colliery to Charles and William Bell on 13th March 1867, though all the leases contained the proviso that their coal should continue to be dispatched via the Railway. A similar attitude was taken with the Shotton branch, which was sold to The Haswell, Shotton & Easington Coal & Coke Co Ltd as from 1st January 1868, though with the traffic agreement continuing. Shotton Colliery closed in 1877, and Belmont, Grange, Kepier Grange and Old Durham Collieries were all officially abandoned in December 1885; probably about the same period the Lady Seaham Pit closed, while Broomside Colliery was abandoned in September 1890. Finally The North Hetton Coal Co closed Pittington Colliery, probably about the same time; it was officially abandoned in June 1891. The closure of Broomside and Pittington Collieries meant the closure of the Railway south of the Robney Engine on the Alexandrina branch.

At Rainton by the late 1880s the producing pits were the Alexandrina, Adventure, Meadows (re-opened after a period of closure) and Nicholson's, though here too output was declining. The reduction in traffic along the Rainton & Seaham section led successive Railway Managers to consider ways of reducing costs, not least the costs of the stationary engines standing in steam with no work. The first to be dispensed with was the Warden Law Engine and the inclines on either side of it. This engine had been rebuilt in 1864 with larger cylinders and reduced steam pressure. Almost certainly in 1877 rope working was replaced by a locomotive working from a small **loco shed** (NZ 366498) built on to the west side of the engine house, with the rails extended into the former engine room to provide a basic inspection and repair facility; the Warden Law Engine's cylinder was put into the beam engine working the south side of the North Dock. The locomotive here thus worked traffic between Copt Hill Bank Head and Seaton Bank Head. Another change was the fitting of brakes to the waggons. Previously waggons had been stopped by pushing a "drag" between the spokes of the wheels. The introduction of brakes both reduced the damage to waggons, and also allowed sets of six, instead of four, to be run on the self-acting inclines.

In 1887 The South Hetton Coal Co Ltd offered to make an agreement with the Marquis under which he would handle all of its rail traffic between its collieries and either Seaham or Sunderland. It would seem that South Hetton was hoping that the Marquis would either build a new line, or at least remove one or more of the rope inclines on the existing line, which the company offered to the Marquis, together with its locomotives. Although some consideration was given, and the offer made again in 1890, in the end matters stayed as they were, and the South Hetton company continued to own and operate its own line, together with its staff at the staiths at the harbour.

By 1892 Nicholson's Pit had ceased production; Old Durham Colliery closed in 1892, and in March 1893 the Meadows Pit also closed, to be followed by the end of coke production at the Rainton beehive ovens on 9th April 1893. These closures, together with a strike of the wagon riders on the inclines, led the Railway Manager (George Hardy from 1883) to

173. The bank head of the self-acting incline down to North Dock, Seaham, in 1879, with 16, Head Wrightson 16/1870, shunting on the left.

174. The foot of the same incline, with a full set arriving to be unloaded. Note how small the North Dock was when it was opened in 1831.

bring in further changes. During the strike, in 1892, the gradient on the west side of the Londonderry Engine was eased considerably by infilling, enabling the Londonderry Engine to be abandoned and locomotive working to be introduced between Seaton Bank Foot and the Seaham/Polka Bank Heads. So far as is known no locomotive shed was built, so perhaps the locomotive here was stabled somewhere at Seaham Colliery. This was not the first time that locomotives had worked this section, two having been used for five days whilst the Londonderry Engine was being modified in 1861. Shortly afterwards the Rainton Engine was abandoned, the Copt Hill bank being extended half way down the former Rainton bank and the lower half added to the existing locomotive working. So by 1893 the only rope haulage still in use on the Rainton & Seaham line comprised the Copt Hill, Seaton and Seaham Inclines. The end of coke production at last enabled the locomotives to use coal instead, at half the cost.

The closure of the Rainton & Seaham Railway

It was then announced that production at the Adventure and Alexandrina Pits would cease in 1896, the Marquis giving up his royalty leases in

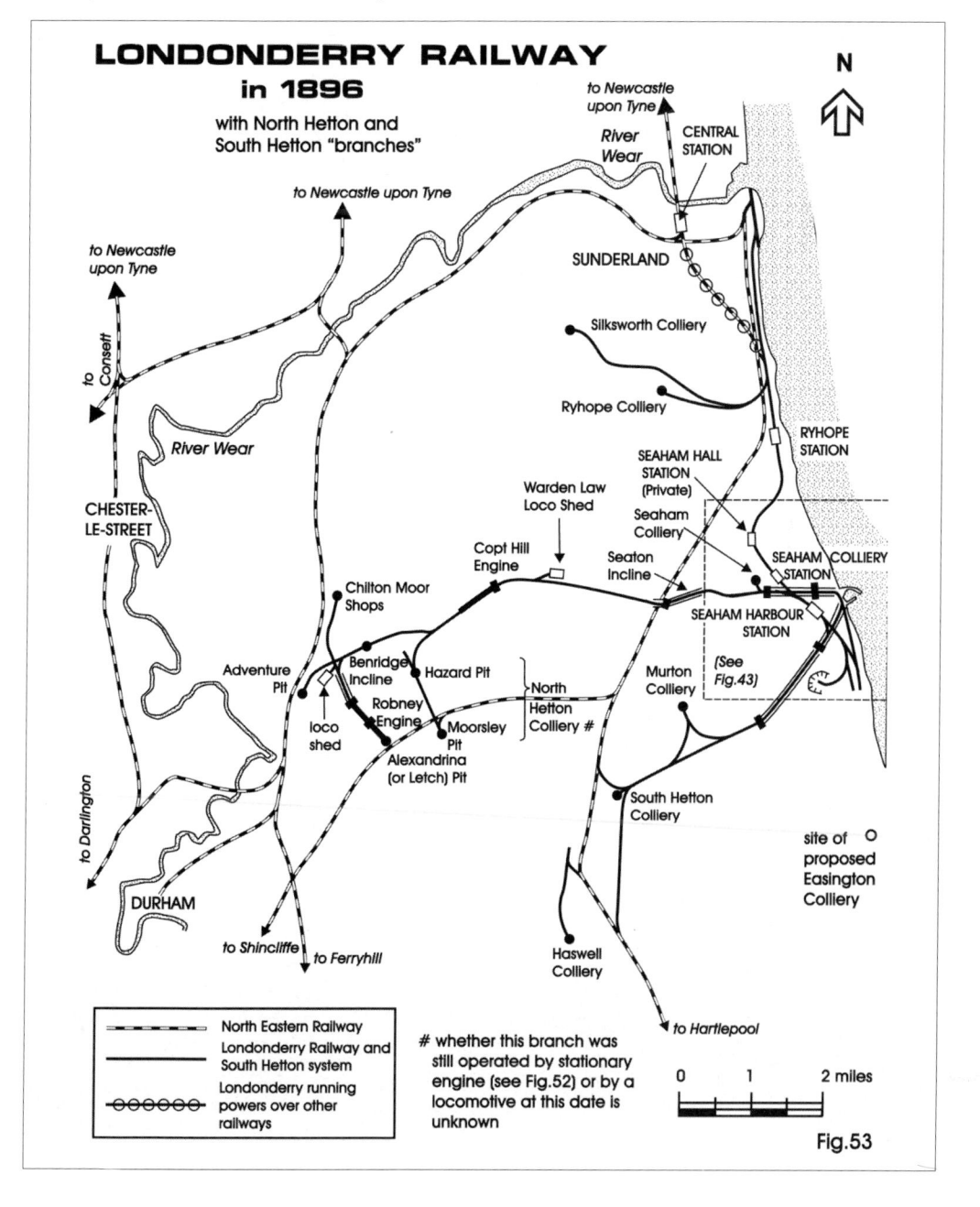

Fig.53

September 1896. This meant the closure of the Rainton line west of Seaham Colliery. Lifting and salvaging, by the Marquis' men, began immediately, and was completed by 18th December 1896. Four locomotives and 1500 waggons ceased to work. In March 1897 there was a major sale of surplus material; for further details see the notes to the locomotive list. The closure of the Railway deprived The North Hetton Coal Co Ltd of its outlet to Seaham for its North Netton Colliery coal, and instead it built a short link from Rainton Bridge to join the Copt Hill Incline on the Hetton Railway.

The year 1896 was a landmark year in the Durham coal industry, with not only the end of the Londonderry control of Rainton and its area, but also the closure of Haswell Colliery and most importantly of all, the withdrawal from the coal trade of the Earl of Durham, who sold his huge undertaking to Sir James Joicey in June.

The Adventure Pit was subsequently re-opened by The Rainton Colliery Co Ltd and re-commenced production about 1914; it survived to pass to the National Coal Board in 1947. The remaining royalties were subsequently taken over by The Lambton & Hetton Collieries Ltd, and for the subsequent history of the other pits and some of the railway trackbed see the chapter on the Lambton Railway.

Improvements on the Seaham & Sunderland Railway

From 1st October 1868 Londonderry trains ran into the Hendon Station of the North Eastern Railway, situated near to the now-abandoned Londonderry Station, just south of the junction with the Pensher branch. However, it would appear that the Londonderry family obtained running powers for their own use over the Pensher branch in order to run their private train into the NER's Fawcett Street Station at Sunderland, a more convenient connection when travelling to or from London. The arrangements at Sunderland were altered again on 4th August 1879, when the NER opened its new line from Ryhope Grange Junction, where the Londonderry Railway built a signal box, across the River Wear to Monkwearmouth. Londonderry trains were now allowed to work into the new **Sunderland Central Station** (NZ 397570). On at least one occasion Londonderry trains ran further afield; at Easter 1898 four trains were run to South Shields and another to High Shields, whilst one set of LR coaches was worked through to South Shields by a NER engine. It is also thought that on occasion the Marquis' special train was allowed to run through to Newcastle Central Station for him to board a London train. Ryhope was also the place for Londonderry passengers to change for connections to Hartlepool and destinations further afield. There was also a fear that the NER would insist on Londonderry locomotives being turned at Sunderland – the LR did not have any turntables after the very small examples provided for the opening of the line were removed – and so Nos.8 and 9 locomotives were rebuilt as tank engines to overcome this situation, while all Londonderry locomotives were also fitted with steam brakes, an innovation for the period. The final major improvement was an impressive new station at Seaham, opened without ceremony on 28th December 1886. This station also had a public house attached to it.

In 1879 the Londonderry Railway carried over a million tons of coal for shipment at Sunderland, more than the NER carried there. Until 1887 mineral trains did not use guards, though at night

175. The second Seaham Station, manufactured at the Wagon Works and opened on 28th December 1886.

176. General view of Seaham from the north, with the Station Hotel on the far left, the station, the carriage shed and the Londonderry Engine Works on the far right.

177. Seaham Hall Station, the Marquis of Londonderry's private station, possibly in the 1930s.

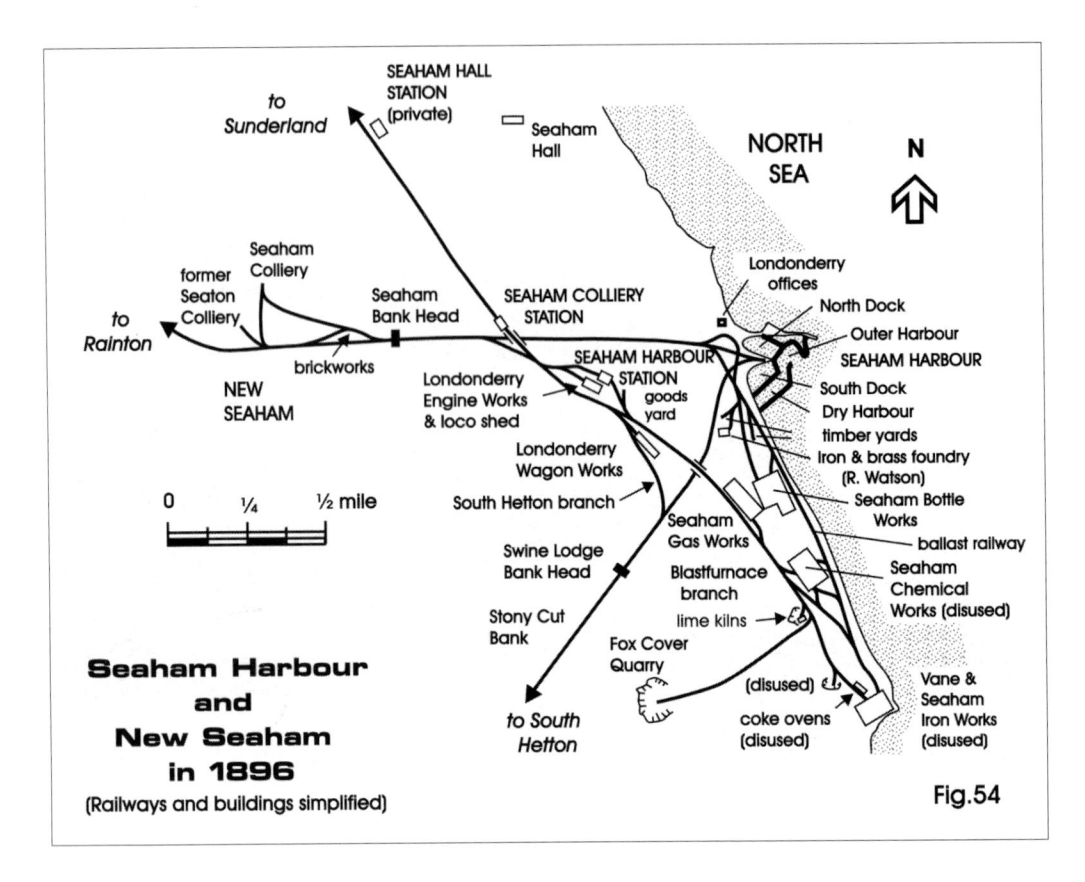

Seaham Harbour and New Seaham in 1896
(Railways and buildings simplified)

Fig.54

a man holding a lamp travelled on the last waggon. After questions in Parliament the first guard's brake van was introduced on 21st December 1887. Westinghouse air brakes were introduced on all passenger rolling stock and passenger locomotives by 28th May 1888, with No.15 being similarly fitted later, although a mineral engine. In the following year the line's signalling was up-graded and block instruments introduced, with full block working commenced on 23rd July 1891. As this was a public railway, a wide range of goods was carried, with appropriate waggons provided, while the Wagon Works built new passenger carriages and the Engine Works new locomotives.

The re-organisation of 1898-1900

It was abundantly clear to the 6th Marquis by the mid-1890s that a complete review of all of his activities was critically urgent. The end of mining at Rainton had left him with only two collieries, Seaham and Silksworth, and it was clear that the future of mining in the area would be on his land at the coast. The harbour was nearly seventy years old and unable to handle modern shipping adquately; if it was to continue in business a larger dock had to be built. Both the Vane & Seaham Iron Works and the Seaham Chemical Works had closed, victims of the depression in trade after 1875. His town needed employment, and prosperity for its inhabitants required investment on a massive scale. The Londonderry Railway was making money, but its facilities were now too large for what was left of the system, resulting in more unemployment. Equally, his liability was unlimited in law. Curiously, he did begin one new venture during the 1890s, when he opened **FOX COVER QUARRY** (NZ 429479) not far from the derelict iron works at Dawdon, served by a ½ mile branch westwards from the Blastfurnace branch. This was certainly working by 1897, and continued, under the Marquis' personal ownership, for quite a time; it is believed to have been closed about 1919.

The Marquis began by intending to merge the collieries, harbour and Railway into one limited company, but this proved impossible when he was advised that the proposed new dock would require an Act of Parliament. This was passed on 12th July 1898 and created The Seaham Harbour Dock Co. The Marquis became the company's chairman and a major shareholder. The new company took over the harbour and its sidings on 1st January 1899, and work on the extended South Dock began almost immediately.

Next to be dealt with were the two collieries and the Londonderry Brickworks at Seaham Colliery, which were transferred to another new company, The Londonderry Collieries Ltd. This was registered on 31st May 1899, again with the Marquis as chairman and primary shareholder. Here too new development began at once, with the sod-cutting ceremony for Dawdon Colliery on 26th

178. A train of spotless Londonderry Railway coaches stands at Seaham Station. The nearest vehicle is one of a pair of Brake 3rds built for the railway in 1893, one of which survived to pass to the NER.

179. A train of four-wheeled stock at Seaham Station, with a "birdcage" brake 3rd, built in 1883, at the rear. The Station Hotel is in the background.

180. Brake van 2, with a "birdcage" lookout. Note the snow plough in the background.

181. The last Seaham passenger engine: 21, built in 1895, stands at Seaham Station on a train from Sunderland on the last day of Londonderry ownership, 6th October 1900.

LONDONDERRY RAILWAY.

SEAHAM AND SUNDERLAND.

Time Table from AUGUST 1st, 1900. Until Further Notice.

FROM SEAHAM TO SUNDERLAND.

STATIONS.	WEEK DAYS.										SUNDAYS.				
	A.M.	A.M.	A.M.	A.M.	MAIL P.M.	P.M.	P.M.	P.M.	MAIL P.M.	MAIL P.M.	A.M.	A.M.	P.M.	MAIL P.M.	P.M.
SEAHAM	5 10	7 25	9 0	10 50	12 50	2 15	3 50	5 0	†5 27	6 35	8 40	10 15	7 35	9 0	1 30	4 0	7 45	8 50
Seaham Colliery	5 12	7 32	9 2	10 52	12 52	2 17	3 52	5 2	5 29	6 37	8 42	10 17	7 37	9 2	1 32	4 2	7 47	8 52
Ryhope	5 18	7 38	9 8	10 58	12 58	2 23	3 58	5 8	5 35	6 43	8 48	10 23	7 42	9 8	1 38	4 8	7 53	8 58
SUNDERLAND	5 25	7 30	9 18	11 8	1 8	2 33	4 8	5 18	5 45	6 53	8 58	10 33	7 50	9 18	1 48	4 18	8 3	9 8

FROM SUNDERLAND TO SEAHAM.

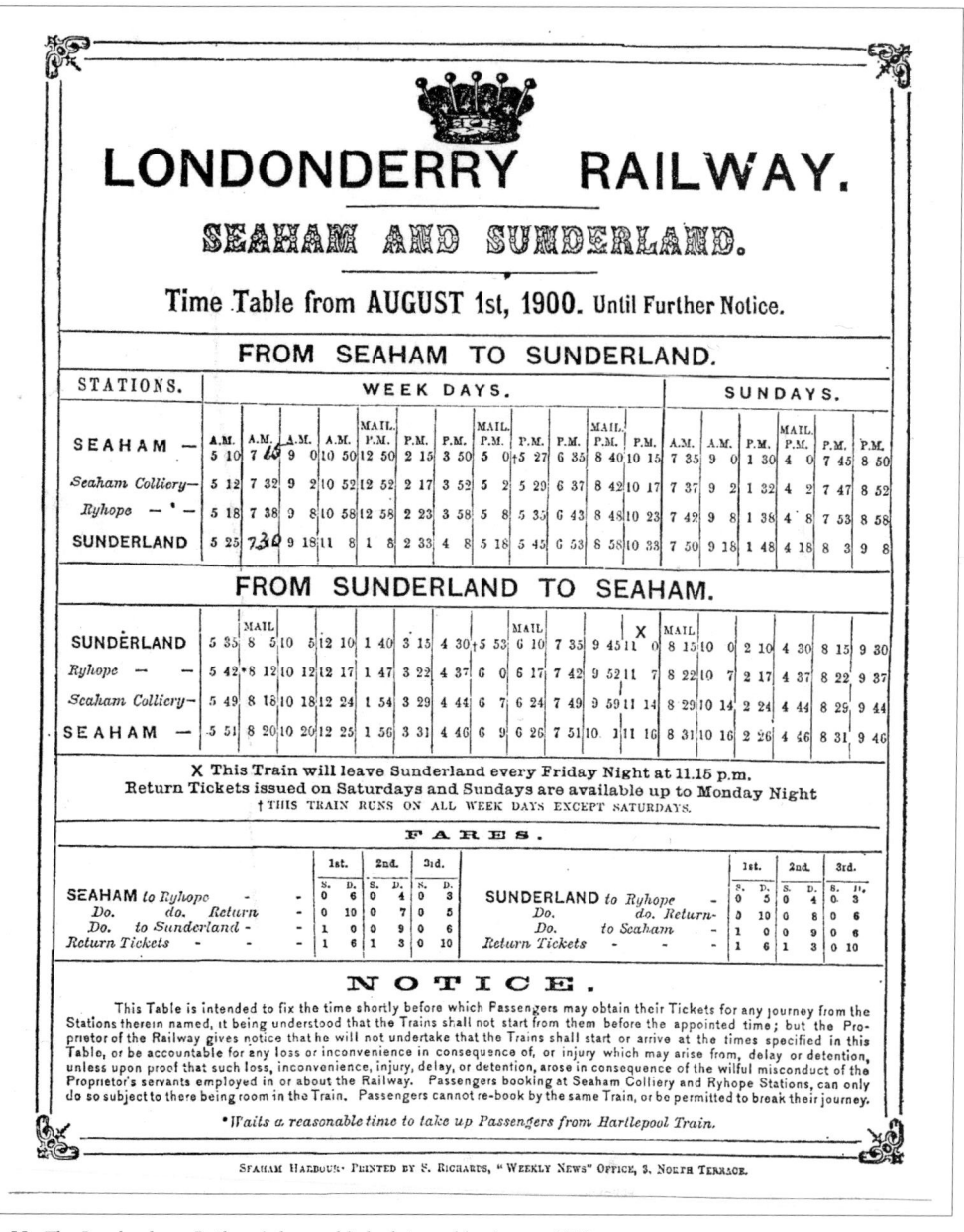

	MAIL							MAIL			X	MAIL					
SUNDERLAND	5 35	8 5	10 5	12 10	1 40	3 15	4 30	†5 53	6 10	7 35	9 45	11 0	8 15	10 0	2 10	4 30	8 15	9 30
Ryhope	5 42	*8 12	10 12	12 17	1 47	3 22	4 37	6 0	6 17	7 42	9 52	11 7	8 22	10 7	2 17	4 37	8 22	9 37
Seaham Colliery	5 49	8 18	10 18	12 24	1 54	3 29	4 44	6 7	6 24	7 49	9 59	11 14	8 29	10 14	2 24	4 44	8 29	9 44
SEAHAM	5 51	8 20	10 20	12 25	1 56	3 31	4 46	6 9	6 26	7 51	10 1	11 16	8 31	10 16	2 26	4 46	8 31	9 46

X This Train will leave Sunderland every Friday Night at 11.15 p.m.
Return Tickets issued on Saturdays and Sundays are available up to Monday Night
† THIS TRAIN RUNS ON ALL WEEK DAYS EXCEPT SATURDAYS.

FARES.

	1st.	2nd.	3rd.		1st.	2nd.	3rd.
	S. D.	S. D.	S. D.		S. D.	S. D.	S. D.
SEAHAM to Ryhope	0 6	0 4	0 3	SUNDERLAND to Ryhope	0 5	0 4	0 3
Do. do. Return	0 10	0 7	0 5	Do. do. Return	0 10	0 8	0 6
Do. to Sunderland	1 0	0 9	0 6	Do. to Seaham	1 0	0 9	0 6
Return Tickets	1 6	1 3	0 10	Return Tickets	1 6	1 3	0 10

NOTICE.

This Table is intended to fix the time shortly before which Passengers may obtain their Tickets for any journey from the Stations therein named, it being understood that the Trains shall not start from them before the appointed time; but the Proprietor of the Railway gives notice that he will not undertake that the Trains shall start or arrive at the times specified in this Table, or be accountable for any loss or inconvenience in consequence of, or injury which may arise from, delay or detention, unless upon proof that such loss, inconvenience, injury, delay, or detention, arose in consequence of the wilful misconduct of the Proprietor's servants employed in or about the Railway. Passengers booking at Seaham Colliery and Ryhope Stations, can only do so subject to there being room in the Train. Passengers cannot re-book by the same Train, or be permitted to break their journey.

*Waits a reasonable time to take up Passengers from Hartlepool Train.

SEAHAM HARBOUR: PRINTED BY S. RICHARDS, "WEEKLY NEWS" OFFICE, 3, NORTH TERRACE.

Fig. 55. The Londonderry Railway's last published timetable, August 1900

August 1899 on the site of the former Vane & Seaham Iron Works.

This left only the Londonderry Railway, which the Marquis still owned personally. Here the position was more complicated. In 1893 a proposal for a railway between Seaham and Hartlepool was brought forward by various business interests, but it was opposed by both the Marquis and the NER and failed to obtain its Act. This stimulated the NER, which in 1895 obtained an Act for the same purpose, gaining at the same time running powers over the Londonderry Railway to allow direct running between Sunderland and Hartlepool. However, the NER then took no action, to the increasing frustration of The Easington Coal Co Ltd, which wanted rail access to its proposed new colliery at Easington, four miles south of Seaham. This company then approached the Marquis with a request that he build a branch of the Londonderry Railway to Easington. By this time the NER had decided that it wished to alter the route of the Seaham – Hartlepool line to the east of Hawthorn Tower, two miles south of Seaham – only to find that this route was already to be occupied by the proposed new branch, whose intended joint owners, the Marquis, The Seaham Harbour Dock Co and The Easington Coal Co Ltd, strongly opposed the new NER route. The proposal for the branch may well have been a political move to force the NER to negotiate; if so, it was successful, for the NER agreed to buy out the opposition and purchase the Londonderry Railway. Terms were agreed, together with a price of £400,000, and confirmed in the North Eastern Railway Act of 30th July 1900. The NER took possession at midnight on 6th October 1900. Besides the Londonderry "main line", the railway taken over included the Ryhope branch (but not its extension to Silksworth), the Polka Bank and the whole of the Blastfurnace branch.

In its last full year of operation the Londonderry Railway carried 532,366 passengers, in three 1st, two 2nd and 13 3rd class carriages, painted lake and lined in gold. 869,351 tons of coal and other minerals, and 42,450 tons of general goods, including mail and livestock, were carried, the goods stock consisting of 2,866 vehicles, including four brake vans. The locomotives were painted green and lined out in orange, carrying the initials "L.R." and a coronet.

Specifically excluded from the NER takeover were all the goods stock, the Londonderry Wagon Works, the equipment of the Londonderry Engine Works (including a partially-completed new locomotive), the two hotels at Seaham and Hendon, the Seaham Hall Station (though the NER agreed to maintain the platforms) and the lines south of Seaham Station, together with the Seaham Incline from Seaham Colliery and the branch to the new sinking at Dawdon. The Ryhope section of the Ryhope/Silksworth branch was to pass to the NER but the ownership of the Ryhope – Silksworth section was to remain with the Marquis, though all the traffic would be worked by the NER. In return, The Londonderry Collieries Ltd and The Seaham Harbour Dock Co were given running powers which in practice applied over any NER lines in the Seaham Harbour area.

Brief subsequent history under the NER/LNER
The Londonderry Railway's passenger stock and thirteen of the locomotives were included in the take-over. Only three, those mostly recently built, were included in the NER Capital Stock list; these were Nos.2, 20 and 21, which became NER Nos.1113, 1335 and 1712 respectively; the others were placed in the NER Duplicate List (indicating a short life expectancy), Nos. 1, 5, 8-15 becoming NER Nos.2267-2276 in the same order. All thirteen had been withdrawn by the end of 1906, though some were subsequently sold. The last passenger vehicle remained in service with the LNER until April 1928.

The NER's new railway from Seaham to Hartlepool, starting from a junction, Seabanks Junction, with the former Blastfurnace branch near South Hetton Junction, was opened on 1st April 1905. Together with this line a short branch was built to Dawdon Colliery from the Blastfurnace branch, and the branch itself was extended around the east side of the colliery to a junction (Hawthorn Junction) with the Hartlepool line two miles south of Seaham: this extension was known as the Seaham Dock branch.

Turning to the former Londonderry "main line" the NER now had two stations at Ryhope, and so the former Londonderry Station was re-named Ryhope East Station. An NER branch up to Seaham Colliery was opened by 1903, leaving the self-acting incline to link the colliery purely to the docks. The loco shed at Seaham was closed by the NER on 1st October 1913. In 1924 the LNER wished to end the right of the Marquis to have trains "other than express trains" stopped at Seaham Hall Station for his personal use (only exercised four times between 1900 and 1923) and their maintenance agreement brought to an end, and this was agreed, subject to Seaham Colliery Station being re-named Seaham and Seaham Station being renamed Seaham Harbour. These changes were implemented on 1st March 1925. Seaham Harbour Station was closed on 11th September 1939, though it continued to stand until August 1971.

The Engine Works, Wagon Shops and wagons
The equipment in Londonderry Engine Works was partially dismantled and some of it was installed in premises next to the foundry of Robert Wright & Son (NZ 432493), both sites being served by sidings near the South Dock. This done, Hardy retired, on 30th December 1902 at the age of 77. At this point the works, now called the Seaham Harbour Engine Works, was still owned by the Marquis personally, together with the Wagon Shops and certainly all of the coal waggons, for the hire of which The Londonderry Collieries Ltd paid the Marquis. This continued until 30th December 1911, when the colliery company issued shares to the Marquis in lieu of the value of the Engine Works (valued at £7,500), the Wagon Shops (£11,442) and 2,426 wagons (£41,057). It would seem that The Seaham Harbour Dock Co initially did not acquire any coal wagons, though it certainly did so later. According to the directories for Seaham, the Engine Works, which supplied seven steam (road) wagons to the NER in 1905-1906, was by 1910 owned by the Seaham Harbour Engine Works Co Ltd. This title cannot be explained, for the details that The Londonderry Collieries Ltd owned it are clearly given in its Annual Reports. It consistently lost money, and was closed in the autumn of 1925.

The remaining branches
The branches to Seaham Colliery, to Dawdon Colliery and to Fox Cover Quarry were not included in the take-over by the NER and remained in the ownership of the Marquis. The NER soon objected to the existence of an "intermediate party" between their lines and the Dock Company, and so in January 1901 the Dock Company agreed to lease them from the Marquis, almost certainly purchasing them later. The self-acting incline from Seaham Colliery, the only surviving section of the Rainton & Seaham Section, although owned by the Dock Company, was rebuilt by the National Coal Board in 1959 to allow 21-ton wagons to be

introduced to replace the chaldron waggons still in use. Six years later rope working was replaced by locomotive working, although in practice it was rarely used, with most traffic using the adjacent British Railways branch. It was leased to the NCB from 25th March 1967 and finally lifted in January 1988.

Notes on the locomotives
Hardy gives details of all of the Londonderry locomotives except for the harbour locomotives, about which he says nothing at all, despite them being numbered in the Londonderry list and being (presumably) repaired at the Engine Works. Unfortunately, he does not list all of the locomotive builders, and some of these are still unknown. There is also an invaluable document in the DCRO Londonderry Collection, D/Lo/B/385, entitled *Report on the Locomotive Engines to J.H.Ravenshaw* [one of the Marchioness' Agents] by S.J.Green [then Railway Manager], dated 27th July 1860. This gives dates of acquisition and price, together with each locomotive's current condition and location. At that date No.1 was working ballast for the construction of the Blastfurnace branch; Nos.2, 5, 6 and 9 were all under repair (later in 1860 No.9 went to work the Shotton branch – see above); Nos.3 and 4 were working between Rainton Bridge and Rainton Meadows and Nos.7, 8 and 10 were working between Seaham and Sunderland.

Green lists the locomotives by number (10 at that date), so clearly the numbering system was in use by then. This also shows that all the locomotives were numbered in one list, regardless of which part of the system they were working on. He also gives names for some locomotives, these being confirmed in Hardy's draft. All those given were on second-hand engines, and it would appear that they arrived on the Londonderry Railway carrying them. The Green/Hardy names are given below. There is no Londonderry evidence that No.1 was named FRANCIS ANNE, while the name DAWDON was almost certainly not carried by No.3 until after it ceased to be a Londonderry Railway engine. It would appear that no names survived the 1860s.

At much the same date, about 1860, one of the earliest-known colliery photographs in the North-East shows Ryhope colliery from the south, the picture including two locomotives, always captioned as "probably Londonderry Railway locomotives". One is a 0-6-0 tender loco with inside cylinders, which could well have been one of the Londonderry locomotives. The other is a 0-6-0ST with inside cylinders and outside frames, and a very tall, flared chimney; at this date the Railway did not have a 0-6-0ST, unless this is CARADOC.

Oral tradition from 1950 stated that from the 1880s 0-6-0 No.1 was the usual engine working from the engine shed at Warden Law.

There are also considerable difficulties concerning the disposal of the locomotives between 1896 and 1901, apart from those that went to the NER. On 20th November 1896 an advertisement naming Hardy was published in the *Colliery Guardian* offering Nos.1, 3 and 4 for sale. Hardy then describes in his draft a sale held at Rainton on 31st December 1896 in which he says that Nos.4 and 6 were sold, the latter to "Samuelsons" (Sir B. Samuelson & Co Ltd of the Newport Ironworks in Middlesbrough). Notwithstanding this, a major auction was held at Rainton by A.T. and E.A.Crow of Sunderland in March 1897. As advertised in the *Colliery Guardian* of 12th February 1897, this was scheduled for 9th-12th March, and included the Meadows, Alexandrina (Letch), Adventure, Nicholson's, Lady Seaham and Resolution Pits (presumably those where coal production had ceased were being used for pumping or man-riding), together with five locomotives; but a report of it in the *Newcastle Daily Journal* of 18th March 1897 says that it had then lasted for six days, so that it would appear that the sale began later than advertised. Very unusually, the newspaper gives full details of the sale of the locomotives, though sadly it does not give their numbers. These are listed as follows:

Locomotive and tender by Black, Hawthorn, 16½inx24in [cylinders], 5ft 5½in [wheels; the size is an error; Hardy gives 55½in, or 4ft 7½in], sold for £680 to Millfield Grange Co. This is clearly No.1. This sale must have collapsed, for the locomotive was subsequently taken over by the NER.

Saddletank by T.Richardson, £670 to Godfrey & Liddells of London (this should be Liddels). This is clearly No.3. This sale too must have collapsed, for it was still present when the NER took over, but it was not included in the transfer.

Saddletank by R.Stephenson, to North Walbottle Coal Co for £335. This entry is a major problem. The only Stephenson locomotive rebuilt to a saddletank was No.12, but this was one of the locomotives taken over by the NER. It is much more likely to have been No.4, which was built by R & W Hawthorn, and for which no other disposal is known. This loco was over fifty years old, which could be the reason for the low price. Assuming that the purchaser was the North Walbottle Coal Co in Northumberland, that company had an unidentified 0-6-0ST called EDDIE, which may have been this locomotive.

Saddletank, for £455 to Sir B.Samuelson, Middlesbrough. This would appear to be No.6, the difficulty here being its alleged sale to the same purchaser four months earlier (see above).

Saddletank by R.Stephenson, to J.H.Denton, Middlesbrough, £670. The problem here is the same as described for the third loco in the list, though the price is considerably higher. This newspaper list appears to deal with the locomotives in numerical order, and indeed the only loco this one can be is No.7, which was a Stephenson engine. Here too the sale seems to have collapsed, for the loco is believed to have stayed at Seaham until about 1901, when it too was sold to Sir B.Samuelson & Co Ltd at Middlesbrough.

On 1st January 1899 The Seaham Harbour Dock Company took over the harbour and its plant, including locomotives. These certainly included Nos.16-18. For many years it was believed that No.19, also used at the docks, was sold to The Rainton Colliery Co Ltd, only to return to The Seaham Harbour Dock Co after a short time. However, research shows that this firm did not begin production until 1912, while the Directors' Minutes for the Seaham Harbour Dock Co record No.19 as being under repair on 2nd May 1906, and thus it would seem almost certain that No.19 was acquired by the Dock Company at the same time as the others.

In October 1900 Nos.1, 2, 5, 8-15, 20 and 21 were taken over by the NER. About the same time No.7 was sold to Sir B. Samuelson & Co Ltd (see above). This left two locomotives, No.3 and the locomotive then under construction at the Londonderry Engine Works. Hardy in his locomotive summary describes No.3 as working at Dawdon Colliery in 1912, and it is possible, although there is no supporting evidence, that it may have passed to The Londonderry Collieries Ltd in 1900 and been used during the sinking of Dawdon Colliery. The locomotive which was under construction in the Londonderry Engine Works when the NER took over in October 1900 was allegedly intended to be an 0-4-4T, presumably similar to No.21, for use on the passenger service, though why it should have been authorised in such circumstances is not clear. It is also curious that Hardy does not mention it in his text, although it appears in his list of engines. However, an authoritative later source said that it was "not quite complete at the take-over", which would suggest that it was already an 0-6-0T at this stage, and perhaps always had been. The work was transferred to the Seaham Harbour Engine Works, and the engine was completed in 1902. It was then transferred to the Wagon Shops, still in grey paint, where it stood for a number of years, still the personal property of the Marquis. Eventually the Seaham Harbour Dock Company's Directors' Minutes of 11th January 1906 record that "the offer of a suitable locomotive [of greater power to cope with the coal traffic], which had been tried successfully, for £1500 [and] built at the Londonderry Engine Works was accepted".

Gauge : 4ft 8½in

1	(STOCKTON)	0-4-0	OC	RS	753	1849	(a)	(1)
1		0-6-0	IC	BH	34	1868	New	(2)
2	(CHEAPSIDE)	0-4-2	IC	HF	46	1841	(b)	(3)
		reb		Seaham		1860	(c)	(4)
2		2-4-0T	IC	Seaham		1889	New	(5)
3		0-6-0	IC	TR	254	1855	New	
		reb 0-6-0ST	IC	Seaham		1876		(6)
4	"NORTH BRITISH"	0-6-0	IC	RWH	479	1846	(d)	
		reb 0-6-0ST	IC	Seaham		1875		(7)
5	SEFTON	0-4-2	OC	CT	320?	1848	(e)	(8)
5		0-6-0	OC	F&H		1861	New	(9)
5		0-6-0	IC	Seaham		1885	New	(10)
6	(CARADOC)	0-6-0T+t	OC	reb TR	182	c1851	(f)	(11)
6		0-4-0ST	OC	Harris		1867	New	(12)
6		0-6-0ST	IC	Seaham		1883	New	(13)
7		0-6-0	IC	RS	1073	1856	New (g)	
		reb 0-6-0ST	IC	Seaham			(h)	(14)
8		0-6-0	IC	RS	1075	1856	New (g)	
		reb 2-4-0T	IC	Seaham		1879		(15)
9		0-6-0	IC	RS	1096	1857	New	
		reb 2-4-0T	IC	Seaham		1880		(16)
-		4-4-0	OC	RS	1206	1859	(j)	(17)
10		0-6-0	IC	RS	1217	1859	New	(18)
11		0-6-0	IC	RS	1326	1860	New	(19)
12		0-6-0	IC	RS	1327	1860	New	
		reb 0-6-0ST	IC	Seaham		1877		(20)
13		0-6-0	IC	RS	1416	1862	New	(21)
14		0-6-0	IC	RS	1417	1862	New	(22)
15		0-6-0	IC	Blair		1868	New	(23)
16		0-4-0VBT	VC	HW	21	1870	New	(24)
17		0-4-0VBT	OC	HW	33	1873	New	(24)
18		0-4-0WT	OC	Lewin	683	1877	New	(24)
19		0-4-0ST	OC	BH	203	1871	(k)	(24)
20		0-6-0	IC	Seaham		1892	New	(25)
21		0-4-4T	IC	Seaham		1895	New	(26)
-		0-6-0T	IC	Seaham			(m)	(27)

Additional notes
According to NER records, a locomotive was hired from the NER in August 1856.
A locomotive is believed to have been hired by the River Wear Commissioners between 1895 and 1899, presumably for working at the South Dock in Sunderland. Whether the same locomotive was used for the whole period, and which locomotive(s) were involved, is not known.
The rebuilds of Nos.2, 8 and 9, together with new loco 21, were all carried out for the passenger service.

(a) ex Forster & Lawton, contractors for the Seaham-Sunderland section, 2/1854; described as a "firetube type with diagonal cylinders"
(b) ex Lancashire & Yorkshire Railway, 139, 5/1854; originally Manchester & Leeds Railway, 35
(c) "renewal" of 2 Haigh 1841, but actually a new locomotive, including new boiler, motion and tender, and (mentioned by Hardy only in his summary) "new framing"
(d) ex North British Railway, 32, 8/1855
(e) ex J.Blundell, Warrington, Lancashire, 10/1855; originally Liverpool, Crosby & Southport Railway, who sold the loco in 1/1850
(f) ex East Hetton Coal Co, East Hetton Colliery, Kelloe, 9/1855; makers unknown, but believed to have been a York, Newcastle & Berwick Railway engine; described as a tank engine with a tender at the back, a firetube type with diagonal cylinders
(g) RS 1073 was originally ordered by C.M.Palmer of John Bowes, Esq., & Partners for the Pontop & Jarrow Railway, an order subsequently cancelled in favour of a larger engine, RS 1074. John Bowes, Esq., & Partners also owned as a subsidiary company The Northumberland & Durham Coal Company in London, which operated what when sold in 1859 became the North London Railway. Hardy claimed that RS 1075 was originally ordered for the "North London Railway", a confusion with RS 1073 and also an error
(h) there is no mention in any of Hardy's writing that this loco was rebuilt as a saddletank; however, when C.H.A.Townley was collecting information about the locomotives at Seaham in the late 1940s he was twice told that 7 had been rebuilt as a saddletank – which would also appear to be confirmed by the 1897 sale details above
(j) hired from RS, /1859, whilst waiting for delivery of RS 1217; this loco was ordered by the Ottoman Railway Company of Turkey; Hardy gives Cairo in Egypt as its destination, which could be true as Turkey ruled Egypt at this time
(k) one version says ex a contractor (unknown) building a dock on the River Tyne, c/1890; another states that it was acquired from a scrapyard at Jarrow; originally owned by The Felling Coal, Iron & Chemical Co Ltd, Felling
(m) new locomotive, completed in 1902

(1) frame, cylinders and motion used in the construction of a stationary engine on the Railway at Pittington about 1863 (see text); remainder scrapped
(2) to NER, 7/10/1900; allocated NER 2267; to R.Frazer & Sons (Newcastle) Ltd, Hebburn, dealers, 29/3/1901; apparently not re-sold and presumably scrapped
(3) withdrawn from traffic in 1856 and used in 1857-1858 to drive the machinery in the workshops being developed at Polka Bank Foot, Seaham; this use was subsequently terminated and the locomotive "renewed" (see footnote c above)
(4) withdrawn from traffic in 1884; cylinders and motion incorporated into a horizontal engine operating a crane to draw ballast from ships at Seaham Harbour; later this was modified and installed in the Engine Works to drive machinery; the tender was used as a water tank at the Harbour, and later as a tank to store sand; all eventually scrapped
(5) to NER, 7/10/1900; became NER 1113; withdrawn from traffic, 28/12/1906 and cut up at Percy Main workshops, Percy Main, North Shields, Northumberland, 13/1/1910
(6) see notes above; to The Londonderry Collieries Ltd, date unknown
(7) believed to be the loco sold to The North Walbottle Coal Co Ltd, Northumberland, 3/1897 (see notes above)
(8) dismantled by 1858; scrapped after 27/7/1860
(9) described as "a firetube type with diagonal cylinders"; withdrawn from traffic by 1873 and parts used to drive a sawmill at Seaham Harbour, with the remainder being scrapped
(10) to NER, 7/10/1900; became NER 2268; sold, /1902
(11) almost certainly it was this locomotive ("a six wheeled loco & tender with 14½in x 18in cylinders") which was offered for sale in the *Colliery Guardian* on 25th May 1867; to John Harris, Hopetown Foundry, Darlington, in part payment for new 0-4-0ST built by him and delivered c9/1867
(12) scrapped by /1883
(13) to Sir B.Samuelson & Co Ltd, Newport Ironworks, Middlesbrough, Yorkshire (NR), either in 12/1896 or 3/1897 (see notes above)
(14) to Sir B. Samuelson & Co Ltd, Newport Ironworks, Middlesbrough, Yorkshire (NR), c/1901; see notes above
(15) to NER, 7/10/1900; became NER 2269, and worked at Scarborough, Yorkshire (ER); replaced, /1920
(16) to NER, 7/10/1900; became NER 2270; withdrawn from traffic, /1902

(17) returned to RS; RS 1217 was delivered new in 11/1859
(18) to NER, 7/10/1900; allocated NER 2271; to R.Frazer & Sons (Newcastle) Ltd, Hebburn, dealers, 29/3/1901; apparently not re-sold and presumably scrapped
(19) to NER, 7/10/1900; allocated NER 2272; withdrawn from traffic, /1902
(20) to NER, 7/10/1900; allocated NER 2273; to R.Frazer & Sons (Newcastle) Ltd, Hebburn, dealers, 29/3/1901; to The Seaton Burn Coal Co Ltd, Seaton Burn, Northumberland, almost immediately; scrapped, /1923
(21) to NER, 7/10/1900; allocated NER 2274; replaced, /1920
(22) to NER, 7/10/1900; allocated NER 2275, withdrawn from traffic, /1902
(23) to NER, 7/10/1900; allocated NER 2276. withdrawn from traffic, /1902
(24) to The Seaham Harbour Dock Co , 1/1/1899
(25) to NER, 7/10/1900; became NER 1335; withdrawn from traffic, 30/6/1906; to The Seaton Delaval Coal Co Ltd, Seaton Delaval, Northumberland, 4/1907; to Hartley Main Collieries Ltd on its formation on 16/5/1929; scrapped, 9/1936
(26) to NER, 7/10/1900; became NER 1712; withdrawn from traffic, 21/12/1906; to Isle of Wight Central Railway, Isle of Wight, 8/6/1909, where it became WCR No.2; to Sir W.G.Armstrong, Whitworth & Co Ltd, Elswick Works, Newcastle-upon-Tyne, 7/1917; scrapped, c/1922
(27) remained unused and the personal property of the Marquis of Londonderry until sold to The Seaham Harbour Dock Co, Seaham, 1/1906

Coaching stock taken over by the North Eastern Railway

Built	Type	Wheels	Seats 1st	Seats 3rd	1st NER	2nd NER	Disposal number number
1893	Brake Third	6	-	40	2940	-	Condemned 13/4/1922
1893	Brake Third	6	-	40	2941	-	Condemned 18/4/1925
1894	Third	6	-	60	2942	-	Condemned 7/4/1928
1894	Third	6	-	60	2943	-	Condemned 12/5/1923
1885	Third	4	-	50	2944	-	Replaced by 12/1906
1885	Third	4	-	50	2945	-	Replaced by 6/1912
1882	Third	4	-	50	2946	-	Replaced by 9/1909
1883	Brake Third	4	-	30	2947	-	Condemned 26/9/1901
1883	Brake Third	4	-	30	2948	-	Condemned 29/8/1901
1885	Composite	4	16	20	2949	-	To Third, 6/1901; condemned, 14/12/1905
?	Third	4	-	50	2950	3593	Replaced by 12/1905
?	Third	4	-	50	2951	3594	Replaced by 12/1905
?	Third	4	-	50	2952	3595	Replaced by 12/1905
?	Third	4	-	50	2954	3596	Replaced by 4/1906
?	Third	4	-	40	2955	3597	Condemned 14/3/1901
?	Third	4	-	40	2956	3598	Condemned 21/2/1901
?	Third	4	-	40	2957	3599	Condemned 21/2/1901
?	Third	4	-	40	2958	3600	Condemned 21/2/1901
?	Third	4	-	40	2959	3601	Condemned 21/2/1901
?	Third	4	-	40	2960	3602	Condemned 21/2/1901
?	Composite	4	16	20	2961	3603	To Third, 6/1901; condemned 11/6/1903
?	Composite	4	16	20	2962	3604	Condemned 21/2/1901
?	Van	4	-	-	383	-	Condemned 5/12/1901

Nos. 2947 and 2948 were reputed to have been built at Birmingham. No building dates are given in NER records for Nos. 2950-1962, nor for the van.

The former Londonderry Railway between Seaham and Sunderland continues in use, now owned by Network Rail. The collieries once owned by Londonderry Collieries Ltd, Seaham, Dawdon and Vane Tempest, have all closed, The former Londonderry Offices, near to the North Dock at Seaham, survive, as does The Seaham Harbour Dock Company, albeit having passed through various ownerships since 1899. Its rail traffic ceased in 1992 and the remaining track was lifted; but having subsequently sold its former onshore area for re-development, it acquired the large area once occupied by the Bottle and the Chemical Works and then developed "CargoDurham", a major storage and distribution centre, and to serve this a new rail connection was laid in 2001 from the former Seabanks Junction along part of the former Blastfurnace branch. Of the former Rainton & Seaham section, almost nothing survives – except for the buildings of the former Warden Law Engine House, pump house and loco shed, which, with the cells of the former coal depot here and the railwaymen's cottages, are now incorporated into a private small-holding.

182. On the Rainton & Seaham route, closed in 1896, most buildings have been demolished and the trackbed ploughed out; but at Warden Law the engine house building (1831), the loco shed built on to its western end (1880) and the adjacent well-house (on left) not only survived to 1950, as here, but survive into the 21st century too (albeit surrounded by additional buildings) as part of a privately-owned smallholding, together with some stone sleeper blocks, a few rail chairs, the cells of the coal depot and sections of the trackbed.

Chapter Eleven
The Pelaw Main Railway

OWNERS BEFORE 1947
The Pelaw Main Collieries Ltd until 1/1/1947
The Birtley Iron Co until 26/5/1926; see also below

Like several of the other major private railways in Durham, the Pelaw Main Railway was developed from eighteenth century waggonways. For many years it was operated by an iron company whose owners were very different from The Consett Iron Co Ltd, and in its final years before nationalisation it was controlled by French owners. Equally, it became a unique mix of second-hand locomotives and rope haulage, both fascinating and very varied.

The Birtley Iron Company was founded in 1827 by Benjamin Thompson (1779-1867), a Sheffield man already involved with the iron trade elsewhere in the country, who in 1811 had come to Co.Durham to manage Urpeth Colliery, near Chester-le-Street, for the assignees of the bankrupt company of Harrison, Cooke & Co (see below). Thompson became a prominent advocate of rope haulage, and a minor figure on the national stage of railway development in the late 1820s and 1830s. He was the engineer for the Brunton & Shields colliery railway in Northumberland, and in 1828 he became the contractor to Shakespeare Reed for the construction of the new section of the Londonderry Railway between Rainton Bridge and Seaham. He was also a director of both the Brandling Junction and Newcastle & Carlisle Railways. In 1838 he sold his share of the Birtley Iron Company to a new group of partners headed by a London businessman, Frederick Perkins. The latter died in 1871 and was succeeded by his son, Charles Perkins, who died in 1905. Throughout this period the ironworks and colliery businesses, though legally the same, were kept separate for trading purposes, the latter operating under various titles : **Pelaw Main Collieries**, **The Owners of Pelaw Main Collieries**, **Charles Perkins & Partners** and then **Pelaw Main Collieries** for a second time, are all found. The origin of the title "Pelaw Main" is unclear; Pelaw was a hamlet near Bill Quay on the River Tyne, but there was no colliery there.

The Birtley Iron Co fell on bad times in the depression of the early 1920s and the collieries were closed. In 1926 they and their accompanying royalty of about 6000 acres were acquired by new owners under the title of **The Pelaw Main Collieries Ltd**. In 1930 the iron works site was re-opened by a new company, The Birtley Co Ltd, which concentrated on fabricated products. The colliery company passed into the ownership of the Paris, Lyon & Mediterranean Railway, the only example of foreign ownership in the North-East coalfield. During the Second World War French control could not be exercised, and the collieries were managed from the Mining Offices at Birtley by the company's Agent; French control resumed with the end of the War.

The iron works and all of the company's collieries, together with quite a number of other businesses, were served by what became called the **PELAW MAIN RAILWAY**.

The Railway was basically a combination of two old waggonways, the **Ouston Waggonway** and the **Team Colliery Waggonway**. The title "Pelaw Main Railway" is found as early as 1843, on Bell's Map of the Great Northern Coalfield, though the old names continued in use until about the beginning of the twentieth century. When compared with other colliery railways, the Pelaw Main Railway was unusual in two respects. Firstly, whilst the others replaced their rope inclines with locomotive working either partially or completely, the Pelaw Main Railway became a piecemeal mixture of not only rope and locomotive haulage but also gravity and horse haulage, with rare or unique types of rope operation surviving into the NCB period. Because of this, rather more description of the rope haulage has been included here. Secondly, whilst most of the others basically ran full coal trains to the staiths and empties back to the collieries, the Pelaw Main Railway not only ran full traffic in both directions, mainly for dispatch via its various links to the public system but also carried a considerable volume of other traffic, both for the company's use – workmen's coal, loco coal, colliery materials, timber for the company's Property Department and a weekly stores van - but also for the businesses established alongside it. This was due in part to the lack of public railways for many years in the company's area; the NER main line between Newcastle upon Tyne and Durham down the Team valley, the present East Coast Main Line, was not opened until 1868.

The Ouston Waggonway/Railway
The first waggonway to be built in the Birtley area of Co.Durham was also the first-ever to incorporate a stationary steam engine to haul waggons. This was opened about 1805 to carry coal to the River Wear at Fatfield, the **stationary engine** being sited on Black Fell on the eastern side of the valley of the River Team. The final section, down to the river at Fatfield, was a **self-acting incline**. Soon afterwards, probably about 1807-1808, the line passed to the control of Messrs. Harrison, Cooke & Co, who were

254

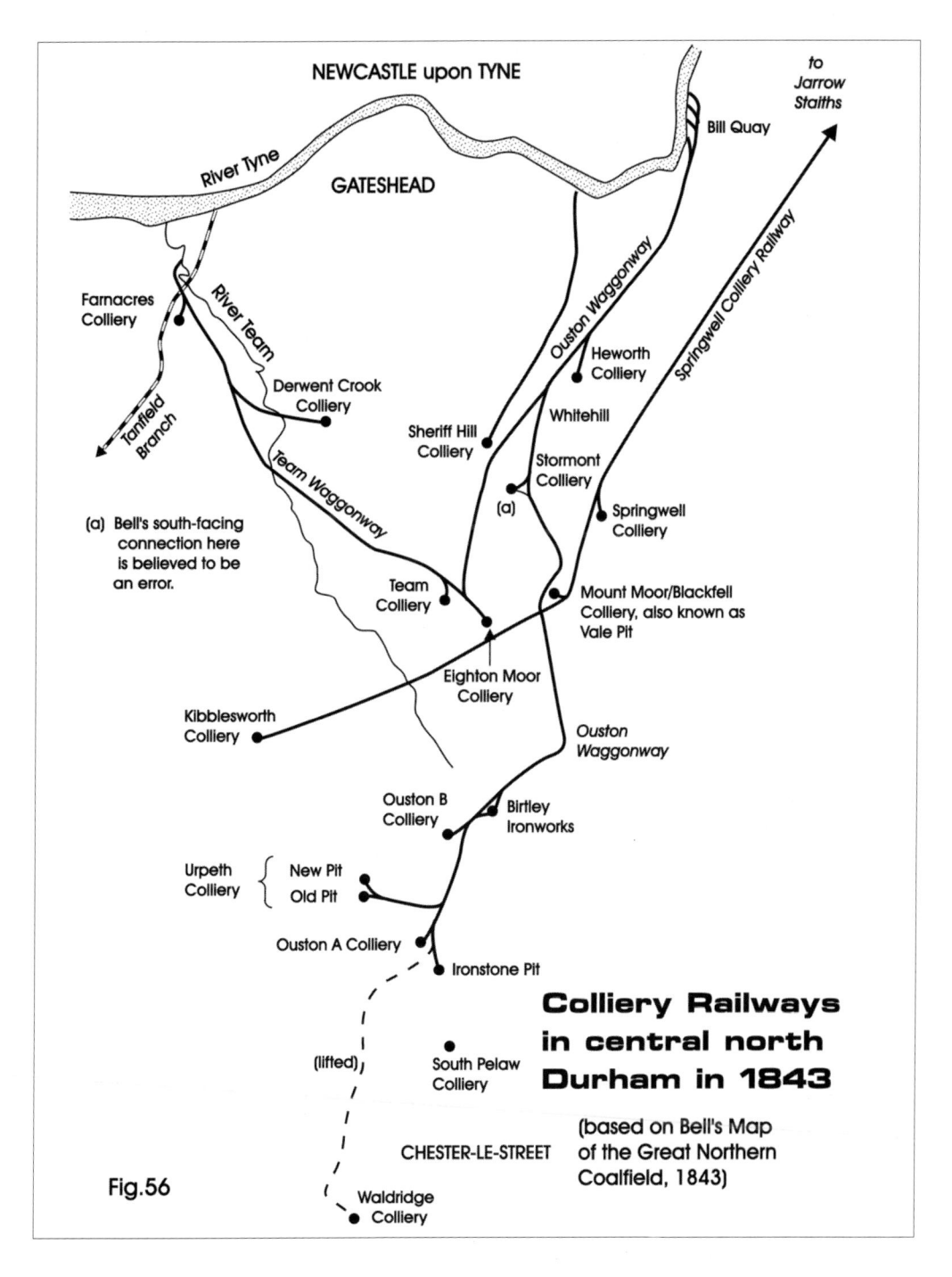

Colliery Railways in central north Durham in 1843

(based on Bell's Map of the Great Northern Coalfield, 1843)

Fig.56

(a) Bell's south-facing connection here is believed to be an error.

sinking a colliery at Urpeth, north-west of Chester-le-Street. They kept the old route but also built a new one, known as the **Bewicke Main Waggonway**, to staiths on the River Tyne at Bill Quay, which was opened on 17th May 1809. A description in the *Newcastle Courant* states that the line took 76 days to construct. It ran from the colliery in a north-easterly direction up to the top of the eastern side of the Team valley, using two **stationary engines**. These totalled 4,375 yards, replaced 203 horses and men and worked waggons at 9 m.p.h. From the summit the *Courant* states that "descending planes" took the line down to the River Tyne, but in fact this section was worked entirely by horses until the following year, when part of this length, at Whitehill, south-east of Windy

Nook, was replaced by the **self-acting Heworth Incline**, 1337 yards long, which was brought into use on 15th March 1810.

However, the cost of all this development rendered the company bankrupt soon afterwards. As noted above, Benjamin Thompson was brought north to sort out the affairs of the bankrupt company. He subsequently acquired the assets, sank a new colliery at Ouston, about a mile from Urpeth, and completely rebuilt the southern end of the waggonway. This line, now called the **Ouston Waggonway**, opened on 17th November 1815.

The waggonway is described in *Des Chemins de Fer en Angleterre, Notamment a Newcastle*, compiled by M.de Gallois, the Engineer in Chief to the Royal Mines in France, and published in *Annales des Mines, 1818*. When de Gallois visited the line in 1817 the section to the River Wear was still in use, and he describes it as four miles long and having two descending inclined planes. Also in 1817 this section attracted the attention of the Board running the colliery interests of John George Lambton (see The Lambton Railway), which considered acquiring it as an outlet for coal from Harraton Colliery, but in the event took no action.

The next detailed description of the line is found in a large-scale book of plans entitled *Ouston Colliery – The Waggonway and Farms*, surveyed by John Bell between 1819 and 1824, which survives in Tyne & Wear Archives (T&W DT/BEL/2/287). This makes no mention of the section to the River Wear, so presumably it had been closed by this time. Bell's plans start at **OUSTON COLLIERY** (NZ 264536), from where there was a short **self-acting incline** down to the valley floor. Then comes what was obviously a horse-worked section for about a mile to the foot of the next incline. The text on the plans gives the **Turnpike Inclined Plane** and the **Birtley Inclined Plane** coming next, with a short length dividing the two; but the drawing seems clearly to show that these were one incline, about 470 yards long, worked by the **Birtley Engine** (NZ 274555). This worked two sets simultaneously that passed just above the Durham Turnpike road. The waggons travelled the next forty yards by gravity. Then came the **Blackhouse Inclined Plane**, up to the **Black House Engine** (NZ 280560) (25 h.p.), working sets alternately. Here a "stable" is marked, presumably for the horses that worked the next 1¼ miles to the foot of the **Ayton Inclined Plane**, near which the route of the original Urpeth Waggonway is shown. The **Ayton Engine** (later **Eighton Engine**) (NZ 281582) also worked two sets at once on this short bank, which was only 334 yards long. The existence of three inclines, all worked by stationary engines, is also confirmed by de Gallois, who gives the total rise as 406 feet and adds that "the combined force of the three engines equals sixty nine horses."

In describing the section between the top of the Ayton Incline and the River Tyne the sources disagree. De Gallois states that this included three descending inclined planes, with one of nearly a mile long (presumably the Heworth Incline); but Bell's plans appear to show that the section to the top of the **Heworth Inclined Plane** was worked by horses, as was the 1¼ mile section between Heworth bank foot and the staiths, where a final **self-acting incline**, the **Tyne Inclined Plane** (225 yards) took the waggons down to the loading points. Bell gives the distance between the colliery and the river as 7 miles 14 yards.

As noted above, Benjamin Thompson was a leading advocate of rope haulage, and it is believed that during the 1820s he converted all of the horse-worked sections on the Ouston Waggonway to rope working. According to his own account in his book *Inventions, Improvements and Practice of a Colliery Engineer*, published in 1847, in 1821 he replaced the ten horses working the 1992 yards between Blackhouse bank head and Eighton bank foot, together with the Eighton Incline itself, with what he called "reciprocating haulage", which was a version of what was later known as main-and-tail haulage. This involved fitting "rope wheels" to the two stationary engines, which operated the system in tandem, working six sets of waggons at a time and producing considerable savings in costs. However, this did not prove entirely satisfactory, and within a short time the **Eighton Incline** (later the **Eighton Banks Incline**) was re-instated and a new **stationary engine** was installed at **Eighton bank foot** (NZ 277576) to operate, still by main-and-tail, the section between there and Blackhouse. The next horse-worked section ran between Eighton (Banks) bank head and Whitehill. One has to assume that Thompson converted this to reciprocating haulage too, but no evidence has been found to confirm this or how it was done. Over the final section, between Heworth bank foot and the top of the staiths' incline, there was a gradient in favour of the load, but insufficient for a self-acting incline. So Thompson retained the single line and installed a **stationary engine** (NZ 287613) at the bank foot, the fulls travelling to the staiths by gravity, dragging the rope, and the empties being hauled back by the engine. At the other end of the line the original self-acting incline at Ouston was replaced by the **Ouston Engine** (NZ 264535) near the colliery; but how it participated in railway operation can be no more than conjecture. This problem is further complicated by a new sinking which Thompson completed in 1824. This was **OUSTON B COLLIERY** (NZ 266547), west of the line about ¾ mile north of what was now Ouston A Colliery. Whether the Ouston Engine worked traffic in and out of both collieries is not known.

Other collieries join the line

As the modern waggonway in its area, with access to deepwater staiths on the River Tyne and so by-passing the need to use keels to trans-ship to colliers, the waggonway soon attracted other traffic. Very little would be known about this, were it not for a very informative letter written during the dispute between the Marquis of Londonderry and the Birtley Iron Co in 1840 about the valuation of the section of the Londonderry Railway between Rainton Bridge and Seaham (which see). The letter, written to the "umpire" by George Johnson,

Birtley & Ouston 1857

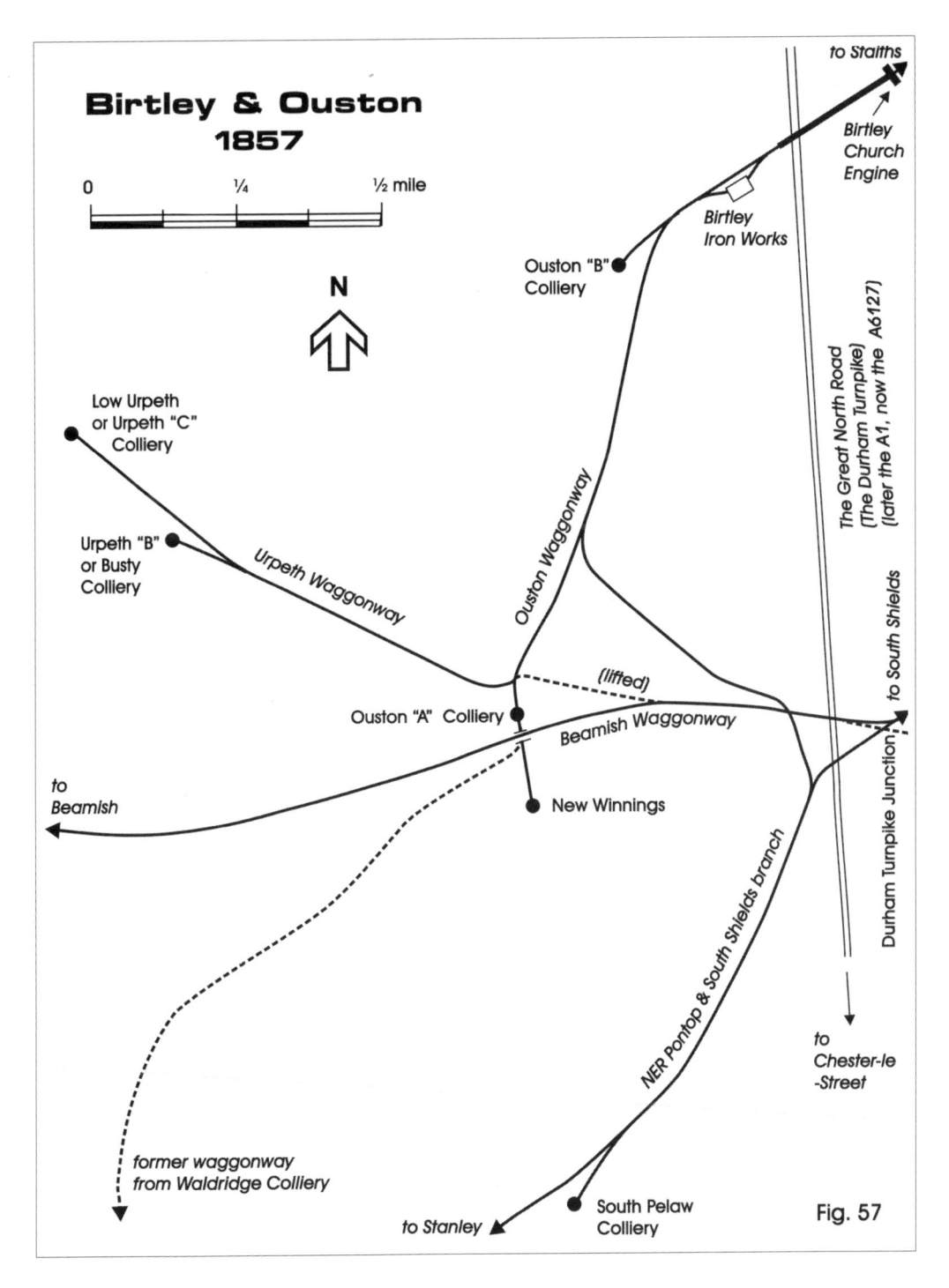

0   ¼   ½ mile

N ⬆

to Staiths
Birtley Church Engine
Birtley Iron Works
Ouston "B" Colliery
Low Urpeth or Urpeth "C" Colliery
Urpeth "B" or Busty Colliery
Urpeth Waggonway
Ouston Waggonway
The Great North Road (The Durham Turnpike) (later the A1, now the A6127)
to South Shields
Ouston "A" Colliery
(lifted)
Beamish Waggonway
Durham Turnpike Junction
to Beamish
New Winnings
NER Pontop & South Shields branch
to Chester-le-Street
former waggonway from Waldridge Colliery
to Stanley
South Pelaw Colliery

Fig. 57

representing the Iron Company, is dated 28th August 1840, and a copy survives in the Johnson papers in the Northumberland Record Office (NRO 3410/JOHN/9/145). Johnson lists five collieries which had sent their coal down the Ouston line, the first four all making their agreements in 1828 and 1829, finding their own waggons and paying wayleave charges. However, his list is not without its difficulties.

1. **Heworth Colliery, Heworth** (NZ 284605)
The first colliery here was sunk in 1701 by the Blackett family; but in 1821 a new shaft was sunk

near to the eastern side of the Whitehill Incline. By 1828, and probably earlier, it was linked to the bottom of the Whitehill Incline by the **self-acting Heworth Incline**, ½ mile long. By the middle of the nineteenth century the colliery was owned by **The Heworth Coal Company**, which became **The Heworth Coal Co Ltd** in 1902. For a time it was called **Upper Heworth Colliery**, but later it became simply **Heworth Colliery**. How its traffic was worked is described below.

2. **Eighton Moor Colliery, Low Fell, near Gateshead** (NZ 271575)

This colliery lay at the southern end of the **Team Colliery Waggonway**. Sometime during the 1820s its owners built a new line north-eastwards to join the Ouston line near Whitehill Bank Head. This was very important, because it led to the merger of the Ouston and Team lines into one ownership.

3. **Blackfell Colliery, Eighton Banks, near Gateshead**

This name must clearly refer to **Mount Moor Colliery** (NZ 279577), owned by Lord Ravensworth & Partners (see chapter 3), which was originally linked by a waggonway to the River Wear at Washington. It lay close to the bank foot of the Eighton Incline, to which it was presumably linked, with its traffic being worked by the Eighton Banks Engine. Johnson continues "The Blackfell owners have since laid a way for themselves", which must refer to the Springwell Colliery Railway; but this was extended to Mount Moor Colliery in June 1826, so Johnson's memory in dating an agreement to 1828-1829 is presumably in error. However, a link between the two lines continued here for many years (see below).

4. **Waldridge Colliery, Waldridge, near Chester-le-Street** (NZ 253502)

Here too Johnson's memory betrayed him a little, for this colliery was opened in August 1831. It was linked to the Ouston waggonway by a line about 2¾ miles long to a junction just north of Ouston A Colliery. The first ½ mile from the colliery was worked by horses, and then the Waldridge Engine (NZ 252505) worked a 1 mile long incline down to Pelton Fell, from where, almost certainly, horses took over for the remaining length to Ouston. This link was equally short-lived, for in 1834 the Stanhope & Tyne Railway was opened, passing through Pelton Fell, about 1½ miles north of the colliery, and its owners promptly linked their line to it and abandoned the remaining section to Ouston.

Johnson goes on to list a fifth colliery that was linked to the Ouston line by 1840:

5. **Stormont Colliery, near Gateshead** (NZ 276592)

Johnson describes its agreement as having been made "lately", presumably dating it to the latter half of the 1830s. It was linked to the line about half way between Eighton Banks bank head and Whitehill (Bell's map of 1843 shows a south-facing link, but this must surely be an error for a north-facing link). Johnson continues "From the Stormont Pit the work is done by self-acting planes"; but even this direct statement has difficulties, discussed below.

The gauge of the railway

The gauge of the Ouston Waggonway as built is not known. For the Team Colliery Waggonway to have been linked to it the two must clearly have been built to the same gauge. It may well be that the original gauge was not 4ft 8½in; if so, then nothing is known of any conversion of the system to standard gauge.

So within a few years of its opening the Ouston line was being altered, a process that was to continue constantly over the next 125 years, with branches added or closed, together with new collieries and businesses, as well as changes to motive power. The complexity of these suggests that it would be better to deal with these linearly, from south to north, rather than chronologically. In doing this it should also be noted that the Iron Company also allocated letters in alphabetical order to its collieries, as well as names, probably in the 1880s.

From Urpeth C Colliery to Ewe Hill

Besides the additions above the Ouston line was also extended to serve collieries at Urpeth. The changes of nomenclature are a problem, but almost certainly there were only two collieries here. It would seem that the pit opened in 1805 was subsequently re-opened by Thompson. This is presumably the pit shown on Bell's map of 1843, reproduced as Fig.56, as **Urpeth Old Pit**, later called **URPETH B COLLIERY** and then **URPETH BUSTY COLLIERY** (NZ 249536). On 1st July 1835 (another version gives 1831) another shaft was begun ½ mile to the north-west. This was called **Urpeth New Pit**, then **LOW URPETH COLLIERY** and finally **URPETH C COLLIERY** (NZ 248535). Bell's map shows the two linked separately to the line, but the 1st edition of the O.S. maps shows the two to have been served by the same line. It also shows what appears to be an extension of the Urpeth waggonway near Ouston A Colliery eastwards for just under ¼ mile to join the Beamish Waggonway, but lifted by 1857, when the O.S. survey was carried out.

When the line was extended from Ouston to the Old Pit it was worked by a stationary engine to the west of the latter, the **Urpeth Engine** (NZ 248536). The Engine Book for R & W Hawthorn of Newcastle records that Works Nos.125 and 126 were stationary engines ordered by Thompson for the Ouston Railway. The list at this time does not record the dates of ordering or manufacture, but these would have been built about 1829-1830. No.125 was a 40 h.p engine, No.126 a 15 h.p. engine, and these may be the Urpeth and Ouston Engines (see above for the latter). At the beginning it would seem likely that the Urpeth Engine hauled empties up to the back of the pit, whence they were worked through the screens by gravity back to the bank head for the rope to be attached for the bank down to Ouston A Colliery. When Low Urpeth Colliery was opened this clearly had to change. In the event a **new Urpeth Engine** was built at the Old Pit on the south side of the line, working the inclines on either side of it, but unusually with the

183. A set of empties, with a NER wagon next to the rope end, leaving Ouston Bank Foot for Urpeth, probably in 1904. Note the line from Ouston A Colliery entering from the right, apparently worked by horses.

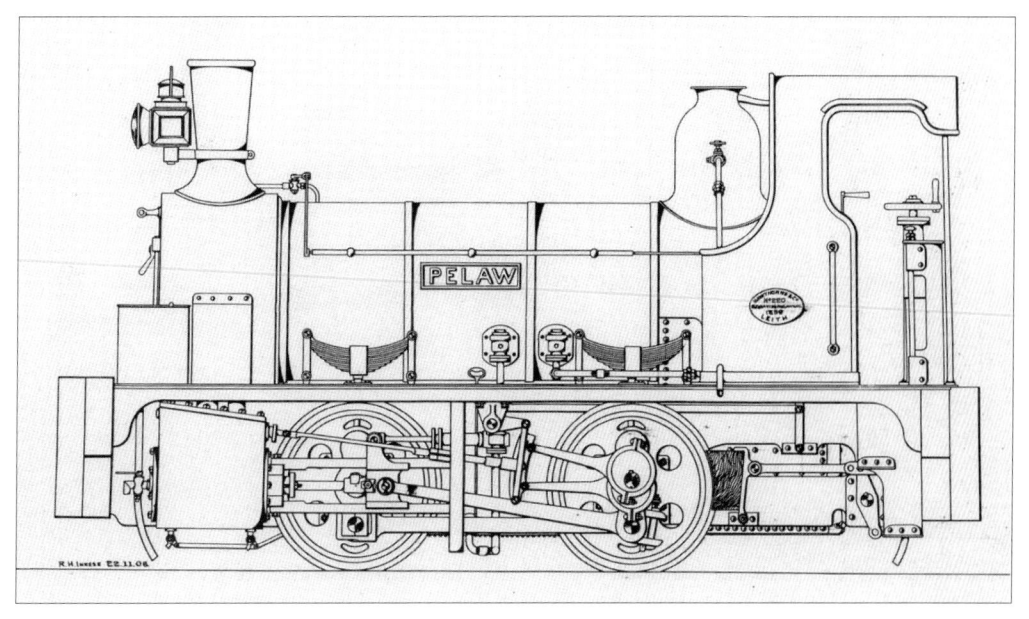

Fig. 58. Line drawing by R.H.Inness of PELAW, 0-4-0WT built H(L) 220/1859, possibly the first locomotive to work at Birtley.

same rope. A set of empty wagons, six in later years, was run down the 750 yard, 1 in 22 bank, to the C Pit at speed, and at "the mark" the rope was slipped for the set to be fly-shunted up to the back of the pit and then run through the screens by gravity to be filled. The Engine then hauled a set of six fulls up to the engine house, where again the rope was slipped and the wagons run past and braked to a halt. The same rope was then attached to the rear end of the set for it to be lowered down to the sidings at Ewe Hill, which were developed about ¼ mile north of Ouston A Colliery. Then six empties would be hauled back to the engine house, where the rope would be slipped and then re-attached as before. Alternatively, the empties could be run into Urpeth Busty Colliery, followed by a set of fulls from here to Ewe Hill.

Ouston A Colliery
Bell's 1843 map shows an "Ironstone Pit" (NZ 265535) just to the south-east of Ouston A Colliery, but curiously there appears to be no sign of it on the 1st edition O.S. map. However, the map does show that by 1857 a ¼ mile extension of the spur to Ouston A Colliery had been built underneath the Beamish Waggonway to serve the **NEW WINNINGS** (NZ 264532). From the O.S. map it would appear this link was standard gauge; the method of haulage is not known. On Airey's *Railway Map of the County of Durham and District*, published in 1876, a second line is shown, branching south of the Beamish Waggonway bridge, to additional workings, but no confirmation of this has been found.

The "Ouston Branch Waggonway"
It was clearly essential for the Birtley Iron Works to be linked to the public railway system, and undoubtedly this was why this line, just over ½ mile long, was built. The northern end left the main line at Ewe Hill, where sidings were constructed later, crossed the Beamish Waggonway, apparently on the level, and joined the NER Pontop & South Shields line at what was almost certainly the southern end of the bank foot of the Vigo West Incline. One of the reasons for the south-facing junction here may well have been to bring traffic on to the Ouston line from **SOUTH PELAW COLLIERY** (NZ 264523), which the firm probably opened in the 1840s; later it was the first colliery to be allocated letter E. The colliery was closed in 1886 due to the exhaustion of the seams that it was working; however, it was re-let in 1890 to different owners to work the lower seams and was re-opened in 1892, using a different rail link.

However, by this time there had been radical changes in the area. The NER line southwards from Gateshead down the Team Valley to Durham had been opened in 1868, and the former junction between the Beamish Waggonway and the Pontop & South Shields branch at the northern end of the former Vigo Bank Foot had been replaced by a new, but northern-facing junction where the Ouston branch junction had been, the two private railways joining just west of the bridge carrying them over the NER Team Valley line. For many years the junction with the NER Pontop & South Shields line was called Durham Turnpike Junction, from the adjacent "Durham Turnpike" – the Great North Road, later the A1 – a few yards away, and this was the name always given to it by the Pelaw Main men, although it was subsequently renamed Beamish Junction.

184. VICTORY, built by John Harris of Darlington in 1863, used by B.C.Lawton, the contractor for the construction of the Team Valley line for the North Eastern Railway, and then acquired for the Railway, also probably for working at Birtley.

185. PELAW II, which was built in 1847 by Charles Todd of Leeds as a 0-6-0 tender engine for the York & Newcastle Railway and was rebuilt to this form by the NER in 1879, seen here, probably at Birtley, on 2nd May 1922.

186. The Railway acquired four of the NER 964 class in 1905 from dealers Robert Frazer & Sons Ltd of Hebburn, of which SALISBURY, RS 2244/1875, was one.

The link to the NER at Durham Turnpike Junction allowed coal to be dispatched this way and materials for the collieries to be brought in, as well as to service various businesses that were started alongside the branch and shunted by Pelaw Main locomotives. On its eastern side was situated the **Birtley Grange Brick & Tile Works** (NZ 268541), which was opened in 1890. From 1925 this was owned by J.O.Scott & Co Ltd and called the **Pelaw Grange Brickworks**. It closed in 1938. On the opposite side of the line lay the **Pelaw Grange Sawmills** (NZ 266540). These had been opened by 1890, and appear to have been closed in the late 1920s; latterly they were owned by Joseph Smith.

Birtley Iron Works and "Birtley Tail"
At the end of the incline from Ouston lay **BIRTLEY IRON WORKS** (NZ 271550 approx.). As noted above, Thompson set up The Birtley Iron Company in 1827. This decision was almost certainly based on the discovery of iron ore above the Hutton seam at the collieries, a similar situation to that found at Consett, whilst the site chosen lay south of the line between the Ouston and Birtley Church Inclines but still close to the collieries. In 1828-1829 two blast furnaces were built and by 1830 the works was producing 3,000 tons of iron per year. A third furnace had been added by 1847. By then iron ore was being brought from a mine which the company had developed on the Yorkshire coast near Whitby. The ore was unloaded at Pelaw Main Staiths and brought to the works down the Railway, which of course was also handling the iron produced by the works. The furnaces ceased production in 1866 and the works then concentrated on foundry and general engineering work, However, it continued to be known colloquially as the "Iron Works", and this use has been continued in these notes. By 1894 the slag from the iron works was being worked by a man called McGregor, though it was a short-lived venture; once again Pelaw Main locomotives handled the traffic.

With the iron works alongside the line and the branches from the collieries joining together to the west and the bank foot of the Birtley Church Incline to the east, a major complex of sidings grew up here, known for many years as **"Birtley Tail"**.

The Bewicke Main branch
To work the coal in the north-west area of the royalty the company sank **BEWICKE MAIN COLLIERY** (NZ 254556), later **BEWICKE MAIN D COLLIERY**. This was opened in August 1862. It was served by a branch 1 mile long from Birtley Tail. This line was probably never rope-worked, though whether horses or locomotives were used initially is not known. About half way along on its eastern side was another brickworks, latterly called the **Station Brickworks** (NZ 265556). This was owned by the Blythe family, latterly Blythe & Sons (Birtley) Ltd, a business started in 1858. How long Pelaw Main locomotives shunted this works is not known. In 1902 to the west of Bewicke Main Colliery the company opened the **RIDING DRIFT** (NZ 245553) and built a narrow gauge line to serve it. How this line was worked before the arrival of a locomotive in 1905 is not known. In 1907 the **MILL DRIFT** (NZ 246555) was added, with the line extended to it. This was closed in April 1915, to be followed by the Riding Drift at the beginning of the General Strike in April 1926. How the line was worked after the disposal of the locomotive is also not definitely known, though it is believed to have been by some form of rope haulage. Bewicke Main Colliery itself closed on 2nd January 1932, but with the shaft retained for pumping and a coal depot serving the adjacent village, the branch remained open, at least until the Second World War.

The Birtley Station branch
On its Team Valley line, opened for goods on 2nd March 1868 and for passengers on 1st December

187. Later the Railway acquired three LNER Y7 locomotives, again from Frazers, all of which had spells at Birtley; 1308, Gateshead 37/1891, festooned with equipment, is almost certainly standing outside the Ouston E Pit loco shed.

188. Birtley Church Incline bank foot at Birtley Tail, looking west, probably in 1904, with the East Coast main line crossing in the background. Note the 'sampson' for moving wagons by hand lent against the wall, the sprags through the wheels, the horse and the very early electric lighting, supplied by the power station at Ouston E Colliery in the distance. The locomotive is an 0-6-0ST, very probably BH 48 or 52, both built in 1868.

189. Birtley Tail looking east, with the line to Birtley Station in the foreground and the former Birtley Iron Works on the right, taken probably on 13th June 1950.

1868, the NER included a station at Birtley. To give itself a link to the station the company built a ¾ mile branch from the Bewicke Main branch, passing under the NER to reach the eastern side of Birtley Station. This link was used mainly for iron works traffic, though a reverse was needed on each trip. Later a link to this line was built from Birtley Tail, thus forming a triangle, which the company used to turn locomotives after repair to equalise tyre wear before dispatching them back into traffic.

From the line to Birtley Station there was a link on the eastern side into the **Ravensworth Brick & Tile Works** (NZ 258556). Various opening dates have been quoted, but it is shown on the NER Siding Map of 1894. This works was owned latterly by the Ravensworth Brick & Tile Co, and it eventually extended southwards right to the Tail. It was closed in 1938 (1940 is also given).

To the south of the iron works the company constructed **BIRTLEY GAS WORKS** (NZ 271552); its date of opening is not known. This supplied not only the iron works but the whole of Birtley village. This works was served by a ½ mile link from near Ouston B Colliery. Maps show that by 1900 this link had been extended round to the eastern end of the iron works to join the "main line", though by the 1920s it had been removed.

The introduction of locomotives
The first locomotive known to have been owned by The Birtley Iron Company arrived in 1859. On 1st April 1859 the company put an advertisement in *The Engineer* seeking a 13in to 15in [cylinder] locomotive for heavy work and tight curves, "with machinery 10in above the rails to clear the sheaves on the railway." In the event the locomotive purchased, from Hawthorn's of Leith, had outside eccentrics (see Fig.59). One has to assume that this locomotive was acquired for working at Birtley Tail. If so, one wonders whether the use of rope haulage between Ouston A Pit and the Tail was abandoned about this time; the gradient between Ewe Hill and the colliery was not severe. DCOA Return 102 lists three locomotives and six stationary engines under Ouston A Pit for both April 1871 and November 1876; presumably the three were those used at the Tail and on its branches at those dates. A photograph taken at the site of Ouston A Colliery after the Second World War shows a large brick loco shed, capable of holding two or three locomotives. When it was built, and how it related to the loco shed known to have existed at the Iron Works, is not known; perhaps the shed at the latter housed only the loco used for shunting the works.

Further developments at Ouston
Ouston B Colliery was closed in 1875, but in the 1890s the site was re-developed as the **Birtley Brick & Tile Works** (its owners are not known and it should not be confused with a later Birtley Brick & Tile Works south of Birtley village); rather surprisingly, it was not connected to the Railway. This brickworks was short-lived and by 1914 the site had been cleared and re-developed, this time as a central disposal point for all the waste from collieries in the area. In the 1950s a link with British Railways was installed here for the colliery stone, now purchased by BR, to be taken northwards to provide the foundations for the large new Tyne Marshalling Yard being built at Lamesley.

Also included on the same site were two depots, one for household coal and the other the **DUSTON MANURE DEPOT**, where the manure from the pit ponies was brought to be disposed of to local farmers.

Ouston E Colliery and its branch
On 19th July 1888 near the western end of the Tail the company cut the first sod for **OUSTON E COLLIERY** (NZ 256548), sunk to work the deeper seams and opened in 1893. It was linked to the Tail by a ½ mile branch. This was locomotive-worked from the beginning, the locomotive pushing the wagons up to the back of the pit for them to be fed down through the screens by gravity. The company also built here an **ELECTRICITY STATION** (later replaced by another) and a coal **DRY-CLEANING PLANT**, and in the 1930s it also built the Railway's **LOCOMOTIVE & WAGON REPAIR WORKSHOPS** here (NZ 266547).

Between the First and Second World Wars, and possibly afterwards briefly, the E Pit also had a short-lived drift, though this was not designated as operationally separate. It was served by an endless rope system, operated by a hauler inside the E Pit winding house for the shaft, which brought the tubs out of the hillside straight on to the E Pit screens.

In 2002 a magnificent set of photographs of the Ouston line came to light. From internal evidence they can be dated to 1904. They begin at Ouston Bank Foot and show the line through to the staiths at Bill Quay, although the section between Blackhouse Fell, Eighton Banks and Whitehill is not covered. This is only the third such set known, the others being the *Mines de Lambton* set, taken in 1891, copies of which are held by Tyne & Wear Museums in Newcastle, and the Londonderry Railway set, deposited by the North Eastern Railway Association in the Ken Hoole Study Centre at Darlington Railway Centre & Museum. The Ouston set is particularly important for its illustrations of the rope haulage. Whereas photographs of rope haulage taken from 1950 onwards show nineteenth century technology being used with twentieth century wagons and methods, the Ouston set show nineteenth century technology and waggons probably very little changed since the 1830s, and in the illustration of operational detail and methods they are unique in North-East England. A selection of them has been included here.

The later years at Birtley and Birtley Tail
By 1919 the loco shed at the iron works had been cleared to make way for new developments, and a new 2-road shed was built near the beginning of the branch to Bewicke Main Colliery, superceding the shed at Ouston A Colliery. Despite its location, this shed was always referred to as the **E PIT SHED** (NZ 270537). Normally four locomotives were kept here. They shunted Birtley Tail, the iron works and the

gas works, the link to Birtley Station, the Urpeth line as far as Ewe Hill (where DERWENT was the normal loco) and then down to Durham Turnpike Junction, Ouston E Colliery and its various additional enterprises and the Bewicke Main branch, together with the various independent businesses which the branches also served.

By the beginning of the twentieth century the New Winnings Drift at Ouston A Colliery is believed to have been linked to the colliery by a narrow gauge line worked by endless rope haulage. The drift was closed in 1915. The colliery was finally closed in August 1924, although the shaft was retained for pumping and the railway to it remained open, with a small winch installed at the site to shunt wagons when needed.

After the separation of the iron works and the collieries in 1926 Pelaw Main locomotives continued to shunt both the former and the gas works and their traffic to Birtley Station. Although a very minor contributor to the Durham coke industry, the firm had maintained 74 beehive ovens at Urpeth B Colliery for many years; these ceased production during the third quarter of 1928. By May 1930 the steam hauler at Urpeth had been replaced by a 120 b.h.p. electric hauler. As noted above, Bewicke Main Colliery closed in January 1932, and during 1933 Urpeth Busty Colliery ceased to exist as a separate colliery, its workings being merged with Urpeth C Colliery, whose management was then combined with Ouston E Colliery, though officially the two collieries remained separate. The gas works had closed by 1939. Because of Pelaw Main Collieries Ltd's French ownership and the fall of France in 1940, mining at Ouston E Colliery was suspended in July 1940, to be followed by Urpeth C Colliery in October 1940, although the Annual Report of the Mines Inspectorate gives the "discontinued" date as January 1941. This did not entirely close this section of the Railway, for locomotives and wagons continued to travel to the workshops at Ouston E Colliery for repair and coal continued to be supplied to the landsale depots on this section. However, it did compel The Birtley Co Ltd, now the owner of the former iron works premises, to purchase its own locomotive (0-4-0DM JF 22900/1941) to shunt the works and work its traffic to and from Birtley Station.

The Birtley Tail sidings lay about 80 yards from the bank foot of the next incline eastwards. Empty wagons arriving at the bank foot were slipped off the rope and then run down to the Tail sidings by gravity. However, when the sidings were empty the speed of the set did not carry it far enough, so **a horse**, provided with its own stable nearby, was kept to pull the wagons down below the bridge over the NER/LNER. As the sidings filled up the arriving wagons ran down to buffer up to those already there and the horse could have a rest.

The Blackhouse Incline

As indicated above, when the Ouston waggonway was built the long haul up to Black Fell was originally divided into two inclines. The first incline was worked by the **Birtley Church Engine** (formerly

190. The ruins of Birtley Church Engine House, which housed a vertical-cylinder engine and was abandoned in 1904, on 16th May 1964.

191. What was then called Black Fell in 1904, with the engine house in the background and 0-6-0ST PELAW II setting off with a train for Eighton Banks bank foot. The line on the far right led to the small wooden loco shed.

the Birtley Engine) (NZ 274555), so called because St.John's Church was subsequently built nearby. Over the next forty yards to the foot of the Blackhouse Incline the wagons were worked by gravity. From here they were hauled up to the top of the fell by the **Blackhouse Engine** (NZ 280560), which worked full and empty sets alternately. However, in 1904 these two inclines were completely re-modelled. The Birtley Church Engine was taken out of use and the bank converted into one huge incline, worked by the Blackhouse Engine. The 1st edition O.S. map gives the name as the **Blackfell Engine**, and this name is still recorded on the 3rd edition of 1921; but it was dropped in favour of the original name, apparently about the beginning of the First World War and almost certainly because of confusion with the engine of the same name on the Pontop & Jarrow Railway nearby. A new meetings was put in to allow fulls and empties to be run simultaneously, while the two level crossings, near the Church Engine and over the Durham Road through the centre of Birtley – the sets at the latter appear to have been received and dispatched actually on the road – were replaced by bridges. The hauler was re-used at Eighton Banks, while the redundant engine house initially became Birtley's first fire station, and after a new fire station had been built it became a store for the colliery company's Property Department; the shell survived well into the 1960s.

At the bank foot, now just below the bridge over the Durham Road, there was latterly a flat four-road dish for fulls and a kip for empties. Fulls would be marshalled by a loco into sets of 18, with a slip coupling on the back of the sixth wagon from the rope end. All 18 wagons would then be hauled until the back twelve had reached the mark, when the slip coupling was knocked off, leaving the front six to be hauled up the incline and the slip coupling put behind the sixth wagon again for the same procedure to be followed again. This process ensured that the set was always in the correct place for the rope to be attached.

Just above the Durham Road bridge, on the north side, there was a coal depot serving Birtley, which of course had to be shunted by the Blackhouse Fell Engine. A set of five fulls would be hauled up above the depot and then dropped back into it. Here they were immediately emptied, and then hauled out and dropped back to the bank foot. In parallel with this, as two sets had to be run simultaneously, the empty set at the bank head was being lowered and raised again, before finally descending the bank. In the 1950s stone from the collieries was run into this depot for onward transhipment by road to the former Birtley Quarry, being filled in to provide a car park for the Caterpillar Tractor Co Ltd's premises.

Here too electricity had replaced steam by May 1930, the hauler here being 500 b.h.p.

Blackhouse bank head to Eighton Banks bank foot
When the description of this section was left above, it was being worked by main-and-tail rope haulage between the Blackhouse Engine and the engine at Eighton Banks bank foot, whose name has not survived. In May 1869 a boiler at this latter engine exploded, whereupon the directors decided to replace the main-and-tail haulage with locomotive working. The **BLACKHOUSE LOCO SHED** (NZ 282562), a wooden building, was then built to house the two locomotives normally kept here.

In 1913, near the top of the fell, the company opened **BLACKHOUSE H COLLIERY**, known locally as the **Wash Houses Pit** (NZ 280556), building a ½ mile branch behind the rear of the engine house to serve it, worked by a locomotive. This was closed in July 1914 and did not re-open until 1920. It in turn was linked to a drift further down the hillside by a long, curving 2ft 0in gauge line about a mile long. This was worked by a stationary engine at the Blackhouse screens, which hauled the tubs from underground and up to Blackhouse using main-and-tail haulage. As at Ouston E Pit, the drift here was not given a separate identity. Both Blackhouse Colliery and its drift closed in July 1932.

From Blackhouse Fell one loco would haul a set of 18 wagons as far as a loop about 300 yards south of the bridge carrying the Pontop & Jarrow Railway over the Pelaw Main line. Here waiting would be the second locomotive, which would come on to the rear of the set, wait for one of the rare Pelaw Main signals to be cleared and then push the set into the bank foot. As there was no run-round loop at Blackhouse Fell, the empties would be run past the first loco, which would then attach to the rear end to push them to Blackhouse Fell, either on to the bank head or into the H Pit. Because of the heavier work and the distance involved, a larger locomotive was required here. Both BIRTLEY and MOSELEY worked here, followed by HENRY C. EMBLETON and one of the former Metropolitan Railway 4-4-0Ts.

The Eighton Banks Incline
As noted above, this was a short incline, only about 330 yards, with a dish at the bottom for fulls and only one kip at the top for empties, where the **Eighton Banks Engine** (formerly the Eighton Engine) (NZ 281582) lay offset on the eastern side. About half way up was a level crossing (ungated and controlled only by a flagman, the standard Pelaw Main practice), with the meetings being sited just below this. Because of the shortness of the bank and its meetings sets could not exceed three wagons. The bank foot was another place on the Railway where a slip coupling was used. With the set of 18 fulls in the dish, a slip coupling would be attached behind the third wagon. The rope would then haul all 18 up the steep gradient out of the dish, with the back 15 being slipped when they had reached the mark. This was repeated each time a set was run until only three were left.

As noted earlier, the Pontop & Jarrow Railway crossed the Pelaw Main here on a bridge, and certainly by the 1870s a link between the two had been installed. Its main use seems to have been to transfer bricks made at Birtley on to the P&JR, so presumably the Eighton Banks Engine hauled these wagons up from the bank foot and dropped them into the link. This connection had been removed by 1923.

The operation at the bank head was also unusual. The engine had only one drum, and to run sets simultaneously both ends of the rope had to be used, one end coming off the top of the drum and the other off the bottom, both coming out of the front of the engine house. There were also only two roads at the bank head, the kip (nearest the engine house) for empties and one road for fulls, which meant that on alternate sets the two ropes crossed, an unusual and dangerous situation. Equally unusually for an incline running fulls and empties simultaneously, the top section of the incline had only two, rather than three, rails. This meant both ropes, with two sets of rollers, had to be accommodated within the "four foot", with the empty wagons running over the top of the rope hauling up the fulls.

The beam engine installed here for the opening of the line in 1809, with its 18ft diameter flywheel, did duty for exactly 100 years, being replaced in 1909 by the redundant hauler from the Birtley Church Engine. A new, brick, engine house was also provided at some stage. Like the other Pelaw Main haulers, it was replaced in the 1930s by an electric hauler, the motor here being 250 b.h.p., though the old engine house was retained.

Eighton Banks to Whitehill
As noted above, it is believed that the horses originally used on this section were replaced by Thompson with main-and-tail haulage in the 1820s, but no evidence of this has survived. Well before the 1890s the rope haulage, assuming that it was used, had been replaced by a locomotive housed in another wooden loco shed, the **EIGHTON BANKS LOCO SHED** (NZ 281583). But once again the railway operation was far from orthodox, again because no run-round loop was provided at Eighton Banks. The loco would haul 18 empties from Whitehill attached to the wagons by a heavy chain about 20 feet long, travelling quite quickly.

192. The second Blackhouse Fell loco shed, a replacement built in NCB days, with its egg-ended water tank, on 16th May 1964. For many years HENRY C. EMBLETON, HL 3766/1930 (see photo 53), worked from here.

193. One of HENRY C. EMBLETON's predecessors here was BIRTLEY, which is believed to have been built as a 2-4-0WT by Hawthorns of Leith and rebuilt at the Railway to the 0-6-0ST shown here, on the section between Blackhouse Fell bank head and Eighton Banks bank foot in 1920.

194. The remains of the Eighton Banks Engine House, with the Blackham's Hill Engine House on the Bowes Railway in the distance, on 16th May 1964.

When the loco was approaching the siding to the loco shed the chain was detached from the wagons, the loco would accelerate into the loco shed siding, the points would be changed and the wagons following would (hopefully) go past the points. The loco would then come out of the siding and push the wagons on to the kip. There were of course occasions when the wagons failed to clear the points; when this happened a large pole would be jammed between the locomotive's rear buffer beam and the frame of the nearest wagon on the adjacent track, and the set pushed forward until the loco could get out.

195. In the 1920s the Railway acquired three Metropolitan Railway 4-4-0Ts, hardly the ideal colliery railway locomotive; they were used mainly on the two loco-worked sections to Whitehill. 26, BP 772/1867, stands outside the ramshackle wooden shed at Eighton Banks (the only known photograph of one of the Railway's wooden loco sheds) in the 1930s, with the stout wooden pole used for "parallel shunting" lying in front of the smokebox.

Whitehill

This was the site, from about 1828, of the trailing junction with the extension of the Team Colliery Waggonway, to be described below. A few yards further north were three branches. The first, on the north-west side and shown on Bell's Plans of the Ouston Waggonway of 1819-1824, served **Thieves Close Quarry** (NZ 278605), which was closed by 1850 and then merged into Windy Nook Quarry. By then **Whitehouse Quarry** (NZ 280602) had been opened on the opposite side of the line, while a third short branch ran down to a further small quarry near the southern boundary of Heworth Colliery. All the quarries produced sandstone, and their owners are unknown. However, by the beginning of the twentieth century working on both sides of the line was being carried on under the collective title of **Windy Nook Quarries**, which were owned by Richard Kell & Co (later a limited company). It employed over 100 men and dispatched a sizeable output via the Railway. The same firm was still working them in 1937, but it is believed to have closed down around the beginning of the Second World War.

The Whitehill Incline

This was formerly called the Heworth Incline (see above). Although this was a self-acting incline, the bank head incorporated kips on the outer roads and fulls running through the middle (Photo 204), while the bank foot was unusual in Durham in being duplicated. Some time around the beginning of the twentieth century the bankhead was extensively rebuilt; one source gave the date as 1890, but a brake cabin alongside a kip is shown on photographs in the Ouston Waggonway set, attributed to 1904, so it would seem that the rebuilding came after this date. The position of kips on the sides and the centre road for fulls with a return wheel beneath was retained; but set back from the bank head and at right-angles to it was a drum house, with the rope ends coming off the drum and going to the wheel in gulleys, or "cundies". This was done in the belief that a braked drum was more effective than a braked wheel, and a drum house at ground level would suffer from less vibration than one that was elevated. The system proved very effective, although the gulleys got choked with slurry and it was more difficult to change the rope. With the introduction of 10-ton wagons sets of six were usually run, although this was reduced if a locomotive was being worked from Pelaw Main Staiths through to Ouston for repairs.

Heworth Bank Foot to Pelaw Main Staiths and Heworth Staiths

Despite the incline being known as the Whitehill Incline, to distinguish it from the Heworth Incline from Heworth Colliery, the joint bank foot was known as Heworth Bank Foot. The juxtaposition of two bank foots, both of self-acting inclines, is rare, the only other example in Durham being at Waldridge Bank Foot on the Sacriston Railway (see chapter 12). Originally the section between Heworth Bank Foot and the top of the incline to the staiths was worked by horses, but they were soon replaced by a stationary engine, presumably by Thompson. The original engine house was situated in the space between the two bank foots, but it was subsequently replaced by a new engine on the western side of the Pelaw Main line. At first this was called the **Heworth Engine** (NZ 287613), but later it became known as **Fox's Engine**, from the

196. Another loco that worked at Whitehill was MOSELEY, formerly a Great Northern Railway engine and acquired from the Darlington dealer J.F.Wake in 1920.

name of the family that drove it. The building housed two stationary engines, again possibly uniquely, one for Pelaw Main traffic and one for Heworth traffic. By May 1930 this was a 500 b.h.p. hauler. A large wooden frame was constructed over the Pelaw Main line to carry the rope over the wagons beneath, while the Heworth rope went underground and round a large return wheel to come on to the bank foot (see photo 207).

If Heworth fulls were being run to their staiths a set of ten (two sets of five combined) was run out below the Old Sunderland Road level crossing, ¼ mile from the bank foot. The Heworth rope was then detached and a set of 18 Pelaw Main fulls was then run out. The two sets were coupled up and the 28 wagons run to the staiths, where they were split and dispatched accordingly. Coming back, the Heworth empties would be attached to a Pelaw Main set of 18. When nearing the Old Sunderland Road crossing the Heworth set would be slipped and the Pelaw Main set would continue into its bank foot and on to its kip, where its rope would be slipped and wound up on to the frame to keep it clear of the set. Then, as at Birtley Tail, a slip coupling was inserted behind the sixth wagon, the Whitehill Incline rope was attached to the front end, and the back twelve slipped once they had reached the mark. Meanwhile, the Heworth rope was attached to the Heworth set standing out near the level crossing for the second stationary engine in the engine house to haul them into Heworth bank foot, where both the main rope and the back five were slipped. Momentum carried the first five into the first road, while the main rope was attached to the back five and then slipped for momentum to take them into the second road. Up at Heworth Colliery itself a horse was used for shunting, right up to the end of rail traffic in 1959.

Heworth Colliery also had its own link to the NER Gateshead – South Shields line (originally the Brandling Junction Railway), which crossed over the Pelaw Main Railway without any connection. This link was purely for Heworth Colliery traffic, both for materials for the colliery and some outgoing coal traffic. It diverted from the Pelaw Main Railway immediately north of the bridge carrying the New Sunderland Road over the line, than ran alongside the Pelaw Main but at a higher level, and divided into two tracks, one for incoming and one for outgoing traffic (see photo 208). The Heworth Engine ran wagons down into the southern end of this link and then hauled wagons back. The link itself was operated by an endless rope system, which took the wagons right round alongside the NER, where it is believed the small hauler was situated.

There was a long-standing tradition amongst the Pelaw Main railwaymen that the charges for Heworth traffic paid all the wages on the Railway.

In almost every respect the company operated the Railway with long-lived, second-hand equipment – but with one major exception; in the 1930s the Urpeth, Blackhouse, Eighton Banks and Heworth Engines were all given new electric haulers in place of the steam engines, together with the two stationary engines on the former Team waggonway. This was a significant major investment, and in doing it the company was years ahead of the other private railways that retained inclines.

Pelaw Main Staiths, Bill Quay

The railway came to the river bank high above the river, and so from the beginning a steep, **self-acting incline**, called initially the **Tyne Incline**, but latterly just known as the **Staiths Incline**, was used to get the waggons down to the staiths for unloading. Originally loading was done using the cradle method common at that time, and then by spouts; but in the 1930s these were, unusually, replaced by a tippler, which turned the wagons about 80 degrees for the coal to slide out.

On Bell's map of 1843 four sets of staiths are shown here, but latterly there were only three, two for Pelaw Main traffic and a little further downstream one for Heworth Colliery. All three had short self-acting inclines to take the waggons down to the ships, though it would seem that the Heworth incline worked only one waggon at a time, whereas the Pelaw Main inclines worked two.

The Ouston Waggonway photographs show that at the end of the nineteenth century both of the Pelaw Main inclines had only one kip. As can be seen on photo 212, this meant that the descending full set left the bank head over the top of the rope bringing the empties up, which in turn had to cross the rope behind the fulls in order to get on to the kip. To make all this possible, slots for the ropes had to be made in the rails and the ropes themselves were constantly moving laterally, quite a dangerous situation. Subsequently the inclines were built to a more orthodox layout, though still only running two wagons at a time (see photo 213).

In 1940 the Heworth Staith was destroyed by a fire, and thereafter Heworth coal was shipped through the Pelaw Main Staiths.

It is not known when locomotive working replaced horses here, but it was probably in the last quarter of the nineteenth century. **PELAW MAIN STAITHS LOCO SHED** (NZ 300632), unusually for the Railway a stone building (and a very large one too), was built alongside the staiths' sidings. In order to pass through the narrow bridges between the staiths and Heworth bank foot when en route over the inclines for repairs at the Ouston E Workshops, the locomotives used here had to be no more than 8ft 6in high. A locomotive was worked over the inclines by taking out four of the six wagons in the set in which it was to travel. At Pelaw Main Staiths too wagons were fly-shunted using a long, heavy chain.

The northern arm of the Pelaw Main Railway had its origins in the

The Team (or Teams) Colliery Waggonway

The Team, Waggonway, one of several developed to convey coal to the River Tyne from pits south of the river, was built in 1669. Its history is discussed fully in *A Fighting Trade – Rail Transport in Tyne*

Fig.59

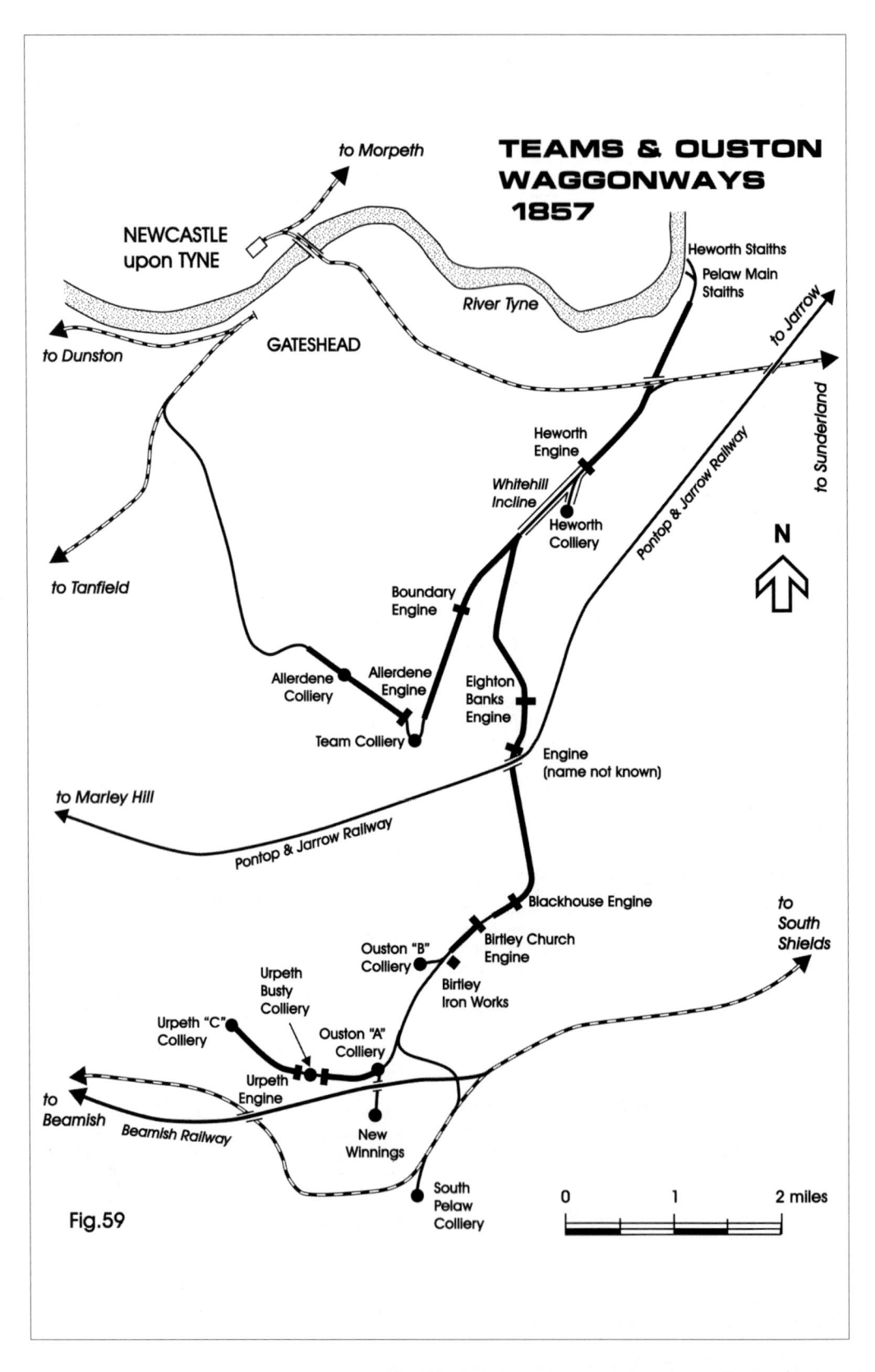

coal, 1600-1800, Vol.1 – History, Vol.2 – Data by G.Bennett, E.Clavering and A.Rounding, published by the Portcullis Press in 1990. Two names are found for this waggonway; firstly, it brought coal to staiths on the River Team, about ½ mile from its confluence with the River Tyne, in a district to the west of Gateshead known as The Teams; the word "Colliery" is also sometimes omitted. Almost certainly it was built to a gauge less than 4ft 8½in, though as noted above, to be joined to the Ouston waggonway in the later 1820s must mean that the two were of the same gauge by then. When wooden rails were replaced by iron, and when standard gauge was adopted, are not known.

By the first quarter of the nineteenth century the waggonway ran from the **Team Staith** (NZ 237624 approx.) for 3½ miles southwards to **TEAM COLLIERY** (NZ 265578). For most of its length the line followed the route of the River Team before climbing steeply up the side of the valley to reach Team Colliery, which lay south of Gateshead alongside the Great North Road. Bell's map of 1843 shows the line serving three other collieries. The nearest to the staith was **Farnacres Colliery** (NZ 234617), situated just south of the crossing with the Tanfield Branch, rebuilt in 1839 by the Brandling Junction Railway. Then came **Derwent Crook Colliery** (NZ 251600), owned by Lord Ravensworth & Partners and served by a ½ mile branch, and finally **Eighton Moor Colliery** (NZ 271575), served by a short extension from Team Colliery (see Fig 56).

As noted above, about 1828-1829 the owners of Eighton Moor Colliery linked their pit to the Ouston Railway. This meant climbing for a mile to the top of the eastern side of the valley at Wrekenton, then a much shallower climb for a further ½ mile to the summit of the line, before descending for the final ¼ mile to a junction just south of Whitehill bank head. The initial link to the Team Waggonway faced south towards Eighton Moor Colliery, which suggests that originally only this colliery's coal used the new line, and this position is the same on Bell's map of 1843; but by the time of the surveying for the 1st edition of the O.S. map was carried out everything had changed.

Almost certainly during the middle 1840s a new colliery was sunk on the north side of the Tanfield Branch crossing. This was **Norwood Colliery** (NZ 234618), which had a link to the Team Colliery waggonway, but dispatched its output to the Tanfield Branch. The opening of Norwood Colliery seems to have caused the closure of Farnacres Colliery, though the latter's branch is still shown in situ on the 1st edition O.S. map. About October 1849 Norwood Colliery, with Farnacres, was taken over by John Bowes, Esq., & Partners, and its link to the Team waggonway was eventually removed. (It should also be mentioned that the 1st edition map shows a second Team Colliery at Dunston (NZ 234625); but this was not linked to the waggonway and whether it shared the same ownership as the Team Colliery 3½ miles away is unknown.) It was probably about this time that a south/east curve

197. A very rare view of the Railway's line to Dunston, in May 1920, where it crossed the LNER Tanfield Branch (left to right), controlled by the Teams Crossing signal box; the line to the right linked the Railway to the Branch, whilst on the far right is the closed Dunston Colliery (not owned by The Birtley Iron Co).

was put in to link the Team waggonway to the Tanfield line.

The Team Staith had closed by 1850, but at almost the same place the **Teams Fire Brick Works** (NZ 235621) was established in 1850, linked to the waggonway and latterly situated at the end of the line.

Derwent Crook Colliery and its branch had also closed by 1857, but a new colliery had been sunk further south, about a third the way up the valley side on the eastern side of the line. Its original name was **ALLERDEAN COLLIERY** (NZ 257586). Meanwhile Eighton Moor Colliery (called the Street Pit in various contemporary publications) had also closed, with production concentrated at Team Colliery, though "Eighton Moor/Team" is found in *Mineral Statistics* for some time afterwards. So by the mid-1850s there were effectively only two collieries linked to the Team Colliery waggonway, Allerdean and Team, and both they and the waggonway were owned by **William Wharton Burdon**, whose ancestors had worked Team Colliery since 1796.

The operation of the system in the 1850s

The first 2½ miles from the Team Staith lay in the floor of the valley, and since there is no evidence for locomotives at this date, this section was presumably worked by horses. Sending coal to Pelaw Main Staiths for shipment rather than the Team Staith reversed the coal flow, which meant that full waggons now had to be hauled out of the Team valley, and with the severity of the grades stationary engines were unavoidable. The 1st edition O.S. 25in map shows an **engine house** at the uphill end of Team Colliery, and perhaps it was this engine which first worked the incline up from the Team valley. However, the later engine house at the northern entrance to the pit yard is also shown, perhaps leaving the first to shunt only the colliery itself; it had been removed by the 1890s. The second, known for many years as the **Allerdene Engine** (NZ 264581), worked not only the single line **Allerdene Incline**, but also had to shunt Allerdean/Allerdene Colliery.

At Team Colliery itself the link to Whitehill had been altered to join from the north, creating a severe 110 degree curve, which meant a combination of sheaves, guides and pulleys to accommodate the curving, rising rope. Once round the curve it was a straight climb to the Old Durham Road at Wrekenton, another single line incline worked by the **Boundary Engine** (NZ 273594), so called because the level crossing beyond it marked the boundary of the Gateshead County Borough. The final section to Whitehill was also worked by the Boundary Engine, this time using main-and-tail haulage with a return wheel.

Changes between 1860 and 1900

The first locomotive known to have been owned by "The Owners of Teams Colliery" was ordered in 1868, presumably to replace the horses north of Allerdene bank foot. In later years a loco shed was provided at Allerdene Bank Foot (see below). Airey's map of 1876 shows that the northern end of the line had been altered by this date. This now ran to staiths on the River Tyne at Dunston, but these seem to have been short-lived. The line had also now been linked to the NER Redheugh Branch 1 mile west of Redheugh Station, which allowed coal to be dispatched via this route if required. Finally, it would seem that some time during this period the original **Sheriff Hill Colliery** (NZ 273596)(see above)

198. In 1910 the Railway acquired four NER 1350 class locomotives and one of the routes on which they were used was the line through the Team Valley, where VICTORY, RWH 1669/1875, was recorded in the 1920s.

was linked to the line about half way between the Boundary Engine and Whitehill, though how its traffic was worked is not known.

However, the biggest change was in ownership. W.W.Burdon died in 1872, and after passing to his trustees the two collieries and the line passed to A.E.Burdon; but in 1882 he sold out to The Birtley Iron Co, a decision said to have been forced on him by a lost horse-racing wager. So the Iron Company now possessed a system with two long "arms" which joined at Whitehill to go north to Bill Quay. It would seem that the title **PELAW MAIN RAILWAY** came into general use about this time. Allerdean Colliery had become **ALLERDENE COLLIERY**, and then became collectively part of Team Colliery, being better known as the **Shop Pit**, while the original Team Colliery became known as the **Betty Pit**. According to the Lists of Mines produced by H.M.Inspectorate of Mines & Quarries, the latter became **RAVENSWORTH BETTY COLLIERY** in 1893, while Allerdene Colliery was re-named **RAVENSWORTH SHOP COLLIERY** four years later; but the old names continued in use, even on Ordnance Survey maps, for another forty years, and the new names did not come into common use until NCB days. Under the company's lettering scheme for its collieries the Betty Pit was allocated F and the Shop Pit G. In turn the loco shed at Allerdene bank foot became known as the **SHOP PIT LOCO SHED** (NZ 253587).

Change at Wrekenton

In 1903 the Gateshead & District Tramways Co's system reached the level crossing next to the Boundary Engine, any further progress being prevented by the main-and-tail haulage to Whitehill. By 1909 there was a growing demand to extend the tram system to Wrekenton, and so the Iron Company agreed to replace the rope haulage with locomotive working. Level crossing gates were installed, rare on the Railway, operated by a large signal box-type building, and with a semaphore signal, believed to be the only signal ever used on the system and curiously designed with the arm on the right-hand side of the post – to guard the crossing on the Whitehill side. To house the locomotive a wooden loco shed, the **STARRS LOCO SHED**, was built near the engine house; but to save space it straddled the fulls road, so that the wagons actually passed through it until the day's work was completed and the locomotive was put away for the night. At the same time the Engine's former name fell into disuse and it became known as the **Starrs Engine**, from the Seven Stars public house on the opposite side of the road (the reason for the spelling using two r's is not known).

Change at Ravensworth Betty Colliery, 1930/1937

In the late 1920s the company decided on a major re-organisation of its mining. It was decided to sink a new shaft, the **Ann Pit**, at "Team Colliery", to gain access to the deeper seams, and to close Bewicke Main Colliery. The Ann Pit opened in August 1930, greatly increasing the rail traffic on this section. Until 1937 the colliery, now officially called **RAVENSWORTH ANN COLLIERY**, was shunted entirely by rope or gravity. The bank foot of the Starrs Incline was situated alongside the colliery yard on its eastern side, but with the sinking of the Ann Pit the incline ran between the two shafts, past the screens. The colliery's empties sidings were built at a slightly higher level than the main line, which was hollowed out to form a shallow dish. But the colliery had only restricted empty standage above the shaft, so that empties had to be stored below the shaft. Working the colliery below the shaft was straightforward – the rope dropped empties in and hauled fulls out; but when empties were required above the screens working became more complicated. A set of five fulls was first hauled out, and then dropped back on to a set of five empties, to which they were coupled with a slip coupling. The Starrs Engine – a mile away, of course – then hauled all ten out. When they were above the pit points the second set-rider slipped the back five and ran them down to the screens by gravity. Similar working was required to work full wagons of landsale coal into the colliery's coal depot near the Ann Pit shaft and also a second, privately-owned coal depot in the colliery yard alongside the A1 road.

The original arrangement at Allerdene Bank Head was very unusual, in that a road divided the engine house from the bank head. The rope was detached at the bank head and the wagons crossed the road into Team Colliery yard by impetus. However, the road was the A1 and the increase in car and lorry traffic was making the operation increasingly undesirable by the mid 1930s. So in 1937 it was decided to re-model the whole of the bank head and the colliery yard, which would now be shunted by a locomotive. A short tunnel was built under the road and the incline re-routed past the old bank head, under the road and round the back of the old engine house. Here, squeezed into a cutting just above the tunnel was the new, short bank head, with its one steep kip. The sharp curve which followed it meant the up-coming set had to be run quite fast, and this made the working quite dangerous, especially the timing of the release of the rope. A new engine house (NZ 265581) was built in line with the new route but much higher than track level and set back above the curve round into the colliery yard. It had a 225 b.h.p. electric hauler built jointly by Metropolitan-Vickers Ltd and John Wood & Co Ltd of Wigan (Wood's makers no. N376 of 1937). The engine soon became known as **King's Engine**, again after its haulerman. The old engine house was converted into the **ANN PIT LOCO SHED**. The locomotive here now did all of the colliery's shunting, leaving the Starrs Engine to handle only traffic to and from the colliery itself or on the main line. All of these new arrangements were brought into operation on 14th November 1937.

The installation of an electric hauler here was not the first example on the Railway. The Starrs Engine had been replaced by May 1930 with a 500 h.p. hauler also built by John Wood & Co Ltd of Wigan, makers no. N176. It *may* be that a new engine house was provided there too, but this is unconfirmed.

Fig.60

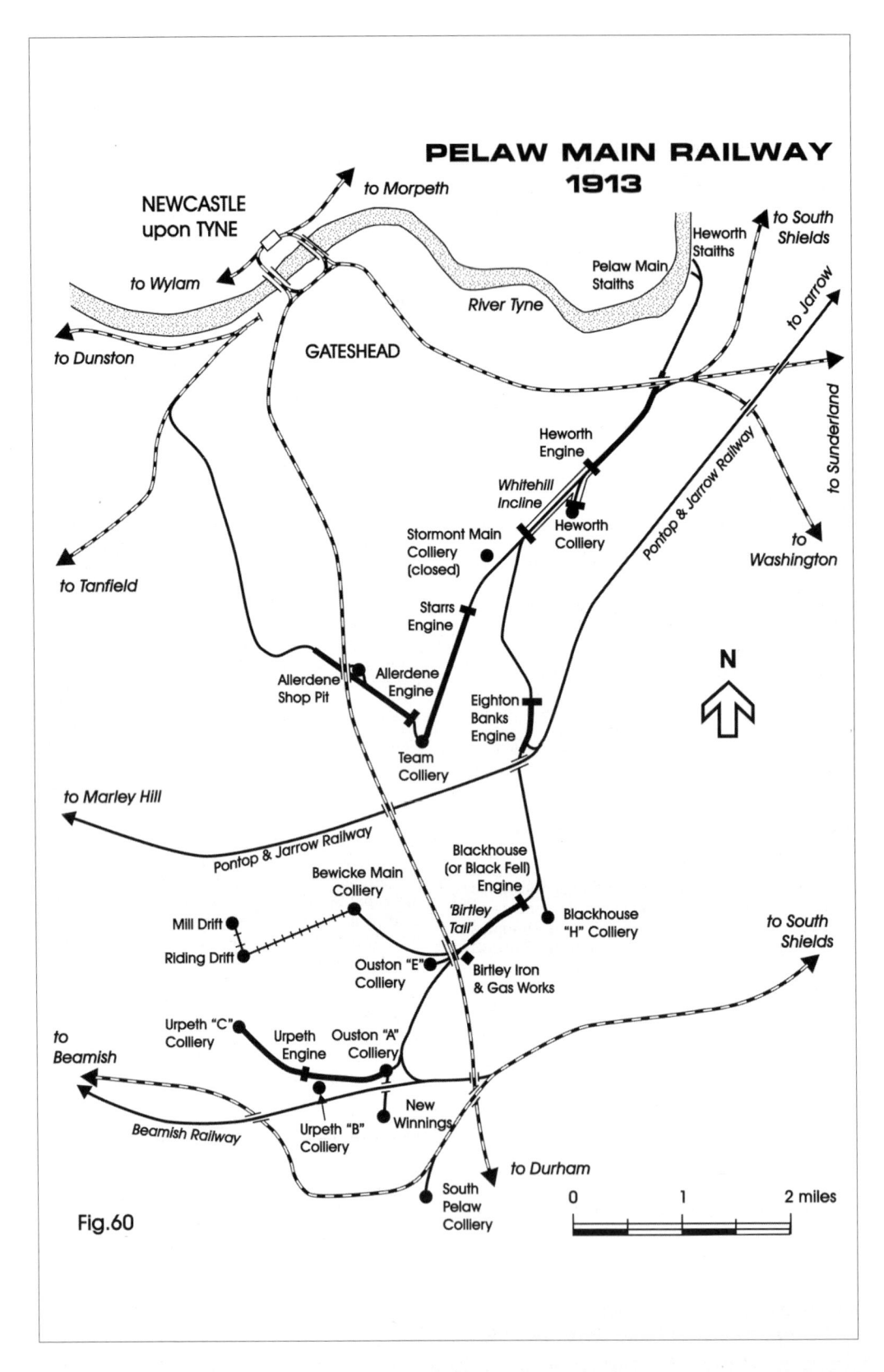

Fig.61 — Birtley & Ouston 1921

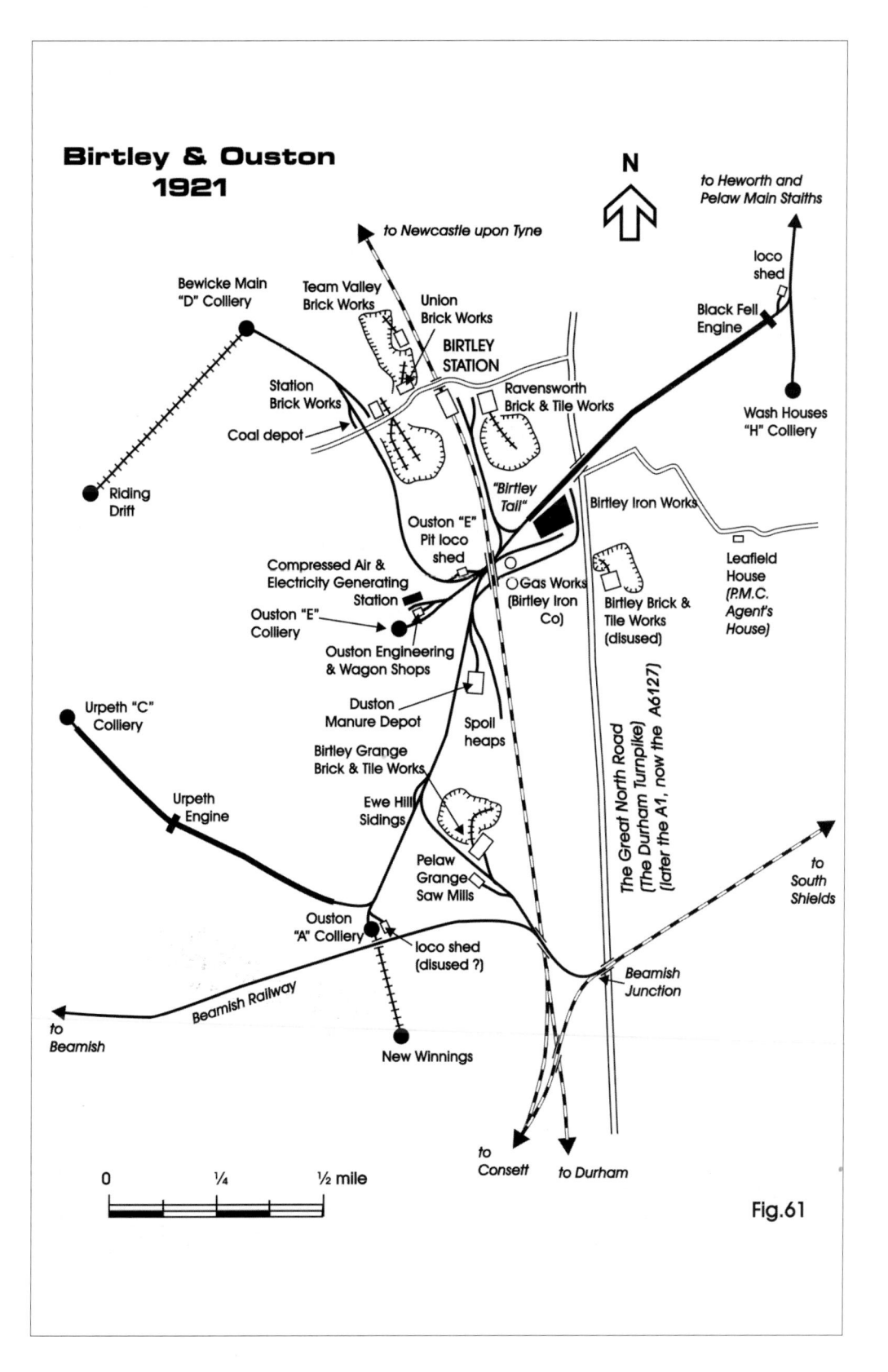

199. The line crossed the Team Valley Trading Estate on a long double track viaduct. Here CHARLES NELSON, P 1748/1928, heads for the Shop Pit sidings with four fulls from the Park Drift in 1968.

200. The fulls were then pushed up past the loco shed to chocks at Allerdene Bank Foot, which comprised only a downhill gradient, with no kip. Here a full set leaves the bank foot on 21st October 1968, only a short distance from the NCB North East Area's headquarters, on the far left.

201. The full set from Allerdene Bank Foot crosses the road south of Low Fell by gravity into Ravensworth Ann Colliery yard, having had its rope slipped on the bank head off to the left, with not even a red flag, let alone crossing gates - and the road was the A1.

202. So the company decided to build a tunnel under the road, together with a new engine house and bank head; the first set and its set-rider coming through the new tunnel on 14th September 1937.

203. The view the other way: King's Engine House, with its electric hauler, and the very constricted bank head on 22nd June 1965.

The operation of the Allerdene Incline
The changes at the bank head in 1937 are described above. The incline itself was single line, and of course two-thirds of the way down, on its eastern side, was the Shop Pit, which was also shunted entirely by rope or gravity. When empty coal wagons were destined for the pit a set of five was run down the incline and stopped below the colliery on the bridge over the NER (LNER from 1923) Gateshead-Durham main line, where the brakes were pinned down and the rope detached. A set of five fulls was then run out from the pit by gravity to join them and be coupled up. The set of ten was then hauled up above the points into the pit. Here the empties were uncoupled and run down by gravity into the roads required, while the fulls were hauled up to the bank head. Wagons of materials for the colliery were run in the same way, but when these were empty they were run by gravity right down to the bank foot for outward dispatch to the LNER at Dunston.

Latterly the working of the incline was further complicated by the development of the Meadows stone disposal point. This was situated on the site of the former Meadows shaft just below the tunnel and consisted of two sidings above hoppers, to which stone waste had to be worked for disposal on the heap here. For the Shop Pit this meant a variation in the working above. To get the rope down to the Shop Pit once again coal empties were run down to the LNER bridge and the rope detached. Next the wagons of stone were run out to join them, followed by one wagon of coal, and the rope re-attached. The coal and the stone was then hauled up above the Meadows points and the stone wagons put back into whichever siding was vacant. The full coal wagon was hauled out and then dropped back into the other siding where stone empties were waiting to be coupled up. The new set was then hauled out and lowered back down the incline, either to be stopped for the stone empties to be run into the Shop Pit or to be coupled

204. Starrs at Wrekenton on 18th July 1972, with the engine house on the right, with its rope attached to empties, and the NCB loco shed in the distance on the left; the former wooden shed stood approximately in the gap between the wagons. The kip lay off to the left.

up to the coal empties still waiting on the bridge, to be run through to the bank foot for working through to the Lady Park Drift (see below), Its stone was worked through to the Ann Pit, whose stone also had to be worked out through the bank head in a similar way. The Railway often had to work well into the weekend running only stone if it could not be fitted into normal traffic during the week. At the bottom of the incline, known as the Shop Pit sidings, there was a fairly steep gradient down towards the valley floor. Descending sets simply had the rope detached before being braked to a halt. On the fulls road, with no kip, there was simply a set of chocks, used to prevent the wagons rolling back once they were above them. A set of 18 wagons was pushed up to the rope end, with the first wagon above the chocks. The rope was attached and then the whole set drawn forward until the first seven were past the chocks. The back twelve were then detached and the first six hauled up the incline, with the process being repeated for the remaining wagons.

The construction of the Team Valley Trading Estate
In 1937 the Team valley was chosen as the site of the country's first "Trading Estate", the Government's response to the Jarrow March of 1936 and the need to create employment in areas of high unemployment. The Team Valley Trading Estate, owned by North Eastern Trading Estates Ltd, was developed with its own railway system, and this meant the Pelaw Main line had to be re-routed. The new line left the old route about 100 yards north of the Shop Pit shed, curving sharply westwards. Here there was a link with the TVTE's eastern line, which in turn was linked to the LNER East Coast main line at Low Fell, but no Pelaw Main traffic used this link. The Pelaw Main and TVTE lines then crossed the southern end of the new estate on a long viaduct. At its western end a ¼ mile branch was built to serve the new Lady Park Drift (see below), while the two lines joined to go northwards down the western side of the estate, dividing to flank both sides of Princesway before re-uniting for the Pelaw Main line to cross Lobley Hill Road (the A692). To the north of the road the Pelaw Main line ran past the eastern side of the **Norwood Coke Works** (NZ 238613 approx.), opened in 1913 and from 1930 owned by The Priestman Collieries Ltd. After passing under the LNER north of this works the line served Eslington Road coal depot at Dunston, to be followed by the link to the Tanfield Branch before going on to terminate at the Teams Fire Brick Works. This works, latterly owned by Lucas Bros Ltd, closed in 1938. This northern link with the LNER was well used, with up to 3000 tons of coal a week being dispatched to firms like Stewarts & Lloyds Ltd, as well as being used for incoming materials for the local collieries.

Following the abandonment of Ravensworth Castle it was possible to mine under it, and so in October 1936 the company opened a new drift (NZ 242588), known locally as the **LADY PARK DRIFT**, but known officially to the Inspectorate as **RAVENSWORTH PARK DRIFT**. It was served by a link to the Team valley line, modified as noted above with the construction of the Team Valley Trading Estate, and shunted by a loco from the Shop Pit shed.

Consideration of a link to the Bowes Railway
Also in 1937 the company gave detailed

205. Whitehill Bank Head, probably in 1904, with its brake cabin and the rapper equipment immediately beyond, and a set of fulls leaving for Heworth Bank Foot. Note the sprags, ready to slow down the empties - chaldron brakes were not very effective - and the metal slide on the edge of the kip so that the rope would fall into the middle road without damaging the stonework.

206. Heworth Bank Foot, probably in 1904, with a set of empties for Pelaw Main coming along the outer road of the double kip and its rope rising to the gantry in the next picture. Note the hoist for the fire-basket (with the basket itself lying on the ground) and the can hanging on the end chaldron. Beyond stand the Heworth Colliery chaldrons, with their own bank foot.

207. The remains of the wooden gantry used for carrying the ropes at Heworth Bank Foot (see text), five years after closure in 1959.

208. Looking north to Heworth Bank Foot from near the bridge under the BR Gateshead-South Shields line at Pelaw on 17th May 1959; on the left is the Heworth Colliery link to the BR line, which was worked by its own small electric hauler.

consideration to the construction of a new link between its railway and what was now called the Bowes Railway, formerly the Pontop & Jarrow Railway, of John Bowes & Partners Ltd. The link at Black Fell, where the lines had crossed, had long gone, but thereafter the lines ran almost parallel to the River Tyne, only a mile or so apart. The new link would have run from Heworth bank foot on the Pelaw Main Railway to Wardley on the Bowes Railway, the intention presumably being to ship Pelaw Main and Heworth coal at the new Jarrow Staiths (owned by the Tyne Improvement Commission), opened the year before. This would use locomotive haulage throughout and allow three rope inclines on the Pelaw Main Railway to be abandoned. Considerable surveying was undertaken, but the proposal was eventually abandoned, apparently because some of the land involved was scheduled for domestic housing.

The Second World War

A flat was maintained in the company's Mining Offices at Birtley for use when a French director visited the company. But following the fall of France in 1940 French control could not be maintained, and so the company was run by its Agent, Henry Hornsby. As noted above, coal production at Urpeth and Ouston was suspended in January 1941, though the southern arm of the Railway remained operational to handle locomotive and wagon repairs at Ouston and coal for the landsale depots. Ouston E Colliery was re-opened in August 1946, but Urpeth C Colliery did not re-open until after nationalisation. One unusual working for a colliery railway was that every Friday a stores van was sent out from Ouston to service all the locations along the system.

A summary

Thus from 1937 the Railway was operated as follows: from Urpeth C Colliery there were two inclines, both worked by the Urpeth Engine, which took traffic as far as Ewe Hill. Locomotives from the E Pit shed then worked the link to Durham Turnpike Junction, the Ewe Hill disposal point, Ouston E Colliery, its workshops, The Birtley Co Ltd (until 1940), the link to Birtley Station and Birtley Tail, where the horse was still in daily use. Next came the Blackhouse Incline, worked by the Blackhouse Engine, following which a loco at Blackhouse loco shed worked the traffic to Eighton Banks bank foot. Then came the Eighton Banks Incline, worked by the Eighton Banks Engine, following which the locomotives at Eighton Banks loco shed worked traffic as far as Whitehill.

On the northern arm the locomotive at the Shop Pit loco shed worked traffic to Dunston and shunted the Lady Park Drift and Allerdene Bank Foot. Then came the Allerdene Incline, worked by King's Engine, which also shunted the Shop Pit and the Meadows disposal point. The locomotive from the Ann Pit shed shunted Team/Ravensworth Ann Colliery. Then came the Starrs Incline, worked by the Starrs Engine, which also assisted in the working of Ravensworth Ann Colliery, following which locomotives from the Starrs loco shed worked traffic as far as Whitehill.

From Whitehill the Whitehill self-acting incline took traffic down to Heworth Bank Foot, where the self-acting incline from Heworth Colliery joined. Fox's Engine then worked the section down to Bill Quay, and also the Heworth link to the LNER at Pelaw Station. At Bill Quay locomotives from Pelaw Main Staiths shed sorted the traffic on to the self-acting inclines which served the Pelaw Main Staiths and, until 1940, the Heworth Staiths.

The Railway and its collieries were all vested in NCB Northern Division No.6 Area on 1st January 1947.

The locomotives

The locomotives acquired for the Pelaw Main Railway were easily the most varied of any of Durham's private railways. Studying the list shows three distinct periods of acquisition. In the first period, up to 1903, the locomotives were all industrial designs. Then in 1904 the Agent, Philip Kirkup, purchased an 0-6-0ST from the NER and found it so ideal that he purchased four more in 1905, all given the names of British Prime Ministers, and five more locomotives from main line companies came before the First World War. The third period came between 1927 and 1933, and a more varied collection would be difficult to imagine, from Metropolitan Railway 4-4-0T's with 5ft 9in driving wheels to three small 0-4-0T's of the LNER's Y7 class.

A powerful locomotive was always kept at Blackhouse loco shed, latterly HENRY C. EMBLETON. At least one Y7 loco also normally worked from the Shop Pit shed, with another at the E Pit shed, and from 1937 a four-coupled engine was also allocated to the Ann Pit. At least one Metropolitan tank was normally kept at Eighton Banks shed, whilst at Pelaw Main Staiths CHARLES PERKINS was the normal locomotive. The following observations were recorded between 1924 and 1939:

On 16/8/1924   BYRON, PELAW II, SALISBURY and VICTORY at Birtley
On 30/10/1938   TYNE at Starrs (Wrekenton)
On 1/8/1939   Starrs had 900 and 1310; TYNE was at Ravensworth Ann Colliery; DERWENT and CHARLES NELSON were at Ouston E Pit, with the latter recorded as dismantled, so that it may well have been in Ouston E Pit workshops; 44 and HENRY C. EMBLETON were at Blackhouse Fell; 26 was at Eighton Banks and CHARLES PERKINS was at the staiths. 1308 was not recorded.

The closure of Ouston and Urpeth Collieries in 1940 resulted in the two ex-Metropolitan tanks retiring into their sheds, and during the War 900 was also withdrawn from traffic. The fate of all three was not decided until after nationalisation.

209. The sidings for fulls and empties south of Pelaw Main Staiths at Bill Quay, probably in 1904. The loco, with its hinged chimney and (almost certainly) home-made cab, may be URPETH, AB 277/1884. Its large stone shed can be seen to the left of the brick chimney.

210. One of the two regular locomotives at Pelaw Main Staiths in later years was TYNE, AB 786/1896, here almost certainly brand new; she and CHARLES PERKINS, HL 2986/1913, were only 8ft 3in and 8ft 6in high so that they could pass through the bridges on the inclines to reach the Ouston E Workshops for repairs.

211. To the rear of the staiths loco shed were the two self-acting inclines down to the staiths. Here, probably in 1904, a set of empties has just arrived up the steep bank to the left and the rope is being detached, ready to go on the rear of the set of fulls waiting to be run forward by gravity. Note beyond it the long side of the rope and the O (= Ouston) on the waggons.

212. The second self-acting incline, probably in 1904. The next set of empties will ascend the right-hand side and to reach the kip will have to cross over the fulls descending past the chock in the foreground. Note the slots in the rails, in several places, for the rope and the changes of rope direction which are necessary. The masts of sailing ships are just visible in the distance.

213. *Pelaw Main Staiths, probably in the first twenty years of the twentieth century, but after rebuilding from the system shown in photo 212, and to be rebuilt again in the 1930s. These were the last staiths in the north-east incorporating a rope incline to reach the loading point.*

Gauge : 4ft 8½in

PELAW		0-4-0WT	OC	H(L)	220	1859	(a)	(1)
BEWICKE		0-6-0ST	OC	BH	52	1868	New	Scr 12/1929
VICTORY		0-4-0ST	OC	John Harris		1863	(b)	Scr c/1900
DERWENT		0-4-0ST	OC	John Harris		1865	(b)	Scr c/1900
BYRON		0-4-0ST	OC	John Harris		1868	(b)	Scr c/1900
BIRTLEY		2-4-0WT	OC	H(L)			(c)	
	reb	0-6-0ST	OC	Birtley		1871		(2)
PELAW		0-6-0T	OC	BH	60	1868	(d)	(3)
OUSTON		0-6-0ST	OC	BH	602	1881	New	Scr 12/1929
BURDON		0-6-0ST	OC	BH	48	1868	(e)	Scr c/1920
URPETH		0-4-0ST	OC	AB	277	1884		
	reb			AB	9410	1915	(f)	(4)
TYNE		0-4-0ST	OC	AB	786	1896	New	
	reb			AB		1940		(5)
DERWENT		0-6-0ST	OC	AB	970	1903	New	
	reb			RSHN		1945		(5)
PELAW II		0-6-0	IC	Todd		1847		
	reb	0-6-0ST	IC	Ghd		1879	(g)	(6)
ROSEBERY		0-6-0ST	IC	RS	2139	1873	(h)	Scr 7/1932
BALFOUR		0-6-0ST	IC	RS	2239	1875	(j)	Scr /1925
GLADSTONE		0-6-0ST	IC	RS	2240	1875	(k)	Scr /1929
SALISBURY		0-6-0ST	IC	RS	2244	1875	(m)	Scr /1925
EAST CLIFF		0-6-0ST	IC	P	774	1899	(n)	Scr /1928
OUSTON		0-6-0ST	IC	RWH	1657	1875	(p)	Scr /1928
BYRON		0-6-0ST	IC	RWH	1662	1875	(q)	(7)
LEAFIELD		0-6-0ST	IC	RWH	1666	1875	(r)	Scr c/1930
VICTORY		0-6-0ST	IC	RWH	1669	1875	(s)	(8)
MOSELEY		0-6-0ST	IC	Don	213	1876	(t)	Scr 8/1932
CHARLES PERKINS		0-4-0T	OC	HL	2986	1913	New	(5)

24	4-4-0T	OC	BP	770	1867			
	reb				1880			
	reb				1900	(u)	(9)	
26	4-4-0T	OC	BP	772	1867			
	reb				1901			
	reb		Neasden		1920	(v)	(10)	
44	4-4-0T	OC	BP	868	1869			
	reb				1888			
	reb				1902			
	reb		Neasden		1920	(w)	(10)	
BUSTY	0-4-0ST	OC	BH					
	reb		Ridley Shaw		1928	(x)	Scr /1936	
CHARLES NELSON	0-4-0ST	OC	P	1748	1928	New	(5)	
HENRY C. EMBLETON	0-6-0T	OC	HL	3766	1930	New	(5)	
-	4wVBT	VCG	S	6936	1927	(y)	Scr /1935	
900	0-4-0T	IC	Ghd	35	1888	(z)	(11)	
1308	0-4-0T	IC	Ghd	37	1891	(aa)	(5)	
1310	0-4-0T	IC	Ghd	38	1891	(ab)	(5)	
-	0-4-0ST	OC	RS	3057	1904	(ac)	(12)	

In 1946 the company ordered a new 0-4-0ST from Peckett & Sons Ltd, Bristol (Makers No.2093), but this had not been delivered by Vesting Day, 1st January 1947.

On 1st January 1947 locomotives were allocated to the following loco sheds:

Ouston E Pit	AB 970/1903
Blackhouse	BP 868/1869, HL 3766/1930
Eighton Banks	BP 772/1867, AB 786/1896
Shop Pit	Ghd 37/1891
Ann Pit	Ghd 35/1888, Ghd 38/1891
Starrs	P 1748/1928
Pelaw Main Staiths	HL 2986/1913

The horse used for shunting at Birtley Tail was also transferred to NCB No.6 Area.

(a) New; see also note above in text
(b) ex B.C.Lawton, contractor for the construction of the NER Team valley line, /1869
(c) origin unknown; reputed to have been purchased from the Caledonian Railway, Scotland, /1871, but this appears to be unsupported in fact
(d) a loco very likely to be this one was offered for sale in *The Engineer* of 13/12/1878 by The Darlington Forge Co Ltd, Darlington
(e) New to "Owners of Teams Colliery", i.e. W.W.Burdon; ex A.E.Burdon, with Team Colliery and railway, /1882
(f) ex AB, 1884, as a new loco, but alleged to have been a rebuild by AB of a loco as yet unidentified
(g) ex Robert Frazer & Sons Ltd, dealers, Hebburn, 1/1904; NER 2289, 287 class, until 2/7/1903; this loco was built new by Charles Todd of Leeds in 1/1847 as a 0-6-0 tender engine with 15in x 24in cylinders and 4ft 9in wheels for the York & Newcastle Railway, No.107; it kept the same number under the York, Newcastle & Berwick Railway and again when this railway was merged into the NER in 1854; it was rebuilt at the NER's Gateshead Works about 3/1862 and again there in 12/1879, when it was converted into a 0-6-0ST using miscellaneous parts from other locomotives. It was re-numbered into the NER Duplicate List in 12/1890 as 1903 and to 1716 in 1/1894; it was withdrawn from traffic by 4/1903, but was nevertheless allocated 2289 in another re-numbering in 7/1903; presumably it never carried this last number. It was sold to Robert Frazer & Sons Ltd in 12/1903
(h) ex Robert Frazer & Sons Ltd, dealers, Hebburn, /1905; previously NER, 1670, 964 class, until 3/1905
(j) ex Robert Frazer & Sons Ltd, dealers, Hebburn, /1905; previously NER, 1673, 964 class, until 3/1905
(k) ex Robert Frazer & Sons Ltd, dealers, Hebburn, /1905; previously NER, 1674, 964 class, until 30/6/1904
(m) ex Robert Frazer & Sons Ltd, dealers, Hebburn, /1905; previously NER, 1676, 964 class, until 30/6/1904
(n) ex J.F.Wake, dealer, Darlington, 9/1908; previously S.Pearson & Son Ltd, Admiralty Harbour contract, Dover, Kent, until 9/1908
(p) ex Robert Frazer & Sons Ltd, dealers, Hebburn, 1/1910; previously NER 1350, 1350 class, until 1/1910
(q) ex Robert Frazer & Sons Ltd, dealers, Hebburn, 2/1910; previously NER 1355, 1350 class, until 22/2/1910
(r) ex NER, 1359, 1350 class, 9/9/1910
(s) ex NER, 1362, 1350 class, 9/9/1910
(t) ex J.F.Wake, dealer, Darlington, /1920; previously Great Northern Railway, 606, J6 class, until 3/1920
(u) ex Robert Frazer & Sons Ltd, dealers, Hebburn, /1927 (by 7/6/1927); previously Metropolitan Railway, A class, 24; Metropolitan records apparently give the date of sale to Robert Frazer as /1913, which would cast doubt on the date of /1927 above

(v) ex Robert Frazer & Sons Ltd, dealers, Hebburn, /1927; previously Metropolitan Railway, A class, 26
(w) ex Robert Frazer & Sons Ltd, dealers, Hebburn, /1927; previously Metropolitan Railway, A class, 44
Note : whilst on the Metropolitan Railway these locomotives carried a small A below the number to identify the class to which the locomotive belonged; these letters were not a suffix to the number, and so have been omitted from their numbers here.
(x) ex Ridley, Shaw & Co Ltd, dealers, Middlesbrough, Yorks (NR), 17/4/1928; identity and previous owners unknown
(y) New from the makers, but believed not to have been delivered until 1930
(z) ex Robert Frazer & Sons Ltd, dealers, Hebburn, 5/1932; previously LNER 900, Y7 class, withdrawn from traffic, 2/1931 and sold to Frazer
(aa) ex Robert Frazer & Sons Ltd, dealers, Hebburn, 5/1932; previously NER 1308, Y7 class, withdrawn from traffic, 2/1931, sold to Frazer, and moved 9/1931
(ab) ex Robert Frazer & Sons Ltd, dealers, Hebburn, /1933; previously NER 1310, Y7 class, withdrawn from traffic, 2/1931, sold to Frazer, and moved 9/1931
(ac) ex U.A.Ritson & Sons Ltd, Burnhope Colliery, Burnhope, loan, in 1930s

(1) s/s, but a drawing of this loco by R.H.Inness was dated 22/1/1906, so the loco may have survived until this period
(2) sources disagree on the Scr date, giving /1925, /1928, /1929 and withdrawn /1930
(3) to United National Collieries Ltd, Risca Colliery, Monmouthshire, /1881
(4) to Steetley Lime & Basic Co Ltd, Coxhoe, c /1930
(5) to NCB No.6 Area, with the Railway, 1/1/1947
(6) Scr /1925, after 5/1925
(7) sources disagree, giving both /1928 and /1930 as Scr dates
(8) probably Scr /1932, though /1929 is also found
(9) one version gives Scr c/1929, another gives Scr /1932; spares from this loco were kept to repair BP772 and BP 868
(10) these locomotives did not work after coal traffic on this section ceased in 1940, and were left in their sheds; to NCB No.6 Area, with the Railway, 1/1/1947
(11) latterly dismantled at Ravensworth Ann Colliery; to NCB No.6 Area, with the Railway, 1/1/1947
(12) returned to U.A.Ritson & Sons Ltd, Burnhope Colliery, Burnhope, in 1930s

Additional notes
In the edition of the *Colliery Guardian* for 24/7/1903 Philip Kirkup, Agent for The Birtley Iron Co Ltd, advertised for sale a 12in 0-4-0ST "done for work" at "Ravensworth Colliery", possibly meaning the Shop Pit shed. Its identity and disposal are unknown; possibly it was one of the John Harris locomotives.

In the *Colliery Guardian* for 16/2/1906 Kirkup offered for sale a 12in six-wheeled coupled locomotive, lying at Ouston. This loco would appear not to be any of the six-wheeled locomotives listed above, and its identity and disposal are unknown.

About 1908 The South Hetton Coal Co Ltd acquired a Metropolitan Railway A class 4-4-0T, No.6 (which see). There was an oral tradition at South Hetton that its loco had previously worked on the Pelaw Main Railway. However, there was no parallel tradition on the Pelaw Main Railway supporting this.

Gauge : 1ft 11½in

As noted above, a narrow gauge line was built from Bewicke Main Colliery to serve the new Riding Drift when it opened in 1902. How this line was worked before the arrival of the locomotive below is unknown, though it was very likely to have been by some form of rope haulage. This line was extended to the Mill Drift in 1907. This drift was closed in 1915, co-incidentally with the departure of the locomotive below. It is assumed that rope haulage was then resumed, until the Riding Drift closed in April 1926; but see also the footnote below.

      -                    0-4-0ST   OC   AB   703   1893   (a)   (1)

(a) ex William Jones, dealer, Greenwich, London, by 5/1905; previously James Nuttall, contractor for the Lynton & Barnstaple Railway, Devon

(1) to J.F.Wake, dealer, Darlington, c/1915

Additional notes
In the edition of *Contract Journal* for 20/1/1909 Philip Kirkup advertised for what was presumably intended to be a second locomotive for this line, seeking a locomotive as near as possible with 5in x 10in cylinders and a 3ft 0in wheelbase. Nothing further is known.

In June 1924 the Coast Road Joint Committee, responsible for the construction of a new road between South Shields and Whitburn, acquired from N.E.Potts, described as a dealer at Boldon, a 2ft 0in gauge 4wPM locomotive, MR 429/1917, which was described as being "free on rail at Ravensworth Colliery". Whether this locomotive had any connection with The Birtley Iron Co is not known.

NATIONAL COAL BOARD
Durham Division No.6 (North-West Durham) Area from 1/1/1950
Northern Division No.6 (North-West Durham) Area from 1/1/1947

The re-opening of Ouston E Colliery in August 1946 was followed by the re-opening of Urpeth C Colliery in the spring of 1947. These brought the Railway back to normal operating conditions, albeit with less coal than before the War. One early change was the Area's decision to confirm the three collieries on the northern arm as Ravensworth Park Drift, Ravensworth Shop Colliery and Ravensworth Ann Colliery.

As mentioned elsewhere, the NCB management structure at nationalisation was very hierarchical. The eight Divisions were divided into Areas, and each Area was divided into Groups. The Pelaw Main collieries were allocated to No.6 Area's E Group, together with Watergate Colliery, near Sunniside, formerly owned by The Priestman Collieries Ltd. Because of the large number of locomotives that it inherited, No.6 Area introduced an Area numbering scheme in 1949, allocating numbers to the locomotives in each Group in Group alphabetical order. E Group was allocated Nos.61 to 72, which included the non-Pelaw Main locomotive at Watergate Colliery, which became 68. However, the early scrapping of the two Metropolitan Railway tanks and the combination of two of the Y7 0-4-0Ts into one locomotive meant that 70-72 were never carried by the locomotives to which they were allocated. Each Group's Mechanical Engineer was in charge of his Group's locomotives and the livery to be used, and so all the Pelaw Main locomotives continued in plain unlined light green with white numbers. When Area No.54 arrived in the Group in 1953 it was given the prefix D to indicate that it was a D Group locomotive. With the delivery of a 0-4-0ST ordered before nationalisation the NCB needed to add only one more 0-4-0ST to the Railway's stock, and the Railway did not receive any of the new steel wagons, well over 1000, which the Area ordered between 1952 and 1961.

With the installation of electric haulers in all of the stationary engines before 1939, the most important NCB investment in the Railway in the early years following nationalisation saw the end of all the old wooden locomotive sheds. Single-road brick sheds capable of holding two locomotives were built at Allerdene Bank Foot (the Shop Pit sidings) and at Blackhouse Fell, while the unusual shed at Starrs, which the full wagons passed through during the day, was replaced by a lofty brick building on the side of the bank head capable of holding the three locomotives needed here to work the traffic between Starrs, Whitehill and Eighton Banks, together with facilities for repair work. The already-abandoned Eighton Banks shed was demolished once the Metropolitan tank inside it had been cut up.

In the 1950s the rope inclines, which all had to begin together, started work at 7.00am, with the locomotive shifts as follows:

Ouston E Pit	2 locos	6.00a.m.-2.00p.m., 2.00p.m.-10.00p.m. day shift 7.00a.m.- 4.00p.m.	
Blackhouse Fell	1 loco	7.00a.m. - 4.00p.m.	Overtime as required
Shop Pit	1 loco	7.00a.m.-4.00p.m.	Overtime as required
Ravensworth Ann Colliery	1 loco	6.00a.m.-2.00p.m., 2.00p.m.-10.00p.m.	
Starrs	2 locos	7.00a.m. – 4.00p.m.	Overtime as required
Pelaw Main Staiths	2 locos	6.00a.m.-2.00p.m., 2.00p.m.-10.00p.m.	Overtime as required

Whether overtime was worked depended on the position at the staiths; if coal was needed in order to complete the loading, then the railway would continue beyond 4.00p.m. The Railway Manager would make this decision as soon after midday as possible, and it would then be telephoned to the various places.

However, with the exception of Ravensworth Park Drift, all of the Pelaw Main collieries were old and nearing the end of their productive life, and in the light of this the NCB revived the plan to combine the Pelaw Main and Bowes Railways. In 1949 the Board revived the 1937 scheme for a line between Heworth Bank Foot and the Bowes Railway at Wardley, but planning permission was refused because it would have passed close to land scheduled for domestic housing. The NCB then adopted a much simpler scheme, a link between Eighton Banks and the Blackham's Hill East Incline, where the two lines were only about 200 yards apart. The East Incline had a gradient of only 1 in 70, which would allow a locomotive from the Pelaw Main Railway to work full wagons into Springwell Yard whilst the Blackham's Hill Engine was working sets on its West Incline. Furthermore, at this point the two Railways were scarcely more than 100 yards apart, so that a single line on an embankment (made from small coal) was all that was needed to join them. This work was undertaken in 1955, though for a while the new link was hardly used.

The section of the Beamish Railway between West Pelton and Beamish Junction was closed in 1955, and it seems likely that the Pelaw Main link between Ewe Hill and the Beamish line was closed at the same time, though this has not been confirmed. On 30th March 1957 Urpeth C Colliery was merged with Ouston E Colliery, thus closing

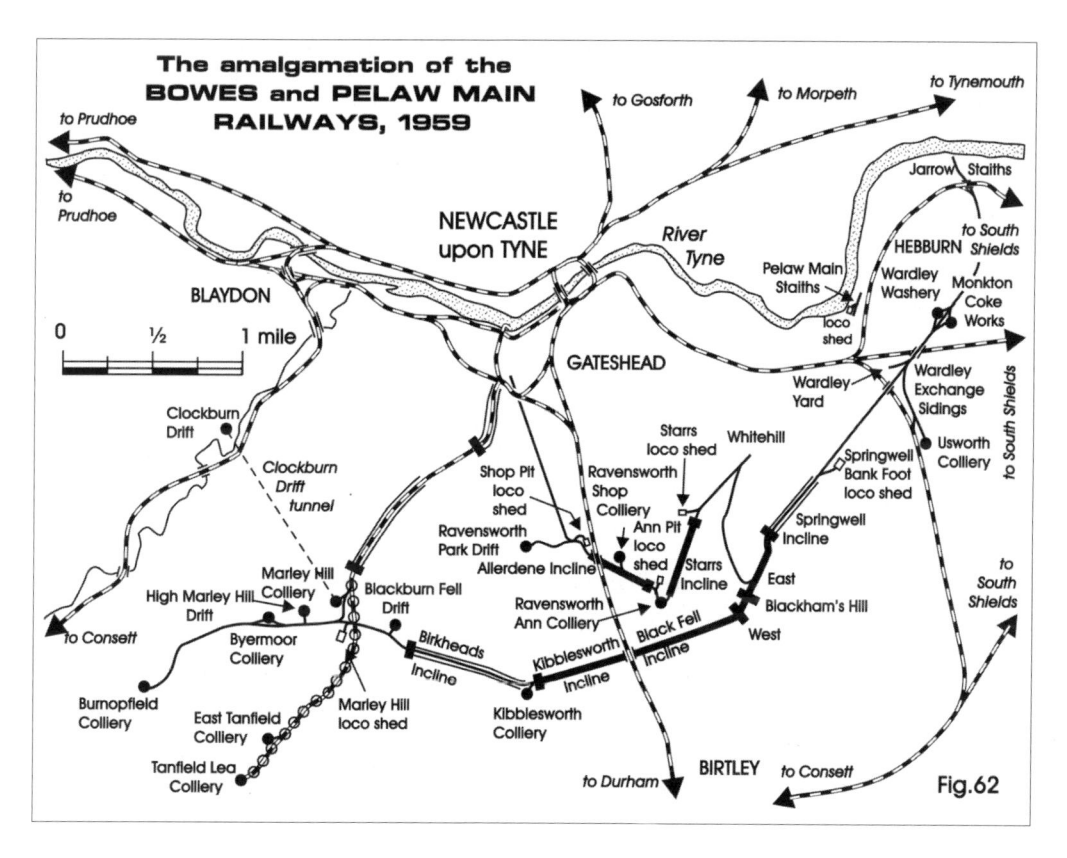

214. 101, 4wDM FH 3922/1959, propelling fulls from the Pelaw Main branch, waits to go on to the Blackham's Hill East Incline of the Bowes Railway to leave them in Springwell Yard on 2nd December 1967.

the southern arm altogether west of the latter. Then on 31st January 1959 Ouston E Colliery was closed, and with it came both the end of the Railway as a separate organisation, with its merger with the Bowes Railway and the closure of major sections of the system. The first of these ran from Ouston up to Blackhouse Fell, then on and up to and including the Eighton Banks Engine, closing the Ouston and Blackhouse Fell loco sheds and the Blackhouse Fell and Eighton Banks Engines. The second ran from Whitehill to just short of Pelaw Main Staiths at Bill Quay, closing the Whitehill and Heworth sef-acting inclines and Fox's Engine at Heworth Bank Foot; coal from Heworth Colliery was transferred to road transport. The staith and its rail system, with its locomotives and self-acting incline, would still be required, but all coal would have to be taken there by road and transferred into railway wagons retained there for the short journey to the staith; 488 wagons were retained there for this work. As part of these changes, NCB No.6 Area ordered two 4-wheeled "Planet" diesels for the section between Starrs and Springwell Yard. These were the Area's first diesels, and a new numbering scheme was started for them, beginning at 101.

The next nine years saw almost continuous piecemeal closures. The workshops at Ouston were retained until about the end of 1960, when they were closed and the responsibility for the repair of Pelaw Main locomotives was transferred to the Bowes Railway's Springwell Bank Foot shed at Wardley. On 23rd February 1962 Ravensworth Shop Colliery was closed, to be followed soon afterwards by the closure of Whitehill Washery, with all Pelaw Main coal now sent to the Wardley Washery on the Bowes Railway. This resulted in changes to the locomotive shift times, as follows (with the inclines still starting at 7.00 a.m.):

Shop Pit	1 loco	6.00 a.m. – 5.00 p.m.
Ravensworth Ann Colliery	1 loco	2.00 a.m. – 10.00 a.m., 10.00 a.m. – 6.00 p.m.
Starrs	1 loco	7.00 a.m. – 5.00 p.m.

In May 1963 the line to Dunston, little used latterly, was closed, and traffic between Ravensworth Park Drift and Allerdene Bank Foot was handed over to a loco from North Eastern Trading Estates Ltd. The Shop Pit shed continued to be used for repair work until August 1964, when it was closed. Meanwhile, the Pelaw Main Staiths finally closed in May 1964.

Curiously, the Shop Pit shed closure proved only temporary. In September 1965 slippage on a Trading Estate embankment meant the temporary re-instatement of a NCB locomotive at the Shop Pit, and with the Trading Estate withdrawing from the hire arrangement altogether in May 1966, the NCB was obliged to resume full control of the traffic. A further re-organisation was introduced in 1968. From 11th March all Ravensworth Ann coal was to be drawn at Ravensworth Park Drift, now to be re-named Ravensworth Ann Colliery. This eliminated locomotive working at the former Ann Pit, but introduced two-shift working at the Shop Pit shed, with the fore-shift driver signing on at midnight and the back-shift driver finishing at 6.00 p.m. The end of coal winding at the Ann Pit also altered the working of the Starrs Incline. Empties were run through to the middle of the yard, where the rope was detached and put on to the fulls, while the empties were run by gravity round to Allerdene Bank Head with some of the brakes pinned down.

This new system lasted just over five years, until it was decided to merge Ravensworth Ann Colliery into the nearby Kibblesworth Colliery on the Bowes Railway. So on 18th April 1973 the last coal was hauled on the Pelaw Main Railway, the Shop Pit shed retaining a steam locomotive to the end. Thus the last section of the old Ouston Waggonway, between Whitehill and Eighton Banks, closed after 168 years of operation.

One of the Y7 locomotives, 1310, had already been preserved before the final closure, and both the main Ouston Workshops building and the former Pelaw Main Mining Offices at Birtley survive. The Bowes Railway preservation scheme acquired "Planet" 101 in 1979, and has subsequently relaid track from the now preserved Blackham's Hill East Incline near Eighton Banks round the curve on to the Pelaw Main route from Eighton Banks towards Whitehill, with the intention of offering its visitors a longer passenger ride, and thus re-using a length of railway first constructed in 1805.

It is clear from observations of the locomotives after 1947 that transfers between locations occurred quite frequently, and it may very well be that not all have been listed below. In addition, the nomenclature of locations can give rise to confusion: "Allerdene" for the Shop Pit loco shed; "Bill Quay" for Pelaw Main Staiths; "Birtley" for Ouston E Pit; "Eighton Banks" and "Wrekenton" for Starrs (although a locomotive from Starrs may well have been seen at Eighton Banks, since they worked there) and "Team(s) for Ravensworth Ann Colliery, were all commonly used. In addition, observations at "Ouston E Pit" do not always distinguish between the loco shed and the workshops. Nevertheless, the locomotive list and the transfers below are believed to be as accurate as these circumstances allow, with allocations abbreviated as follows:

	BF	Blackhouse Fell loco shed, Birtley							
	EB	Eighton Banks loco shed, Wrekenton (closed)							
	OE	Ouston E Pit loco shed, Ouston							
	OEW	Ouston E Pit Workshops							
	PMS	Pelaw Main Staiths, Bill Quay							
	RA	Ravensworth Ann Colliery, Low Fell							
	S	Starrs loco shed, Wrekenton							
	SP	Shop Pit loco shed, near Lamesley							

Gauge : 4ft 8½in

[71] 26   4-4-0T   OC   BP   772   1867
                            reb   1901
                            reb   Neasden   1920   (a)
      EB   (1)

[72] 44   4-4-0T   OC   BP   868   1869
                            reb   1888
                            reb   1902
                            reb   Neasden   1920   (a)
      BF   (1)

[70] 900   0-4-0T   IC   Ghd   35   1888   (b)
      RA-OEW c1948   (2)

 63   1308   0-4-0T   IC   Ghd   37   1891   (c)
      SP-RA by 17/3/1950-OEW by 13/6/1950-RA by 6/1951
      -S (repairs) after 7/1952, by 1/2/1953-RA by 9/8/1953
      -Watergate Colliery, near Sunniside, by 30/8/1954
      -RA after 9/1954, by 4/1955-OEW? after 9/1956, by 6/1957
      -RA after 9/1957, by 6/1958   (3)

 64   1310   0-4-0T   IC   Ghd   38   1891   (c)
                            reb Ouston Shops   1950   (d)
      RA-S by 19/9/1948-OEW by 13/6/1950-RA by 6/1951-S by 6/1951
      -OEW (new boiler) after 8/1951-RA by 12/1952-S by 1/2/1953-SP 2/1953
      -RA by 8/1953-OEW by 4/1955-S by 7/1955-OEW by 7/1956-S by 1/8/1956
      -RA by 16/4/1957-OE by 6/1958   (3)

 62   TYNE   0-4-0ST   OC   AB   786   1896
                            reb   AB   1940   (c)
      S-RA by 13/6/1950-S by 9/1950-RA (repairs) by 4/1951
      -OE after 8/1951, by 4/1952-PMS after 8/1953, by 4/1955   (3)

 61   DERWENT   0-6-0ST   OC   AB   970   1903
                            reb   RSHN   1945   (c)
      OE-SP by 6/1952-OEW by 1/2/1953-SP by 30/8/1954   (3)

 69   CHARLES PERKINS   0-4-0T   OC   HL   2986   1913   (c)
      PMS-OEW by 3/1949-PMS by 6/1952-OEW by 4/1955-PMS by 6/1957   (3)

 66   CHARLES NELSON   0-4-0ST   OC   P   1748   1928   (c)
      S-OEW by 6/1952-RA after 1/2/1953, by 30/8/1954-S by 4/1955   (3)

 65   HENRY C.EMBLETON   0-6-0T   OC   HL   3766   1930   (c)
      BF-OEW by 8/1953-BF by 4/1955-OEW 31/1/1959   (4)

 67   NCB-PELAW   0-4-0ST   OC   P   2093   1948   (e)
      OE-SP by 7/5/1949-S by 6/1/1950-OE after 9/1950, by 6/1951
      -S after 8/1951, by 7/1952   (3)

 81   0-4-0ST   OC   RSHN   7604   1949   New
      OE according to makers, S according to men-SP c12/1949, by 29/4/1950-S by 7/1952
      -OE by 8/1953-S by 7/1955   (3)

D54   (54 HAMSTERLEY No.1 until /1954)
                            0-4-0ST   OC   HL   3467   1920   (f)
      BF-OEW c/1954-OE by 4/1955   (3)

(a)   ex The Pelaw Main Collieries Ltd, with Railway, 1/1/1947; loco believed not to have been used since 1939-1940
(b)   ex The Pelaw Main Collieries Ltd, with Railway, 1/1/1947; loco dismantled at this date and believed not to have been used for some time

(c) ex The Pelaw Main Collieries Ltd, with Railway, 1/1/1947
(d) fitted with the frame from 900; although strictly the "new" loco should have been numbered 900, 1310 continued to be carried; the frame of 1310 was still at Ouston Workshops in 1956, though it is assumed that it was eventually scrapped
(e) ordered by The Pelaw Main Collieries Ltd, but New to NCB, 9/1948
(f) ex Hamsterley Colliery, Hamsterley, 7/1953

(1) one source gave Scr 12/1948; both NCB and oral report gave Scr /1949
(2) the frame of this engine was combined with the boiler, tanks and cab of 1310; although strictly this combined loco should have been 900, it actually became 1310; the other parts (e.g. boiler) of 900 were apparently scrapped in 1949 (by 13/6/1950)
(3) to control of Bowes Railway, 31/1/1959; for further history see chapter 3
(4) withdrawn from traffic, 31/1/1959; re-instated on 4/2/1959 and transferred to Derwenthaugh Loco Shed, Swalwell, on same day; scrapped by D.Sep. Bowran Ltd, Gateshead, 2/1971

215. The slip pin with its release chain and hook and the shackles leading to the rope, used on the inclines of the Bowes and Pelaw Main Railways from the 1960s onwards. Note the flat on the buffer-guide for the set rider to stand on.

Chapter Twelve
The Sacriston Railway

Like the Pelaw Main Railway, this system had two distinct parts, but unlike the Pelaw Main, the parts remained in quite separate ownership until well into the twentieth century.

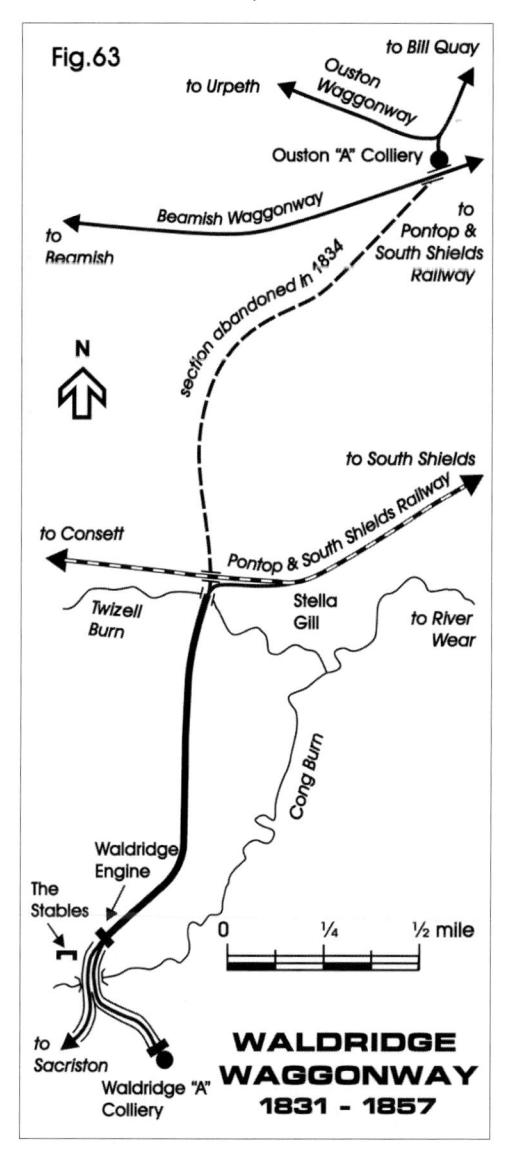

Fig.63

WALDRIDGE WAGGONWAY 1831 - 1857

the River Tyne and the lack of modern waggonways. One of the new collieries here was **WALDRIDGE COLLIERY** (NZ 253502), which was opened in August 1831. Preferring a shipping outlet on the River Tyne to the River Wear, its owners negotiated an agreement to link it to the Ouston Waggonway (see chapter 11), opened fifteen years earlier.

No documentary evidence describing the operation of the Waldridge line seems to have survived, and there is only scant oral tradition on record. Horses shunted waggons at the colliery. In later years the first 600 yards from the colliery down to the embankment which carried the line over the Cong Burn was a self-acting incline, and this may well have been the case from the beginning. The next section, just under a mile, between the Cong Burn and the bridge over the Twizell Burn, was said to have been worked initially by horses and dandy carts – a set of fulls with a carriage (the "dandy cart") at the rear end for the horse to ride in, which was then braked downhill to the bottom of the bank, with the horse pulling the empties back uphill. The remaining section, northwards for just under 1½ miles to Ouston A Colliery, was almost certainly worked by horses too.

However, hardly had the line been opened when proposals for a railway between Stanhope and South Shields were announced. This would cross the waggonway just north of the Twizell Burn bridge, and provide shipping staiths on the River Tyne very close to the mouth of the river. The eastern section of the Stanhope & Tyne Railroad, from Annfield [Plain] to South Shields, was opened on 10th September 1834, and the owners of Waldridge Colliery lost no time in connecting their waggonway to it and abandoning the northern section to Ouston. The obvious junction was at Stella Gill, at the foot of the Waldridge or Howlett Incline. The first Waldridge coal, 410 tons, was conveyed to South Shields on 20th November 1834.

The Sacriston Waggonway
Meanwhile, in 1833, 3¼ miles to the south of Waldridge, the sinking of **SACRISTON COLLIERY** (NZ 237479) and **CHARLAW COLLIERY** (NZ 233477) was begun. Sacriston was a new colliery, but for Charlaw a shaft dating back to 1733 was re-opened, as well as a new shaft being sunk. The ownership of the two collieries was separate, but they worked together to transport their coal. The only way for the owners to gain the benefits of shipping at a deep-water staith on the Tyne was to construct a link to the Waldridge Waggonway, so that their coal too could travel down to South Shields. This link,

The Waldridge Waggonway
As has been noted earlier, the area of the coalfield from Chester-le-Street westwards towards Stanley began to be opened up in the 1820s, although this was hampered by its considerable distance from

SACRISTON WAGGONWAY 1857

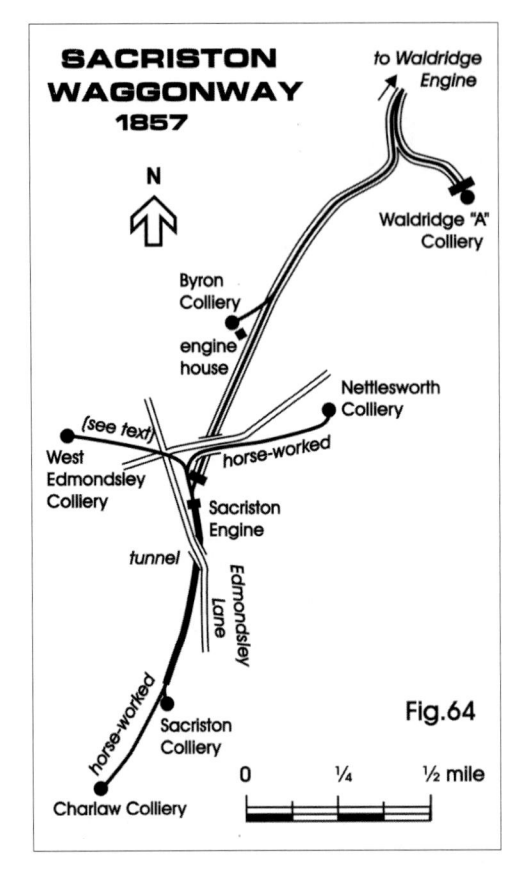

Fig.64

called the Sacriston Waggonway, was opened on 29th August 1839. Waggons from the two collieries were brought by horses to a point just north of Sacriston Colliery, from where the **Sacriston Engine** (NZ 238488) hauled them for ½ mile to the top of Daisy Hill at Edmondsley, passing under Edmondsley Lane in a short tunnel. From the engine a **self-acting incline** about 1¼ miles long took the wagons down to the junction with the Waldridge line, the two self-acting inclines crossing the embankment over the Cong Burn together to reach their bank foots. From Sacriston to Stella Gill was 3¼ miles.

Beehive coke ovens were built at Sacriston Colliery in 1845, and similar ovens were built at Waldridge too, though when this was done is not known. Five years later the Sacriston owners opened **NETTLESWORTH COLLIERY** (NZ 244491), about half-way between Sacriston and Waldridge Collieries. This was served by a ½ mile branch from a junction near the Sacriston Engine, which ran north and then crossed over the "main line". Subsequently another branch from this line turned westwards to serve **WEST EDMONDSLEY COLLIERY**, later **EDMONDSLEY COLLIERY** (NZ 234491), which for many years in the second half of the nineteenth century was operated by **Samuel Tyzack & Co**, the owners of Monkwearmouth Ironworks in Sunderland. At some point the Sacriston Engine was modified by the addition of a second drum, the rope on it being used to work wagons to and from Nettlesworth and Edmondsley Collieries as required, although when this was done, and whether horses were used prior to it being done, is not known.

The Waldridge Engine and Stables

The addition of the Sacriston line meant a major increase in traffic over the Waldridge line from what was now called Waldridge Bank Foot (not to be confused with the Waldridge Bank Foot at Stella Gill on what was now the Pontop & South Shields line nearby). In response, the Waldridge owners converted the bank down to Stella Gill to rope haulage, not with a self-acting incline, as might have been expected, but with the stationary **Waldridge Engine** (NZ 252505). The use of a stationary engine to work one bank lowering fulls was quite rare, the best-known example nearby being the Kibblesworth Engine on the Pontop & Jarrow Railway. Its adoption here was probably because the route, already built, had various curves, which would have made the use of a self-acting incline very difficult. When it was installed is not known, but it is shown on the 1st edition Ordnance Survey map, surveyed in 1857. The map shows the bank to have been single line, which must mean that the full and empty sets were worked alternately.

Horses were used to shunt the waggons at Waldridge Bank Foot, a considerable number being needed because of both the volume of waggons and their varied destinations. So a large three-sided stable block was built a few yards to the north of the Waldridge Engine, where all the horses could be fed and cleaned and looked after properly.

The unique "auxiliary cylinder"

The O.S. map also shows **BYRON COLLIERY** (NZ 243498), situated alongside the western side of the self-acting incline down from the Sacriston Engine. The colliery had a short trailing link to the incline, and an "engine house" is shown near to the colliery, which may have been the means by which waggons were hauled in and lowered out of its yard. However, oral tradition many years later stated that the colliery had been worked in a completely different way, using a method believed to be unique in the North-East coalfield. At right-angles to the return wheel for the self-acting incline to Waldridge Bank Foot a small cylinder was built, supplied with steam from the Sacriston Engine and linked to the top of the wheel by a crank. Using the rope end on the western side of the incline, empty waggons could be lowered into Byron Colliery, and then by operating the cylinder the fulls could be drawn up to the bank head, for running down the main bank. Presumably a set had to be attached to the rope end at Stella Gill to provide a counterbalance when this system was operating, although there is no record to confirm this. When the colliery closed, the auxiliary cylinder was retained, to be used to free the set when it became stuck, for example at the bank head in frosty weather.

In 1859 the owners of Charlaw Colliery began the sinking of **WITTON COLLIERY** (NZ 233474), about

180 yards south of Charlaw Colliery, and had the railway extended to it. In the following year William Hunter set up a brickworks adjacent to Sacriston Colliery to manufacture common bricks, although there may have been a brickworks here before this. Charlaw Colliery closed in 1884, and Byron Colliery followed afterwards.

Ownership

The ownership of the collieries above is extremely complex. Up to 1860 all of the collieries had different owners, and the ownership of Sacriston Colliery alone changed hands six times between 1839 and 1859. Sometimes the partners owning a colliery traded under the title, common in Durham, of "The Owners of XXX Colliery". Of all these owners, the partnership of George Elliot and William Hunter, who owned Sacriston and Nettlesworth Collieries for some years after 1860, was perhaps the most important. George Elliot, M.P. and baronet from 1874, once the Marchioness of Londonderry's Agent, had various business interests, including the ownership, either alone or with a partner, of North Biddick, Felling, Pensher, Usworth and Wardley Collieries, as well as these two. However, at no time were Sacriston and Waldridge held by the same owners, so the ownership and operation of the two sections of the railway remained separate for the whole of the nineteenth century.

Eventually the owners of the collieries around Sacriston combined to form **The Charlaw & Sacriston Collieries Co Ltd**, which was registered on 12th August 1890. The new company owned Witton, Sacriston, Nettlesworth and Edmondsley Collieries. The last was soon sold on, to **The Edmondsley Coal Co**, although The Charlaw & Sacriston Collieries Co Ltd continued to work its rail traffic.

In 1890 Waldridge Colliery was owned by the partnership of **Thiedmann & Wallis**, which also, on the same royalty, owned Chester South Moor Colliery (NZ 268494) at Chester Moor, alongside the NER Darlington-Newcastle line about a mile south of Chester-le-Street. This partnership amalgamated about 1893 with the owners of Victoria Garesfield Colliery at Rowlands Gill, south-west of Gateshead, to trade as The Owners of Victoria Garesfield Colliery, only to change to The Owners of the Waldridge Collieries about two years later. Then on 1st January 1899 this firm became one of several small companies which amalgamated to form **The Priestman Collieries Ltd**. However, the firm's main activities lay around Blaydon, west of Gateshead, and Waldridge and Chester South Moor Collieries were not physically linked to the Blaydon system.

The introduction of locomotives

The introduction of locomotives on the system would seem to have taken place rather later than was usually the case. The Sacriston owners ordered no fewer than three standard gauge 0-4-0ST's with outside cylinders from Black, Hawthorn & Co Ltd - BH 188 and 189 in 1871 and BH 234 in 1873, but all of them were cancelled before delivery and no locomotives are listed at any colliery in 1871 or 1876, according to Durham Coal Owners Association Return No.102. The first place to use a locomotive would seem to have been Waldridge Colliery, which purchased a locomotive from Black, Hawthorn & Co Ltd in 1881. This was followed by a locomotive at Sacriston, though the exact date is not known. By 1939 the **loco shed** (NZ 234476) for this section was situated about 50

216. Charlaw & Sacriston Collieries Co Ltd : 2, CHARLAW, P 1180/1912, arriving at Sacriston in May 1912, hauled by the traction engines ALICE and JESMOND.

yards north of Witton Colliery, and this shed may well have dated back to the introduction of locomotives. Finally, in 1897 the Waldridge owners decided to dispense with the horses at Waldridge Bank Foot and the rope haulage down to Stella Gill. The Waldridge Engine was demolished and a **loco shed** built on the site, long enough to house the two six-coupled locomotives always kept here.

Developments around Sacriston
In 1891 the company built a new coke works at Sacriston, though it closed Nettlesworth Colliery in 1894. At some date about this time a branch about ¾ mile long was built south-eastwards from Sacriston Colliery to carry household coal to a coal depot in Sacriston village. In 1897, to the rear of the coke works, the company opened **SHIELD ROW DRIFT** (NZ 234479), together with a short branch to serve it. This was later re-named the **SACRISTON SHIELD ROW DRIFT**, and further drifts were driven between here and Witton to work further areas of the Shield Row seam – **SHIELD ROW CORONATION DRIFT** (NZ 234476), **SHIELD ROW No.2 DRIFT** (NZ 233475) and **SHIELD ROW No.1 DRIFT** (NZ 233473), all collectively called Shield Row Drift.

In 1902 the Sacriston Engine was replaced by a new engine straddling the track, believed to be the last of this design to be built in Durham. The actual engine was built by The Birtley Iron Company. Like its predecessor, this engine hauled sets up from Sacriston to the south and Edmondsley to the north, while the auxiliary cylinder mentioned above was retained. Like all steam stationary engines, its work included working coal in for its boilers and the removal of boiler ash, which in 1950 was described as being done "by ropes attached to [the] self-acting bank"; short lengths of rope were used at many bank heads to perform short-distance shunting.

The closure of Waldridge Colliery
By the 1890s production at Waldridge was centred on **WALDRIDGE D COLLIERY** (NZ 253500), which was situated a short distance to the south-east of the A Pit. Later the **WALDRIDGE SHIELD ROW DRIFT** (NZ 244497) and working the same seam as at Sacriston, was opened about a mile to the south-west of the D Pit. Curiously, the screens were built about half way between the two sites, with a standard gauge line from the D Pit and narrow gauge rope haulage bringing the tubs from the drift.

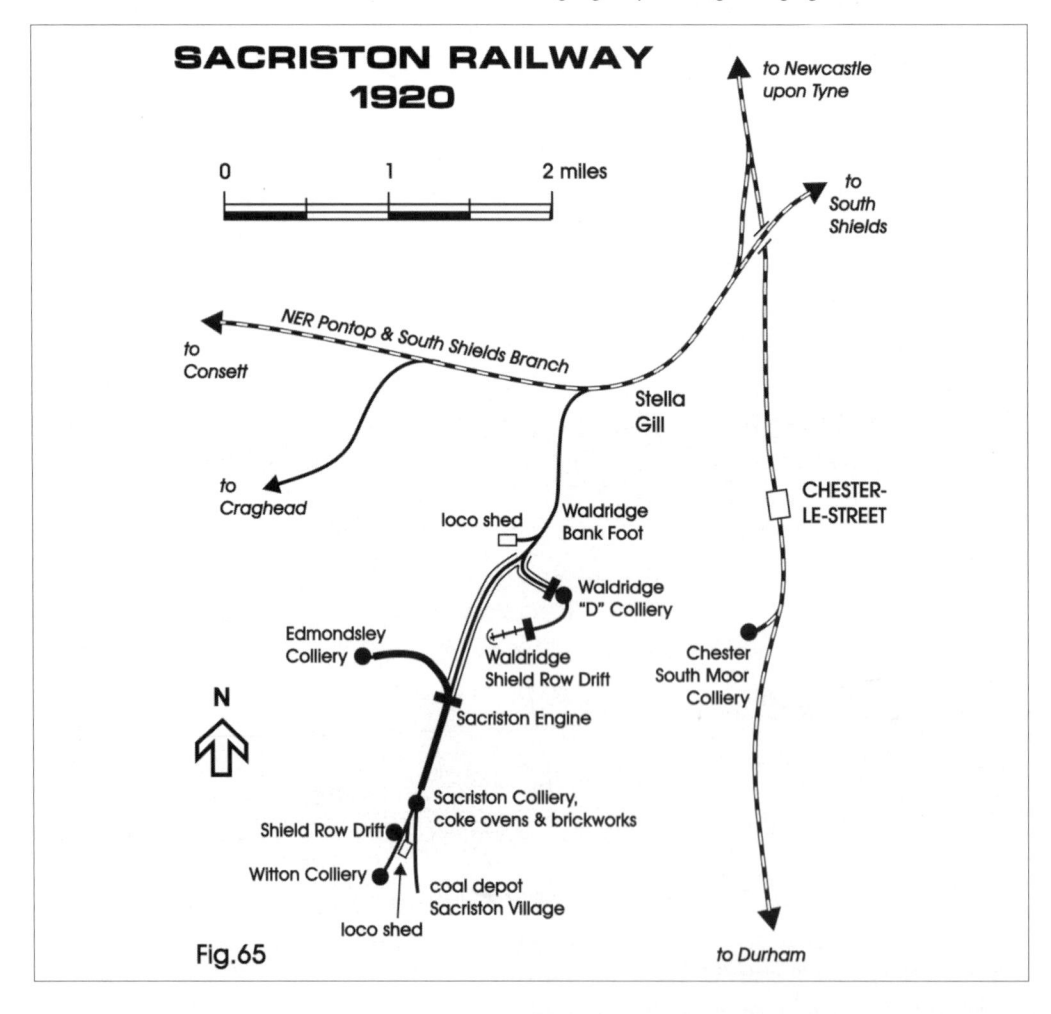

Fig.65

217. The southern side, facing Sacriston, of the Sacriston Engine House at Daisy Hill, on 28th August 1955, six months after closure. At the summit of the line and replacing the original engine in 1902, it hauled wagons up from Sacriston Colliery and also worked the branches to Nettlesworth and Edmonsley Collieries.

218. The Sacriston Engine had a unique auxiliary steam cylinder, seen here on 31st August 1955, which could be used to operate the return wheel of the Waldridge self-acting incline when the wagons became stuck on the bank.

219. *The northern side of the Sacriston Engine House and the bank head of the self-acting incline down to Bank Foot, Waldridge, on 6th November 1949. Note the old incline rope coiled round on the right. The RSHN 0-4-0ST delivered here new two days earlier can be seen in photo 12.*

220. *Priestman Collieries Ltd: CLAUDE, HL 2349/1896, a standard HL design, with 12in x 18in cylinders and 3ft 0in diameter wheels, working at Waldridge Colliery.*

Fig.66

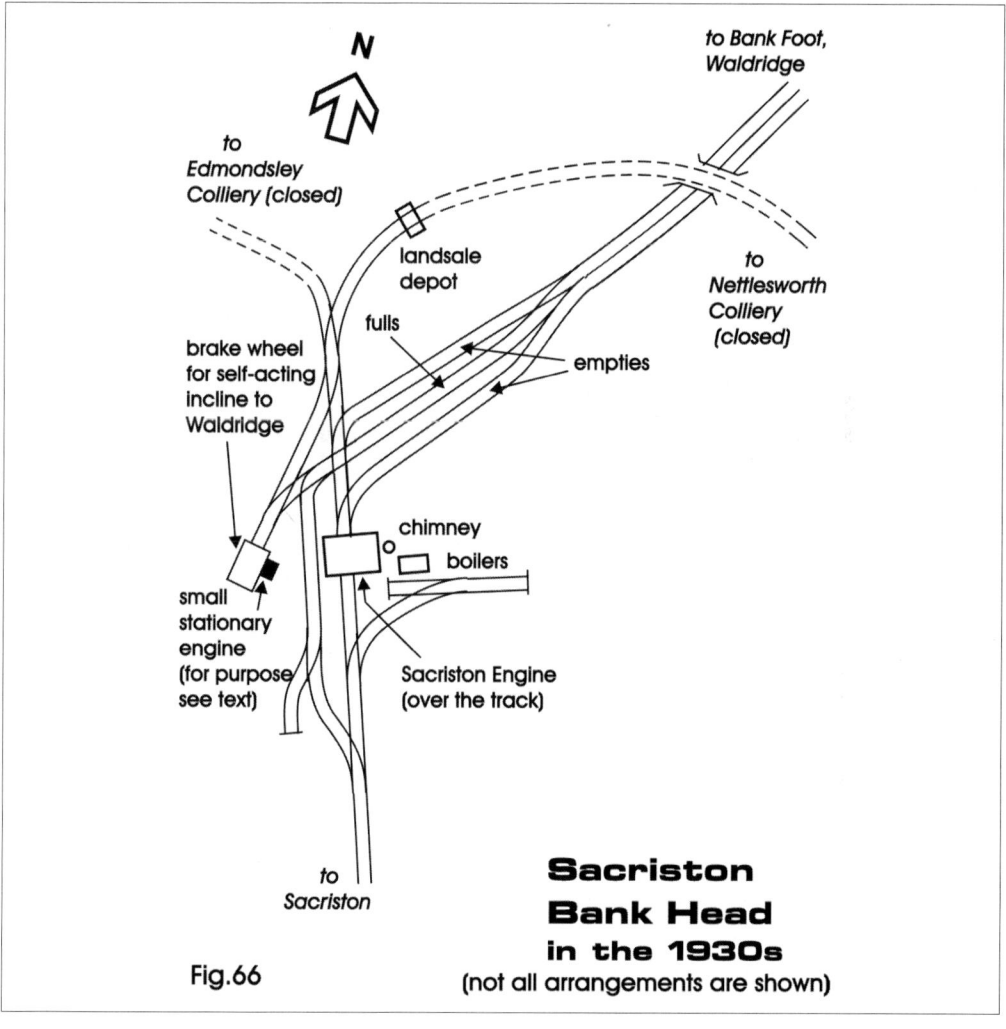

Sacriston Bank Head in the 1930s
(not all arrangements are shown)

The beehive coke ovens closed in March 1922, the D Pit followed in 1925 and Waldridge Shield Row Drift closed at the beginning of the Miners' strike in March 1926 and did not re-open, the company preferring to work the remaining coal to Chester South Moor Colliery. With no Priestman Collieries coal now being worked here, about November or December 1926 the company handed over control of the railway between Bank Foot, Waldridge, and Stella Gill to The Charlaw & Sacriston Collieries Ltd. The two locomotives here were to work on together here, with no help so far as is known, for over thirty years.

Locomotives known to have worked at Waldridge Colliery
Gauge : 4ft 8½in

WALDRIDGE	0-4-0ST	OC	BH	546	1881	New	(1)
WALDRIDGE No.2	0-4-0ST	OC	HC	674	1903	New	(2)
CLAUDE	0-4-0ST	OC	HL	2349	1896	(a)	(3)
FAITH	0-4-0ST	OC	HC	1201	1916	New	(4)

(a)   ex Blaydon Burn Colliery, Blaydon Burn (also owned by The Priestman Collieries Ltd), /1916

(1)   to Hudswell, Clarke & Co Ltd, Leeds, /1903, in part payment for HC 674
(2)   to R & W Hawthorn, Leslie & Co Ltd, Newcastle-upon-Tyne, for repairs, /1925, and then to Watergate Colliery, near Sunniside (also owned by The Priestman Collieries Ltd)
(3)   returned to Blaydon Burn Colliery, Blaydon Burn, /1917; borrowed again subsequently, and again returned

(4) is said to have worked at least once at Waldridge Bank Foot in an emergency; Scr c/1926

Locomotives believed to have worked at Waldridge Bank Foot
Gauge : 4ft 8½ in

	VICTORIA	0-6-0ST					(a)	s/s
	CECIL	0-6-0ST	IC	AB	803	1897	New	Scr /1924
	MARGARET	0-6-0ST	IC	AB	1005	1904	New	
		reb		AB	8833	1924		(1)
	FAITH	0-4-0ST	OC	HC	1201	1916	(b)	(2)
	CECIL	0-6-0T	IC	HC	1524	1924	New	(1)

(a) said to have been the first locomotive to work here; oral tradition claimed that it was ex The Ashington Coal Co Ltd, Ashington, Northumberland (with which the Priestman family were connected): given its name, it may have been a locomotive from Victoria Garesfield Colliery at Rowlands Gill, also owned by the Waldridge owners
(b) came from Waldridge Colliery to work here at least once in an emergency

(1) to The Charlaw & Sacriston Collieries Co Ltd, with this section of the Railway, c11-12/1926
(2) returned to Waldridge Colliery

1926-1947

Back at Edmondsley Colliery the beehive coke ovens closed in October 1920. The colliery itself, latterly called **EAST EDMONSLEY COLLIERY**, was abandoned in March 1929. Although this removed the main purpose of the north drum on the Sacriston Engine, also although now sometimes known as the **Edmondsley Engine**, although it continued to be used to work a landsale depot on the stub of the Nettlesworth branch. The Sacriston Coke Works, still comprising solely of beehive coke ovens, closed in 1939, while the Shield Row Drift closed nominally in 1942, though in fact the workings were absorbed into Witton Colliery.

The Railway employed 21 men in 1930, which had fallen to 11 in 1938, but risen to 14 by 1945. Like the Beamish Railway, it never had any wagons of its own; private owner wagons, and later those of British Railways, were worked in for loading.

Together with Sacriston and Witton Collieries and Sacriston Brickworks, it was vested in NCB Northern Division No.5 Area on 1st January 1947.

NATIONAL COAL BOARD
Durham Division No.5 (Mid-West Durham) Area from 1/1/1950
Northern Division No.5 (Mid-West Durham) Area from 1/1/1947

A visitor to the Railway in March 1950 recorded that both inclines worked sets of either six 10-ton wagons or four 20-ton wagons. The advent of the NCB brought a much-needed new locomotive to Sacriston, but with both collieries going deeper to work thinner seams, less and less coal was being sent along the Railway, and it was decided that from February 1955 all coal would be transported by road. It was thus the first of the railways inherited by the NCB to be closed. The track and buildings remained in situ for some time before being cleared.

Locomotives at Sacriston Colliery
Gauge : 4ft 8½in

	-		0-4-0ST	OC	MW	455	1874	(a)	(1)
	CHARLAW		0-4-0ST	OC	BH	1037	1891	New	(2)
1	(SACRISTON)	C614	0-4-0ST	OC	CF	1210	1901	New	(3)
(2)	(CHARLAW)	C615	0-4-0ST	OC	P	1180	1912	New	(4)
503	"SACRISTON"		0-4-0ST	OC	RSHN	7605	1949	New	(5)

(a) ex R.H. & H.Hodgson, contractors, Workington, Cumberland

(1) to Raine & Co Ltd, Blaydon
(2) to W.Whitwell & Co Ltd, Thornaby, Yorks (NR), /1912
(3) loaned to Ministry of Works (location unknown) during 1914-1918 War, and returned; dismantled by /1947; Scr /1951
(4) to Langley Park Colliery, Witton Gilbert, 12/1955; to Stella Gill Coke Ovens, Pelton Fell, 4/7/1961; recommended for scrap, 5/12/1961; Scr /1962
(5) to Beamish Railway, Beamish, after 7/1955, by 7/1956; for subsequent history see chapter 2

221. Waldridge Bank Foot, on 28th August 1955, with the incline curving away up the hill and the former line to Waldridge Colliery branching off to the left.

222. Waldridge Bank Foot, loco shed on 28th August 1955, built in 1897 on the site of the former Waldridge Engine House.

223. MARGARET, AB 1005/1904, shunting at Waldridge Bank Foot, on 4th July 1951.

224. The other long-term loco at Waldridge Bank Foot - CECIL, HC 1524/1924, taken here just before the Second World War.

Locomotives at Waldridge Bank Foot
Gauge : 4ft 8½in

MARGARET	0-6-0ST	IC	AB	1005	1904		
		reb	AB	8833	1924	(a)	(1)
CECIL	0-6-0T	IC	HC	1524	1924	(a)	(2)

(a) ex The Priestman Collieries Ltd, c11-12/1926

(1) to Beamish Railway, Beamish, 11/1955; for subsequent history see chapter 2
(2) to Ridley, Shaw & Co Ltd, Middlesbrough, Yorkshire (NR), for repairs, by 28/7/1951; returned to Waldridge Bank Foot after 29/9/1951; to Beamish Railway, Beamish, 16/5/1955; for subsequent history see chapter 2

Sacriston Brickworks closed in 1958, and Witton Colliery followed on 8th January 1966. To work the remaining coal in the Nettlesworth and Waldridge areas the NCB opened **Nettlesworth Drift** (NZ 254493) and the **Dene Drift** at Waldridge (NZ 247502); these were eventually merged, and closed in September 1974. In addition, a private company company, the Smithy-Dene Quarry Co Ltd, opened **Waldridge Fell Mine** (NZ 244498), begun in 1950. This was originally a quarry worked for barytes but from 1952 this was abandoned and drifts opened up to work coal instead. The first drift was closed in 1968, but the final drift, No.3, was not closed till 1990.

However, Sacriston Colliery itself survived for many years because its high quality coking coal was needed for blending with the poorer quality coal from the coastal collieries. It was the last colliery in Durham to work seams thinner than 20 inches, which men hewed with pneumatic drills, and it was the last in Durham to use pit ponies underground. It ceased production on 16th November 1985 and was closed altogether on 20th December 1985.

Chapter Thirteen
The South Hetton Colliery Railway

OWNERS BEFORE 1947
The South Hetton Coal Co Ltd; latterly this company, re-registered on 7/5/1898, was a subsidiary of
The South Durham Steel & Iron Co Ltd of West Hartlepool
The South Hetton Coal Co until 18/7/1874

Compared with many of the other private railways in Co. Durham, the history of the South Hetton system was one of the more straightforward; but it stretched over 160 years and it had an extremely varied and interesting range of locomotives.

One of those from whom the Marquis of Londonderry had sought financial backing for the construction of the Seaham Harbour was Colonel R.G.Braddyll, who proved more interested in developing the coalfield to the south-west of the harbour. On 1st March 1831, just under four months before the harbour was opened, Braddyll and his partners began the sinking of **SOUTH HETTON COLLIERY** (NZ 383453) and the construction of a railway four miles long to link it to the new dock. The colliery was opened, with the railway, on 5th August 1833. The partners subsequently traded under the title of The South Hetton Coal Company. Meanwhile various of the partners next formed The Haswell Coal Company and began the sinking of **Haswell Colliery** (NZ 374423), extending the railway to serve it. This colliery was opened, with the extension, on 2nd July 1835. The section between Haswell and South Hetton is shown on the 1st edition O.S. map as the **Haswell & Seaham Waggonway**, and the section between South Hetton and Seaham as the **South Hetton Colliery Railway**, though whether either of these titles was official is not known.

The whole line as built, 1833-1835
The majority of the section between Haswell and South Hetton was operated by a **stationary engine** (NZ 373432) (name not known) about 800 yards north-east of Haswell Colliery, from which it hauled up full waggons and then, using the same rope, lowered them down to Low Fallowfield, about ¼ mile from South Hetton. The stationary engine was owned by the Haswell company, but most, if not all, of this line between the engine house and South Hetton was owned by the South Hetton Coal Company, the two companies making an agreement regarding the handling of the traffic. The next ¼ mile, from Low Fallowfield to South Hetton Colliery was fairly level, and this continued after the line left South Hetton and turned north-eastwards for about a mile. Possibly horses were used for the ¼ mile to South Hetton, as well as to shunt waggons at both collieries; but whether any of the early locomotives (see below) also worked traffic over this section is not known. From the northern-eastern end of this section, near Murton, the waggons were hauled up the **Hesleden Bank** to the **Cold Hesleden Engine** (NZ 415469) at the summit of the line (Hesleden was the spelling in the mid-nineteenth century, superceded by Hesledon by 1900). From Hesleden Bank Head two **self-acting inclines**, the **Stony Cut** and **Swine Lodge Inclines**, took the waggons down to Seaham Harbour, 5¼ miles from Haswell. The company used the staiths on the south side of the Dock, employing its own men here. Later, when the South Dock was opened, and in 1905 extended, the South Hetton company continued to operate staiths on the northern side with its own men.

Traffic to Hartlepool
Other railways also saw the South Hetton and Haswell traffic as a potential source of income. The Hartlepool Dock and Railway Company was the first on the scene. It had planned to build a line from Hartlepool north-westwards to serve as many collieries as possible en route for Moorsley and Hetton; but the owners there having declined to send their coal over it, it eventually terminated at Haswell, with the first South Hetton coal being shipped at the company's Tide Dock at Hartlepool on 23rd November 1835.

When the HD&R was first opened several major lengths were worked by rope inclines, and it would seem that the remaining sections may well have been initially worked by horses. Equally, it is clear that by the second half of 1838 the South Hetton company was working its own traffic over the HD&R and using its own locomotives. This is given added credence by the fact that at least one of the Hackworth engines first in the list below is believed to have been built in the late 1830s. This system, of the colliery owners operating their own trains using their own locomotives and waggons, was much the same as that operated by the HD&R's neighbour, the Clarence Railway. However, when it began and ended, and whether locomotives worked right through from Haswell to Hartlepool or for only part of that distance, remains unknown.

Interestingly, the South Hetton traffic to Hartlepool soon brought trouble at Haswell, graphically described by John Buddle, who was appointed as arbitrator between the two companies (NRO 3410/Bud/50/3b). When the extension to Haswell, followed by the connection to the Hartlepool Dock & Railway Co, was opened in 1835, both companies decided to ship coal via Hartlepool. This meant that the Haswell stationary engine now had to haul South Hetton traffic up from Low Fallowfield for it to pass on to the Hartlepool line, which initially it did with "great indifference" (= impartiality). However, after August 1836, when the Durham & Sunderland Railway opened its branch, the Haswell company decided to transfer its Hartlepool shipments to Sunderland, while the South Hetton company continued to send coal to Hartlepool. Buddle continues "the Haswell co's engine was now chiefly engaged on their own traffic and the work of the S.H.Co became neglected", so neglected that the South Hetton company built their own **stationary engine** and claimed against the Haswell company for the cost! Despite this unequivocal reference, research has failed to find any further evidence of this engine. The South Hetton company also built its own branches to both railways, a ½ mile line known as **Dobson's branch** running north-westwards to join the Durham & Sunderland line at South Hetton Colliery Junction, and a 1¾ mile branch going southwards, known as the **Pespool** or **Pesspool branch** (both spellings are commonly found) to join the Hartlepool line at Pespool Junction.

Traffic to Sunderland
Not only the HD&R wanted South Hetton/Haswell traffic. The Durham & Sunderland Railway also had eyes on it, and on 9th August 1836 it opened its own branch from the north to Haswell. Needless to say, there was no connection between the two; not until 1877 did the North Eastern Railway build the link at Haswell to connect them. Although the first shipment of Haswell coal at Sunderland was made on 9th August, the first coal, to depots at Hendon, was dispatched four days earlier. The whole of the D&SR was rope-worked. The South Hetton owners then made their own branch to the D&SR, as noted above, and their first coal was shipped at Sunderland on 6th October 1836. One is left to wonder how much coal was still going down the company's own line to Seaham Harbour.

Murton Colliery and its branches
The South Hetton partnership next turned to the sinking of **MURTON COLLIERY** (NZ 399473). This proved an immense undertaking. Two shafts were begun on 19th February 1838, but in June 1839 a thick layer of waterlogged quicksand was reached. A third shaft was started in July 1840 and more and more pumps were brought in, until over 1600 h.p. was employed. The sinking was not completed until 22nd April 1843, after expenditure estimated to approach £400,000, a huge sum by Victorian standards. The new colliery was linked to the original railway by two ¾ mile branches, one, called the **Murton branch**, joining towards South Hetton and the other, called the **Murton Dene branch**, joining towards Seaham. As the bank foot of the Hesleden Incline lay between these two junctions, it would seem that the Cold Hesleden Engine must also have worked the Murton Dene branch, with coal for Seaham leaving this way and coal for Sunderland and Hartlepool leaving via the Murton branch.

The company played hardly any part in the coking industry, though it did have 173 beehive ovens at Murton by the beginning of the twentieth century.

Links with the Londonderry Railway
Meanwhile, the Haswell partnership had gone on to sink **Shotton Colliery** (NZ 398412), opened in 1841 and linked to the HD&R line. Some ten years later, the 3rd Marquis of Londonderry was planning his own line between Seaham and Sunderland, which was to be opened for coal traffic on 3rd August 1854 (see chapter 10). The Marquis clearly wanted to attract as much coal traffic on to the line as he could, and he made new agreements with both the South Hetton and Haswell companies before the construction of the new line was begun. Initially the only link between the South Hetton line and the Londonderry Railway belonging to the Marquis had been near the Seaham South Dock, but in order for South Hetton coal to be conveyed to the South Dock at Sunderland over the Marquis' new line, a ¼ mile link was put in at Stony Cut bank foot, 1320 yards from the harbour. Here alongside the original bank foot a second was constructed on the northern side to connect with the Londonderry Railway's Blastfurnace branch. This enabled South Hetton coal to avoid the harbour when destined for Sunderland. This link, to South Hetton Junction, was known as the Londonderry Railway's South Hetton branch.

The Marquis clearly wanted the Haswell company's Shotton Colliery traffic too, and on 5th February 1853 he made an agreement with The Haswell Coal Company (D/Lo/E/378), presumably with the South Hetton Coal Company's agreement, in which he undertook to construct what was called the **Londonderry (Pespool branch) Railway**, a line estimated at 600 yards long between the South Hetton Coal Company's Pespool branch (to the Hartlepool Railway & Dock Company's line) and Shotton Colliery. Construction would seem to have been delayed, for in a new agreement dated 17th March 1860 (D/Lo/E/378/1) between the Marchioness, the 3rd Marquis' widow, and the Haswell Company the branch is described as "recently constructed". The line as built was 1½ miles long, running from near the southern end of the South Hetton company's branch to the northern end of Shotton Colliery. Under the agreement the Haswell company was to bear the cost of working its coal from Shotton and over the South Hetton company's railway to the South Hetton Junction with the Londonderry Railway at Seaham, be responsible for repairs to the branch and to find locomotives and waggons to work it. This was clearly altered in part almost immediately, for in his history of the Londonderry Railway its then locomotive foreman George Hardy says (p.77 of draft) that "at this period [1860] No.9 Engine was leading coals from Shotton Colliery by the Pesspool branch to So[uth] Hetton". This can only mean that the Londonderry Railway was working the Haswell company's traffic from the branch over the South Hetton company's line as far as South Hetton, where presumably the locomotive was serviced and housed in the latter's loco shed.

SOUTH HETTON COLLIERY RAILWAY 1865

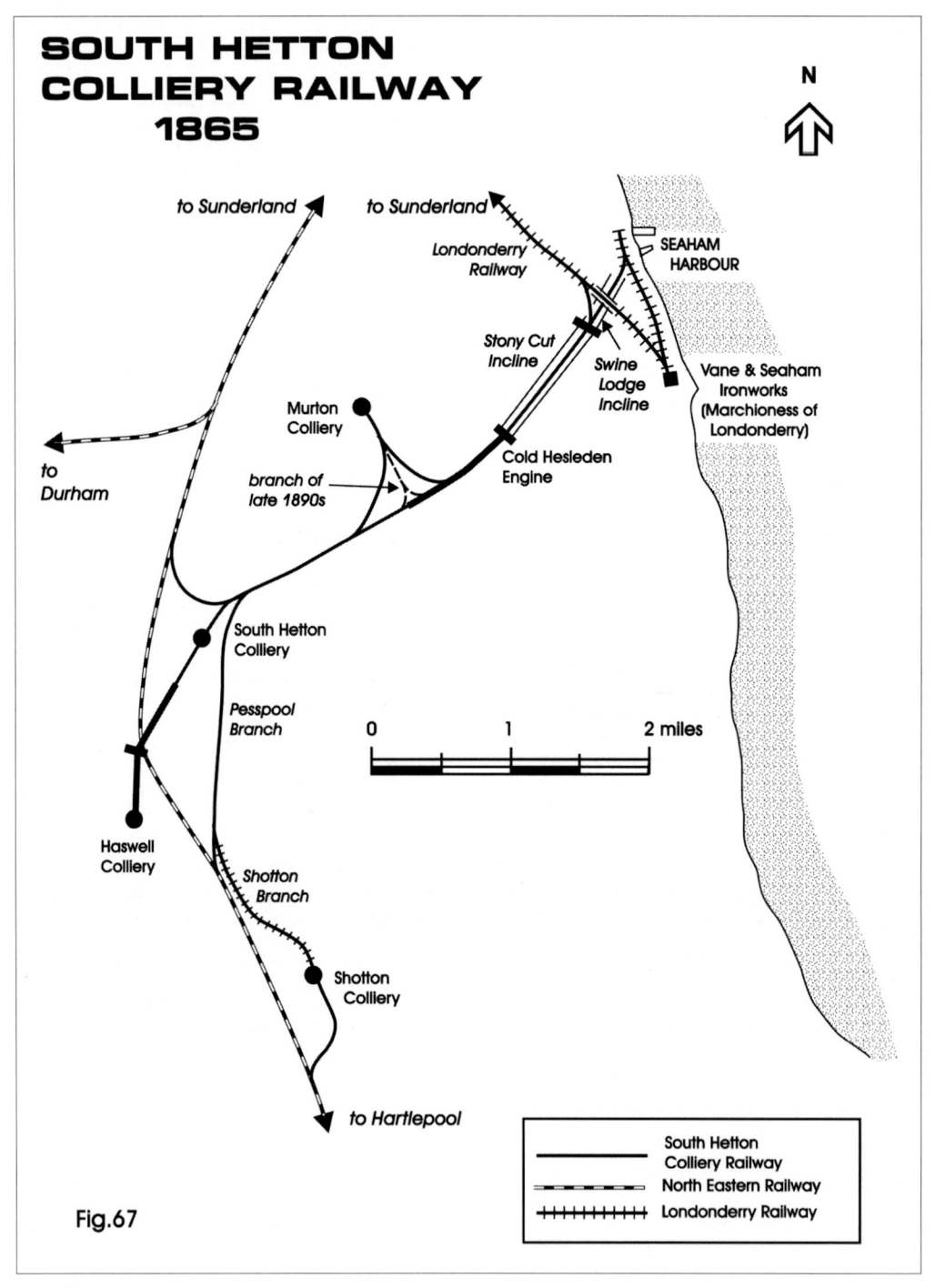

Fig.67

This agreement was short-lived, for under another agreement dated 24th July 1868 but back-dated to 1st January 1868, the branch was sold to the Haswell company, though with the traffic agreement still continuing. The Haswell company now purchased its own locomotives, and so far as is known, at least some Shotton traffic continued to travel to Seaham via South Hetton, though whether the interchange point between the two companies was near Pespool Junction or at South Hetton is not known. Shotton Colliery closed in November 1877.

However, by 1882 the **Tuthill Limestone Quarry Co** had opened **Tuthill Quarry** (NZ 388426), linking it to the Pespool branch by a ½ mile line using part of the trackbed of the former line to Shotton. It is assumed that the NER worked the traffic, travelling over the Pespool branch to do so. In 1899 the quarry was taken over by **Pease & Partners Ltd**. It was closed after the First World War, and in 1923 it was taken over for the production of explosives by **The Northern Sabulite Co Ltd**, later part of Imperial Chemical Industries Ltd, which was still using it for this purpose when the coal industry was nationalised in 1947.

The closure of the Haswell branch

By about 1880 it would seem that **The Haswell, Shotton & Easington Coal & Coke Co Ltd**, as the Haswell owners had become, had drifted away from the South Hetton/Londonderry association, and was sending all its coal via the North Eastern Railway. As a result the branch from South Hetton to Haswell became disused, except for a short spur retained to provide access to the South Hetton locomotive sheds and workshops. It is still shown in place on the 2nd edition O.S. map of 1896, but was lifted soon afterwards. Haswell Colliery itself closed in September 1896.

In 1887 The South Hetton Coal Co Ltd offered to make an agreement with the Marquis under which he would take over its railway and its locomotives and handle all of its rail traffic between its collieries and either Seaham or Sunderland. It would seem that South Hetton was hoping that the Marquis would either build a new line, or at least remove one or more of the rope inclines on the existing line. Although some consideration was given, in the end matters stayed as they were, almost certainly because the Marquis was unwilling to increase his financial liabilities. About the same time the company also tried to persuade the NER to construct a branch to Murton Colliery, but the NER similarly declined, presumably on the basis that the existing links to the South Hetton system provided sufficient capacity. So despite its efforts the South Hetton company continued to have to own and operate its railway.

By 1896 the company had built a new branch from Murton Colliery, in between the earlier two and joining at Hesledon Bank Foot, with junctions in both directions. On the 2nd edition O.S. map of this year the two original branches are still shown in use, but it would seem likely that they were lifted soon afterwards. It would seem likely that the Cold Hesleden Engine was dispensed with about this time too and locomotive working introduced up to Hesleden Bank Head, giving a 1 in 35 gradient for about ¾ mile against the load.

In 1905 what was now The Seaham Harbour Dock Company opened its major extension of the South Dock, where the South Hetton company operated the No.2 (The "Pole") Berth. To serve this a south-turning link was built from Swine Lodge bank foot to the Dock Company's lines, with the latter continuing to work South Hetton traffic to the berth. The South Hetton company relinquished its operating rights on this berth from 9th April 1923.

After this the line remained unaltered until nationalisation. In 1910 a brickworks, making common bricks, was established adjacent to Murton Colliery. The beehive ovens here closed soon after the First World War, and the company never built a by-product coke oven plant, nor even a coal washing plant. During the Second World War, two sidings were laid ½ mile east of South Hetton, ostensibly to store petrol tank wagons, though it is not clear whether they were actually used for this. South Hetton Colliery, Murton Colliery and its brickworks, and the railway, were vested in NCB Northern Division No.2 Area on 1st January 1947.

The company followed the normal nineteenth century practice and developed workshops around a central courtyard near the eastern end of South Hetton Colliery yard, with the **loco shed** on its eastern side (NZ 384453). Later further sheds were added, with the access to these being from the stub end of the former branch to Haswell. Here too there was virtually no up-grading of the workshop facilities after 1900.

The locomotives

A great deal of uncertainty surrounds some of the South Hetton locomotives, and despite extensive discussion over the years it is unlikely now that an absolutely definitive identity can ever be given for these. As noted above, the company's first locomotives were used to work the company's own trains over the Hartlepool Dock & Railway Co. The first four are all said to have been built by Timothy Hackworth at his Soho Works at Shildon.

Gauge : 4ft 8½in

BRADDYLL	0-6-0	OC	Hackworth	New	see below
KELLOE	0-6-0	OC	Hackworth	New	see below
NELSON	0-6-0	OC	Hackworth	New	see below
WELLINGTON	0-6-0	OC	Hackworth	New	see below

Even the names are disputed. One source gives BRADDYLL as BUDDLE, but since the former is confirmed in the HD&R minutes, this would seem to be an error. KELLOE is sometimes given as KELLOR; but Kelloe is the name of a Durham village, which in Durham dialect would sound like Kellor, which is otherwise unknown, so this would seem to be a mis-writing of someone recording oral tradition. NELSON is also recorded as PRINCE ALBERT, but the former could well be correct, as Prince Albert did not marry Queen Victoria until 1840, some years after the locomotive was probably built. All four locomotives were almost certainly built with two tenders, one at each end.

The remains of BRADDYLL survive, now at the Timothy Hackworth Victorian & Railway Museum at Shildon, and in 1995 she was carefully examined

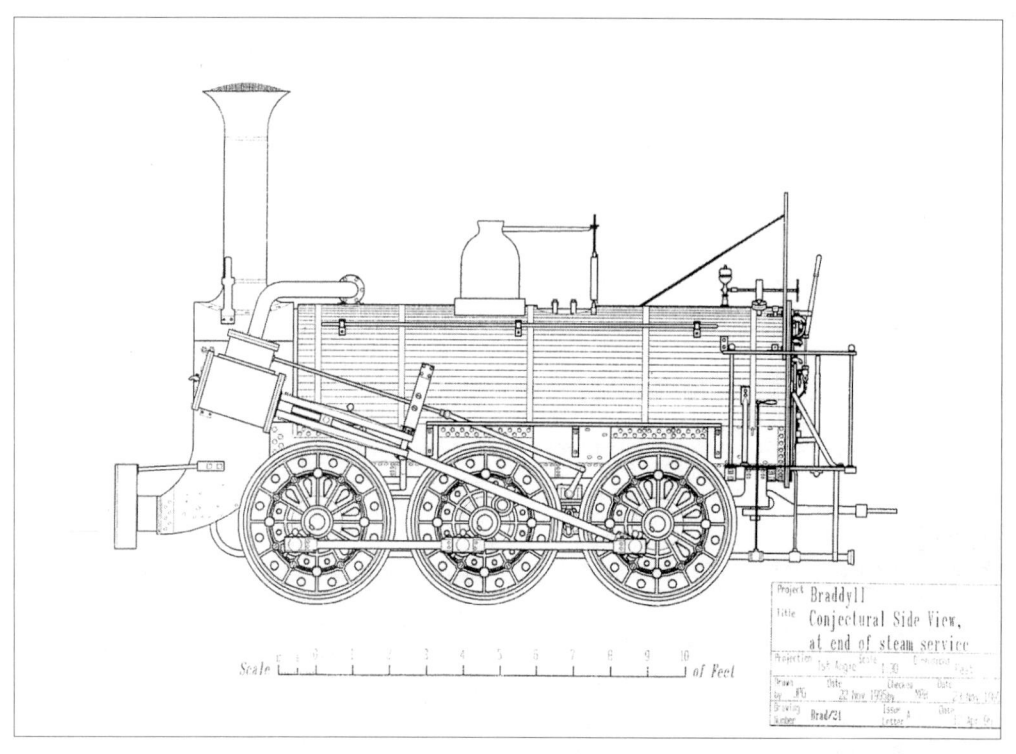

Fig.68. A reconstruction by Dr.M.Bailey and J.Glithero of how BRADYLL may well have looked at the end of her service as a locomotive about 1875

225. *The remains of BRADDYLL being used as a snow plough, at South Hetton in July 1935; the "plough" is believed to have been made from old boiler plates.*

by the expert team of Dr.Michael Bailey and John Glithero. It was their opinion that she was built in the late 1830s. It does not, of course, follow that the other three were built at the same time, or were even identical.

According to *British Locomotive Catalogue, 1825-1923, Vol.5A, the North Eastern Railway & the Hull & Barnsley Railway*, compiled by B.Baxter and edited by D.Baxter, two South Hetton locos found their way on to the NER. The first is listed as built at South Hetton in June 1840, the second as built at South Hetton in June 1841. They came to the NER in 1854 as Nos. 117 and 118 from the York, Newcastle & Berwick Railway, where they had carried the same numbers. According to Baxter, 118 was named KELLOE and was rebuilt by Thomas Richardson of Hartlepool about 1848. It was replaced in 1875, whilst 117 was replaced in 1873.

The route by which this might have come about is tortuous. As noted above, The South Hetton Coal Co had running powers over the Hartlepool Dock & Railway Company's line. The Newcastle & Darlington Junction Railway, or more accurately, George Hudson, the "Railway King", wanted to acquire the HD&R in order to control Hartlepool Docks and negotiated a provisional lease. In 1845 the N&DJR and the HD&R jointly leased the Great North of England, Clarence & Hartlepool Railway; but on 27/7/1846 the Newcastle & Darlington Junction Railway alone purchased the GNoEC&HR, the new company being called the York & Newcastle Railway. On 12/8/1846 the Y&NR finalised its lease of the HD&R, only for the Bill authorising it to be rejected by Parliament. On 9/8/1847 the York & Newcastle Railway amalgamated with the Newcastle & Berwick Railway to form the York, Newcastle & Berwick Railway, and the proposed lease of the HD&R eventually received Parliamentary sanction on 22/7/1848, but was backdated to 1/7/1846. In the York, Newcastle & Berwick loco list Nos.114 and 119 were locomotives acquired by the Newcastle & Darlington Junction Railway in 1844 from the Midland Railway. How, when and by whom, through all of this maze, the South Hetton locomotives might eventually have come into YN&BR stock, is unknown, as is whether any surviving primary source confirms the information Baxter gives. Indeed, all of the above was dismissed by the earliest researcher into NER locomotives, R.H.Inness, who stated that no South Hetton locomotives ever came to the NER. It has not proved possible to resolve these difficulties.

BRADDYLL is said to have worked until about 1875, when it was converted into a snowplough. In this form, and increasingly derelict, it survived to pass to NCB Durham No.2 Area on 1st January 1947. Although not strictly included in this list, it seems more appropriate to give its subsequent history here. It was scheduled to be cut up with other South Hetton locomotives in 1948, but was saved by a senior NCB official, who instead decided that it should be preserved. It was taken to Lambton Engine Works at Philadelphia (see chapter 9), where two new wheels were fitted to replace two that were "damaged" (believed to be the middle pair of wheels). It was then mounted on a plinth at the northern entrance to the works. As recorded above, it is now housed in the Timothy Hackworth Victorian & Railway Museum at Shildon, and carefully restored in the colours which Bailey & Glithero showed it had once carried.

The other Hackworth locomotives were said at South Hetton to have been "scrapped", though since this was widely used within the coal industry to mean any of, 'stopped working', 'disposed of' and 'cut up for scrap', its actual definition here cannot be known.

In a description of South Hetton Colliery in the Supplement to the *Mining Journal* of 29th April 1871 there were said to be six locomotives here,

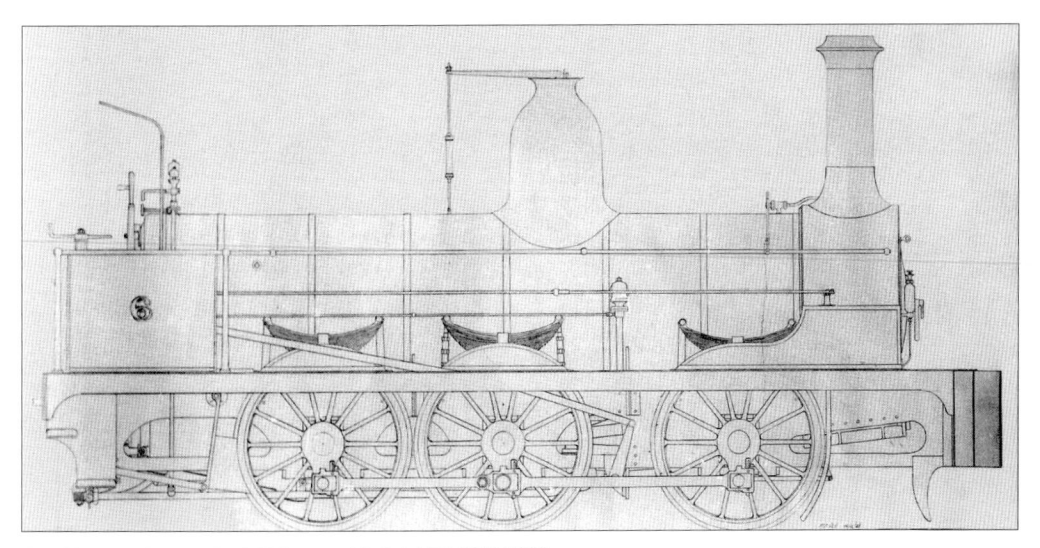

Fig.69. Line drawing by R.H.Inness of 6, 0-6-0 RS 1913/1868

226. 0-6-0ST 1, BH 355/1875, at South Hetton on 10th October 1947.

227. 0-6-0T 2, HAVERHILL, SS 2358/1873, shunting chaldron waggons at South Hetton on 17th July 1945.

228. 0-6-0T GLAMORGAN, HE 396/1886 - it never seems to have carried its number - at South Hetton on 30th June 1936.

229. 0-6-0ST No.4, MW 697/1878, (Manning Wardle O class), at South Hetton in June 1935. The upper part of the entrance to the cab has been narrowed to increase the crews' protection in bad weather.

230. 6, a Metropolitan Railway A class 4-4-0T, purchased about 1908, probably from the dealers R.Frazer & Sons Ltd of Hebburn – but not destined to last long in this form.

231. The same locomotive as rebuilt to 0-6-0T in 1909, at South Hetton in July 1935.

232. 0-6-0ST 7, Joicey 305/1883, at South Hetton in 1935.

though how many of the first five below survived to this date is unknown. However, the April 1871 section of DCOA Return 102 gives five locomotives here, while the November 1876 section gives only four, noting that "2 work night and day". It could be that the company misunderstood the Return, and entered only locomotives at work, rather than locomotives owned.

It would seem that a numbering scheme was in use by 1868, given that there is a drawing by R.H.Inness of 6 0-6-0 on which he records the date 14/11/1868; but which locomotives carried those numbers is unknown. The sources appear tentative as to TR 265 being No.1, and whether RS 1913 was 2 or 6; given the date of 1868 on the Inness drawing, it would seem more likely that this loco was 6. A book started in January 1895 by the South Hetton boilersmith came to light in 2004. This records work done to No.3 loco and then new No.3 loco, so that there was clearly a No.3 before BP 190. There is no photographic evidence of GLAMORGAN ever carrying its number. Even the identities of some of the later locomotives are disputed, as the footnotes show. Very unusually, the Railway never had any 0-4-0STs.

At nationalisation the company handed over the most elderly and worn out fleet of locomotives in the North East; apart from two War Department locomotives acquired eight months earlier, the newest loco was built in 1886, five were not in working order and two of those which were capable of working had frames that were 99 years old. A large number of 4½ ton chaldron waggons were also still in use.

Gauge : 4ft 8½in

	DILIGENCE	0-4-0	VC	RS		1826		
		reb 0-6-0	OC	Hackworth		1834	(a)	s/s
No.1		0-6-0	IC	TR	265	1856	New	
		reb 0-6-0ST?						s/s
1		0-6-0ST	OC	BH	355	1875	New	(1)
2	HAVERHILL	0-6-0T	OC	SS	2358	1873	(b)	(1)
3							(c)	(2)
3	(HALSTEAD?)	0-4-2ST	IC	BP	190	1860	(d)	Scr /1902
(No.3)	GLAMORGAN	0-6-0T	IC	HE	396	1886		
		reb		Baker		1907	(e)	
		reb		South Hetton		1926	(f)	(1)
No.4		0-6-0ST	IC	MW	697	1878	New	
		reb		South Hetton		1913		(1)
No.5		0-6-0ST	IC	MW	758	1881	New	
		reb		South Hetton		1910		(1)
6		0-6-0	IC	RS	1913	1868	New	Scr /1903
	-	4-4-0T	OC	BP	425	1864	(g)	(3)

			4-4-0T	OC	BP	417	1864	(h)	
No.6		reb	0-6-0T	OC	South Hetton		1909		(1)
No.7			0-6-0ST	IC	Joicey	305	1883	New	
		reb			South Hetton		1908		
		reb			M.Coulson		1935		(1)
No.8			0-6-0	IC	RS	625	1848		
		reb	0-6-0ST	IC			1866	(j)	
		reb	0-6-0T	IC	South Hetton		1923		(1)
No.9	SIR GEORGE		0-6-0	IC	RS	624	1848		
		reb	0-6-0ST	IC			1865	(j)	
		reb			South Hetton		1911		(1)
10	WHITFIELD		0-6-0	IC	SS		1857		
		reb	0-6-0ST	IC			1870	(k)	(1)
	JAMES WATT		0-6-0ST	IC	SS	1768	1866	(m)	(4)
11			0-6-0ST	IC	VF	5308	1945	(n)	(1)
12			0-6-0ST	IC	VF	5309	1945	(p)	(1)

(a) ex Stockton & Darlington Railway, No.4, DILIGENCE, 2/1841; this was the fourth locomotive built by RS, though whether it had a works number and if so what it was is disputed

(b) ex Colne Valley & Halstead Railway, /1889; previously Cornwall Minerals Railway, 10

(c) identity, origin and date of arrival unknown; here by 6/1/1895

(d) ex Colne Valley & Halstead Railway, 2; previously North London Railway, 42. The BP works number has been questioned, depending on which NLR loco was sold to the Colne Valley & Halstead Railway. The loco would appear to have arrived at South Hetton in 1/1895; the boilersmith's book mentioned above states that work overhauling it began on 25/1/1895, and then that 'loco entered work, 27/3/1895'

(e) ex P.Baker & Co Ltd, dealers, Cardiff, Glamorgan, c/1907; previously T.A.Walker, contractor, and used on his Barry Railway contracts in Glamorgan

(f) rebuilt with new frames, new boiler and firebox, new cylinders and new valve gear (= effectively a new locomotive)

(g) ex Metropolitan Railway, 14, /1905

(h) ex Metropolitan Railway, 6, /1908 (?), via R.Frazer & Sons Ltd, dealers, Hebburn; there was an oral tradition at South Hetton that this loco came from the Pelaw Main Railway of The Birtley Iron Co, but there was no parallel tradition there, and it seems likely the tradition has become confused with the Metropolitan Railway engines which the Pelaw Main Railway acquired in 1927

(j) considerable dispute surrounds the identity of these locomotives. The traditional view was that both were ex Alexandra (Newport & South Wales) Docks & Railway in 1898, where RS 624 had been No.1 and RS 625 No.2. RS 624 had been built for the London & North Western Railway (Southern Division) as No.216, renumbered 816 in 1862, 1156 in 8/1864 and 1805 in 11/1871, being also named SIR GEORGE ELLIOT; it was sold by the LNWR to ADR in 3/1875, who numbered it 1. RS 625 was built for the LNWR (S.D.) as 220, renumbered 820 in 1862, 1199 in 8/1864 and 1807 in 11/1871, being also named LORD TREDEGAR. It too was sold to the ADR in 3/1875, who numbered it 2. In the RCTS *Locomotives of the Great Western Railway* Part 10, page K10, it is suggested that the minutes of the ADR indicate that a new No.23 was built in 1900 using parts of Nos. 1 and 2, while ADR No.4 (RWH 709/1849) and 7 (a SS loco, possibly 1012/1857), both also ex LNWR, were sold in 1900 to the dealer C.D.Phillips, and so might have been, although this is not stated, the locomotives acquired by The South Hetton Coal Co Ltd. However, after the RCTS book was published, E.R.Mountford, the noted historian of railways in South Wales, came to the view that ADR No.23 was actually built from parts of ADR Nos. 3 and 4, and that Nos. 1 and 2 were sold to South Hetton as previously believed. There are certainly similarities in both appearance and dimensions between ADR Nos. 1 and 2 and the South Hetton engines, as well as the otherwise curious co-incidence of the name of RS 624.
According to South Hetton tradition, No.9 was fitted about 1915 with the tank and cab from JAMES WATT (see below).

(k) considerable uncertainty has surrounded this locomotive too. Almost certainly it was one of seven locomotives built for the London & North Western Railway (Northern Division) by Sharp Stewart in 1857, this one numbered 308 and named BOOTH. If this batch was delivered in works number sequence and given sequential numbers by the LNWR in order of delivery then 308 would be SS 1014; however, this seems not to have been the case, and instead 308 was given to the second SS loco to arrive, making it probably SS 1010. 308 was re-numbered 1814 in 9/1870 and 1154 in 12/1871. In 7/1874 it was put on the Duplicate List as 1933, but in the same month it was sold to The Chatterley Whitfield Collieries Ltd in Staffordshire, who named it WHITFIELD. Towards the end of 1877 it was sold to the Ebbw Vale Steel, Iron & Co Ltd, Monmouthshire. It was one of the locomotives earmarked for disposal by EVSIC in a list of 7/1903 and offered for sale in the *Colliery Guardian* on 6/5/1904. Despite this, the South Hetton loco carried a plate saying rebuilt by EVSIC in 1904, the loco being said to have come to South Hetton in 1907, almost certainly via C.D.Phillips Jnr, dealer, Cardiff, Glamorgan

(m) this locomotive is said to have arrived at South Hetton in 1911. Almost certainly it was the JAMES WATT also owned by the Ebbw Vale Steel, Iron & Coal Ltd, Monmouthshire. This loco was purchased new by the firm as one of a batch of three built in 1865-1866, and research now shows that it was almost certainly SS 1768/1866. It was also on EVSIC's disposal list dated 7/1903, and offered for sale in the *Colliery Guardian* advertisement of 6/5/1904. Where it was between 1904 and 1911 is not clear. It too may well have been acquired through a dealer. However, another source recorded that it was scrapped at South Hetton in 1904; presumably this is inaccurate

(n) ex War Department, 75318, Longmoor Military Railway, Hampshire, 4/1946; arrived by 11/5/1946; loco had to be fitted with dumb buffers in order to shunt the chaldron waggons
(p) ex War Department, 75319, Longmoor Military Railway, Hampshire, 4/1946; arrived by 11/5/1946; loco had to be fitted with dumb buffers in order to shunt the chaldron waggons

(1) to NCB No.2 Area, with the Railway, 1/1/1947
(2) boiler repairs to this loco ceased on 15/2/1895; s/s
(3) it is believed that parts of this loco were used in the rebuilding of 6, BP 417/1864, and the remainder was scrapped c/1909
(4) the tank and cab of this loco are said to have been fitted to No.9 about 1915, with the remainder being scrapped

In March 1871 the company offered for sale a six-coupled saddletank with 12inx20in cylinders and 3ft 0in diameter wheels; its origin, identity and disposal are unknown.

Other work
The book which the South Hetton boilersmith began on 5/1/1895 gives details of boiler work done regularly to "locos 1 and 2" and also to a traction engine at Tuthill Quarry, which was owned by The Tuthill Limestone Co Ltd and was situated near the end of the Pespool branch. A new firebox was fitted to No.2 in 1896. The identity of these locomotives is uncertain and when this contract began and ended is unknown, as is whether only boiler work was involved and where this work was undertaken. The quarry was sold to Pease & Partners Ltd in 1899.

One source records that WINGATE 0-4-0ST OC AB 675/1891, from Wingate Quarry, Wingate and owned by The Wingate Limestone Co Ltd, was repaired at South Hetton. The first record of this loco at Wingate is dated 6/1906 and she had left there by 6/1921, so the repair at South Hetton must have fallen between these dates.

NATIONAL COAL BOARD
North East Group from 1/1/1989
North East Area from 1/4/1974
South Durham Area from 26/3/1967
Northumberland & Durham Division No.3 Area from 28/3/1965
Northumberland & Durham Division No.2 Area from 1/1/1964
Durham Division No.2 (Mid-East Durham) Area from 1/1/1950
Northern Division No.2 (Mid-East Durham) Area from 1/1/1947

At nationalisation the South Hetton unit became controlled by No.2 Area, dominated by its powerful and well-organised former neighbour, The Lambton, Hetton & Joicey Collieries Ltd, whose Chief Engineer, Walter Tulip, was now the Area Mechanical Engineer. The South Hetton locomotives were allocated Nos. 61-72, in the same order as their South Hetton numbering, in the new Area list, but most of them never carried these numbers. As a temporary measure, various Lambton Railway locomotives were drafted in to help, and following a scathing inspection, a mass clear-out of the out-of-use locomotives soon followed. Gradually a locomotive fleet based on the 'Austerity' design was developed, with locomotives being transferred to Lambton Engine Works at Philadelphia for major overhauls.

Coal continued to be dispatched via both the north and south branches. Besides coming in via South Hetton Junction, British Railways' locomotives also worked in and out to South Hetton via the Pespool branch, and handled explosives traffic from the Haswell Works of Imperial Chemical Industries Ltd in Tuthill Quarry.

But everything was soon to be completely changed by the biggest development scheme ever undertaken in the Durham coal industry. After an assessment of the coal reserves in mid-east Durham and factors such as the elderly Hetton Railway, it was decided to develop a huge new complex at Hawthorn, about a mile south of Murton village on the northern side of the railway. Here a large new shaft, coal-drawing only, was to be sunk, to be known as the **HAWTHORN COMBINED MINE** (NZ 390458). This would wind in skips all the coal produced by Elemore, Eppleton and Murton Collieries, which would then wind only men and materials. Two locomotive horizons would be driven to serve Murton (linked to both levels) and Eppleton, linked to the Bottom Level only. The two levels, with some twenty miles of new 2ft 0in gauge track, would serve no fewer than 24 coal loading points. Man-riding trains and sets of 24 two-ton mine cars would be operated by 35

233. One of the few South Hetton engines to survive 1948 - and this one allegedly went back over 100 years, starting life as a six-coupled tender engine built by RS, 625/1848: 68 (formerly No.8) at South Hetton in 1949.

234. Originally a sister engine, but again much rebuilt: No.9, SIR GEORGE, RS 624/1848, outside the original and rather decrepit loco sheds after a major overhaul, on 10th October 1947.

235. Another locomotive with a long and unclear history: 10, WHITFIELD, built as a six-coupled tender engine by Sharp Stewart in 1857, at South Hetton in June 1936.

236. South Hetton was the last major system to use chaldron waggons: Nos. 576, 1150, 275 and 165 stand near the South Hetton landsale depot.

237. With locomotives needed desperately, the NCB obtained the War Department's 70205, last used at the Longmoor Military Railway in Hampshire; she had been built by the Taff Vale Railway at Cardiff in 1897 as a member of the O1 class, and passed to the GWR in 1922. Becoming No.67, she was sympathetically repaired at Lambton Engine Works in 1955, and is seen here near the sheds at South Hetton on 31st March 1957.

238. An empty set arrives on the kip and the rope is released at Stony Cut bank head, Hesledon, on 26th October 1973.

239. Swine Lodge Bank Head, Dawdon, with the remains on the right of the bank head, with its kip, for the link round to British Rail, formerly the Londonderry Railway, on 30th May 1974.

240. A set of fulls carrying waste destined for Seaham Harbour approaching the meetings on the Swine Lodge Incline at Dawdon on 25th August 1970. Note the 14-ton steel hoppers rebuilt by Seaham Wagon Works with wooden planks.

241. The main replacements for the old locomotives were 'Austerities'. Here 69, HE 3785/1953, fitted with a Hunslet underfeed mechanical stoker in 1964 (hence the unusual chimney), stands as spare loco inside one of the old sheds on 20th March 1975.

242. The construction of the Hawthorn Combined Mine, Washery and Coke Works to the south of Murton transformed the South Hetton system. This view looks towards the Hawthorn complex from near the control cabin east of South Hetton on 24th February 1987. Note the colour light signalling.

243. 68, HE 3784/1953, shunts near the Washery, with the coke works, and its coke car loco on the far right, beyond, 19th August 1970.

244. The construction of Hawthorn also saw the introduction of three 440 H.P. diesel locomotives, which took numbers formerly allocated to steam locomotives. 66, NBQ 27765/1959, shunts at Hawthorn on 24th September 1959, five months after delivery.

245. 'Austerities' 68, HE 3784/1953, and 61, HE 3821/1954, stand alongside the steam shed at lunch time with 66, NBQ 27765/1959, and 65, NBQ 27764/1959 (right), on 19th August 1970.

246. At South Hetton new workshops (on the left) and a new diesel loco shed (far right) were built. The old sheds lie at right-angles behind the workshops building, with the weigh cabin in the middle and South Hetton Colliery beyond. The line curving across to the bottom left corner led to the former coaling and watering point for the steam locomotives, 28th July 1982.

SOUTH HETTON RAILWAYS 1970

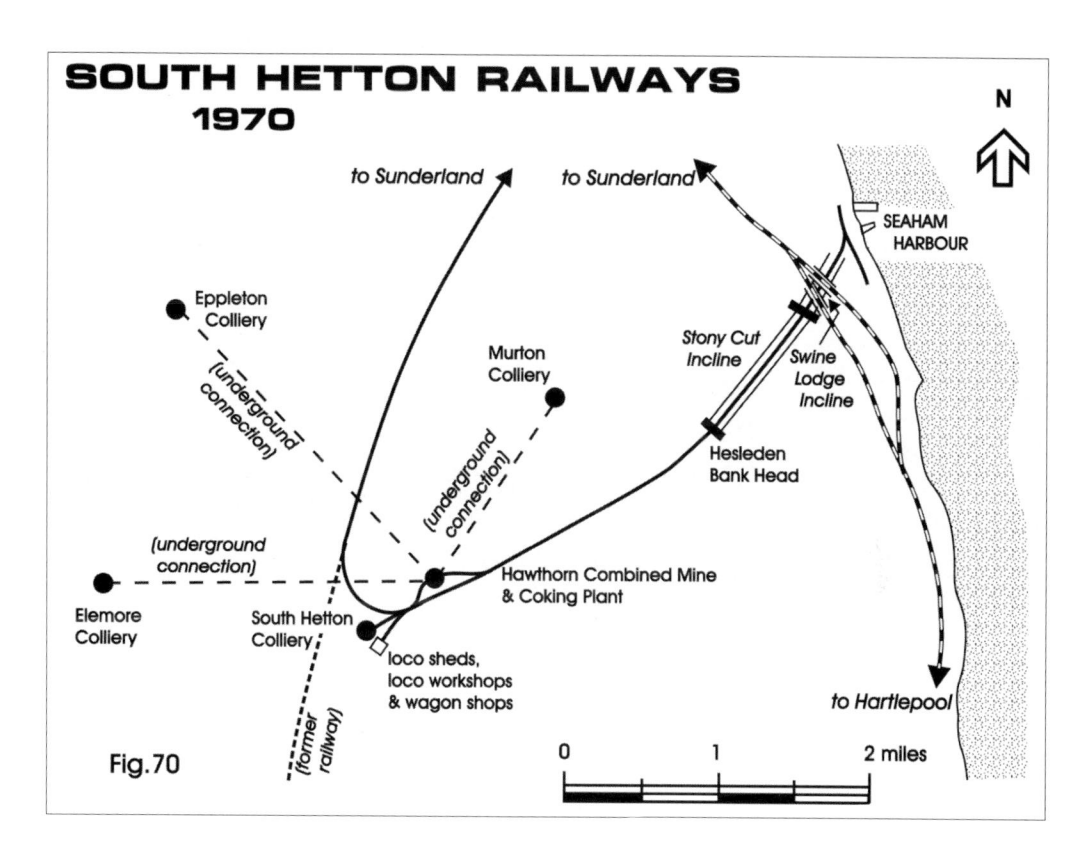

Fig. 70

battery locomotives, controlled by an extensive signalling system. Only Eppleton and Murton Collieries were included in the initial scheme. When it was decided to link Elemore to the Top Level as well, Elemore's original 2ft 3½in gauge system had to be converted to 2ft 0in, but instead of battery locomotives, diesel locomotives were purchased. When the scheme was fully operational it was planned that Hawthorn would raise 8,000 tons of coal per day. The three collieries would remain under separate management, with the Hawthorn curtilege limited to 200 yards.

Next to the Combined Mine a large coal washing plant was to be built, capable of handling 750 tons per hour, most of which would then be carried by conveyor to a large new coking plant, the **MURTON COKING & BY-PRODUCT PLANT** (NZ 3845/3945/3946), whose construction would allow the obsolete plants at Shotton Colliery and at Horden Colliery on the coast to be closed. Most coal and coke would be dispatched via the link with BR at South Hetton, to go northwards, although some coal and all the washery waste would be dispatched eastwards to Hesledon and down the inclines to Seaham Harbour. The majority of the Hetton Railway, made redundant, would close, together with the South Hetton's branch to Murton Colliery and the Pespool branch. The South Hetton system would receive three new 440 h.p. diesel locomotives, and a new loco shed would be built for them at South Hetton, together with new repair shops. The number of new steel wagons already sent to South Hetton would be increased considerably, and their repair shared between the Seaham Wagon Works and a new wagon shop at South Hetton. A sizeable new rail system was needed to serve the mine, the washery and the coking plant, and because of the complexity of the shunting, a colour light signalling system would be installed around the Hawthorn area, controlled from a large cabin to the east of South Hetton. This huge development would cost over £60 million.

Work began in 1952. The coking and by-products plants, including 50 Woodall-Duckham Becker regenerative combination ovens, were commissioned in November 1958, with the Shotton plant closing in May 1958 and the Horden plant in January 1959. The plant was re-named the **HAWTHORN COKING & BY-PRODUCT PLANT** about 1961. Meanwhile, the Combined Mine was officially opened on 2nd January 1960, although it had actually begun production some months earlier and the Hetton Railway had closed on 9th September 1959. The link with BR at Swine Lodge Bank Foot at Seaham was retained until 1964.

The last working steam locomotive and rope inclines in North-East England

The three new North British diesels purchased in 1959 had supplemented the existing steam fleet. From 1973 diesels began to replace the steam locomotives at South Hetton, which eventually became the last place in North-East England where a steam locomotive was in daily commercial use.

247. 62, HE 3687/1949, became the last steam locomotive to work commercially in Durham. Here she descends from Hawthorn towards the bridge over the A19 with fulls to go down the inclines to Seaham on 8th June 1976.

248. The miners' strike of 1984-1985 saw the large-scale excavation of small coal from the inclines and made them unsafe. It was uneconomic to repair them, and after the strike washery waste was disposed of in Tuthill Quarry, near the end of the Pesspool Branch, where one of the later 400 h.p. diesels built by Andrew Barclay is being attached to some empties on 13th July 1989. Note the rotating wagon tippler in the background.

**"HAWTHORN RAILWAYS"
at closure, 1991**

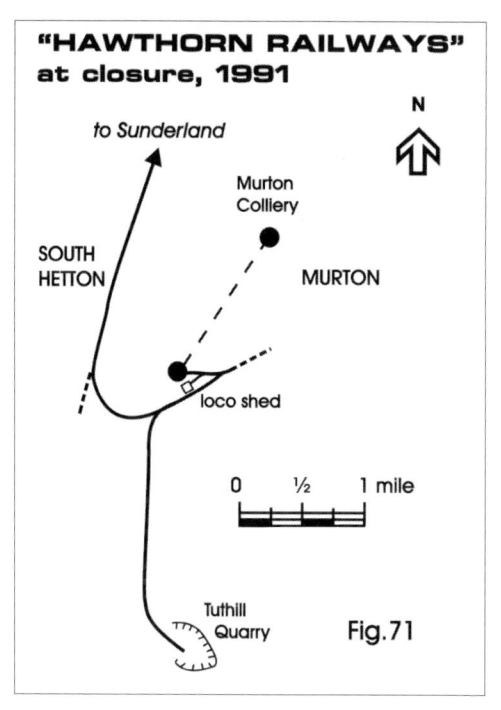

Fig. 71

This ended in 1976. The Plant Pool organisation at the NCB's North East Area followed the policy of re-organising its stock of locomotives to concentrate as far as possible on only one type of loco at each location. This brought to South Hetton most of the Area's other 440 b.h.p. North British diesels, together with the six-coupled Barclay diesel hydraulics, although at 400 b.h.p the men thought the latter were underpowered for the work. Equally, Plant Pool concentrated all surface standard gauge locomotive overhauls at Lambton Engine Works, which left the South Hetton workshops to carry out only running repairs. The two self-acting inclines on the line to Seaham became the last of their type in Britain, and the last inclines of any type in commercial use in the North-East, albeit they were latterly only used to carry washery waste. They ceased work at the beginning of the miners' strike on 5th March 1984, and were then destroyed by people excavating their foundations for the small coal of which these were constructed. This meant that when the long strike was over, British Coal had to find a new way of disposing of the washery waste. This was solved by re-laying the Pespool branch and connecting it to the former **TUTHILL QUARRY** (NZ 388426), where the waste was tipped. The inclines were finally dismantled and the track lifted in the autumn of 1985.

The long decline
Elemore Colliery was the oldest of the three linked to Hawthorn, and it closed on 2nd January 1974. Output at South Hetton, which had been falling for some years, was suspended on 24th August 1979, and although it was resumed during the winter of 1979-1980, it was not for long, and in October 1982 it was linked to Hawthorn Combined Mine and its coal drawn there. The miners' strike, starting on 5th March 1984, forced the Hawthorn Coking Plant to close, although the ovens were kept warm, in the

249. On 15th January 1989 the two working locomotives, 20/104/997, AB 594/1974, and 20/110/89, AB 647/1979, stand outside the locomotive bay opened at Hawthorn Combined Mine in 1987.

event for over a year, in the hope that production could be resumed. But the foreign markets had been irretrievably lost, and although the plant was 'mothballed' for a time, its closure was formally approved early in 1988.

The last major re-organisation occurred on 1st April 1986, when Eppleton Colliery was closed and Hawthorn and Murton were combined under the name of the latter. The extensive underground railway system at Murton had been replaced by conveyors in July 1982. With South Hetton Colliery being demolished, the retention of the loco sheds and workshops there became unviable, and in March 1987 they were closed and a new loco shed was opened by converting part of a building near the screens at Hawthorn. Officially this shed was never given a name; although at Hawthorn, it was officially part of Murton Colliery, whilst after the closure of South Hetton Colliery, Plant Pool regarded the system as 'Hawthorn Railways'. Unofficially it became **HAWTHORN LOCO SHED** (NZ 392460). Murton Colliery, with Hawthorn, finally closed on 29th November 1991, thus bringing to an end the very last of the private railways in County Durham.

Numbers carried by locomotives

In 1948 No.2 Area allocated Nos.61-72 in its Area numbering scheme to locomotives at South Hetton, and as new locomotives were purchased and sent to South Hetton, they were allocated gaps in the same list. This continued with the introduction of diesels from 1959. By this date the Area had introduced the national Plant Numbering scheme. This gave each item of plant a lengthy number, which in the case of the South Hetton locomotives was abbreviated to simply the number of the colliery – 2235 – and the loco number; so 61 was Plant No. 2235/61. Some of the locomotives carried these numbers, painted very small, in addition to their Area numbers. 2235 ceased to be used after No.2 Area was abolished, and a different system was introduced. In the list below, from AB 582/1973 the Area locomotive numbers are shown in the first column and the Area Plant numbers in the second column.

From 1974 North East Area concentrated solely on Plant numbers, whose "method of construction" had also changed again, although Plant numbers issued before 1974 were retained. As locomotives were repainted, only the Plant numbers were put on.

It is a curious co-incidence that the Railway should have the last commercially-operated steam locomotive in the North-East, should have the last commercially-working rope inclines in the North-East, should be the last private railway in the area to close and that one of the locomotives that worked on it should become the last standard gauge locomotive to be used at a British colliery.

South Hetton Loco Sheds

All locomotives in the list below were based at South Hetton Loco Sheds. Locomotive transfers are shown only if the locomotive returned to South Hetton.

Bl	Blackhall Colliery, Blackhall
Bt	Bates Colliery, Blyth, Northumberland
E	Easington Colliery, Easington
EH	East Hetton Colliery, Kelloe
H	Hetton Loco Shed, Hetton
Ho	Horden Colliery, Horden
LEW	Lambton Engine Works, Philadelphia
P	Lambton Railway Loco Sheds, Philadelphia
SH	South Hetton Loco Sheds, South Hetton
Wt	Whittle Colliery, Newton-on-the-Moor, Northumberland

Gauge : 4ft 8½in

[69]	(No.9) SIR GEORGE		0-6-0	IC	RS	624	1848		
		reb	0-6-0ST	IC			1865	(a)	(1)
68	No.8		0-6-0	IC	RS	625	1848		
		reb	0-6-0ST	IC			1866		
		reb	0-6-0T	IC	South Hetton		1923	(a)	(1)
[70]	10		0-6-0	IC	SS		1857		
		reb	0-6-0ST	IC			1870	(a)	(2)
[66]	No.6		4-4-0T	OC	BP	425	1864		
		reb	0-6-0T	IC	South Hetton		1909	(a)	(2)
[62]	2 HAVERHILL		0-6-0ST	OC	SS	2358	1873	(a)	(2)
[61]	1		0-6-0ST	OC	BH	355	1875	(a)	(3)
64	(No.4)		0-6-0ST	IC	MW	697	1878		
		reb			South Hetton		1913	(b)	(4)
[65]	No.5		0-6-0ST	IC	MW	758	1881		
		reb			South Hetton		1910	(a)	(2)
[67]	No.7		0-6-0ST	IC	Joicey	305	1883		
		reb			South Hetton		1908		
		reb			M.Coulson		1935	(a)	(2)

[63]	(3) GLAMORGAN	0-6-0T	IC	HE	396	1886	(a)	(2)
71	(11)	0-6-0ST	IC	VF	5308	1945	(a)	

SH-LEW 12/1960-SH 5/8/1961 (5)

72	(12)	0-6-0ST	IC	VF	5309	1945	(a)	

SH-LEW /1954-P by 29/1/1955, almost certainly awaiting repairs-LEW by 4/1955 -SH after 11/1955, by 4/1956H after 7/1958, by 3/1959-SH c10/1959? -LEW by 4/1961-SH c10/1961-LEW repairs, begun 2/6/1964-SH 9/1965 (6)

19		0-4-0ST	OC	MW	344	1871	(c)	(7)
67	(70205) GORDON	0-6-2T	IC	Cdf	306	1897	(d)	

SH-believed to LEW, /1955, and returned (8)

36		0-4-0ST	OC	P	615	1896	(e)	(9)
62		0-6-0ST	IC	HE	3687	1949	New	

SH-LEW after 5/1956, by 8/1956-SH after 5/1957, by 22/7/1957 -P after 8/1960, by 4/1961-SH after 4/1961, by 10/1961 -LEW 20/12/1965-SH /1966 (10)

No.63		0-6-0ST	OC	RSHN	7600	1949	New	(11)
45		0-6-0ST	IC	HL	2932	1912	(f)	(12)
27		2-4-0	IC	RS	491	1845		
	reb	0-6-0	IC	Ghd		1864		
	reb	0-6-0ST	IC	Ghd		1873		
	reb	0-6-0T	IC	LEW		1904	(g)	(13)
51		0-6-0ST	IC	RSHN	7101	1943	(h)	(14)
68		0-6-0ST	IC	HE	3784	1953	New	

SH-LEW 10/1959-P 10/1960-SH 25/1/1961 (15)

69		0-6-0ST	IC	HE	3785	1953	New	

SH-P, to await repairs, 1/4/1963, but seen at work on 29/4/1963-LEW 30/5/1963; to Hunslet Engine Co Ltd, Leeds, 17/10/1963; boiler from 61 HE 3821/1954 sent to HE, Leeds, 11/11/1963, to be fitted with new tubes, firebox and HE mechanical stoker and to be fitted to this loco; rebuilt HE 59222/1964 (carried plate); records gave returned from HE, 2/5/1964-P (trials), 5/1964-SH 20/5/1964 N.B. mechanical stoker disconnected by 1/1967 (16)

61		0-6-0ST	IC	HE	3821	1954	New	

SH-P, to await repairs, 15/9/1961-LEW 8/1/1962-SH 17/12/1962 (15)

48		0-4-0ST	OC	HL	3544	1923	(j)	(17)
64		0-6-0DH		NBQ	27763	1959	New	

SH-BI 26/9/1968-Wt 9/3/1977-LEW 30/11/1979-SH 12/7/1980 -LEW 10/6/1982-SH 24/3/1983-LEW 26/8/1983-SH 10/11/1983 (18)

65		0-6-0DH		NBQ	27764	1959	New	

SH-LEW 23/3/1983-SH 31/1/1984 (18)

66		0-6-0DH		NBQ	27765	1959	New	

SH-LEW 12/1980-SH 24/8/1981-LEW 26/4/1982-SH 2/7/1982 (18)

59		0-6-0ST	IC	VF	5300	1945	(k)	(19)
67	(BETA)	0-6-0DH		NBQ	27717	1959	(m)	

SH-LEW 10/11/1976-SH 10/7/1978-LEW 15/7/1982-SH 8/12/1983 (18)

No.61	2100/519	0-6-0DH		AB	582	1973	New	(20)
(No.72)	2100/520	0-6-0DH		AB	583	1973	New	

SH-LEW 26/7/1981-Bt 18/12/1981-Ho 31/5/1985-SH, for spares, 30/9/1986 (21)

No.71	2100/521	0-6-0DH		AB	584	1973	New	(22)
No.69	2100/522	0-6-0DH		AB	585	1973	New	(23)
101		4wDM		FH	3922	1959	(n)	(24)
	20/110/705	0-6-0DH		AB	604	1976	New	

SH-LEW 20/9/1979-E 2/11/1979-EH 18/1/1980-LEW 26/3/1982-P 25/6/1982 -SH 27/9/1982 (21)

	20/110/706	0-6-0DH		AB	612	1976	New	

SH-LEW 11/11/1983-SH 10/7/1985 (21)

	2505/79	0-6-0DH		NBQ	27592	1957	(p)	(25)
	20/110/701	0-6-0DH		NBQ	27588	1957	(q)	

SH-LEW 25/6/1980-SH 28/1/1981 (26)

	20/109/08	0-6-0DH	AB	647	1979	(r)		
	SH-LEW 11/8/1983-Wa 20/1/1984-SH 11/7/1985							(21)
	20/110/712	0-6-0DH	AB	616	1977	(s)		
	SH-LEW 13/10/1983-E 1/4/1985							(27)
No.53		0-6-0DE	Dar		1961	(t)		(28)
	20/110/711	0-6-0DH	AB	615	1977	(u)		(29)
	20/110/708	0-6-0DH	AB	609	1976	(v)		(21)
No.594	20.110.997	0-6-0DH	AB	594	1974	(w)		(21)

(a) ex The South Hetton Coal Co Ltd, with the railway, 1/1/1947
(b) ex The South Hetton Coal Co Ltd, with the railway, 1/1/1947; at this date this loco was under repair at M.Coulson & Co, Spennymoor; returned to South Hetton, c7/1947
(c) ex Lambton Railway Loco Sheds, Philadelphia, 5/11/1947
(d) ex War Department, Longmoor Military Railway, Hampshire, 70205, 27/1/1948, per J.N.Connell, Coatbridge, Glasgow, Scotland, dealer, who purchased it in 12/1947; built originally by the Taff Vale Railway at their West Yard Works, Cardiff, Glamorgan, as 28 in its O1 class; became GWR 450 in 1922; withdrawn, 30/12/1926 and placed on Sales List; to Woolmer Instructional Military Railway, Hampshire, later the Longmoor Military Railway, 12/1927, and became WD 205, later WD 70205, and named GORDON; withdrawn by WD in 1945
(e) ex Lambton Railway Loco Sheds, Philadelphia, 17/3/1948
(f) ex Lambton Railway Loco Sheds, Philadelphia, 30/11/1949
(g) ex Lambton Railway Loco Sheds, Philadelphia, 17/3/1952
(h) ex Lambton Railway Loco Sheds, Philadelphia, 16/7/1952
(j) ex Hetton Loco Shed, Hetton Railway, Hetton, 8/4/1957
(k) ex Lambton Railway Loco Sheds, Philadelphia, 15/1/1959
(m) ex Brandon Pit House Colliery, near Meadowfield, 5/4/1968
(n) ex East Hetton Colliery, Kelloe, 10/1973; used to replace broken down creeper equipment which moved wagons under the screens at Hawthorn Combined Mine until equipment was repaired
(p) ex Horden Colliery, Horden, 2/4/1979
(q) ex Lambton Railway Loco Sheds, Philadelphia, 5/12/1979
(r) ex Lambton Railway Loco Sheds, Philadelphia, 5/6/1980
(s) ex Lambton Engine Works, Philadelphia, 19/5/1982
(t) ex Lambton Railway Loco Sheds, Philadelphia, 7/6/1982
(u) ex Lambton Engine Works, Philadelphia, 18/5/1983
(v) ex Lambton Engine Works, Philadelphia, 18/6/1985
(w) ex Lambton Engine Works, Philadelphia, 21/11/1986

(1) scrapped on site by D.Sep. Bowran Ltd, Gateshead, 11/1953
(2) locos 2, (3), 5, 6, 7 and 10 were scrapped on site by J.C.Wight Ltd, Pallion, Sunderland, between 18/5/1948 and 20/7/1948
(3) scrapped on site by D.Sep. Bowran Ltd, Gateshead, 3/1950
(4) scrapped on site by J.C.Wight Ltd, Pallion, Sunderland, 9/1954
(5) sold for scrap to D.Sep.Bowran Ltd, Gateshead, 17/3/1976; scrapped on site, 4/1976
(6) sold for scrap to C.Herring & Son Ltd, Hartlepool, 8/1973; sale rescinded; to Colne Valley Railway Preservation Society Ltd, Castle Hedingham, Essex, for preservation, 12/1973
(7) withdrawn from traffic, 11/1952 and cut up on site by D.Sep. Bowran Ltd, Gateshead, 8/1954
(8) boiler condemned, 10/1959. but not officially withdrawn until 10/1960; donated by NCB to British Transport Commission for preservation as the last surviving Taff Vale Railway locomotive in more or less original condition, 12/1961; left South Hetton on 29/1/1962 and arrived at British Railways, Western Region, Caerphilly Works, Caerphilly, Glamorgan 26/2/1962; to Caerphilly Railway Society; to Dean Forest Railway, Parkend, Gloucestershire, 16/5/1996
(9) to Lambton Railway Loco Sheds, Philadelphia, after 9/1950, by 6/1951; for subsequent history see chapter 9
(10) scrapped by C.Herring & Son Ltd, Hartlepool, 1/1977
(11) to Lambton Railway Loco Sheds, Philadelphia, 11/1958; for subsequent history see chapter 9
(12) to Lambton Railway Loco Sheds, Philadelphia, after 8/1951, by 6/1952; for subsequent history see chapter 9
(13) to Lambton Railway Loco Sheds, Philadelphia, 4/9/1953; for subsequent history see chapter 9
(14) to Lambton Railway Loco Sheds, Philadelphia, 12/1955; for subsequent history see chapter 9
(15) scrapped on site by C.Herring & Son Ltd, Hartlepool, 6/1974
(16) to Yorkshire Dales Railway, Embsay, North Yorkshire, for preservation, 5/1977; moved, 20/5/1977
(17) to Hetton Loco Shed, Hetton Railway, Hetton, 11/4/1957
(18) sold for scrap to C.H.Newton Jnr & Co Ltd, Durham, 20/9/1985; cutting up on site was completed as follows: 64/67, 29/11/1985, 65, 11/12/1985 and 66, 13/12/1985

(19) to Lambton Staiths Loco Shed, Sunderland, Lambton Railway, 4/4/1962; for subsequent history see chapter 9
(20) to Lambton Engine Works, Philadelphia, 24/9/1981; to Bates Colliery, Blyth, Northumberland, 25/2/1982; to Lambton Engine Works, Philadelphia, 16/7/1985; to Whittle Colliery, Newton-on-the-Moor, Northumberland, 6/9/1985; to Ellington South Coal Preparation Plant, Lynemouth, Northumberland, 25/3/1987; to Westoe Colliery, South Shields, 10/5/1988; sold for scrap to Booth Roe Metals Ltd, Rotherham, South Yorkshire, 6/1989
(21) to Hawthorn Loco Shed, 3/1987 (see below)
(22) to Wardley Loco Shed, Wardley, Monkton Railways, 6/12/1983; to Lambton Engine Works, Philadelphia, 19/1/1984; to Wardley Loco Shed, Wardley, Monkton Railways, 6/3/1985; to Whittle Colliery, Newton-on-the Moor, Northumberland, 16/7/1985; to Andrew, Barclay, Sons & Co Ltd, Kilmarnock, Ayrshire, Scotland, for rebuilding, 23/3/1987; rebuilt AB 6718/1987; to Lynemouth Coal Preparation Plant, Lynemouth (part of Ellington Colliery), Northumberland, 29/2/1988; to Hunslet-Barclay Ltd, Kilmarnock, for rebuilding, by 10/8/1990; rebuilt AB 6917/1990; to Ellington South Coal Preparation Plant, Lynemouth, c12/1990; to RJB Mining (UK) Ltd, with Ellington Colliery, 30/12/1994; to Harworth Stores, Harworth, Nottinghamshire, c/1997, to be used as source of spares for AB 615 (see 29 below); to Booth Roe Metals Ltd, Rotherham, South Yorkshire, for scrap, 8/2001 (arrived there, 27/8/2001, and cut up soon afterwards)
(23) to Bates Colliery, Blyth, Northumberland, 1/2/1981; to Lambton Engine Works, Philadelphia, 31/3/1981; to Lambton Railway Loco Sheds, Philadelphia, 29/9/1981; to Seaham Colliery, Seaham, 12/1981; to Dawdon Colliery, Seaham, 6/1/1982; to Ashington Colliery, Ashington, Northumberland, 7/10/1982; to Lambton Railway Loco Sheds, Philadelphia, 2/11/1982; to Bates Colliery, Blyth, Northumberland, 1/5/1983; to Ashington Colliery, Ashington, Northumberland, 2/10/1985; to Seaham Colliery, Seaham, 29/3/1986; to Vane Tempest Colliery, Seaham, for repairs, 23/1/1987; to Seaham Colliery, Seaham, 3/1987, by 11/3/1987; sold for scrap to C.F.Booth (Rotherham) Ltd, Rotherham, South Yorkshire, 9/1987, and moved to Rotherham for cutting up, 4/11/1987
(24) to Thornley Coal Preparation Plant, Thornley, 31/10/1974; for subsequent history see chapter 3
(25) transmission, springs and side rods stripped off, 2/1980, and frame (with main drive) and wheels sent to Lambton Engine Works, Philadelphia, for further stripping, 2/1980; salvage cancelled by 12/1980; scrapped, c1/1981
(26) stripped for spares; remainder scrapped on site by D.Short Ltd, North Shields, Tyne & Wear, 12/1983
(27) to Douglas Engineering Services Ltd, Middlesbrough, North Yorkshire. 2/1989, where it was stored, and then subsequently re-purchased by British Coal North East Group, for Hawthorn Loco Shed (see below)
(28) to Lambton Engine Works, Philadelphia, 27/9/1982; for subsequent history see chapter 9
(29) to Lambton Engine Works, Philadelphia, 17/6/1985; to Whittle Colliery, Newton-on-the-Moor, Northumberland, 13/9/1985; to Andrew Barclay, Sons & Co Ltd, Kilmarnock, Ayrshire, Scotland, for rebuilding, 25/3/1987; rebuilt AB 6719/1987; to Lynemouth Coal Preparation Plant (part of Ellington Colliery), Lynemouth, Northumberland, 3/2/1988; to RJB Mining (UK) Ltd, with Ellington Colliery, 30/12/1994; to Gascoigne Wood Colliery, South Milford, North Yorkshire, 12/3/1996; still there in June 2004, the last standard gauge locomotive in use at a British colliery.

Hawthorn Loco Shed
Gauge : 4ft 8½in

	2120/520	0-6-0DH	AB	583	1973	(a)	(1)
No.594	20.110.997	0-6-0DH	AB	594	1974	(b)	(2)
	20/110/705	0-6-0DH	AB	604	1976	(b)	(1)
	20/110/708	0-6-0DH	AB	609	1976	(b)	(1)
	20/110/706	0-6-0DH	AB	612	1976	(b)	(3)
	20/109/089	0-6-0DH	AB	647	1979	(b)	(4)
	2120/211	0-6-0DH	AB	514	1966	(c)	(1)
	20/110/712	0-6-0DH	AB	616	1976	(d)	(5)

(a) ex South Hetton Loco Sheds, South Hetton, 3/1987; being used as source of spares
(b) ex South Hetton Loco Sheds, South Hetton, 3/1987
(c) ex Ashington Colliery, Ashington, Northumberland, 15/2/1988, for cannibalisation only
(d) ex Douglas Engineering Services Ltd, Middlesbrough, North Yorkshire, in store, 4/1990; this loco had previously worked at South Hetton – see list above

(1) scrapped on site by M.J.K.Demolition Ltd, Esh Winning, near Durham, in week ending 29th May 1992
(2) to Shropshire Loco Collection, near Wellington, Shropshire, for preservation, 4/1992; moved between 28/4/1992 and 30/4/1992; to S&D Locomotive Co Ltd, c6/2000 (did not move from site); to Harry Needle Railroad Co, and moved to Barrow Hill Loco Shed, Staveley, Derbyshire, 24/1/2001
(3) to Shropshire Loco Collection, near Wellington, Shropshire, for preservation, 4/1992; moved between 28/4/1992 and 30/4/1992; to S&D Locomotive Co Ltd, c6/2000 (did not move from site); to Harry Needle Railroad Co, and moved to Barrow Hill Loco Shed, Staveley, Derbyshire.

(4) to Shropshire Loco Collection, near Wellington, Shropshire, for preservation, 4/1992; moved between 28/4/1992 and 30/4/1992; to S&D Locomotive Co Ltd, c6/2000 (did not move from site); to Harry Needle Railroad Co.
(5) to Shropshire Loco Collection, near Wellington, Shropshire, for preservation, 4/1992; moved between 28/4/1992 and 30/4/1992; to S&D Locomotive Co Ltd, c6/2000 (did not move from site); to Harry Needle Railroad Co, and moved to Barrow Hill Loco Shed, Staveley, Derbyshire, in week ending 5/7/2002

Locomotives used at Hawthorn Coking Plant, but only to shunt the coke car
National Smokeless Fuels Ltd from 1/4/1973
NCB Coal Products Division from 1/1/1963
previously **NCB Durham Division No.2 (Mid-East Durham) Area**

Gauge : 4ft 8½in

		0-4-0WE	RSHN	7886	1958	New	(1)
		0-4-0DH	HE	6263	1964	(a)	(2)

(a) ex Norwood Coking Plant, Dunston, 1/1973

(1) to Avenue Coking Plant, Wingerworth, Derbyshire, 12/1988
(2) to Bowes Railway Co Ltd, Bowes Railway Centre, Springwell, Gateshead, 11/1988, for preservation; moved, 7/12/1988

250. The numberplate for No.7, Joicey 305/1883, 10th October 1947.

Chapter Fourteen
The South Shields, Marsden & Whitburn Colliery Railway
called the Marsden Railway until about 1894

OWNERS BEFORE 1947
The Harton Coal Co Ltd until 1/1/1947 (**The Harton Coal Co** until 6/8/1885)
subsidiary of Stephenson, Clarke & Co Ltd from 1927, which became Stephenson, Clarke & Associated Companies Ltd in 1928 and which was acquired by Powell Duffryn Steam Coal Co Ltd from 21/12/1928
The Whitburn Coal Co Ltd (formed in 1873) until 1891

Coal mining in the South Shields area was begun in 1810 by Simon Temple, who sank the Manor Wallsend Colliery, sometimes known as the Templetown Pit (NZ 356656) and shipped his coal at his Templetown Staiths (NZ 354662) via a ½ mile waggonway. This was a short-lived venture, and in 1819 the large royalty passed to the brothers John and Robert Brandling. In 1822 they began sinking **ST. HILDA COLLIERY** (NZ 361667), named after a nearby church and much closer to the centre of the town. This was opened in 1825 and linked to the erstwhile Templetown Staiths, now St.Hilda's Staiths, by a winding waggonway about a mile long, joining the former Templetown waggonway near to the staiths. This waggonway was 3ft 6in gauge and worked by horses. The site of the old colliery was retained for some years, latterly used as a coal depot. On 30th August 1835 the brothers opened their public railway, the Brandling Junction Railway, its main line running from Gateshead to

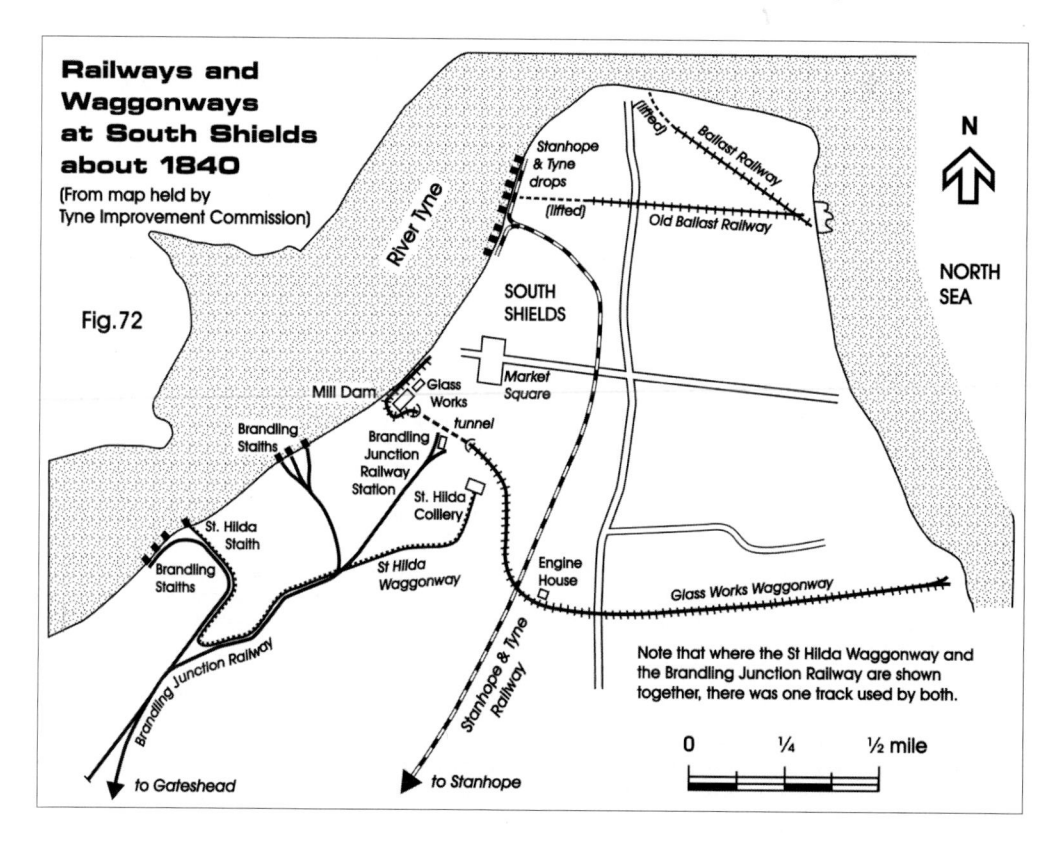

Fig.72 Railways and Waggonways at South Shields about 1840 (From map held by Tyne Improvement Commission)

South Shields, with the station at the latter, known as High Shields Station, being adjacent to the St.Hilda's Staith. Various branches were either acquired or built, the most important being a line to Monkwearmouth (Sunderland), opened in August 1839.

With their railway opened the brothers returned to the development of their mining interests, the royalty covering 9,000 acres. They joined Nicholas Wood (see Chapters 2 and 8), Nicholas Anderson and Ralph Philipson, and on 10th May 1841 began the sinking of **HARTON COLLIERY** (NZ 362642). During the sinking the Brandlings sold their share to the other partners, who having first begun trading as Wood, Philipson & Co, changed their title in 1842 to The Harton Coal Co. Coal was won on 8th July 1844 at 215 fathoms, then the deepest pit on the Tyne. The colliery lay alongside the Brandling Junction Railway's Monkwearmouth line, about a mile south of the subsequent Tyne Dock Station. The 1st edition Ordnance Survey calls the colliery Harton & Whitburn Colliery, though this appears to be the only reference to such a name.

Meanwhile the Brandling Junction Railway was faced with an increasing demand for better facilities in South Shields. To provide a better passenger service a new line was built in 1842 from a junction near the former Templetown Colliery to a new station called South Shields, closer to the centre of the town. From this new line the Railway intended to provide sidings and new coal staiths; but, unable to do so immediately, the Railway came to an agreement with the Harton Coal Co for the use of St.Hilda Staith. To do this a link was put in from near the 1835 station, the Railway company also converting the St.Hilda waggonway to 4ft 8½ in gauge to avoid two gauges at the staith. This rebuilding included four passing loops for its horse-drawn traffic.

The southern area of the royalty was too far away to reach from Harton Colliery, so to work this area a new colliery, **BOLDON COLLIERY** (NZ 347623), was opened on 26th July 1869. This lay alongside the NER Pontop & South Shields Branch near to Brockley Whins South Junction, and its traffic was worked by the NER. At least some of this was worked to St.Hilda Staith. This was the standard nineteenth century design in the North-East, where the waggon was run on to a balanced platform, lowered out over the ship, the bottom doors opened to discharge the coal into the hold and then brought back to the riverbank. This meant that the staith became increasingly congested.

Huge reserves of coal were believed to lie along the coast and for at least three miles out to sea, but a major geological fault east of St.Hilda Colliery meant two new coastal collieries would be needed to work them, one at the Bents, not far from the mouth of the River Tyne, and one north of Whitburn, about three miles to the south. The Harton partners appear to have anticipated an expensive sinking because of the likely depth of the coal, and so to safeguard the rest of the business they set up in 1873 **The Whitburn Coal Co Ltd**. One recent researcher has suggested that the partners set up a second company, The Harton & Hilda Coal Co, to run St.Hilda, Harton and Boldon Collieries, with the original company becoming, presumably, simply a holding company. On balance, it would seem that this was not the case, and that The Harton Coal Co continued to manage its other collieries as before.

On 14th July 1874 The Whitburn Coal Co Ltd began sinking **WHITBURN COLLIERY** (NZ 408637), in exposed, thinly-populated countryside with a few country lanes. Although the most direct route to reach the NER was directly west to Harton Colliery, this was obstructed by the Cleadon Hills, and so to serve the new colliery the company made a wayleave agreement with the Dean & Chapter of Durham, the owners of the land, to construct a single line branch from a point on the NER Pontop & South Shields Branch north of Tyne Dock, to be called Whitburn Colliery Junction, to run north-eastwards and then curve round south of South Shields to run south-eastwards to the colliery, a distance of 3 miles 7 furlongs and 1½ chains, virtually four miles. One source has suggested that the line was still under construction in 1878; but given that the sinking had then been underway for four years and the company had also to construct a new village, called Marsden, adjacent to the new colliery, it would seem more likely that the railway was built during 1874 but that the formalities between the Harton and Whitburn companies to cover it were not agreed until 1878. The locomotives acquired for the new line were of course owned by The Whitburn Coal Co Ltd – indeed, at this time the Harton company did not own any locomotives.

Around the new colliery there were large outcrops of magnesian limestone. Two small quarries between the colliery and the sea were almost worked out, and could be used for colliery waste; but about ½ mile to the north was a very large area of stone. So in 1874 the company leased all this, and developed what was at first known as **MARSDEN QUARRY** (NZ 405641) to the west of the line, together with a battery of seven large kilns.

The original sinking proved very difficult because of water and quicksand, justifying the company's original caution. After a halt, it was re-commenced in 1877, with the pumps raising 12,000 gallons a minute, and Whitburn Colliery eventually produced its first coal on 1st May 1879. Soon afterwards the railway to it was given the title of **THE MARSDEN RAILWAY**.

On 13th November 1885 the company's solicitors wrote to the Railway Department of the Board of Trade enquiring what "preliminaries might be requisite" regarding the carrying of passengers on the railway. The letter is vague, perhaps deliberately, as to whether passengers were actually being carried, but it would seem almost certain that they were, and perhaps had been for some time. Many men from South Shields worked at the colliery and would clearly not have taken kindly to walking three or four miles to and from work, quite apart from the families at Marsden wishing to travel to South Shields. Curiously, it took the Board of Trade 19 months before Major General Hutchinson was instructed to inspect the 2¾ miles over which the passenger service ran. His report, dated 20th June 1887, fails almost every aspect of the line; although there would appear to have been platforms at the termini, there were no buildings at all on them, there was no signalling, mile posts or gradient posts, the track and its ballasting was inadequate, and there were not even any operating rules.

The passenger service ceased while all the improvements were made, and Major General Hutchinson gave his approval eight months later. The two stations, **SOUTH SHIELDS** (NZ 369666) and **MARSDEN** (NZ 404645), now had station buildings with shelters, booking offices and toilets and also had signal boxes, that at South Shields having 12 levers and that at Marsden 15 levers. The first passenger train following approval ran on 19th March 1888, and a Sunday service was added in September 1888. The earliest surviving timetable, dated January 1890, lists the service as follows:

Weekday trains depart South Shields
8.15, 10.00 am, 12.50, 1.00 (NS), 3.15, 4.35, 6.15, 9.30 pm
Weekday trains depart Marsden
9.15, 11.55 am (NS), 12.35, 2.45, 4.15, 5.35, 9.00 pm
(NS = Not Saturdays)
Sunday trains depart South Shields
2.00, 3.00, 5.00, 6.00, 7.00, 9.30 pm
Sunday trains depart Marsden
1.00, 2.30, 4.30, 5.30, 6.30, 9.00pm

The basic fares were 3rd class adult return 6d, single 4d, with children half fare. A generous time of ten minutes was allowed for the 2¾ journey.

However, these were only the times and charges for the general public. For pit and quarry workers separate trains were run, travelling a further 1,200 yards beyond Marsden Station to a platform (NZ 406638) at Whitburn Colliery itself, situated on the eastern side of the northern end of the colliery yard. Since workmen travelled free, neither these trains nor the Whitburn Colliery platform came within the Board of Trade approval. Just to the west of the platform was a two-road **loco shed** (NZ 406637). At this period the traffic was handled by 0-6-0STs, although a 0-6-2T was added to the fleet in 1898. So far as is known, the locomotives worked coal trains as far as the sidings at Whitburn Colliery Junction, where the NER took over for the short distance on to Tyne Dock.

In 1889 a small chemical works was opened ½ mile to the south of Whitburn Colliery, and the railway was extended to serve it. In 1895 this became the **North Eastern Paper Mills** (NZ 411632) of **The North Eastern Paper Co Ltd**. This company was owned by The Harton Coal Co Ltd, an unusual venture for a North-East colliery company. This works took coal from the colliery and dispatched newsprint to be distributed all over the British Isles, whilst its workers also increased the passenger service numbers. So far as is known, the Railway shunted the works, although a photograph of 1934 shows a mysterious AB 0-4-0ST at Marsden which may have worked at the paper mill, which closed in that year.

Trains on the Railway were initially controlled by the staff and ticket system, but about 1900 the company installed electric staff instruments, with each machine capable of of accommodating 18 staffs at a time in a long vertical slot. About the same time many of the points affecting main line working but too far to be controlled from the signal boxes were fitted with Annett's locks, with the keys for these locks attached to the train staffs by brass rings, so that they could only be used to operate the points with the knowledge of the signalman.

Meanwhile, back in South Shields, where the NER now controlled all the public railways, the NER in 1879 extended the former Brandling Junction line to link to the former Pontop & South Shields line and opened a third new station. This extension left the Pontop & South Shields line just north of Harton Junction and made a junction with the St.Hilda line at St.Hilda Junction, where interchange sidings known as the Hilda Hole Sidings were built. After crossing over this line three times and through yet another station (High Shields), a 14-arch viaduct over the east end of St.Hilda Colliery yard was needed to rejoin the Pontop & South Shields line, in return for which the NER linked the colliery to the new line at Garden Lane Junction.

In 1891 The Harton Coal Co Ltd dissolved The Whitburn Coal Co Ltd and merged the Whitburn business into its other activities. By this date the company had four excellent collieries, but was facing severe transport and shipping problems. None of the collieries had any connection with any of the others; the St.Hilda Staiths were unable to handle all the coal to be shipped and large sums were being paid to the NER to handle the traffic, including shipment at Tyne Dock.

Then came a way forward, offered by the demise of the Tyne Plate Glass Co Ltd. This company's works, with its quay, was situated about 300 yards downstream of St.Hilda Staith and, equally importantly, the firm had also owned a single track railway which ran from the quay, then through a narrow tunnel before passing alongside St.Hilda Colliery to a sand quarry on the Bents. This had latterly been operated by two locomotives, very much cut down to pass through the tunnel. The Harton Coal Co Ltd purchased all of this, including the two locomotives, in 1892. The company then opened negotiations with South Shields Corporation, which led in February 1896 to the "Harton Agreement", incorporated later that year in the South Shields Corporation Act. The huge modernisation and railway programme now agreed may be summarised as follows, with the stages of completion:

Rebuilding of the four collieries, 1895-1910

The Harton Coal Co Ltd's position in 1891

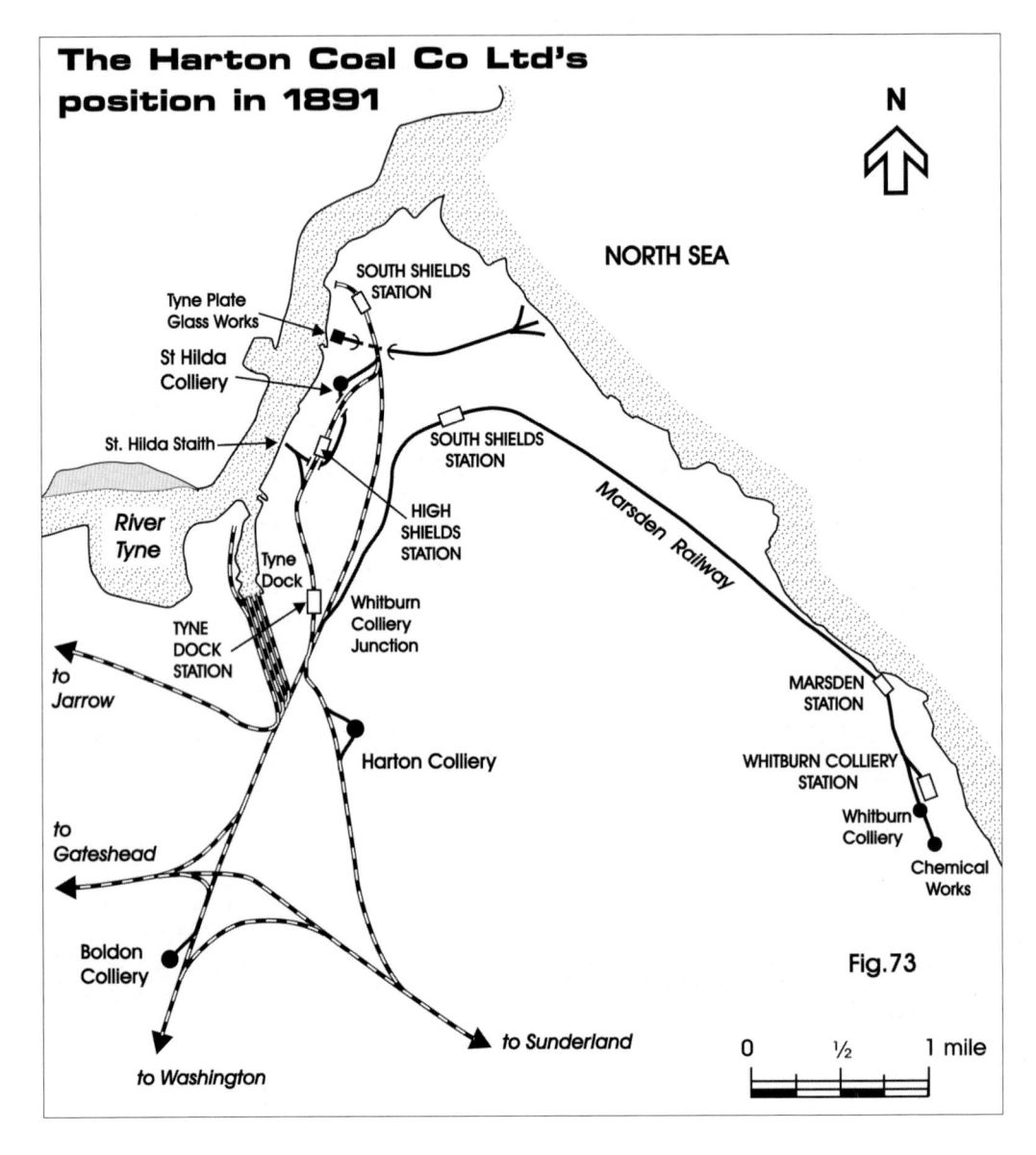

Fig.73

Up-grading of the Marsden Railway, 1900
Reconstruction of the Tyne Plate Glass Co's railway, 1902-1903
Construction of new staiths on the Tyne Plate Glass Co's quay, 1903-1904
Conversion of the St.Hilda waggonway to railway operation, 1906-1908
Widening of part of the railway between Dean Road sidings and Westoe Lane to accommodate double track, 1907-1908
Construction of a new railway from Harton Colliery to Whitburn Junction, 1908-1910
Construction of a new colliery at Bent House Farm, 1909-1913

To this new St.Hilda Staiths had to be added when the old staiths were destroyed by a fire spreading from a ship in 1894.

In 1895 a major rebuilding of the surface of Whitburn Colliery was begun. As part of this the passenger platform and its adjacent locomotive shed were demolished to make way for new sidings. To replace them a **WHITBURN COLLIERY platform** (NZ 406636) was built on the western side of the colliery, near the offices, and a **new 2-road loco shed** was built at the southern end of the colliery (NZ 407635).

Some time during the 1890s the company renamed the line the **SOUTH SHIELDS, MARSDEN & WHITBURN COLLIERY RAILWAY** (SSM&WCR); this name is shown on the 2nd edition O.S. map, published in 1897. Although this name was not carried on the coaches and locomotive tenders,

251. Whitburn Colliery, with 10, formerly Blyth & Tyne Railway No.3 and acquired from the NER in April 1900, on a coal train and 2, BH 504/1879, on a passenger train in the original platform. The original loco shed stood on the site of the four-arched building behind the passenger train.

which were simply painted HCC, it was included around the perimeter of the cast locomotive number plates carried on the sides of the cabs. When this practice was introduced is not known. The name was also printed on the tickets. It did not catch on with local people, who always referred to the passenger service as the 'Marsden Rattler'. It was not always used by the company either, which as late as 1936 still included "The Marsden Railway" on its letterhead!

The Railway itself was considerably up-graded. Both local people and holiday makers were using the Railway to visit Marsden Bay, which included a grotto built into the cliffs, sea bird nesting sites, Marsden Rock and a small hotel. So in 1900 the company completely rebuilt the station buildings at South Shields to provide a fine new station, now called **WESTOE LANE**, although South Shields, or rather 'Shields', was still used on the tickets. A small halt, called **MARSDEN COTTAGE** (NZ 392655), was built about ¾ mile north of Marsden itself, a slightly curious choice of site as there was little local population and also left visitors quite a walk to reach Marsden Bay. The platform – a

252. Westoe Lane Station in 1907, looking north before the overhead wires were erected for the electric system. The small building with the pitched roof in the centre of the station is the signal box.

'request stop' - was only long enough for one carriage, and for many years its only building was a brick shelter 6 feet long, 4 feet wide and 8 feet high. For many years it enjoyed, correctly or otherwise, the title of 'the smallest station in Britain'.

It was also in 1900 that the first tender locomotives were purchased for the line, second-hand from the North Eastern Railway, like all the tender locomotives to follow. The tender locomotives handled all the traffic, passenger and coal, between Whitburn and South Shields, with the tank locomotives used to shunt Marsden Quarry and Whitburn Colliery.

There was clearly a great deal of development to undertake in South Shields. Almost certainly the first was to link the SSM&WCR to the former Tyne Plate Glass Co Ltd's line. This was done by constructing a short line from just north-east of Westoe Lane Station, then skirting the eastern boundary of Westoe Cemetary to join its neighbour at the top of Erskine Bank, a gradient once worked by a stationary engine, which ran alongside Erskine Road. This had also been done by 1897. St. Hilda Colliery was also linked to the line by this date, after some difficult engineering. As noted above, the NER line to South Shields ran past the eastern side of the colliery yard on a viaduct, the two being connected to the north at Garden Lane Junction, while the St. Hilda waggonway passed underneath the viaduct en route to the St.Hilda Staiths. The colliery was also now surrounded by town development and space was severely restricted. The only way to link the yard to the former Glass Co's line was to construct a very tight 360 degree spiral down to it, joining just to the north of the tunnel which took it underneath the yard.

The re-modelling of the line itself involved some major engineering work, done mostly by R.W.Ridley & Sons (Contractors) Ltd, with work starting about 1902. The original waggonway tunnel up from the glass works was reduced from 216 yards to 172 yards and re-bored to give a new height of 10ft 7in, in order for the 10½ ton hopper wagons, now being purchased from the NER to replace the chaldron waggons, to pass through. Even so, the gradient in part of the tunnel was 1 in 28. This was followed by the St.Hilda tunnel mentioned above, already rebuilt, and the junction of the link to St.Hilda Colliery. Beyond this the original railway climbed at various gradients up Erskine Bank, mentioned above, passing under five bridges, to reach the junction with the SSM&WCR before continuing on to the Bents. To accommodate modern traffic the bridges were rebuilt and the cutting widened, though still single line, and deepened, to give a steady gradient of 1 in 38.

With this work nearing completion, work began on the river frontage, extending it 50 feet out into the river, with a berth length of 635 feet and allowing ships up to 10,000 tons to berth regardless of the tide. Much of the former glass works was demolished, but instead of staiths with spouts, the now-standard design in the North-East, the company installed two huge steam cranes. These were mounted on a track 330ft long with a gauge of 21 feet, ran on two sets of twelve wheels and used

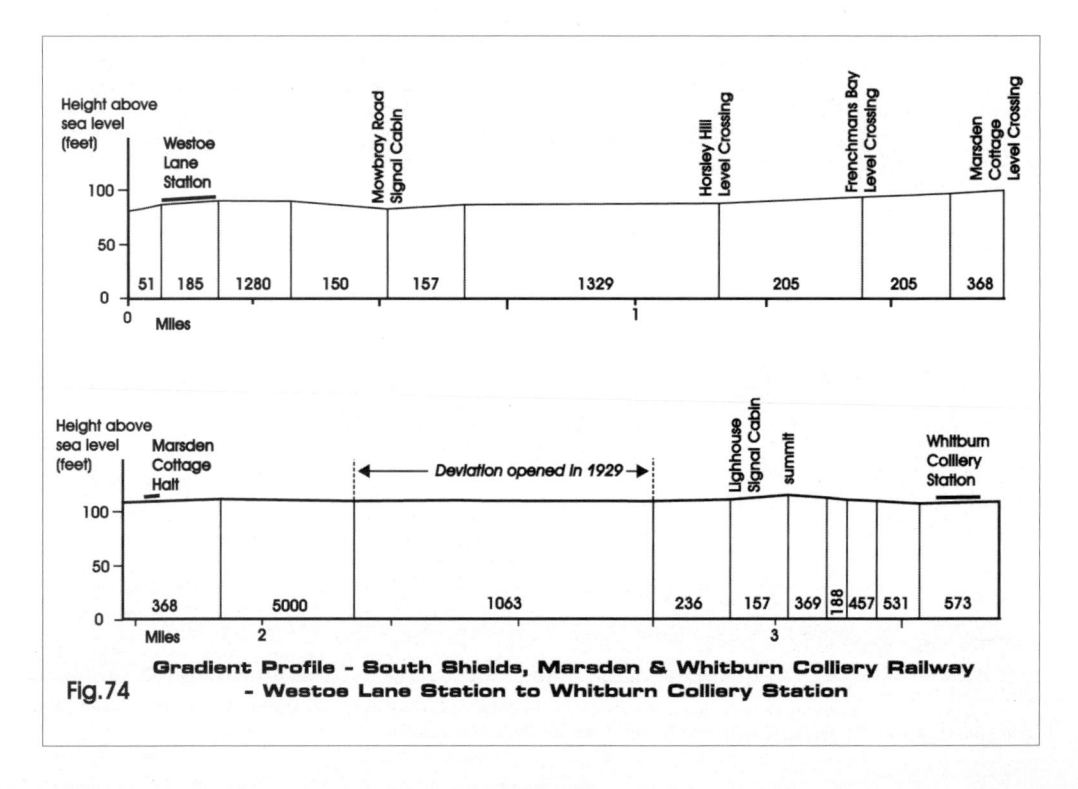

Fig.74 Gradient Profile - South Shields, Marsden & Whitburn Colliery Railway - Westoe Lane Station to Whitburn Colliery Station

253. 6, RS 2056/1872, formerly NER 786, on a passenger train at Westoe Lane Station on 22nd July 1912, a month after she was purchased.

no fewer than four steam engines to undertake all the operations. Wagons were run one at a time on to a cradle and then lifted out over the ship's hold and emptied, before being returned to their rails and running forward by gravity to a headshunt. They soon became known as **Harton Low Staiths** (NZ 359670). The first vessel was loaded at these staiths on 9th March 1904. Although such cranes were used at some Scottish ports, here the system proved too slow to handle the volume of traffic, and in 1913 the company decided to replace them with electrically-operated flight conveyors. This work had not been completed when the staiths were burned down, on 25th January 1914. Apart from installing new conveyors, the rebuilding allowed the company to introduce a very much better gravity-fed railway system, with the wagons discharging into hoppers which fed the conveyors. This system was so much better that on good days over 5,000 tons could be shipped. A few of the Glass Co's buildings were retained, one near the bottom of the tunnel being converted into a **WAGON SHOP** (NZ 359669).

The new staiths operational, the company could next turn to the rebuilding of the St.Hilda waggonway. The first step was to construct exchange sidings laid out for steam locomotive operation to the north of the St.Hilda Junction with the NER to allow steam locomotive working between what became known as the Hilda Hole sidings and the newly-named **HARTON HIGH STAITH**. Horses were still being used on the line from St.Hilda Colliery to Hilda Hole Sidings, 17 horses working a nine-hour shift. Later in 1906 this was closed and rebuilt by South Shields Corporation, using the contractor Gustavus Bailey. The biggest job was the replacement of the level crossing over Station Road, adjacent to the colliery, by a new tunnel, Slaughterhouse Tunnel, which was 60 yards long and constructed by the cut-and-cover method. A new spur was also built at Portberry Street to give St.Hilda Colliery traffic direct access to the Hilda Hole sidings. The rebuilt line finally re-opened in November 1908, 16 months late and over budget.

Work was still in progress on the St.Hilda line when work was also started on converting the section between Benthouse, Westoe Lane and Whitburn Colliery Junction to double track. Originally this was intended to be double track throughout, but in the event a deep and narrow cutting 366 yards long near Laygate Lane remained single track. At the end of this section the former Whitburn Colliery Junction was closed and extensive sidings, known as the Dean Road Sidings, were built for the exchange of Boldon Colliery and NER traffic, with a new junction being installed a short distance south called simply Whitburn Junction.

Serious problems – the adoption of electrification
Even before all this work was completed it was becoming increasingly clear to the company that the sections already in use were causing very serious problems. With the development of steam working in South Shields, a 2-road **loco shed** had been built at St.Hilda Colliery. The two locomotives taken over from the Tyne Plate Glass Co Ltd were too small to work other than at the colliery and, needing locomotives to work at the Low Staiths, Nos.3 and 4 were rebuilt in cut-down format to pass through the tunnel to work there. But they

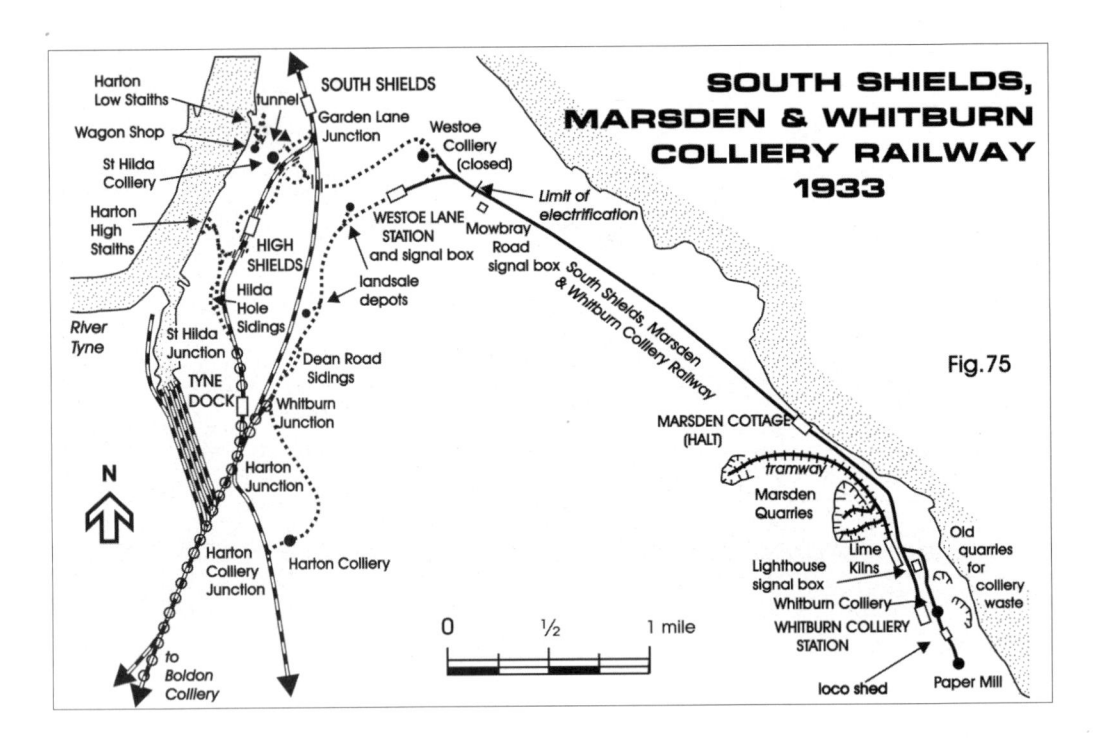

Fig.75 SOUTH SHIELDS, MARSDEN & WHITBURN COLLIERY RAILWAY 1933

proved underpowered for the work, whilst the need to return to the shed for re-fuelling caused shunting to be held up. Some of the gradients were proving too severe, the curves were very tight in places, the cuttings, in deep shadow, frequently suffered from wet rails, while local residents complained about noise and dirt. To design a steam locomotive with a height limit of less than 10ft 7in, capable of negotiating severe curves and sufficiently powerful to work over the steep gradients with lengthy trains seemed unlikely; the only feasible solution was electrification.

The leading electrical engineers at this time were in Germany, and the company approached Siemens-Schuckert Elektricitats AG in Munich. The decision was made to electrify the whole system from Benthouse southwards, although the passenger service would be allowed under wires to reach Westoe Lane Station. Now that Benthouse would become the interchange point between steam and electric working, new exchange sidings would be needed here. Work began early in 1908 and the first electrically-hauled revenue-earning train ran from Benthouse to the Low Staiths on 14th December 1908.

The subsequent history of the electrified section can be found in Chapter 15.

The company thus developed an extensive electric system around South Shields, which was served by its steam trains from Whitburn over the South Shields, Marsden & Whitburn Colliery Railway and also from Boldon Colliery. Boldon Colliery lay two miles south of the main system, and the company decided, perhaps because of the very heavy financial outlay elsewhere, not to build its own branch down to the colliery. Instead it obtained running powers over the NER Pontop & South Shields branch between Boldon and Harton Junction, whence trains could be routed along the former Brandling Junction Railway to reach Hilda Hole Sidings for shipment at the High Staith or continue along the Pontop & South Shields line to Whitburn Junction to reach Dean Sidings for shipment at the Low Staiths.

With electrification well underway, the company announced on 21st May 1909 that the construction of its fifth colliery, at Benthouse, would commence immediately. The sinking of a single shaft was completed in 1911. This was originally called **BENTHOUSE COLLIERY** (NZ 373368), but before long this name had been replaced by **WESTOE COLLIERY**. With both exchange sidings and a colliery now at Benthouse, it was clearly essential to control the traffic safely, and so a new signalbox was installed, sanctioned by the Board of Trade on 3rd November 1911. This box, built and equipped like all the others used on the system by the Railway Signal Co Ltd of Fazackerley in Lancashire, was called **Mowbray Road Bridge Signalbox** (NZ 375666). This had 12 levers, although four were spare. A zero mile post 120 yards west of Westoe Lane Station marked the official beginning of the Railway, and latterly the first 1,140 yards were also electrified. Steam locomotives from Whitburn had therefore to work "under the wires" to bring their trains in to the sidings at Benthouse, where the electric locomotives took over. However, the platform road at Westoe Lane Station remained un-wired.

254. The Chapman & Furneaux catalogue photograph of No.7, CF 1158/1898. She was sold to John Bowes & Partners Ltd for the Pontop & Jarrow Railway in 1912.

It may well have been that initially both steam and electric locomotives were stationed at the St.Hilda loco shed; but this was clearly an unsatisfactory arrangement, only to be continued until all of the electric locomotives had been delivered. Three steam locomotives were disposed of in 1910, and it would seem likely that this was also when St.Hilda shed became all electric.

Thus matters remained until 1923, when South Shields Borough Council and South Shields Rural District Council resolved to construct a new road 2½ miles long between South Shields and Marsden, to be undertaken with Government support to reduce local unemployment. To manage the project the two councils set up the Coast Road Joint Committee, which was constituted on 13th May 1924. To accommodate the route of the road The Harton Coal Co Ltd agreed to let the route of the Railway be moved inland about 100 yards for a distance of 1050 yards. This would involve the construction of a cutting, the Grotto cutting, as it became known, 700 yards long, 80 feet wide and 18

255. 10, RWH 1564/1873, formerly NER 827 of the 398 class, at Marsden Station on 8th May 1923 with what appears to be a train of thirteen coaches.

WESTOE LANE

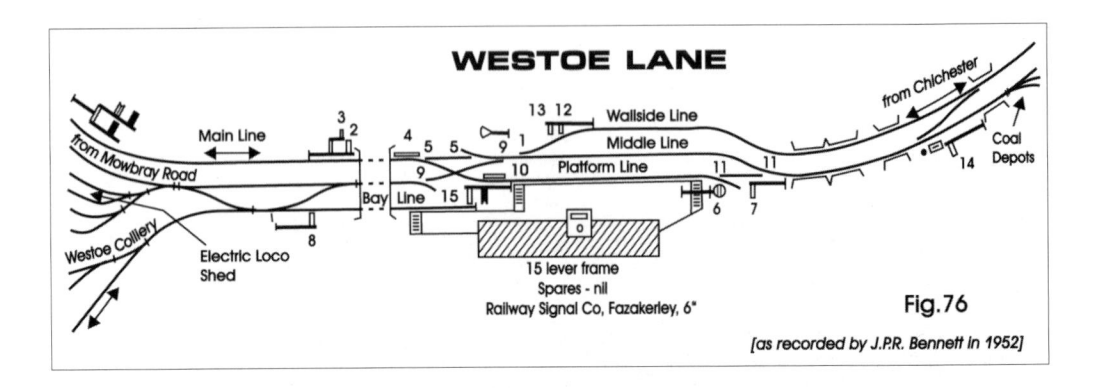

Fig. 76

[as recorded by J.P.R. Bennett in 1952]

feet deep. Work began on 23rd June 1924. Construction was closed down on 11th September 1926 through lack of materials, but was then unable to re-start due to financial problems, not least the increasing cost of the Lighthouse bridge to carry the railway over the road south of Marsden. Eventually the Ministry of Transport agreed to fund the outstanding cost, together with a ½ mile extension to Whitburn village. Work recommenced in November 1928 and the road was officially opened on 2nd November 1929. It is now part of the A183.

For the Railway much more was involved than the re-alignment of 1050 yards. Marsden Station was cleared to make way for the road, and the former miners' platform became **WHITBURN COLLIERY STATION** (NZ 407635), with the public passenger service extended to it. Apart from improving the actual platform, made of timber and earth and 40 feet long, it would seem that the only other change from what had been there previously was the provision of a ticket booth. With miners' baths being opened in 1930 on the opposite side of the road to the station, a concrete footbridge was built from the baths, over the road and the track to the platform. The now-demolished Marsden signal box was replaced by a larger and very substantial building to the south of the lime kilns, known as the **Lighthouse Signalbox** (NZ 406641). This had 26 levers, and controlled the link into Marsden Quarry and a landsale depot, as well as the northern end

256. 8, RS 1973/1870, formerly NER 718 of the 708 class, at Whitburn Colliery on 3rd August 1924.

257. 6, RS 2587/1884, formerly LNER 1486 of the J22 class, approaches Marsden Cottage Station, "the smallest station in England" in the early 1930s.

of Whitburn Colliery. To cover these changes, and to be able to run its new route officially as a Light Railway when it was completed, The Harton Coal Co Ltd applied for a Light Railway Order from the Ministry of Transport, which was issued on 7th August 1926. With the proposed extension of the passenger service to Whitburn Colliery Station, this section was at last inspected on 28th March 1929, and all railway traffic, including the passenger service, began using the new route on 9th April 1929. With the new passenger route now ½ mile longer the journey time for passenger trains was increased from 10 to 12 minutes.

The passenger timetable for 1930 was as follows:

Weekday trains depart Westoe Lane
6.05, 6.35, 9.05, 9.50, 10.50 am, 12.30, 2.15, 4.20, 5.05, 8.40, 10.15 pm

Weekday trains depart Whitburn Colliery
6.20, 7.20, 10.10 am, 12.15, 1.00, 1.35, 2.40, 4.45, 5.25, 9.10 pm

Saturday trains depart Westoe Lane
5.30 am, 12.35, 1.30, 5.30, 8.40, 9.30 pm

Saturday trains depart Whitburn Colliery
5.15, 7.20, 11.30 am, 1.15, 4.20, 6.00, 9.15 pm

Sunday trains depart Westoe Lane
7.10, 10.15 am, 12.30, 1.30, 3.40, 5.30, 8.40, 9.30 pm

Sunday trains depart Whitburn Colliery
6.05, 9.45 am, 12.10, 2.10, 4.30, 6.10, 10.00 pm

In fact, the opening of the new road and the Corporation bus service along it, had already reduced the number of passengers using the service, which dwindled still further with the introduction of trolleybuses in stages down to Marsden. The Railway must also surely have been

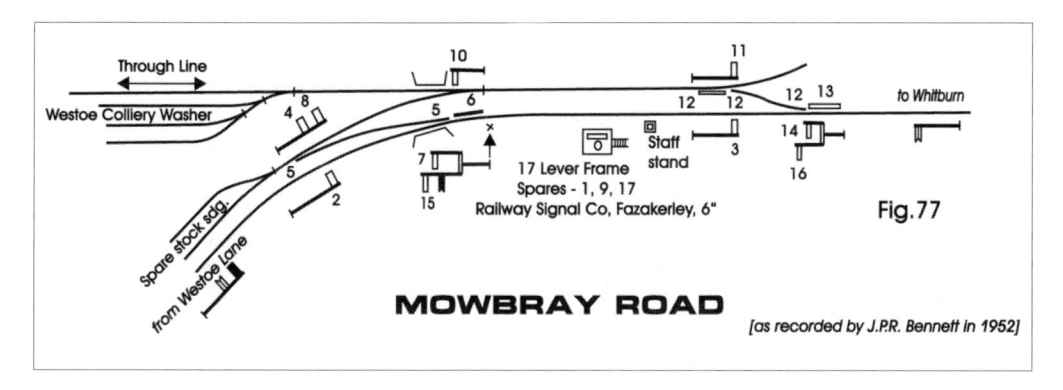

MOWBRAY ROAD

Fig.77

[as recorded by J.P.R. Bennett in 1952]

343

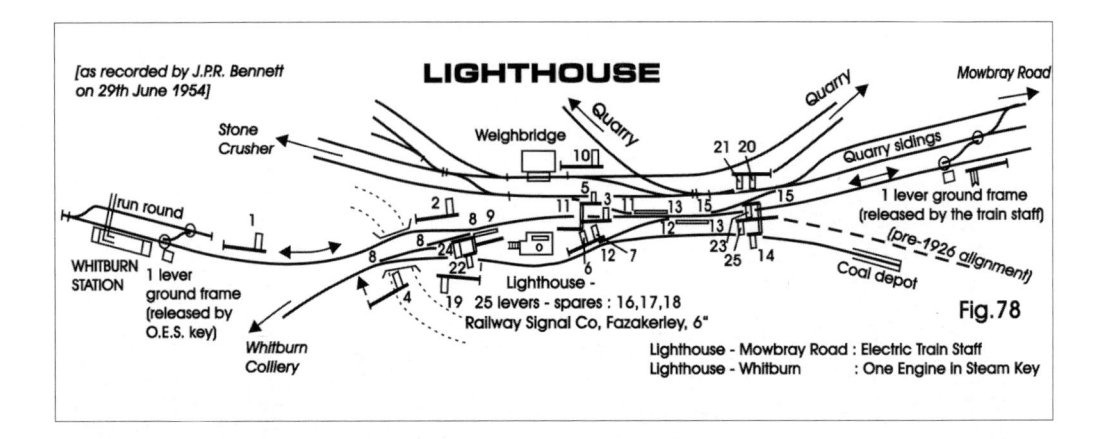

[Figure 78 — Lighthouse signalbox diagram, as recorded by J.P.R. Bennett on 29th June 1954]

Labels visible on diagram:
- LIGHTHOUSE
- Stone Crusher
- Weighbridge
- Quarry
- Mowbray Road
- Quarry sidings
- run round
- WHITBURN STATION — 1 lever ground frame (released by O.E.S. key)
- Whitburn Colliery
- 1 lever ground frame (released by the train staff)
- (pre-1926 alignment)
- Coal depot
- Lighthouse – 25 levers – spares: 16,17,18 – Railway Signal Co, Fazakerley, 6"
- Lighthouse – Mowbray Road : Electric Train Staff
- Lighthouse – Whitburn : One Engine in Steam Key

Fig.78

---

unique, in that whilst the names on its terminus station nameboards were Westoe Lane and Whitburn Colliery, the tickets for the journey between them read South Shields to Marsden!

In 1933 the company constructed a coal dry-cleaning plant at Westoe, and the extra sidings needed for this meant the demolition of Mowbray Road Bridge Signalbox and its replacement by a new box 225 yards further south, called simply **Mowbray Road Signalbox** (NZ 376665). This had 17 levers, with three spare. Two years later the increased traffic in this area also saw the Westoe Lane signalbox fitted with a new 15-lever frame, with all the levers working. One oddity here was a "point indicator", a semaphore signal operated in a vertical arc and worked directly from the points, which showed loco crews which route was set. Both Westoe Lane and the Lighthouse signalboxes were manned for 24 hours a day, but Mowbray Road was manned only between 6.00 am and 10.00 pm. When this box was open train staffs were exchanged here, but outside those hours the length between the other two was operated under one staff. The run-round points at Whitburn Colliery were not operated from the Lighthouse box, the crew having to pick up an Annett's key from the box to unlock the ground frame which operated the points.

At Marsden eventually three quarries were developed, called Marsden Harbour, Marsden Lighthouse and Marsden No.2. In 1937 these were modernised, with the installation of a stone crushing, screening and storing plant and the replacement of the horses on the 2ft 0in gauge system by locomotives, for which a new loco shed and workshop facilities were built. Stone from the 90ft high faces was loaded by steam excavators into narrow gauge tubs, which were then hauled to the standard gauge rail terminals. The quarry engine hauled the standard gauge wagons out for weighing, and then put the stone for crushing into the crushing plant. Output increased to 2000 tons of stone per week, most stone being dispatched via the High Staith. In addition, between 400-500 tons of lime were produced. This was intended for the farming, building and chemical industries, and also for use underground in collieries, where it was used to help prevent the spread of carbon dioxide. Later it was also used to help stop carbon monoxide speading in the event of a fire or explosion. Most of the lime was dispatched in LNER or private owner wagons worked through Dean Road sidings.

Despite having steam locomotives both at Whitburn and at Boldon Colliery and the electric locomotives based at Westoe, the company never developed a central engineering workshops. This meant that all locomotive overhauls had to be carried out in the locomotive sheds, often with fairly basic facilities. At Whitburn shed maintenance was carried out by three fitters with apprentices and two labourers.

The advent of the Second World War saw the closure of the St.Hilda/Westoe complex in 1940, together with the High Staith. St.Hilda never re-opened, but the High Staith resumed shipments in 1948. The Ministry of War also closed the coast road on 20th August 1941, which meant an increase in passengers on the Railway, so that more trains were run than at any time in its history. The closure remained in force until 24th June 1944.

On 1st January 1947 the Railway, together with Whitburn Colliery and Marsden Quarries, were vested in NCB Northern Division No.1 (North-East Durham) Area, The Harton Coal Co Ltd being the Area's largest constituent company.

The locomotives

Although the first No.7 was purchased new, thereafter all locomotives acquired for the Railway up to nationalisation were second-hand. Some were acquired through the dealers Robert Frazer & Sons Ltd of Hebburn, but quite a number were acquired direct from the NER and then the LNER. They may well have been acquired quite cheaply, for it would certainly seem that the company worked its locomotives hard, wore them out and then approached the LNER for another, rather than spend money on locomotives for which they had no spares, other than what they salvaged from locomotives already scrapped.

258. Former Great North of Scotland Railway coach No.78, built by the Metropolitan Railway Carriage & Wagon Co in 1866, at Marsden on 1st April 1934. Despite its condition, it was repaired and survived at Westoe until at least 1953.

259. The Railway had to undertake locomotive repairs in very basic conditions at Whitburn, where No.5, built at the NER's Gateshead Works in 1881, is seen on 9th June 1934.

260. 7, built at the NER's Gateshead Works in 1892 and one of the LNER J21 class purchased by the company, stands outside Whitburn loco shed about 1937, carrying a painted number and letters. Note the Westinghouse air brake apparatus.

261. No.4, BH 826/1884, stands outside Whitburn loco shed about 1938; with LALEHAM, she was one of the locomotives which shunted Marsden Quarries and its kilns.

Gauge : 4ft 8½in

Locomotives acquired from The Tyne Plate Glass Co Ltd and used at St.Hilda Colliery only

ST.HILDA No.1	0-4-0ST	OC	BH	515	1879	(a)	Scr c/1910
ST.HILDA No.2	0-4-0ST	OC	BH	516	1897	(a)	Scr c/1910

(a) ex The Tyne Plate Glass Co Ltd, /1892

Locomotives acquired by The Whitburn Coal Co Ltd (absorbed into The Harton Coal Co Ltd in 1891)

1		IC	MW					
		reb	Grange I.W.		1875	(a)	Scr /1895
2	0-6-0ST *	OC	BH	504	1879	New	Scr /1905
3	0-6-0ST	OC	BH	716	1882	New	
	reb				1906		(1)
No.4	0-6-0ST	OC	BH	826	1884	New	
	reb				1906		
	reb				1923		(2)
No.5	0-6-0ST	IC	RS	2629	1887	New	Scr /1922

* fitted with Westinghouse brakes for the passenger service

(a) origin and date of arrival unknown; one source listed it as a 0-4-0T, another as a 0-6-0ST; the latter would seem more likely

(1) to James W.Ellis Ltd, Swalwell, /1910; to Leversons Wallsend Collieries Ltd, Usworth Colliery, Usworth; to The Ryhope Coal Co Ltd, Ryhope Colliery, Ryhope; s/s
(2) to NCB No.1 Area, with the Railway, 1/1/1947

Locomotives acquired by The Harton Coal Co Ltd
The Railway's method of locomotive numbering would suggest that there should have been a No.6 before the first 6 listed next; if so, no information seems to have survived.

5		0-6-0 *	IC	Ghd		1881	(a)	(1)
6		0-6-0	IC	RS	2160	1874	(b)	Scr /1912
6		0-6-0	IC	RS	2056	1872	(c)	(2)
6		0-6-0 *	IC	RS	2587	1884	(d)	Scr /1936
6		0-6-0 *	IC	Ghd	23	1889	(e)	(1)
No.7		0-6-2T	IC	CF	1158	1898	New	(3)
7		0-6-0 *	IC	Ghd	38	1892	(f)	Scr /1935
7		0-6-0 *	IC	Ghd	43	1889	(g)	(4)
7		0-6-0	IC	Dar	631	1898	(h)	Scr /1946
8		2-2-2WT	IC	SS	1501	1864	(j)	Scr /1907
8		0-6-0 *	IC	RS	1973	1870	(k)	Scr /1929
8		0-6-0 *	IC	Ghd	3	1889	(m)	(1)
9		0-6-0	IC	Blyth & Tyne		1862	(n)	Scr /1913
10		0-6-0	IC	Blyth & Tyne		1862	(p)	Scr /1914
10		0-6-0	IC	RWH	1564	1873	(q)	Scr /1931
11		0-4-0ST	OC	MW			(r)	Scr /1920
	LALEHAM	0-6-0ST	OC	AB	1639	1923	(s)	(1)
	BOWES No.9	0-6-0ST	IC	SS	4051	1894		
	reb	0-6-0PT	IC	Caerphilly		1930	(t)	(5)

* fitted with Westinghouse brakes for the passenger service

(a) ex Robert Frazer & Sons Ltd, Hebburn, dealers, 10/1929; LNER, 396, formerly NER 398 class, until 8/1925
(b) ex NER, 786, 398 class, per R.Frazer & Sons Ltd, Hebburn, dealers, 12/1907; sold by NER, 18/12/1907
(c) ex NER, 827, 398 class, per R.Frazer & Sons Ltd, Hebburn, dealers, 3/1912
(d) ex LNER, 1486, J22 class, formerly NER 59 class, 21/1/1930
(e) ex LNER, 1509, J21 class, formerly NER C class, 2/8/1935; withdrawn by LNER, 8/1935
(f) ex LNER, 1616, J21 class, 10/10/1929; withdrawn by LNER, 10/1929
(g) ex LNER, 776, J21 class, 17/5/1935; withdrawn by LNER, 5/1935
(h) ex LNER, 1953, J24 class, 20/5/1939; previously NER, P class
(j) ex Robert Frazer & Sons Ltd, dealers, Hebburn, c/1899; previously Furness Railway, 22A, until 8/1899
(k) ex NER, 718, 708 class, per Robert Frazer & Sons Ltd, dealers, Hebburn, 12/1907; sold by NER, 18/12/1907

(m)   ex LNER, 869, J21 class, 29/1/1931; withdrawn by LNER, 1/1931
(n)   ex NER, 2255, 4/1900; built by Blyth & Tyne Railway at Percy Main, North Shields, Northumberland, as 3; railway acquired by NER, 7/8/1874, and loco re-numbered 1303; re-numbered 1923 in 8/1891, 1733 in 1/1894 and 2255 in 3/1899
(p)   ex NER, 1712, 11/1900; built by Blyth & Tyne Railway at Percy Main, North Shields, Northumberland, as 14; re-numbered 1314 in 8/1874, 1729 in 7/1892 and 1712 in 1/1894
(q)   ex NER, 827, 398 class, 31/8/1914
(r)   identity and origin unknown; possibly acquired in 1908; it was fitted up by 10/1914 as part of an armoured train on the Railway to guard against a German invasion (*The Locomotive Magazine*, 15/10/1914)
(s)   ex Boldon Colliery, Boldon Colliery, 7/1931, to share with No.4 the Marsden Quarries duty
(t)   ex Boldon Colliery, Boldon Colliery, c4/1943; on hire from John Bowes & Partners Ltd, Bowes Railway (see chapter 3)

(1)   to NCB No.1 Area, with the Railway, 1/1/1947
(2)   withdrawn from traffic in /1927; scrapped, 1/1930
(3)   to R.Frazer & Sons Ltd, Hebburn, dealers, /1912 (after 22/7/1912); to John Bowes & Partners Ltd, Pontop & Jarrow Railway (see chapter 3)
(4)   to Boldon Colliery, Boldon Colliery, c/1937, and returned; dismantled at Whitburn shed by 3/8/1939; scrapped, /1939
(5)   to Boldon Colliery, Boldon Colliery, c7/1943

NATIONAL COAL BOARD
North Durham Area from 26/3/1967
Northumberland & Durham Division No.1 Area from 1/1/1964
Durham Division No.1 (North-East Durham) Area from 1/1/1950
Northern Division No.1 (North-East Durham) Area from 1/1/1947

On the Railway it was clear that it was certainly time to phase out the aging tender locomotives that had worked so hard for so long. After the usual hurried measures that many of the private railways saw, the decision was made to approach Robert Stephenson & Hawthorns Ltd at Newcastle upon Tyne for a powerful design, capable of handling both heavy mineral trains and the passenger service. The result was a large 0-6-0ST with 18in x 24in outside cylinders and 4ft 0in diameter wheels, working at 180 p.s.i, and of course fitted with Westinghouse air brakes for the passenger service. The first was delivered to Whitburn on 13th December 1949, and proved deceptively powerful for its size, being able to haul a train of 2,102 tons on the level, 1,116 ton trains on a gradient of 1 in 200 and 399 ton trains on a gradient of 1 in 50. Two more were delivered in 1951-52 and a fourth, without Westinghouse equipment, in 1954. At this period four engines were in steam daily, one handling the passenger service in addition to coal traffic, while another shunted at Marsden Quarries.

Curiously, "the smallest station in the world" also found itself being developed. After the War large new housing estates were being developed at Horsley Hill, leading to far more miners using Marsden Cottage Station to reach work. So in 1950 two new shelters of corrugated iron were erected each side of the original brick shelter, utilising the whole length of the platform.

In 1948 Westoe Colliery at last opened as a coal-drawing colliery; but in 1953 it was announced that it was to be developed into a large modern colliery, one of series of high-production collieries being developed all down the North-East coast. A large new shaft would be sunk and two locomotive horizons driven well out under the North Sea into the huge coal reserves there. On the surface, the old dry-cleaning plant was to be swept away and replaced by a modern coal washery, to which all local coal would be brought. This would bring increased traffic from British Railways into Dean Road Sidings and through Westoe Lane Station to reach the new plant.

It was essential to ensure that Westoe Lane Station could handle the increased traffic flow, and in such circumstances, the operation of a little-used and uneconomic passenger service with worn out coaching stock was doomed. The weekday service during 1953 was as follows:

Monday-Friday trains depart Whitburn Colliery [Marsden]
12.30, 2.00, 4.55, 6.00, 7.10, 10.40 am, 1.35, 2.15, 3.05, 4.48, 6.35, 9.20 pm
Monday-Friday trains depart Westoe Lane [Shields]
1.45, 4.25, 5.43, 6.25, 9.28 am, 12.05, 2.00, 2.48, 3.27, 5.15, 8.03, 9.58 pm

Passengers wishing to travel on Saturdays or Sundays had to find out locally what trains were running. Incredibly, third class tickets were still for sale at the 1888 prices of 4d. single and 6d. return! It was announced that the service would close on Sunday 22nd November 1953, the fleet of buses for carrying the miners having been introduced on 14th November. Railway enthusiasts had been promised a commemorative train – which was never organised – and so the last train, the 9.58 pm from Westoe Lane, probably left empty. Thus closed the only passenger service in England

262. Whitburn loco shed on 29th June 1954, with the then quarry engine, RSHN 7339/1947, standing outside. The doors, once of arched construction, were rebuilt to allow more air to circulate.

263. RSHN 7603/1949, with the Westinghouse brake apparatus mounted on the frame, stands at Whitburn Colliery Station with a six-coach train of six-wheelers on 7th August 1952.

264. In 1961 the NCB's Whitburn Workshops fitted a Giesl ejector to 'Austerity' HE 3191/1944 to explore the possibility of burning small coal without smoke. She stands outside Whitburn shed on 11th August 1965.

whose trains did not connect with British Railways.

In fact, rather than disappearing, the relics of the passenger service survived for many years. It seems very likely that tender locomotives ceased working before the closure of the service. The stations survived. Tickets could still be bought as souvenirs. Some coach bodies, in time-honoured fashion, became cabins for the railwaymen. The electric train staff instruments were taken out of use in 1957 and replaced by single line staffs operated manually. Communication between the signal boxes was abandoned soon afterwards and the signalmen removed, leaving the boxes to be operated as required by the train crews. For many years Whitburn Colliery's output averaged between 450,000 and 550,000 tons, so there was still plenty of work for the Railway.

Together with the development of Westoe Colliery, NCB No.1 Area had acquired the site of the former paper mill south of Whitburn Colliery, and this was re-developed as a much-needed **AREA CENTRAL WORKSHOPS** (NZ 411632), with the Area Headquarters nearby. The works was of course rail-linked, and some major steam locomotive overhauls were undertaken. Locomotive work at the workshops ceased in the autumn of 1965, and thereafter locomotives needing overhaul had to be sent elsewhere.

The lime kilns at Marsden Quarries were closed down about 1954, and in September 1965 the quarries themselves were sold to a Wakefield firm, Slater & Co (Limestone) Ltd. This firm immediately replaced all rail traffic, both within the quarries and on the Railway, by road transport. This reduced the number of locomotives required daily at Whitburn to three, and in the same year the Area sent three new diesel locomotives to replace the remaining steam engines. At 311 b.h.p. these had more than enough power to handle the coal traffic, but their top speed of 15 m.p.h. did not impress the men, who with a steam locomotive had frequently exceeded 40 m.p.h. on the downhill gradient towards Westoe.

However, the Railway owed its continuation solely to Whitburn Colliery, and the colliery became one of many closed in the 1960s. The last shift was worked on 7th June 1968 and the Railway was officially abandoned on the next day. A celebratory rail-tour was run for enthusiasts on 7th September 1968, and lifting and demolition began soon afterwards. The Whitburn workshops survived until 31st October 1985. With its buildings in use as offices, the last feature of the Railway to survive was Westoe Lane Station, which could still be seen until the demolition of Westoe Colliery in the spring of 1994.

The rolling stock : 1. wagons

Given the number of chaldron waggons on other private railways in the North-East, there were probably several thousand of this design used by the company. In 1909 there were still nearly 800 of them left, with 30 allocated to Harton Colliery, 12 to Boldon Colliery and the remainder divided between St.Hilda and Whitburn Collieries. For many years the company made separate allocations to the collieries, and the colliery's name was painted on the wagons. The first NER-designed 'P4' 10½ ton wooden hopper wagons

265. *No.505, HE 6616/1965, shunts BR 21-ton wagons for the Marsden Coal Depot near the redundant Lighthouse signalbox at Whitburn on 16th April 1968. Note the remains of a coach body near the signalbox.*

which were to replace the chaldrons arrived in 1900, and more were purchased over the years following. The number of chaldrons declined steadily after 1911, but in June 1921 there were still 112 left, the 12 being ex Lambton Railway waggons allocated to Boldon Colliery. By this date 1,151 of the 10½ ton hoppers were allocated to Whitburn Colliery. There was also the usual miscellany of vans, for breakdowns, carrying weights and "choppy" (chopped hay for the pit ponies), together with bolster wagons for carrying materials, and finally a few hopper wagons with dumb buffers used for landsale depot work only.

In 1951 the NCB announced that the entire 'P4' fleet was to be replaced by 1,021 new 21-ton steel hopper wagons, to be built by Charles Roberts & Co Ltd of Wakefield and Hurst, Nelson & Co Ltd of Motherwell. The allocation of wagons to individual collieries had long vanished, and these worked down to Whitburn as required, as did British Railways 21-ton wagons.

The rolling stock : 2. coaches
The coaching stock used on the Railway was always second-hand and usually life-expired when it arrived. The wagon shop at the Low Staiths had very limited capacity, and from the photographs it would seem that many of the coaches received little or no maintenance, merely being replaced when they had become truly awful.

The stock was too numerous to list in detail here; full details are given in the reference below. However, some photographs before the First World War show 13 coach trains – the reasons for such a length are not known – which would suggest that there were more coaches then than given in the list. Suffice to say that while most were bought from the NER and LNER, they were built for a very wide variety of sources, including the Hull & Barnsley Railway, the Great Eastern Railway and the North British Railway, although the biggest number were formerly owned by the Great North of Scotland Railway, including the most of the final coaching stock used on the Railway.

The main set of coaches comprised six 6-wheeled, non-corridor 3rd class coaches built by the Ashbury Railway Carriage & Wagon Co Ltd for the GNoSR in 1893, Nos. 200/2/6/9/13/14. They were 31ft wide, 8ft 11in high and 12ft 6½in high, weighed 13¾ tons and had 50 seats. The LNER added 7000 to the numbers and withdrew them from traffic in 1937, selling them on to the North Shields builders and dealers, Watts, Hardy & Co Ltd, who in turn resold them in 1938 to The Harton Coal Co Ltd. These were used only for miners. Most, if not all, eventually had all the compartments removed and the existing seating replaced by longitudinal seating running the length of the coach. As all of the platforms were on the seaward side of the train, doors on the landward side were locked, the doorhandles removed and all the windows boarded up. Also in 1938 the company bought 6-wheeled two brake thirds, built by the GNoSR themselves in 1895. The guard's compartment and van end had a wider body and was equipped with double doors and duckets. These two were used for braking purposes and to carry the general public and white collar workers. These were usually coupled at each end of the train. Most coaching stock was never repainted and continued to carry its old livery and numbering. Incredibly, the NCB also purchased two 6-wheeled brake thirds in 1952. These had been built by the Great Eastern Railway in 1892-3, and were sold by the LNER in 1937 to the North Sunderland Railway, which ran from Chathill to Seahouses in Northumberland. This railway closed in 1951 and the coaches were sold to Watts, Hardy & Co Ltd, who gutted them and sold them on to the NCB. They had 60 seats each. This purchase seems to have stirred the NCB management, for even more incredibly, also in 1952, the whole fleet was repainted in mid-grey, with no numbers but with NCB on the central panels!

Reference : *The South Shields, Marsden & Whitburn Colliery Railway*, by W.J.Hatcher, Oakwood Press, 2002

The locomotives
The Railway's numbering scheme was continued with the two locomotives that arrived in 1947; after that new arrivals were referred to by their works numbers. RSH 7339/1947 was purchased to take over the Marsden Quarries duty vacated by BH 826/1884. Each NCB Area was sub-divided into Groups, and in the North-East these had much more influence on locomotive operation than elsewhere in the country. In 1963 No.1 Area's 'B' Group introduced a numbering scheme for the non-electric locomotives in the Group, in practice those at Boldon and Whitburn Collieries. However, some locomotives never carried their numbers, whilst the two locomotives intended to be 8 and 9 had 9 and 10 painted on in error. The full scheme was:

[1]	AB 1639/1923	[6]	RSH 7603/1949
2	HE 3191/1944	7	RSH 7695/1951
[3]	RSH 7339/1947	9	RSH 7749/1952
[4]	RSH 7294/1945	10	RSH 7811/1954
5	RSH 7132/1944		

The diesels that arrived in 1965-66 were part of a larger Divisional order, for which a new numbering scheme was introduced, starting at No.501. No.505 was the final locomotive to work over the Railway, hauling the commemorative railtour on 7th September 1968.

266. Alongside the A183 road that marks the original route of the Railway, No.506, HE 6617/1965, with the former Marsden Quarry kilns in the background, toils towards the Marsden Grotto footbridge with coal for Westoe and eventually Harton Low Staiths on 11th April 1968, some seven weeks before the closure of the Railway.

In the list below the following abbreviations are used:

B	Boldon Colliery, Boldon Colliery
LEW	Lambton Engine Works, Philadelphia, for repairs
WCW	Area Central Workshops, Whitburn
Wh	Whitburn Colliery, Whitburn

All locomotives without transfers shown in italics were shedded at Whitburn Colliery.

Gauge : 4ft 8½in

No.5		0-6-0 *	IC	Ghd		1881	(a)	Scr 2/1953
No.4		0-6-0ST	IC	BH	826	1884	(a)	Scr c8/1948
8		0-6-0 *	IC	Ghd	3	1889	(a)	Scr 7/1954
6		0-6-0 *	IC	Ghd	23	1889	(a)	Scr 6/1951
LALEHAM [1] from 1963		0-6-0ST	OC	AB	1639	1923	(a)	(1)
"9"	2 from 1963	0-6-0ST	IC	HE	3191	1944	(b)	

Wh-LEW c6/1951 (by 8/1951)- Wh 4/1952-LEW 30/5/1952-Wh 2/6/1952
-B, after 7/1956, by 9/1957-WCW /1960 (after 7/1960); fitted with Giesl ejector system
- Wh 21/2/1961-WCW 10/12/1963, ejector removed-Wh 7/5/1965 (2)

"10"	[3]	0-6-0ST	OC	RSHN	7339	1947	New	

Wh-WCW 5/7/1961; repairs suspended, to Wh to stand, 1/5/1962;
boiler removed for repair, /1964, frame & wheels to WCW by 11/1964
-frame and wheels to Wh, 17/12/1964 (3)

	-	0-6-0ST	IC	HC	1513	1924	(c)

Wh-B c5/1948 (by 9/1948)-Wh by 2/1949-B /1949-Wh for repairs, 1/1950 (4)

No.4		0-6-0	IC	Ghd		1883	(d)	Scr 6/1952
(75182)	"7132"	0-6-0ST	IC	RSHN	7132	1944	(e)	
5 from 1963	Wh-B 6/5/1954-W.G.Bagnall Ltd, Stafford, for repairs, /1961							

-Wh 20/12/1961-WCW 28/9/1963; fitted with HE underfeed mechanical stoker
-Wh 14/6/1964; stoker out of use by 11/8/1965-WCW c9/1965-Wh 25/9/1965 (5)

"7603" [6] from 1963		0-6-0ST	* OC	RSHN	7603	1949	New	

Wh-B 21/9/1961-Wh 17/11/1962 (6)

"7695"	7 from 1963	0-6-0ST	* OC	RSHN	7695	1951	New	

Wh-B 11/2/1958-Wh 8/7/1959 (7)

"7749"	9 from 1963	0-6-0ST	* OC	RSHN	7749	1952	New	

Wh-B 24/7/1958-Wh 11/2/1959-B 21/2/1961-WCW 22/5/1962-B 19/11/1962
-Wh 5/12/1962-B 13/5/1963-Wh, 4/1965, to await repairs; WCW 2/6/1965;
dismantled by 11/8/1965 ;frame & wheels to Wh by 4/7/1966, boiler at WCW (8)

"7811"	10 from 1963	0-6-0ST	OC	RSHN	7811	1954	New	

Wh-B 8/7/1959-LEW 3/2/1960-B 5/1960-WCW 12/1/1961-Wh 7/2/1961
-B 7/8/1962-Wh 10/9/1962; between 9/1962 and 12/1962 there were several
transfers between Wh-WCW-Wh, dates not available; -B 12/1962; withdrawn, /1964;
-Wh, 4/1965, to await repairs-WCW 25/6/1965; dismantled by 11/8/1965;
frame and wheels to Wh by 4/7/1966. boiler at WCW (8)

	4	0-6-0	IC	Ghd	28	1897	(f)	(9)
"7294"	[4] from 1963	0-6-0ST	IC	RSHN	7294	1945	(g)	

Wh-WCW 21/7/1961-Wh 21/9/1961-B 4/1962-WCW 18/5/1962-Wh 26/5/1962
-B 30/5/1962-WCW c7/1962-B 10/9/1962-WCW 22/11/1962-Wh 27/11/1962 (10)

No.505	0-6-0DH	HE	6616	1965	New	(11)
No.506	0-6-0DH	HE	6617	1965	New	(12)
No.507	0-6-0DH	HE	6618	1965	New	(13)
509	0-6-0DH	AB	514	1966	New	(14)

* fitted with Westinghouse brakes for the passenger service

(a) ex The Harton Coal Co Ltd, with the Railway, 1/1/1947
(b) ex War Department, 75140, Central Ordnance Depot, Lockinge, Berkshire, 6/1947
(c) ex War Department, 70069, Bicester Central Workshops, Bicester, Oxfordshire, via repairs at Hudswell Clarke & Co Ltd, Leeds; arrived 1/1/1948
(d) ex Boldon Colliery, Boldon Colliery, by 19/9/1948
(e) ex Boldon Colliery, Boldon Colliery, 20/9/1948
(f) ex Boldon Colliery, Boldon Colliery, 30/3/1956; loco already withdrawn from traffic
(g) ex Boldon Colliery, Boldon Colliery, 11/2/1959

(1) to Boldon Colliery, Boldon Colliery, 3/2/1960; for subsequent history see chapter 15
(2) to Lambton Railway loco sheds, Philadelphia, 21/12/1965; to Wearmouth Colliery, Sunderland, 17/6/1966; scrapped on site, 3/1969
(3) to Washington 'F' Colliery, Washington, 2/3/1966; withdrawn, 4/1969, and taken to Washington Glebe Colliery to stand; scrapped on site, 8/1970
(4) to Boldon Colliery, Boldon Colliery, 2/1950; for subsequent history see chapter 15
(5) to Boldon Colliery, Boldon Colliery, 25/12/1965; for subsequent history see chapter 15
(6) to Boldon Colliery, Boldon Colliery, 14/7/1964; for subsequent history see chapter 15
(7) to Boldon Colliery, Boldon Colliery, 4/1965; for subsequent history see chapter 15
(8) sold for scrap to Bowburn Engineering Co Ltd, Bowburn, 4/1968
(9) engine section scrapped on site by D.Sep. Bowran Ltd, Gateshead, 7/1956; tender retained, and at some date after 26/8/1960 its frame and wheels were used in the contruction of a pressurised tank wagon for weed-killing
(10) to Washington 'F' Colliery, Washington, 10/2/1963; to Wearmouth Colliery, Sunderland, 28/3/1966; to Lambton Engine Works, Philadelphia, 1/1968; to Wearmouth Colliery, Sunderland, 11/1968; to Morrison Busty Colliery, Annfield Plain, 3/2/1970; scrapped, 7/1974
(11) to Westoe loco shed, South Shields, 6/1968; for subsequent history see chapter 15
(12) to Boldon Colliery, Boldon Colliery, 6/1968; for subsequent history see chapter 15
(13) to Boldon Colliery, Boldon Colliery, 19/5/1966; for subsequent history see chapter 15
(14) to Springwell Bank Foot loco shed, Bowes Railway, for repairs, 3/1968; to Boldon Colliery, Boldon Colliery, 5/5/1968; for subsequent history see chapter 15

267. The starter signals and water crane at Westoe Lane Station on 1st April 1934.

Chapter Fifteen
The Harton Electric System

OWNERS BEFORE 1947
The Harton Coal Co Ltd until 1/1/1947
subsidiary of Stephenson, Clarke & Co Ltd from 1927, which became Stephenson, Clarke & Associated Companies Ltd in 1928 and was taken over by Powell Duffryn Steam Coal Co Ltd from 21/12/1928

The railway network that had been developed up to 1908 to serve The Harton Coal Co Ltd's collieries at **ST.HILDA** (NZ 361667) in South Shields, **HARTON** (NZ 362642) near Tyne Dock, **BOLDON** (NZ 347623) and **WHITBURN** (NZ 408637) has been described in Chapter 14. The company did now have two sets of staiths at South Shields, the **HARTON HIGH STAITHS** (NZ 354662) and the **HARTON LOW STAITHS** (NZ 359670), but the company's own railway system only linked two of the collieries, St. Hilda and Whitburn, directly to them; traffic from the other two was worked by the NER. Moreover, whilst the line from Whitburn Colliery Junction at Tyne Dock on the NER Pontop & South Shields branch had been opened only in 1879 and was locomotive-worked throughout, the lines to the two sets of staiths had been built between 1810 and 1832 and had been designed for horses and rope haulage respectively. They not only suffered collectively from severe gradients, tight curves, a tunnel with very restricted clearance and cuttings where the rails were always damp and leaves collected, they ran through the streets and along the backs of houses, and were of course worked by steam locomotives; the residents complained about noise and dirt, and the the capacity of the staiths was limited by the locomotives' need to return to the loco shed at St.Hilda Colliery for coal. All these factors presented the company with a major problem, quite apart from that of attempting to design steam locomotives with a prohibitively-limiting height limit of less than 10ft 7in yet capable of not only overcoming the physical restrictions but also handling lengthy trains. The only feasible solution was electrification.

In the first decade of the twentieth century Tyneside and Durham led the way with the adoption of electricity in industry and transport, in much the same way that it had done with the development of steam locomotives almost a century earlier. Power stations to generate electricity began to develop, some by private companies, some by the leading colliery companies, such as The Lambton & Hetton Collieries Ltd (at Philadelphia), The Birtley Iron Co (at Ouston) and Pease & Partners Ltd at Crook. Electric trams were beginning to replace the steam trams; the Tyneside Tramways opened their first route, from Gosforth, north of Newcastle upon-Tyne, to North Shields, in the autumn of 1902. Faced with a serious loss of traffic to the trams, the NER responded by electrifying 37 miles of its Tyneside system, its first section, between New Bridge Street Station in Newcastle upon Tyne and Benton to the east, opening in March 1904. Set in this context, the decision of the The Harton Coal Co Ltd to adopt electrification was not an isolated venture into the unknown. Nor were they alone; at the same time that the Harton company made its decision, The Consett Iron Co Ltd decided to adopt electric traction on its new line between Chopwell and Whittonstall, although this was to be narrow gauge (see Chapter 5). Equally, the decision of the two companies can, from the perspective of a century later, be seen as the step which in turn led the NER to electrify their 18½ miles between Shildon and Newport (Middlesbrough), heavily used by coal traffic. This work began in June 1913; if it had not been interrupted by the First World War the history of Britain's national railway system might well have been very different.

It was not just on its railway system that the company was investing in electrical equipment; all of the colliery winders were converted to electric operation too, as was much of the colliery equipment and lighting. The company did not build its own generating station, so that its consumption had to be purchased. By the First World War there were seventeen generating stations in the North-East, and over a quarter of the output available for mining was purchased by the Harton company alone, or 6% of the total output nationally, making it one of the country's biggest single consumers.

The NER had used British contractors for their Tyneside scheme; but the leading electrical engineers at this time were in Germany, and both the Harton and Consett companies approached Siemens-Schuckert Elektricitats AG in Munich. This firm had already established itself in Britain, with headquarters in London and a manufacturing works at Stafford. In view of the extreme variation in height, from 10ft 6in to 21 feet, Siemens recommended an overhead wire system supplied at 550 volts direct current. The first stage was to electrify the section from the junction with the South Shields, Marsden & Whitburn Colliery Railway at Benthouse, down Erskine Road bank and thence the lines to the two sets of staiths, including St.Hilda Colliery. Six electric locomotives were ordered, three for heavy freight and three for shunting. To balance the demands of the locomotive weight required (17 tons) and the

268. Looking from the exit lines from St. Hilda loco shed in 1910; E4 (Siemens 457/1909) is standing on the St.Hilda-Hilda Hole line, E2 (Siemens 455/1908) and E5 (Siemens 458/1909) on the stores siding and E1 (Siemens 451/1908) and E3 (Siemens 456/1909) at the northern end of the St.Hilda Colliery sidings, with the NER viaduct in the background.

269. E1, Siemens 451/1908, with temporary L-section buffers, hauls a mixed train of chaldron waggons and former NER P4 wagons through Benthouse sidings in 1911. Note that she has two pantographs.

270. E4 (Siemens 457/1909) standing at the Portberry Street Crossing in South Shields on the branch to Harton High Staiths in 1911, with the branch to the North Eastern Foundry running alongside and the St.Hilda-High Staiths spur in the foreground. Note the extreme height of the wires.

271. The only known photograph of the St.Hilda locomotive shed, with E5 outside.

severe curves at St.Hilda Colliery, the last two locomotives were articulated. All locomotives had to be capable of hauling 110-ton trains up the 1 in 38 gradient of Erskine Road bank without wheel slip. The first revenue-earning train ran from the Benthouse sidings to the Low Staiths on 14th December 1908.

The operational success and low working costs of the new traction soon convinced the company to initiate a second stage. To bring Harton Colliery coal directly into the system, a new branch ¾ mile long was to be built from Dean Road sidings. These would now be handling coal from both Boldon and Harton Collieries, and to accommodate this they were to be considerably extended. This in turn would mean the replacement of Whitburn Colliery Junction by a new junction with the NER about ¼ mile to the south, entitled simply Whitburn Junction. Together with all this new construction the whole of the section between Harton Colliery and Benthouse was to be electrified, bringing the total electrified mileage to just over 14¼ miles. For this two more locomotives would be needed, and as fulls were to be hauled up Chichester bank, the specification laid down was for locomotives weighing a minimum of 40 tons and capable of hauling a 165-ton train, and the decision was that these should also be articulated. Although the electrical equipment was to be supplied by Siemens, the assembly was sub-contracted to Kerr, Stuart & Co Ltd at Stoke-on-Trent. Although the Harton Colliery branch was opened in 1910, the two locomotives were not delivered until the spring of 1911.

In May 1909 the company began the sinking of its fifth colliery at Benthouse, whose name it initially took. At first this single shaft was only to be the upcast shaft for St.Hilda Colliery, but in 1914 it was decided to develop it as a coal-drawing shaft, working the area east of St.Hilda and down towards Whitburn Colliery, and also out under the North Sea, and to mark this it was re-named **WESTOE COLLIERY** (NZ 373368). Its sidings too were wired. With production from the company's collieries already approaching 2½ million tons a year, it was decided to order an extra freight and an extra shunting locomotive. Although Siemens built the latter, the first was constructed by Allgemeine Elektricitats Gesellschaft at Berlin, based on a design adapted from a 900mm lignite mine underground locomotive. This brought the locomotive fleet to ten, with the first nine based at the former steam locomotive shed at St.Hilda Colliery and the last at a new, one-road, shed at Harton Colliery. They were numbered E1 to E10, which was carried on plates with THE HARTON COAL CO LTD around the perimeter.

The locomotive duties in 1913 were as follows:

Locomotive	Duty
E1	Benthouse Sidings
E2	Hilda Hole sidings * to Harton High Staiths
E3	St.Hilda Colliery to Harton Low Staiths
E4	St.Hilda Colliery to Hilda Hole sidings *
E5	St.Hilda Colliery (shunting)
E6	St.Hilda Colliery (shunting)
E7	Harton Colliery – Dean Road sidings – Benthouse sidings
E8	Harton Colliery – Dean Road sidings – Benthouse sidings
E9	Benthouse sidings to St. Hilda Colliery
E10	Harton Colliery

* interchange point for traffic destined for Harton High Staiths

Boldon Colliery thus became the company's only colliery not directly worked by the company's own railway systems. Its coal was worked northeastwards over the NER Pontop & South Shields branch, going to the Hilda Hole sidings alongside the line to South Shields Station if destined for the High Staith and into Dean Road sidings via Whitburn Junction if destined for the Low Staiths. By the mid-war period virtually all coal went to the Low Staiths, with the High Staiths reduced to one conveyor point used for loading colliery waste for dumping at sea or stone from Marsden Quarries, brought there via the South Shields, Marsden & Whitburn Colliery Railway. For many years the Boldon traffic was handled by the NER, but eventually it was taken over by the company, using running powers over the NER. When this change occurred is not known; the first known Harton locomotive likely to have been used between Boldon and Dean Road did not arrive until 1928.

When the first electric locomotives arrived, the majority of the system's coal waggons were 4-ton chaldrons, hence the photographs showing this unusual combination; nearly 800 were still in use in 1909. To the 200 10½-ton NER 'P4' type hopper wagons already purchased were added over 600 more between January 1909 and September 1911. However, by June 1921, out of a total wagon fleet of 2,009, 1,671 were 10½ tonners, with only 112 chaldrons left. For many years the coal wagons had been allocated to a named colliery, and the 1921 allocations show that much of the output from Harton and Boldon Collieries must have been

Fig.79 The electric system in the 1930s

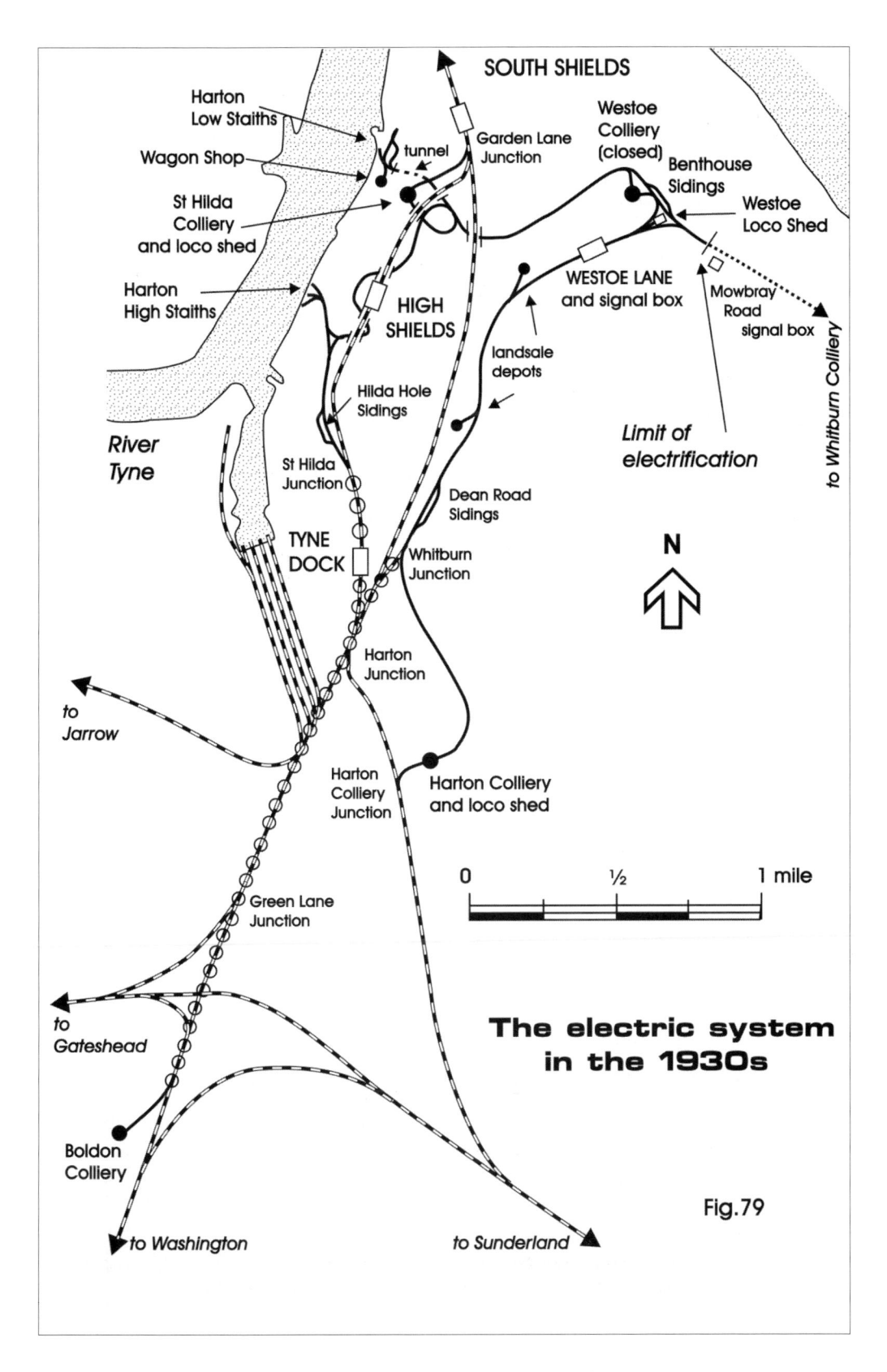

carried in NER wagons, presumably for destinations other than the Low Staiths. Repairs were undertaken in a small **WAGON SHOP** (NZ 349669) near the foot of the Low Staiths tunnel, in a building formerly part of the Tyne Plate Glass Co's premises.

The system was operated as if it were entirely single line, double track sections being regarded as a main line and a loop. It was thus essential to control this single line working, which was done by using the One Engine in Steam(!) system and train staffs (the metal staffs resembled large keys) and a time interval system based on both loaded and light running time. There were initally five sections - Harton Colliery-Whitburn Junction, Dean Road Sidings-Westoe Lane Station, Benthouse (later Bents) Sidings-St.Hilda Sidings (later to Claypath Sidings), St.Hilda Sidings (later Oyston Street Bridge)-Low Staiths and St.Hilda Colliery (later Claypath Sidings) to Hilda Hole Sidings. Staffed single line working was strictly observed in the Low Staiths tunnel; even maintenance staff walking through the tunnel had to be in possession of the staff. A full Railway Rule Book was issued in 1908, revised in 1921 to over 100 pages. In later years it would seem that staff working over the Harton Colliery branch was abandoned.

In 1920 a new loco shed, **WESTOE LOCO SHED** (NZ 374667), was built near Westoe Colliery, to re-house the majority of the electric locomotive fleet.

In 1930 this was enlarged to a four-road shed, and then doubled in size three years later in order to accommodate new English Electric rotary converters. All loco maintenance was now carried out here, the St.Hilda shed being retained only for locomotives on duties in its immediate area. The company never developed a central workshops for its colliery and railway maintenance work, leaving locomotive repairs to be undertaken in the locomotive sheds, at Westoe, Whitburn (on the SSM&WCR) and at Boldon. Latterly there were two locomotives sheds at the last, facing each other at opposite ends of the colliery yard.

In 1933 a coal dry-cleaning plant was built at Westoe and the locomotive duties were re-organised, with E1 becoming the locomotive shunting the new plant. However, with the onset of the Second World War St.Hilda Colliery and its Westoe shaft were closed on 6th September 1940, the former never to resume coal production, and shipments from the High Staith were also suspended. As a result E2, E5 and E6 were stored, (although E2 did come out when E10 at Harton needed repairs), while there was also little work for E1.

At Vesting Day, 1st January 1947, the system and its collieries became part of NCB Northern Division No.1 (North-East Durham) Area.

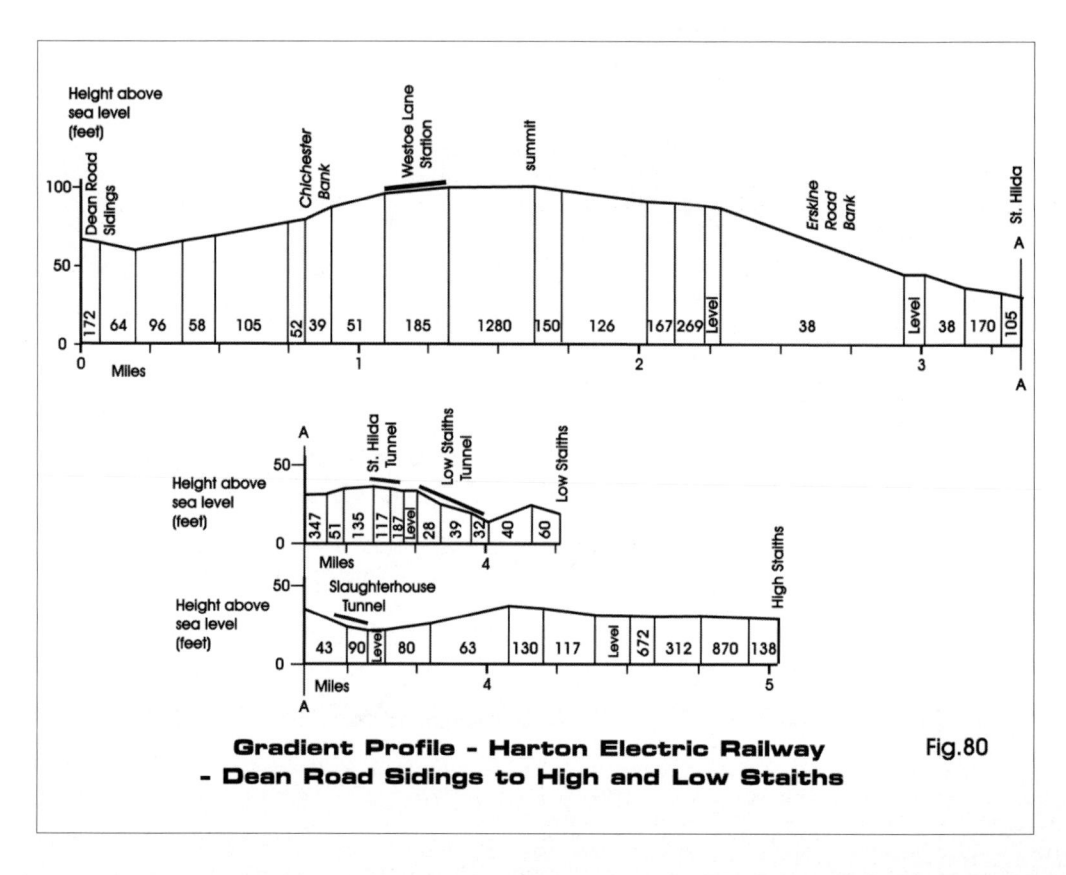

Gradient Profile - Harton Electric Railway - Dean Road Sidings to High and Low Staiths　　Fig.80

272. Now with a single pantograph and hauling empties back from the High Staiths, 1 crosses Laygate near its junction with Commercial Road in South Shields with only a flagman for protection on 7th March 1956. The BR line from Tyne Dock reached High Shields Station just off picture to the left.

273. Westoe Lane Station on 12th March 1957, with a Siemens loco standing at the home signal on the now-wired platform road and a 1951 English Electric loco, either 11 or 12, passing the route indicator signal and gliding down the Wallside road. The Westoe Lane signal box is on the platform.

BRITISH COAL from 5/3/1987
NATIONAL COAL BOARD
North East Group from 1/1/1989
North East Area from 1/4/1974
North Durham Area from 26/3/1967
Northumberland & Durham Division No.1 Area from 1/1/1964
Durham Division No.1 (North-East Durham) Area from 1/1/1950
Northern Division No.1 (North-East Durham) Area from 1/1/1947

In the early years of the National Coal Board there was a national coal shortage, and in 1948 Westoe Colliery was at last brought into coal production. The High Staith was also re-opened in that year, on 20th September. Since 1913 there had been little major investment, and the first major decision came in 1951, with the announcement that all the 10½ ton wagons were to be replaced by 21-ton steel wagons. This meant major work had to be carried out on the railway. The biggest job was the enlargement of the Low Staiths tunnel, closing the street involved temporarily and using the cut and cover technique, to increase the height to 13 feet. The St. Hilda loco shed, latterly only used as a stabling point, was closed, and its area modified to remove the tight curves, while to accommodate all the locomotives the front of the Westoe shed was enlarged by 34 feet. In addition, a turnout was installed to give a direct link between Westoe and the route to the High Staiths via St. Hilda. The delivery of the 21-ton wagons, from Charles Roberts & Co Ltd of Wakefield and Hurst, Nelson & Co Ltd of Motherwell, began in 1954, although the last of the 10½-ton wagons survived into the early 1960s. The new wagons were painted in the standard Durham Division vermilion with white lettering, with HARTON in large letters in the top right-hand corner and with a 3-link coupling painted on a centre panel, with the outer links enclosing NCB1 (the number of the Area) and the month/year of the latest overhaul. Finally, to cope with the increased weight of 21-ton wagon trains up Chichester Bank, two new 400 h.p. locomotives were ordered from The English Electric Co Ltd, though in fact they were sub-contracted to E.E.Baguley Ltd of Burton-on-Trent. These continued the original numbering, becoming Nos. 12 and 13.

The next major investment was a new £1 million coal preparation plant at Westoe, to replace the ageing dry-cleaning plant. The plant, opened in July 1954, was designed to handle 500 tons of coal per hour, and although coal from Westoe Colliery was to be brought there via underground conveyor, coal from Boldon, Harton and Whitburn Collieries would arrive by rail in the new wagons.

The biggest investment was announced in 1957 – a 10-year programme to develop Westoe into one of the collieries to take British coal production into the twenty-first century. With some faces already producing 1000 tons per day, coal reserves proved by drilling to at least six miles out and a major contract between the NCB and the Central Electricity Generating Board to supply coal by sea to the new power stations on the banks of the Thames, Westoe was to receive £6.6 million. A new shaft was to be sunk, the Crown Shaft, to be coal-drawing only, and two horizons for locomotive working driven out under the North Sea, in order to bring Westoe up to a million tons per year. Major changes to the railway would be needed. One of the biggest was the clearing of the St.Hilda area and the installation of a major sidings area, taken right up to the entrance of the Low Staiths tunnel. The heavily-used section between Westoe and the Low Staiths was fitted with colour light signalling, controlled from a **signal box** (NZ 364666) at the foot of Erskine Bank, under the Crossgate bridge. The former Westoe triangle was removed in order to accommodate vastly increased siding accommodation at the colliery, and to cope with the extra traffic and heavier trains, three more 400 h.p locomotives were ordered from English Electric, one in 1957 and two in 1959. These, built to a lower height in order to work through the Low Staiths tunnel, were numbered 13 to 15. Their arrival made it possible to schedule trains of twenty-four 21-ton wagons between Westoe and the St.Hilda Sidings, while the articulated locomotives Nos. 5 and 6 could be withdrawn. In addition, the electricians at Westoe at last received a purpose-built diesel-driven tower wagon for overhead maintenance, built by E.E.Baguley Ltd and delivered in November 1960; this replaced the home-made, hand-pushed vehicle that they had previously used.

With the end of trolleybus systems in the region the NCB took the opportunity to purchase surplus equipment at scrap prices, firstly from the former Sunderland system in 1954, and then when the South Shields system closed down ten years later. This allowed much of the German equipment to be replaced, and a new 750 kW sub-station to be built at Westoe. In 1971 a large stock of ex-Newcastle Corporation fittings were acquired, and these were used to replace any life-expired overhead items. In 1978 the first catenary equipment was installed, using components manufactured in bulk for British Rail.

Towards the end of the investment programme further changes were made. Firstly, the Low Staiths discharging point and the area's sidings were re-modelled to make the handling of wagons quicker and more efficient. The second came about because of the end of BR traffic over the Pontop & South Shields line in 1966, leaving the NCB trains between Boldon Colliery and Whitburn Junction the only traffic on the line. This gave the NCB the opportunity to take over part of the route north of Tyne Dock to instal a single line track between Dean Road and the St.Hilda sidings. This diverged

274. E10, Siemens 862/1913, in green with red lining, stands outside the shed at Westoe, still carrying all her plates, on 6th June 1962.

275. The last of the electrics – No.15, EE 2600/1959 but actually built by Bg, 3520/1959, in royal blue livery and yellow lining and lettering, at Harton Low Staiths on 10th July 1963.

276. 8, KS 1203/1911, at Westoe on 10th June 1964, painted black with red lining and gold letters shaded red.

277. 7, KS 1202/1911, originally identical to 8, but rebuilt with new motors and superstructure at Westoe in 1953, also in royal blue with yellow lining, at Westoe on 10th June 1964.

278. No.9, AEG 1565/1913, near the Mowbray Road signal box south of Westoe on 10th June 1964.

279. Westoe Lane loco shed, with an old passenger coach body from the South Shields, Marsden & Whitburn Colliery Railway acting as a store, on 11th August 1965.

280. BOLDON No.1, HC 332/1889, formerly GWR 782 and originally a Barry Railway 'E' class, stands alongside Boldon brickworks in 1949.

from the Dean Road-Westoe line just below the Victoria Road bridge and then used the Pontop & South Shields route for about ¼ mile before diverging to reach the Westoe-St.Hilda line at the bottom of Erskine Road Bank. The new route, named by the men 'The Pontop', meant that even if both Chichester and Erskine Banks became blocked, traffic from BR still had direct access to the Low Staiths. However, because it was rarely used, a locomotive had to be sent down about once a month to keep the overhead wire polished.

The loco roster from 1959 required ten locomotives, as follows:

Locomotive	Duty
1	Standby/spare
2	Harton High Staith (working alternate weeks with E10)
3	Westoe Washery – raw coal end
4	Westoe Washery – raw coal end
7	Standby/spare
8	Harton Colliery
No.9	Relief for Westoe – St. Hilda Sidings
E10	Harton High Staith (working alternate weeks with 2)
11	Harton Colliery – Dean Road Sidings – Westoe
12	Harton Colliery – Dean Road Sidings – Westoe
13	Westoe Washery, washed coal end (a 3-shift duty)
14	Westoe – St. Hilda sidings
15	Harton Low Staiths

281. One of the RSHN 0-6-0STs, en route between Boldon Colliery and Dean Sidings, is held at Pontop Crossing while a British Rail DMU set from Sunderland to Newcastle passes, in 1962.

282. AB 478/1963 and AB 646/1979 on the BR line once the Stanhope & Tyne Railway cross the bridge over the River Don with a train from Boldon Colliery to Dean Sidings, 24th July 1980.

283. No.505, 0-6-0DH HE 6615/1965, approaches Dean Sidings with coal from Harton Colliery on 22nd July 1969. An electric locomotive worked this turn at night because of diesel noise waking nearby residents. Note the replacement overhead equipment.

The development of Westoe Colliery had hardly been completed before the pit closure programme hit the area. The first to go was Whitburn Colliery, served by the South Shields, Marsden & Whitburn Colliery Railway (see Chapter 14), which was closed on 7th June 1968. This left three diesel locomotives needing new work, and one was transferred to Westoe shed, thus beginning the combination of electric and diesel locomotives on the system which was to last till its end. The closure of Whitburn Colliery was soon followed by the end of Harton Colliery, where rail traffic ceased on 25th July 1969, with the colliery closing on 1st August 1969. Whilst No.8 was the usual locomotive here, the first diesel locomotive to arrive on the system, after the closure of the SSM&WCR, HE 6616/1965, was also used here, and E3 was used for the pit's final weeks; neither electric locomotive worked again after the colliery closed.

Westoe shed found itself with new occupants in September 1974. The main stockyard at the colliery was situated near the Crown shaft, but all materials were sent underground via the Westoe shaft. The two areas were connected by a tunnel, operated by rope haulage and a "dilly" truck, which took the rope down to the bottom of the tunnel. Originally the shunting of the two areas was done by tractor, but in 1974 the original 2ft 6in gauge ½ ton tubs were replaced by 3½ ton mine cars, and it was decided that these would need to be shunted by locomotives, two old Ruston & Hornsby diesels being obtained from Lambton Engine Works at Philadelphia. To service them part of one of the wall-side locomotive roads in the shed was rebuilt, with an entrance from the rear of the shed. This continued until the system was abandoned in January 1988.

Next came the closure of the High Staith. As described above, this had been used for any years solely for the shipment of waste. The improvements to the Low Staiths and the rebuilding of the 21-ton wagons with four doors instead of eight, following an experimental rebuild of a Harton wagon at the Philadelphia Wagon Shops, meant that waste shipments could be integrated with coal shipments there. The branch was also very labour-intensive, with no fewer than six level crossings, two controlled by barriers, three controlled by flagmen and one by a hand-operated boom. So the High Staith and its branch were closed on 28th February 1976.

The closure of Whitburn and Harton raised questions about the long-term future of Boldon Colliery. Westoe shed's first diesel locomotive had soon been dispatched to Boldon Colliery, and Westoe then remained diesel-free until August 1976, when, with traffic declining, it was decided to close Boldon Colliery's locomotive shed and to transfer its one remaining duty and the diesel locomotives kept to cover it, to Westoe. With plenty of spare ground at Boldon, it had also been

284. E3, Siemens 456/1909, at Harton Colliery on the day of its closure, 25th July 1969, in the white livery adopted in 1966 after a fatality on the railway..

decided to develop the area as a coal stocking site, where either coal awaiting shipment or sale could be temporarily dumped. Hardly had the shed closed when a national seaman's strike looked likely, and in case Boldon had to be used intensively, a spare locomotive was brought by road from Wearmouth Colliery in Sunderland. In the event, the strike did not take place and the locomotive never left the shed, returning to Wearmouth in April 1977. Despite this, Boldon became a major stocking site, and such was the volume of traffic that two locomotives were sometimes needed on this duty, hence the arrival of AB 478/1963 to act as a spare loco for this turn. The colliery eventually closed on 26th June 1982, but the coal stocking site remained open until the major re-organisation of March 1988 (see below).

The public electrified systems initiated by the NER had been abandoned in 1967, only for growing road transport congestion to bring the whole concept forward again less than fifteen years later. With the creation of Tyne & Wear County Council in 1974 came the creation of the Tyne & Wear Passenger Transport Executive, which saw the development of a major tramway system – the "Metro" – as an essential contributor to public transport on Tyneside, and eventually also to Wearside. Having taken over the local infrastructure previously operated by British Rail, the PTE's proposed development included an electrified line from Heworth to South Shields – but not via the 1879 line, which was closed, together with the demolition of the viaduct at St.Hilda; instead, the PTE decided to utilise the former Pontop & South Shields route from Tyne Dock, which it then compulsorily purchased northwards from a point near the former Harton Junction. This in turn meant accommodating the Harton electric system alongside the new double-track Metro lines north of Dean Road sidings, now more commonly known as "The Deans", for about ¾ mile. Both the Dean Road and Victoria Road coal depots were removed, together with sidings at Laygate, while the Laygate cutting was opened out and a new Metro station, called Chichester, built there, with the Harton line, completely separate, passing alongside. Much of the NCB section was rebuilt on a new alignment, though it remained in full use throughout, albeit using diesel locomotives to work the traffic.

By 1983 the Westoe engineers had realised that in the event of one of the three low-height locomotives Nos.13-15 being unavailable, the remaining two would not be able to handle all of the traffic. It was thus decided to rebuild No.12 to match the later locomotives, or, more accurately, to have Baguley-Drewry Ltd build a new locomotive, including new frames, but utilising as many parts from No.12 as possible, including the motors. No.12 went to Burton-on-Trent in June 1983, with No.9 being given a new lease of life in her absence. However, the national miners' strike, which began on 12th March 1984, delayed the delivery of the new No.12 until February 1985.

285. The Tower Wagon, much rebuilt at Westoe, at Harton Low Staiths on one of the last Sunday inspection duties, 25th June 1989.

Its return allowed the five working electric locomotives to be rotated between the Westoe Washery washed coal end (normally No.11, as she could not be used elsewhere), two working between Westoe and St.Hilda sidings and one at the Low Staiths, with the fifth in for maintenance, whilst one of the two resident diesels worked the concentration sidings at Westoe, including the raw coal end of the Washery. Volumes remained high, with 7,000 tons of coal and 1,500 tons of waste being handled daily between Westoe and the Low Staiths. The Wagon Shop near the bottom of the Low Staiths tunnel was fully occupied, although wagons from now-closed railways such as

286. The interior of the Wagon Shop at Harton Low Staiths, with its turntable, on 15th February 1988. A former BR 21-ton wagon is receiving attention.

287. 12 in green livery shunting in the Westoe Colliery sidings on 29th March 1983; two of the railway's second-hand brake vans stand beyond the loco.

288. 12 leaving the Wagon Shop "loco shed" on 18th July 1989, the railway's penultimate day; her construction in 1984 included new frames, a re-designed bonnet and cab, welded superstructure and round buffers, but re-used the original No 12's motor and other parts. She was the last new locomotive built for a private railway in County Durham.

Monkton and Lambton now began to appear.

The death-knell for the railway came with the opening of the new Tyne Coal Terminal at Tyne Dock, a mile upstream from the Low Staiths, on 7th November 1985. This was a joint venture between the Port of Tyne Authority, the NCB, the Central Electricity Generating Board and British Rail, and was designed to handle ships of up to 30,000 tons and trains of 1,000 tons, in high-capacity BR wagons. In February 1988 it was announced that under a £4.2 million investment the line between the Deans and Westoe would be brought up to BR standard in order for BR to operate merry-go-round trains between Westoe, where a rapid loader would be installed, and the Terminal. The original plan envisaged BR also handling the waste, and working it through to Dawdon Colliery, near Seaham, where there was a waste disposal point that discharged on to the beach. This would render the Low Staiths redundant, and the area was to be cleared and landscaped. In the event, dumping waste on to the beach became environmentally unacceptable, and as a result the Low Staiths would have to remain open to continue to handle waste for dumping at sea. Although British Rail would work the coal trains, British Coal would still own the track northwards from the Deans. All of the siding accommodation on this section was to be removed, including the concentration sidings at Westoe, together with the link between Victoria Road and St.Hilda ('The Pontop'). The new line was a simple, single track with passing loops, although it was fitted with track circuits and two-aspect colour signals controlled from a new signal box at Westoe looking like a two-storey detached house.

Entrance to the "Westoe branch" was controlled from the Gateshead power box, the Westoe box only being manned when trains were using the branch. Together with these changes, the working down to the Boldon coal stocking site came to an end, while the Westoe shed exit lines terminated in a headshunt in order to prevent a runaway gaining access to the new running line.

The decision to continue to ship waste through the Low Staiths meant that the railway would continue to be needed, although for how long was clearly debatable. The railway operation would be re-organised. Electric working would be confined to the section between St.Hilda sidings and the Low Staiths, with two locomotives being required, one being spare. The Wagon Shop would be used as their **loco shed** (NZ 349669), although in practice there was scarcely enough room for two locomotives, and the working locomotive was usually housed just inside the tunnel. Between Westoe and St.Hilda sidings work would be handled by three diesels from the fleet of seven working from Westoe shed, though enough overhead wires would be retained in case an electric locomotive stored there needed to be brought out in an emergency, such as assisting a struggling diesel up Erskine Road bank. 700 wagons remained, far more than were needed; 380 were sent for scrap, and minor repair work needed to any of the remainder was to be done in the open air.

Full electric working ended on 18th March 1988, with Nos.12 and 13 then being allocated to the Low Staiths section and the others stored. The last collier to be loaded at the Low Staiths, the *Warrenpoint*,

289. 12's erstwhile twin, 13, leaving Hilda Sidings with empties for Westoe in 1987.

290. 13 collects empties for Hilda sidings at Harton Low Staiths on the railway's last day, 19th July 1989.

left on 18th July 1988 and BR traffic for the Tyne Coal Terminal began on 8th August 1988.

It soon became clear that this rather fragmented system would be replaced by a waste conveyor system, to be installed during the next pit holidays. The last stone train was worked on 19th July 1989, and the last section of the last of Durham's private railways was closed.

De-wiring began the same afternoon and was completed within 24 hours, and the conveyor system began operation on 8th August 1989 as planned. The remaining 300 wagons, 210 at Westoe and 90, now trapped, at St.Hilda, were removed by road to the scrapyard of C.Herring & Son Ltd at Hartlepool, apart from one acquired for preservation by the Bowes Railway. One diesel locomotive was retained to facilitate maintenance on the Westoe-Deans section, but this work was soon taken over by British Rail. Two of the diesels were returned to the makers, one was preserved, as was the tower wagon, whilst all of the remainder, including the last four electric locomotives, were sold for scrap to Booth Roe Metals Ltd at Rotherham. Westoe shed and the Low Staiths "shed" were demolished during January 1990.

In the event the reduction in the demand for coal and the availability of cheaper coal from Europe meant the end of the coal industry in Durham, and despite the recent investment, Westoe Colliery ceased production on 7th May 1993.

Locomotive liveries
At the end of the Second World War the electric locomotives were painted in unlined black. In 1950 an experiment was tried with two different liveries; E8 was painted in olive green, with red and yellow lining and yellow lettering shaded red, while E10 was painted slate grey, with black edging to the bonnet and cab. In the event neither was adopted and the black livery was retained, but with yellow lettering shaded red. In 1958 this was changed to royal blue, with the same lettering, but also with red lining, buffer beams and pantographs. However, the blue tended to fade in the sun.

In 1966 a child was fatally injured at a level crossing, and the NCB ordered a change to all white, though with the lettering as before. In the event, all white proved a dangerous colour against the sky, and to counter-act this black chevrons were added to the nose-ends and an inverted black V painted on the cab sides. Some locomotives had their chevrons supplemented by 'day-glo' orange strips. The white livery was retained until 1972, when it was replaced by olive green, with the lettering and chevrons as before. This lasted until 1984, when during the miners' strike the locomotives were repainted in royal blue, with inverted V symbols and yellow lettering, with the window surrounds also painted yellow and the buffer beams red. About February 1988 the diesel locomotives present all had their works numbers painted on the cab doors in yellow.

Reference : W.J.Hatcher, *The Harton Electric Railway*, Oakwood Press, 1994.

Fig.81 — The electric system 1981 - 1989

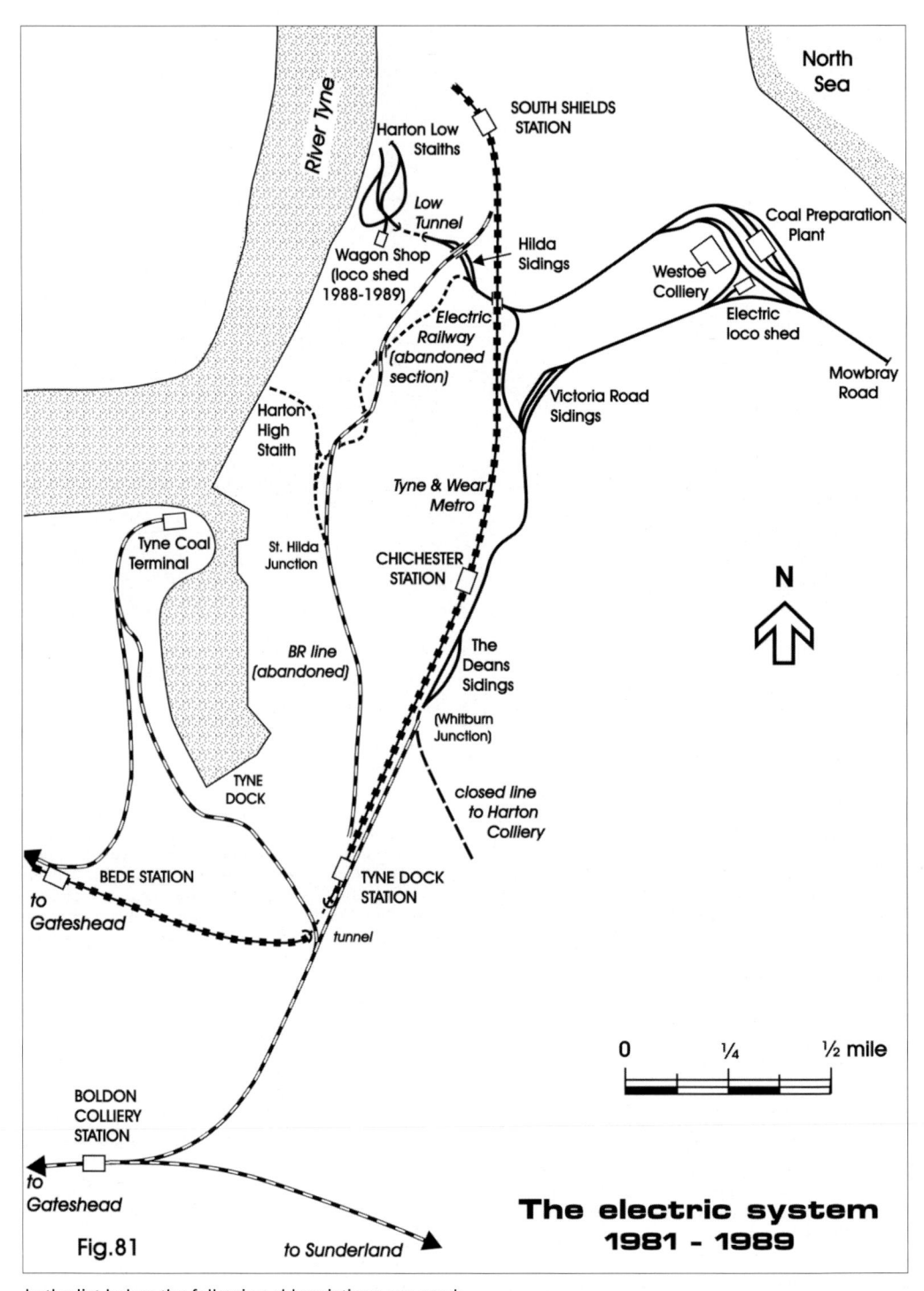

In the list below the following abbreviations are used:

B	Boldon Colliery, Boldon Colliery
Da	Dawdon Colliery, Seaham
LEW	Lambton Engine Works, Philadelphia
Se	Seaham Colliery, Seaham
We	Westoe loco shed, South Shields

Gauge : 4ft 8½in

E1	later 1	4wWE	Siemens	451	1908	New	(1)
E2	later 2	4wWE	Siemens	455	1909	New	(2)
E3	3 on opposite side of loco	4w-4wWE	Siemens	456	1909	New	(3)
E4	later 4	4w-4wWE	Siemens	457	1909	New	(4)
E5		0-4-4-0WE	Siemens	458	1909	New	(5)
E6		0-4-4-0WE	Siemens	459	1910	New	(6)
E7	later 7	4w-4wWE	KS	1202	1911	New	
			reb NCB		1953		(7)
E8	later 8	4w-4wWE	KS	1203	1911	New	(7)
E9	later No.9	4w-4wWE	AEG	1565	1913	New	(8)
E10		4wWE	Siemens	862	1913	New	(9)
No.11	later 11	4w-4wWE	EE	1795	1951		
			Bg	3351	1951	New	(10)
No.12	later 12	4w-4wWE	EE	1794	1951		
			Bg	3350	1951	New	(11)
No.13	later 13	4w-4wWE	EE	2308	1957		
			Bg	3469	1957	New	(12)
No.14	later 14	4w-4wWE	EE	2599	1959		
			Bg	3519	1959	New	(13)
No.15	later 15	4w-4wWE	EE	2600	1959		
			Bg	3520	1959	New	(14)
-		2w-2DM(R)	Bg	3565	1960	New	
	reb	2w-2DH(R)	NCB				(15)
(No.505)	21201/208 *	0-6-0DH	HE	6616	1965	(a)	
	We-B 11/1970-We 8/1976						(16)
	2120/211	0-6-0DH	AB	514	1966	(b)	(17)
	-	0-4-0DH	AB	478	1963	(c)	
	We-LEW 27/8/1979-We 18/4/1980						(18)
(20/110/733)		0-6-0DH	AB	646	1979	(d)	
	We-Da 19/1/1984-We 12/2/1988						(19)
No.2		0-6-0DH	AB	423	1958	(e)	Scr 8/1981
-	No.623 from c2/1988	0-6-0DH	AB	623	1977	(f)	
	We-LEW 18/5/1981-Se 19/6/1981-We 10/9/1986-Se c2/1987-We 10/3/1987						(20)
(9101/0067)	549 from c2/1988	0-6-0DH	AB	549	1967	(g)	(20)
No.12		4w-4wWE	BD		1984	New (h)	(21)
No.504		0-6-0DH	HE	6615	1965	(j)	(22)
-	No.613 from c2/1988	0-6-0DH	AB	613	1977	(k)	(23)
-	No.491 from c2/1988	0-6-0DH	AB	491	1964	(m)	(24)
-	659 from c2/1988	0-6-0DH	AB	659	1982	(n)	(25)
-	582 from c5/1988	0-6-0DH	AB	582	1973	(p)	(26)

* carried incorrectly for 2120/208 (its NCB Plant number)

(a) ex Whitburn Colliery, Whitburn, 6/1968; for previous history see chapter 14
(b) ex Boldon Colliery, Boldon Colliery, 8/1976 (see below)
(c) ex Monkton Railways, Wardley loco shed, Wardley, 4/10/1978; for previous history see chapter 3
(d) ex Bates Colliery, Blyth, Northumberland. 8/9/1979
(e) ex Wearmouth Colliery, Sunderland, 10/2/1980
(f) ex Ashington Colliery, Ashington, Northumberland, 1/9/1980
(g) ex Lambton Engine Works, Philadelphia, 15/5/1981; at Bates Colliery, Blyth, Northumberland, until 8/10/1980
(h) incorporated motors and bogies from EE 1794/Bg 3350 above
(j) ex Monkton Railways, Wardley loco shed, Wardley, 22/7/1985; for previous history see chapter 3
(k) ex Hunslet-Barclay Ltd, Kilmarnock, Ayrshire, Scotland, 3/12/1986, following rebuild (heavy repairs); at Ashington Colliery, Ashington, Northumberland, until 8/1986
(m) ex Hunslet-Barclay Ltd, Kilmarnock, Ayrshire, Scotland, 22/12/1986, following rebuild (heavy repairs), but carried 1987 on rebuild plate; at Ashington Central Workshops, Ashington, Northumberland, until 8/1986
(n) ex Seaham Colliery, Seaham, 23/12/1987
(p) ex Ellington South Coal Preparation Plant, Lynemouth, Northumberland, 10/5/1988

(1) withdrawn from traffic by 30/10/1970; to North of England Open Air Museum, Marley Hill loco shed store, near Sunniside, for preservation, 10/8/1973; scrapped on site by K.Thomas, Lanchester, 2/1981

(2) sold for scrap to L.Marley, Stanley, c2/1984; to West Yorkshire Transport Museum Trust, for preservation at Spen Valley Railway Project, 7/3/1984; moved from Westoe to former BR Hammerton Street loco shed, Bradford, West Yorkshire, 20/6/1985; to National Museum of the Working Horse, Halifax, West Yorkshire (but privately owned), 19/6/1989; to North of England Open Air Museum, Beamish, 26/3/1991

(3) from time to time used at Harton Colliery deputising for 8; usually stored from 26/7/1969; scrapped on site, 4/1978

(4) withdrawn from traffic, 18/11/1981; to Tyne & Wear County Council, Museum of Land Transport, North Shields, for preservation, 16/6/1982 (loaded at Boldon Colliery); now Tyne & Wear Museums, North Tyneside Steam Railway; to Heritage Engineering, Lanark, Lanarkshire, 4/1998; returned, 25/11/1998; rebuilt to 4w-4wBE and restored to working order, using batteries carried in a replica Harton Coal Co Ltd wagon, with sponsorship by Siemens, 6/2001

(5) withdrawn from traffic, /1959, and stripped for spares; frame and wheels scrapped on site, 10/1965

(6) withdrawn from traffic, /1959, and stripped for spares; to Area Central Workshops, Whitburn, for conversion to a diesel-powered maintenance vehicle, 11/10/1962; plan abandoned; remains scrapped on site, 1/1966

(7) scrapped on site by "Laing, Sunderland", 8/1974; this is believed to refer to the former shipyard of J.L.Laing & Co Ltd at Sunderland, by that date part of Doxford & Sunderland Ltd

(8) to Tanfield Railway, Marley Hill loco shed, near Sunniside, for preservation, for preservation, 23/4/1988 (privately owned)

(9) sold for scrap to L.Marley, Stanley, c2/1984; to West Yorkshire Transport Museum Trust, for Spen Valley Railway Project, 7/3/1984; moved from Westoe to former BR Hammerton Street loco shed, Bradford, West Yorkshire, 18/6/1985; to Ludlam Street bus garage store, Bradford, West Yorkshire, 7/7/1989; to Tanfield Railway, Marley Hill loco shed, near Sunniside, 28/6/1995 (owned by Tyneside Locomotive Museum Trust)

(10) stripped for spares, 3/1988; to J.McClachlan, Bishop Auckland, for scrap, 4/1988; moved to Tyne Dock, 12/4/1988, and scrapped there

(11) to Baguley-Drewry Ltd, Burton-on-Trent, Staffordshire, for motors and bogies to be used in the construction of a new locomotive; frames scrapped there, 1/1984

(12) to Booth Roe Metals Ltd, Rotherham, South Yorkshire, for scrap, 10/1989; moved to Rotherham, 4/11/1989 and cut up immediately

(13) to Booth Roe Metals Ltd, Rotherham, South Yorkshire, for scrap, 10/1989; moved to Rotherham, 14/11/1989 and cut up the next day

(14) to Booth Roe Metals Ltd, Rotherham, South Yorkshire, for scrap, 10/1989; moved to Rotherham, 7/11/1989; cut up, 22/2/1990

(15) to Tanfield Railway, Marley Hill loco shed, near Sunniside, for preservation (privately owned), 3/1990, by 16/4/1990

(16) to Lambton Engine Works, Philadelphia, 5/10/1978; to Derwenthaugh loco shed, Swalwell, 2/2/1979; for subsequent history see chapter 4

(17) to Lambton Engine Works, Philadelphia, 3/4/1980; to Monkton Railways, Wardley loco shed, Wardley, 17/11/1980; for subsequent history see chapter 3

(18) to C.F.Booth (Steel) Ltd, Rotherham, South Yorkshire, 21/10/1985; moved to Rotherham, 9/11/1985, and put to use as works shunter; to Shropshire Loco Collection, near Wellington, Shropshire, for preservation, c11/1991, and moved on 20/12/1991; to S&D Locomotive Co Ltd, (not moved from site); to McLaren Antiques, Oswestry, Shropshire, by 8/6/2002

(19) to Hunslet-Barclay Ltd, Kilmarnock, Ayrshire, Scotland, 8/1989; rebuilt HAB 6767/1990 and named LAURA; contracted to British Steel Corporation, Ebbw Vale Works, Ebbw Vale, Gwent, /1990 (British Steel Corporation became Corus plc in 10/1999); to Llanwern Works, Newport, (still on hire from HAB), c8/2001

(20) sold for scrap to C.Herring & Son Ltd, Hartlepool, Cleveland, 8/1989; moved to Hartlepool, 6/9/1989

(21) to Booth Roe Metals Ltd, Rotherham, South Yorkshire, for scrap, 10/1989; moved to Rotherham, 30/10/1989; cut up by 6/11/1989

(22) to Wearmouth Colliery, Sunderland, to be used as source of spares for similar locomotives, 2/1988; to Booth Roe Metals Ltd, Rotherham, South Yorkshire, for scrap, 8/1990; moved to Rotherham, 9/1990 and cut up in same month

(23) to P.Dawe for preservation, 8/1989, and moved to Bowes Railway Centre, Springwell, near Gateshead, 7/9/1989

(24) to Booth Roe Metals Ltd, Rotherham, South Yorkshire, for scrap, 10/1989; moved to Rotherham, 20/11/1989, and scrapped within days of arrival

(25) to Hunslet-Barclay Ltd, Kilmarnock, Ayrshire, Scotland, 8/1989; rebuilt HAB 6768/1990 and named TRACEY; contracted to British Steel Corporation, Ebbw Vale Works, Ebbw Vale, Gwent, /1990 (British Steel Corporation became Corus plc in 10/1999); to Port Talbot Works, Port Talbot, (still on hire from HAB), 7/2002

(26) to Booth Roe Metals Ltd, Rotherham, South Yorkshire, for scrap, 6/1989; moved to Rotherham in same month and cut up soon afterwards

Locomotives at Boldon Colliery

Return No.102 of the Durham Coal Owners Association (DCRO/NCB/Co/86/102) lists one locomotive here in both April 1871 and November 1876, but no details are known. The earliest locomotive recorded here arrived in 1922; whether there were other locomotives here between 1876 and 1922, or whether the NER worked the traffic, is also unknown. The final locomotives and their duty were transferred to Westoe loco shed, South Shields, in August 1976.

In the list below the following abbreviations are used:

B	Boldon Colliery, Boldon Colliery
LEW	Lambton Engine Works, Philadelphia
P	Lambton Railway loco sheds, Philadelphia
SBF	Springwell Bank Foot loco shed, Wardley, Bowes Railway
WCW	Area Central Workshops, Whitburn
We	Westoe loco shed, South Shields
Wh	Whitburn loco shed, Whitburn

Gauge : 4ft 8½in

-		0-4-0ST	OC	HE	286	1883	(a)	s/s
1		0-6-0	IC	Ghd		1882	(b)	Scr /1944
4		0-6-0	IC	Ghd		1883	(c)	(1)
LALEHAM	[1] from 1963	0-6-0ST	OC	AB	1639	1923	(d)	
	B-Wh 7/1931-B 3/2/1960							(2)
3		0-4-0T	IC	Ghd	38	1888	(e)	(3)
2		0-6-0	IC	Ghd	43	1889	(f)	(4)
(1)	later BOLDON No.1	0-6-0T	IC	HC	332	1889	(g)	Scr 3/1958
	BOWES No.9	0-6-0ST	IC	SS	4051	1894		
	reb	0-6-0PT	IC	Caerphilly		1930	(h)	(5)
(75182)	("7132") 5 from 1963	0-6-0ST	IC	RSHN	7132	1944	(j)	

B-Wh 20/9/1948-B 6/5/1954-W.G.Bagnall Ltd, Stafford, for repairs, /1961
-Wh 20/12/1961-WCW 28/9/1963 for fitting with Hunslet mechanical stoker
-Wh 14/6/1964-WCW c9/1965-Wh 25/9/1965-B 25/12/1965 (6)

71485		0-6-0ST	IC	RSHN	7294	1945	(k)	(7)
-	later BOLDON No.1513	0-6-0T	IC	HC	1513	1924	(m)	
	B-Wh by 2/1949-B-Wh for repairs, 1/1950-B 2/1950							Scr 12/1959
No.4		0-6-0	IC	Ghd	28	1897	(n)	(8)
"9"		0-6-0ST	IC	HE	3191	1944	(p)	(9)
"7695"	7 from 1963	0-6-0ST	OC	RSHN	7695	1951	(q)	
	B-Wh 8/7/1959-B 4/1965							Scr 3/1970
"7749"	9 from 1963	0-6-0ST	OC	RSHN	7749	1953	(r)	

B-Wh 11/2/1959-B 21/2/1961-WCW 22/5/1962-B 19/11/1962
-Wh 5/12/1962-B 13/5/1963 (10)

"7811"	10 from 1963	0-6-0ST	OC	RSHN	7811	1954	(s)	
	B-LEW 3/2/1960-B 5/1960-WCW 12/1/1961-Wh 7/2/1961-B 7/8/1962							(11)
"7603"		0-6-0ST	OC	RSHN	7603	1949	(t)	(12)
(No.507)	2120/211 from 8/1969	0-6-0DH		HE	6618	1965	(u)	
	B-We /1968-B /1968-We 5/1968-P 2/1969-B c5/1969-P 4/1/1971-B 2/3/1971							(13)
(509)	2120/211 from 6/1972	0-6-0DH		AB	514	1966	(v)	
	B-SBF, for repairs, 11/3/1971-B 25/5/1972							(14)
No.506		0-6-0DH		HE	6617	1965	(w)	(15)
(No.505)	2120/208 from 11/1970	0-6-0DH		HE	6616	1965	(x)	
	B-We 10/1968-B 11/1970							(14)
	(D)3516	0-6-0DE		Derby		1958	(y)	(16)
506		0-6-0DH		Sdn		1964	(z)	(17)

In addition to the locomotives in the list above, the spares orders of the Hunslet Engine Co Ltd, Leeds, record an order from The Harton Coal Co Ltd dated 13/1/1915 for 0-4-0ST OC HE 361/1885. The order does not record a delivery address, so whether the locomotive worked here or on the South Shields, Marsden & Whitburn Colliery Railway is not known.

The following locomotive was sent to Boldon Colliery in anticipation of a national seaman's strike and coal needing to be stocked here. In the event this did not take place, and the locomotive never left the shed.

No.3D		0-6-0DM	HE	5302	1958	(aa)	(18)

(a) probably ex R.Frazer & Sons Ltd, dealers, Hebburn, 10/1922; previous owners unknown; new to Lucas & Aird, contractors, Kingston-upon-Hull, Yorkshire (ER)
(b) ex LNER, 1453, 3/1927; previously NER, 398 class
(c) ex R.Frazer & Sons Ltd, dealers, Hebburn, /1928; previously LNER, 1333, originally NER, 398 class, until 8/1925
(d) ex George Cohen & Co Ltd, contractors, /1929, who offered the locomotive for sale in the *Colliery Guardian* on 8/3/1929; previously S.Pearson & Son Ltd, Queen Mary Reservoir contract, Sunbury, Middlesex
(e) ex LNER, 24, Y7 class, per R.Frazer & Sons Ltd, dealers, Hebburn, 2/2/1931
(f) ex South Shields, Marsden & Whitburn Colliery Railway, 7, c/1937; for previous history see chapter 14
(g) ex GWR, 782, 11/1939; previously Barry Railway, 34, E class
(h) ex John Bowes & Partners Ltd, Bowes Railway, Springwell Bank Foot loco shed, Wardley, 20/2/1943, on hire
(j) ex War Department, 75182, location unknown, 7/1947; previous known location was South Wales Electric Power Co Ltd, Upper Boat Power Station, Treforest, Glamorgan
(k) ex War Department, 71485, Longmoor Military Railway, Liss, Hampshire, 9/1947
(m) ex South Shields, Marsden & Whitburn Colliery Railway, by 9/1948
(n) ex BR, 5626, J24 class, 10/3/1949 (per LNER/BR official Locomotive Register); originally NER, 1931
(p) ex Whitburn Colliery, Whitburn, after 7/1956, by 9/1957; for previous history see chapter 14
(q) ex Whitburn Colliery, Whitburn, 11/2/1958; for previous history see chapter 14
(r) ex Whitburn Colliery, Whitburn, 24/7/1958; for previous history see chapter 14
(s) ex Whitburn Colliery, Whitburn, 8/7/1959; for previous history see chapter 14
(t) ex Whitburn Colliery, Whitburn, 21/9/1961; for previous history see chapter 14
(u) ex Whitburn Colliery, Whitburn, 19/5/1966; for previous history see chapter 14
(v) ex Springwell Bank Foot loco shed, Bowes Railway, after repairs, 5/5/1958
(w) ex Whitburn Colliery, Whitburn, 6/1968
(x) ex Westoe loco shed, South Shields, 9/1968, after 7/9/1968
(y) ex British Rail, Doncaster Motive Power Depot, Doncaster, Yorkshire (NR), hire, 16/4/1973, while AB 514 was under repair
(z) ex Lambton Railway loco sheds, Philadelphia, 2/1974
(aa) ex Wearmouth Colliery, Sunderand, 13/9/1976

(1) to South Shields, Marsden & Whitburn Colliery Railway, by 19/9/1948; for subsequent history see chapter 14
(2) scrapped on site by J.Wight & Co Ltd, Pallion, Sunderland, 6/1964
(3) to Usworth Colliery, Usworth, by 26/10/1947; scrapped there, /1952
(4) returned to South Shields, Marsden & Whitburn Colliery Railway, by 3/8/1939; for subsequent history see chapter 14
(5) to South Shields, Marsden & Whitburn Colliery Railway, c4/1943; returned, c7/1943; returned to John Bowes & Partners Ltd, Bowes Railway, Springwell Bank Foot loco shed, Wardley, 14/8/1943
(6)) to Wearmouth Colliery, Sunderland, 5/7/1966; scrapped on site, 4/1969
(7) to Robert Stephenson & Hawthorns Ltd, Newcastle upon Tyne, for repairs, by 30/7/1955, and returned; to Whitburn Colliery, Whitburn, 11/2/1959; for subsequent history see chapter 14
(8) to Whitburn Colliery, Whitburn, 30/3/1956, by which date withdrawn from traffic; for subsequent history see chapter 14
(9) to Area Central Workshops, Whitburn, /1960, after 16/7/1960; for subsequent history see chapter 14
(10) to Whitburn Colliery, Whitburn, 4/1965, to await repairs; for subsequent history see chapter 14
(11) to Whitburn Colliery, Whitburn, 10/9/1962; for subsequent history see chapter 14
(12) to Whitburn Colliery, Whitburn, 17/11/1962; for subsequent history see chapter 14
(13) to Derwenthaugh loco shed, Swalwell, 12/6/1972; for subsequent history see chapter 4
(14) to Westoe loco shed, South Shields, 8/1976, on closure of shed
(15) to Bowes Railway. Springwell Bank Foot loco shed, Wardley, for repairs, 31/10/1968; to Lambton Railway loco sheds, Philadelphia, 13/2/1969; for subsequent history see chapter 9
(16) returned to British Rail, Doncaster Motive Power Depot, Doncaster, Yorkshire (NR), 24/4/1973
(17) to Backworth Colliery, Backworth, Northumberland, 17/12/1974; to Burradon Colliery, Burradon, Northumberland, 29/1/1975; to Weetslade Coal Preparation Plant, Weetslade, 3/1/1976; to Lambton Engine Works, Philadelphia, for repairs, 23/4/1981; to Ashington Colliery, Ashington, Northumberland, 11/9/1981; to Tenterden Railway Co Ltd (Kent & East Sussex Railway), for preservation, 26/9/1987
(18) to Wearmouth Colliery, Sunderland, 18/4/1977; scrapped here by D.Short Ltd, North Shields, 1/1984

Although the routes of the railway in South Shields can still be traced, heavy landscaping has obliterated much of the detail; for example, the entrances of the Low Staiths tunnel are completely buried. The electric locomotives saved for preservation have had difficult fortunes; one was scrapped; two have changed hands three times, and neither they nor No.9 have to date (2004) had any restoration work done to them. Only E4 has been restored to working order, albeit powered by batteries carried in a replica Harton wagon.

Chapter Sixteen
The Towneley Colliery Railway
The Stella Unit Railway from 1947

OWNERS BEFORE 1947
The Stella Coal Co Ltd until 1/1/1947
The Stella Coal Co until 2/2/1903; see also below

Coal was being mined in the Ryton area of north-west Durham by the second half of the 14th century. In the second half of the 16th century the Bishop of Durham granted a large area comprising Whickham, Winlaton, Ryton and Stella to Queen Elizabeth I, who sublet what was then called the Stella Grand Lease to "a powerful company". By the 17th century a large shareholder in the Lease was the Vane family (see chapter 10), while by the end of the 18th century another major shareholder was George Silvertop of Minsteracres, although in 1800 he sub-let his interests. By 1820 the main leaseholder was Peregrine Towneley, who sub-let to George Dunn of Newcastle upon Tyne and his sons, one of whom was the leading viewer Matthias Dunn, who lived at Stella Hall. Their lease terminated in 1831 and failed to be renewed due to legal disputes. Mining thus ceased for some years, until in the mid-1830s the southern area was acquired by the 2nd Marquis of Bute (see chapter 4). Then in 1839 the northern area was let to a partnership of John Buddle (see chapters 9 and 10), T.Y.Hall and A.L.Potter, who traded under the name of The Stella Coal Company. However, this title may well have also been used by previous lessees. The partnership was subsequently joined by Robert Simpson and his son John Bell Simpson, who played a major part in the firm's affairs. The partnership became a limited company in 1903, by which time the directors were F.Buddle Atkinson, W.R.Lamb and the Browne and Simpson families. A large volume of company material survives, most of it now in the Durham Record Office (NCB/I/SC and others).

Nomenclature in this area is confusing. The royalty names were sometimes used as colliery names. The two chief colliery names, Towneley Colliery and Stella Colliery, were also used collectively to represent various separate pits. In the 20th century the pits became collieries in their own right.

In the 19th century the company also owned two other collieries not on the Grand Lease – **BLAYDON MAIN COLLIERY**, near Blaydon (NZ 188632), which it had acquired by 1883 and sold in 1908, and **CLARA VALE COLLIERY**, Clara Vale (NZ 132651), which it opened in 1893 and which passed to the NCB in 1947. These had rail provision separate from the Towneley Main Waggonway.

In the account below no attempt has been made to discuss the pits in the area and their waggonways before 1800; this is described in *A Fighting Trade – Rail Transport in Tyne coal, 1600-1800, Vol.1 – History, Vol.2 – Data* by G.Bennett, E.Clavering and A.Rounding, published by the Portcullis Press in 1990. The waggonway/railway system begun in the first half of the 19th century to serve the pits on the Grand Lease was called at first the **Towneley Main Waggonway**, and then from at least 1858 the **Towneley Colliery Railway**. This name fell into disuse in the early 20th century, and for many years the system seems not to have had a formal name. Under NCB ownership it was designated the **Stella Unit Railway**.

The first of the 19th century collieries to be sunk was what became the **TOWNELEY COLLIERY, Stargate Pit**, later **STARGATE COLLIERY** (NZ 162635), to the south-east of Ryton. Sinking began in 1800 and was completed on 16th June 1803. An undated map in the Durham Record Office (NCB I/P 5) shows that this pit was originally linked to what the map calls the 'Old White Field Waggonway to Stella', which ran from a pit called the C PIT (NZ 154629) about ¾ mile to the southwest to staithes on the River Tyne just east of Stella Hall (NZ 175639). The sequencing of collieries/pits and waggonways/railways now becomes extremely problematic. The next pit to be sunk was certainly the **STELLA FREEHOLD PIT**, sometimes called the **Bog Pit** (NZ 166634), whose sinking was completed on 28th April 1835. This is not shown on the map above, which would suggest that the latter predates 1835, and also that the proposed new waggonway which the map shows was not proceeded with at that time. It may well be that this new line was contemporary with the sinking of the next pit, at first called **TOWNELEY MAIN COLLIERY**, then **TOWNELEY COLLIERY, Emma Pit**, and latterly **EMMA COLLIERY** (NZ 145640), at Bar Moor, near Ryton. Although a sinking was made here in 1823, the sinking of the modern colliery here began on 17th March 1845 and was completed on 20th April 1847. This was to work the western area of the royalty. The first coal seam, six feet thick, was only 50 feet from the surface (although it had been worked by earlier miners) and as the shafts were sunk deeper it was found that there were more than a dozen coal seams here, although some were too thin to work. This lay 1¼ miles west north-west of Stargate, and a new line was certainly needed to serve it, and so it may be that this was part of the entirely new line built to new staiths on the River Tyne about ¼ mile downsteam of the old waggonway's staiths.

Shunting of waggons at the Emma Pit was done by a '**Jack Engine**' at the colliery, a small stationary engine situated to the west of the screens, through which the waggons would then run by gravity. The section to Stargate was worked by the **Stargate Engine** near the Stargate Pit. Curiously, it is not shown on any O.S. map. The 1st edition of the Ordnance Survey maps shows two signal posts on this section, though their purpose on a rope incline is not known. The Stargate Engine then lowered the fulls down to the **STELLA STAITHS** (NZ 176638). These staiths were the furthest upstream on the River Tyne, some fifteen miles from the sea. From the Emma Pit to the staiths was about 2½ miles. Presumably the engine also had to work traffic in and out of the Freehold Pit. However, it would seem that the Stargate Pit had been closed by 1845.

Amongst the records of the company in the Durham Record Office are various documents detailing the costs of the railway at various dates between 1860 and 1877 (NCB I/SC 462). These show that in 1861 the staiths handled 39,794 waggons of Emma Pit coal, 7,237 waggons of Freehold Pit coal and 2,445 tons of clay. The overall costs of the railway were £2,220-18s-4d, or 10.96d per chaldron. The costs for the previous year note that a rope lasted about 3½ years, and that one rope, possibly both, was 1,870 yards, or nearly 1¼ miles, the two costing £178 new.

The next new colliery to be sunk worked the coal in the north-eastern sector of the royalty. This was **STELLA COLLIERY, Addison Pit**, later **ADDISON COLLIERY** (NZ 167634) at Hedgefield. Sinking began on 1st February 1864 and was completed on 26th January 1865. It lay alongside the NER Newcastle-Carlisle line, to which it was connected, 1 mile east of Ryton Station.

Beehive coke ovens were built at all three collieries, but instead of taking the colliery name, they were known collectively as the **HEDGEFIELD OVENS**. Latterly production was concentrated at Addison Colliery, where the last ovens were put out in the quarter ending 31st March 1922. There was also a **brickworks** on the northern side of Stargate Colliery, almost certainly using seggar clay from the pit, but its history is unclear.

The Freehold Pit closed during the 1860s, and in 1871 the Stargate Pit was sunk deeper and re-opened. This done, the firm clearly decided that the restrictions on the size of ships using the Stella Staiths was such that the railway needed to be linked to the North Eastern Railway in order for at least some of its coal to be shipped further downstream, almost certainly at the NER's Tyne Dock (opened in 1859). Rather than construct a link near the staiths, where the railway crossed the NER on bridges, the firm decided to build a self-acting incline, initially called in the records the **Stella & Hedgefield bank**, from north of the Stargate Pit down to the eastern end of the sidings serving the Addison Pit. Unusually for Durham in the second half of the 19th century, the incline had a drumhouse at the bank head (NZ 164636) that straddled the track, while most of the bottom section below the meetings ran in a tunnel, believed to be unique in the North-East. Almost certainly, a major factor in the decision to build this incline was that it would undoubtedly have handled a larger volume of traffic than the incline down to the Stella Staiths. Since the bank head lay

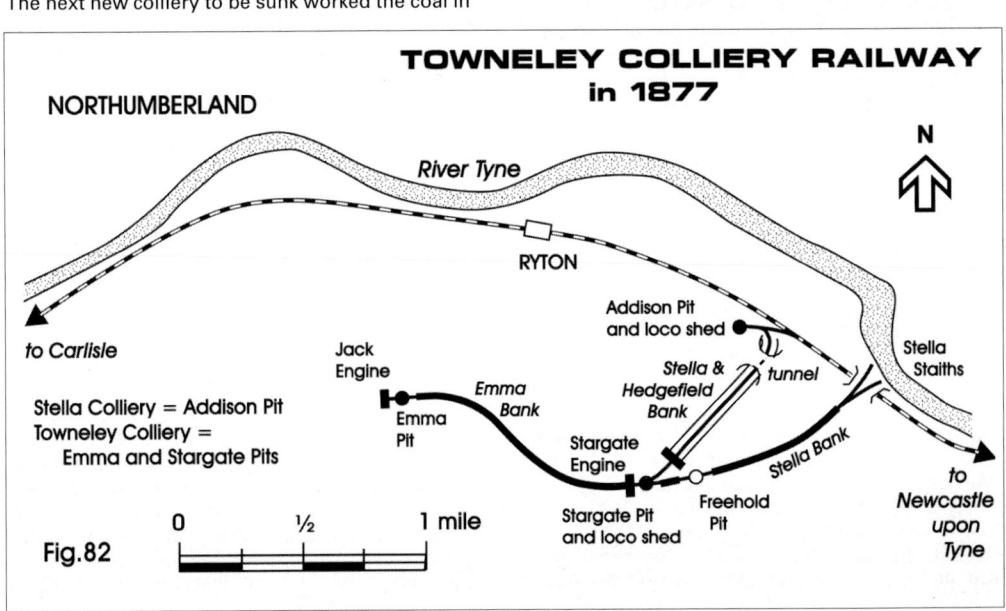

Fig.82 TOWNELEY COLLIERY RAILWAY in 1877

Stella Colliery = Addison Pit
Towneley Colliery = Emma and Stargate Pits

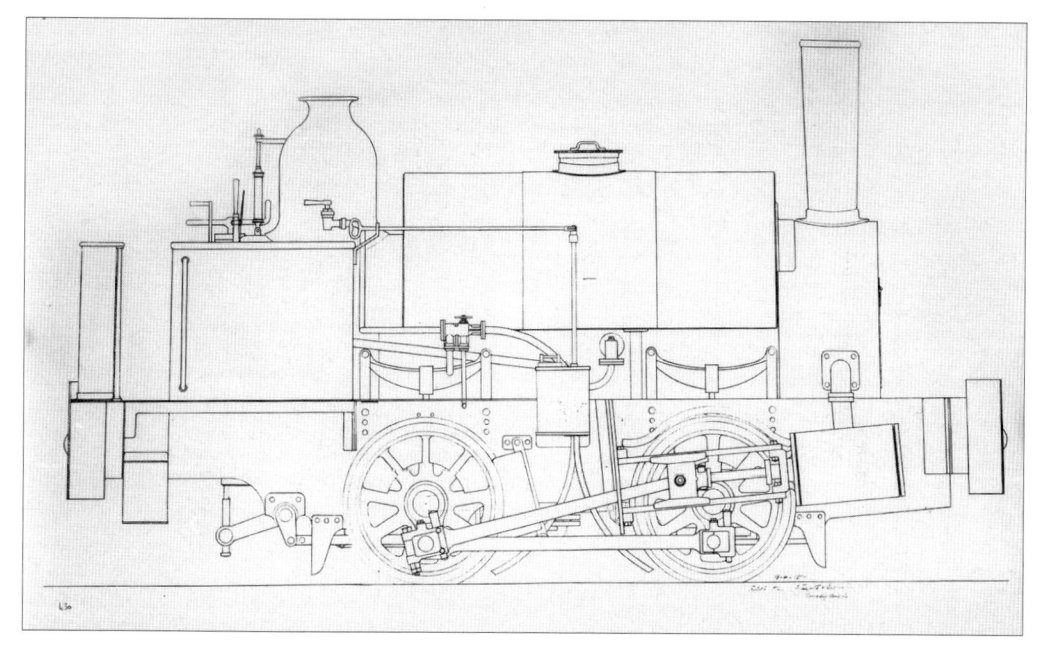

Fig.83. Line drawing by R.H.Inness of TOWNELEY, 0-4-0ST RWH 1726/1875

about ¼ mile north of the Stargate Pit, the waggon traffic would need to be shunted. The surviving annual costs for the railway in 1874 make no mention of this line or a locomotive, but both are listed in those for 1877, and as a locomotive was delivered in 1875, it must clearly have worked here and may also be the year in which the incline began work. The 1874 accounts list 150 chaldron waggons, and the accounts for 1877 give the operating costs as 6.48d per ton.

A detailed description of the railway is recorded in the *Colliery Guardian* of 2nd February 1894. This states that the Stargate Engine had two drums, 6ft and 9ft in diameter, and that it hauled "fulls from Emma to Stargate. These are then run by gravity down to Stella Staiths and the empties are brought up from the Staiths to Stargate, then run down to Emma". This would suggest that the inclines were worked alternately, although this does not have to have been the case, as both could have been worked simultaneously if one was worked by gravity whilst the other was in gear and hauling.

In 1902 the original stationary engine was replaced by a new one, built at Kilmarnock, in a new engine house (NZ 156634) further to the west of the colliery yard than the old one. CHA Townley recorded a workman's memory of how it worked on a visit to Stargate Colliery in 1950: "The set was taken from the kip [about ¼ mile to the east of the colliery], on a rope which went round a return wheel at the top of the incline [approx. ¼ mile on the Emma side of the engine]. When the set reached the top of the incline it was lowered on the rope to Emma Bank Foot. This engine also worked the bank down to Stella Staith, also a single [line] bank. At Emma [Colliery] the trucks were hauled up [to the west end of the colliery] and the shunting done by a small hauling engine." The two inclines were known as the Emma and Stella banks. He continued that latterly "the Emma bank ran 3 or 4 twenty ton trucks. The Stella bank only used black waggons" [the local name for 4-ton chaldron waggons, so called because of their invariable colour].

The final colliery to be linked to the system was **GREENSIDE COLLIERY**, Greenside (NZ 139619), sunk to work the lower seams on the southern side of the royalty. A colliery was worked here in the 18th century, but its shafts were ½ mile from the new pit. The line to serve this, begun on 16th May 1906, was built by a contractor (name unknown) who borrowed an "old engine" from the company to help him. From a junction with the Stargate-Addison line just to the north of the loco shed, it crossed the line to Stella Staith just east of the kip on a bridge, and then ran 2 miles southwestwards to the new colliery. Much of the branch was in cutting to allow easier locomotive working. Given the distance from Stargate, a **loco shed** was built at the southern end of the colliery to house the one locomotive to be kept here. The first train of coal was worked on 7th May 1907.

Also early in the 20th century, perhaps at much the same time as the opening of Greenside Colliery, the railway also received other major investment. A new shed to house the locomotives working at Stargate was built about half way along the spur between Stargate Colliery and the bank head. Much of what was now called the **Stargate bank** was rebuilt, with a longer meetings (presumably to allow the running of longer sets) and a new tunnel on the bottom section on a larger radius curve

291. Like South Hetton, the Stella system was still using chaldron waggons into National Coal Board days; Nos. 84, 16 (a rare example of a NCB-lettered chaldron), 33, 50 and 51 stand at Stargate Colliery, 4th March 1950. Note the differences in design from the South Hetton chaldrons shown on photo 236.

round to the NER. **WORKSHOPS** (NZ 169643) were built at Addison Colliery, to which the company's locomotives came for repair, and a new loco shed replaced the original one here.

Being so far upstream, shipments from Stella Staith eventually became limited only to wherries. Almost certainly this trade ceased between the two World Wars, although an older employee of Tyne Improvement Commission, whose records have been lost, thought that the last shipment could have been about 1942. However, the line itself remained open to handle landsale and workmen's coal, still using black waggons. It may well be that this traffic was handled by a locomotive, but there is no evidence to confirm this.

The company thus joined The South Hetton Coal Co Ltd in still using chaldron waggons when the coal industry was nationalised in 1947, and for the same reason: they were used only for internal traffic. Coal dispatched via the LNER was carried in LNER wagons, latterly in 20-ton hoppers, so that the colliery screens must have been made capable of handling this larger and higher design.

At the end of the Second World War major changes were made. The rope working to Emma Colliery, and the hauler shunting there, was replaced by locomotive working. Part of the old route near the colliery was replaced by a new line with easier gradients. At the same time the old route to the former staiths was also closed, and subsequently lifted. The engine house, its horizontal engine removed, was converted into new premises for the colliery fitters.

On 1st January 1947 Stargate, Emma, Addison and Greenside Collieries, together with the railway, were vested into NCB Northern Division No.6 (North-West Durham) Area.

NATIONAL COAL BOARD

Durham Division No.6 (North-West Durham) Area from 1/1/1950
Northern Division No.6 (North-West Durham) Area from 1/1/1947

Upon being taken over by the National Coal Board, the collieries were entitled the Stella Unit and the railway was called the Stella Unit Railway; they were allocated to No.6 Area's 'A' Group. In 1949 the Area drew up an Area numbering scheme, the only locomotive acquired in 1947 and not included in the list being ADDISON HL 2702/1907. Numbers were allocated in descending order of Groups. The Stella engines were allocated 12 to 17, with the Group Mechanical Engineer ordering that when numbers were applied the nameplates should be removed. In this Area each Group decided its own locomotive livery, and the 'A' Group locomotives were painted in middle green and lined out in red, with yellow numerals shaded red painted high on the

STELLA UNIT RAILWAY in 1950s

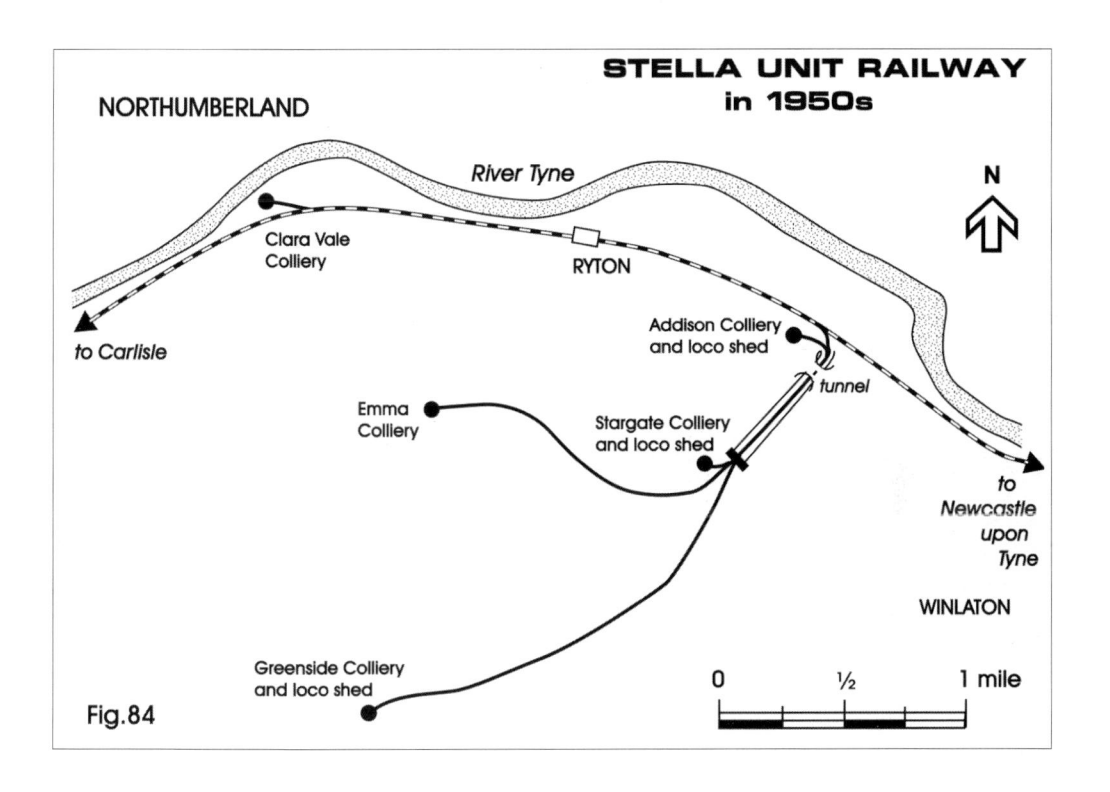

Fig. 84

292. Looking towards the drumhouse of the Addison self-acting incline at Stargate, with the unusual balanced level-crossing gate and a coal depot entered by road vehicles at the end, on 4th March 1950.

293. The drumhouse from the bank head on 31st August 1960.

294. Looking north down the Stargate Incline from the drumhouse, with its small and steeply-graded kips and the rodding on the right to operate the runaway switches, 4th March 1950.

295. From 1875 The Stella Coal Co Ltd purchased all of its locomotives from R. & W. Hawthorn and then R. & W. Hawthorn, Leslie & Co Ltd. Here 14, formerly named JOAN, HL 2617/1905, with two sets of dumb buffers, shunts the Addison Colliery sidings in front of the BR signal box here on 28th September 1955.

cab side sheets, a livery which looked attractive, even when faded.

The Group managed to obtain one new locomotive, 78 RSHN 7538/1949, a 16in x 24in 0-4-0ST. Although first allocated to Blaydon Burn Colliery, this was soon transferred to Greenside for the Greenside-Stargate work, the biggest engine to work on the railway.

It has been possible to re-construct the locomotive movements from 1947 onwards, and these show locomotives regularly moving around, probably in much the same way that they had done for years beforehand. Locomotives which worked at Clara Vale Colliery and never came to the main system have been omitted. Repairs continued to be carried out at the workshops at Addison Colliery, although no records for this works survive. Whilst two locomotives came to the railway from Derwenthaugh loco shed on the Chopwell & Garesfield Railway (see chapter 4), these were short-term transfers. The others that came – Nos. 4/7/9-11 – were all former Priestman Collieries Ltd locomotives, whose royalty lay immediately to the east of the Stella collieries, so they travelled only a few miles to their new home. 4 was also a 16in engine, and shared the Greenside work with 78. As in pre-Vesting days, the only locomotives to work on the system after 1947 were four-coupled saddletanks.

The system survived until August 1961, when, except at Addison Colliery, it was replaced by road transport, to save money. Presumably because of its link with BR, Addison Colliery retained a locomotive until it closed on 22nd February 1963, though latterly output was so low that the one locomotive worked only between 1.00 pm and 3.30 pm. Stargate Colliery closed on 29th June 1963, Greenside Colliery on 23rd July 1966 and Emma Colliery on 19th April 1968.

The locomotives

The system was unusual compared with others in Durham, in that it used only four-coupled saddletanks, in that no second-hand locomotives were ever purchased for it and that apart from the first locomotive, all the locomotives were purchased from R & W Hawthorn & Co and its successors, R & W Hawthorn, Leslie & Co Ltd. In the list below, the company's locomotives working at Blaydon Main and Clara Vale Collieries have been omitted.

The first locomotive listed below almost certainly worked at the Addison Pit, as no locomotive was recorded at Stargate in the early 1870s. The second locomotive below was almost certainly the first at Stargate. Locomotive allocations and transfers below have been given from 2nd September 1947. The following abbreviations have been used:

	A	Addison Colliery, Hedgefield						
	BB	Blaydon Burn Colliery, near Blaydon						
	CV	Clara Vale Colliery, Clara Vale						
	D	Derwenthaugh loco shed, Swalwell (see chapter 4)						
	G	Greenside Colliery, Greenside						
	S	Stargate Colliery, Stargate						

Gauge : 4ft 8½in

	STELLA	0-4-0ST	OC	AB	70	1868	New	(1)
	TOWNELEY	0-4-0ST	OC	RWH	1726	1875	New	s/s
	HEDGEFIELD	0-4-0ST	OC	RWH	1817	1880	New	s/s
	TOWNELEY	0-4-0T	OC	HL	2199	1891	New	s/s
12	(STELLA)	0-4-0ST	OC	HL	2583	1904	New	(2)
		reb		HL		1931		

A-S by 19/9/1948-A by 15/5/1949-S by 4/2/1950-A by 9/1950
-CV by 6/1952-D (repairs?) after3/1953, by 4/1954-A by 4/1956 (3)

| 14 | (JOAN) | 0-4-0ST | OC | HL | 2617 | 1904 | New | |

G-S by 15/5/1949-A after 4/2/1950, by 22/3/1953-S 3/1953
-A after 25/4/1956, by 25/7/1956-S by 6/1957 (4)

| 15 | (MURIEL) | 0-4-0ST | OC | HL | 2694 | 1907 | New | |

St-A after 15/5/1949, by 4/2/1950-S by 9/1950-A after 4/1958, by 8/1959
-S by 4/60-A after 4/1961, by 8/1961 (5)

	ADDISON	0-4-0ST	OC	HL	2702	1907	New	(6)
13	(EMMA)	0-4-0ST	OC	HL	2740	1909	New	
	A							(7)
16	(VICTORY)	0-4-0ST	OC	HL	3438	1920	New	

S-G by 15/5/1949-A (workshops) by 4/2/1950-G by 9/1950
-S by 9/1952-A after 7/1960, by 4/1961 Scr 8/1962

| 78 | | 0-4-0ST | OC | RSHN | 7538 | 1949 | (a) | |

G-S after 9/1955, by 25/4/1956-A by 21/5/1957-G by 27/8/1958
-A after 4/1960, by 7/1960 (8)

59		0-4-0ST	OC	HL	3003	1913	(b)	
	S							(9)
57		0-4-0ST	OC	CF	1158	1898	(c)	
	A							(10)
4		0-4-0ST	OC	HC	1514	1923	(d)	

S-G by 8/5/1957-A by 1/10/1958-S by 2/1959
-A (workshops) by 8/1959-G 3/5/1960-A by 8/1961 (11)

11		0-4-0ST	OC	HL	2330	1896	(e)	
	S-A by 4/1958							(12)
9		0-4-0ST	OC	HL	2426	1899	(f)	

A-BB by 4/1958-A by 9/1958-S by 1/10/1958
-A (workshops) by 4/1960-S after 7/1960, by 4/1961-A by 8/1961 (13)

7		0-4-0ST	OC	RS	3376	1909	(g)	
	A							(14)
10		0-4-0ST	OC	HC	674	1903		
		reb		HL	4161	1925	(h)	
	A							Scr 1/1962

(a) ex Blaydon Burn Colliery, near Blaydon, by 6/1952
(b) ex Derwenthaugh loco shed, Swalwell, 1/1955
(c) ex Derwenthaugh loco shed, Swalwell, 7/5/1956
(d) ex Derwenthaugh loco shed, Swalwell, 12/1956
(e) ex Lilley Drift, near Rowlands Gill, after 7/1955. by 6/1957
(f) ex Blaydon Burn Colliery, near Blaydon, after 2/1957, by 6/1957
(g) ex Blaydon Burn Colliery, near Blaydon, after 8/1959, by 4/1960
(h) ex Clara Vale Colliery, Clara Vale, after 4/1961, by 8/1961; possibly brought to Addison Colliery for repairs in the workshops

(1) oral tradition said that this locomotive was sold to "Winter of Winlaton" (no one of that name is listed at Winlaton in any Durham directory between 1890 and 1938), then re-sold to a steelworks in Scotland
(2) hired to Synthetic Ammonia & Nitrates Ltd, Billingham, /1928; this firm was absorbed by Imperial Chemical Industries Ltd in 1931 and the works became operated by I.C.I. (Fertilizers & Synthetic Products) Ltd; loco returned, /1934
(3) to Clara Vale Colliery, Clara Vale, by 6/1957; scrapped on site, 7/1960
(4) to Clara Vale Colliery, Clara Vale, after 7/1960, by 4/1961; scrapped on site, 7/1963
(5) dismantled in Addison Colliery workshops by 5/12/1962; scrapped on site by D.Sep Bowran Ltd, Gateshead, 7/1963
(6) seen out of use at Emma Colliery, Bar Moor, on 18/9/1948; believed scrapped by 15/5/1949
(7) to Leadgate loco shed, Leadgate, 22/5/1956; scrapped on site, 2/1959
(8) to Derwenthaugh loco shed, Swalwell, 19/1/1961; scrapped on site by Thos W Ward Ltd, Middlesbrough, Yorkshire (NR), 3/1971
(9) to Derwenthaugh loco shed, Swalwell, 3/1956; scrapped on site by Thos W Ward Ltd, Middlesbrough, Yorkshire (NR), 5/1960
(10) to Victoria Garesfield Colliery, near Rowlands Gill, c12/1956; to Derwenthaugh loco shed, Swalwell, 3/4/1962; scrapped on site by D Sep Bowran Ltd, Gateshead, 10/1962
(11) to Clara Vale Colliery, Clara Vale, 12/11/1962; to Bowes Railway, Marley Hill loco shed, near Sunniside, for repairs, 23/12/1964; to Morrison Busty Colliery, Annfield Plain, 5/7/1965; scrapped on site, 9/1973
(12) scrapped on site by D Sep Bowran Ltd, Gateshead, 5/1961
(13) to Clara Vale Colliery, Clara Vale, 2/6/1961; scrapped on site, 5/1966
(14) scrapped on site by D Sep Bowran Ltd, Gateshead, 12/1963

296. 7, RS 3376/1909, one of the relatively few industrial locomotives built by this firm in the twentieth century, awaits scrap at Addison Colliery in May 1963. Note the single slide bar and the hole at the bottom of the backplate that allowed tubes to be withdrawn from the boiler. The only plate still carried was the locomotive's Railway Executive plate, giving it permission to run over BR lines.

Chapter Seventeen
The Weatherhill & Rookhope Railway and The Rookhope & Middlehope Railway

OWNERS
The Weardale Steel, Coal & Coke Co Ltd
The Weardale Iron & Coal Co Ltd until 28/9/1899
The Weardale Iron Co until 23/7/1863

These railways, forming one system, were very different from any of the other private railways in Co.Durham. They were constructed over some of the bleakest and most remote country in England, rising over 1600 feet, barren, windswept and frequently blocked by snow in winter; and although the system was built for its owners to convey minerals, it was not coal but iron ore which provided the economic stimulus. With the public railway initially declining to develop into the area, the owners had to take the initiative themselves, and inevitably the system became a general carrier, handling local goods traffic and also running a passenger service. Equally, because it closed in 1923, few of its records, or those of its owners, survive, and because it was so remote and closed soon after the First World War, it had no known visitors to record it while it was working.

The Upper Pennines, and in particular Upper Weardale, had long been known for its lead deposits, worked chiefly by the London Lead Company and the Blackett-Beaumont family, latterly trading as W B Lead Co. Lead mining had revealed the existence of iron ore, and as industrial activity developed further east in Durham, so various people began to explore the mineral deposits in Weardale. One of these was Charles Attwood (1791-1875), an entrepreneur who had previously operated a soap works at Gateshead. In 1845 he founded The Weardale Iron Co, intending to take over a part-finished iron works at Stanhope. This was the **Stanhope Burn Iron Works** (NY 989399). Its construction was begun, probably in 1844, by a local landowner, Cuthbert Rippon, and included one blast furnace. There were ironstone deposits alongside Stanhope Burn, but no coal. It was served by a ½ mile link to the foot of the Crawleyside Incline at Stanhope on what until the beginning of 1845 had been the Derwent Railway (see chapter 6), formerly the Stanhope & Tyne Railway and now owned by the Stockton & Darlington Railway, and the only railway thus far penetrating the upper end of the valley. In the valley itself the railway had reached only as far as Bishop Auckland, and although the Wear Valley Railway, effectively a subsidiary of the Stockton & Darlington, had obtained its Act in 1845, this would only bring the railway as far as Frosterley. In 1843 Bishop Auckland had been linked to Crook by the Bishop Auckland & Weardale Railway, and two years later the Wear & Derwent Junction Railway (W&DJ) had opened its line between Crook and what became Waskerley on the former Stanhope & Tyne Railway between Stanhope and Consett. Effectively all of these lines were controlled by the Stockton & Darlington Railway.

Although the Stanhope Burn Ironworks was put into blast, its location was clearly unsuitable economically. Attwood thus decided to build a large iron works alongside the W&DJ about 3¼ miles north-west of Crook, at a location which became known as Tow Law. Coal was available here, and it had rail access to both Tyneside and south-west Durham. The **Tow Law Iron Works** (NZ 118389 approx.) had six blast furnaces and was opened about April 1846.

At the same time Attwood was clearly hoping that the W&DJ would build a branch westwards across the moors and into the valley of the Rookhope Burn, with its hamlet of Bolt's Burn, one of the centres of the local lead industry. There was no iron ore here, but at least a railhead could be established to which iron ore from further west could be brought by horse and cart, as the lead ore was also brought. Whittle, in his *Railways of Consett & North-West* Durham, states that Attwood began work on his own line to Bolt's Burn at the same time as he was trying to persuade the Wear & Derwent Junction Railway to build a branch to Rookhope, but this would seem very unlikely. Nevertheless, Attwood was to be disappointed, for in August 1846 the railway's engineer reported unfavourably on this proposal, quoting the "nature of the country", "considerable works" and gradients as severe as 1 in 6. He was thus left with no alternative but to build his own line. Either from the beginning, and certainly from soon after it was opened, it was known as the

WEATHERHILL & ROOKHOPE RAILWAY

This ran from a junction with the Wear & Derwent Junction Railway's line from Stanhope to Consett (later known as the NER Stanhope & Tyne branch)

297. The line west of Parkhead ran through some of the bleakest and most remote country in England. This view was taken in 1939 after it had been abandoned.

at Parkhead, 2 miles north of Stanhope and ½ mile north of the Weatherhill Engine, and ran for 5½ miles to Bolt's Burn, or Rookhope, reaching 1670 feet above sea level, the highest railway ever built in Britain, across bleak, treeless, windswept moorland. Construction began in 1846 and the line was opened either in the following year or in 1848. To keep the initial section virtually level the line made a lengthy detour around Stanhope Common, but a tremendous incline from Bolt's Law down to Bolt's Burn was unavoidable. This was approximately 2,000 yards long on a gradient of 1 in 12, although sections at the top and bottom were as steep as 1 in 6. At the top was built the **Bolt's Law Engine** (NY 949442), together with houses for the railway workers and their families to live in. It may well be that locomotives were used between Bolt's Law and Parkhead from the beginning; it would seem inconceivable to expect men and horses to work traffic over four miles of level track in frequently severe weather conditions. A **loco shed** was built on to the eastern end of the engine

298. The ruins at Bolt's Law in 1955, facing east, with the remains of the loco shed here alongside the kip at the bank head. Beyond from left to right lay the drumhouse, the engine and the boiler house.

299. Bolt's Law Incline looking from Rookhope village, about 1900. The link into Rookhope Depot can be seen.

300. Bolt's Law Bank Foot at Rookhope. It has not been possible to identify the locomotive, although it has a stovepipe chimney, a Black Hawthorn/Joicey type saddletank and a Weardale Iron Co cab.

301. The Bolt's Law Incline crossed Rookhope Burn near the bank foot on a wooden trestle viaduct, where this accident occurred about 1910-1911.

house. The Bolt's Law Incline was built with a "meetings", allowing ascending and descending sets to be run simultaneously. Near the bottom the incline crossed Bolt's Burn on a wooden trestle bridge before reaching the bank foot on an isthmus between the Rookhope Burn and the Bolt's Burn. Nearby was **Boltsburn Mine** (NY 936428), owned by W B Lead Co, while about ½ mile further up Rookhope Burn lay the **Rookhope** (or Lintzgarth) **Smelt Mill** (or Smelter) (NY 926428). Although no documentary evidence is known, it would seem very likely that the railway was extended to serve these in order to handle the lead traffic, which may well have been handled in Wear & Derwent Junction Railway wagons, of which there were 200 in 1847. It would seem equally likely that the first **loco shed** (NY 927436) here dates from the opening, or soon afterwards; a locomotive was recorded here in 1854. To serve Bolt's Burn village quite a large **Depot** (NY 930431) was built just uphill of the trestle viaduct.

Two branches were subsequently built from the Weatherhill & Rookhope Railway. The first was

"Dead Friars branch"
This was a ¼ mile line from a junction about ¾ mile east of Bolt's Law Engine House, which served gravel pits on the north side of the "main line" near Dead Friars. One source says it was opened in 1848. How long it remained open is not known. The second was

The Sikehead branch
To the north of Bolt's Law lay the Ramshaw valley, where lead mining had begun in the eighteenth century. In 1857 the mines at Sikehead and Whiteheaps were taken over by the **Derwent Lead Mining Company**, who engaged the firm of **John Taylor & Sons** to manage them. At this date Sikehead Mine (NY 955465) consisted of two shafts, and the lead produced was taken down a narrow-gauge self-acting incline about 400 yards long to the smelter on the valley floor, to which a tramway also ran from the **Whiteheaps Mine** (NY 948473). About 1862 the Iron Company was persuaded to lay a branch from the same point as the "Dead Friars" branch to Sikehead, a distance of about 600 yards and nearly level. From here the narrow gauge self-acting incline was rebuilt to standard gauge and a **stationary engine** was built at Sikehead to work traffic (lead and coal) down to the valley floor, and haul lead back. Who owned this incline is unclear. The mines appear to have closed down about 1872, and the branch probably closed about the same time. The mines were re-opened in the twentieth century to mine fluorspar.

Having reached Bolt's Burn, the company paused; but the railway was not yet connected to the ironstone deposits, which lay to the west and north-west. The extensions to reach them may well have both begun about the same time, about 1850-51.

The Groove (Grove) Rake branch
This was developed north-westwards from Bolt's Burn Mine up Rookhope Burn, another extensive mining and opencasting area. As mentioned earlier, this may well have been done by 1847-48, when the railway was soon opened. However, one source says that this line began in 1851 with a short line to serve **FOULWOOD MINE** (NY 933429), to be extended to the **Smelt Mill** (NY 926427) in 1859. Construction to Groove Rake, 2½ miles away, then began in earnest, serving en route **RISPEY MINE** (NY 911428) before reaching **GROOVE RAKE MINE** (NY 896442). Beyond Groove Rake were extensive ironstone deposits at **FRAZER'S HUSH** (NY 884446 approx.), which were worked by opencasting, and most sources believe that the line was extended for a further mile to reach them; but the O.S. maps show no evidence of this, and it may be that the output was brought to Groove Rake by horse and cart. Similar opencasting was carried out around Groove Rake itself. The principal mining rights were held by W B Lead Co, who owned the mines, but sub-let the ironstone rights to the Iron Company, as it was always called.

The line westwards from Rookhope was much longer, and gained its own title:

ROOKHOPE & MIDDLEHOPE RAILWAY
Details of the construction of this line are scant and contradictory, and it may well have been opened in three or four sections. It is possible that the first stage took the line as far as Heights, just under 3 miles from Bolt's Burn. The first, short, section was level, serving the **Boltsburn Washing Mill** (NY 938425), owned by W B Lead Co; but then the line needed to rise to 1300 feet. With the majority of the loaded traffic travelling towards Rookhope, a self-acting incline 1½ miles long, the **Smailsburn Incline**, was adopted, but it was worked in an unusual way in order to accommodate coal and other traffic travelling westwards. In 1857 a number of old Stockton & Darlington Railway locomotive tenders were purchased and kept at the bank head full of water, to be used as the descending set when full waggons had to ascend the incline. At the bottom the water was drained off and the tenders worked back to the top. Latterly only one tender and three wagons of scrap were used to form the downwards set. Near the meetings was the **SMAILSBURN MINE** (NY 941415); how its traffic was incorporated into the working of the incline is not known.

JF 1142/1868
This was an extraordinary locomotive about which very little is known. It was based on a patent application for a locomotive to ascend rope inclines – Patent 1016 of 1867. To enable it to do this, a cable laid in the centre of the track was taken round a clip drum, said to have been 7ft in diameter, mounted in the centre of the locomotive frames. The boiler had two barrels from a single firebox to accommodate this. The drum was driven off a transversely-mounted crankshaft, apparently also geared to drive the front axle. One can only speculate as to where the company considered using such a machine, but the Smailsburn Incline, with its loaded traffic travelling in both directions, seems the most likely possibility. If so, the tenders must have proved a simpler and cheaper solution.

The next 1½ miles to Heights was virtually level, but initially a main-and-tail system was installed, operated by the **Bishop's Seat Engine** (NY 936405). This may well have been the 40 h.p. engine with 20in x 24in cylinders, described as "for hauling incline", ordered from R & W Hawthorn of Newcastle (RWH 789/1851) in August 1851. At Heights, **HEIGHTS MINE** (NY 925388) was developed, producing lead and iron. Subsequently the company decided to abandon the mine and instead quarry the large limestone deposits here, thus developing **HEIGHTS QUARRY**. This was still quite small when the O.S. survey of 1895 was undertaken, so it would seem reasonable to assume that quarrying began in the 1880s.

By the time the survey for the 1st edition O.S. map was undertaken in 1858 the line had been extended for a further 1¼ miles to run up Middlehope Burn, north of Westgate village, to **SLIT PASTURE MINE**

302. The former locomotive sheds at Rookhope on 25th July 1939, with behind them the headgear of Bolt's Burn Mine, owned by The Weardale Lead Co Ltd.

303. 4, Joicey 210/1869 – originally a 0-4-0ST, but like a number of the company's 0-4-0ST's, it was rebuilt to a six-wheeled engine. She was the regular engine working between Bolt's Law and Parkhead, but here is at Rookhope, about 1912.

393

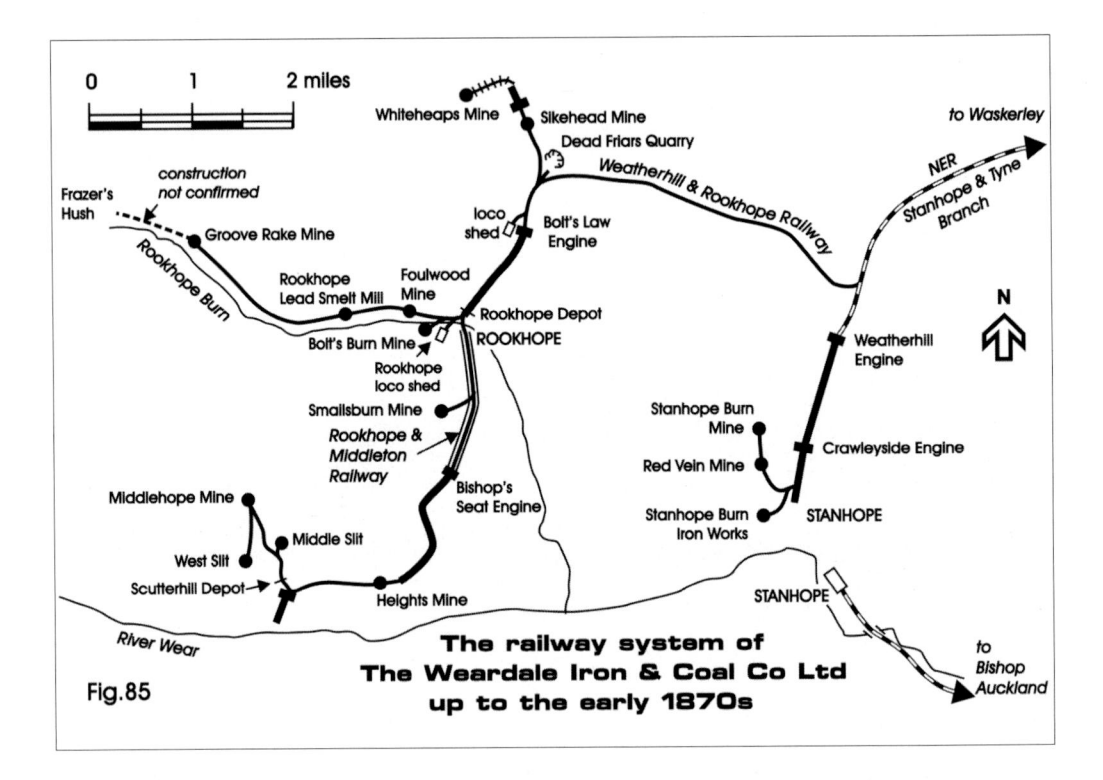

Fig.85 The railway system of The Weardale Iron & Coal Co Ltd up to the early 1870s

(NY 909384), though here the ironstone was opencasted. Adjacent to this area, but without a link to the railway, was **WEST RIGG MINE** (NY 912393 approx.) By the 1850s there was an extensive area of levels and opencasting for both ironstone and lead on both sides of Middlehope Burn (Low Slit Mine, Middle Slit Mine and the Middlehope Shield Level all lay to the west of the burn), and for the output of these mines to be brought to the railway by horse and cart the company opened the **SCUTTERHILL DEPOT** (NY 909390), 300 feet above Westgate. The lead, mined for W B Lead and then The Weardale Lead Co Ltd, was taken back to Bolt's Burn for processing and smelting at the Rookhope Smelter.

At some point the line was extended for a further ¾ mile up the burn to **MIDDLEHOPE MINE** (NY 904402), from which a reverse ran back down the western side of the burn for ½ mile to **WEST SLIT MINE** (NY 903393). This gave a total distance of about 5¾ miles from Bolt's Burn, or about 11 miles from Parkhead. One source dates this extension to the mid/late 1860s, but the company was working West Slit Mine by 1863 (Hunt's *Mineral Statistics*), so the line may have been in place by then.

With no other railway in the area the Scutterhill Depot rapidly became the railhead not only for the upper parts of Weardale, but also Teesdale, Tynedale and Allendale. Thousands of tons of goods, such as food, drink, coal, animal feed and ironmongery, all nothing to do with the company's business, came to be handled through the depot, all taken away by horse and cart struggling up the 1 in 5 hill from Westgate. To relieve this, the company decided on a further short branch.

The Scutterhill Incline
This was built from a junction about ½ mile east of the depot down to Westgate village near the church, ½ mile at 1 in 6. It was operated by the **Scutterhill Engine** (NY 912389) at the junction, which allowed full loads to be worked in either direction. It was probably not a very powerful engine, as normally only one waggon was run at a time.

When locomotive working was introduced on the Rookhope & Middlehope section is not known. As the line was extended west of Heights locomotive working was introduced, presumably causing the demise of the Bishop's Seat Engine; the first locomotives known on this section arrived in 1868. However, none of the Ordnance Surveys show any building on this far western section which might have been a loco shed, though there must surely have been one.

The passenger service
Although the Stockton & Darlington Railway eventually reached Stanhope on 22nd October 1862, this was some way from the communities which the Iron Co's lines served. This undoubtedly led to a demand for a passenger service. When the company began to operate this is not known. However, in 1863 the company purchased an old Stockton & Darlington Railway 4-wheeled passenger carriage from the NER, followed by another in 1871. These are reported to have been used in a three times a week passenger service

between Rookhope and Parkhead to allow local people to shop at Stanhope. Since the carriages are unlikely to have worked over the Bolt's Law Incline, the hardy travellers presumably had to use open trucks. Equally, the carriages are unlikely to have worked down to Stanhope over the Stanhope & Tyne inclines; perhaps the Weardale train was met at Parkhead by horses and carts. Later it would seem that the carriages were laid aside and passengers travelled the whole way between Rookhope and Parkhead in open waggons.

A working timetable

Colliery railways normally ran trains as required, to meet the demands of collieries for empties and the staiths for shipment. Unusually, the Weardale system, with of course no colliery at all, actually had a working timetable, a fragment of which, dating from about 1898, is quoted in the reference below, and is reproduced here. There was no Sunday working.

Weatherhill & Rookhope Railway

Depart Bolt's Law	Depart Parkhead	Notes
7.05am	8.20am	
9.10am		Passenger, Saturdays only
10.30am		Passenger, Mondays and Thursdays only
10.40am		Mondays and Thursdays excepted
-	11.30am	Coal inwards, Saturdays excepted
-	11.50am	Return Passenger, Saturdays only
12.10pm	1.30pm	Satudays excepted
2.10pm	3.20pm	Saturdays excepted
-	4.02pm	Passenger, Thursdays only
4.50pm	5.45pm	Saturdays excepted

Notes: presumably a light engine working from Bolt's Law to Parkhead was necessary for the 4.02pm passenger on Thursdays. How passengers returned from Parkhead on Mondays is not clear.

Trains from Rookhope

These departed from Rookhope at 6.45am, 8.45am, 11.10am, 1.45pm, 3.00pm (Saturdays excepted) and 4.45pm (Saturdays excepted). No destinations or return times are given.

Rookhope & Middlehope Railway

Depart Bishop's Seat	Depart Heights	Depart Scutterhill
6.30am	7.50am	
9.10am	10.05am	
11.10am	12.05pm	
1.30pm		2.35pm
3.17pm	4.20pm	
5.30pm (except Saturdays)	6.10pm (except Saturdays)	

The last quarter of the nineteenth century

In 1863 The Weardale Iron & Coal Co Ltd owned seven ironstone sites in various places throughout Upper Weardale; some were mines, shared with W B Lead Co, others were "quarries", or opencast sites. These had risen to 13 by 1875. Those served by the railway are noted above; others had no connection. The company also obtained iron ore from North Yorkshire, but it continued to use Weardale ironstone as long as it was economic. Production at Groove Rake was abandoned in 1875, Stanhopeburn and West Slit were closed in 1878 and other sites were closed in the 1880s. At Stanhopeburn and West Slit the Iron Co and W B Lead Co had separate entrances. By 1891 the number of mines had declined to seven, including three not on the 1875 list; but most were "standing", never to work again, and it is clear that most production was now being obtained from quarrying; five are listed in 1891. The 2nd edition O.S. map, surveyed in 1896, shows the line to Groove Rake in situ, presumably for The Weardale Lead Co Ltd's traffic, and the line to West Slit is also still in place, though with the connection to Middlehope Mine lifted; this mine had been abandoned on 9th April 1894.

After opening Tow Law Iron Works in 1846, the company opened **Tudhoe Iron Works** (NZ 206338), further east again, at Spennymoor in 1853. The first steel rails to be rolled in North-East England were made at Tow Law in 1862, but the works became obsolete and was closed in 1887. Tudhoe Works suffered an uneasy existence. It was the first works in the North-East to instal, in 1861, a Bessemer converter for the production of steel, and eventually four were installed. Despite this, the works was closed between 1875 and 1881, when it was rebuilt and re-opened. There were also coke ovens here. The Bessemer converters were not a success, and were derelict by the 1890s. By this date the company owned collieries around both Tow Law and Tudhoe, and also around Thornley in east Durham, which it acquired in 1888.

By the end of the nineteenth century the company's iron and steel production had been overtaken by

304. Also known to have been taken at Rookhope, this unidentified engine appears to be a J.& G. Joicey loco in original condition. Because chaldron waggons were not used on the line, there was no need to fit the usual lower buffers.

cheaper plants nearer the coast, especially on Teesside. In 1899 the London bankers Baring Brothers sold their interest to Sir Christopher Furness (1852-1912), the Teesside shipping and ship-building magnate, who set up a new company, The Weardale Steel, Coal & Coke Co Ltd, with an issued capital of £1,025,000. In the following year he became chairman of The South Durham Steel & Iron Co Ltd. In 1901 the Weardale company acquired control of The Cargo Fleet Iron Co Ltd of Middlesbrough. A complicated re-organisation of shares followed, so that it is far from clear which company was a subsidiary of another, and whether this remained constant; but the South Durham company under Lord Furness, as he became, controlled the group.

Despite the company's new title, Furness soon decided that the Weardale company's steel-making was uneconomic, and that its future contribution to the group would be coal, coke and limestone. Steel production at Tudhoe ceased abruptly in November 1901. The works' subsequent history is not clear. Dismantling of the steel plant began in 1908, and more was dismantled between 1910 and 1912. However, it would seem that one furnace was still in blast, and that iron production continued until at least 1920, possibly until 1926. The company's head office was still at the works, which received new by-product coke ovens between 1907 and 1909.

Decline and closure
Against this background the continued operation of a remote railway system in Upper Weardale could clearly be questioned, yet it seems that the company decided to continue there as long as it served a purpose for the local community. With the end of ironstone mining north of Westgate the only company traffic being handled by the system was the limestone output from Heights Quarry; the remainder consisted of traffic for The Weardale Lead Co Ltd (successors to W B Lead Co) and coal and general merchandise for the local inhabitants. The opening of the NER line between Stanhope and Wearhead in 1895 seriously reduced the latter, and the Scutterhill Incline was closed in 1897. However, Scutterhill Depot remained open, served in 1898 by one train per day. The Depot at Rookhope also continued in use.

It would seem clear from the 1898 operating timetable quoted above, with loco working on the Rookhope & Middlehope section commencing at Bishop's Seat, that at that time the Smailsburn Incline was still working. It was said that in later years the rope was abandoned and a locomotive was allowed to work over it, presumably subject to restrictions, but this is not confirmed.

The First World War brought a minor revival to the mining industry, and output from Heights Quarry actually rose beyond the capacity of the railway to handle it. So in 1915 German prisoners of war were used to construct a **self-acting incline** ¾ mile long, known as the **Heights** or **Cambo Keels Incline**, from the quarry down to the NER Wearhead line, 1½ miles east of Westgate Station. At the bank foot there was, curiously, a connection in both directions, perhaps to provide sufficient capacity

305. Oral tradition stated that 9 was new to Rookhope and she was also there when the line closed. It also claimed that she was built by Joicey in 1874; but if so, she presents major detail differences from the usual Joicey design, not least the unusual raised running plate over the cylinders. The rounded cab was a feature of later company rebuilding.

306. The company acquired BH 31/1867 when it took over Thornley Colliery in east Durham in 1888; but she too, as 21, found her way to Rookhope.

307. 19, BH 704/1882. Note the rail lifting jack resting against the smokebox. After many years of service in Weardale and then twenty years abandoned in the shed at Heights Quarry, she ended her days at Easington Colliery on the Durham coast.

308. German prisoners of war, with their cap-badges removed, loading spoil for the construction of the Cambokeels Incline in September 1915, again with 19.

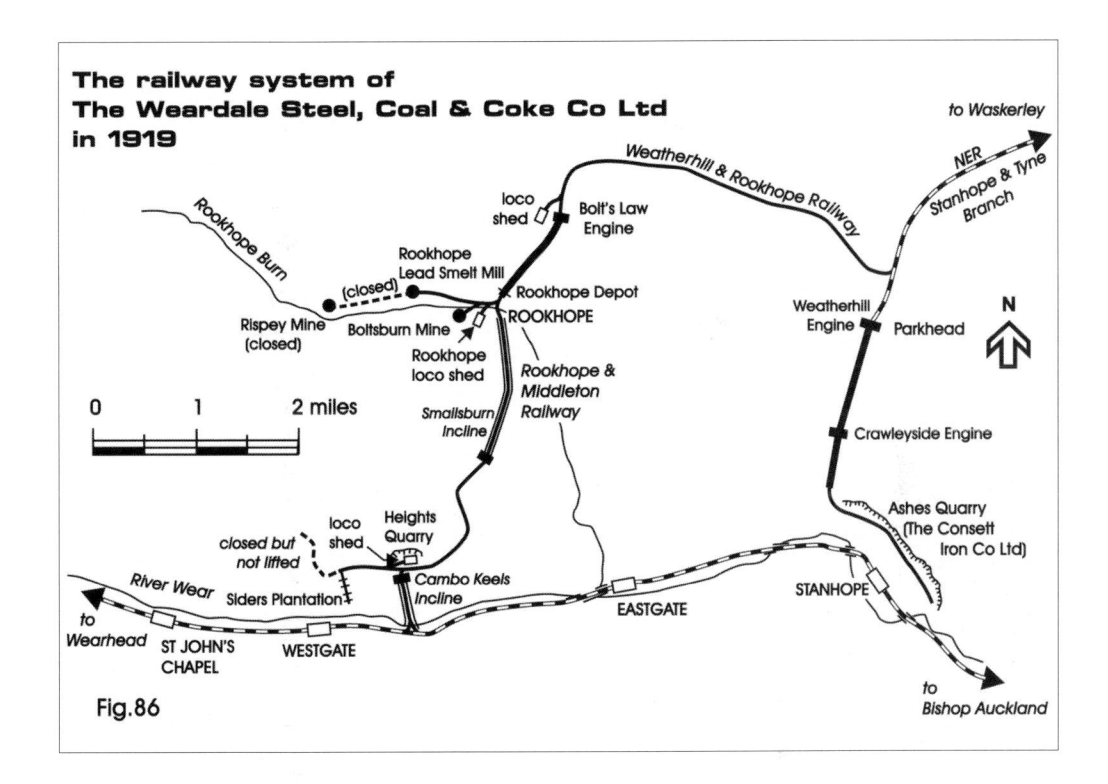

The railway system of The Weardale Steel, Coal & Coke Co Ltd in 1919

Fig.86

when the NER delivered a train of empties.

After the War decline set in rapidly. The Rookhope Smelt Mill closed in May 1919, and the 3rd edition O.S map, revision for which was undertaken in 1919, shows the Groverake branch in place only as far as Rispey Mill, also shown as disused, though the lifted section was not officially closed until March 1921. The remaining section, between Rookhope and Rispey, continued to receive a service until its closure on 20th February 1923.

In the far west, the section west of Scutterhill Depot was officially closed about 1915, though the Depot continued to receive a twice-weekly train, mainly to convey local timber. By 1919, although the track is

309. The unusual bi-directional foot of the Cambo Keels Incline over the River Wear near Eastgate, on the LNER Wearhead Branch, 25th July 1939.

310. Heights Quarry, closed in 1923, with 19 left in its shed, on 25th July 1939.

still shown as in place as far as the Middle Slit Level, its actual operation had been cut back to ½ mile east of Scutterhill, the end of the line being served by a tramway from the adjacent **Siders Plantation** (NY 917387 approx.), presumably to carry felled timber from the plantation. Presumably the Scutterhill Depot had by now been closed. Curiously, Heights Quarry would appear from the map to be served only by the Cambo Keels Incline, though clearly this was not the case, as the locomotive which worked the line here was kept in a loco shed at the quarry. In 1922 an aerial flight was built between Heights Quarry and the NER, which in turn brought the closure both of the incline and of the railway between Bolt's Burn and Heights. Heights Quarry itself was closed in 1923, although it was worked much later by different owners. With the closure of the Rookhope-Rispey section in February 1923, this left only the section between Rookhope and Parkhead, and with the commissioning of an aerial flight for The Weardale Lead Co Ltd between Rookhope and Eastgate, this last section of the system closed on 15th May 1923.

After the closure
Even despite the closures, the system was maintained, apparently in the forlorn hope that one day traffic might be resumed. The track remained in place, while locomotives were repaired and kept in their sheds and only after some time were they eventually removed for use elsewhere; the loco at Heights Quarry stayed there until 1943 before being winched down the Cambo Keels Incline for further use. From 1st June 1923 a twice-weekly horse drawn truck was operated between Parkhead and Bolt's Law to provision the inhabitants of the cottages there. In addition there was the unique service offered by "The Stanhope, Rookhope & District Railway". The grouse shooting rights on Stanhope Common were owned by A.E.Bainbridge, of Stanhope Castle at Stanhope, and to assist his guests in their shooting parties between 12th August and December he brought to the line between Parkhead and Rookhope a wooden-bodied four-wheeled battery operated truck, even issuing (humorous) tickets, including dog tickets, and railway rules. During the close season the gamekeepers used the truck to carry supplies used in managing the moor. This "service" had almost certainly ceased by 1939. The trestle viaduct at Bolt's Burn was dismantled in 1942 and the line between Bolt's Law and Parkhead was eventually lifted in June 1943, though the derelict truck remained at Parkhead until removed by British Railways in 1958. The last remaining section of track was at Heights and the Cambo Keels Incline, but with the company not resuming production at the quarry (though it has since been worked by various owners), the track was lifted between October 1945 and May 1946.

Reference: *The Remarkable Rookhope Railway*, by L.E.Berry, BackTrack, August and September 1996.

The locomotives
With much of the company's activity concentrated in the second half of the nineteenth century, and also located in the most remote area of west Durham, the surviving information about its locomotives is very limited. Unfortunately from a historian's point of view, the company purchased a number of its locomotives from J & G Joicey & Co Ltd of Newcastle upon Tyne, whose records are not

311. The battery-powered trolley operated by A.E.Bainbridge of Stanhope Castle between Bolt's Law and Parkhead for his shooting parties up to the Second World War, lying derelict at Parkhead in October 1951.

known to have survived. The company's workshops at Tow Law Iron Works were more than capable both of building their own locomotives and undertaking major rebuilds of others, a practice continued both at Tudhoe Iron Works and later still at the workshops at Thornley Colliery, all of them removing the original makers' plates. Such photographs as survive do so because the originals were taken for family reasons, and with family connections now lost they cannot be dated.

The usual locomotive allocation was two engines at Bolt's Law, two at Rookhope and one for Bishop's Seat to Middlehope.

It would seem that at first locomotives carried only names, but that a numbering scheme was then introduced, although on what basis is not known. The two ran parallel for a time, but eventually the names were removed. Repairs are known to have been carried out both at Bolt's Law and Rookhope loco sheds, but it is clear that for major overhauls locomotives were sent to Tow Law or Tudhoe. Whilst it is possible from some of the photographs to say that a locomotive was working at a particular location about a certain time, not only are precise dates of transfers not known, even the sequence of transfers is unknown in some cases. Because of this, it is impossible to produce a locomotive list based on the date of arrival on the system; instead, the locomotives are listed below in numerical order. Only the company's locomotives which are known to have worked on the system are included.

Gauge : 4ft 8½in

-		0-4-0	IC	Fairbairn	1842		
	reb	0-4-2	IC			(a)	
at Rookhope in 12/1854							(1)

-		0-4-0	IC	Fairbairn	1842		
	reb	0-4-2				(b)	
at Bolt's Law, /1856; to Rookhope by late 1860s							(2)

-		0-6-0	OC	Hackworth	1842	(c)	
said to have worked at Middlehope and Rookhope and then Bolt's Law, its final shed							(3)

-		0-6-0	OC	Shildon	1845	(c)	
said to have worked at Middlehope and Rookhope and then Bolt's Law, its final shed							(3)

4	(WEARDALE)		0-4-0ST	OC	Joicey	210	1869	(d)	
		reb	0-6-0ST	OC			1876		
			reb		HL	7409	1897		

believed to be still at Bolt's Law in the later 1870s; is said to have worked at Middlehope, Heights Quarry and Rookhope, though in what sequence is not known; at the closure in 1923 she was at Bolt's Law, where she was repaired in 1924 and then stored (4)

(9)	(SEDGEFIELD)	0-4-0ST	OC	Joicey		1874	(e)	

where this locomotive worked is not clear; a photograph of her was taken at Rookhope, where she was situated when the system closed in 1923 (5)

19		0-6-0ST	OC	BH	704	1882	(f)
		reb		Tudhoe		1909	

all the known photographs show her on the Rookhope & Middlehope Railway. Was at Heights Quarry when transferred to Tudhoe Iron Works for repairs c12/1899; is believed to have returned to Heights Quarry c12/1907; to Tudhoe Iron Works for repairs, /1908; to Heights Quarry, /1909 (6)

20		0-6-0ST	OC				(g)
		reb		Tudhoe		1908	

at Rookhope; to Heights Quarry, /1899; to Tudhoe Iron Works for repairs, /1908, and returned to Rookhope in the same year; at Rookhope when the system closed in 1923, and stored in the loco shed there (7)

21	(QUEEN)	0-6-0ST	OC	BH	31	1867	(h)	
		reb		Tudhoe		1896		

at Rookhope; appears to have been sent twice to Tudhoe Iron Works for repairs, at dates unknown, and returned to Rookhope (8)

No.22	PRINCESS	0-4-0ST	OC	MW	466	1873	(j)	

said to have worked at Middlehope, Heights Quarry, Rookhope and Bolt's Law, although in what sequence is not known (9)

23	(ALBERT)	0-4-0ST	OC	MW	492	1874	(j)	

normally located at Hedley Hill Colliery, near Waterhouses, but said to have been used briefly at both Heights Quarry and Rookhope (10)

25		0-4-0ST	OC	P	521	1891	(k)
		reb		Thornley		1922	

said to have worked at both Bolt's Law and Heights Quarry in 3/1916; at Rookhope when the system closed in 1923, and stored in the loco shed there (11)

-		2w-2wTG	IC	JF	1142	1868	(m)	s/s

(a) built new for the Manchester & Leeds Railway, No.43, RHINE; became Lancashire & Yorkshire Railway No.143 in /1850; rebuilt to 0-4-2 in 1850; purchased by Stockton & Darlington Railway, 8/1854; on loan to The Weardale Iron Company by 12/1854

(b) built new for the Manchester & Leeds Railway, No.41, ELBE; became Lancashire & Yorkshire Railway No.141 in /1850; rebuilt to 0-4-2; ex Lancashire & Yorkshire Railway, 1/1855; delivered to Tow Law Iron Works, 5/1855; if this loco was later allocated or carried a number it is not known

(c) these were both built new for the Stockton & Darlington Railway, as No.8 LEADER (Hackworth 1842) and No.31 REDCAR (Shildon Works Co 1845). In 1863 they passed to the NER, from whom they were purchased in 11/1868; here they were named JENNY LIND and BELLEROPHON, but it is not known which engine carried which name. It would appear likely that these locomotives were allocated/carried numbers, but what they were is not known

(d) New; the Joicey works number is believed to have been 210, although 240 has been quoted; delivered to Bolt's Law, 16/1/1870

(e) oral tradition claimed that this locomotive was New to the system

(f) BH records show New to Tow Law Iron Works, but she may have been there only briefly before coming to the system

(g) New to the company; believed built by the company at Tow Law Iron Works in the 1880s, possibly with parts supplied by BH

(h) New to The London Steam Collier & Coal Co Ltd, Thornley Colliery, Thornley; the company was re-named The Original Hartlepool Collieries Co Ltd from 9/4/1868; this company went into liquidation on 18/1/1877, and the locomotive remained at the colliery until passing to a new company, The Thornley Colliery Co, on 16/7/1881; this owner closed the colliery on 4/4/1884 and went bankrupt; the colliery and the locomotive were taken over by The Weardale Iron & Coal Co Ltd, the chief creditor, in 4/1885; when the locomotive was transferred to Rookhope is not known

(j) New to The Original Hartlepool Collieries Co Ltd, Thornley Colliery, Thornley. This company went into liquidation on 18/1/1877, and the locomotive remained at the colliery until passing to a new company, The Thornley Colliery Co, on 16/7/1881; this owner closed the colliery on 4/4/1884 and went bankrupt; the colliery and the locomotive were taken over by The Weardale Iron & Coal Co Ltd, the chief creditor, in 4/1885; when the locomotive was transferred to Weardale is not known

(k) New to Christopher Rowland, the contractor operating Swansea Docks, Swansea, Glamorgan; when she was acquired by The Weardale Steel, Coal & Co Ltd and from whom is not known, neither is when she was sent to Weardale. The loco was also owned by The Broomhill Collieries Ltd, Broomhill, Northumberland; but how this ownership fits together with the Weardale ownership is not known

(m) New; see note in text

(1) had left Rookhope by /1859; presumably returned to the Stockton & Darlington Railway
(2) believed to have been sent to Tudhoe Iron Works, Spennymoor, about 12/1879, and scrapped there about /1880
(3) JENNY LIND (see note c above) was taken out of service in /1900 and sold for scrap (no details are known). BELLEROPHON was taken out of service in /1902; its disposal is unknown
(4) to Thornley Colliery, Thornley, c/1930, and rebuilt there, /1931; to The New Brancepeth Colliery Co Ltd (a subsidiary of The Weardale Steel, Coal & Coke Co Ltd), New Brancepeth Colliery & Coke Ovens, New Brancepeth, after 12/1933; to NCB Northern Division No.5 Area, with the site, 1/1/1947; to Brancepeth Colliery, Willington, 13/1/1953; scrapped on site by Donkins Ltd, Sunderland, 3/1955
(5) scrapped in /1924, although whether at Rookhope or at Thornley Colliery, Thornley, is unclear
(6) at Heights Quarry when the system closed in 1923; stored in the shed here until /1943, when she was transferred to The Easington Coal Co Ltd (a subsidiary of The Weardale Steel, Coal & Coke Co Ltd), Easington Colliery, Easington Colliery; to NCB Northern Division No.3 Area, with the colliery, 1/1/1947; to Blackhall Colliery, Blackhall, by 4/1950 (loan); returned to Easington Colliery by 10/1950; scrapped on site, /1958
(7) taken to Thornley Colliery, Thornley, at a date unknown, and scrapped on site there c/1939
(8) sold to an unknown purchaser at Liverpool, /1921
(9) to Hedley Hill Colliery, near Waterhouses, c/1901; hired to Wake & Hollis Ltd, contractors; this firm had agreement to remove ballast and other materials from both Tow Law and Tudhoe Ironworks, and from 1903 the firm was also controlled by Sir Christopher Furness; returned from Wake & Hollis Ltd, and then normally used at Hedley Hill Colliery; said to have been sent to Thornley Colliery for scrapping
(10) scrapped at Tudhoe Iron Works c /1906, although one source stated that she was sent to Thornley Colliery for scrapping
(11) scrapped in /1941, but whether at Rookhope or Thornley Colliery, Thornley, is not known

The routes of much of the system can still be traced, although the Sikehead branch has largely disappeared beneath the undergrowth. The section from Rookhope to Parkhead is now both a footpath and part of the C2C (Coast-to-Coast) long distance cycle route between Whitehaven and Tynemouth.

The Indexes

Index 1 **Important people and companies**
(a) important people
(b) companies/people in business whose premises were served by private railways
(c) other companies and organisations mentioned

Index 2 **Locations**
(a) collieries
(b) coke ovens & by-product plants
(c) iron and lead mines
(d) locomotive sheds, other than at collieries
(e) miscellaneous
(f) passenger stations
(g) signal boxes
(h) quarries
(j) staiths
(k) workshops

Index 3 **References to Public Railways**

Index 4 **Locomotives**

Index 5 **Synopsis of chapters**

Index 1

Important people and companies

(a) important people

Charles Attwood (1791-1875)	388
John Blenkinsop (1783-1831)	5
John Bowes (1811-1885)	27
William Brunton (1777-1851)	11
John Buddle (1773-1843)	9, 14, 145, 149, 150, 151, 159, 219, 220, 227, 306, 379
2nd Marquis of Bute (1793-1848)	63
3rd Marquis of Bute (1847-1900)	65
William Chapman (1749-1832)	3, 5, 9, 14, 115, 225
George Elliot (1815-1893)	40, 234, 297
Christopher Furness (1852-1912)	396
John Grimshaw (c1762-1840)	11
Timothy Hackworth (1786-1850)	7
George Hardy (1825-1912)	219, 222, 232, 235, 239, 248, 249, 250, 307
George Hudson (1800-1871)	i, 27, 28
William Hedley (1779-1843)	7
James Joicey (1806-1863)	17, 125
James Joicey, 1st Baron Joicey (1846-1936)	19, 125, 173
John George Lambton, 1st Earl of Durham (1792-1840)	145
John George Lambton, 3rd Earl of Durham (1855-1928)	173
Charles Stewart, 3rd Marquis of Londonderry (1778-1854)	127, 219, 307
Francis Anne, Marchioness of Londonderry (1800-1865)	219, 229, 232, 307
Charles Stewart Vane-Tempest, 6th Marquis of Londonderry (1852-1915)	219, 244
Matthew Murray (?1765-1826)	5
Charles Mark Palmer (1822-1907)	27, 28, 39
Shakespear Reed	225, 226
George Stephenson (1781-1848)	12, 14
Benjamin Thompson (1779-1867)	220, 225, 254
Richard Trevithick (1771-1833)	3
Lindsay Wood (1834-1920)	19, 125
Nicholas Wood (1795-1865)	11, 27, 28, 116, 334

(b) companies/people in business whose premises were served by private railways

Berkley, John	28
The Birtley Co Ltd	254, 265
Blythe & Sons (Birtley) Ltd	262
The British Electrozone Corporation Ltd	231
A.E. Burdon	275
William Wharton Burdon	275
Candlish, Robert, & Son(s) Ltd	231
Crowley, Millington & Co Ltd	65
Edmonsley Coal Co	297
Elliot & Hunter	297
Foster, Blackett & Wilson Ltd	40
The Haswell Coal Co	232, 306
The Haswell, Shotton & Easington Coal & Coke Co Ltd	239
The Heworth Coal Co Ltd	260
Hopper, George (later Hopper & Radcliffe)	227, 239
Kell, Richard, & Co Ltd	270
The Londonderry Collieries Ltd	243
Marley Hill Coke Co	29
Marley Hill Coke & Chemical Co Ltd	32, 42
National Smokeless Fuels Ltd	59, 81, 206
The Newcastle upon Tyne Electric Supply Co Ltd	173
The North Eastern Paper Co Ltd	335
North Eastern Trading Estates Ltd	281
The North Hetton Coal Co Ltd	118, 127, 242

Palmers Shipbuilding & Iron Co Ltd	40
Pease & Partners Ltd	309
Pensher Foundry Co	168
The Priestman Collieries Ltd	281, 297
Raine & Co Ltd	65
Ravensworth Brick & Tile Co Ltd	264
Ryhope Coal Co Ltd	231
Scott, J.O., & Co Ltd	262
Seaham Gas Co	231
The Seaham Harbour Dock Co	244, 250, 309
Seaham Iron Co	231
Smith, Joseph	262
South Hetton Coal Co Ltd	238
Southern, George	28, 52
Sunderland Corporation	124, 176
Thiedman & Wallis	297
Tuthill Limestone Quarry Co Ltd	308
Tyzack, Samuel, & Co Ltd	296
Watson, Kipling & Petrie	231
Watson, Kipling & Co Ltd	231
Weardale Lead Co Ltd	394, 396, 400
W B Lead Co	388, 392, 395

(c) other companies and organisations mentioned

Armstrong, Sir W.G., Whitworth & Co (Ironfounders) Ltd	40
Bedlington Coal Co Ltd, Northumberland	40
Beamish, The North of England Open Air Museum	53, 144
Bowes Railway Co Ltd	53
Bowes Museum, Barnard Castle	40
The Consett Iron Co Ltd	113, 118, 254
Derwent Lead Mining Co	392
The Easington Coal Co Ltd	247, 248
Fenton, Murray & Wood, Leeds	5
Gateshead & District Tramways Co	275
Hall & Blenkinsop Ltd	144
Jarrow Metal Industries Ltd	40
Jarrow Tube Works Ltd	40
Losh, Wilson & Bell, Newcastle upon Tyne	12
The Northern Sabulite Co Ltd	309
The Owners of Coxlodge Colliery	6
The Owner of Wylam Colliery	7
Paris, Lyon & Mediterranean Railway	257
The Rainton Colliery Co Ltd	250
Samuelson, Sir B., & Co Ltd	127, 162
Seaton Burn Coal Co Ltd, Northumberland	40
Seaton Burn Coal Syndicate, Northumberland	40
Smithy-Dene Quarry Co Ltd	305
'The Stanhope, Rookhope & District Railway'	400
Stewarts & Lloyds Ltd	281
Stephenson & Hawthorn Locomotive Trust	53
Tanfield Railway	53
The Tyne Plate Glass Co Ltd	335
The Washington Coal Co Ltd	43, 44

Index 2

Locations

(a) collieries (smaller drifts excluded)
rounded brackets indicate a change of name
squared brackets indicate ownership or location

Addison..380, 385	Grange..227, 239
Alexandrina 220, 239, 241	Greenside 381, 385
Alma..22	
Allerdean/Allerdene..28, 40	Handen Hold 20, 22
Andrews House...	Harraton 15, 16, 148, 199
	Harton 334, 355, 368
Beamish 15, 17	Haswell 224, 241, 306
Beamish Air 18	Hawthorn Combined Mine..135, 137, 199, 317, 328
Beamish Mary 19, 20, 23	Hetton (Lyons)...................................114, 135, 176, 199
Beamish Second (& Park) 18, 20, 22	Heworth 257
Beamish South Moor..15	High Marley Hill Drift..48, 52
Belmont 227	Holmside 102
Bewicke Main 262	(New) Herrington 165, 206
Bourn Moor 146	Houghton..150, 206
Blackburn Fell Drift 42, 52	
Blackhouse..267	Kepier Grange..227, 239
Blaydon Main 379	Kibblesworth 28, 52
Boldon 334, 340, 355, 369	Kibblesworth Grange Drift 33, 40
Brasside 158, 165	
Broomside 222, 239	Lady Ann 165
Burnhope 102	Lady Park Drift...281
Burnopfield...28, 57	Lady Seaham..228
Byermoor..28, 57	Lambton 'D' 165, 199
Byron...296	Langley Park 103
	Lee Field...15
Charlaw...295	Letch...220
Chopwell...66, 79	Littletown..154, 222
Clara Vale 379, 385	Lumley 146, 152
Clockburn Drift 48, 74, 81	Lumley 2nd...152, 165
Cocken..152, 165	Lumley 3rd/Lumley New Winning.....152, 173, 189
Craghead 101	Lumley 6th..164, 199
Crookbank...28	Lumley 9th..152
Dawdon...244	Manor Wallsend 333
Deanry Moor 15	Marley Hill 27, 52, 74
Dene Drift...305	Medomsley 112
Derwent Crook 273	Millwellburn 65
Dipton (Delight)..28, 29, 43	Mill Drift 262
Dunston 40	Mount Moor 26, 29, 258
	Murton 137, 199, 307, 317, 328
East Edmonsley..302	
East Stanley..18, 20	Nettlesworth 296, 298
East Tanfield...20, 48	Nettlesworth Drift..305
Edmonsley...296	Newbottle 148
Eighton Moor 258, 273	(Newbottle) Dorothea 148, 168
Elemore.....................................116, 137, 176, 199, 317	(Newbottle) Margaret 148, 168, 189
Emma..379, 385	(Newbottle) Success 148, 168
Eppleton 116, 137, 176, 199, 317	New Winnings 260
	North Biddick...168, 189
Farnacres 273	North Hetton 118, 133, 176, 189, 222
Felling..40	Norwood...40, 273
Follonsby (Wardley No.1/Usworth).........38, 43, 57	
Framwellgate 158, 227, 232	Old Durham..227, 239
Frankland 158, 165	Ouston 15, 256
	Ouston 'A' 256, 260, 265
Garesfield (Bute) 63, 79	Ouston 'B' 256

408

Ouston 'E'	50, 264, 284, 290, 292
Pensher [Lambton]	146
Pensher [Londonderry]	146, 168, 220, 227, 234, 239
Pittington	129, 220, 239
Pontop	32, 63
Rabbit Warren Drift	103
Rainton	220
Rainton Adventure	220, 239, 241
Rainton Meadows	178, 189, 220, 227, 239
Rainton Nicholsons	178, 239
Ravensworth Ann	51, 52, 275
Ravensworth Betty	275
Ravensworth Park Drift	50, 281
Ravensworth Shop	51, 275, 292
Riding Drift	262
Ryhope	231
Sacriston	295, 305
Seaham	228, 244
Seaton	228
Sheriff Hill	274
Sherburn (Lady Durham)	162
Sherburn House	154
Sherburn Hill (orig. Sherburn)	154, 162
Shield Row Drift [Sacriston]	298, 302
Shield Row Drift [Waldridge]	298, 301
Shotton	232, 239, 307, 308
Silksworth	133, 175, 179, 199, 231, 244
Spen	63
Springwell	26, 40, 43
Springwell Vale Pit	38, 40
South Hetton	224, 306
South Medomsley	32
South Moor	101
South Pelaw	260
South Tanfield	17, 20
(South) Pontop	32
St.Hilda	333, 338, 344, 355, 360
Stargate	379, 385
Stella	379
Stella Freehold	379, 380
Stormont (Main)	258
Tanfield Lea	17, 20, 48
Tanfield Moor	20, 28
Team(s)	273
Towneley	379
Twizell	17
Twizell Burn Drift	20
Urpeth	15
Urpeth 'B'	258, 265
Urpeth 'C'	258, 265, 284, 290
Usworth	40
Waldridge	258, 295
Waldridge 'A'	295, 298
Waldridge 'D'	298, 301
Waldridge Fell Drift	305
Wardley, later Wardley No.2	38
Watergate	290
Washhouses	267
Westoe (orig. Benthouse)	340, 344, 348, 358, 373
West Edmonsley	296
West Pelton	20
Whitburn	334, 350, 355, 368
Whittonstall Drift	69, 76, 79, 91, 97
Witton	296

(b) coke ovens & by-product plants (beehive ovens only where noted)

Chopwell (beehives)	68
Derwenthaugh	69, 76, 77, 81
Hawthorn (orig. Murton)	325, 327
Hedgefield (beehives)	380
Hetton (beehives)	131
Horden	325
Lambton	173, 206
Marley Hill	30, 42
Monkton	42, 59, 60
Murton (beehives)	307, 309
Norwood	76, 206, 281
Sacriston (beehives)	298, 301
Shotton	325

(c) iron/lead mines (shaft and opencast)

Bolts Burn	391
Foulwood	392
Frazers Hush	392
Groove Rake	392
Heights	392
Middlehope	394, 395
Rispey	392
Sikehead	392
Slit Pasture	392
Smailsburn	392
West Rigg	394
West Slit	394, 395
Whiteheaps	392

(d) locomotive sheds, other than at collieries

Allerdene/Shop Pit......................50, 51, 52, 275, 290
Beamish Engine Works......................................22, 23
Blackhouse 267, 290
Bolt's Law..389
Derwenthaugh..64, 81
Eighton Banks..267, 290
Harton Wagon Shop..372
Hetton...123, 176, 189
Lambton Sheds, Philadelphia......................180, 206
Lambton Staiths, Sunderland......................180, 199
Marley Hill..29, 48, 53
Ouston 'E' 264
Pelaw Main Staiths, Bill Quay...................................271

Rainton Meadows (?)..227
Rookhope...391
Sacriston..297
Seaham (Londonderry Engine Works) 238
Springwell Bank Foot, Wardley 38, 54
South Hetton 234
Starrs, Wrekenton 51, 275, 290
Sunderland (Hetton Railway)..............123, 180, 184
Waldridge Bank Foot...298
Warden Law...239
Wardley..59
Westoe 360, 373

(e) miscellaneous

Birtley Brick & Tile Works.......................................264
Birtley Gas Works..264, 265
Birtley Grange Brick & Tile Works.......................262
Birtley Iron Works..262
Bishopwearmouth Iron Works............111, 118, 151
Black Fell Underground Locomotive Training Site
....52
Bolts Burn Washing Mill...392
Bowes House Farm, Bournmoor.......................168
Caerphilly Tar Works, Glamorgan 81
Chopwell Electricity Station............................69, 79
Consett Iron Works..70, 76
Craghead Brickworks..103
Duston Manure Depot, Ouston..........................264
Great Lumley village 153, 165
Heaton Colliery Waggonway, Northumberland
....9, 10
Killingworth Colliery Waggonway 12
Lambton Brick & Tile Works, Fencehouses173, 189
Lambton Firebrick Works, Fencehouses............173
Lambton Waggonway..9
Londonderry Bottle Works, Seaham...................231
Londonderry Brickworks, Seaham 228, 239
Lumley Brickworks...189
Lumley Sixth Brickworks...189
Newbottle Coal Washery..180
Newbottle Choppy Store..168
North Eastern Paper Works, Marsden................335
Ouston Dry Cleaning Plant....................................264
Ouston Electricity Station 264
Pelaw Grange Brick Works 262
Pelaw Grange Sawmills..262
Pensher Foundry 168, 227, 234
Pensher Stables 220

Philadelphia Power Station.........................173, 189
Ravensworth Brick & Tile Works 264
Rispey Mill...399
Robertson's Slate Yard..152
Rookhope Depot 391, 396
Rookhope/Lintzgarth Smelt Mill 391, 399
Sacriston Brickworks 302, 305
Scutterhill Depot, Westgate 394, 396, 399, 400
Seaham Bottle Works..231
Seaham Chemical Works...........................231, 244
Seaham Gas Works..231
Seaham Harbour [the port].......................225, 244
Sherburn Hill village..173
Siders Plantation..400
Stanhope Burn Iron Works....................................388
Stanhope Lead Smelter..111
Stargate Brickworks...380
Sunderland Glass Works.......................................118
Sunderland Power Station 124, 176
Tadcaster Brewing Co store 152
Teams Firebrick Works, Dunston................274, 281
Tow Law Ironworks...388
Trimdon Iroworks, Sunderland 118
Tudhoe Ironworks, Spennymoor.........................395
Vane & Seaham Iron Works, Dawdon........231, 244
Wardley Dry-Cleaning Plant 42
Wardley/Monkton Washery..........................48, 292
Washington Colliery Waggonway..........................9
Wear Glass Works, Sunderland..........................118
Westoe Dry-Cleaning Plant, South Shields360, 362
Westoe Washery, South Shields 362, 362
Winlaton Iron Works, Winlaton Mill.......................65
Whitehill Washery..51, 292
Wylam Colliery Waggonway, Northumberland....9

(f) passenger stations

Hendon Burn 230
Jarrow..38
Marsden...335
Marsden Cottage 337, 349
Ryhope...230, 231
Seaham Harbour (later Seaham)..............230, 248

Seaham Colliery..230, 248
Seaham Hall 230, 248
South Shields 335
Springwell..28, 38
Westoe Lane..337, 349
Whitburn Colliery 335, 336, 342, 250

(g) signal boxes

Bournmoor 186
Copt Hill 135, 189
Deptford Branch 135
Erskine Bank Foot 362
Harraton 189
Herrington Crossing ? 189
Hendon 242
Junction Bank Top (prev. Crossing Minders) ... 189
Junction Bank Foot 186
Lighthouse, Marsden 342, 344
Lumley 189
Marsden 335, 342
Mowbray Road 344
Mowbray Road Bridge 340
Philadelphia Crossing 186
Penshaw ? 189
South Shields (Marsden Railway) 335
Sunderland Central 242
Westoe 372
Westoe Lane, South Shields 342, 344

(h) quarries

Cross Rigg/Long Pasture, Pensher 152
Dead Friars, near Bolt's Law 392
Fox Cover, Dawdon 244
Heights, near Eastgate 392, 400
High Downs/Eppleton 121, 176, 189
Lanehead. Stanhope 111
Marsden 334, 350
Newbottle 168
Pensher 152, 220, 225
Sherburn Hill 168
Springwell 38
Thieves Close, Windy Nook 270
Toad Hole, near Lumley 153
Tuthill, near Shotton 308, 327
Windy Nook 270
Whitehouse, Windy Nook 270

(j) staiths

Derwenthaugh 66, 69, 77, 79
Fatfield 159, 165
Garesfield, Derwenthaugh 64
Harton High, South Shields 339, 344, 368
Harton Low, South Shields 339, 372, 373
Hetton 115, 128, 131, 176, 199
Heworth 271
Jarrow 39, 41
Lambton, Sunderland 131, 151, 176, 180, 189
.... 199, 224
Low Lambton, Pensher 145, 152, 154, 165
Painshaw 173, 224
Pelaw Main, Bill Quay 42, 51, 272
Pensher 220, 227
St.Hilda, South Shields 333
Springwell, Jarrow 26
Stella, near Hegdefield 380, 382
Team, Dunston 273, 274
Templetown, Jarrow 323
Tyne Coal Terminal 372

(k) workshops

Addison Workshops, Hedgefield 382
Beamish Engine Works .... 18, 176 .
Birkheads Wagon Shop 44
Chilton Moor Workshops 227, 235
Garesfield Wagon Shop 68
Derwenthaugh Wagon Shop 68, 81
Harton Wagon Shop, South Shields 339, 351
.... 360, 370, 372
Hetton Engine Works .117, 124, 131, 133, 176, 184
Hetton Wagon Shop 133, 176, 184, 199
Lambton Engine Works, Philadelphia 133, 184
.... 185, 206
Lambton Staiths Wagon Shop, Sunderland 185, 199
Lambton Wagon Shops, Philadelphia 184, 185
.... 199, 206
Littletown Workshops 184
Londonderry Engine Works, Seaham ..239, 244, 248
Londonderry Wagon Shops, Seaham..235, 244, 248
Lumley Workshops 153
Pensher Colliery E Pit 222
Ouston Workshops 264, 292
South Hetton Workshops 325, 327
South Hetton Wagon Shop 325
Springwell Engineering Shops 44, 53, 54
Springwell Wagon Shops 44, 53, 54
Wardley Wagon Shop 53, 59
Whitburn Central Workshops 350

411

Index 3

References to Public Railways

Bishop Auckland & Weardale Railway 112
Brandling Junction Railway 112, 332, 334
    - Tanfield Branch 28, 112, 273
British Railways
    - Leamside Branch 59
    - Pelaw-South Shields 59
    - Pontop & Shields Branch 22, 362, 369
    - Silksworth Branch 137
    - Tanfield Branch 48, 50
Clarence Railway 306
Durham Junction Railway 224
Durham & Sunderland Railway 159, 226
Great North of England, Clarence & Hartlepool Railway 311
Hartlepool Dock & Railway 306, 311
London & North Eastern Railway
    - Penshaw Branch 178
Newcastle & Darlington Junction Railway 162, 311
North Eastern Railway
    - Annfield Plain deviation 19
    - Blackhill Branch 32, 65
    - Castle Eden-Stockton Branch 230
    - Deptford Branch 165
    - Durham & Sunderland Branch 129, 131, 176, 229, 307
    - Newcastle-Darlington 297
    - Pelaw-South Shields 40
    - Pensher (Penshaw) Branch 152, 165, 176, 180
    - Pontop & South Shields Branch 16, 17, 32, 159, 165, 260, 334
    - Redheugh Branch 64
    - Seaham-Hartlepool 248
    - Stanhope & Tyne Branch 388
    - Team Valley Branch 262
    - Washington-Ferryhill 162
Pontop & South Shields Railway 111, 112
Stanhope & Tyne Railway 16, 101, 109, 110, 111, 158, 258, 295, 388
Stockton & Darlington Railway 112, 113, 388, 394
Wear Valley Railway 388
Weardale & Derwent Junction Railway 113, 388, 391
Weardale Extension Railway 113
York & Newcastle Railway 311
York, Newcastle & Berwick Railway 311
    - Pensher Branch 162

312. The weighted lever safety valve on one of the boilers of the Warden Law Engine on the Hetton Railway, built by Thomas Murray of Chester-le-Street in 1836.

Index 4

Locomotives & Rail Cranes

NOTES : Information normally relates to the locomotive as built.

Column 1 — Works Number (or original company running number for locomotives built in main line workshops without a works number).

Column 2 — Date ex-works where known - this may be a later year than the year of building or the year recorded on the works plate

Column 3 — Gauge

Column 4 — Wheel arrangement

Steam Locomotives :

Column 5 — Cylinder position

Column 6 — Cylinder size in inches

Column 7 — Driving wheel diameter in feet and inches

Column 8 — Either the Manufacturers type designation OR the working weight as given in National Coal Board records. The weight shown for tender locomotives includes the tender.

Column 9 — Page references

Diesel and Electric Locomotives :

Column 5 — Horse power.

Column 6 — Engine type

Column 7 — Driving wheel diameter in feet and inches

Column 8 — Weight in working order, as recorded in manufacturers' records

Column 9 — Page references

(a) locomotives

ANDREW BARCLAY, SONS & CO LTD, Caledonia Works, Kilmarnock, Ayrshire.　　　　　　**AB**
(member of Hunslet group from 21/8/1972)

70	3.2.1868	4ft8½in	0-4-0ST	OC	9 x 18	3ft0in		386
277	24.6.1884	4ft8½in	0-4-0ST	OC	11 x 18	3ft0in		287
703	21.1.1893	1ft11⅝in	0-4-0ST	OC	5 x 10	1ft10in		289
786	#25.9.1896	4ft8½in	0-4-0ST	OC	12 x 20	3ft2in	23t	56, 287, 293
803	26.8.1897	4ft8½in	0-6-0ST	IC	16 x 24	3ft9in		302
970	1.4.1903	4ft8½in	0-6-0ST	OC	14 x 22	3ft5in	33t	56, 84, 287, 293
1005	13.4.1904	4ft8½in	0-6-0ST	IC	16 x 24	3ft9in	38t	25, 302, 305
1639	29.12.1922	4ft8½in	0-6-0ST	OC	14 x 22	3ft5in	32t6cwts	347, 353, 377
1659	3.3.1920	4ft8½in	0-4-0ST	OC	14 x 22	3ft5in	27t10cwts	55
1724	7.3.1922	4ft8½in	0-4-0ST	OC	14 x 22	3ft5in	27t15cwts	143
1883	7.10.1927	4ft8½in	0-4-0ST	OC	16 x 24	3ft7in	33t	55, 106
1885	12.1.1926	4ft8½in	0-4-0ST	OC	14 x 22	3ft5in	27t15cwts	212
2274	26.10.1949	4ft8½in	0-4-0ST	OC	14 x 22	3ft5in	29t	55

\# date of invoice

423	25.7.1958	4ft8½in	0-6-0DM	310hp	Natl M4AAU6	3ft2in	43t	375
478	10.12.1963	4ft8½in	0-4-0DH	233hp	R-R C6SFL	3ft2in	32t	57, 60, 85, 375
491	8.4.1964	4ft8½in	0-6-0DH	380hp	Dorman 6QAT	3ft5in	48t	375
498	9.3.1965	4ft8½in	0-6-0DH	380hp	Dorman 6QAT	3ft5in	48t	85
514	13.5.1966	4ft8½in	0-6-0DH	311hp	R-R C8SFL	3ft9in	46t	57, 60, 331, 353, 375, 377
523	23.1.1967	4ft8½in	0-4-0DH	233hp	R-R C6SFL	3ft9in	32t	213
524	30.1.1967	4ft8½in	0-4-0DH	233hp	R-R C6SFL	3ft9in	32t	60
549	14.10.1967	4ft8½in	0-6-0DH	311hp	R-R C8SFL	3ft9in	46t	375
582	23.3.1973	4ft8½in	0-6-0DH	400hp	R-R C8TFL	3ft9in	52t	329, 375
583	28.3.1973	4ft8½in	0-6-0DH	400hp	R-R C8TFL	3ft9in	52t	329, 331
584	18.6.1973	4ft8½in	0-6-0DH	400hp	R-R C8TFL	3ft9in	52t	60, 329
585	25.7.1973	4ft8½in	0-6-0DH	400hp	R-R C8TFL	3ft9in	52t	213, 329
594	4.12.1974	4ft8½in	0-6-0DH	400hp	R-R C8TFL	3ft9in	52t	330, 331
604	7.6.1976	4ft8½in	0-6-0DH	400hp	R-R C8TFL	3ft9in	52t	213, 329, 331
609	3.12.1976	4ft8½in	0-6-0DH	400hp	R-R C8TFL	3ft9in	52t	330, 331
612	15.12.1976	4ft8½in	0-6-0DH	400hp	R-R C8TFL	3ft9in	52t	329, 331
613	5.2.1977	4ft8½in	0-6-0DH	400hp	R-R C8TFL	3ft9in	52t	375
615	30.3.1977	4ft8½in	0-6-0DH	400hp	R-R C8TFL	3ft9in	52t	330, 375
616	30.4.1977	4ft8½in	0-6-0DH	400hp	R-R C8TFL	3ft9in	52t	330, 331
623	25.3.1978	4ft8½in	0-6-0DH	400hp	R-R C8TFL	3ft9in	52t	375
646	3.7.1979	4ft8½in	0-6-0DH	400hp	R-R C8TFL	3ft9in	52t	375
647	14.8.1979	4ft8½in	0-6-0DH	400hp	R-R C8TFL	3ft9in	52t	60, 213, 330, 331
659	24.2.1982	4ft8½in	0-6-0DH	400hp	R-R C8TFL	3ft9in	52t	375

ALLGEMEINE ELEKTRICITATS GESELLSCHAFT, Berlin, Germany **AEG**

1565	24.7.1913	4ft8½in	4w-4wWE	244hp		3ft1½in	40t	375

BARCLAYS & CO, Riverbank Engine Works, Kilmarnock, Ayrshire **B**

303	1883	4ft8½in	0-4-0ST	OC	12½ x18⅝	3ft1in	20t6cwts	84

(cylinders, wheel diameter and working weight as per NCB records)

E.E. BAGULEY LTD, Burton on Trent, Staffordshire **Bg**

3350	18.12.1951	4ft8½in	4w-4wWE	400hp		3ft0in	50t	375
3351	11.1.1952	4ft8½in	4w-4wWE	400hp		3ft0in	50t	375
3469	15.6.1957	4ft8½in	4w-4wWE	400hp		3ft0in	48½t	375
3519	8.4.1959	4ft8½in	4w-4wWE	400hp		3ft0in	48½t	375
3520	29.4.1959	4ft8½in	4w-4wWE	400hp		3ft0in	48t	375
3565	23.11.1960	4ft8½in	2w-2DM(R)	22hp	Lister JP2			375

All the electric locomotives were built under sub-contract from English Electric Co Ltd (EE), as EE works numbers 1795, 1794, 2308, 2599 and 2600 respectively.

BAGULEY-DREWRY LTD, Burton-on-Trent, Staffordshire **BD**

	#25.2.1985	4ft 8½in	4w-4wWE	400hp	3ft 0in	375

\# date of invoice

BLACK, HAWTHORN & CO LTD, Gateshead, Co. Durham **BH**

This company was formed in 1865 to take over the engine works in Quarry Lane formerly operated by Ralph Coulthard. The firm's main output was to industrial customers, though they also supplied main line railways and customers abroad. Besides locomotives, the firm also built other types of steam engine, such as colliery pumping engines, and these were also allocated numbers in the makers' serial list. Although serial numbers were issued up to No. 1143, the last locomotive built was No. 1138. However, with rare exceptions, the company did not issue works numbers ending in zero. The company went into voluntary liquidation In January 1897, and the business was subsequently taken over by Chapman & Furneaux (which see).

Perhaps more than many firms, Black, Hawthorn frequently built locomotives for stock, and the actual customer's order might come as much as three years later. To try to avoid too much confusion, the date of first ordering is given in the list below, with customers' order dates (if different) shown in a footnote. Very few delivery dates are recorded, but those known are also given. The same problem also gives rise to uncertainty about many dates carried on the maker's plate; the date given in the main text is that believed to have been carried.

17	16.3.1866	4ft8½in	0-6-0 %	IC	16 x 24	4ft6in		190, 209
31	12.3.1867	4ft8½in	0-6-0ST	OC	14 x 20	3ft4in		402
32	12.3.1867	4ft8½in	0-6-0ST @	OC	15 x 20	4ft0in		191, 209
34	23.5.1867	4ft8½in	0-6-0	IC	16 x 24	4ft8in		250
48	8.1.1868	4ft8½in	0-6-0T	OC	14 x 20	3ft6in		287
52	8.1.1868	4ft8½in	0-6-0ST	OC	14 x 20	3ft6in		287
60	11.6.1868	4ft8½in	0-6-0T	OC	14 x 20	3ft6in		287
203	#20.4.1871	4ft8½in	0-4-0ST	OC	9 x 16	2ft9in		250
304	9.10.1873	4ft8½in	0-6-0ST	IC	14 x 20	3ft6in		45
326	3.2.1874	4ft8½in	0-4-0ST	OC	12 x 19	3ft2in		72
355	#25.2.1875	4ft8½in	0-6-0ST	OC	14 x 20	3ft6in		315, 328
504	11.6.1879	4ft8½in	0-6-0ST	OC	14 x 20	3ft6in		347
515	12.9.1879	4ft8½in	0-4-0ST	OC	9 x 18	2ft8in		347
516	12.9.1879	4ft8½in	0-4-0ST	OC	9 x 18	2ft8in		347
546	#23.3.1879	4ft8½in	0-4-0ST	OC	12 x 19	3ft2in		301
602	3.8.1880	4ft8½in	0-6-0ST	OC	17 x 26	4ft6in		287
688	9.3.1882	4ft8½in	0-4-0ST	OC	15 x 20	3ft7in	27t5cwts	142, 191, 210
692	17.4.1882	4ft8½in	0-6-0ST	IC	14 x 20	3ft6in		45
698	22.6.1882	4ft8½in	0-4-0ST	OC	12 x 19	3ft2in		73
704	#24.8.1882	4ft8½in	0-6-0ST	OC	14 x 20	3ft6in		402
716	15.9.1882	4ft8½in	0-6-0ST	IC	15 x 22	3ft9½in		347
826	27.5.1884	4ft8½in	0-6-0ST	IC	15 x 22	3ft9½in	30t	347, 353
832	20.11.1884	4ft8½in	0-4-0ST	OC	15 x 20	3ft7in	27t5cwts	142, 191, 210
854	#17.5.1885	4ft8½in	0-4-0ST	OC	12 x 19	3ft2in		65, 72
888	#9.11.1886	4ft8½in	0-6-0ST	OC	14 x 20	3ft7in	25t	106
891	#9.11.1886	4ft8½in	0-6-0ST	OC	12 x 19	3ft2in		45
937	7.3.1888	4ft8½in	0-6-2ST	IC	16 x 24	4ft6½in		45
938	+4.1888	4ft8½in	0-6-2ST	IC	16 x 24	4ft6½in	40t	45, 54
971	#1889	4ft8½in	0-6-0ST	OC	14 x 20	3ft7in	28t	106
1037	#9.6.1891	4ft8½in	0-4-0ST	OC	12 x 19	3ft3in		302
1051	+18.8.1891	4ft8½in	0-4-0VBCr	OC	12 x 21½	3ft0in	7t capy.	74
1071	21.7.1892	4ft8½in	0-6-2ST	IC	16 x 24	4ft6⅞in		46
1113	#5.4.1894	4ft8½in	0-4-0ST	OC	12 x 19	3ft3in		72
1115	#17.5.1895	4ft8½in	0-6-0ST	IC	12 x 18	3ft0½in		66
1116	#17.5.1895	4ft8½in	0-6-0ST	IC	12 x 18	3ft0½in		66
		4ft8½in	0-4-0ST	OC			[BUSTY]	288

% built from material supplied by the Earl of Durham
@ "Reconstruction of loco engine"
+ 938 was delivered on 26.10.1888 and 1051 in 6.1892
# date ordered for stock

BLAIR & CO, Norton Road, Stockton-on-Tees **Blair**

George Blair had been the works manager for the firm of Fossick & Hackworth (see below), and when the latter retired in 1865 Blair joined George Fossick and the firm traded briefly as Fossick & Blair. When Fossick died in 1866, Blair took over the business. So far as is known, no locomotives were built after 1868, and the firm concentrated on marine work. It closed in 1920.

	c1865	4ft8½in	0-6-0	IC				190
	1868	4ft8½in	0-6-0	IC	16¾x24	4ft9in		250

BLYTH & TYNE RAILWAY, Percy Main, North Shields, Northumberland **Blyth & Tyne**

	4.1862	4ft8½in	0-6-0	IC	16 x 24	4ft6in	[later NER 2255]	387
	9.1862	4ft8½in	0-6-0	IC	16 x 24	4ft6in	[later NER 1712]	387

BEYER, PEACOCK & CO LTD, Gorton, Manchester **BP**

190	3.8.1860	4ft8½in	0-4-2ST	OC	16 x 24	5ft0in		315
417	29.6.1864	4ft8½in	4-4-0T	OC	17 x 24	5ft9in		316
425	5.8.1864	4ft8½in	4-4-0T	OC	17 x 24	5ft9in		315, 328
550	8.6.1865	4ft8½in	0-6-0	IC	17 x 24	4ft6in	59t4cwts	190, 209
770	20.7.1868	4ft8½in	4-4-0T	OC	17 x 24	5ft9in		288, 293
772	31.7.1868	4ft8½in	4-4-0T	OC	17 x 24	5ft9in		288
868	15.3.1869	4ft8½in	4-4-0T	OC	17 x 24	5ft9in		288, 293
7859	18.9.1958	4ft8½in	0-4-0DE	230hp	McLaren LES6		34t [BT 102]	58

BRUSH ELECTRICAL MACHINES LTD, Loughborough   BT

| 102 | 18.9.1958 | 4ft8½in | 0-4-0DE | 230hp | McLaren LES6 | 34t [BP 7859] | 58 |

WEST YARD LOCOMOTIVE WORKS, Cardiff, Glamorgan, Taff Vale Railway   Cdf

302	11.1894	4ft8½in	0-6-2T	IC	17½ x 26	4ft6½in	62t	191, 211
306	5.1897	4ft8½in	0-6-2T	IC	17½ x 26	4ft6½in	56t8cwts	329
311	10.1897	4ft8½in	0-6-2T	IC	17½ x 26	4ft6½in	56t8cwts	142,191, 211

CHAPMAN & FURNEAUX, Quarry Lane, Gateshead   CF

This firm was formed in 1897 to take over the business of Black, Hawthorn & Co Ltd (which see) which had gone into voluntary liquidation. It continued the Black, Hawthorn serial numbers, its first locomotive being No.1144. The firm closed down in 1902, the last locomotive to be built at Gateshead being No.1212, although Nos.1213-1215 were built by Hudswell, Clarke & Co Ltd, Leeds as its Nos. 617, 618 and 631. The goodwill of the firm was taken over by R & W Hawthorn, Leslie & Co Ltd (which see) of Newcastle upon Tyne.
As with Black, Hawthorn, the dates given in the list below are those of first ordering.

1158	+4.3.1898	4ft8½in	0-6-2T	IC	17 x 24	4ft3in	45t4cwts	46, 346, 386
1163	+16.5.1898	4ft8½in	0-4-0ST	OC	13 x 19	3ft4in	25t6cwts	72, 83
1203	16.10.1900	4ft8½in	0-4-0ST	OC	15 x 22	3ft8in	29½t	45
1204	31.10.1900	4ft8½in	0-6-0ST	OC	16 x 24	3ft8in	45t	106
1210	#18.4.1901	4ft8½in	0-4-0ST	OC	14 x 19	3ft2in	33t	302

+1158 was delivered on 29.12.1898 and 1163 on 16.12.1898
#date of order for stock; customer's order was dated 15.1.1902

COWANS, SHELDON & CO LTD, Carlisle   CoS

| 4101 | 4.11.1920 | 4ft8½in | 0-4-0VBCT | OC | | | | 74 |

CREWE WORKS, Crewe, Cheshire (British Railways)   Crewe

| [BR D3744] | 6.1959 | 4ft8½in | 0-6-0DE | 350hp | EE 6KT | 4ft6in | 48t 08577 | 90 |

CHARLES TAYLEUR & CO, Newton-le-Willows, Lancashire   CT

| ? 320 | 1848 | 4ft8½in | 0-4-2 | OC | 16 x18 | 4ft7in | | 250 |

DARLINGTON WORKS, Darlington (North Eastern Railway/London & North Eastern Railway/British Railways)   Dar

[NER 1953] 347	6.1898	4ft8½in	0-6-0	IC	18½ x 24	4ft7¼in		
[BR 12119]	9.1952	4ft8½in	0-6-0DE	350hp	EE 6KT	4ft0½in	47t2cwts	213
[BR 12120]	9.1952	4ft8½in	0-6-0DE	350hp	EE 6KT	4ft0½in	47t2cwts	213
[BR 12133]	12.1952	4ft8½in	0-6-0DE	350hp	EE 6KT	4ft0½in	47t2cwts	213
[BR 13140]	4.1955	4ft8½in	0-6-0DE	350hp	Blackstone ER6T	4ft6in	47½t	217
[BR 13227]	12.1955	4ft8½in	0-6-0DE	350hp	EE 6KT	4ft6in	48t 08159	62
[BR 13232]	1.1956	4ft8½in	0-6-0DE	350hp	EE 6KT	4ft6in	48t 08164	218
[BR 13238]	2.1956	4ft8½in	0-6-0DE	350hp	EE 6KT	4ft6in	48t 08170	90
[BR 13244]	3.1956	4ft8½in	0-6-0DE	350hp	EE 6KT	4ft6in	48t 08176	62, 218
[BR 13324]	11.1956	4ft 8½in	0-6-0DE	350hp	EE 6KT	4ft6in	48t 08254	90
[BR D4070]	6.1961	4ft8½in	0-6-0DE	350hp	Blackstone ER6T	4ft6in	47t	213
[BR D4072]	7.1961	4ft8½in	0-6-0DE	350hp	Blackstone ER6T	4ft6in	47t	213, 330

DERBY WORKS, Derby (British Railways)   Derby

[BR 12050]	1.1949	4ft8½in	0-6-0DE	350hp	EE 6KT	4ft0½in	47t2cwts	213
[BR 12060]	11.1949	4ft8½in	0-6-0DE	350hp	EE 6KT	4ft0½in	47t2cwts	85, 213
[BR 12078]	10.1950	4ft8½in	0-6-0DE	350hp	EE 6KT	4ft0½in	47t2cwts	217
[BR 12084]	12.1950	4ft8½in	0-6-0DE	350hp	EE 6KT	4ft0½in	47t2cwts [514]	144, 213
[BR 12098]	2.1952	4ft8½in	0-6-0DE	350hp	EE 6KT	4ft0½in	47t2cwts [513]	85, 213, 218
[BR 13088]	10.1954	4ft8½in	0-6-0DE	350hp	EE 6KT	4ft6in	48t 08073	213
[BR 13110]	3.1955	4ft8½in	0-6-0DE	350hp	EE 6KT	4ft6in	48t 08085	62
[BR 13216]	3.1956	4ft8½in	0-6-0DE	350hp	EE 6KT	4ft6in	48t 08148	90
[BR D3516]	3.1958	4ft8½in	0-6-0DE	350hp	EE 6KT	4ft6in	48t 08401	217, 377
[BR D3965]	5.1960	4ft8½in	0-6-0DE	350hp	EE 6KT	4ft6in	48t 08797	62

[BR D3970]	6.1960	4ft 8½in	0-6-0DE	350hp	EE 6KT	4ft 6in	48t	08802	62
[BR D3976]	7.1960	4ft 8½in	0-6-0DE	350hp	EE 6KT	4ft 6in	48t	08808	62

DONCASTER WORKS, Doncaster (Great Northern Railway/London & North Eastern Railway/British Railways)   Don

213	10.1876	4ft 8½in	0-6-0ST	IC	17½x26	4ft 8in			287
[BR D2099]	9.1960	4ft 8½in	0-6-0DM	204hp	Gardner 8L3	3ft 7in	30¼t	03099	61
[BR D2102]	9.1960	4ft 8½in	0-6-0DM	204hp	Gardner 8L3	3ft 7in	30¼t		217

DICK, KERR & CO LTD, Preston, Lancashire   DK

	1918	4ft 8½in	4wBE		[51]	191

EARL OF DURHAM, Lambton Engine Works, Philadelphia   Earl of Durham

[9]	1877	4ft 8½in	0-6-0	IC	17 x 24	4ft 6in	55t 14cwts	190, 209
[25]	1890	4ft 8½in	0-6-0	IC	17 x 24	4ft 6in	56t	191, 210
[26]	1.1894	4ft 8½in	0-6-0	IC	17 x 24	4ft 6in	56t	191, 210

ENGLISH ELECTRIC CO LTD, Preston, Lancashire   EE

The construction of all of the locomotives below was sub-contracted to E.E.Baguley Ltd, Burton-on-Trent, Staffordshire (which see).

1794	18.12.1951	4ft 8½in	4w-4wWE	400hp	3ft 0in	50t	375
1795	11.1.1952	4ft 8½in	4w-4wWE	400hp	3ft 0in	50t	375
2308	15.6.1957	4ft 8½in	4w-4wWE	400hp	3ft 0in	48½t	375
2599	8.4.1959	4ft 8½in	4w-4wWE	400hp	3ft 0in	48½t	375
2600	29.4.1959	4ft 8½in	4w-4wWE	400hp	3ft 0in	48½t	375

ENGLISH ELECTRIC CO LTD, Vulcan Works, Newton-le-Willows, Lancashire   EEV

D1121	1966	4ft 8½in	0-6-0DH	305hp	Cummins NHRS6B1	38t	213

W FAIRBAIRN & SONS, Canal Street Works, Manchester   Fairbairn

	10.1842	4ft 8½in	0-4-0	IC	14 x 20	4ft 6in	401
	12.1842	4ft 8½in	0-4-0	IC	14 x 20	4ft 6in	401

F C HIBBERD & CO LTD, Park Royal, London   FH

3852	6.4.1957	4ft 8½in	4wDM	75hp	Dorman 4DL	3ft 1½in	18t#	212
3922	29.12.1959	4ft 8½in	4wDM	134hp	Dorman 6KD	3ft 0in	24t	56, 213, 329
3923	4.1.1960	4ft 8½in	4wDM	134hp	Dorman 6KD	3ft 0in	24t	56

weight as built; the loco was subsequently ballasted to 20t

FOSSICK & HACKWORTH, Norton Road, Stockton on Tees   F&H

This firm was established in the spring of 1840 by Thomas Hackworth, the brother of Timothy Hackworth (see chapter 1) and George Fossick. Besides the construction of locomotives and other types of steam engine, foundry work was also undertaken. In addition, the firm operated under contract the Stockton & Hartlepool Railway and the Clarence Railway (1844-1854) and the Llanelly Railway & Dock Co in South Wales (1850-1853). Hackworth retired in 1865, and Fossick was joined by George Blair (see Blair & Co above). The firm is known to have built about fifty locomotives and the total is probably not many more than this.

	1861	4ft 8½in	0-6-0	OC	250

FLETCHER, JENNINGS & CO LTD, Lowca Engine Works, Whitehaven, Cumberland   FJ

125	26.11.1874	4ft 8½in	0-4-0WT	OC	12 x 20	3ft 6in	45

GREENWOOD & BATLEY LTD, Armley, Leeds   GB

2047	19.2.1947	4ft 8½in	0-4-0WE	80hp	17t	61

GATESHEAD WORKS, Greensfield, Gateshead, North Eastern Railway   **Ghd**

	8.1881	4ft8½in	0-6-0	IC	17 x 24	5ft0in	[NER 396]	347, 353
	11.1882	4ft8½in	0-6-0	IC	17½x24	5ft0in	[NER 1453]	377
	4.1883	4ft8½in	0-6-0	IC	17 x 24	5ft0in	[NER 1333]	353, 377
35	12.1888	4ft8½in	0-4-0T	IC	13 x 20	3ft6¼in	[NER 900]	288, 293
38	12.1888	4ft8½in	0-4-0T	IC	13 x 20	3ft6¼in	[NER 24]	377
3	2.1889	4ft8½in	0-6-0	IC	18 x 24	5ft1¼in	[NER 869]	347, 353
23	6.1889	4ft8½in	0-6-0	IC	18 x 24	5ft1¼in	[NER 1509]	347, 353
43	2.1889	4ft8½in	0-6-0	IC	18 x 24	5ft1¼in	[NER 776]	347, 377
37	10.1891	4ft8½in	0-4-0T	IC	14 x 20	3ft6¼in	[NER 1308]	55, 288, 293
38	10.1891	4ft8½in	0-4-0T	IC	14 x 20	3ft6¼in	[NER 1310]	55, 288, 293
38	12.1892	4ft8½in	0-6-0	IC	18 x 24	5ft1¼in	[NER 1616]	347
7	3.1897	4ft8½in	0-6-0T	IC	14 x 20	3ft6¼in	[NER 1787]	45
28	12.1897	4ft8½in	0-6-0	IC	18 x 24	4ft7¼in	[NER 1931]	353, 377

GRANT, RITCHIE & CO LTD, Kilmarnock, Ayrshire   **GR**

| 769 | 1920 | 4ft8½in | 0-4-0ST | OC | 16 x 24 | 3ft8in | 35t | 142, 191, 210 |

TIMOTHY HACKWORTH, Soho Works, Shildon   **Hackworth**

Timothy Hackworth was appointed to have "the superintendence of the permanent and locomotive engines" on the Stockton & Darlington Railway in 1825. In 1833 he took over this work under contract, and for this purpose he developed an engine works at Shildon, putting in his brother Thomas as its manager. This allowed him to undertake other work, including the construction of a number of locomotives. In 1840 he relinquished the Stockton & Darlington Railway contract, his brother left to set up in business at Stockton with George Fossick (see Fossick & Hackworth above), leaving Timothy to run the business at Shildon until his death in 1850. The works buildings that remain, together with Hackworth's house nearby, are now part of the Timothy Hackworth Victorian & Railway Museum.

		4ft8½in	0-6-0	OC	15 x 18	4ft0in	[BRADDYLL]	309
		4ft8½in	0-6-0	OC			[KELLOE]	309
		4ft8½in	0-6-0	OC			[NELSON]	309
		4ft8½in	0-6-0	OC			[WELLINGTON]	309
	1842	4ft8½in	0-6-0	OC			[PRINCE ALBERT]	190
	c1842	4ft8½in	0-6-0	OC				401

HANNOVERSCHE MASCHINENBAU-AG (vormals Georg Egestorff), Hannover-Linden, Germany   **Hano**

| 5968 | 1910 | 2ft2in | 0-4-0+0-4-0WE | 120hp | [Siemens 460] | 97 |

JOHN HARRIS, Hope Town Foundry, Darlington   **Harris**

John Harris (1812-1869) set up his business in 1840, north of Darlington (North Road) Station on the Stockton & Darlington Railway. At first he concentrated on contracting for railway track, but by the 1860s he had expanded into the repair and construction of tank locomotives and wagons. After his death the premises were taken over by the Whessoe Foundry.

	1863	4ft8½in	0-4-0ST	OC	[VICTORY]	287
	1865	4ft8½in	0-4-0ST	OC	[DERWENT]	287
	1867	4ft8½in	0-4-0ST	OC	[6]	250
	1868	4ft8½in	0-4-0ST	OC	[BYRON]	287

HUDSWELL & CLARKE (until /1870)   **H&C**
HUDSWELL, CLARKE & RODGERS (from /1870 until /1880)   **HCR**
HUDSWELL CLARKE & CO LTD (1880-1972)   **HC**
HUDSWELL BADGER LTD (from 1972), all at the Railway Foundry, Leeds   **HB**

21	3.4.1865	4ft8½in	0-6-0ST	IC	13 x 18	3ft6in		190
30	30.9.1864	4ft8½in	0-6-0	IC	17 x 24	5ft0in		190
71	9.8.1866	4ft8½in	0-6-0	IC	17 x 24	4ft0in	59t4cwts	190, 209
72	30.10.1866	4ft8½in	0-6-0	IC	17 x 24	4ft0in		190
76	7.5.1866	4ft8½in	0-6-0ST	IC	13 x 18	3ft0in		190
78	8.8.1866	4ft8½in	0-6-0ST	IC	13 x 18	3ft0in		190
79	7.2.1868	4ft8½in	0-4-0ST	OC	14 x 20	3ft6in		190
96	28.6.1870	4ft8½in	0-4-0ST	OC	15 x 20	3ft6in	27t5cwts	142, 191, 209
98	9.9.1870	4ft8½in	0-6-0ST	IC	17 x 24	4ft0in		190

130	28.6.1873	4ft8½in	0-4-0ST	OC	15 x 20	3ft6½in			142, 191
169	26.10.1875	4ft8½in	0-4-0ST	OC	15 x 20	3ft6½in	26t14cwts		190, 209
230	8.8.1881	4ft8½in	0-4-0ST	OC	15 x 20	3ft6½in	27t5cwts		142,191, 209
332	23.9.1889	4ft8½in	0-6-0T	IC	14 x 20	3ft3in	31t		377
674	14.8.1903	4ft8½in	0-4-0ST	OC	12 x 18	3ft1½in	22t18cwts		301, 386
702	23.6.1904	4ft8½in	0-4-0ST	OC	13 x 19	3ft4½in			73
749	31.1.1906	4ft8½in	0-4-0ST	OC	16 x 24	3ft8in	34t2cwts		84
764	23.4.1906	4ft8½in	0-4-0ST	OC	16 x 24	3ft8in	34t2cwts		84
809	29.6.1907	4ft8½in	0-6-0PT	IC	18 x 26	4ft2⅜in	43t6cwts		71
1190	13.1.1916	4ft8½in	0-4-0ST	OC	14 x 20	3ft3½in	25t		84
1201	25.8.1916	4ft8½in	0-4-0ST	OC	14 x 20	3ft3½in			301,302
1251	15.2.1917	4ft8½in	0-6-0T	IC	15½x20	3ft4in	34t		84
1255	27.7.1917	4ft8½in	0-6-0T	OC	16 x 24	3ft9in	42t		55, 84
1412	20.8.1920	4ft8½in	0-4-0ST	OC	16 x 24	3ft9in	36½t		141, 143, 190, 209
1448	26.5.1921	4ft8½in	0-6-0PT	IC	18 x 26	4ft2⅜in	43t6cwts		84
1449	26.5.1921	4ft8½in	0-6-0PT	IC	18 x 26	4ft2⅜in	43t6cwts		71, 83
1513	20.3.1924	4ft8½in	0-6-0ST	IC	13 x 20	3ft3½in	24t16cwts		353, 377
1514	19.12.1924	4ft8½in	0-4-0ST	OC	16 x 24	3ft8in	34t2cwts		56, 84, 386
1524	30.6.1924	4ft8½in	0-6-0T	IC	18 x 24	4ft0in	45t		25, 302, 305
DM632	30.5.1947	3ft6in	0-6-0DMF+100hp		Gardner 6LW	2ft2½in	15t		87
DM639	18.12.1947	3ft6in	0-6-0DMF+100hp		Gardner 6LW	2ft2½in	15t		87
DM709	4.2.1955	3ft6in	0-6-0DMF+100hp		Gardner 6LW	2ft2½ in	15t		87
DM993	29.10.1956	3ft6in	0-6-0DMF+100hp		Gardner 6LW	2ft2½in	15t		87
DM1063	30.7.1957	3ft6in	0-6-0DMF# 100hp		Gardner 6LW	2ft2½in	15t		87
DM1428	28.10.1977	3ft0in	0-6-0DMF# 100hp		Gardner 6LW	2ft2½in	15t [HE 8525]		87

+ single-ended (i.e., with a cab only at one end)
# double-ended (i.e., with a cab at both ends)

HUNSLET ENGINE CO LTD, Hunslet, Leeds   HE

286	7.5.1883	4ft8½in	0-4-0ST	OC	10 x 15	2ft9in			377
361	8.1.1885	4ft8½in	0-4-0ST	OC	9 x 14	2ft8½in			377
396	9.4.1886	4ft8½in	0-6-0T	IC	15 x 20	3ft4in			315, 329
1506	6.6.1930	4ft8½in	0-6-0T	IC	18 x 26	4ft0in	48t		46, 55
3191	28.10.1944	4ft8½in	0-6-0ST	IC	18 x 26	4ft3in	48t3cwts		353, 377
3215	23.5.1945	4ft8½in	0-6-0ST	IC	18 x 26	4ft3in	48t3cwts		56
3686	18.1.1949	4ft8½in	0-6-0ST	IC	18 x 26	4ft3in	48t3cwts		56, 143, 212
3687	3.1.1949	4ft8½in	0-6-0ST	IC	18 x 26	4ft3in	48t3cwts		329
3688	8.2.1949	4ft8½in	0-6-0ST	IC	18 x 26	4ft3in	48t3cwts		55
3689	17.2.1949	4ft8½in	0-6-0ST	IC	18 x 26	4ft3in	48t3cwts		84, 212
3784	30.6.1953	4ft8½in	0-6-0ST	IC	18 x 26	4ft3in	48t3cwts		212, 329
3785	30.6.1953	4ft8vin	0-6-0ST	IC	18 x 26	4ft3in	48t3cwts		212, 389
3820	1.7.1954	4ft8vin	0-6-0ST	IC	18 x 26	4ft3in	48t3cwts		85, 212
3821	16.7.1954	4ft8½in	0-6-0ST	IC	18 x 26	4ft3in	48t3cwts		329
3833	30.9.1955	4ft8½in	0-6-0ST	IC	18 x 26	4ft3in	48t3cwts		55, 84
4551	1956	4ft8½in	0-6-0DM	325hp	Mirrlees J4		44t		58
5302	13.10.1958	4ft8½in	0-6-0DM	204hp	Gardner 8L3	3ft4in	29t19cwts		377
5382	29.12.1958	4ft8½in	0-6-0DM	204hp	Gardner 8L3	3ft4in	29t19cwts		218
5647	30.6.1960	4ft8½in	0-6-0DM	204hp	Gardner 8L3	3ft4in	30t15cwts [D2598]		213
6263	30.12.1964	4ft8½in	0-4-0DH	195hp	Gardner	3ft4in			90, 332
6611	5.4.1965	4ft8½in	0-6-0DH	311hp	R-R C8SFL	3ft9in	55t		56, 60
6612	8.4.1965	4ft8½in	0-6-0DH	311hp	R-R C8SFL	3ft9in	55t		57, 85
6613	9.6.1965	4ft8½in	0-6-0DH	311hp	R-R C8SFL	3ft9in	55t		56, 60
6614	21.6.1965	4ft8½in	0-6-0DH	311hp	R-R C8SFL	3ft9in	55t		56, 60
6615	29.7.1965	4ft8½in	0-6-0DH	311hp	R-R C8SFL	3ft9in	55t		57, 60
6616	31.8.1965	4ft8½in	0-6-0DH	311hp	R-R C8SFL	3ft9in	55t		85, 353, 375, 377
6617	30.9.1965	4ft8½in	0-6-0DH	311hp	R-R C8SFL	3ft9in	55t		57, 85, 353, 377
6618	5.11.1965	4ft8½in	0-6-0DH	311hp	R-R C8SFL	3ft9in	55t		85, 353, 377
6662	6.12.1966	4ft8½in	0-6-0DH	311hp	R-R C8SFL	3ft9in	55t		85, 213
6676	26.6.1967	4ft8½in	0-4-0DH	233hp	R-R C6SFL	3ft9in	35t		85, 144
6688	5.12.1968	4ft8½in	0-4-0DH	252hp	R-R C6SFL	3ft9in	35t		90
7305	20.2.1973	4ft8½in	0-6-0DH	400hp	R-R C8TFL		45t		61, 218
8525	28.10.1977	3ft6in	0-6-0DMF	100hp	Gardner 6LW	2ft2½in	15t [HB DM1428]		87

HETTON COAL CO, Hetton Engine Works, Hetton **Hetton**

	1852	4ft8½in	0-4-0	VC	9 x 24	3ft9in	[LYON(S)]	139
	c1854	4ft8½in	0-4-0	VC			[LADY BARRINGTON]	139
		4ft8½in	4wVBT	VC		6½x 8	[LYONS]	141
		4ft8½in	4wVBT	VC			[EPPLETON]	141

HAIGH FOUNDRY CO, Wigan, Lancashire **HF**

46	5.1841	4ft8½in	0-4-2	IC	14 x 18	5ft0in		250

HENRY HUGHES & CO, Falcon Works, Loughborough, Leicestershire **HH**

		4ft8½in	0-6-0ST?				[HOLMSIDE]	106

HAWTHORNS & CO, Leith Engine Works, Leith, Edinburgh **H(L)**

220	1859	4ft8½in	0-4-0WT	OC				287
		4ft8½in	2-4-0WT	OC			[BIRTLEY]	287

R & W HAWTHORN, LESLIE & CO LTD, Forth Banks Works, Newcastle upon Tyne **HL**

This company was formed in March 1886 by the amalgamation of R. & W. Hawthorn Ltd (which see) and Andrew Leslie & Co Ltd, shipbuilders, of Hebburn, Co. Durham. The numbering scheme of R. & W. Hawthorn was continued, but which locomotive was the first to carry a HL plate is uncertain. Whereas R. & W. Hawthorn had built chiefly main-line locomotives, the new firm concentrated more on industrial customers, and soon became the main suppliers of industrial locomotives in North-East England. In 1902 it took over the goodwill of Chapman & Furneaux of Gateshead (which see), successors to Black, Hawthorn & Co Ltd (which see).

The locomotive business was sold in May 1937 to Robert Stephenson & Co Ltd (which see), which changed its name in the following month to Robert Stephenson & Hawthorns Ltd (which see). Despite this, locomotives continued for a time to be turned out with HL plates, the last being No.3953 in March 1938.

2199	6.1891	4ft8½in	0-4-0ST	OC	12 x 18	3ft0½in		386
2330	6.1896	4ft8½in	0-4-0ST	OC	12 x 18	3ft0½in	18t15cwts	386
2349	11.1896	4ft8½in	0-4-0ST	OC	12 x 18	3ft0½in	18t15cwts	56, 301
2377	1.7.1897	4ft8½in	0-4-0ST	OC	13 x 19	3ft4½in	25t6cwts	72, 83
2426	9.1899	4ft8½in	0-4-0ST	OC	14 x 20	3ft6in	25t	386
2481	12.2.1900	4ft8½in	0-4-0ST	OC	14 x 20	3ft6in	21½t	55
2515	19.12.1901	4ft8½in	0-6-0ST	OC	15 x 22	3ft9in	32t9cwts	45, 54
2530	22.8.1902	4ft8½in	0-4-0ST	OC	14 x 20	3ft6in	26t	191, 210
2545	24.12.1902	4ft8½in	0-6-0ST	IC	17 x 26	4ft6in	40t	46, 55, 84
2583	11.5.1904	4ft8½in	0-4-0ST	OC	14 x 20	3ft6in	24t8cwts	84, 386
2617	21.6.1905	4ft8½in	0-4-0ST	OC	14 x 22	3ft6in	24t15cwts	386
2639	20.2.1906	4ft8½in	0-4-0ST	OC	13 x 19	3ft4½in	25t6cwts	72, 83
2640	26.2.1906	4ft8½in	0-4-0ST	OC	13 x 19	3ft4½in		73
2641	17.4.1906	4ft8½in	0-6-0PT	IC	18 x 26	4ft2⅝in	43t6cwts	71, 83
2694	17.7.1907	4ft8½in	0-4-0ST	OC	15 x 22	3ft9in	31t5cwts	386
2701	2.5.1907	4ft8½in	0-4-0ST	OC	14 x 22	3ft 6in	27t10cwts	212
2702	7.5.1907	4ft8½in	0-4-0ST	OC	14 x 22	3ft6in		386
2719	7.11.1907	4ft8½in	0-6-0ST	OC	15 x 22	3ft9in	33½t	46, 55, 84
2740	25.2.1909	4ft8½in	0-4-0ST	OC	14 x 22	3ft6in	24t15cwts	386
2789	.1909	4ft8½in	0-4-0ST	OC	16 x 24	3ft10in	37t14cwts	142, 143, 190, 209
2826	10.8.1910	4ft8½in	0-4-0ST	OC	15 x 22	3ft8in	29t17cwts	142, 143, 191, 210
2827	18.8.1910	4ft8½in	0-4-0ST	OC	15 x 22	3ft8in	29t17cwts	142, 143, 191, 210
2932	31.7.1912	4ft8½in	0-6-0ST	IC	15 x 22	3ft9in	33t3cwts	142, 143, 211, 329
2954	31.8.1912	4ft8½in	0-4-0ST	OC	15 x 22	3ft8in	29t17cwts	142, 143, 191, 210
2956	29.11.1912	4ft8½in	0-6-0ST	OC	16 x 24	3ft8in	41½t	56, 84, 106
2984	19.1.1914	4ft8½in	0-4-0VBCr	OC	12x21½	3ft0in	44t	74, 83
2986	19.4.1913	4ft8½in	0-4-0T	OC	14 x 22	3ft6in	26½t	56, 287, 293
3003	19.9.1913	4ft8½in	0-4-0ST	OC	13 x 19	3ft4½in	25t 6cwts	84, 386
3004	23.9.1913	4ft8½in	0-4-0ST	OC	13 x 19	3ft4½in		73
3022	3.11.1913	4ft8½in	0-4-0ST	OC	13 x 19	3ft4½in		72
3023	17.11.1913	4ft8½in	0-4-0ST	OC	13 x 19	3ft4½in		73
3024	12.12.1913	4ft8½in	0-4-0ST	OC	15 x 22	3ft8in	29t17cwts	191, 210
3055	6.4.1914	4ft8½in	0-4-0ST	OC	16 x 24	3ft10in	37t14cwts	141, 143, 190, 209
3056	22.4.1914	4ft8½in	0-4-0ST	OC	16 x 24	3ft10in	37t14cwts	141, 143, 190, 209
3080	9.12.1914	4ft8½in	0-6-0PT	IC	18 x 26	4ft2⅝in	43t6cwts	71, 83

3103	9.4.1915	4ft8½in	0-6-0ST	OC	17 x 24	3ft10in	45t		46, 55
3251	2.10.1917	4ft8½in	0-4-0ST	OC	13 x 19	3ft4½in			73
3391	24.11.1919	4ft8½in	0-4-0ST	OC	14 x 22	3ft6in	28t		73, 83
3438	27.10.1920	4ft8½in	0-4-0ST	OC	15 x 22	3ft9in	31t5cwts		386
3467	30.10.1920	4ft8½in	0-4-0ST	OC	14 x 22	3ft6in	28t		56, 84, 293
3471	1.6.1921	4ft8½in	0-4-0ST	OC	16 x 24	3ft10in			72
3472	8.6.1921	4ft8½in	0-4-0ST	OC	16 x 24	3ft10in			73
3474	16.11.1920	4ft8½in	0-4-0ST	OC	14 x 22	3ft6in	28t		57, 84
3476	21.12.1920	4ft8½in	0-4-0ST	OC	14 x 22	3ft6in			73
3496	22.7.1921	4ft8½in	0-4-0ST	OC	16 x 24	3ft10in			72
3528	17.8.1922	4ft8½in	0-6-0ST	OC	16 x 24	3ft8in	41½t		25, 106
3543	11.9.1923	4ft8½in	0-4-0ST	OC	15 x 22	3ft8in	29t17cwts		142, 143, 191, 211
3544	11.9.1923	4ft8½in	0-4-0ST	OC	15 x 22	3ft8in	29t17cwts		142, 143, 191 211, 329
3569	6.11.1923	4ft8½in	0-6-0ST	IC	18 x 26	4ft6in	50t		46, 55
3745	12.7.1929	4ft8½in	0-4-0ST	OC	16 x 24	3ft10in			73
3752	21.2.1930	4ft8½in	0-4-0ST	OC	16 x 24	3ft10in			73, 83
3753	21.2.1930	4ft8½in	0-4-0ST	OC	16 x 24	3ft10in			73
3766	13.3.1930	4ft8½in	0-6-0T	OC	18 x 24	4ft0in	53t		84, 288
3834	18.9.1934	4ft8½in	0-6-2T	IC	18½x26	4ft6in	61t		191, 211, 293
3891	14.10.1936	4ft8½in	0-6-0P	IC	18 x 26	4ft2⅝in	43t6cwts		71, 83
3951	21.2.1938	4ft8½in	0-6-0PT	IC	18 x 26	4ft2⅝in			71, 83

HEAD, WRIGHTSON & CO LTD, Thornaby, Yorkshire (NR) **HW**

21	1870	4ft8½in	0-4-0VBT	VC	6 x 12	2ft6in	250
33	1873	4ft8½in	0-4-0VBT	OC	9 x 14	2ft5½in	250

JOHN FOWLER &, CO, Hunslet, Leeds **JF**

1162	12.1868	4ft8½in	2w+2wTG	IC	8 x 12	402

J & G JOICEY & CO LTD, Pottery Lane, Newcastle upon Tyne **Joicey**

This firm of general engineers commenced operations in 1855, and concentrated on various types of steam engine, mainly for winding, hauling and pumping. Locomotives were numbered into a general list of products, but how many were built is not known. The firm closed down in 1926.

210	1869	4ft8½in	0-6-0ST	OC	14 x 20	3ft4¾in	33t		402
	1874	4ft8½in	0-4-0ST	OC				[9 SEDGEFIELD]	402
305	1883	4ft8½in	0-6-0ST	IC					316, 328
377	1885	4ft8½in	0-4-0ST	OC					25

KITSON & CO LTD, Airedale Foundry, Leeds **K**

1844	18.10.1872	4ft8½in	0-6-0ST	IC	16 x 24	3ft10in		71
1998	23.1.1875	4ft8½in	0-6-0ST	IC	16 x 24	4ft0in		71
2509	28.7.1883	4ft8½in	0-6-0PT	IC	17½x26	4ft2in	42½t	71, 83
2510	24.8.1883	4ft8½in	0-6-0PT	IC	17½x 26	4ft2in	42vt	71, 83
3069	2.12.1887	4ft8½in	0-6-2T	IC	17½x 26	4ft6in	51t	143, 191, 211
3580	22.11.1894	4ft8½in	0-6-2T	IC	17½x 26	4ft6in	51t	191, 211
3905	13.10.1899	4ft8½in	0-6-0PT	IC	18 x 26	4ft2⅝in	43t6cwts	71
3906	6.11.1899	4ft8½in	0-6-0PT	IC	18 x 26	4ft2⅝in		71
4051	26.6.1901	4ft8½in	0-6-0PT	IC	18 x 26	4ft2⅝in	43t6cwts	71, 83
4263	18.3.1904	4ft8½in	0-6-2T	IC	19 x 26	4ft6in	60½t	191, 210
4294	27.10.1904	4ft8½in	0-6-0T	IC	17½x 26	4ft6in	45t	25, 84
4532	24.10.1907	4ft8½in	0-6-2T	IC	19 x 26	4ft6in	60½t	191, 210
4533	24.10.1907	4ft8½in	0-6-2T	IC	19 x 26	4ft6in	60½t	191, 210

KERR STUART & CO LTD, California Works, Stoke-on-Trent, Staffordshire **KS**

1202	18.5.1911	4ft8½in	4w-4wWE# 300hp			2ft 9½in	40t		375
1203	30.6.1911	4ft8½in	4w-4wWE# 300hp			2ft 9½in	40t		375
3074	14.9.1917	4ft8½in	0-6-0T	OC	17 x 24	4ft0in	49t	VICTORY	143, 191, 210
4030	23.5.1919	4ft8½in	0-4-0ST	OC	15 x 20	3ft3in	27t6cwts	MOSS BAY	45, 54

Motors and electrical equipment by Siemens Brothers Dynamo Works Ltd, Stafford

NATIONAL COAL BOARD, Lambton Engine Works, Philadelphia   **LEW**

[6]   30.7.1958   4ft8½in   0-6-0PT   IC   16 x 24   4ft7in   42t   212

313. The works plate for Lambton Railway 0-6-0 9, built at "Lambton Colliery Works, Philadephia, 1877", photographed on 10th October 1947.

314. From 1978 Lambton Engine Works began fitting rebuild plates to locomotives passing through the workshops. This is the plate for Job No. 9-601-001, fitted to 0-6-0DH HE 6612/1965 in 1979, 102 years after the previous plate was made, photographed on 28th August 1987.

STEPHEN LEWIN, DORSET FOUNDRY, Poole, Dorset   **Lewin**

683   1877   4ft8½in   0-4-0WT   OC   9 x 18   2ft6in   250

JOHN BOWES, ESQ., & PARTNERS, Marley Hill   **Marley Hill**

   1854   4ft8½in   0-4-0ST   IC   [DANIEL O'ROURKE]   45

MANNING, WARDLE & CO LTD, Boyne Engine Works, Leeds   **MW**

152	9.5.1865	4ft8½in	0-6-0ST	IC	13 x 18	3ft0in	M	190
344	21.4.1871	4ft8½in	0-4-0ST	OC	12 x 18	3ft0in	H	191, 209, 329
455	20.8.1874	4ft8½in	0-4-0ST	OC	10 x 16	2ft9in	F	302
466	8.9.1873	4ft8½in	0-4-0ST	OC	12 x 18	3ft0in	H	402
492	20.4.1874	4ft8½in	0-4-0ST	OC	12 x 18	3ft0in	H	402
697	7.5.1878	4ft8½in	0-6-0ST	IC	15 x 22	3ft9in	O	315, 328
758	7.3.1881	4ft8½in	0-6-0ST	IC	15 x 22	3ft9in	O	315, 328
1313	17.6.1896	4ft8½in	0-6-0ST	IC	12 x 17	3ft1⅜in	K	66
1813	7.4.1913	4ft8½in	0-6-0T	IC	18 x 24	4ft2in	Spl	141, 143, 191, 211
1934	29.9.1917	4ft8½in	0-6-0ST	OC	17 x 24	3ft9in	17in Spl	191, 210
2023	9.4.1923	4ft8½in	0-4-0ST	OC	15 x 22	3ft9in	15in Spl	143, 191, 209
2035	19.5.1924	4ft8½in	0-4-0ST	OC	15 x 22	3ft9in	15in Spl	143, 191, 211
2036	28.5.1924	4ft8½in	0-4-0ST	OC	15 x 22	3ft9in	15in Spl	191, 211

NORTH BRITISH LOCOMOTIVE CO LTD, Glasgow.

A   North British Locomotive Co Ltd, Atlas Works, Glasgow   **NBA**
Q   North British Locomotive Co Ltd, Queen's Park Works, Glasgow   **NBQ**

A16628	2.1905	4ft8½in	0-6-0ST	IC	18 x 26	4ft3in	46t14cwts	46, 55
Q27410 #	10.7.1956	4ft8½in	0-6-0DH	400hp	Paxman 12RPH	3ft6in	51t	143, 212
Q27588	13.5.1957	4ft8½in	0-6-0DH	440hp	MAN W8V	3ft9in	51t	329
Q27592	4.11.1957	4ft8½in	0-6-0DH	440hp	MAN W8V	3ft9in	51t	329
Q27717 #	c10.1957	4ft8½in	0-6-0DH	520hp	MAN W6V	3ft9in	51t	58, 329
Q27763	27.2.1959	4ft8½in	0-6-0DH	440hp	MAN W8V	3ft9in	51t	329
Q27764	11.3.1959	4ft8½in	0-6-0DH	440hp	MAN W8V	3ft9in	51t	329
Q27765	27.4.1959	4ft8½in	0-6-0DH	440hp	MAN W8V	3ft9in	51t	329

\#   Demonstration locomotive   The dates given for locos 27410 to 27765 are invoice dates.

NEW LOWCA ENGINEERING CO LTD, Whitehaven, Cumberland — NLE

249	1908	4ft8½in	0-6-0PT	IC	18 x 26	4ft2⅝in	43t6cwts	71

NEILSON, REID & CO LTD, Glasgow — NR

5408	5.1899	4ft8½in	0-6-2T	IC	17½x26	4ft6½in	61½t	142, 143, 191, 211

PECKETT & SONS LTD, Atlas Engine Works, Bristol — P

521	28.7.1891	4ft8½in	0-4-0ST	OC	14 x 20	3ft2in	W4	402
615	20.5.1896	4ft8½in	0-4-0ST	OC	14 x 20	3ft3¾in	W4	130, 142, 191, 210, 329
774	23.2.1899	4ft8½in	0-6-0ST	IC	16 x 22	3ft10in	X	287
1180	#3.5.1912	4ft8½in	0-4-0ST	OC	15 x 21	3ft7in	E	302
1748	7.6.1928	4ft8½in	0-4-0ST	OC	14 x 22	3ft2½in	W6	56, 288, 293
2093	22.9.1947	4ft8½in	0-4-0ST	OC	14 x 22	3ft2½in	W7	56, 293

\# Peckett records suggest this loco was built in 1909

RUSTON & HORNSBY LTD, Lincoln. — RH

243081	19.2.1948	4ft8½in	0-4-0DM	165hp	165DS	3ft2½in	28t	61
313391	4.6.1952	4ft8½in	0-4-0DM	165hp	165DS	3ft2½in	28t	61
319295	14.12.1953	4ft8½in	0-4-0DM	165hp	165DS	3ft2½in	28t	61
384141	18.11.1955	4ft8½in	0-4-0DE	155hp	165DE	3ft2½in	28t	217
421438	9.5.1958	4ft8½in	0-6-0DE	155hp	165DE	3ft2½in	30t	217

ROLLS ROYCE LTD, Sentinel Works, Shrewsbury — RR

This firm was the successor to Sentinel (Shrewsbury) Ltd, which had built diesel locomotives to Rolls Royce design. The works numbers continued in the Sentinel series - see under the Sentinel entry.

ROBERT STEPHENSON & CO LTD, Newcastle upon Tyne & Darlington — RS

This firm was founded in June 1823 with Robert Stephenson, the son of George Stephenson, as managing partner. At first its works was at South Street, Newcastle upon Tyne, but this was soon extended to Forth Banks. The company's reputation was always firmly based as a manufacturer of main line stock, and the majority of its products in industrial service were ordered new by the chief colliery railways or obtained second-hand from the North Eastern Railway. In 1901 the firm removed from Newcastle to a large new works at Darlington, and thereafter industrial orders were few. The firm's former works at Newcastle upon Tyne was taken over by R & W Hawthorn, Leslie & Co Ltd and absorbed into their existing premises. The firm also operated a shipyard at Hebburn-on-Tyne, Co. Durham, which it disposed of in 1912.

In May 1937 the company purchased the locomotive business of R. & W. Hawthorn, Leslie & Co Ltd (which see), and in the following month changed its title to Robert Stephenson & Hawthorns Ltd (which see). The firm had built 4155 locomotives.

Parts of the firm's premises at South Street, Newcastle upon Tyne, are now preserved and being developed as a museum.

Built at Newcastle upon Tyne

	12.4.1826	4ft8½in	0-4-0	VC	10 x 24	4ft0in	[No.1]	27, 44
	26.4.1826	4ft8½in	0-4-0	VC	10 x 24	4ft0in	[No.2]	27, 45
	5.1826	4ft8½in	0-4-0	VC	10 x 24	4ft0in	[DILIGENCE]	315
491	22.12.1845	4ft8½in	2-4-0	IC	14 x 22	5ft8in		191, 210, 329
624	24.7.1848	4ft8½in	0-6-0	IC	18 x 24	5ft0in		316, 328
625	4.9.1848	4ft8½in	0-6-0	IC	18 x 24	5ft0in		316, 328
753	20.9.1849	4ft8½in	0-4-0	OC	14 x 22	4ft5in		250
795	4.7.1851	4ft8½in	0-4-0	OC	14 x 22	4ft4½in		45
816	5.12.1851	4ft8½in	0-4-0	OC	14 x 22	5ft0¾in		45
1073	8.12.1856	4ft8½in	0-6-0	IC	16¾x24	4ft6in		250
1074	10.9.1856	4ft8½in	0-6-0	IC	16 x 24	4ft7½in		45
1075	29.9.1856	4ft8½in	0-6-0	IC	15½x22	5ft0in		250
1096	31.8.1857	4ft8½in	0-6-0	IC	15½x22	5ft0in		250
1100	19.8.1857	4ft8½in	2-4-0	OC	15 x 24	4ft7½in		139
1206	5.8.1859	4ft8½in	4-4-0	OC	16 x 22	5ft0in		250
1217	17.11.1859	4ft8½in	0-6-0	IC	16¾x24	4ft6in		250
1313	17.8.1860	4ft8½in	0-6-0	IC	16 x 24	4ft6in		46
1326	17.10.1860	4ft8½in	0-6-0	IC	16¾x24	4ft6in		250

1327	5.11.1860	4ft8½in	0-6-0	IC	16¾x24	4ft6in		250
1416	2.4.1862	4ft8½in	0-6-0	IC	16¾x24	5ft0in		250
1417	4.4.1862	4ft8½in	0-6-0	IC	16¾x24	5ft0in		250
1516	13.5.1864	4ft8½in	0-6-0	IC	16x24	4ft6in		45
1611	1.9.1864	4ft8½in	0-6-0	IC	16 x 24	4ft6in		46
1612	10.6.1864	4ft8½in	0-6-0ST	IC	13 x 18	3ft6in		46
1649	7.6.1865	4ft8½in	0-6-0	IC	13 x 18	3ft6in		139
1800	21.7.1866	4ft8½in	0-6-0ST	IC	14 x 22	3ft7in		46
1913	6.2.1869	4ft8½in	0-6-0	IC	17 x 24	4ft7in		315
1919	21.12.1869	4ft8½in	0-6-0ST	IC	14 x 20	3ft3in	28½t	25, 141, 191
1973	29.11.1870	4ft8½in	0-6-0	IC	17 x 24	5ft0in		347
2013	9.2.1872	4ft8½in	0-6-0ST	IC	14 x 20	3ft7in		24
2014	9.2.1872	4ft8½in	0-6-0ST	IC	14 x 20	3ft7in	30t	24
2056	11.6.1872	4ft8½in	0-6-0	IC	17 x 24	5ft0⅜in		347
2139	24.10.1873	4ft8vin	0-6-0ST	IC	14¾x22	4ft0in		287
2160	20.2.1874	4ft8½in	0-6-0	IC	17 x 24	5ft0⅜in		347
2239	17.6.1875	4ft8½in	0-6-0ST	IC	14¾x22	4ft0in		287
2240	23.6.1875	4ft8½in	0-6-0ST	IC	14¾x22	4ft0in		287
2244	24.7.1875	4ft8½in	0-6-0ST	IC	14¾x22	4ft0in		287
2260	31.7.1876	4ft8½in	0-6-0	IC	17 x 24	4ft6in	55t14cwts	191, 209
2308	20.11.1876	4ft8½in	0-4-0ST	OC	15 x 20	3ft8in	27t5cwts	142, 191, 209
2587	29.12.1884	4ft8½in	0-6-0	IC	17 x 26	5ft1in		347
2629	15.12.1887	4ft8½in	0-6-0ST	IC	15 x 22			347
2730	17.3.1891	4ft8½in	0-6-0T	IC	17 x 24	4ft0in	41t	24
2822	5.1895	4ft8½in	0-6-0T	IC	17 x 24	4ft0in	41t	25
Built at Darlington								
3057	20.5.1904	4ft8½in	0-4-0ST	OC	14 x 20	3ft3in		103, 288
3376	31.5.1909	4ft8½in	0-4-0ST	OC	15 x 22	3ft6in	31t	386
3377	5.11.1909	4ft8½in	0-6-2T	IC	18½x26	4ft6in	61½t	190, 209
3378	12.11.1909	4ft8½in	0-6-2T	IC	18½x26	4ft6in	61½t	190, 209
3801	28.2.1921	4ft8½in	0-6-2T	IC	18½x26	4ft6in	61½t	191, 210
4112	23.8.1935	4ft8½in	0-6-0ST	OC	16 x 24	3ft10in	39t15cwts	213
		4ft8½in	2-4-0	IC			[GIBSIDE]	44

ROBERT STEPHENSON & HAWTHORNS LTD, Darlington and Forth Banks, Newcastle upon Tyne

This company was formed in June 1937 after the purchase during the previous month by Robert Stephenson & Co Ltd of the locomotive business of R. & W. Hawthorn, Leslie & Co Ltd, which gave the firm works at both Darlington and Newcastle upon Tyne. The Darlington works continued to concentrate on main line and export orders, while the Newcastle works handled industrial work.

In 1938 the company took over the goodwill of Kitson & Co Ltd of Leeds and, through them, of Manning, Wardle & Co Ltd, also of Leeds. In 1944 the company became a subsidiary of Vulcan Foundry Ltd of Newton-le-Willows, Lancashire, itself a subsidiary of the English Electric Co Ltd. In general the firm concentrated on a standard range of products based on Hawthorn Leslie designs. In later years Newcastle concentrated on steam locomotive work, while the Darlington Works handled mainly diesel and battery-electric locomotives sub-contracted from English Electric. The Newcastle Works closed in 1961, and in 1962 the parent company took over full control of the Darlington Works, which closed in March 1964, marking the end of industrial locomotive building in North-East England.

The 4155 locomotives built by Robert Stephenson & Co Ltd were added to the 2983 locomotives built by R. & W. Hawthorn, Leslie & Co Ltd and their predecessors, R. & W. Hawthorn & Co, making the first RSH locomotive Works No. 6939.

All the locomotives in the following list were built at the Newcastle Works (RSHN).

6943	22.4.1938	4ft8½in	0-6-0ST	OC	16 x 24	3ft8in	43t6cwts	57
7028	24.3.1941	4ft8½in	0-6-0PT	IC	18 x 26	4ft2⅝in		71
7101	13.9.1943	4ft8½in	0-6-0ST	IC	18 x 26	4ft3in	48t3cwts	212, 329
7132	14.4.1944	4ft8½in	0-6-0ST	IC	18 x 26	4ft3in	48t3cwts	353, 377
7294	30.8.1945	4ft8½in	0-6-0ST	IC	18 x 26	4ft3in	48t3cwts	212, 353, 377
7339	8.10.1947	4ft8½in	0-6-0ST	OC	16 x 24	3ft8in	43t6cwts	353
7538	8.4.1949	4ft8½in	0-4-0ST	OC	16 x 24	3ft8in	36t13cwts	84, 386
7546	4.7.1949	4ft8½in	0-6-0ST	OC	16 x 24	3ft8in	40t	106
7599	17.8.1949	4ft8½in	0-6-0ST	OC	16 x 24	3ft8in	43t6cwts	212
7600	24.8.1949	4ft8½in	0-6-0ST	OC	16 x 24	3ft8in	43t6cwts	212, 329
7603	13.12.1949	4ft8½in	0-6-0ST	OC	18 x 24	4ft0in	53t	84, 353, 377
7604	1.11.1949	4ft8½in	0-4-0ST	OC	16 x 24	3ft8in	36t13cwts	56, 293

7605	4.11.1949	4ft8½in	0-4-0ST	OC	16 x 24	3ft8in	36t13cwts		25, 302
7687	19.10.1951	4ft8½in	0-6-0ST	OC	18 x 24	4ft0in	53t		212
7688	19.11.1951	4ft8½in	0-6-0ST	OC	18 x 24	4ft0in	53t		212
7691	1.5.1952	4ft8½in	0-6-0ST	OC	18 x 24	4ft0in	53t		212
7695	19.12.1951	4ft8½in	0-6-0ST	OC	18 x 24	4ft0in	53t		353, 377
7749	17.12.1952	4ft8½in	0-6-0ST	OC	18 x 24	4ft0in	53t		353, 377
7751	23.7.1953	4ft8½in	0-6-0ST	IC	18 x 26	4ft3in	48t3cwts		55, 84
7755	10.4.1953	4ft8½in	0-4-0ST	OC	15 x 22	3ft8in	31t		212
7756	15.4.1953	4ft8½in	0-4-0ST	OC	15 x 22	3ft8in	31t		212
7757	22.4.1953	4ft8½in	0-4-0ST	OC	15 x 22	3ft8in	31t		148, 212
7804	15.11.1954	4ft8½in	0-4-0WE	80hp		2ft9in			218
7811	1.11.1954	4ft8½in	0-6-0ST	OC	18 x 24	4ft0in	53t		353, 377
7882	4.11.1957	4ft8½in	0-4-0WE	80hp		2ft9in			90
7886	21.5.1958	4ft8½in	0-4-0WE	80hp		2ft9in			332
8093	15.10.1959	4ft8½in	0-4-0WE	80hp		2ft9in			51

R & W HAWTHORN LTD, Forth Banks, Newcastle upon Tyne   RWH

This firm was founded by Robert and William Hawthorn in 1817, and soon entered locomotive building as the railway age developed, though they continued to produce other types of steam engine. Like their near-neighbours, Robert Stephenson & Co, they concentrated on main line locomotives. In 1886 the firm amalgamated with Andrew Leslie & Co Ltd, shipbuilders, of Hebburn-on-Tyne, Co. Durham, to form R & W Hawthorn, Leslie & Co Ltd (which see)..

171	c1833	4ft8½in							127
308	1840	4ft8½in	0-6-0		14 x 18	4ft0in			190
476	1846	4ft8½in	0-6-0	IC	15 x 24	4ft3in			44
479	1846	4ft8½in	0-6-0	IC	15 x 24	4ft3in			250
1422	1867	4ft8½in	0-6-0ST	IC	15 x 22	3ft9in	28t2cwts#46, 414, 191, 210		
1430	1868	4ft8½in	0-6-0ST	IC	14 x 18	3ft0in			141, 191, 210
1478	1870	4ft8½in	0-6-0ST	IC	17 x 24	4ft6in	42t		141, 191
1564	7.1873	4ft8½in	0-6-0	IC	17 x 24	5ft0in			347
1657	10.1875	4ft8½in	0-6-0ST	IC	15 x 22	4ft0in			287
1662	12.1875	4ft8½in	0-6-0ST	IC	15 x 22	4ft0in			287
1666	2.1876	4ft8½in	0-6-0ST	IC	15 x 22	4ft0in			287
1669	2.1876	4ft8½in	0-6-0ST	IC	15 x 22	4ft0in			287
1726	1877	4ft8½in	0-4-0ST	OC	11 x 18	3ft0in			386
1817	26.4.1880	4ft8½in	0-4-0ST	OC	10 x 15	2ft9in			386
1969	9.2.1884	4ft8½in	0-6-0ST	IC	16 x 24	4ft6in			141, 190
1986	19.3.1886	4ft8½in	0-6-0ST	OC	15 x 20	3ft6in	35t		45

as given in records at Lambton Engine Works, though it seems rather low

SENTINEL (SHREWSBURY) LTD, Battlefield Works, Shrewsbury, Shropshire   S
(form. Sentinel Wagon Works (1936) Ltd; orig. Sentinel Wagon Works Ltd)

6936	1927	4ft8½in	4wVBT	VCG	6¾x 9			288
9581	1.3.1955	4ft8½in	4wVBT	VCG	6¾x 9	200hp	34t	84
9583	23.3.1955	4ft8½in	4wVBT	VCG	6¾x 9	200hp	34t	84
9584	29.3.1955	4ft8½in	4wVBT	VCG	6¾x 9	200hp	34t	84

Diesel locomotives (built to Rolls Royce design, and from 1964 marketed as Rolls Royce)

10072	9.6.1961	4ft8½in	0-6-0DH	311hp	R-R C8SFL		48t	58, 217
10097	8.2.1962	4ft8½in	4wDH	230hp	R-R C6SFL		34t	217
10157	28.3.1963	4ft8½in	0-6-0DH	310hp	R-R C8SFL	3ft6in	48t	56, 60, 217
10158	19.4.1963	4ft8½in	0-6-0DH	310hp	R-R C8SFL	3ft6in	48t	56, 60

ROLLS ROYCE LTD, Sentinel Works, Shrewsbury, Shropshire   RR

10201	30.11.1964	4ft8½in	0-4-0DH	325hp	R-R C8SFL		31t	60, 85, 90, 213

SWINDON WORKS, Swindon, Wiltshire (Great Western Railway/British Railways)   Sdn

[BR D2139]	4.1960	4ft8½in	0-6-0DM	204hp	Gardner 8L3	3ft7in	30t4cwts	61
[BR D9504]	7.1964	4ft8½in	0-6-0DH	650hp	Paxman 6YJX	4ft0in	50t	212, 377
[BR D9525]	1.1965	4ft8½in	0-6-0DH	650hp	Paxman 6YJX	4ft0in	50t	213
[BR D9540]	4.1965	4ft8½in	0-6-0DH	650hp	Paxman 6YJX	4ft0in	50t	213

MARQUIS OF LONDONDERRY, Londonderry Engine Works, Seaham Harbour — Seaham

[6]	1883	4ft8½in	0-6-0ST	IC			250
[5]	1885	4ft8½in	0-6-0	IC	17½x26	4ft9½in	250
[2]	1889	4ft8½in	2-4-0T	IC	15x24	4ft11in	250
[20]	1892	4ft8½in	0-6-0	IC	17½x26	4ft9in	250
[21]	1895	4ft8½in	0-4-4T	IC	17 x 24	5ft4½in	250
	1902	4ft8½in	0-6-0T	IC			250

SHILDON WORKS CO, Shildon — Shildon

[S&DR 31]	9.1845	4ft8½in	0-6-0	OC	15 x 24	4ft0in	401

SIEMENS-SCHUCKERT ELEKTRICITATS AG, Munich, Germany
Siemens

450	1908	2ft2in	0-4-4-0WE	66hp			97
451	1908	4ft8½in	4wWE	300hp		27t	375
454	1909	2ft2in	0-4-4-0WE	66hp			97
455	1908	4ft8½in	4wWE	93hp		17t	375
456	1909	4ft8½in	4w-4wWE	186hp	2ft9¼in	35t13cwts	375
457	1909	4ft8½in	4w-4wWE	186hp	2ft9¼in	35t13cwts	375
458	1909	4ft8½in	0-4-4-0WE	280hp	2ft9¼in	44t	375
459	1909	4ft8½in	0-4-4-0WE	280hp	2ft9¼in	44t	375
460	1910	2ft2in	0-4-4-0WE	120hp	[Hanomag 5968]		97
862	1913	4ft8½in	4wWE	93hp	2ft7¼in	17t	375

SHARP, STEWART & CO LTD, Manchester & Atlas Works, Glasgow — SS

	1857	4ft8½in	0-6-0ST	IC	18 x 24	5ft0in	40t4cwts	316, 328
1501	18.4.1864	4ft8½in	2-2-2WT	IC	15 x 18	5ft6¼in		347
1768	15.1.1867	4ft8½in	0-6-0ST	IC	18 x 24	5ft0in		316
2260	10.1872	4ft8½in	0-6-0ST	IC	17 x 24	4ft7in		71
2358	1873	4ft8½in	0-6-0T	OC	16½x20	3ft6in	33t5cwts	315, 328
4051	12.1894	4ft8½in	0-6-0ST	IC	17½x26	4ft3in	46t14cwts	46, 54, 347, 377
4594	3.1900	4ft8½in	0-6-0ST	IC	17½x26	4ft3in		45

THOMAS HILL (ROTHERHAM) LTD, Vanguard Works, Kilnhurst, South Yorkshire — TH

105V	22.1.1961	4ft8½in	4wDH	178hp	R-R C6NFL		30t	217
135C	31.1.1964	4ft8½in	4wDH	308hp	R-R C8SFL	3ft2in	35½t	84
313V	13.4.1985	4ft8½in	4wWE	132hp			25t	65

CHARLES TODD, Leeds — Todd

	1847	4ft8½in	0-6-0	IC	15 x 24	4ft 9in	287

THOMAS RICHARDSON & SONS, Hartlepool Ironworks, Middleton, Hartlepool — TR

Thomas Richardson (c1795-1850) entered business in 1832, when he took a 21-year lease on land at Castle Eden in south Durham on which to start an iron-working business. In 1847 he took a lease of the Hartlepool Ironworks at Middleton, which had been started about 1838, and moved much of his work here, although the Castle Eden works continued until April 1853. It would seem that the construction of locomotives began at Castle Eden about 1835 and was subsequently transferred to Hartlepool, where it was continued by his son, also Thomas Richardson (1821-1890). No locomotives are known after 1858, when the firm concentrated on marine work. The firm failed in April 1875, and the engineering side of the business was re-constituted as Thomas Richardson & Sons Ltd. This formed one of the constituents of Richardsons, Westgarth & Co Ltd when it was formed in 1900, which in 1977 became part of the nationalised British Shipbuilders. The works closed in 1981.

182	c1851	4ft8½in	0-6-0T+t#	OC			250
213	1852	4ft8½in	0-6-0#	IC			190
236	1853	4ft8½in	0-6-0	IC			190
251	10.1854	4ft8½in	0-6-0	IC	17 x 24		190
252	1854	4ft8½in	0-6-0	IC	15 x 22	4ft6in	46
254	6.1855	4ft8½in	0-6-0	IC	15 x 22		250
265	1856	4ft8½in	0-6-0	IC			315

\# rebuild of an earlier locomotive by an unknown builder

WEARDALE IRON & COAL CO LTD, Tow Law Iron Works, Tow Law, Co Durham — Tow Law

[20]		4ft8½in	0-6-0ST#	OC	402

believed built in the 1880s, possibly with parts supplied by BH

VULCAN FOUNDRY LTD, Newton-le-Willows, Lancashire — VF

5288	6.1945	4ft8½in	0-6-0ST	IC	18 x 26	4ft3in	48t3cwts	46, 55, 84
5298	7.1945	4ft8½in	0-6-0ST	IC	18 x 26	4ft3in	48t3cwts	46, 55
5299	7.1945	4ft8½in	0-6-0ST	IC	18 x 26	4ft3in	48t3cwts	84, 142, 143 191, 211
5300	7.1945	4ft8½in	0-6-0ST	IC	18 x 26	4ft3in	48t3cwts	85, 143, 191 211, 329
5307	7.1945	4ft8½in	0-6-0ST	IC	18 x 26	4ft3in	48t3cwts	46
5308	9.1945	4ft8½in	0-6-0ST	IC	18 x 26	4ft3in	48t3cwts	316, 329
5309	9.1945	4ft8½in	0-6-0ST	IC	18 x 26	4ft3in	48t3cwts	143, 212, 316, 329

W. G. BAGNALL LTD, Castle Engine Works, Stafford, Staffordshire — WB

3123	6.12.1957	4ft8½in	0-6-0DM	308hp	National M4AA7	38t	58
3160	30.11.1959	4ft8½in	0-6-0DM	304hp	Dorman 6QT	38t	58

THE OWNERS OF WYLAM COLLIERY, Wylam Colliery, Wylam, Northumberland — Wylam

	1827-1832	5ft0in	4w	VCG	[WYLAM DILLY]	103

YORKSHIRE ENGINE CO LTD, Meadow Hall Works, Sheffield, Yorkshire (WR) — YE

2668	# 1958	4ft8½in	0-6-0DE	400hp	2xR-R C6SFL	48t	58

demonstration locomotive

UNIDENTIFIED BUILDERS

	4ft8½in	0-6-0ST	OC	[BURLEY]	65, 72
	4ft8½in			[BETTY]	66

RAIL CRANES

Rail cranes, as opposed to crane tank locomotives, are not normally included in locomotive indexes. However, those below were included in the D Class of the Consett Iron Co Ltd.

THOMAS SMITH & SONS (RODLEY) LTD, Rodley, Yorkshire (WR) — TS

5784	1900	4ft8½in	4wCr	5t capy.	74
9586	18.12.1920	4ft8½in	4wCr	5t capy.	74

Index 5
Synopsis of chapters

The Beamish Railway
Beamish Waggonway, 16; James Joicey, 17; James Joicey, 1st Baron Joicey, 19; amalgamation into Lambton, Hetton & Joicey Collieries Ltd, 19; National Coal Board, 22; closure of railway, 23.

The Bowes Railway
Springwell Colliery Railway, 26; passenger service, 26; Marley Hill Railway, 27; work of 1853-1855, 28; *John Bowes,* 29; Northumberland & Durham Coal Co, 29; Dipton to Birkheads, 29; branches on the western section, 32; Birkheads to Springwell Bank Foot, 32; Springwell Bank Foot to Jarrow, 38; links at Jarrow, 40; company history, 1870-1900, 40; company history, 1920-1940, 40; workshops, 43; wagons, 44; liveries, 44; National Coal Board, 47; major investment, 47; amalgamation with Pelaw Main Railway, 50; working of Pelaw Main branch, 50; Pelaw Main Staiths, 51; introduction of diesel locomotives, 52; closures west of Kibblesworth, 52; closures of 1973-74, 52; preservation schemes, 53; Monkton Railways, 59.

The Chopwell & Garesfield Railway
Garesfield Waggonway, 63; conversion of waggonway into Chopwell & Garesfield Railway, 65; locomotive sheds, 68; wagons, 68; passenger service, 68; Chopwell Coke Ovens, 68; developments up to 1947, 69; coke making, 69; locomotives and locomotive transfers, 70; National Coal Board, 74; Clockburn Drift, 74; Derwenthaugh Staiths, 77; the closure of Garesfield and Chopwell collieries, 79; locomotive working from Derwenthaugh shed, 79; final closures, 81.

Craghead and Burnhope
Railway to Craghead, 101; extension to Burnhope, 102; National Coal Board, 105; closure of Burnhope section, 105; final closure, 105.

The Derwent Railway
Construction of Stanhope & Tyne Railway, 109; collapse of Stanhope & Tyne Railway, 110; description of route, 111; survey of railway and sale of line to Stockton & Darlington Railway, 112.

The Early Industrial Locomotives
Background to locomotive development, 1; Richard Trevithick, 3; John Blenkinsop and Matthew Murray, 5; William Hedley and Timothy Hackworth, 7; William Chapman and John Buddle, 9; William Brunton, 11; John Grimshaw, 11; George Stephenson, 12; the reasons why North-East England became the centre of locomotive development, 14; the problems faced, 14.

The Hetton Railway
The significance of both Hetton Colliery and the Hetton Railway, 114; the early years, 114; opening of Elemore and Eppleton Collieries, 115; rope haulage replaces locomotives on northern section, 1827, 115; Hetton Staiths, 116; links with other railways, 117; maintenance of the line by contractors, 120; use of horses, 120; changes to the railway and its route after 1832, 120; Hetton Workshops and loco sheds, 124; sale of the company to Lord Joicey, 125; North Hetton branch and its collieries, 127; the locomotive of 1833, 128; integration with the Lambton Railway, 131; branch to Silksworth Colliery, 133; signalling, 135; locomotives, 137; National Coal Board, 135; the development of Hawthorn Combined Mine, 136; final closure, 137.

The Lambton Railway
The Lambton family, 145; Lambton Waggonway, 145; Lumley Waggonway, 146; Newbottle Waggonway, 148; the new route to Sunderland, 150; gauge differences, 151; old route to Low Lambton Staiths, 151; Cross Rigg branch, 152; Pensher Quarry branch, 152; Wapping branch, 152; Lumley branch, 152; Cocken branch, 152; developments at Littletown and Sherburn, 153; collaboration with Marquis of Londonderry, 154; Frankland branch, 158; Harraton Colliery, 159; development of Lambton Engine Works, 159; development of public railways in the area, 159; introduction of locomotives, 162; Pensher branch (York, Newcastle & Berwick Railway), 162; other changes in the 1850s, 162; "Union Railway", 165; Deptford branch (North Eastern Railway), 165; branch and colliery closures, 1877-1883, 165; North Biddick Colliery, 168; Pensher Foundry branch, 168; Bowes House Farm branch, 168; more quarrying activities, 168; Littletown & Sherburn branch, 168; acquisition by Sir James Joicey, 173; by-product coke making, 173; Philadelphia Power Station branch, 173; Lord Joicey's plans for expansion, 175; acquisition of the Hetton Coal Co Ltd, 175; sale of the Sherburn collieries, 175; creation of Lambton, Hetton & Joicey Collieries Ltd, 175; the Hetton Railway in 1911, 176; the North Hetton branch, 176; the union of the Lambton and Hetton Railways, 178; Silksworth Colliery and its branches, 179; the wagon fleet and its repair, 184; new locomotive sheds and repair facilities, 180; signalling on the railway, 184; closures of the 1920s and 1930s, 189; locomotives, 189; National Coal Board, 193; early years of nationalisation, 193; end of the Hetton Railway, 199; the closures of the 1960s, 199; locomotive rosters and the introduction of diesel locomotives, 202; the run-down to final closure in 1986, 206; the closure of Lambton Engine Works, 206.

The Londonderry Railway
Charles Stewart, 3rd Marquis of Londonderry, 219; Vane Tempest Waggonway, 220; original "main line" to Pensher Staiths, 220; developments of Pensher route, 220; collaboration between

Londonderry and Lambton, 222; the line between Pittington and Pensher, 222; development of Seaham Harbour, 225; the railway to Seaham Harbour, and its construction, maintenance and operation by contractors, 225; passenger service over it?, 226; conversion to standard gauge, 227; re-organisation of original line, 227; introduction of locomotives, 227; beginning of mining at Seaham, 227 ; Londonderry (Seaham & Sunderland) Railway, 228; Framwellgate Colliery, 232; Shotton Colliery, 232; "Union Railway", 234; Londonderry Engine Works and Wagon Shops, 235; retraction, 239; closure of Rainton & Seaham Railway, 241; improvements on Seaham & Sunderland Railway, 242; re-organisation of 1898-1900, 244; brief subsequent history under North Eastern Railway, etc, 248; Engine Works, Wagon Shops and wagons, 248; remaining branches, 248; notes on locomotives, 249.

The Marsden Railway – see South Shields, Marsden & Whitburn Colliery Railway

The Pelaw Main Railway
Ouston Waggonway, 254; other collieries join the line, 256; gauge of waggonway, 258; from Urpeth C Colliery to Ewe Hil, 258; Ouston A Colliery, 260; Ouston branch waggonway, 261; Birtley Iron Works and Birtley "Tail", 262; Bewicke Main branch, 262; Birtley Station branch, 262; introduction of locomotives, 264; further developments at Ouston, 264; Ouston E Colliery and its branch, 264; later years at Birtley and Birtley Tail, 264; Blackhouse Incline, 265; Blackhouse bank head to Eighton Banks bank foot, 267; Eighton Banks Incline, 267; Eighton Banks to Whitehill, 269; Whitehill Incline, 270; Heworth Bank Foot to Pelaw Main Staiths, 270; Team(s) Waggonway, 271; operation in 1850s, 274; changes between 1860 and 1900, 274; change at Wrekenton, 275; changes at Ravensworth Betty Colliery, 1937, 275; operation of Allerdene Incline, 280; construction of Team Valley Trading Estate, 281; consideration of link to Bowes Railway, 281; Second World War, 284; summary, 284; locomotives, 284; National Coal Board, 290; amalgamation with Bowes Railway, 290.

The Pontop & Jarrow Railway – see The Bowes Railway

The Sacriston Railway
Waldridge Waggonway, 295; Sacriston Waggonway, 295; Waldridge Engine and Stables, 296; unique "auxiliary cylinder", 296; ownership, 297; introduction of locomotives, 297; developments around Sacriston., 298; closure of Waldridge Colliery and sale of section, 301; 1926-1947, 302; National Coal Board, 302; final closure, 304.

The South Hetton Colliery Railway
Whole line as built, 1833-35, 306; traffic to Hartlepool, 306; Dobson's branch, 307; Pespool branch, 307; traffic to Sunderland, 307; Murton Colliery, 307; Murton branch, 307; Murton Dene branch, 307 ; links with Londonderry Railway, 307; use of Pespool branch to serve Shotton Colliery, and then Tuthill Quarry, 308; closure of the Haswell branch, 309; new Murton branch, 309; locomotives, 309; National Coal Board, 317; the development of Hawthorn Combined Mine and Washery, 317 and Coking Plant, 325; the last working steam locomotive and rope inclines in North-East England, 325; the long decline, 327; numbers carried by locomotives, 328.

The South Shields, Marsden & Whitburn Colliery Railway
Early years of Harton Coal Co, 333; Whitburn Colliery and the Marsden Railway, 334; introduction of passenger service, 335; developments, 1895-1913, 335; signalling, 335 ; serious problems in South Shields, 329; re-alignment arising from construction of South Shields-Whitburn Colliery road, 341; Marsden Quarries, 344; National Coal Board developments, 348 ; end of passenger service, 348; closure of railway, 348; wagons, 350; coaches, 351; locomotives, 352.

The Harton electric system
Electrification in North-East England after 1900, 355; reasons for adoption of electrification in South Shields, 355; operation of system, 1908-1913, 358; changes of 1913-1947, 360; National Coal Board, 362; the development of Westoe Colliery, 362; take-over of part of former Pontop & Shields route, 362; closure of Harton High Staith, 368; closure of Boldon Colliery, then of Boldon coal stocking site, 369; final closure of railway, 372; locomotive liveries, 373.

The Towneley Colliery Railway
Stella Grand Lease, 379; development of railway and its collieries, 379; chaldron wagons, 381; the final system, 382; National Coal Board, 382, and closure, 385.

The Weatherhill & Rookhope and Rookhope & Middlehope Railways
Stanhope Burn Iron Works, 388; the need for a railway in Weardale, 388; Weatherhill & Rookhope Railway, 388; "Dead Friars" branch, 392; Sikehead branch, 392; Groove Rake branch, 392; Rookhope & Middlehope Railway - extension from Rookhope to Middlehope, 392; Scutterhill Incline, 394; the passenger service, 394; working timetable, 1898, 395; last quarter of the nineteenth century, 395; Tudhoe Iron Works, 396; take-over by Sir Christopher Furness, 396; Cambo Keels Incline, 396; decline and closure, 396; after the closure, 400; locomotives, 400.

The Whittonstall Railway
Its construction, 91; development during First World War, 93; failure of the locomotives and adoption of rope haulage, 93; National Coal Board, 97; improvements to system, 97; run-down in mid-1960s, 98; tubs used on the line, 98; closure, 100.